empire in *De tumultibus horum temporum querela.*

1529	Publishes *In P. Virgilii Maronis Bucolica ac Georgica adnotationes.*
1530	Publishes *Psalmus CXVIII et sedecim alii* and *Imper. Caes. Carolo V. Germaniam ingredienti urbis Norimbergae gratulatoria acclamatio.*
1531	Publishes *Theocriti Idyllia XXXVI* and a set of *Epicedia*; also a revision of his dietetic poem, now entitled *Bonae valetudinis conservandae rationes aliquot.*
1532	Publishes *Urbs Noriberga illustrata.* Also brings out his revised heroic epistles, entitled *Heroidum libri III recogniti*, and an *Epicedion in funere Hieronymi Ebneri.*
1533	Early in the year publishes *Salomonis Ecclesiastes.* At the beginning of May returns to teach at Erfurt.
1534	Publishes a translation from the Greek, *Coluthi Lycopolitae de raptu Helenes*; also publishes a poem in praise of Landgrave Philip's victory in Württemberg, *De victoria Wirtembergensi.*
1535	Publishes his occasional verse in *Sylvarum libri VI.*
1536	Leaves Erfurt to become professor of history at the University of Marburg, arriving there on September 1.
1537	Publishes the mock-encomium *Podagrae ludus*, versified from the German; also publishes *Epicedion in funere Erasmi* and the complete versified Psalter, *Psalterium universum.*
1538	Elected rector of the University of Marburg (January 1 to July 1). Publishes *Elegia de Calumnia* in defense of Philip Melanchthon.
1539	Collects his major works in *Operum farragines duae.* Publishes *Ad Philippum Nidanum in morte Barbarae uxoris consolatio* as well as an *Epithalamion* for Justus Studaeus.
1540	Publishes *Homeri Ilias.* Dies in Marburg on October 4.

THE POETIC WORKS OF
HELIUS EOBANUS HESSUS

VOLUME 1

RENAISSANCE TEXT SERIES

VOLUME 18

THE RENAISSANCE SOCIETY OF AMERICA

MEDIEVAL AND RENAISSANCE TEXTS AND STUDIES

VOLUME 215

Helius Eobanus Hessus in 1526
Silverpoint by Albrecht Dürer
*Reproduced by kind permission of the Trustees
of the British Museum, London*

THE POETIC WORKS OF
HELIUS EOBANUS HESSUS

Edited, translated, and annotated by

Harry Vredeveld

Volume 1
STUDENT YEARS AT ERFURT, 1504-1509

Published by: Arizona Center for Medieval and Renaissance Studies, PO Box 872508, Tempe, AZ 85287-2508.

MRTS Volume 215
Renaissance Text Series Volume 18

ISBN: 0-86698-257-4

Hessus, Helius Eobanus, 1488–1540
    [Poems. English & Latin]
    The poetic works of Helius Eobanus Hessus / edited, translated, and annotated by Harry Vredeveld.
                v. cm. –(Medieval and Renaissance texts and studies ; 215)
        Contents: v. 1. Student years at Erfurt, 1504–1509
        ISBN: 0-86698-257-4 (alk. paper)
        1. Hessus, Helius Eobanus, 1488–1540 — Translations into English. 2. Latin poetry, Medieval and modern — Germany — Erfurt — Translations into English. 3. Vredeveld, Harry. II. Title. III. Medieval & Renaissance Texts & Studies (Series) ; v. 215.

PA8527.H4A28 2004
971'.04–dc22   2003070860

Digitally printed on acid-free paper by Yurchak Printing, Inc. of Lancaster, PA.

FOR HANS-GERT ROLOFF

Ut meminisse iuvat!

TABLE OF CONTENTS

PREFACE

The poetic texts presented in volume 1 of this edition – most of them now exceedingly rare and hitherto unedited – derive from Eobanus Hessus's student years at the University of Erfurt, where he matriculated in 1504 and earned his B.A. in 1506, his M.A. in 1509. Subsequent volumes will carry the story forward in chronological order. Thus volume 2 will offer the poems of Eobanus's journeyman years in Prussia, Frankfurt an der Oder, and Leipzig (1509-1514), volume 3 the works produced during his "kingship" in Erfurt (1514-1526). Further volumes will cover the years at Nuremberg (1509-1533), Erfurt (1533-1536), and Marburg (1536-1540) and bring an edition of *Sylvarum libri IX* and the uncollected minor poems. Metrical translations from the Greek (Theocritus, Coluthus, and Homer's *Iliad*) as well as the verse paraphrases of the Psalms and Ecclesiastes are to be edited in separate volumes.

The base text for each edition is normally the *editio princeps*, unless a later redaction presents a significant improvement over the earlier version. For example, the dietetic poem *Bonae valetudinis conservandae praecepta* of 1524 was superseded in 1531 by the better-organized *Bonae valetudinis conservandae rationes aliquot*; and the *Bucolicorum idyllia* of 1528 were augmented with informative headnotes and marginalia in the *Operum farragines duae* of 1539. In such cases I plan to use the later version as the copy text. Poems that Eobanus revised so extensively as to become new works in their own right will be printed as parallel editions in separate volumes. Hence the *Bucolicon* (1509) and the *Heroidum Christianarum epistolae* (1514) will appear in volumes 1 and 2 respectively, while the *Bucolicorum idyllia* of 1528/39 will find a place in volume 4, the *Heroidum libri tres* of 1532/39 in volume 5. The many verse letters that were brought out posthumously by Eobanus's friends cannot be included in the present edition. They are to appear within the framework of his correspondence.

Editorial Principles

To meet the requirements and expectations of present-day readers, I have normalized the Latin texts according to the following principles:

1. The orthography of the copy-texts has been retained, except as indicated below. Consonantal and vocalic *u* and *v* have been distinguished; the various forms of *s* have been standardized; *j* (generally in *ij*) has been printed

as *i*; and *e*-caudata (*ę*) has been rendered as *ae*. Contractions and abbrevia-
tions have been silently expanded. Ligatures and diacritical marks (dieresis
and accents) have not been reproduced. Enclitic *-ne* and *-ve*, often printed as
separate words in the originals, have been joined to the preceding word. The
use of lower and upper case has been modernized. Obvious misprints (for ex-
ample, turned letters) have been tacitly corrected. The spelling and
abbreviation of speakers' names in dialogic poems (for example, *Bucolicon*)
has been standardized. Greek inserts have been printed according to modern
conventions.

2. The punctuation has been modernized throughout.

3. The various verse forms have been indented according to present
practice. The paragraphing of prose and verse texts has also been brought
into line with modern standards.

4. The editor is responsible for the numbering of poems and verses as
well as for the paragraph and sentence numbers in the prose texts. Front mat-
ter, other than the dedicatory letter, is marked with the letter *A*, followed by
a number. Back matter is indicated with *B*, followed by a number. The sig-
natures and folio or page numbers of the copy texts have been added at the
appropriate locations in the margin of this edition.

The apparatus criticus contains only substantive variants from editions
that appeared during Eobanus's lifetime. Obvious typographical errors and
purely orthographical variants have been excluded.

Translation and Commentary

The translation aims to be a companion to the Latin text as well as an intro-
duction to Eobanus's work. Accordingly I aim to stay as close to the original
as English idiom permits. But whenever the ideals of faithfulness and read-
ability clash, as they inevitably will, I resolve the conflict in favor of a more
understandable, idiomatic text. Hard-to-understand allusions are translated
freely, with an eye to making the intended meaning clear; unfamiliar patro-
nymics are replaced with more familiar names. I use prose throughout,
except in the prosimetric *De amantium infoelicitate*; but even there the verse
is decidedly prosaic and unbound, being intended merely to suggest the in-
terplay of prose and verse in the Latin.

The commentary consists of two parts. Footnotes to the translation offer
information of interest to the general reader. A supplementary set of notes,
keyed to the Latin text, provides additional information, attempts to account
for the manifold sources and models on which Eobanus drew, and builds a
network of cross-references to other works of his. Lines and phrases that oc-
cur in such parallel texts as *Bucolicon* and *Idyllia* (or *Heroidum Christianarum*

epistolae and *Heroidum libri tres*) are normally cited according to the first version of the work; lack of a reference to the later version, therefore, does not necessarily imply that the phrase does not occur there too. In citing verbal parallels to ancient, medieval, and Renaissance texts or to other works by Eobanus, I normally point only to the earliest instances known to me. Proper names not explained in the notes are identified in the Glossarial Index. In the lemmata preceding the supplementary notes I use the following symbols:

A dash (–) indicates "from ... to"; the words omitted are to be supplied by the reader.

Suspension points (...) signify that the words omitted are to be ignored for the purposes of the note.

An equal sign (=) means that the words in the lemma are identical to the words referred to in the note and occupy the same metrical position in the verse.

An approximation sign (≈) indicates that the words in the lemma differ slightly from the words referred to in the note, but occupy the same metrical position.

Acknowledgments

This edition has been long in the making. As a dissertation writer abroad in West Berlin during the tumultuous years 1968/70, I sought out Professor Hans-Gert Roloff at the Free University. With a kindness that I cannot ever hope to repay, that eminent scholar took me under his wing, placed the resources of his Center for Early Modern German Literature at my disposal, and unstintingly offered me his counsel and encouragement. Indeed, it was he who without a moment's hesitation suggested that I produce an annotated edition of Eobanus's *Heroides* and followed up with so much enthusiasm that he in effect became my unofficial *Doktorvater*. And when he thereupon proposed that I publish an edition of Eobanus's works under his aegis, I gladly accepted his more than generous offer. Our hopes for orderly publication, however, came to naught in the following years. Neither Professor Roloff's "Ausgaben Deutscher Literatur des XV. bis XVIII. Jahrhunderts" nor his series "Mittlere Deutsche Literatur in Neu- und Nachdrucken" was ultimately in a position to bring out the planned edition. Only one of the projected volumes ever appeared in print: *Helius Eobanus Hessus, Dichtungen: Lateinisch und Deutsch. Dritter Band: Dichtungen der Jahre 1528-1537* (Bern, 1990). And so it was that after more than two decades of collaboration I was faced with the dismal prospect of having to cut my publishing ties with an esteemed friend, to discard my German-language translations of the works from the period 1506-1528, and to start afresh for an English-reading audience. I daresay, however, that the storm and stress of these years, though a trial for me personally, has nevertheless proved a boon to the edition itself. As always, I feel immensely grateful to my old mentor, without whom this project would never have gotten off the ground. To him, therefore, I dedicate this volume.

It remains for me to thank other good friends and colleagues who cheerfully lent me their expertise, especially Gerlinde Huber-Rebenich, Tonya Knudsen, Clarence H. Miller, John Monfasani, Richard J. Schoeck, Claudia Sode, Terence O. Tunberg, and Ulman Weiß. To Erika Rummel, who critiqued this edition and recommended its publication in the Renaissance Texts Series, I owe a special debt of gratitude. Over the years I have benefited from numerous grants-in-aid provided by the College of Humanities, the Center for Medieval and Renaissance Studies, and the Department of Germanic Languages and Literatures at The Ohio State University, Columbus. Thanks are likewise due to the libraries that so generously supplied me with photocopies and photographs. Anyone who knows the current scholarship in this field will be aware that all research on Eobanus Hessus builds on Carl Krause's nineteenth-century biography. For the history of the University of Erfurt we can rely on Erich Kleineidam's magisterial *Universitas studii Erffordensis*. I am deeply indebted to both.

Vera, Harmon, and Albert have been my *portus et aura*. They are beyond thanks.

The Life of Eobanus Hessus

Several years ago, just as I was settling in to write a brief life of Eobanus for this edition, my colleagues Jim Hardin and Max Reinhart asked me to produce precisely such an essay for a biographical volume they were planning. The article has since appeared under the heading "Eobanus Hessus (6 January 1488 – 4 October 1540)" in: *Dictionary of Literary Biography*, vol. 179, *German Writers of the Renaissance and Reformation, 1280-1580* (Detroit, 1997), pp. 97-110.[1] That reference work now being widely available, I have opted instead for a "Chronology of Eobanus's Life," immediately followed by an edition and translation of Joachim Camerarius's splendid biographical essay, first published in 1553.

The standard biography is Carl Krause's *Helius Eobanus Hessus, sein Leben und seine Werke: Ein Beitrag zur Cultur- und Gelehrtengeschichte des 16.*

---

[1] As the Greek inserts in this essay resurfaced in rather worse shape than when I had bade them farewell, I herewith offer the necessary balm. On p. 98, column 1, read "παράκλησις." On the same page, column 2, read "ἐκφώνησις." On p. 100, column 1, read "ἐσσήν." And on p. 105, column 2, read "ἐκφώνησις."

Jahrhunderts, 2 volumes (Gotha, 1879; repr. Nieuwkoop, 1963). Ingeborg Gräßer-Eberbach's recent booklet *Helius Eobanus Hessus: Der Poet des Erfurter Humanistenkreises* (Erfurt, 1993) is a lively, but not always reliable epitome of Krause's work.

Chronology of Eobanus's Life

1488	Born on 6 January in the village of Halgehausen, not far from Frankenberg in Hesse, as the son of Hans Koch and Katharina of Gemünden.
1495?-1501	Attends the monastery school at nearby Haina for a few years, then (until his 14th year) the Latin school of his kinsman Johann Mebessen in Gemünden.
1501-1504	Attends the Latin school of Jakob Horle in Frankenberg.
1504	In the autumn matriculates at the University of Erfurt.
1505	In mid-summer leaves Erfurt with a group of instructors and students in order to escape the plague; studies with them in Frankenberg until the following spring.
1506	Having returned to Erfurt by Easter, he writes *De recessu studentum* in the spring and *De pugna studentum* in August. Introduces himself to Mutianus Rufus in mid-August by sending him a manuscript of *De pugna*. Overjoyed by Mutianus's praise, he publishes both poems in September. Receives his B.A. in the early autumn of 1506. In October he celebrates the university in *De laudibus et praeconiis incliti gymnasii litteratorii apud Erphordiam*.
1507	Revises *De laudibus et praeconiis* and publishes it in the late summer. Appointed rector of the chapter school of St. Severi, he receives free board at the residence of Bishop Johann Bonemilch.
1508	Publishes *De amantium infoelicitate* in the late summer. Having by now lost his right to free board at the bishop's residence, he resigns as schoolmaster.
1509	Receives his M.A. in early February. Publishes his *Bucolicon* in Erfurt at the end of September and then goes to Leipzig. In ca. November signs on as chief secretary to Bishop Job von Dobeneck in Riesenburg, Prussia.
1512	In early February accompanies the bishop to Cracow to attend the nuptials of King Sigismund of Poland and Barbara Zápolya of Hungary. Publishes *Encomium nuptiale divo Sigismundo, regi Poloniae* on February 29. At Cracow writes *Victoria Christi ab inferis* in a poetic competition with Johannes Dantiscus. Turns

down an academic position at the University of Cracow, but continues to search for a teaching post elsewhere.

1513   In the spring matriculates at the University of Frankfurt an der Oder to study law; in the autumn takes up studies in Leipzig.

1514   Early in the year publishes *Sylvae duae* (in which he styles himself "Helius" for the first time); in the summer publishes *Heroidum Christianarum epistolae*. Returns to Erfurt in July and quickly establishes himself as "king" of the local humanists. Marries Katharina Später in late 1514 or early 1515.

1515   Publishes *Hymnus paschalis* and *De vera nobilitate*.

1516   Publishes *De vitanda ebrietate elegia* and *Maximilianus Augustus Italiae*.

1517   Publishes *Victoria Christi ab inferis*.

1518   Appointed professor at Erfurt on July 6,[2] he visits Erasmus in Louvain early in the autumn.

1519   Publishes *A profectione ad Des. Erasmum hodoeporicon*.

1520   Leads other Erfurt humanists in a satiric attack on Edward Lee, who had criticized Erasmus's work on the Greek New Testament: *In Eduardum Leeum epigrammata*. Also publishes *Praefaciuncula in Enchiridion Christiani militis*.

1521   After Luther's visit to Erfurt on April 6-8 he publishes *In evangelici Doctoris M. Lutheri laudem elegiae*.

1523   Increasingly at odds with the evangelical preachers in Erfurt, whom he blames for the collapse of humanistic studies at the university, he publishes *Ecclesiae afflictae epistola ad Lutherum* and *De non contemnendis studiis humanioribus aliquot clarorum virorum ad E. Hessum epistolae*. Begins to study medicine. In late 1523 or early 1524 publishes *In poetam Sarmatam invectiva*, directed at an anonymous Polish poet (Johannes Dantiscus).

1524   Publishes *Dialogi tres*, a defense of medicine and an attack on the obscurantist reformers in Erfurt; also publishes the dietetic poem *Bonae valetudinis conservandae praecepta*.

1526   Leaves Erfurt at the beginning of May to teach poetics at the Gymnasium of St. Aegidius in Nuremberg. Publishes *Elegiae tres* in support of the school; also an introduction to versification, *Scribendorum versuum maxime compendiosa ratio*.

1527   Publishes *Venus triumphans*, celebrating the wedding of Joachim Camerarius and Anna Truchseß on March 7; also publishes *In hypocrisin vestitus monastici* and *Psalmi IV*.

1528   Brings out a thoroughly revised version of his pastorals, with five new idylls, in *Bucolicorum idyllia*. Laments the turmoil in the

[2] For this date see Kleineidam, vol. 2, p. 227.

DE H. EOBANO HESSO NARRATIO

Ioachimi Camerarii Pabebergensis

THE STORY OF H. EOBANUS HESSUS

by Joachim Camerarius of Bamberg

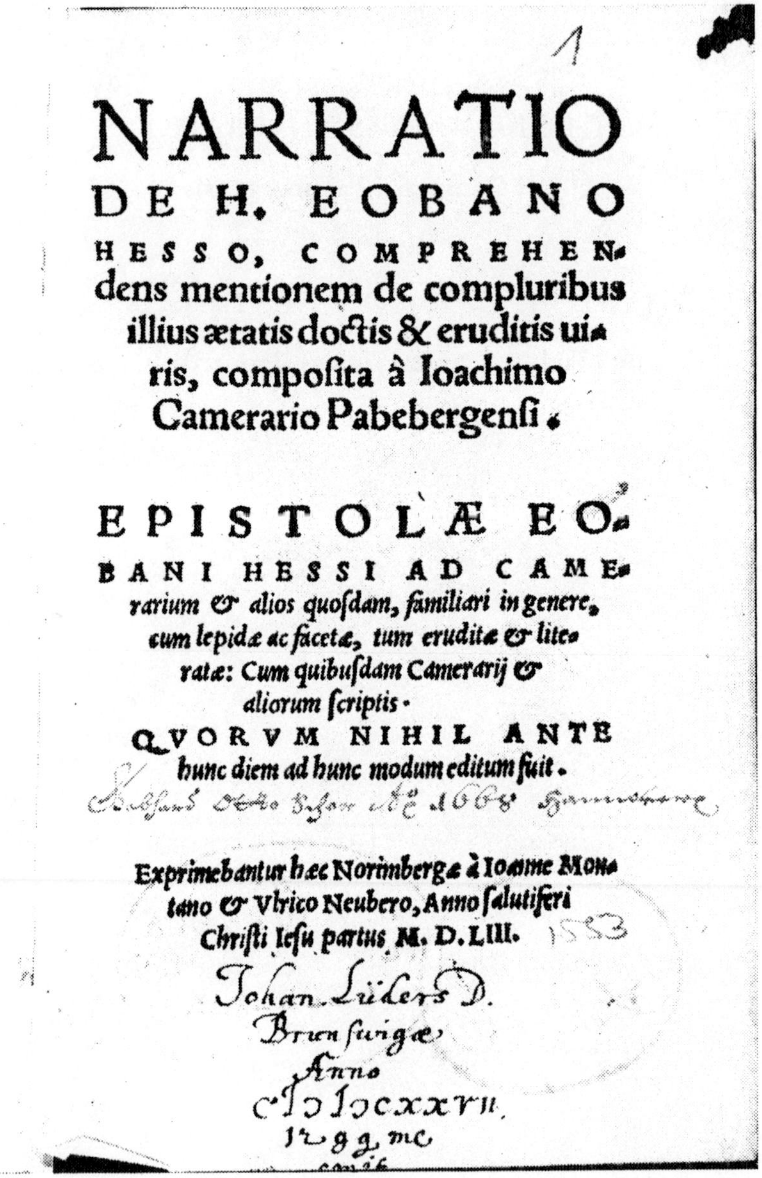

1

NARRATIO
DE H. EOBANO
HESSO, COMPREHEN-
dens mentionem de compluribus
illius ætatis doctis & eruditis ui-
ris, composita à Ioachimo
Camerario Pabebergensi.

EPISTOLÆ EO-
BANI HESSI AD CAME-
rarium & alios quosdam, familiari in genere,
cum lepidæ ac facetæ, tum eruditæ & lite-
ratæ: Cum quibusdam Camerarij &
aliorum scriptis.
QVORVM NIHIL ANTE
hunc diem ad hunc modum editum fuit.

[handwritten annotation]

Exprimebantur hæc Norinbergæ à Ioanne Mon-
tano & Vlrico Neubero, Anno salutiferi
Christi Iesu partus, M. D. LIII. *1553*

Johan. Lüders D.
Brunsuigæ
Anno
cↃ Ↄↄcxxvii.

Title page of Joachim Camerarius's *Narratio de H. Eobano Hesso*
Nuremberg: Johann vom Berg and Ulrich Neuber, 1553
Niedersächsische Staats- und Universitätsbibliothek, Göttingen

SIGNVM EOBA-
NICVM CVM ELO-
GIO IPSIVS.

Nubila scandentem Lauri de stipite cygnum,
Hesso stemma suum libera Musa dedit.

Eobanus Hessus's emblem as depicted in
Narratio de H. Eobano Hesso Ioachimi Camerarii (Nuremberg, 1553), sig. A1ᵛ
Niedersächsische Staats- und Universitätsbibliothek, Göttingen

DE H. EOBANO HESSO NARRATIO
IOACHIMI CAMERARII

Introduction

The following sketch of Eobanus's life was composed by one of his closest friends and greatest admirers, Joachim Camerarius – himself a humanist of the first rank. Camerarius wrote it to introduce a large collection of Eobanus's correspondence that he had retrieved from his own papers or obtained from mutual friends.[1] First published in 1553, the biography was adapted and partially reprinted in Melchior Adam's "Helius Eobanus Hessus," in his: *Vitae Germanorum philosophorum qui seculo superiori ... floruerunt* (Heidelberg, 1615), pp. 105-118. Thereafter it was edited, if somewhat carelessly and freely, by Johann Benedict Carpzov in: *Narratio de Helio Eobano Hesso, comprehendens mentionem de compluribus illius aetatis doctis et eruditis viris, composita a Ioachimo Camerario Pabepergense* (Leipzig, 1696). Johann Theophil Kreyssig produced a more accurate edition in the mid-nineteenth century, with many philological notes that I have found useful. See: *Ioachimi Camerarii narratio de Helio Eobano Hesso. Accesserunt Christ. Theoph. Kuinoelii oratio de Helii Eobani Hessi in bonas literas meritis et Helii Eobani Hessi carmina: De pugna studentum Erphordiensium cum quibusdam coniuratis nebulonibus et in bonarum artium detractorem* (Meissen, 1843). The latest edition is Georg Burkard and Wilhelm Kühlmann's *Joachim Camerarius,*

---

[1] Camerarius began working on the *Narratio* in 1544 (see note at *Nar.* 5, 1) and completed a first draft by 18 January 1551, for he mentions the work in the letter to Peter von Suaven that prefaces the letter collection itself. (The letter itself bears no indication of year; but cannot be later than 1551, the year Peter von Suaven died.) See Eob. *Epp. 1*, sig. D6ʳ. The composition date is confirmed in Johann Stigel's letter of 19 September 1551, in which he warmly thanks Camerarius for sending him the "scriptum de Eobano" and compliments him not only on his delightful portrait of Eobanus and his times but also on his pure and elegant style. See *Epp. 1*, sig. b5ʳ-b6ʳ. Camerarius must have continued to revise and update the biography later on, for in *Nar.* 2, 2 he reminds Adam Krafft that it has been 34 years since they first met in Erfurt (in the spring of 1518); and in *Nar.* 24, 17 he alludes to the destruction that Nuremberg suffered in May and June of 1552. The book itself seems to have been published in late 1553. At any rate, the dedicatee Adam Krafft thanks Camerarius for it in a letter of 10 February [1554]. See *Epp. 4*, sig. M7ᵛ-M8ʳ.

Narratio de Helio Eobano Hesso .... *Das Leben des Dichters Helius Eobanus Hessus* .... *Lateinisch und deutsch*, Bibliotheca Neolatina 10, trans. Georg Burkard (Heidelberg, 2003). Essentially a reprint of Carpzov's text, the book adds an informative introduction, a thorough translation (the first in any language), and concise annotations. I am grateful to Wilhelm Kühlmann for kindly sending it to me when the present volume was already in proof, and happily acknowledge that it inspired several last-minute improvements and corrections.

Joachim Camerarius (Kammermeister) of Bamberg (1500-1574) matriculated at Leipzig in 1512, where he studied with Georg Helt. After obtaining his B.A. in 1514, he learned Greek from Richard Croke and Petrus Mosellanus. In 1518 he enrolled at Erfurt. Introduced to Eobanus by Adam Krafft, Camerarius quickly established himself as a leading member of Eobanus's circle. His M.A. in hand, he left Erfurt in 1521 to continue his studies at Wittenberg with Philip Melanchthon. At the latter's recommendation Camerarius was appointed rector of the newly founded Gymnasium of St. Aegidius at Nuremberg in 1526. Eobanus joined him on the faculty that same year. The two were inseparable until 1533, when Eobanus returned to Erfurt. Two years later Camerarius himself left Nuremberg to accept a position as professor of classics at Tübingen. In 1541 Duke Ulrich of Württemberg invited him to reorganize the University of Leipzig. There he remained until the end of his life, repeatedly serving as the university's rector and dean of arts. In addition to numerous annotated editions and translations of ancient Greek and Latin authors, Camerarius produced works on grammar and style, exegetical and theological books, monographs on contemporary history, as well as biographical essays – the most famous being the ones on Eobanus Hessus (1553) and Philip Melanchthon (1566). Two large collections of his correspondence were published posthumously in 1583 and 1595.

Camerarius's biography of Eobanus Hessus is addressed to Adam Krafft of Fulda (1493-1558), who matriculated at Erfurt in 1512. While working toward his B.A. (1514) and M.A. (1519), Krafft became good friends with Mutianus Rufus, Euricius Cordus, Eobanus Hessus, and Camerarius. He got to know Luther and Melanchthon at the Leipzig Disputation in 1519. During the next two years Krafft was a spirited advocate of reformation in Erfurt. Thereafter he served as vicar and preacher at Fulda, in 1525 also at Hersfeld. That same year Philip of Hesse named him court preacher and visitor. Appointed professor of theology at the University of Marburg in 1527, he became its rector in 1529, 1540, and 1553. His dominant role in the Hessian Church eventually earned him the sobriquet "the Reformer of Hesse."

For a study of Camerarius's biographical writings see Friedrich Stählin, *Humanismus und Reformation im bürgerlichen Raum: Eine Untersuchung der biographischen Schriften des Joachim Camerarius,* Schriften des Vereins für Reformationsgeschichte 53, part 1 (Leipzig, 1936). See further: Frank Baron, ed., *Joachim Camerarius (1500-1574): Beiträge zur Geschichte des Humanismus im Zeitalter der Reformation / Essays on the History of Humanism during the Reformation* (Munich, 1978), with a full list of Camerarius's publications; and Stephan Kunkler, *Zwischen Humanismus und Reformation: Der Humanist Joachim Camerarius (1500-1574) im Wechselspiel von pädagogischem Pathos und theologischem Ethos,* Theologische Texte und Studien 8 (Hildesheim, 2000).

Another contemporary life of Eobanus Hessus, entitled "Von des erleuchten vnd hoch begabten Poeten Helij Eobani hessi leben vnd absterben," was composed by the Hessian historiographer Wigand Lauze. This biography is contained in Lauze's enormous *Hessische Chronik,* part two: *Leben und Thaten des Durchleuchtigsten Fursten und Herren Philippi Magnanimi, Landgraffen zu Hessen,* book 2, chapter 8. Written around 1560, Lauze's account of Eobanus's life was first published in *Zeitschrift des Vereins für hessische Geschichte und Landeskunde: Zweites Supplement* (Kassel, 1841), pp. 426-441. Since it is virtually everywhere dependent on Camerarius's *Narratio,* I see no point in reprinting it here.

In the following edition of the *Narratio* the section numbers are the ones introduced by Carpzov and retained by Kreyssig. The sentence and line numbers are my own; so is the numbering of the concluding epitaphs. The phrase "Sit igitur hic istorum finis," which Carpzov and Kreyssig print at the end of section 1, is now placed at the start of section 2.

Camerarius' biographical essay appeared once during his lifetime:

A

NARRATIO | DE H. EOBANO | HESSO, COMPREHEN= | dens mentionem de compluribus | illius ætatis doctis & eruditis vi= | ris, composita à Ioachimo | Camerario Pabebergenſi. | EPISTOLÆ EO= | BANI HESSI AD CAME= | *rarium & alios quoſdam, familiari in genere,* | *cum lepidæ ac facetæ, tum eruditæ & lite=* | *ratæ: Cum quibuſdam Camerarij &* | *aliorum ſcriptis.* | QVORVM NIHIL ANTE | *hunc diem ad hunc modum editum fuit.* | *Exprimebantur hæc Norimbergæ à Ioanne Mon=* | *tano & Vlrico Neubero, Anno ſalutiferi* | *Chriſti Ieſu partus* M.D.LIII.

Collation: 8°: A-Z⁸, a-b⁸, [\$5 (– E3) signed, H5 missigned G5], 200 leaves

Contents: A1ʳ title page; A1ᵛ *Signum Eobanicum cum elogio ipsius,* with a woodcut and the elegiac distich: "Nubila scandentem lauri de stipite cygnum, / Hesso stemma suum libera Musa dedit"; A2ʳ-D5ᵛ *De H. Eobano Hesso narratio*; D6ʳ-D8ʳ Camerarius's preface to the correspondence, addressed to Peter von Suaven and dated 18 January [1551]; D8ᵛ-T3ᵛ *Epistolae diversis temporibus ac locis ad Ioachimum Camerarium, familiariter ab Eobano Hesso perscriptae*; T4ʳ-b7ᵗ *Epistolae Ioachimi Camerarii*; b7ᵛ-b8ʳ list of errata; b8ᵛ blank

Catchwords: Used on versos and rectos

Running titles: A2ᵛ-D5ʳ: NARRATIO DE EOBANO HESSO; D6ᵛ-D8ʳ: PRAEFATIO IN EPIST. EOBANI HESSI; E1ʳ-T3ʳ: EPISTOLAE EOBANI HESSI; T5ᵛ-b7ʳ: EPISTOLAE IOACH. CAMERARII

Copy-text: Göttingen, Niedersächsische Staats- und Universitätsbibliothek
Call number: Hist. lit. biogr. IV, 1245

I have checked this copy against the one in the Universitäts- und Landesbibliothek Münster (call number: X 1938). There are further copies in: Amberg, Staatliche Provinzialbibliothek; Augsburg, Staats- und StadtB; Bamberg, SB; Basel, UB; Berlin, SB; Cambridge (Mass.), Harvard University Library; Cambridge (U.K.), University Library; Chicago, University of Chicago Library; Rochester, N.Y., Colgate Rochester Divinity School; Dresden, Sächsische Landesbibliothek; Erfurt, Wissenschaftliche Allgemeinbibliothek; Freiburg/Breisgau, UB; Göttingen, SUB (a second copy); Greifswald, UB; Halle, UB; Heidelberg, UB; Jena, UB; Leipzig, UB; London, BL; Lüneburg, Ratsbücherei; Mannheim, StadtB; Marburg, UB; Munich, SB; Münster, UB; New Haven, Yale University Library; Nuremberg, Germanisches Nationalmuseum; Nuremberg, StadtB; Oldenburg, Landesbibliothek; Oxford (U.K.), Oxford University Library; Salzburg, UB; Strasbourg, BNU; Trier, StadtB; Tübingen, UB; Ulm, StadtB; Vienna, ÖNB; Wittenberg, Lutherhalle; Wolfenbüttel, Herzog-August-Bibliothek; Wrocław, Biblioteka Uniwersytecka; and Wuppertal, StadtB.

DE H. EOBANO HESSO NARRATIO
Ioachimi Camerarii Pabebergensis
Ad clarissimum virum Adamum Cratonem Fuldensem, amicum summum

1, 1 Recordanti mihi, Adame, studia iuventutis nostrae, quae nos singulari usu coniunctos tenuerunt, multae suaves cogitationes excitantur animo meo, in quibus tristissimis rebus et durissimis his temporibus interdum soleo acquiescere. **2** Ut autem qui in febre frigidam biberunt, se nonnihil in praesentia sublevari sentiunt, mox vero gravius affliguntur, ita mihi quoque saepenumero usu venit ut iucunditatem illam maiores molestiae excipiant, non modo cum hanc aetatem et superiorem nostram confero et egre fero tantam contentionem tam celeriter repressam et ardorem istum extinctum esse, sed cum, ut necesse est, de iis quae "ante oculos interque manus sunt," ut poeta ait, coniecturam facio quae deinceps consecutura esse videantur. **3** Atque sunt priora illa quidem eiusmodi ut morsus habeant sane acerbos, hoc vero posterius non solum maximos dolores, sed ingentem etiam metum commovet, de quo quidem neque pos- | sum in acerrima aegritudine neque in tanta hominum improbitate plura scribere debeo.

A2ᵛ

    4 De altero si tecum disputem, et offensione ad plaerosque hoc cariturum esse spero, et ita aberraverit aliquantulum mens a curis et anxietatibus quibuscum conflictatur quoties vel in praesentis miseriae quasi tempestatem intuetur vel futurae calamitatis naufragia prospicit. **5** Quae quidem sola via est declinandi impetum perturbationis, cui si veluti directa fronte et, ut Graeci aiunt, ἀντιπρόσωπος occurrere velis, celeriter perculsus et eversus prosternaris. **6** Iam de studiis nostris disserere, ut nobis dulce, ita ad alios neutiquam invidiosum esse potest. **7** Quis enim illa vel colit vel admiratur vel iam omnino respicit atque curat? **8** Nugae hae esse ducuntur et in vita communi ἀθύρματα tanquam lusuum puerilium. **9** Habent enim iam homines quod expetiverunt, summam statuendi et agendi licentiam. **10** Nihil tam absurdum est quin animus concipere et lingua proferre, nihil tam audax quin aggredi cupiditas et manus conari ausint. **11** "Non ratio, non modus, non lex, non mos, non officium valet, non iudicium, non existimatio civium, non posteritatis verecundia," ut ait Cicero. **12** Aperuerunt autem studia nostra iter eruditae

---

Tit. clarissimum virum *Carpzov et Kreyssig*: CL. V. *A.*   **1, 4** quibuscum *Kreyssig*: quibus cum *A.*

THE STORY OF H. EOBANUS HESSUS
by Joachim Camerarius of Bamberg
To that most distinguished gentleman Adam Krafft of Fulda,
his dearest friend

1 Whenever I think back, Adam, on the endeavors of our youth that bound us together in uncommon friendship, my heart is stirred to many sweet thoughts, in which I like to find solace now and then from the utter bleakness of these calamitous times.[1] But just as people who in a fever drink something cold and feel much relieved for the moment, only to find themselves worse off soon after, so it frequently happens in my case too that those charming memories are supplanted by the far greater troubles of the here and now – not just when I compare the present with the bygone years of our youth and am sickened at the thought that all that vigorous rivalry has been checked so swiftly and all that ardor extinguished, but also when I worry, as I must, how the things that are "before our eyes and at our fingertips," as the poet says, are going to turn out in the age to come. And while the former reflections are truly such as engender bitter pangs, the latter not only inflict the deepest distress, but also excite enormous fear, about which indeed I am neither able nor obliged to write anything further, given the grievousness of my heartache and the outrageous shamelessness of our contemporaries.

If I discuss a different topic with you, I hope that will not give offense to most readers. Such a discussion would help divert my thoughts a little from the cares and anxieties with which it is tormented whenever it contemplates the storm of our present-day misery, so to speak, or anticipates the shipwreck of impending disaster. In truth, this is the only way to steer clear of that violent rush of emotion, which, if you wanted to confront it head-on and, as the Greeks say, *face to face,* would quickly overwhelm you and knock you sprawling to the ground. Besides, talking about our endeavors, while a pleasure to us, can in no way be odious to others. For who still cultivates or admires or even pays the slightest attention and respect to things like that? In everyday life they are considered mere trifles, the *playthings,* as it were, of children's games. After all, people now possess what they have always craved: the unbridled freedom to think and do as they please. Nothing is so absurd but there is a mind to embrace it and a tongue to give it voice; nothing is so audacious but there is a passion that dares undertake it and a hand to risk the attempt. "Reason, moderation, law, tradition, duty count for nothing – likewise the judgment and views of the citizen body and respect for the opinion of those who come after us," as Cicero remarks. Our studies, on the other hand, have opened up the

---

[1]In the early 1550's the strongly Lutheran Camerarius had good reason to be depressed and anxious about the turmoil in Germany. The Schmalkald War of 1546/47 had ended in the destruction of the Schmalkald League by the imperial forces. Several Protestant leaders, among them Philip of Hesse, were still being held in prison.

et liberalis vitae, errorum quasi vepribus excisis et bonis artibus atque literis consuetudine humana perculta. **13** In hos tanquam amoenissimos hortos temeritas et petulantia vastatrix subito irruit, et sunt Musarum, | secundum poetam, floribus Austri sane procellosi et liquidis immissi fontibus apri. **14** Sed nescio quo pacto, etiam dum fugit tristia animus, nihilominus ad horum conspectum refertur.

2, 1 Sit igitur hic istorum finis, ac aspiciamus iam ad illa in quibus et laeticiae aliquid et quietis me reperire dixi, id quod et te facere mihi persuadeo, ut libenter memineris tam assiduitatis atque diligentiae discipulorum quam magistrorum attentionis atque sedulitatis quam nos sumus experti et cuius participes quoque fuimus, vel potius, quo tempore ac loco nos etiam aliquam laudemque decusque gessimus. **2** Sunt enim anni ferme XXXIIII cum ego me Erphordiam contuli ibique te florentem aetate et ingenio et fama eruditionis atque doctrinae reperi; quasique natura alter alteri conciliaretur, ita factum tum est ut celeriter inter ignotos prius incredibilis animorum benevolentia existeret nosque in studiorum similitudine amicitia coniungeremur et ex usu mutuae familiaritatis uterque aliquid fructus perciperet. **3** Colebamus eas literas sine quibus persuasum nobis erat nullam doctrinam sapientiae professionem suam tueri posse et autores Graecae et Latinae linguae legere studebamus. **4** In qua parte ego, quanquam admodum adolescens, tamen ferebar in oculis quia audiveram Ricardum Crocum Britannum, qui primus putabatur ita docuisse Graecam linguam in Germania ut plane perdisci illam posse et quid momenti ad omnem doctrinae eruditionem atque cultum | huius cognitio allatura esse videretur nostri homines sese intelligere arbitrarentur. **5** Nos quidem certe ita statuebamus hanc esse viam virtutis atque sapientiae et iter directum cum pietatis et religionis tum humanitatis et laudis in hac vita et in terris, verene an falso non exquiram in praesentia. **6** Nos scilicet ita censebamus, neque spem quae concipiebatur de his rationibus quantivis tum vaenire passi fuissemus. **7** Fuerit hoc erratum, mihi tamen profecto etiam opinio illa iucunda est, neque possum vel hodierno die

A3ʳ

A3ᵛ

[2]In 1518.

[3]Richard Croke of London (ca. 1489-1558) studied at Cambridge (1506-1510) and Paris (1511-1512). Thereafter he taught Greek at Louvain and Cologne. After matriculating at Leipzig in 1515, he was asked to teach Greek there too. In 1516 he published *Tabulae*

path to a life of learning and decency, in which, figuratively speaking, the bri-
ars of delusion are cleared away and human intercourse is adorned with
education and culture. Into these incomparably beautiful gardens, so to
speak, effrontery and destructive impudence have irrupted without warning;
and to paraphrase the poet, the all too tempestuous south winds have been let
loose on the Muses' blossoms, and the wild boars on the crystal springs. But
somehow, even as my mind flies from melancholy thoughts, it returns to
dwell on them all the same.

2 Let us stop this brooding right now, therefore, and dwell rather on
those things in which, as I mentioned, I find a measure of joy and solace – as
indeed I am sure you do too, seeing how gladly you recall not only the stu-
dents' assiduity and diligence, but also the teachers' attentiveness and zeal
that we experienced and in which we too had a share, or more exactly, that
time and place where we ourselves enjoyed some fame and respect. As you
know, it has been some thirty-four years since I first went to Erfurt[2] and there
got to know you in the flower of life, a man endowed with brilliant intellect
and renowned for your scholarship and learning. And as each of us, if I may
say so, was instinctively drawn to the other, so it happened that the two of us,
formerly strangers, swiftly experienced an amazing meeting of minds and
found ourselves joined in friendship through the similarity of our intellectual
pursuits and garnered abundant fruit from associating with each other. We
devoted ourselves to those works of literature without which (or so we were
convinced) no discipline could live up to its promise of wisdom and strove to
read the writers of the Greek and Latin language. In this respect, though still
very much a youth, I was nevertheless looked up to because I had studied with
the Englishman Richard Croke, who was believed to have been the first to
teach Greek in Germany in such a way that our countrymen thought they un-
derstood how fully learnable that language was and what important benefits a
mastery of it appeared to bring to all scholarly learning and culture.[3] We for
our part certainly regarded it in that light, namely as the path of virtue and
wisdom and as the highroad not only of piety and religion, but also of re-
finement and esteem in our lifetime on earth – whether rightly or wrongly, I
shall not examine at this point. We, at least, had no doubts on that score and
were prepared at the time to pay any price to fulfill the hope that these reasons
inspired in us. If we deluded ourselves, that belief is nonetheless even now a
source of delight for me, and to this very day I cannot bring myself to think

---

Graecas literas impendio discere cupientibus sane quam necessariae as well as a translation of book
4 of Theodorus Gaza's Greek grammar. He returned to England in 1517, receiving his M.A.
and becoming reader in Greek at Cambridge in 1518. In 1524 he obtained the degree of doc-
tor of divinity from Cambridge, in 1532 also from Oxford.

animum inducere ut aliter sentiam. 8 "Τò δὲ δοκοῦν καὶ τὴν ἀλήθειαν βιάζεσθαι," aiunt. 9 Et fuerit profecto hic error, si error sit, neque turpior neque nocentior quam est multiplex et varius error inter homines, ut non debeat nos huius nimium pudere, si quis illum exprobret et impedimento fuisse perhibeat, quo minus opes, dignitatem, honores consequeremur.

3, 1 Cum autem illius sanctissimae et optimae vitae consuetudinem animo meo repeto, inprimis ante oculos est Eobanus Hessus, ad quem tu quidem me primum adduxisti. 2 Sed ille tam cupide me complexus fuit ut neque dulcius neque constantius fieri quicquam potuerit. 3 Nam et favebat ardori quo flagrare cernebat animum meum studiorum bonorum et diligebat pene puerilem simplicitatem audaciae in iis profitendis quae tenere me crederem et probabat interdum iudicium mediocris considerationis de iis quae forte disserebantur, | etiam firmitatem animi in simultatibus negligendis et contemnendis obtrectationibus. 4 Meminisse enim te arbitror, quorum invidia me tum impetiverit, cum tu me acerrime defenderes et innocentiam meam tuereris. 5 Erant autem aemulationes illae neque capitales neque omnino culpandae. 6 Alius alio videri doctior volebat. 7 Dum igitur se praeferri studet caeteris, fieri non poterat quin minus commode interdum de iis loqueretur, quorum existimatione suam famam premi suspicabatur. 8 "Ἀγαθὴ δ' ἔρις ἥδε βροτοῖσι," secundum Hesiodum. 9 Absit modo acerbitas contumeliae et odii crudelitas. 10 Sed haec oblivioni, quasi ventis dissipanda, praebeantur.

11 Cum autem annis ferme quinque, postea quam ego Erphordiam reliqui, prospera fortuna me denuo cum Eobano coniunxisset et augescentibus annis in mea vita aliquid mutationis accidisset et mihi nonnihil tristitiae oblatum fuisset, ita sum hoc amico usus ut et consiliis et consolatione ab eo saepenumero adiuvarer. 12 Sed praecipua erat suavitas et oblectatio in studiorum communium cultura, cum uterque alteri aliquid a se in hoc opere semper conferret. 13 Nam ego nunquam dissimulavi quantopere mihi profuerit Eobani familiaritas, et ipse, quo erat candore, non dubitabat interdum praedicare quid commoditatis perciperet de mea.

A4ʳ

2, 9 exprobret A (in erratis): exprobet A (in textu).

---

[4]Camerarius left Erfurt in the summer of 1521. After spending several years in Wittenberg he was reunited with Eobanus in Nuremberg in 1526.

otherwise. "*But it is outward seeming that overpowers the truth,*" they say. Yet even if we were manifestly wrong, even if we are deceiving ourselves, our self-deception is no more shameful or harmful than the other multifarious and motley delusions among men, so that we need not be overly ashamed of ourselves, should someone wish to castigate our error and assert that it hindered us in acquiring riches, status, honors.

3 Now when I conjure up the fellowship we enjoyed in that purest and best kind of life, the person that comes to mind above all is Eobanus Hessus, to whom you, in fact, were the first to introduce me. But then he welcomed me so eagerly into his friendship that I could not possibly have experienced anything quite so charming or steadfast. For he not only valued the ardor for liberal studies that he saw blazing in my heart, but also loved the almost childlike simplicity with which I ventured to teach those subjects that I believed I had mastered. Indeed, every so often he would praise my naive opinion of the questions then being debated, also my firm resolve to stay out of feuds and to pay no heed to disparaging remarks. For I imagine you remember the scholars whose jealousy assailed me in those days, when you defended me with uttermost vigor and stood up for my innocence. Those rivalries, to be sure, were neither dead serious nor altogether reprehensible. Each man wanted to appear more learned than the other. And so, as everyone strove to be exalted above the rest, it was only natural that people would sometimes speak less favorably about those whose reputation they suspected was putting their own in the shade. "*This strife is beneficial for mortal men,*" according to Hesiod. Only let harsh contumely and cruel hatred be absent. But matters like this should be consigned to oblivion, to be scattered, so to speak, by the winds.

About five years after I left Erfurt, however, it was my good fortune to be reunited with Eobanus[4]; and as the advancing years had brought considerable changes in my life and inflicted no small sorrow on me, he and I became such close friends that I would ofttimes turn to him for advice and consolation.[5] But the main thing was the charm and delight we each felt in cultivating our common endeavors, for in this collaboration one of us was always contributing something of himself to the other. Indeed I for one have never concealed how much Eobanus's friendship profited me personally; and he himself, such being his kindness, did not hesitate to acknowledge publicly from time to time what benefit he received from mine.

---

[5]In February 1527 Camerarius's older brother Hieronymus (1490-1545), counselor and secretary to the bishop of Bamberg, was imprisoned on suspicion of Lutheran heresy. Later that year his 81-year-old father died. As the extant correspondence confirms, Eobanus did his best to console his friend during those trying times.

A4ᵛ

4, 1 Cum autem vidissem ante annos aliquot epistolas huius scriptas ad diversos editasque magis studiose quam prudenter, vel ne studiose quidem satis, nam exem- | pla incorrecta et mendosa divulgata sunt (et te non fugit qualis Eobanus scriptor fuerit, qui non modo quicquid in buccam venisset, ut dicitur, efferre et τὸ ἐπιὸν cartis committere, sed saepe admodum in festinatione negligenter exarare literas soleret): huius igitur epistolarum librum cum vidissem, ut non probabam talem editionem, ita factum illa occasione fuit ut respicerem ad cartas meas, inter quas scirem Eobani epistolas ad me iacere. **2** Invenique tunc plures quam omnino putaram, et inter relegendum mirifice fui recordatione illorum temporum et consuetudinis nostrae delectatus. **3** Fuit enim tum mos profecto optimus et humanissimus et huic, quo nunc vivitur, dissimillimus, candor eximius in tribuendo cuique quod illi deberetur, summa reverentia eorum qui virtute et doctrina praestare crederentur, mira facilitas ad reconciliationem gratiae, si quid forte simultatum incidisset, in consuetudinis et familiaritatis usu nihil fucatum aut exulceratum, discendi quod ignoraretur inflammati studio animi et nullus in confitendo pudor, nullum persequendi occasiones toedium neque fastidium audiendi, inprimis autem parata bene meritis grati animi memoria.

A5ʳ

4 Sed ut ad rem redeam: Coeperam iam consilium et has epistolas adhuc delitescentes apud me edendi, de quo statim ad te perscripsi, verum ea tempora inciderunt quae non hoc modo turbarent, sed alias multas | praeclaras res pessundarent. **5** Veni tum forte ad nostrum Sturciadem Erphordiam, qui et ipse de editione epistolarum Eobani nonnihil conquerebatur et cum expressarum tum alia autographa scripta Eobani mihi dedit. **6** Sumsi tum et a Groningo nostro complura. **7** Quae quominus hactenus, ut volueram, in lucem prodierint, multa impedimenta fuerunt.

---

[6] Camerarius alludes to Johann Drach's edition of Eobanus's correspondence in *Helii Eobani Hessi, poetae excellentiss., et amicorum ipsius epistolarum familiarium libri XII* (Marburg, 1543). From comparison with other sources we know that Drach was not always faithful to Eobanus's text, leaving out materials that put his friend and others in a bad light and rewriting Eobanus's sentences to suit his own style. What offended Camerarius, however, is that Drach did not carry the principle of revision far enough, being too often content to leave the letters just as he found them, "uncorrected and riddled with errors." For Drach's life see fn. 55 below, at *Nar.* 16.

[7] Eobanus's dear friend and patron Georg Sturtz of Annaberg (1490-1548) matriculated at Erfurt in 1505. He earned his B.A. in 1506, together with Eobanus. After his return to Annaberg he served several years as mayor and then traveled to Italy. In 1519 he resumed his studies in Erfurt. Receiving the M.A. in 1521, he ranked first in a class of eighteen (including

4 Now several years ago, when I saw that a collection of his letters to various people had been published with more diligence than discreteness, or rather, not even with the necessary diligence, for the transcripts were published uncorrected and riddled with errors[6] (and you know full well what kind of writer Eobanus was, one who was not only in the habit of writing down everything that popped into his head, as they say, and committing to paper *whatever occurred to him,* but one who often penned his letters very carelessly whenever he was in a hurry): well then, when I saw a book of letters by him that had been published in a manner I did not approve of, I took the opportunity to go back to my own papers, among which, I knew, lay the letters that Eobanus had sent me. Hereupon I discovered more of them than I had ever expected; and as I reread them, I was wonderfully pleased to think back on those times and the camaraderie we enjoyed. For that was the tradition back then, the best and most civilized I know of, a way of life diametrically opposed to the one you see nowadays: exceptional frankness in giving everybody the credit due to him, the highest respect for those who were believed to excel in virtue and learning, a remarkable willingness to make up graciously if perchance a quarrel had broken out, nothing glossed over or left to fester in the intercourse and dealings between good friends, no stigma attached to enthusiastically studying what one did not know and no shame to admitting one's ignorance, no weariness in searching out opportunities to learn, no aversion to listening, but above all a ready sense of gratitude for kindnesses shown.

But to get back to the matter at hand: I had already decided to publish those letters too that were still lying hid in my files and in fact immediately wrote you at length about this project; but then came those bad years that not only upset my plan, but also ruined a great many other splendid undertakings. Then one day I happened to be visiting our good friend Sturtz in Erfurt, who was grumbling quite a bit himself about the way Eobanus's correspondence had been brought out and then proceeded to give me more autographs of Eobanus's, some of them already published, others entirely new.[7] At that time I also received a fair number from our acquaintance Gröningen.[8] Despite my good intentions, many obstacles prevented their being published until now.

Camerarius). Later that year he took a second trip to Italy, this time with Euricius Cordus. In the summer semester of 1523 he was rector of the University of Erfurt. The following semester he matriculated at Wittenberg, where he earned his doctorate in medicine in December 1523. Admitted to the medical faculty at Erfurt, he was elected dean on 27 September 1524, a post he was to occupy frequently until his death in 1548.

[8]Johann Algesheim of Gröningen (d. 1553) matriculated at Erfurt in 1512, taking his B.A. in 1514, his M.A. in 1517. Later he earned a bachelor's degree in theology and became a canon at St. Mary's in Erfurt. In 1535 he was elected rector of the university. Thereafter he repeatedly served as dean of the philosophical faculty. A lifelong Catholic, he remained close friends with the Protestant Eobanus.

8 Etsi autem rursum is horror tempestatis se ostendit, ut quid omnino de studiis bonarum artium futurum sit valde metuendum esse videatur, tamen cum nuper incidissem et in hanc congeriem epistolarum Eobani et ea quae tu de hoc composita ad me miseras, cupido me cepit et conscribendi de illo quae comperissem et mihi nota essent et emittendi in publicum epistolas Eobanicas nondum editas, cum ad me tum alios ab illo vere familiariter scriptas, sperabamque hoc opus, si absolveretur, et voluptatem legentibus allaturum et non expers etiam utilitatis futurum esse. **9** Multa enim inerunt et liberalibus iocis quasi condita et utilibus disputationibus de bonis literis aucta et gravibus etiam sententiis referta. **10** Tibi certe scio, ut mihi descriptio et elaboratio fuit iucundissima, ita lectionem gratam et hanc operam studii mei acceptam fore.

5, 1 Scripturus autem de Eobano nostro, ordiar de tuis indicationibus, ut narratio ordine quodam procedat. **2** Fuit igitur, ut significatur cum tuis tum aliorum quorum opera in his perquirendis usus fuisti literis, | Eobani patria ea pars Cattorum quae spectat veteres Angrivarios ad Visurgin, in finibus ditionis Hessiacae. **3** Parentibus natus est non illis quidem opulentis, sed honestis et integritatis ac pudoris laude inter omnes conspicuis. **4** Mater civis fuit oppidi Gemundini; pater in montibus quibus territorium Hessiacum concluditur operam suam dedit conventui Heinensi, qui religione iampridem neglecta et disciplina corrupta dissipatus nunc est, et mutata res ut illo loco pauperes aliquot alantur.

A5^v

5 Quo loco vim quandam admirabilem naturae considerandam esse puto, quae in temporum, locorum, hominum, eventuum maxima dissimilitudine similitudinem tamen semper aliquam exprimit, ut in varietate maxima congruentia summa animadvertatur a diligentibus et attentis. **6** Nam cum Eobanus eam nostra aetate et his rebus praestantiam attigerit quam olim rebus aliis Homerus quasi divinam et suspiciendam omnibus absolvisset, fuerunt inter hos similia permulta. **7** Quemadmodum enim Herodotus tradit in ripa fluminis Meletis partu editum fuisse Homerum, ita sub arbore in gramine mater recubans Eobanum enisa fuit. **8** Et ut patria Homeri ignoratur,

---

[9]Eobanus's mother Katharina was born in Gemünden, a small town on the Wohra River. His father Hans, according to Wigand Lauze (p. 428), was from the nearby county of Wittgenstein.

[10]Originally a Benedictine monastery, the abbey of Haina was turned over to the Cistercians in the twelfth century. At the direction of Landgrave Philip, who had criticized the monks for neglecting the divine service and indulging in lavish banquets, it was dissolved in

But even though the horror of this calamitous age is once again rearing its head, so that the very future of education in the liberal arts seems gravely imperiled, nevertheless, when I recently ran across both this pile of Eobanus's letters and the materials about his life that you had sent me, I felt an overwhelming desire, first, to write an account of what I had found out and personally knew about him, and second, to publish the hitherto unedited letters that Eobanus had written in truly familiar style to me as well as to others, in the hope that this work, if brought to completion, might give pleasure to the readers and at the same time not be without profit either. For there will be many pieces in this collection that are, as it were, seasoned with honorable wit and enriched with useful discussions of good literature and crammed full of wise sayings to boot. Just as I took the greatest delight in the telling and elaboration [of his life story], so I am sure you will enjoy the perusal and will take this labor of love to your heart.

5 Now that I am set to write about our dear Eobanus, I shall take my starting point from the indications you provided, so that the narrative may proceed in some semblance of order. Well then, as comes out both in your letters and in those of others who helped you research this question, Eobanus's homeland was that part of western Germany along the Weser River where the Angrivarii lived in ancient times, in the territories subject to Hesse. He was born to parents who, while certainly not wealthy, were altogether respectable and had a reputation in their community as upright and decent people.[9] His mother was a native of the town of Gemünden. His father, raised in the hills that border on the territory of Hesse, worked for the abbey of Haina, which, owing to long-standing neglect of religion and lax moral standards, has since been dissolved and turned into a poorhouse.[10]

At this point, I think, we should take a moment to reflect on a certain remarkable power of nature, which, for all the dissimilarity in times, places, people, and events, always brings some similarity to the fore, such that diligent and attentive observers can discern the most striking congruity even in the greatest diversity. Indeed, considering that Eobanus in our own day and age rose to that almost divine and universally admired preeminence that Homer achieved long ago under different circumstances, the two of them had very much in common. For example, while Herodotus tells us that Homer was born on the bank of the Meles River, so Eobanus's mother bore her son beneath a tree, as she reclined in the grass.[11] And just as Homer's birthplace is unknown, so too it is impossible to tell for certain where

---

1533 and turned into a home for the indigent and mentally ill. See Johannes Schilling, *Klöster und Mönche in der hessischen Reformation,* Quellen und Forschungen zur Reformationsgeschichte 67 (Gütersloh, 1997), pp. 79-81 and 222.

[11]Cf. *Buc.* 4, 37-40 (*Idyl.* 5, 48-51). Though Eobanus does indeed refer to himself in these pastoral verses, we should not take the words quite as literally as Camerarius does. Eobanus is just saying that he was born in the country, not the big city.

sic non potuit certo cognosci quo loco in lucem editus esset
Eobanus. **9** In pago quidem uno ex eorum numero qui attributi
essent conventui Heinensi natum illum esse satis constat, sed
non eundem omnes nominant. **10** Non | abhorret a vero, in pago
natum esse cui est nomen Teutonicum deductum ab hirco, nam
ille aliquando iocans "Tragocomensem" se appellabat. **11** Fuere
et fortunae origini pares, ac toto vitae tempore non admodum
ille in parte aucta aut luculenta re vixit. **12** Peregrinator etiam
atque oculis hebetibus, hoc uno Homero foelicior quod visum
penitus non amisit.

    13 Sed quamvis parentes haberet pauperculos, curae tamen
illis fuit ut Eobanus liberaliter educaretur. **14** Nam fratrem huius
natu minorem officinae statim delegarunt. **15** Accepimus au-
tem natum eum fuisse, et ita credi ipse postulabat, anno Iesu
Christi 1488, Non. Ianuarii, hora post illius diei meridiem 17, id
est, mane hora quinta diei Dominici quo adscriberentur in fastis
Epiphania. **16** Ad quam si describatur thema genethliacum,
animadvertetur non pauca congruere cum themate Homerico,
exposito a Firmico.

    6, 1 Puer didicit a quodam Ditmaro, qui in illo conventu
primas tum esset ecclesiasticus, prima elementa litterarum.
2 Verisimile est, quod celeriter omnia perciperet et fideliter
retineret, placuisse ut litterarum studia sequeretur. **3** Missus igi-
tur fuit ad propinquos Gemundam, inter quos praecipuo loco
et nomine unus Hartomanus Arnoldus, paulo natu grandior,
qui postea in sua civitate magistratus praecipuos gessit. **4** Una
cum illo audivit ludimagistrum cognatum suum, virum gravem
et satis doctum, Iohannem Mebesium, qui hoc | studeret ut pue-
ri inprimis grammaticas praeceptiones cognoscerent et in-
telligerent.

    5 Hi duo postea Francopergam profecti fuerunt ad spem
doctrinae uberioris, quod ibi ludum aperiret eruditione lite-
rarum tum celebris Iacobus Horlaeus, cum ageret Eobanus
annum decimum quartum. **6** Hic vero magna benevolentia

A6ʳ

A6ᵛ

5, 15 fastis *A (in erratis)*: factis *A (in textu)*.

---

[12]That is, in Bockendorf. Wigand Lauze (p. 428), who as a former superintendent of
Haina may be considered a better authority than either Adam Krafft or Camerarius, states that
Eobanus was born in the village of "Hadelgehausen" (Halgehausen) close to Bockendorf, and
even describes the little house where he was born. Lauze's testimony was corroborated inde-
pendently by Johann Letzener in his description of Haina (1588). See Krause, *HEH,* vol. 1,
pp. 6-8.

Eobanus first saw the light of day. To be sure, it is quite well established that he was born in one of the villages that were under the jurisdiction of the abbey of Haina, but not everybody names the same one. It is plausible that he was born in the village whose name derives from the German word for "he-goat,"[12] for he occasionally referred to himself jokingly as "Tragocomensis" or "Bockendorfer." They were likewise a match in their humble origin; and indeed throughout his lifetime he never truly lived in affluence or splendor. He too was a wanderer, and a weak-eyed one at that, being more fortunate than Homer only in that he did not lose his sight completely.

But though his parents were of small means, they nevertheless took care to provide Eobanus with a liberal education. His younger brother, by contrast, was immediately apprenticed. We have found out moreover (and he himself insisted it was true) that he was born in the year of Jesus Christ 1488, seventeen hours past the noontime of January 5, that is, at five o'clock in the morning, on the Sunday that the calendar assigns to Epiphany.[13] Were you to cast a horoscope for the time of his birth, you would notice that it agrees in not a few particulars with Homer's, as set forth by Firmicus.

6 The boy learned his ABC's from a certain Ditmar, who at the time was abbot of that monastery.[14] It is probable, given his quick mind and retentive memory, that his parents agreed to let him continue his schooling. Accordingly he was sent to his relatives in Gemünden, among whom only Hartmann Arnold, who was somewhat older than Eobanus and later became burgomaster in his town, attained to a distinguished position and reputation. Together with him he attended the classes of his kinsman Johann Mebessen,[15] a respected and quite learned man, who was especially concerned that his pupils should understand and master the rules of Latin grammar.

After this the two boys went to Frankenberg in the hope of gaining a more comprehensive education, because Jakob Horle, famed at that time for his humanistic learning, was opening a Latin school there when Eobanus was thirteen years old.[16] This man did in fact embrace Eobanus

---

[13]In other words: on 6 January 1488 at 5 a.m. For much of his life, however, Eobanus assumed he was born in 1487. See, for example, *Laud.*, ded. 7; *Laud.* 149; *Buc.* 8, 92; 9,9-10; and *Her. Chr.* 24, 63-64. It was not until the early 1530's that he learned the true date of his birth, 1488, for in that year Epiphany fell on a Sunday. See *Her.* 3, 9, 57-58 (revision of 1532 and 1539), where the year is corrected to 1488; *Epp. 1*, sig. M2ʳ (letter to Camerarius, 1535).

[14]Ditmar Wagner (d. 1529) did not become abbot of Haina until 1508. See Johannes Schilling, *Klöster und Mönche in der hessischen Reformation,* Quellen und Forschungen zur Reformationsgeschichte 67 (Gütersloh, 1997), p. 79.

[15]In his biography, Wigand Lauze (p. 429) writes the last name as "Mehessen."

[16]Jakob Horle (Hurle), a native of Frankenberg, matriculated at Erfurt in 1498 and earned his B.A. there in the spring of 1501. That same year he opened the Latin school at Frankenberg that Eobanus attended until 1504. In 1510 he left Frankenberg and was appointed schoolmaster in Marburg. He died in 1519.

complexus Eobanum, quod eluceret in eo indoles eximia, una cum paucis quibusdam aliis impendit illi extraordinarias operas doctrinae et tradidit praecepta versuum faciendorum. **7** Cumque aliquantulum temporis hac institutione consumsisset, iussit eos experiri in componendis versibus vires suas et proposuit sententiam illis Evangelicae narrationis, ita ut tum fere commemorabatur, hanc: "Ego sum lux mundi: qui sequitur me, non ambulat in tenebris." **8** In qua statim notasse ferunt Eobanum quod una pars numerose caderet, ita ut pentameter elegiacus concluderetur. **9** Sic autem accepimus expressisse versibus propositam sententiam, ut iam tum statim magister admiraretur vim promti ingenii et se profectus spem singularem de eo diceret concipere ac arbitrari divinitus sibi in mentem venisse ut illam sententiam tum proponeret, ominisque boni id loco accipere saepeque hortari Eobanum, pergeret quo Deus et natura ipsius eum ducerent, non enim sibi dubium esse quin vir magnus esset futurus.

A7ʳ   **10** Audivi ipse ex Eobano, aliquando sibi dormien- | ti et iacenti in quiete profunda oblatam speciem quasi navigii ad cursum omnibus rebus instructi, quod staret religatum ad littus. **11** Cumque accederet et intueretur illud solicite, incessisse se cupiditatem navigandi et visum fuisse sibi quod funem solveret et conscensa nave proveheretur, ita precatus repente versu composito:

> Da tandem, fortuna, viam! Iuvat ire per altum.

12 Fuisse Horlaeum virum optimum traditur, qui mirificam voluptatem caperet de discipulorum profectu. **13** Isque saepe postea, cum Eobani iam nomen celebrari inciperet, huius exemplo aliis ad discendum calcar cohortatione sua admovere solitus fuit. **14** Inprimis autem placuerat illi et spem singularis excellentiae confirmarat in Eobano assiduum studium scribendi et cura ac solicitudo ut scripta sua emendarentur. **15** Cum enim esset ingenio acri et vehemente, quoties forte versus fecisset, si minus potestas daretur conveniendi magistrum, constat eum tum quaesivisse alios a quibus errata corrigi posse speraret neque repelli se passum fuisse ullis occupationibus horum, quin operam sibi dari peteret. **16** Saepe in coetu exhibuit frequente versus suos aut attulit ad convivium et precibus contendit ut illi statim recitarentur, et si quid vitii in his esset, ut demonstra-

---

6, 7 hac *A (in erratis)*: de hac *A (in textu)*.

with great kindness, for he recognized the uncommon talent that shone forth from him; and along with a few other pupils he offered him extra classes and taught him the principles of versification. And when he had spent a fair amount of time on this instruction, he had them test their skill in composing verses and assigned them this saying from the Gospel story, in the form in which it was practically always quoted then: "Ego sum lux mundi: qui sequitur me, non ambulat in tenebris" (I am the light of the world; whoever follows me will not walk in darkness). Eobanus, they say, instantly noticed the metrical cadence in one part of this sentence, such that it ended with an elegiac pentameter. Moreover, I am told, he went on to versify the assignment so brilliantly that the teacher, right there and then, admired the power of his keen intellect. Declaring that he conceived a special hope of success concerning him, he affirmed his belief that he must have been divinely inspired to assign this particular sentence just then. They say he took it as a good omen and often exhorted Eobanus to keep going wherever God and his own nature might lead him, asserting that there was no doubt in his mind but that he would become a great man someday.

I myself heard from Eobanus that once, when he was lying in a sound sleep, he dreamed he saw a vessel moored alongshore, all rigged as if for a voyage. But when he drew near and inspected it closely, he felt an uncontrollable desire to embark; and in his dream he went on board, cast off the rope, and set sail, saying a little prayer in verse that he composed on the spot:

Show me the way, fortune! I long to traverse the high seas.

Horle is said to have been a wonderful person, who took amazing delight in his pupils' progress. In later years, when Eobanus's name was already beginning to be celebrated, this man would often point to the youth's example so as to spur others to emulate his zeal for learning. But what had pleased him most of all and confirmed his hope in Eobanus's extraordinary promise was the latter's unflagging enthusiasm for writing and his anxious care to have his compositions critiqued. As a matter of fact, being of a passionate and impetuous nature, whenever he happened to be writing verses but did not have an opportunity to get together with his teacher, he evidently used to go around looking for others who, he hoped, would be able to correct his mistakes; and no matter how busy they might be, he would not be deterred from seeking their help. At crowded gatherings he often brought out his verses for examination, or he would take them to a dinner party and earnestly beg someone to read them aloud to him at once, and if there were any mistakes in them, to point them out to him, adding that the matter could brook no delay,

retur: negare rem moram ferre posse, sibi alios versus mox esse faciendos. 17 Hac puerili et liberali importunitate multi tum delectati et istum ardorem studii exosculati in puero Eobano fuerunt et dicere | inter se, fieri non posse quin illa incitatio et tam fervens studium admirabile nomen pariturum illi puero esset, si vita ei concederetur, vereri enim se ne praecox ingenium ad fructum proferendum non perveniret. 18 Quem metum ut Deus inanem esse voluit, ita opinionem ominis illos neutiquam fefellisse exitus probavit.

7, 1 Cum in illo ludo mansisset Eobanus triennium, annos deinde natus sedecim Erphordiam quasi ad uberiorem mercatum bonarum artium profectus fuit, operam studii sui illi navante Magistro Artium Bonarum, patria Francopergensi, qui nominaretur Ludovicus cognomento Christianus, vir pius et innocens ac doctus. 2 Habuisse etiam aliunde adiumenta putatur ad studiorum cultum, et ut in hoc ocio perdurare posset, popularium quorundam qui facultatum copia abundarent. 3 Erphordiae admodum tum iuvenis carmen composuit de infoelicitate amantium et alterum bucolicum.

4 Cum Erphordiae eos honores esset consecutus qui in scholasticis communitatibus tribui solent iis qui doctrina aliis praestare iudicantur, visum illi fuit peregrinationi operam dare, non tam, ut ipse aiebat, consideratione quam impetu quodam animi. 5 Erat illis temporibus in Borussia ad Vistulam praesul Risebergensis, gente nobili Nariscorum Iobus, vir amantissimus omnium studiosorum bonarum literarum et artium. 6 Huic conciliatus Eobanus, qui sibi cognomentum patriae sumserat et ante Eobani nomen Graecum | ponere voluerat, quo "sol" significaretur, ut esset appellatio tota "Helius Eobanus Hessus" (reddidit autem causam, cur Helii nomen ascivisset, carmine quod edidit Erphordiae), Praesuli igitur Iobo conciliatus Eobanus fuit mirum in modum gratus. 7 Admirabatur in adolescente

A7ᵛ

A8ʳ

[17]According to popular belief, precocious people die young. See Walther 12953; 24635; Erasmus, *Adag.* 4, 1, 100.

[18]The eldest son of Christian Stippen, mayor of Frankenberg in 1498 and 1499, Ludwig Christiani was born in 1480. He matriculated at Erfurt in 1501 and took his M.A. in February 1505, together with Martin Luther. Thereafter he served as priest in Frankenberg. After the Reformation he was a Lutheran preacher there from 1528 until 1547. He died in 1553. It was Christiani who in the early autumn of 1504 brought Eobanus to Erfurt. The scene is described allegorically in *Buc.* 1 (where Paniscus is Christiani). See also *Rec.* 84-87.

[19]In particular Auxiliary Bishop Johann Bonemilch of Laasphe. See the introduction to *De laudibus* (p. 137); also cf. *Laud.*, ded. 7. For his life see fn. 4 at *Laud.*, ded.

[20]*De amantium infoelicitate* (Erfurt, 1508); *Bucolicon* (Erfurt, 1509).

[21]Eobanus earned his B.A. in 1506, his M.A. in 1509.

for he had to be off directly to compose other verses. At the time many people were charmed by this boyish and high-minded importunity. Indeed, they greatly admired that passion for literary composition in the young Eobanus and said among themselves that with such enthusiasm and fervent zeal the youth could not fail to make a phenomenal name for himself, if only he could survive into adulthood, for they expressed fear that his precocious mind would not last long enough to bear fruit.[17] Just as God wanted that fear to be baseless, so the event proved that their high expectations were by no means misplaced.

7 When he had spent three years at that school, Eobanus at age sixteen set out for Erfurt – a better-stocked marketplace of the liberal arts, so to speak. There he lived under the tutelage of a Master of Liberal Arts, a native of Frankenberg named Ludwig Christiani, a pious man, at once upright and learned.[18] Additional support for his studies, which allowed him to devote himself full-time to education, is thought to have come from some townspeople of ample means.[19] While still very much a youth at Erfurt, he composed a work on the wretchedness of lovers, and a pastoral poem as well.[20]

After attaining the honors in Erfurt that academic institutions grant those whom they judge superior in learning to others,[21] he took a notion to travel abroad, not so much (as he himself used to say) upon careful reflection as upon impulse. In those days there was a bishop by the name of Job, who resided at Riesenburg on the banks of the Vistula River in Prussia.[22] The scion of a noble family in Vogtland, he was a man who dearly loved all students of good literature and the humanities. Having attached himself to him, Eobanus, who by then had taken the surname from his homeland and wanted the Greek word for "sun" put before the name Eobanus, so that the entire appellation would be "Helius Eobanus Hessus" (his reason for adopting the name "Helius" is explained in a poem he published at Erfurt[23]): well then, having attached himself to Bishop Job, Eobanus became a great favorite of his. Prudent man that he was, he admired the youth's formidable intellect and

[22]Job (Hiob) von Dobeneck was born to a noble family in Vogtland. Having come to Prussia in 1498 as archdeacon and provost at Schillen, he served as bishop of Pomesania from 1501 until his death in 1521. In late 1509 he was in Rochlitz, not far from Leipzig, in order to be with the grand master of the Teutonic Order. Eobanus must have been introduced to him in about November, quite possibly through their mutual friend Sebastian Miricius of Königsberg (d. 1531). At any rate, disappointed at not obtaining an academic post at the University of Leipzig, he signed on as the bishop's chief secretary and before long set out for Riesenburg (now Prabuty). See *Sylv.* 3, 4. Eobanus lauds his patron in the dedicatory letters of *Encomium nuptiale* (1512) and *Heroidum Christianarum epistolae* (1514). As for Riesenburg castle, it was built in 1276/77 by the bishop of Pomesania, but was razed during the seventeenth and eighteenth centuries.

[23]The poem was first printed at the end of *De vera nobilitate* (Erfurt, [1515]), where it is entitled: "Ad Ioannem Osthenium equitem, cur vocetur Helius." It also appears in a somewhat different (and probably earlier) form as *Sylv.* 1, 12. Eobanus used the full name "Helius Eoba-

vir prudens vim ingenii et simplicitatem amabat et perpetuam
sibi illius familiaritatem pollicebatur ideoque beneficiis variis
obnoxium sibi reddere eum studebat. 8 Scripsit tum Eobanus et
alia quaedam et ad imitationem Ovidianam heroidas, quas
postea retexuit et nimis futiles inde fabulas exemit ac multo me-
liora et graviora fecit omnia. 9 Est autem et primum opus
memorabile et eo etiam nomine spectandum quod initia com-
plectitur facultatis poeticae et specimen Eobanici ingenii,
praesertim cum non incubuerit ille in compositionem, sed, ut
mihi saepe retulit, maximam partem animo suo composuerit et
absolverit eques dum comitaretur forte praesulem aut ad vena-
tionem proveheretur aut mandata itinera faceret.

    10 Erat consilium praesulis ut Eobani opera ad scripturas
uteretur et negotia ea quae requirunt civilem prudentiam et ad
obeundas legationes, si quando aliquis ad vicinos principes mit-
tendus esset. 11 Curavit igitur Lipsiae comparari libros, quibus
descriptum ius compraehenditur, studio primum imperatorum,
deinde imitatione pontificum Romanorum, ideoque coepit ius
A8ᵛ   civile et pontificium appellari. 12 Sumtibus etiam | liberaliter
instructum Eobanum ad hoc studium Lipsiam misit. 13 Quo
venit, cum ego in prima pueritia ibidem discipulus essem
optimi et integerrimi viri Georgii Helti Vorhemii, cum vestitu
aulico; ea erat talaris vestis, ut tum consuetudo ferebat,
punicea. 14 Ipsum eo tempore fuisse Eobanum oportet natum
annos viginti quinque, nam incidit hoc in annum Christi Iesu
M.D.XIII.

    8, 1 Erat iuvenis ille pulcherrimus, corpore firmo et procero
et membris elegantibus, facie plane virili et ore severo, barbaque
conspicua ac profunda genae totae vestiebantur. 2 Neque ego
facile existimo fuisse quenquam a primo ortu cuius habitus
atque constitutio ac species cum Eobanico corpore conferri, ne-
dum huic ut illa praeferri possent. 3 Omnia etiam quibus
exercendo corpus reddi solet cum agilius tum robustius studio
sibi habuerat, ut luctaretur, ut illos gestus dimicationum et chi-

---

nus Hessus" for the first time publicly in *Sylvae duae* (Leipzig, early 1514). The name "Helius"
is intended to recall the poet's special affinity to the sun-god Apollo as well as Eobanus's birth-
day on a Sunday.

    [24]The *Heroidum Christianarum epistolae* were first published at Leipzig in July 1514. In
1521 Eobanus revised the work to bring it more in line with Lutheran sensibilities, but was un-
able to find a publisher for it. A rewritten version entitled *Heroidum libri III* was finally
published at Haguenau in 1532 (reprinted with minor improvements in 1539).

    [25]Cf. *Her. Chr.,* ded. 3, 2. For Eobanus's amazing facility in writing Latin verse cf. also
Camerarius, *Nar.* 22, 7-10.

loved his candor and looked forward to enjoying his company for as long as
he lived and hence tried hard to put him in his debt with various acts of kind-
ness. During this period Eobanus wrote among other things a book of heroic
epistles in imitation of Ovid. These he later revised, cutting out some of the
too improbable legends and making everything much better and grander in
style.[24] But the original version is a memorable piece of work in its own right
and all the more worthy of notice in that it contains the essence and epitome
of Eobanus's poetic faculty and genius, particularly when one considers that
he did not labor over the composition. Rather, as he frequently told me, he
composed the bulk of it in his head and finished it on horseback, while he was
accompanying the bishop perhaps or riding out to hunt or traveling on diplo-
matic missions.[25]

It was the bishop's plan to put Eobanus in charge of his correspondence
and of those affairs that require statesmanship and to have him conduct em-
bassies whenever someone had to be sent to the neighboring princes. He
therefore arranged to purchase a set of lawbooks for him at Leipzig, first the
ones encompassing imperial law, then those containing the imitation made
by the Roman popes, which on that account came to be termed civil and pon-
tifical law. In addition, he provided Eobanus with plenty of money and sent
him to Leipzig to study these subjects.[26] When he arrived, I was there myself,
a young teenager studying with that most excellent and high-principled man
Georg Helt of Forchheim,[27] and saw him resplendent in his courtier's cloak.
This was an ankle-length scarlet cloak, as was then the fashion. At the time
Eobanus must have been twenty-five years old, for this took place in the year
of Christ Jesus 1513.

8 He was an unusually handsome young man, of sturdy build and tall
stature, with well-proportioned limbs, a thoroughly manly face, and a grave
demeanor, and his cheeks were entirely covered with an impressive thick
beard.[28] I for one find it hard to imagine that there has ever been anyone who
in physical condition and constitution and appearance could compare with
Eobanus, let alone surpass him in these things. He was also keen on perform-
ing all the exercises that tend to make the body at once more agile and robust.
Thus he liked to wrestle, he learned the techniques of fencing and panto-

---

[26]The bishop actually sent Eobanus to study law in Frankfurt an der Oder in the spring
of 1513. But after being maltreated by a local citizen, Eobanus left after just one semester and
took up studies at Leipzig in the autumn.

[27]Georg Helt of Forchheim near Bamberg (ca. 1485-1545) enrolled at Leipzig in 1501,
where he became B.A. in 1502 and M.A. in 1506. From 1507 to 1518 he taught philosophy
at the university; thereupon he was tutor to Prince George von Anhalt. Following the Leipzig
Disputation (1519) Helt was a respondent to Johann Eck. He eventually became a committed
Lutheran. After Helt's death in 1545 Camerarius published the letters of condolence that
Luther and Melanchthon had sent to Prince George, together with funeral poems by divers
hands (1548).

[28]Cf. Eobanus's self-description in *Her. Chr.* 24, 155-158.

ronomias disceret, ut saltaret, ut nataret, neque in ullo genere facile alteri aequalium caedebat.

4 Est ad Risepurgum piscina spaciosa, neque ulla parte sui non distat ripa una huius ab altera ter mille passibus, quam etiam propter hoc, quod narraturus sum, ipse, cum in Borussiam aliquando venissem et illo in oppido pernoctassem, diligenter fui contemplatus. 5 Solebat in ea interdum natare Eobanus et natando etiam certare cum aequalibus.

B1ʳ   6 Quodam die, cum vestes reposuisset ad ripam | quae oppidum spectaret et demisisset se in piscinam, quod ad alteram illius ripam posse se natando procedere gloriatus inter suos fuisset, illo quidem perrexit. 7 Sed tum demum consideravit animo suo, quam longo ambitu sibi nudo ad vestes redeundum et quod pagi etiam transeundi aliquot essent. 8 Itaque pudore nuditatis demersit se denuo in aquas et continuata natatione confecit ad sexies mille passus potius quam se ullius hominis oculis in via nudum offerret. 9 Erat autem in hoc ingens verecundia, quae etiam senescentem prosecuta ita ingenium hominis temperabat ut moderatio illa ad augendam rem ei, ita ut fit, noceret.

9, 1 Cum autem non posset non sentire quantum et ingenii et corporis viribus valeret et esset in eo animus excelsus, quo fieret ne aliis inferior haberi facile pateretur, non ut se ullis praeponeret aut sua bona ostentaret, id quod ab eius summa humanitate longissime abfuit, sed ne, non praestando quod posset, sibi ipsi contemtus autor existeret, unum vereor ne nimis iuveniliter et incogitanter tum non deliberaverit, sed ausus fuerit facere quo et ingenium debilitaretur divinum et excellentis corporis quasi soliditas labefieret. 2 Putavit enim se etiam inter poculorum certamina, quae maxime tum in aulis certabantur et a nobilitate frequentabantur, non vinci ab altero oportere. 3 Advehuntur in illa loca etiam vina plenissima. 4 Sed potus coquitur cum alibi tum maxime Gedani is qui cerebro infestior sit fumis

B1ᵛ   suis | quam vini cuiuscunque ingurgitatio. 5 Ac est ille quidem hoc quoque consecutus, ut de palma in isto genere cum Eobano contendere vellet nemo. 6 Sed brevi tempore repletione nimia iuvenile corpus graviter afflixit et vires nonnihil enervavit.

7 Narrabo hoc loco, et si mihi res non placet et saepe indignatus fui animo meo hoc etiam malum corripuisse Eobanum et communem cladem nostrorum hominum deploravi, cum illi

8, 4 mille passibus *Carpzov et Kreyssig*: M. pass. *A*.   8, 8 mille passus *Carpzov et Kreyssig*: M. passus *A*.   9, 4 ingurgitatio *Carpzov et Kreyssig*: inurgitatio *A*.

mime, he danced, he swam; and in none of these activities was he easily outdone by any of his comrades.

At Riesenburg there is a spacious pond, some three miles across in every direction (once, when I visited Prussia and spent the night in that town, I took a close look at it myself, just on account of what I am about to relate). It is there that Eobanus used to go swimming from time to time and also competed in swimming contests with companions his own age.

One day, after putting down his clothes on the shore opposite the town and diving into the lake, because he had bragged to his friends that he could swim to the other side, he went on to do precisely that. Only then, however, did he stop to consider how far he would have to walk nude to get back to his clothes and, furthermore, that he would have to pass through several villages. And so, in embarrassment at his nakedness, he once more plunged into the water and, continuing his swim, covered some six miles rather than run the risk of being seen naked by somebody along the way. For I should tell you that he had a highly developed sense of shame, which stayed with him even as he grew older. This innate decency of his, as so often happens, did hurt him when it came to making money.

9 Now since he could not help but be aware of his intellectual and physical prowess, and indeed took great pride in it, the upshot was that he could not easily endure being thought inferior to others – not to put himself ahead of anybody else or to flaunt his gifts, for that was something he in his supreme humanity would never dream of doing, but rather to avoid embarrassing himself if he failed to live up to his potential. In just one respect, I fear, did he not only take an all too puerile and thoughtless decision, but actually dared carry it out – a foolhardiness that eventually debilitated his divine mind and sapped the firmness, so to speak, of his exceptional body. For he believed that even at the drinking bouts that were so popular then at the courts and among many of the nobility he should not allow himself to be defeated by anyone. In that region they import very full-bodied wines too. But in many places and especially in Danzig they brew a drink that with its vapors impairs the brain far more than the guzzling of any wine whatsoever. And yet he proved so accomplished even here that nobody wanted to compete with Eobanus for the palm in this kind of contest. Still, it was not long before his immoderate tippling gravely weakened his youthful body and seriously undermined his health.

At this point in my narrative, even though the matter does not please me at all (to tell the truth, I often felt indignant that this evil had also taken hold of Eobanus and used to deplore this universal scourge of our countrymen,

dicerem ita eum seipsum oppugnasse ut castella et arces solerent tormentis: sed quamvis iucunda mihi mentio non sit, tamen, quia scitum est, narrabo quid inter eum et gloriosum alterum potorem acciderit. 8 Aderat forte Eobanus in convivio. 9 Eodem venit ille quoque et iussit intro ferri vas grande ligneum quo apportari de puteis aqua solet (nos situlam aut urnam possumus, ut opinor, nominare), cuius generis minimum capit ad congios duos. 10 Id posuit in medio repletum Gedanensi cervisia. 11 Ac praefatus quaedam quae comperisse se diceret de strenua potatione Eobani, petiit ut ebiberet illud vas sibique propinaret. 12 Hoc si fecisset, praemium se iam ei tribuere annulum cum gemma preciosa, quem detractum de digito in vas illud abiecit. 13 Eobanus nihil cunctatus neque multa locutus, non enim solebat, arripit vas et non longo tempore assumto evacuat bibendo, et cum everteret sicut fert mos compotantium decideretque annulus in mensam, applaudere illi om- | nes, et inprimis provocator, et annulum donare ac incredibile se factum cognovisse dicere. 14 Tum Eobanus torviore vultu, ut consueverat in commotione, eum intuitus, "Quid? Tu," inquit, "me mercede potare censes?" 15 Ac reiecto ad illum annulo, "Tuum," inquit, "annulum tibi habeto et idem quod ego feci in vase isto evacuando, ut promisisti, facito." 16 Tum ille ostentator inchoatam rem cum perficere non posset, ab omnibus derisus et in convivio obrutus somno relictus fuit. 17 Hoc igitur illi incommodi, vel infelicitatis potius, ab axe Boreo inflictum fuit.

18 Etsi autem me non fugiebat haec futilia visum iri quibusdam, non etiam nullis frugalioribus externorum hominum inepta, tamen ad narrandum hoc me de iuvene Eobano cum Socratis senis exemplum, qui illum in Platonis Convivio psyctera poene congialem exhaurit propinatum ab Alcibiade, invitavit, tum promta simplicitas ad omnia et in experiundo quidvis strenua Eobani cupiditas hac etiam in parte declarare visa fuit ingenii vim et corporis robur, quo utroque eum non fuisse ad ullas res malas et turpes abusum, equidem et memorabile et ipsi gloriosum esse iudico. 19 Sed de his statuat quisque quod voluerit, ac nostra pergat oratio ad alia iucundiora.

10, 1 Erat Gedanensis quidam aequalis ferme aetate Eobano, neque corporis specie longe inferior, inferior tamen, pariter et ingenio minor, qui patria appella- | tione se Dantis-

B2^r

B2^v

telling him he was assaulting his own body in the same way that cannons pound fortresses and citadels): but even though I take no pleasure in mentioning this, I shall nonetheless, because it is common knowledge, take the opportunity to relate what occurred between him and another boastful drinker. Eobanus happened to be at a banquet. The braggart came there too and ordered a large wooden vessel brought in, the kind in which water is drawn from wells (we can call it a bucket or tub, I suppose) and which at a minimum holds twelve pints. This he placed in the middle of the room and had it filled with Danzig beer. And after explaining that he had heard some stories about Eobanus's hard drinking, he asked him to drain that vessel as a toast to his health. If he accomplished this, he would reward him with a ring set with a precious stone, which he then proceeded to take from his finger and toss into that vessel. Without delay or much talking, for that was not his wont, Eobanus grasped the vessel and before long drank it empty; and when he turned it bottom-side up, as the custom of tipplers requires, and the ring fell onto the table, all the onlookers applauded him, especially the challenger, who declared he was giving him the ring in recognition of this incredible tour de force. Then Eobanus glared at him rather fiercely, as he used to do when he was upset, and retorted: "What? Do you think I drink for pay?" And tossing the ring back to him he cried, "Here, take your ring and do what I just did, by draining this vessel as you promised." Then, when that show-off started to carry out his boast but failed miserably, he was ridiculed by everyone and was left at the banquet in a drunken stupor. It was the north country, therefore, that inflicted this trouble or, rather, misfortune on him.

Now even though I am well aware that some readers are bound to regard these anecdotes as pointless and many of the more sober-minded foreigners too will find them quite silly, I nevertheless had several reasons that prompted me to tell this story about the young Eobanus. First, it reminded me of the example of old Socrates, who in Plato's "Symposium" drained the wine cooler that Alcibiades had offered him, for it held almost a gallon. And second, I am of the opinion that Eobanus's naive readiness to try anything and everything and his energetic eagerness to push himself to the limit are, even in this respect, a tribute to his mental power and physical strength. And seeing that he abused neither the one nor the other for any evil and disgraceful ends, I in fact consider it a remarkable and glorious feat on his part. But everybody is entitled to his own opinion here. In any case, my narrative should now move on to other, more pleasant topics.

10 There was a certain companion of his, a native of Danzig, who was about the same age as Eobanus, in physical appearance not far inferior to him, but inferior nonetheless, and likewise his inferior in mental endowment, who

canum nominaret. 2 Inter hos praeclara contentio extitit ingenii et eruditionis, cum alter alterum operibus Musicis, initio sane, ut accepimus, aliquanto infestius provocaret. 3 Sed Dantiscanus vir prudens celeriter sensit quam longe in hoc spacio ab Eobano relinqueretur et ingenua confessione primas Eobano concessit et ipse aliam laudis ac praestantiae viam ingressus fuit. 4 Nam Sarmatico regi se adiunxit, cuius nomine legationibus ad alios reges et principes functus ad dignitatem et opulentiam maximam pervenit, habuitque semper postea animo suo carum Eobanum et nonnihil etiam fortunae suae commoditatis ad eum transtulit, cum interdum munusculis eum augeret, eumque vicissim Eobanus coluit et ornavit scriptis suis.

5 Hic est Dantiscanus, qui constantissime dilexit omnes bonarum artium studiosos et ipse ad extremum usque senium easdem coluit, factus benignitate regis Poloniae praesul Varmiensis. 6 Erat autem homo festivus et perfacetus. 7 De quo aliquando mihi clarissimus vir, virtute et doctrina praestans, summus noster Georgius Sabinus retulit, cum Regiomonte ad eum forte venisset, fuisse se ab eo acceptum perquam humaniter et benigne. 8 Postquam abierant dies aliquot et significasset Sabinus se velle discedere et reverti domum, petiit praesul ut pranderet prius. 9 Coeperat tum fama spargi, in pagis qui redeunti transeundi erant saevire pestilentiam. 10 Tum praesul ecquod haberet contra morborum | contagionem alexipharmacon interrogavit. 11 Sabinus habere se nescio quid respondit. 12 Tum praesul, "Nihil," inquit, "nocuerit a me aliquid etiam te accipere. 13 Habeo enim praesens remedium ad permulta quae iter facienti accidere possunt." 14 Cumque dimitteret Sabinum, tradidit ei ita compositum quiddam ut speciem vasculi haberet in quo solent medicati pulveres asservari ac praedicare coepit usum mirabilem et dicere se esse saepissime beneficium illius medicamenti expertum. 15 Cum in manus accepisset Sabinus, statim sensit quid medicamenti esset pondere. 16 Nam arte com-

B3ʳ

10, 8 Sabinus se *Kreyssig*: se Sabinus *A*.

---

[29]Johannes Dantiscus (Jan Dantyszek), a native of Danzig (1485-1548), traveled widely before settling down to study law and theology in Cracow. After receiving lower orders in 1505, he became secretary and notary at the court of King Sigismund I. He first met Eobanus during the latter's visit to Cracow in February 1512. Though they were at each other's throat initially, the two men did end up the best of friends. See the introduction to *Encomium nuptiale* in vol. 2 of this edition. A gifted diplomat, Dantiscus was often sent on missions abroad. In recognition of his accomplishments, Maximilian I made him doctor of civil and canon law

called himself Dantiscanus after his home town.[29] Between these men there arose a noble rivalry in talent and erudition, as each challenged the other to poetic works, initially at least, as I have heard, in a rather too hotheaded manner. But being a sensible man, Dantiscanus quickly realized how far Eobanus outstripped him in this arena and frankly conceded Eobanus's superiority and entered upon another path to renown and preeminence. For he attached himself to the king of Poland, in whose name he conducted embassies to other kings and princes, and reached the pinnacle of rank and affluence, but always continued to hold Eobanus dear in his heart and also put not a little of his fortune at his disposal by presenting him from time to time with modest gifts, while Eobanus in his turn revered and honored him in his writings.

This Dantiscanus, who never wavered in his love for all students of the liberal arts and himself cultivated these studies into extreme old age was by the benevolence of the king of Poland made bishop of Warmia. He was, moreover, a jovial and very witty man. I heard a story about that once, which our excellent friend Georg Sabinus once told me, outstanding gentleman that he is, preeminent in virtue and learning.[30] Sabinus happened to be visiting Dantiscanus in Königsberg and was most graciously and kindly received by him. After a few days had gone by and Sabinus had indicated that he was planning to take his leave and return home, the bishop asked him to have lunch with him first. At just about that time, rumors had started to spread that a plague was raging in the villages through which he would have to pass on his return journey. Accordingly the bishop wanted to know if he had an antidote against being infected by the disease. Sabinus replied that he did have something or other. Hereupon the bishop said: "It won't hurt to take something along from me too. For I have an effective remedy that will cure a good many of the ills that can befall a traveler." And as he bade Sabinus farewell, he handed him something so constructed that it looked like the small box in which one normally keeps medicinal powders and began praising the marvelous efficacy of this medication and averring that he himself had very often experienced its benefits. No sooner had Sabinus taken it in his hands than he sensed from the weight what kind of medication it was. For the

---

in 1516, crowned him poet laureate, and raised him to the nobility. In 1530 he was elected bishop of Chełmno (Kulm). He became bishop of Warmia (Ermland) in 1537, a position he held until his death.

[30]Georg Sabinus (Schuler) of Brandenburg (1508-1560) studied privately with Philip Melanchthon in Wittenberg from 1523, finally matriculating at the university in 1532. In 1530 he published a set of *Elegiae* (later expanded to six books). A trip to Italy in 1533 brought him the friendship of Pietro Bembo and earned him the laurel wreath. In 1538 he was appointed professor of rhetoric at the University of Frankfurt an der Oder. Invited to Königsberg in 1544 by Albert I of Brandenburg, he became rector of the ducal college and soon-to-be university. But after a dispute with the duke in 1555 he returned to Frankfurt an der Oder. His collected *Poemata* were published at Strasbourg in 1544 (expanded in 1558 and 1563).

pegerat praesul complures argenteos qui de valle ubi primum percussi fuerunt Ioachimici vocantur, quos, ne magnifacere ipse donum suum videretur, cum hac illi festivitate obtulit. 17 Sed exeundum nobis e Borussia est.

11, 1 Lipsiae igitur ego puer et primum vidi Eobanum et de fama admiratus fui atque venerans suspexi. 2 Habebat tum Academia Lipsica doctos viros multos. 3 Unum malevolentia et odium quorundam paulo ante expulerat, qui in vicinia ad Albin postea consenuit et obiit diem suum, vir omnibus bonis carus, Ioannes Aesticampianus. 4 Sed aderant tum eruditionis et humanitatis principes Ioannes Sturnus, Vitus Berlerus, et Georgius Aubanus, Franci ambo. 5 In meo autem magistro Georgio Helto cum neque esset ingenium infelicius quam in quovis alio, studium vero et industria haud scio an admirabilior quam in ullo, tamen et | moderatione animi et metu quorundam quibus eum obnoxium reddebat institutum vitae genus cohercebatur ne familiariter cum iis se coniungeret qui politi et exculti litteris tantum videri volebant. 6 Nam quod aliquando hi etiam liberius exultarent, ut fit, grandiores natu, qui aliam rem et doctrinam illam esse animadverterent quam de qua ad dignitatem et emolumenta ipsi pervenissent, offendi et ex his nonnulli irasci atque repugnare novitati, quidam etiam inventi qui invidia et odio extimularentur et studiis essent iniquiores, id quod omnibus mutationum temporibus antea accidit et post hac eventurum est. 7 Sed illi, quos nominavi, minus curare veluti censuram senum ac sua studia colere et doctrinam horum profiteri alacriter et tum sese cum Eobano cupidissime coniungere. 8 Ibi ille, quem natura etiam a Musis aberrare non pateretur et horror tractationis a studio iuris repelleret, oblitus voluntatis ac mandatorum praesulis sui pecuniam confecit et libros grandes istos legum atque constitutionum divendidit et mox Erphordiam ad incunabula doctrinae suae se retulit.

B3ᵛ

---

[31]The "Joachimstaler" were Bohemian silver coins, struck by the Counts of Schlick since 1519 from the silver mined in Sankt Joachimsthal ("St. Joachim's dale") in Bohemia (now Jáchymov in the Czech Republic).

[32]Johannes Rhagius (Rack), known as Aesticampianus after his native Sommerfeld in the former Mark Brandenburg, was born in ca. 1460. In 1491 he matriculated at Cracow, where he studied with Konrad Celtis and appears to have graduated B.A. and M.A. After traveling to Italy in 1499, he enrolled at Bologna and was crowned poet laureate by the pope. From 1501 to 1505 he was professor of moral philosophy in Mainz; and from 1506 he taught Greek in Frankfurt an der Oder. His polemic advocacy of humanism brought him into conflict with his more conservative colleagues, however, and impelled him and some of his students (Hutten

bishop had craftily concealed several of the silver coins known as "Joachims-taler" after the valley where they were first struck[31] and was offering them to him in this amusing way, lest he seem to be making too much of his gift. But it is time for us to leave Prussia behind.

11 As I mentioned already, I was a boy at Leipzig when I first laid eyes on Eobanus and marveled at his fame and looked up to him with veneration. At that time the University of Leipzig possessed many fine scholars. One of them had just been driven away by the spitefulness and hatred of some of his col-leagues: Johannes Aesticampianus, a man dear to all decent people, who afterwards grew old in a nearby town on the Elbe, where he ended his days.[32] Still present then, however, were those princes of learning and culture, Jo-hannes Sturnus and the two Franconians Veit Werler and Georg Aubanus.[33] But although my own teacher Georg Helt was intellectually no less brilliant than anyone else you can think of and in fact, for all I know, was more ad-mirable in his zeal and industry than any, nevertheless his temperate spirit and his fear of certain people on whom his career depended forced him to keep his distance from those who were so keen on appearing refined and accomplished in literary matters. For because the latter, as happens, sometimes tended to flaunt their learning too freely, the older professors, who noticed a subject matter and erudition different from the one by which they themselves had risen in rank and emoluments, began to take offense. Some of them were en-raged at the avant-garde and fought it tooth and nail; others were motivated by nothing but spite and hatred and were prejudiced against the new studies, something that has happened in all transitional periods of history and will oc-cur again in the future. But the upstarts I spoke of ignored the censure, so to speak, of the senior professors and merrily went on to pursue their studies and teach their subject and subsequently allied themselves to Eobanus with the ut-most enthusiasm. It was in this context that he, whose very temperament did not allow him to stray from the Muses and whom a dread of wrangling re-pelled from the study of law, forgot all about the wish and injunctions of his bishop, squandered his money, sold those huge tomes stuffed with laws and decrees, and before long returned to Erfurt, the cradle of his learning.

---

among them) to leave for Leipzig in the early spring of 1508. Here too he ran into opposition from the conservatives. In October 1511 he was expelled from the university. The scandal is described in *Epistolae obscurorum virorum* 1, 17. Aesticampianus thereupon returned to Italy, earning a doctorate in theology in 1512. In 1513 he taught in Cologne; but as an ardent sup-porter of Johann Reuchlin he soon had to leave that city too. From 1517 until his death in 1520 he taught at Wittenberg, a good friend of Luther and Melanchthon.

[33]The poet laureate Johannes Sturnus (Star) of Schmalkalden matriculated at the Uni-versity of Leipzig in 1510. He was reputed to be a fine poet, but of his work nothing survives. Eobanus addresses him in *Sylv.* 1, 11.

Veit Werler of Sulzfeld in Franconia was born in the early 1480's. After matriculating at Leipzig in 1500, he graduated B.A. in 1502 and M.A. in 1508. Thereafter he taught at the uni-

12, 1 Paulo post venit Lipsiam Euricius Cordus, patria et ipse Hessiacus, natus in viculo cui nomen Simus, unde et Simusii cognomentum aliquando assumebat, attulitque secum bucolica sua, quae Lipsiae volentibus audire explicuit. 2 Eum primum vidi apud meum magistrum Georgium Heltum. 3 Cumque caperetur animus puerilis sermonibus eruditis illius, egre- | giam rem esse suspicari coepi poeticam, nam hos poetas nominari audiebam. 4 Hic Cordus postea medicus factus cum a se tum liberis egregiam laudem doctrinae posteris reliquit. 5 Quae esset immensa, si filio huius Valerio id absolvere quod uterque instituerat licuisset. 6 Qui Romae est cum omnium luctu mortuus et reliquit ingens desiderium non modo peritiae et doctrinae, sed etiam virtutis et humanitatis suae. 7 Cum patre autem mihi singularis usus necessitudinis intercessit Erphordiae, neque illo ego quenquam cognovi magis vel vehementius potius studiosum veritatis et qui peius odisset mendacia et vanitatem. 8 Erat autem natura asperior et paulo impatientior, quaeque dissimulare nihil fere quo offenderetur ac ferre posset. 9 Quod in causa fuit ut in aliquorum interdum indignationem incurreret, a quibus potuisset sublevari si favorem ipsorum ambiret ac retineret. 10 Declaratur id epigrammatis quae edidit, et hoc ipsum studium, quale dixi, tale hominis fuisse ingenium ostendit. 11 Cordum nominarat ille se, nam editus fuerat extremo partu matris suae.

12 Euricium autem de Henrico fecerat Cunradus Mutianus Ruffus, qui in sodalitio ecclesiastico Gothae degebat. 13 Et cum esset nobili familia ortus neque non offerrentur occasiones illi

B4ʳ

---

versity. From 1511 to 1515 he produced school editions of Horace, Cicero, Plautus, and Valerius Maximus. In 1514 he contributed a poem to Eobanus's *Heroidum Christianarum epistolae* (*Her. Chr.* A 3), in which he complains about the hostility to humanistic studies in Leipzig. Eobanus consoles him in *Her. Chr.* B 1 (= *Sylv.* 4, 3). In 1516 the bishop of Bamberg, Georg von Limpurg, appointed him tutor to his nephew Karl. In that capacity Werler moved first to Ingolstadt and two years later to Pavia. Having returned to Germany in 1522, Werler became a canon in Wiesensteig. The year of his death is not known, but must be after 1535, for Camerarius wrote to him in the spring of 1536, not long after the jurist Johann Apel had died on April 27; see *Epp. 2*, sig. E8ʳ-F1ʳ.

Georg (or Gregor) Käl (Zäle) of Aub near Heidelberg, matriculated at Heidelberg, where he received his B.A. in 1503. From 1510 he taught and studied at Leipzig (M.A. 1513). In 1514 he contributed a laudatory poem to Eobanus's *Heroidum Christianarum epistolae*; see *Her. Chr.* A 4. Suffering from ill health, he went back to his homeland, where he died in 1515.

[34]Euricius (= Heinrich, Ritze, Ricius) Cordus was born in 1486 at Simtshausen between Marburg and Frankenberg, the youngest of the thirteen children of the miller Kunz (Cord). After studying at Erfurt he taught from ca. 1509 to 1511 at a grammar school in Kassel and then worked as a tax collector in Felsberg until 1512. By the spring of 1513 he was back in Erfurt. He earned his M.A. in early 1516 and became rector of the school of St. Mary's in 1517. His first major work was a collection of allegorical eclogues, entitled *Bucolicon* (Erfurt, 1514).

12 Not long afterwards Euricius Cordus came to Leipzig.[34] A Hessian himself, he was born in the village of Simtshausen, from which at one time or other he also took the surname "Simusius." He brought along his eclogues, which he explicated to students in Leipzig. I first saw him at the house of my teacher Georg Helt. And as his erudite conversation enchanted my youthful soul, I began to think of poetry as something splendid, for I heard these men being called "poets." This Cordus, who later became a physician, left to future generations an outstanding reputation for learning, and not just he, but also his sons. That fame would have been immense, if his son Valerius could have completed what both of them had set out to accomplish. But he died at Rome, mourned by all, and left behind enormous regret not only for his expertise and erudition, but also for his virtue and gentleness.[35] With the father, however, I established a remarkably close friendship in Erfurt. Never in my life have I met anyone more deeply attached or, rather, more ardently committed to the truth or who hated falsehood and hypocrisy with a greater passion than he. On the other hand, he was quite gruff by nature and a bit too impatient, and when something annoyed him, he could barely conceal his irritation or put up with it. For that reason he sometimes exasperated people who might otherwise have been his backers, had he cultivated them and kept their goodwill. The trait shows up in the [caustic] epigrams he published; indeed, this pursuit of his reveals that the man's temperament was exactly as I described. "Cordus" (late-born) is what he called himself, for he was his mother's last child.

Now the man who changed Cordus's first name from "Heinrich" to "Euricius" was Konrad Mutianus Rufus, who lived in the ecclesiastical community of Gotha.[36] And although he was born into a patrician family and

---

Camerarius probably met him in late 1517 or early 1518, for a second edition of the eclogues appeared in Leipzig on 4 February 1518. Cordus turned to medicine in ca. 1518/19. Accompanied (and financed) by Georg Sturtz, he traveled to Ferrara in the spring of 1521, graduating that same year as doctor of medicine and returning to Erfurt in the autumn of 1521. In 1523 he accepted a position as town physician in Brunswick. Appointed professor of medicine at Marburg in 1527, he was elected rector of the university in 1530 and 1533. In 1534 he moved to Bremen as town physician and teacher at the Gymnasium. He died in 1535. Besides numerous Neo-Latin poems and mordantly satiric epigrams, Cordus published works on botany and medicine.

[35]Valerius Cordus (1515-1544) obtained his B.A. at Marburg in 1531, continuing his studies at Leipzig in 1533. By 1539 he was giving lectures on Dioscurides in Wittenberg. While visiting Nuremberg in 1542 he was asked to prepare a pharmacopoeia or *Dispensatorium* – the first handbook of its kind. He presented it to the city council in 1543. That same year he traveled to Rome to continue his research, but died there in 1544. His botanical and pharmacological researches were published posthumously.

[36]Konrad Mutianus Rufus of Homberg in Hesse (1470-1526) matriculated at Erfurt in 1486, together with his younger brother Johann. He graduated B.A. in 1488 and M.A. in 1492. Two years later he went to Italy, where he studied canon law at Bologna, Rome, and Ferrara (doctorate, 1501). After returning to Germany in 1502 he obtained a position in the

amplissimorum honorum, quod et fratrem haberet in principis
Cattorum aula primo loco et ipse non modo animi ac corporis
donis, sed Italica etiam disciplina commendaretur, splendori et
opulentiae fortu- | nam exilem et infra mediocritatem positam
Gothani collegii praetulit. **14** Abest autem Gotha Erphordia
milibus passuum non multo amplius XII. **15** Ad hunc primum a
te, Adame, adductus, saepe praedicavi, ut scis, me illum co-
gnovisse optimum et sapientia ac virtute praestantissimum vi-
rum. **16** Dignitas in hoc erat summa, gravitas autem ea quae
aetatem et locum quem tenebat deceret, commista illa quidem
cum comitate incredibili. **17** Mirifice autem laetabatur cum
audiret sedulo operam dare literis iuventutem, et quibus rebus
poterat in hoc spacio solebat incitare currentes, superstitionibus
inimicus et hospitalis in re tenui admodum, sed erga studiosos
litterarum tantum. **18** Nam aliorum fere omnium consuetu-
dinem fugiebat, adeo ut nimis fuisse appetens ocii studiorum et
tranquillitatis hac in parte videri alicui possit, quam "beatam"
praescripto aedibus titulo se arbitrari significabat, ubi et hoc
visebatur elogium: "Bonis cuncta pateant." **19** Sed turbarunt
hanc tranquillitatem ea tempora, quorum difficultas ac miseria
iam inchoata ad eam perducta est tristiciam et calamitatem
quam experitur et cum qua conflictatur aetas nostra. **20** Qui au-
tem finis futurus sit, nulla coniectura humana potest prospicere.

13, **1** Solebat Mutianus, tum quidem canus, nam annis
gravis erat cum ad eum primum veni, adolescentibus studiosis
litterarum, qui ad se visendum accessissent, proponere mate-
riam quam scribendo elaborarent et scripta postea emendare et
sae- | pe non admodum digna collaudare, ut hoc pacto ad dili-
gentiam et curam studiorum excitarentur animi illorum. **2** Erat
autem festivissimo ingenio et liberalibus iocis admodum delec-
tabatur. **3** Epistolas ad amicos scribebat libenter. **4** Genus autem
erat sententiosum orationis et incisum, quale est Politianicum,
ad quod in Italia erat assuefactus. **5** Rhythmis etiam ludebat in-

B4ᵛ

B5ʳ

12, 14 milibus passuum *Carpzov et Kreyssig*: mil. pass. *A*.

---

chancellery of Landgrave William II of Hesse, where his brother Johann Muth was chancellor.
Impatient with his new employment, however, he soon retired to Gotha, not far from Erfurt.
There he lived in his "blessed tranquillity" (as he termed it), supported by a prebend as canon
of St. Mary's and other benefices. A wonderfully learned and gifted humanist, Mutianus never
published any works of his own, but did attract and inspire a host of admirers and followers
over the years, among them Eobanus, Crotus Rubianus, Heinrich and Petrejus Eberbach, Her-

had no lack of opportunity to advance to the most distinguished positions, for he had a brother who was chancellor at the court of the landgrave of Hesse and he himself could boast not only intellectual and physical endowments but also an Italian education, he nevertheless rejected a life of splendor and opulence in favor of a slender fortune and a lowly prebend as a canon in Gotha. The town of Gotha, incidentally, is not much more than twelve Roman miles from Erfurt. Having been introduced to him by you, Adam, I have often, as you know, proclaimed that I knew him as the best of men, unsurpassed in wisdom and virtue. He had the utmost dignity about him – the kind of gravity, however, that suited his age and the position he occupied and was in any case combined with an incredible graciousness. Moreover, he was always wonderfully delighted to hear that the younger generation was sedulously applying itself to literary pursuits, and used to do whatever he could to spur on those who were competing in this arena. An enemy of all superstition, he was for someone of modest means exceedingly hospitable, but only towards devotees of literature. For he avoided associating with virtually all other people, so much so, that an outsider might well conclude that he was too hungry for the leisure of intellectual pursuits and tranquillity. A sign on his house, in fact, indicated that he thought tranquillity "blessed." One could also see this inscription there: "To the good let every door stand open." But this tranquillity was disturbed by the advent of those times, the troubles and woes of which led directly to the grief that we are now enduring and to the calamity with which our own age has to contend. How this will all turn out, no human prophecy can foretell.

13 The by then gray-headed Mutianus[37] (for he was getting on in years when I first went to visit him) was fond of challenging the young students of literature who had come to see him by proposing a topic that they were to work out at some length. Afterwards he would correct their writing and frequently extol even the not so good pieces, just to inspire them to work hard and kindle their enthusiasm for those endeavors. I should add that he was a man of great wit, who really enjoyed a good clean joke. He loved to write letters to his friends. His prose style was pithy and incisive, much like Poliziano's,[38] for it was in Italy that he had made it his own. Occasionally he also tried his hand at metrical compositions,[39] and I must say that the verses

---

bord von der Marthen, Ulrich von Hutten, Euricius Cordus, and Johann Lang. Eobanus often exchanged letters with his mentor and addressed poems to him. See especially *Ad Mutianum Rufum elegia* (spring, 1508?), *Buc.* 6, and *Sylv.* 1, 2 (revised as *Sylv. duae*, no. 1, in 1514). Also cf. *Laud.* 261-284 and *Epic.* 4.

[37] His hair used to be red, which is why he called himself "Rufus" (redheaded).

[38] Angelo Poliziano (1454-1494), the great Italian humanist, was famed for his learning and elegant style.

[39] The Latin term "rhythmi" normally denotes medieval-style rhythmic verses and hymns. Mutianus is not known to have written in this form, but he did pen numerous classical-

terdum, cum quidem versus faceret sat bonos. **6** Divulgati quidam fuerunt de improbitate simulantum religionem. **7** Sed ipse neque edidit suorum quicquam neque reliquit (affirmante etiam hoc optimo et doctissimo viro Ioanne Marcello Regiomontano, qui affuit cum moreretur et in sua omnia illius potestate habuit) quod edi recte posset et omnino se sua publicari nolle aiebat. **8** Ac mihi perconctanti aliquando causam quamobrem tam pertinaciter premeret scripta sua, cum omnes arbitrarentur et ego quoque putarem eum scriptionibus operam dare, ita fieri respondit quia sua sibi nunquam satis placerent ideoque malle se frui aliorum stultitia. **9** Erat nimirum ei persuasum non facere sapienter illos qui sua scripta facile emitterent in lucem, praesertim cum illis temporibus non emitterentur, sed evolarent undique omnis generis libri. **10** Mortuus est Mutianus Gothae, rebus turbulentis in Germania, in dolore, ut apparebat, amissae dignitatis et diminutae rei familiaris, anno Christi Iesu M.D.XXVI, tertio Calen. Aprilis, vir magnus et

B5ᵛ   probitate, integritate, virtute, sapientia, humanitate ex- | cellens, decus et ornamentum eorum quibuscum vixit et patriae, immo Germaniae totius et seculi sui.

14, 1 Sed ut ad Eobanum revertar, rediit ille Erphordiam et tum etiam Mutiano, qui antea quoque adolescentem illum favore prosecutus fuisset quemque ipse in quodam carmine Eobanus formatorem studiorum suorum nominat et de quo fecerat versum, qui in ore erat tum plurimis:

> Hesse puer, sacri gloria fontis eris.

2 Huic igitur Erphordiam ille reversus non modo carus, sed admirationi quoque fuit. **3** Saepe igitur ad eum scribebat, saepe ab eo litteras accipiebat, saepe excurrebat Gotham Eobanus ut cum Mutiano versaretur. **4** Audivi tamen de Mutiano offensum se aliquando fuisse Eobani moribus in potu; tum enim erat interdum in hilaritate ferocior, non ut laederet quenquam, sed ut esset paulo saepe incogitantior et minus circumspectus atque animo remissiore. **5** Neque quisquam tamen unquam comperit

---

13, 10 quibuscum *Kreyssig*: quibus cum *A*.

---

style verses, mostly elegiac distichs and hexameters. The poem on religious hypocrisy to which Camerarius alludes in the next sentence is not extant.

he wrote were really quite good. Some of the ones dealing with the depravity of religious hypocrites circulated widely. But he himself neither published works of his own nor left any behind at his death – and this is confirmed by that most excellent and learned man Johann Marcellus Regiomontanus,[40] who was present when he died and had power of attorney over his estate – at least not anything that could be edited in good conscience, for he expressly forbade that any of his work should be printed. When I asked him once what made him so determined to suppress his own writings when everybody, including myself, was under the impression that he was applying himself to literary composition, he responded that he did so because he was never all that happy with his own work and hence preferred to enjoy the folly of others. He was quite obviously convinced that people who did not think twice about letting their writings go out into the world were not acting wisely – particularly not in those times, when books of all stripes did not so much go out as gush out from every quarter. Mutianus died at Gotha, during a time of violent unrest in Germany,[41] in grief, or so it would appear, at the loss of his prebend and his dwindling estate, in the year of Christ Jesus 1526, on the thirtieth day of March, a great man of outstanding probity, integrity, virtue, wisdom, and humanity, the glory and ornament of those with whom he lived and of his homeland, nay, of all Germany and his own generation.

14 But to return to Eobanus, he went back to Erfurt[42] and then also to Mutianus, who had favored him already as an adolescent and whom Eobanus himself in one poem or other calls his intellectual mentor. In fact, he had once written this verse about Eobanus, which was widely quoted back then:

Hessus, young man, you're bound to be Hippocrene's pride![43]

Having come back to Erfurt, then, he found that Mutianus not only regarded him with affection, but admired him as well. Hence Eobanus often wrote to him, often received letters from him in return, often made excursions to Gotha to spend time with him. I have it from Mutianus himself, however, that he was sometimes displeased with Eobanus's behavior when tippling; for then he would sometimes get too ferocious in his jesting, not to the extent that he would actually hurt anyone, but that he would often get a little too thoughtless and inconsiderate and unrestrained. Still, no one ever found him making

---

[40] Johann Marcellus of Königsberg in Franconia (1510-1552) was Mutianus's famulus. After Mutianus's death in 1526 he stayed for a while in Erfurt, but then moved to Wittenberg, where he eventually became professor of philosophy.

[41] Mutianus Rufus died a year after the Peasants' Revolt was put down in Germany and during a time when the Reformation was rending the social and political fabric of the Empire.

[42] In July 1514.

[43] Literally: "the glory of the sacred fountain." The Hippocrene on Mount Helicon was sacred to the Muses. Mutianus had written the verse in August 1506 after reading Eobanus's *De pugna studentum*.

dedecus eum etiam in ista laeticia admisisse, vel dicto vel facto.
6 Verum senescentis illius gravitas iuvenilem huius exulta-
tionem interdum non moleste quidem tulit, sed improbavit
tamen, praesertim cum in flore Eobanus aetatis et vita liberiore
etiam amare coepisset. 7 Amavit autem caste virginem Erphor-
diensem Catharinam, quam postea uxorem duxit et cum qua
multis annis maritus vixit et ex qua utriusque sexus numerosam
B6ʳ   sobolem suscepit. 8 Ea habebat patrem ho- | nestum in civitate
sua hominem (illarum aedium dominum quas postea Georgius
Sturciades emit et Eobanus suis scriptis exornavit ac celebravit),
qui moribus aliquanto erat durior et senecta aetate amarior.
9 Accidit ut de hoc apud Mutianum quereretur Eobanus.
10 Tum ille hoc modo respondit:

> Si tibi nata placet, fer patris imperium.

11 Postea et socerum ille aequo animo tulit et cum coniuge
amanter vixit. 12 Et docuit bonas literas Erphordiae admodum
tenui stipendio, cum neque tum rebus omnibus quae ad victum
et cultum sunt necessariae vilibus opus esset multo neque ipse
partem vel minimam curae impenderet faciendae rei.

    15, 1 Non ita multo post ego annos natus octodecim, qui
Iesu Christi annus fuit M.D.XVIII, Erphordiam et ipse me con-
tuli, cum Lipsiae vixissem annis quinque et duobus operam
dedissem Ricardo Croco Britanno, qui primus explicuit doc-
trinam Graecarum litterarum in Germania, fuissemque etiam
Mezeleri et Petri Moselani auditor. 2 Hanc famam cum attu-

15, 1 Britanno *Carpzov et Kreyssig*: Britano *A*.

---

[44]In late 1514 or early 1515 Eobanus married Katharina, daughter of the Erfurt citizen
Heinrich Später (Speter). As Krause, *HEH,* vol. 1, p. 140, suggests, she may well be the "Fla-
via" with whom Eobanus fell in love during his student days at Erfurt; see fn. 43 at *Ama.* B 2.
The marriage produced five sons, Hieronymus (b. 1519/20), Julius (b. 1520/21), Anastasius
(1527-1532), Heliodorus (1529-1587), and Callimachus (b. 1531), and three daughters. The
first two daughters, the one born in ca. 1523, the other in 1525, seem to have died at a young
age. The third, Norica, was born in Nuremberg, sometime before 8 March 1532. Katharina
died between late 1540 and October 1543.
    [45]Eobanus's father-in-law Heinrich Später owned the house "Zur Engelsburg." Accord-
ing to Mutian. *Ep.* 482 and 497, Eobanus himself lived in that house as late as the spring of
1515. Eobanus's friend Georg Sturtz acquired the property in 1519, shortly after he returned
from Italy. The municipal tax records (*Verrechtsbuch*) for the year 1530 add: "Doctor Johann
[*sic*] Stortz hat das huß zur Engelburgk hinder allen heiligen" (Dr. Johann [*sic*] Stortz has the
house "Zur Engelsburg" behind All Saints' Church). See: Stadtarchiv Erfurt 1-1 XXIIIa, Bd.
7, Bl. 285. (No tax records are available for the years between 1511 and 1530.) I am grateful
to Dr. Ulman Weiss for providing this update to Krause, *HEH,* vol. 1, p. 141, fn. 1 and p. 238,
fn. 4.

a fool of himself even at such a revel, whether in word or in deed. The older man's seriousness, while not taking offense at his friend's youthful exuberance, disapproved of it nevertheless, particularly when Eobanus, then in the flower of youth and living a bachelor's life, also fell in love. And indeed, he chastely loved an Erfurt girl, Katharina by name, whom he afterwards married and with whom he lived as husband for many years and by whom he had numerous children of both sexes.[44] Her father was an honest citizen in his town. (It was he who owned the house that Georg Sturtz was to buy later on and that Eobanus then adorned and celebrated in his writings.[45]) He was a rather crusty man, grown increasingly bitter with age. One day Eobanus happened to complain about this to Mutianus. Thereupon the latter replied:

If you're fond of the daughter, put up with the father's behest.

From that time on he patiently put up with his father-in-law and lived lovingly with his wife. He also taught literature in Erfurt, albeit at a pretty meager salary.[46] But since all the things required for sustenance and clothing were cheap in those days, he really did not need a big income nor was he in the least concerned with making money.

15 Not all that much later, when I was eighteen years old, which was in the year of Jesus Christ 1518, I too went to Erfurt.[47] By that time I had lived five years in Leipzig and studied for two of them with the Englishman Richard Croke, who was the first to teach the Greek language in Germany, and had also attended Metzler's lectures and those of Peter Mosellanus.[48] Since I brought this prestige along with me to Erfurt, I became the center of at-

---

In 1524 Eobanus published a set of epigrams on the noted physicians whose likenesses were displayed in Sturtz's study. See "Chorus nobilium medicorum in Museo Sturtiano Erphurdiae," printed at the end of *Bonae valetudinis conservandae praecepta* (Erfurt, 1524).

[46]During the years leading up to his appointment as professor in 1518 Eobanus lectured at the university and taught privately. An introductory lecture to a course on Cicero and Plautus has been preserved in *Oratio sive praelectio in auspicio Officiorum M. Tullii Ciceronis et M. Accii Plauti comoediarum in Academia Erphurdiensi per Magistrum Eobanum Hessum in eadem Academia bonas litteras publice profitentem habita M.D.XV* [Erfurt, 1515]. A copy of this work, hitherto unknown, is extant in the University Library, Basel.

[47]Just before Easter (April 4); see fn. 49 below. Camerarius turned 18 on April 12.

[48]On Richard Croke see fn. 3 at *Nar.* 2, 4. As for Johann Metzler of Wrocław (ca. 1494-1538), he studied law in Italy. While there, he learned Greek from Richard Croke. Before returning to his native city in 1519 he briefly taught Greek at the University of Leipzig. In Wrocław he continued his scholarly work, giving public lectures and publishing a Greek grammar in 1529 that was based on the system developed by Croke. In 1532 he was elected city councilor and then mayor of his hometown; in 1534 he was named head of the regional government.

Peter Mosellanus (ca. 1493/94-1524) hailed from Bruttig, on the Mosel. After matriculating at Cologne in 1512, he studied Greek with Johannes Caesarius. From 1514 to 1515 he taught Greek in Freiburg (Saxony), but then moved to Leipzig to continue his studies with

lissem mecum Erphordiam, qui concursus ad me adolescen-
tum optimorum complurium factus quaque benevolentia me
plaerique omnes complexi sint, tu optime nosti, Adame,
omnium studiosissimus nominis mei. **3** Sed in meum adventum
incidit discessus Eobani, qui tum adiuncto sibi comite uno,
iuvene egregio, Bonarum Artium Magistro Bertero, rebus
B6ᵛ   atque temporibus non admodum expeditis et secundis, | iter
ingressus fuit ut Erasmum videret ac conveniret in Belgico tunc
degentem. **4** De scriptis enim illius, quae tum crebra prodibant,
mirifica cupiditas erga hunc et ingens favor extiterat omnium.
5 Applaudebatur quasi in scena studiorum actori scito et arti-
ficioso. **6** Cumque eum admirabantur et magnifaciebant et
collaudabant omnes qui a Musis alienos esse se perhiberi nollent,
tum congratulabantur sibi eam felicitatem saeculi in quam delata
esset vita ipsorum. **7** Quod si quis ab Erasmo epistolam ad se
elicere forte posset, illa vero ingens haberi gloria et hic praeclarus
triumphus agi. **8** Si autem accederet veluti cumulus colloquii et
congressus Erasmici et ut ad eum alicui aditus pateret, tum
demum sibi in terris is, cui hoc contigerat, beatus videri.
9 Credebatur enim, ut erat, politioris doctrinae ille esse prin-
ceps, et in uno omnes contra adversationem barbariae satis opis

---

15, 8 accederet *A (in exemplari Goting.), Carpzov, Kreyssig*: accideret *A (in exemplari Monast.).*

Richard Croke. When Croke left for England in 1517, Moseʃlanus took his place as teacher of
Greek at Leipzig. In 1520, after taking his M.A. and a bachelor's degree in theology, he was for-
mally admitted to teach Greek and theology at the university. He was twice elected rector
(1520 and 1523).

⁴⁹The nobleman Johann von Werther, a student of Eobanus's, matriculated at Erfurt in
1511, becoming B.A. in 1513 and M.A. in 1517. After the voyage to Erasmus he boarded with
Eobanus for several years. See *Epp. fam.,* p. 217. As for Camerarius, he had in fact arrived in
Erfurt shortly before Easter 1518. See Stephan Kunkler, *Zwischen Humanismus und Reforma-
tion: Der Humanist Joachim Camerarius (1500-1574) im Wechselspiel von pädagogischem Pathos
und theologischem Ethos,* Theologische Texte und Studien 8 (Hildesheim, 2000), p. 29.

⁵⁰Eobanus left Erfurt on 28 September 1518 to visit Erasmus, arriving in Louvain on Oc-
tober 16 (or 17).

Desiderius Erasmus of Rotterdam (1466-1536) attended school in Deventer and
's-Hertogenbosch before entering the Augustinian monastery of Steyn near Gouda in 1487.
Not long after being ordained priest in 1492 he left the monastery as secretary to Hendrik van
Bergen, bishop of Cambrai. He matriculated at the University of Paris in 1495 to study the-
ology. In 1499 he seized the chance to travel to England where he met John Colet, Thomas
More, and other intellectuals and future patrons. Upon his return to the continent in 1500
Erasmus published an early version of his *Adagia,* which established his fame. Much of his en-

tention for a large number of the best young scholars and enjoyed the warm goodwill of virtually everybody there, as you know better than anyone else, Adam, of all people the most solicitous for my reputation. But my arrival co-incided with Eobanus's departure, for he and one single companion, the outstanding young man and Master of Liberal Arts Werther,[49] had just set off, without much planning and at an inauspicious time of the year, to see and meet Erasmus, then living in Brabant.[50] For the latter's writings, which were then coming out in rapid succession, made him an amazingly fascinating fig-ure and the darling of all Europe. He was applauded, as it were, like a skillful and accomplished actor on the stage of learning. And as all who did not wish to be considered strangers to the Muses admired and praised and extolled him, so they congratulated themselves on being contemporaries with this the pride and joy of their age. Now if one of them managed to coax Erasmus into sending him a letter, this was thought a truly momentous honor and an occa-sion to celebrate a magnificent triumph. But if someone were granted the pinnacle of bliss, so to speak, and got to visit and converse with Erasmus and had access to him, then whoever had this good fortune looked upon himself as the happiest man on earth. For Erasmus was believed to be – as indeed he was – the prince of refined learning, and everyone was convinced that in this

---

ergy during the following years was devoted to the study of Greek, the first fruits of which were translations of Euripides and Lucian. His ideas on Christian piety, which stressed inward re-ligion, were summed up in *Enchiridion militis Christiani* (1503). During a lengthy stay in Italy he obtained a doctorate in theology at Turin (1506) and published a much-expanded edition of the *Adagia* (1508). He returned to England in 1509. There he wrote his most famous work, *The Praise of Folly* (Paris, 1511). By 1518 Erasmus was at the pinnacle of his career. Courted by kings and princes and feted by all the humanists of Europe, he continued to publish at a break-neck pace, even as he moved from one center of learning to another. Taking full advantage of Johann Froben's press at Basel in 1514-1516, for example, he published not only an enlarged version of the *Adagia*, but also a revision of *Moriae encomium*, an edition of the complete works of St. Jerome, as well as the monumental *Novum Instrumentum*, offering a Greek text and Latin translation of the New Testament along with numerous philological notes.

Having returned from his pilgrimage to the "prince of humanists," Eobanus described his experiences in a *Hodoeporicon* (1519; reprinted in Louvain, at Erasmus's instigation). For the next few years he remained one of Erasmus's strongest supporters at Erfurt. In 1519 he lectured on the *Enchiridion*, publishing the introductory address as a *Praefaciuncula* to that "divine" work in 1520. And when Erasmus called on his confederates in Erfurt to help him silence Ed-ward Lee, who had disparaged his philological work on the Greek New Testament, it was Eobanus who led the charge with a barrage of epigrams against Lee (1520). Thereafter Eoba-nus's enthusiasm for Erasmus cooled in inverse proportion to his growing ardor for Luther. For unlike the cautious Erasmus, who steadily distanced himself from Luther until the final break in 1524, Eobanus eagerly supported the German reformer. Erasmus's subsequent failure to mention Eobanus among the elite writers in *Ciceronianus* (1528) severely strained relations be-tween the two men. A year later, when Erasmus slurred the evangelical school in Nuremberg, Eobanus was so infuriated that for a time he considered writing an invective (see *Nar.* 17, 22, with fn. 75). Though they continued to correspond from time to time, the two humanists henceforth kept a wary distance. Indeed, it was not until 1537, a year after Erasmus's death, that Eobanus could bring himself to write an epicedium for the great man who in bygone days had been his idol.

praesidiique esse statuebant. **10** Itaque interpellationes adventantium nonnihil toedii et molestiae illi obiiciebant, praesertim scriptionibus diversis occupato, quae tum a librariis magnopere expetebantur, cum nulli libri libris Erasmicis magis essent vendibiles.

11 Venit igitur ad Erasmum Eobanus apud Grudios tunc commorantem et versibus compositam elegantissimis epistolam ad ipsum ex diversorio misit, quae cum Hodoeporico quo describeretur iter illud et aliis quibusdam postea edita fuit. **12** Erasmus quidem, sive occupationibus aliis abstractus seu propter hu- | militatem adventus Eobanici, qui cum uno comite pedes accessisset, sive in tanta salutantium frequentia, non ille quidem despexit Eobanum, sed neque tribuisse ei tantum iudicio suo neque tam officiosus in ipsum fuisse existimabatur quam pro sua humanitate et Eobani studio esse debuisset. **13** Etiam postea laudavit Erasmus Eobanum remissius, non quod iniquior illius famae esset, sed quod non arbitraretur, ut opinor, eum indigere praedicatione sua qui per se magnus esset, atque illos potius extollendos ornandosque qui vel nullam vel non magnam dignitatem parare possent ipsi sibi. **14** Eobanus quidem et Erasmo diligenter et prolixe gratias egit et nomen illius postea maximopere defendit; et cum a Laeo Erasmus carperetur, autor fuit ut pro illo Erphordiani eruditi contra Laeum scriptis suis propugnarent.

16, **1** Ad Eobanum de Erasmico itinere reversum tu me, Adame, ut recordari potes, cum adduxisses et pro me contra illum nescio quid libere tunc dicentem, de iis quae ad eum fuerant falso delata, multa aliquanto etiam quam ipse liberius locutus esses, tum quidem aditum ad amicitiam ipsius, apud quem plurimum valeres et cui unice esses carus, mihi patefecisti. **2** Sed cum postea meum ingenium certius perspexisset Eobanus, sua sponte me ascivit in gregem suum et pro captu et aetate mea plus honoris habuit mihi initio statim quam deberetur, et quo diuturnior consuetudo et familiaritatis | usus frequentior inter nos intercedebat, eo coniunctio arctior et maior necessitudo extitit,

B7ʳ

B7ᵛ

15, 11 elegantissimis *A (in erratis)*: elegantissimam *A (in textu)*.

---

[51]See *Hod.* B 1 and *Sylv.* 3, 8.

[52]Edward Lee (ca. 1485-1544) earned his B.A. at Oxford in 1501 and his M.A. at Cambridge in 1504. In 1515 he became bachelor of divinity at Cambridge. By 1531 he was doctor of divinity at Oxford and archbishop of York. Anxious to learn Greek, Lee took up studies at Louvain in 1516. Within six months he had advanced sufficiently to write a series of notes on

one man there was strength and protection enough against the onslaught of barbarism. As a result, the interruptions from visitors brought him not a little distress and vexation, especially when he was occupied with various writings, these being in great demand from the booksellers in those years, inasmuch as Erasmus's books outsold all others.

In short, Eobanus came to Erasmus, then staying in Brabant, and from the inn sent him a letter composed in his most elegant verses. This he later published together with his *Hodoeporicon,* in which he described that journey, along with some other poems.[51] Erasmus, for his part, either because he was preoccupied with other business or because Eobanus approached him in the humble way that he did, on foot and with only one companion, or because so many people were always visiting him: Erasmus, for his part, did not exactly look down his nose at Eobanus, but he also cannot be said to have held him in such high regard or have shown himself as courteous to him as he ought to have done, given his own good-heartedness and Eobanus's enthusiasm for him. Even in after years Erasmus offered him only muted praise, not because he had something against Eobanus's reputation, but rather, if you ask me, because he did not think that someone who was great on his own account needed any praising from him; he would rather acclaim and honor those who were unable to attain any, or at least a very high standing for themselves. As for Eobanus, he not only thanked Erasmus assiduously and effusively, but afterwards also did his utmost to defend the man's good name; and when Lee started carping at Erasmus, Eobanus was the one who stirred up the scholars of Erfurt to defend him against Lee with their writings.[52]

16 After Eobanus returned from his journey to Erasmus,[53] it was you, Adam, as you may recall, who introduced me to him. And when he thereupon bluntly brought up something or other about the rumors that had been falsely reported to him, you leaped to my defense with even greater bluntness than his. At all events, you opened the way for me to become friends with Eobanus, with whom you had supreme influence and to whom you were especially dear. But afterwards, when he had gained a surer insight into my character, he spontaneously adopted me into his circle and right from the start held me in higher esteem than my ability and age warranted; and the longer we associated with each other and the more time we spent in each

---

the Greek New Testament. Incensed by Erasmus's refusal to incorporate or even acknowledge these contributions in the second edition of his New Testament (1519), Lee furiously attacked Erasmus's philological work. Erasmus replied at once, in a variety of publications (1520), and privately urged Eobanus and his friends at Erfurt to lampoon Lee. They ebulliently answered the call with *In Eduardum Leeum ... epigrammata* (Erfurt, 1520). For an account of the controversy see Erika Rummel, *Erasmus and His Catholic Critics* (Nieuwkoop, 1989), vol. 1, pp. 95-120, and her introduction to *ASD* 9, 4, pp. 1-12.

[53]In late October 1518.

donec verae et deinceps inviolatae amicitiae societas in con-
sensione et concordia et similitudine perpetua studiorum cum
maxima caritate consummata fuit atque perfecta.

3 Tam autem honorifici tunc fuere sermones Eobani de
Erasmo, tam plena praedicatio, tanta amplificatio virtutis illius,
ut nullius non animus cupiditate visendi Erasmum incendere-
tur, quidam etiam ut commoverentur ad idem iter statim
ingrediendum et proficiscendum eo usque ubi convenire pos-
sent Erasmum, qui in Belgico non uno loco maneret. 4 Inter hos
praecipui fuere iuvenes egregii et multis rebus ornati Iustus Io-
nas et Caspar Schalbus, quorum alter annis aliquot post mortuus
fuit, tum etiam aetate grandior. 5 Ionas autem ingenii bonitate
et assiduitate studii, virtute doctrinaque et humanitate excel-
lens, ea quam sibi peperit claritate nominis nunc etiam vivus
fruitur, ita ut indies ab illius pietate et sapientia existimationi
amplissimae aliquid accedat. 6 De quo minus dicendum nobis
est, ne assentationis aliquam suspicionem incurramus. 7 Etiam
Ioannes Draco Francus ad Erasmum tum profectus fuit, qui et
ipse multis et variis difficultatibus exercitatus pietate et constan-
tia celebre nomen consecutus est, cum litterarum et artium
bonarum scientia iam tum cederet nemini. 8 Uterque horum
summus amicus fuit Eobani, sed Ionas facile inter omnes
B8ʳ   amicos Eoba- | ni principem locum tenebat. 9 Itaque vivebant
coniunctissime familiarissimeque, una crebro deambulabant,
crebro domi confabulabantur, crebro etiam coenitabant.

17, 1 Erat familiae cuiusdam religiosae (Georgiana nun-
cupabatur) curator Erphordiae, vir humanissimus et valde
prudens neque illiteratus, cui Henrico Urbano nomen. 2 Is in
Eobanico grege non ferebat postremas ac saepe illum cum suis
accipiebat, ut res erant ac tempora, satis prolixe. 3 Augus-
tinianae autem Iohannes Langus theologus non modo amicum

16, 2 consensione A *(in erratis)*: consentione A *(in textu)*.

---

[54]Justus Jonas and Kaspar Schalbe visited Erasmus at Louvain in the spring of 1519. On
Justus Jonas see fn. 41 at *Buc.* 5. Kaspar Schalbe of Eisenach, a good friend of Mutianus Rufus
and Euricius Cordus, studied at Erfurt from 1504, earning his B.A. in 1506, his M.A. in 1510.
He died not long after 1526.

[55]Johann Drach (Draco, Draconites), born at Karlstadt in 1494, matriculated at Erfurt in
1509. He obtained his B.A. in 1511 and his M.A. in 1514. From 1514 to 1521 he was a canon
at St. Severi. A great admirer of Erasmus, he visited the Dutch scholar at Louvain in July 1520.
He moved to Wittenberg in 1521 to study Hebrew, graduating as doctor of theology in 1523.
After several years as pastor in Waltershausen, Drach moved to Eisenach in 1528 in order to
devote himself to scholarship. From 1534 to 1547 he was professor and pastor in Marburg. It

other's company, the tighter we were bound together and the closer we became, until we achieved a partnership of true and thenceforth unbroken friendship, perfected in lifelong harmony and concord and similarity of interests, along with the greatest mutual affection.

Now Eobanus spoke so reverentially of Erasmus in those days, he praised him so lavishly and lauded his merit so exuberantly, that not a few people were fired with a passionate desire to go and see Erasmus for themselves. Some indeed were so excited that they immediately set out on the same journey to wherever they might be able to visit Erasmus, for he did not stay in just one place in Brabant. Chief among them were the outstanding and well-to-do young men Justus Jonas and Kaspar Schalbe, the second of whom died several years later; he was after all the older of the two.[54] Jonas, however, a man noted for his sound intellect and tireless zeal for humanistic studies and famed for his virtue and learning and kindness, is alive even today, enjoying the brilliant name that he has made for himself, such that something of his piety and wisdom is daily added to his most distinguished reputation. I have to restrain myself in speaking about him, lest I be suspected of flattery. Another who traveled to Erasmus in those days was the Franconian Johann Drach.[55] Afflicted with all kinds of trouble, he too achieved renown for his devoutness and firmness of purpose; and in his knowledge of literature and the liberal arts he was even then second to none. Both of them were the best of friends with Eobanus; but among all of Eobanus's friends Jonas easily occupied the first place. Accordingly, they lived in the closest and most intimate companionship imaginable, often going for walks together, often conversing at home, often inviting each other to dinner as well.

17 In Erfurt there lived the steward of a religious house (called the "Georgenthaler Hof"), a most kindhearted man, exceedingly prudent and by no means unlettered, whose name was Heinrich Urbanus.[56] He occupied a prominent position in Eobanus's circle and often entertained him and his comrades, and quite lavishly too, considering the situation and the times. As for the Augustinian theologian Johann Lang, he was not only a good friend of

---

was he who delivered the eulogy at Eobanus's death in 1540 (*Ein Trostpredigt von der aufferstehung*, Strasbourg, 1541) and edited his friend's correspondence in 1543 (see fn. 6 at *Nar.* 4, 1). From 1551 to 1560 he taught at the University of Rostock and from 1560 to 1564 served as superintendent of the bishopric Pomesania and preacher in Marienwerder. He died at Wittenberg in 1566.

[56]Heinrich Urbanus (Fastnacht) was a native of Orb, north-east of Frankfurt am Main. He matriculated at Erfurt in 1494, but soon left to become procurator in the Cistercian abbey of Georgenthal, south of Gotha. By 1505 he was a close friend of Mutianus Rufus, with whom he exchanged numerous letters. He resumed his studies at Leipzig in 1508, graduating B.A. that same year and M.A. in 1510. Thereupon he was appointed head of the "Georgenthaler Hof," the house that his monastery maintained in Erfurt. Urbanus died in 1538.

habebat Eobanum, sed doctrinae atque ingenii etiam admiratorem. **4** Huic cum more scholastico autoritas publice docendi solenniter conferretur, invitatus ad eam festivitatem Lipsia advenit Petrus Mosellanus et secum adduxit adolescentem tum suavissimis moribus et litterarum eruditione eximia praeditum, Petrum Suavenium. **5** Apud hos perpetuo Eobanus fuit, quam diu Erphordiae manserunt, et cum de communibus studiis disserendo, tum hilariter una vivendo hoc est consecutus ut ab his ad opinionem iam de ipsius excellenti ingenio et doctrina praestante conceptam summae humanitatis et singularis virtutis persuasio adiungeretur. **6** Quorum alter is vir fuit, ut nemini fere est obscurum, qui sanctitate vitae et cognitione et scientia bonarum artium et litterarum non facile ulli cederet, alter adolescens genere nobili et quem natura sua ad magnificos conatus duceret, difficile et arduum virtutis iter ingressus ad dig- |

B8ᵛ   nitatem et opulentiam maximam pervenit. **7** Cum Georgio Spalatino, sanctissimo et politissimo viro, veteris necessitudinis singularis Eobano usus intercedebat, ut et cum aliis quibusdam, de quibus mihi ignotis quae narrarem non habui. **8** Habebat inter suos et popularem, quem valde diligebat, Ioannem Ortum, integerrimum et spectatissimae fidei hominem, et perquam eruditum et festivum iuvenem Nosenum Silesium, cum quibus libenter et multum versabatur. **9** Christophorus Hacus, qui

---

17, 4 scholastico *Carpzov et Kreyssig*: scolastico *A*.

---

[57]Johann Lang of Erfurt (ca. 1486-1548) enrolled at Erfurt in 1500, obtaining his B.A. in 1503. In 1505 or 1506 he entered the house of the Augustinian friars in Erfurt and was ordained priest in 1508. Transferred to Wittenberg in 1511, he took the opportunity to earn his M.A. the very next year. In 1515 he became *baccalarius biblicus,* which allowed him to lecture on the Bible. From 1516 he was prior of the monastery at Erfurt. He continued his university studies, however, and graduated doctor of theology on 14 February 1519. During these years at Erfurt he was in close contact with Eobanus and his circle. He played a major role in the humanistic reform of the university, teaching Greek in the winter semester of 1519. But after leaving his order in early 1522 and becoming the leading reformer in Erfurt, he had a falling out with Eobanus, who by 1523/24 was publicly accusing the evangelical preachers of undermining humanistic education. It was only when Eobanus began to despair of his position in Erfurt and begged Lang to help him, that a reconciliation between the two old friends became possible.

[58]Peter von Suaven was born in ca. 1496 to a noble family in Stolpen, Pomerania. After studying with Peter Mosellanus in Leipzig (see fn. 48 above), he attended the University of Wittenberg. A devoted follower of Luther, he accompanied the reformer to the diet of Worms in April 1521. In 1523 he was appointed privy councilor to the king of Denmark and in 1543 was named rector of the University of Copenhagen. He died in 1551.

[59]For Georg Spalatin (1484-1545) see fn. 19 at *Buc.* 2.

[60]Heinrich (not "Johann") Ort, of Kaldern near Marburg, was the son-in-law of Adam Krafft. Having taken up studies in Erfurt in 1512, he graduated B.A. in 1514, M.A. in 1517.

Eobanus's, but also a great admirer of his learning and genius.[57] When he received his doctoral degree at a solemn ceremony, complete with the usual academic pomp and circumstance, Peter Mosellanus came at his invitation from Leipzig to attend the festivity and brought along a young man endowed even then with exceptionally suave manners and a superb literary education, Peter von Suaven.[58] Eobanus was with them the whole time they stayed in Erfurt, and what with the serious discussions about their common interests and the joyous partying together, they took back with them not only the high opinion about his excellent mind and peerless erudition that they had already formed, but also a firm belief in his consummate humanity and remarkable virtue. The first-mentioned scholar, as practically everyone knows, was a man who in purity of life and in understanding and knowledge of liberal arts and letters did not easily yield to anyone; the second, a young nobleman whose abilities allowed him to set lofty goals for himself, entered upon the difficult and arduous road of virtue and attained to the highest rank and affluence. With Georg Spalatin, that most godly and cultured of men, Eobanus had a remarkably close friendship that went back a long time.[59] He associated with some others as well, but since I never got to know them, that is all I can tell you. Among his boon companions he also counted his compatriot Johann Ort,[60] a man of great integrity and proven loyalty, of whom he was extremely fond, as well as the highly erudite and jovial youth Nossen of Silesia,[61] with both of whom he loved to spend much time. Christoph Hack, the best lyric poet of his generation,[62] and Valentin Capella, a most gifted and learned young man,[63] together with Gröningen and Eckzell,[64] were all cronies of

He was professor of natural science at Marburg in 1549-1554. Thereafter he served as preacher in Giessen, returning to Marburg as professor of theology in 1566. He died in 1575.

[61] Michael Nossen, a native of Grotkau in Silesia, matriculated at Erfurt in 1515 (B.A. 1517, M.A. 1521). By 1532 he was still living in Erfurt.

[62] Christoph Hack of Jerichow, north-east of Magdeburg, enrolled at Erfurt in 1509, where he graduated B.A. in 1512. Though Camerarius, Cordus, Eobanus, and Hutten all praise his poetry highly, he published very little. Not much is known about his life. He was a monk during his years at Erfurt; in December of 1517 he was in Wittenberg, preparing to lecture on the Gospels; and in 1518 he visited Reuchlin at Bad Zell and Ulrich von Hutten at Mainz. Eobanus addressed an epigram to him at the end of his Luther-elegies of 1521. Leaving Wittenberg in 1522, Hack became a "minister of the Gospel" in Erfurt; and by 1523 he was married.

[63] Valentin Sifridi was born in Cappel, Hesse, and hence adopted the surname Capella. From 1512 he studied at Erfurt, obtaining the B.A. in 1514 and the M.A. in 1519. A great admirer of Luther, he left Erfurt to teach school in Wittenberg in 1521. He died unexpectedly in 1528.

[64] On Johann Gröningen see fn. 8 at Nar. 4, 6. His friend Johann Eckzell matriculated at Erfurt in 1513 under the name Johannes Cluss de Echsel, becoming M.A. in 1517. Thereafter he was a member of the philosophical faculty at Erfurt, serving as dean in 1530 and 1532. A staunch Catholic, Eckzell remained on good terms with the Protestant Eobanus. He died in 1541.

melicis carminibus faciendis praestabat aequalibus omnibus, et
Valentinus Capella, iuvenis ingeniosissimus et eruditissimus,
una cum Groningo et Eccilio asseclae erant Eobanici et ad se
saepenumero eum abducebant. **10** Sed ex omnibus familiaris-
sime complectebatur Martinum Hunum, ad quem Medicinae
encomium in versus de Erasmica oratione translatum conscrip-
sit, et affectione praecipua in prima adolescentia cognitum
constantissime diligebat Petreium Aperbachum Erphordien-
sem, iuvenem ingenii cultu et eruditione doctrinae excellentem,
sed aegrum pedibus et valetudine adversa perpetuo laborantem,
qua impeditus eo, quo natura studioque impellebatur, progredi
non potuit. **11** Hunc, cum per iocum apud suos se "regem" fa-
ceret, "ducem" ipse solebat appellare, significans proximum
locum a se quasi in gubernatione regni Musici illi deberi.

 12 Sed hoc unde natum sit ut "regem" se nominaret, et ipse
ostendit carmine quodam et ego breviter exponam. **13** Opti- |
mus et doctissimus vir Ioannes Capnio in quadam ad ipsum
epistola alludens ad Hessi nomen ἐσσῆνα eum appellaverat et
versum adduxerat Callimachi de Iove, quem hic negat hessena
deorum sorte esse factum, sed virtute et praestantia sua. **14** Ex eo
in sodaliis cum "rex" Hessus vocitaretur, hoc ioco postea ute-
batur, ut se regem et alios regni proceres faceret.

 15 Nullo enim non modo cruento, sed ne dentato quidem
dicto ludere Eobanus solebat. **16** Neque reperietur inter omnia
scripta ipsius ullum quo laedatur fama aut nomen proscindatur

C1ʳ

---

[65]Martin Hune of Gittelde in Brunswick began his studies in 1508 at Erfurt, where he
earned the B.A. in 1509. After a prolonged absence, he came back to Erfurt around 1517
(M.A. 1518). In 1520 he was named professor in the Collegium maius. However, as the
university teetered on the brink of collapse in 1523, Hune (like Eobanus) took up the study of
medicine. Eobanus introduces him as a defender of medical studies in the satiric dialogue
"Melaenus" (*Dial.* 1) of 1524. That same year he addressed the "Medicinae encomion ex
Erasmo" (*Val.* 2) to him. Upon his return from a visit with Erasmus at Basel in early 1524,
Hune was elected dean of arts for the summer semester. He left Erfurt in the autumn of 1525,
traveled to Italy in 1526, and graduated M.D. at Padua in 1531. Thereafter he practised
medicine in Graz.

[66]For Petrejus Eberbach see the introduction to *De amantium infoelicitate* (pp. 197-198).

[67]See *Sylv.* 2, 29.

[68]Johann Reuchlin of Pforzheim (1454/55-1522) matriculated at Freiburg in 1470. His
duties as tutor to one of the sons of Margrave Charles I of Baden took him to Paris in 1473. In
1474 he moved to Basel (B.A. 1474, M.A. 1477). Thereafter he studied Greek at Paris and law
at Orléans and Poitiers. He was promoted to doctor of laws at Tübingen in 1485. In 1482 and
1490 he visited Italy in the service of Count Eberhard of Württemberg. From 1496 to 1498
he lived in Heidelberg; but after a third stay in Italy as envoy of Elector Palatine Philip he
moved to Stuttgart in 1499. During his service on the three-man tribunal of the Swabian

Eobanus and frequently took him to dinner at their home. But of all of them he was closest to Martin Hune,[65] to whom he addressed the "Praise of Medicine" that he had put into verse after the declamation by Erasmus; and with surpassing affection and matchless loyalty he cherished Petrejus Eberbach of Erfurt,[66] whom he had gotten to know in his teens, a young man who excelled in cultivating the mind and pursuing scholarly erudition, but was forever suffering from gout of the feet and bad health, which prevented him from advancing to where his nature and ardor impelled him. Since Eobanus jokingly made himself "king" among his intimates, he used to dub Petrejus "duke," implying that the latter was by rights his second-in-command in administering the realm of the Muses.

But how he took to calling himself "king" is something he himself explained in one of his poems[67] and I shall briefly relate. That best and most learned of men Johann Reuchlin[68] once wrote him a letter in which he, punning on the name Hessus, christened him *hessēn* (king) and adduced Callimachus's verse about Zeus, which says that the latter became king of the gods not by the casting of lots, but by his own merit and excellence. Since people now referred to him as "the king" at social gatherings, he thereupon extended the jest to make himself king and create the others princes of the realm.

As a matter of fact, Eobanus was never in the habit of making cruel jokes, not even barbed ones. Among all his writings you will not find any in which another man's reputation is savaged or his good name torn to shreds, save for the book where he vents some of his anger at Lee and for an elegy where he

---

League from 1502 to 1513 Reuchlin lived in Tübingen. When the tribunal was moved to Augsburg, he decided to retire to Stuttgart. In the final years of his life he was appointed Professor of Greek and Hebrew at Ingolstadt (1520-1521) and at Tübingen (1521-1522). He died in Stuttgart.

Together with Erasmus, Reuchlin was the acknowledged dean of the northern humanists. He edited and translated numerous Hebrew, Greek, and Latin books and created a Latin dictionary, *Vocabularius breviloquus* (1478). Besides Neo-Latin comedies for use in the schools, he published a Hebrew grammar and lexicon (1506) and other aids to the study of that language. His work in Hebrew brought him much fame, but also cost him great anguish, for it embroiled him in a bitter dispute with the converted Jew Johann Pfefferkorn, the Dominicans, and the conservative theologians in Cologne and elsewhere. When Pfefferkorn attacked him in his *Handspiegel* (1511) for promoting Hebrew studies, Reuchlin immediately countered with an *Augenspiegel* and rallied the German humanists to his side. He published their letters of support in the collection *Clarorum virorum epistolae* (1514) and *Illustrium virorum epistolae* (1519). The Erfurt circle of humanists, led by Crotus Rubianus, then published the satirical *Epistolae obscurorum virorum* (*Letters of Obscure Men*) that skewered Reuchlin's opponents (1515; expanded in 1518). Though eventually declared guilty by a court in Rome and enjoined to silence, Reuchlin emerged as the hero of humanist Europe, a Hercules who had slain the Hydra of obscurantism.

alterius, nisi quod nescio quid in Laeum indignationis evomuit suae et quendam poeticantem theologum aliquanto immansuetius retudit elegia quadam. **17** Cum enim Martinus Lutherus accersitus in Vangionas, ubi se coram Imperatore Carolo V, qui primum ibi conventum habere instituisset, sistere deberet, Erphordiam illo itinere forte transiret, Eobanus et ei cum Croto Rubiano, qui tum administrationi Academicae praeerat, aliisque compluribus honoratis viris ac iuvenibus eruditis obviam processit et biduo, quo Erphordiae Lutherus mansit, cum eo suavissime versatus fuit. **18** Cumque placuisset illas res et actiones describi interque elaborationem incidisset in manus ipsius libellus editus ab Emsero, quo Lutherum ille maledictis incesseret, et praepositi essent versus scripto perridiculi et mali, commotus fuit iam incitatus Musico impetu animus Eobani, ut

C1ᵛ   eum, qui poeta esse vellet, theologum tum pau- | lo gravius acciperet et tractaret inclementius. **19** Haec sunt, ac praeterea nihil, quae vel ioco vel serio ad alterum exagitandum scripsit aut dixit. **20** Etiam a Philippo Melanchthone aliquando rogatus ut optimorum versuum pulcerrima opera elaboraret et componeret rem deterrimam et turpissimam et sibi hanc operam daret,

---

[69]On Edward Lee see fn. 52 at *Nar.* 15, 14. The "poeticizing theologian" is Hieronymus Emser of Weidenstetten (b. 1478). Emser studied at Tübingen (1493-1497) and Basel (M.A. 1499). Consecrated priest, he worked as secretary to Cardinal Raimund Peraudi from 1502 to 1504. During the summer semester of 1504 he studied at Erfurt and came in contact with Mutianus Rufus and his circle. After matriculating at Leipzig in the autumn of 1504 he earned a baccalaureate of theology and licentiate of canon law in 1505 and then entered the service of Duke George of Saxony. In 1519 Emser accompanied Johann Eck to the Leipzig Disputation. He now turned against Luther, passionately attacking him in a series of pamphlets, letters, and poems. He died suddenly in 1527.

[70]Martin Luther of Eisleben in Thuringian Saxony (1483-1546) studied humanities at Erfurt from 1501, graduating M.A. in early 1505. Thereafter he read law; but in July 1505 he entered the order of Augustinian Eremites and was ordained priest in 1507. During his years in the monastery he studied the Bible and theology. From 1511 he lived in Wittenberg, where in 1512 he took a doctorate in theology and became professor of biblical studies. His 95 Theses of November 1517, attacking the late-medieval system of indulgences, provoked ever-intensifying controversy and finally brought him into direct conflict with the church. However, neither Cajetan's efforts in Augsburg (1518) nor the Leipzig Disputation with Johann Eck (1519) succeeded in swaying him. Excommunicated by Leo X in January 1521, Luther was summoned to appear before Charles V at the diet of Worms in April 1521. The journey to Worms, which took him through Erfurt on April 6-8, became a triumph. Eobanus, for one, was so moved by the reformer's visit that he immediately wrote a set of elegies in praise and defense of Luther. Refusing to recant at Worms, Luther was forced into hiding at the Wartburg, secure under the aegis of Frederick the Wise. In March 1522 he returned to Wittenberg. There he continued to shape the course of the Reformation through his sermons and writings until his death.

[71]Johannes Crotus Rubianus (Jäger, Venatoris) was born at Dornheim, Thuringia, in ca. 1480 and matriculated at Erfurt in 1498 (B.A. 1500). After studying at Cologne in 1505/06,

rather too ruthlessly cuts a certain poeticizing theologian down to size.[69] The occasion was this. When Martin Luther was summoned to Worms, where he was to appear before Emperor Charles V, who had decided to convene his first diet there, he chanced on his way to pass through Erfurt.[70] Eobanus rode out to meet him, together with the then rector of the university Crotus Rubianus[71] and a host of other distinguished men and young scholars, and in the two days that Luther stayed in Erfurt had the most delightful conversations with him. But as he was happily describing those events and actions and working them out in detail, there came into his hands a booklet published by Emser, in which the latter assailed Luther with taunts.[72] When Eobanus noticed that the pamphlet was prefaced by some utterly ridiculous and shoddy verses, he flew into a rage. On the spot he dashed off a poem in which he treated him, the theologian who had pretensions of being a poet, with a little too much severity and dealt with him somewhat too harshly. These are the only works where he, either in jest or in earnest, wrote or said anything to lampoon another man. He even hesitated when Philip Melanchthon[73] once asked him to write the loveliest poem in his best verses, in order to describe the worst and most disgusting thing on earth, and to do this in his behalf. Puzzled by the request at first, he asked what kind of thing that might be.

---

he went back to Erfurt, where he earned his M.A. in 1507. His first publication was a liminary epigram for Eobanus's *De laudibus* (1507). Later he also contributed some complimentary poems for the *Bucolicon* (*Buc.* B 7 and B 8). Ordained priest, he became headmaster of the monastery school at Fulda (1510-1516). There, in the spring of 1515, he wrote much of the *Epistolae obscurorum virorum* (part 1). In 1517 Crotus took up studies in Bologna, becoming doctor of divinity in 1519. He returned to Erfurt in 1520 as professor of theology, serving as rector of the university in 1520/21. In that capacity he led a delegation of the faculty to welcome Luther to Erfurt. The popular unrest that accompanied the Reformation and the ensuing collapse of the university disgusted him, however. He moved to Fulda, but in 1524 went to Königsberg and entered the service of Albert of Brandenburg. In 1531 he became a canon in Halle and delivered himself of an anti-Lutheran tract, *Apologia qua respondetur temeritati calumniatorum* (Leipzig, 1531). In 1537 he was a canon in Halberstadt. He died in ca. 1545.

[72] Camerarius refers to Emser's *Auff des Stieres tzu Wiettenberg wiettende replica* (Leipzig, [February] 1521). The pamphlet contains three satiric epigrams against Luther (sig. C2ᵛ). These stand at the end of the booklet (not at the beginning, as Camerarius suggests). Eobanus parodies some of those verses in his "In Hieronymum Emserum Lutheromastiga invectiva" (*Luth.* 7).

[73] Philip Melanchthon (1497-1560) of Bretten (Palatinate) matriculated at Heidelberg in 1509, earning his B.A. in 1511. The following year he enrolled at Tübingen (M.A. 1514). In 1518 he was named professor of Greek at Wittenberg. He soon established himself as one of Luther's closest collaborators, publishing the first systematic exposition of the reformed theology in his *Loci communes rerum theologicarum* (1521). Melanchthon took a leading role in the Reformation in Germany. He participated in the Marburg colloquy of 1529, the diet of Augsburg of 1530 (where he wrote the *Confessio Augustana*), and the political meetings at Schmalkalden in 1535 and 1537. He also reorganized universities and helped establish new ones, set up Protestant schools (including the one at Nuremberg where Eobanus taught), wrote numerous textbooks, and so earned the title "Preceptor of Germany."

primum miratus et requirens quidnam rei res illa esset, cum au-
diisset Calumniae descriptionem a Philippo expeti, se quidem
facere non posse dixit quin ei gratificaretur, itaque hunc laborem
se esse suscepturum, quamvis argumentum esset alienum a mo-
ribus et ingenio suo, qui neque ioco neque serio neque monendi
aut praecipiendi etiam caussa soleret insectationes aut reprae-
hensiones usurpare. 21 Usque adeo a toto hoc genere inquirendi
in aliquos et vitia aliorum notandi ac exagitandi animus et vo-
luntas Eobani abhorrebat. 22 Nam post multos annos, cum una
Norimbergae viveremus, quid consilii agitare coeperit cum ad se
tum me defendendum, quod uterque indigne tractari videretur,
a quo minime deberet, quoniam repressus conatus fuit, silentio
tegam, cum nostra tum eorum, ad quos illa res pertinet, causa.

    18, 1 Sed ut redeam ad institutum: Eobanus in hoc so-
dalitio quod augebant Iustus Moenius, cui neque studio
veritatis et bonarum artium neque laude officii facile reperires
quem posses anteponere, et is cum quo ego fraterno animo con-
iungebar, contubernalis meus Ioannes Francus, qui "Portunus"
C2ʳ a nobis cognominabatur, et | Megobachus, neque corpore neque
ingenio admodum dissimilis Eobano, item Iacobus Mycillus et
Antonius, cui "Musae" Eobanus cognomentum fecit, vir postea
in re ecclesiastica illustris, et pueri adhuc Valentinus Paceus,

[74]The poem, 101 distichs long, was published as *Elegia de Calumnia* at Marburg in
1538 (repr. Marburg, 1539; Wittenberg, 1560, together with Melanchthon's epigrams).
Melanchthon wanted it written because he himself was being subjected to much abuse from
Lutherans who suspected him of Catholic leanings.

    [75]Basing himself on information supplied by the conservative humanist Willibald Pirck-
heimer, Erasmus in September 1530 slurred the evangelical school at Nuremberg by accusing
its professors and students of laziness. See his *Epistola ad fratres Inferioris Germaniae, ASD* 9, 1,
p. 344, lines 396-401. Incensed, Eobanus fired off a private letter of protest (no longer extant),
in which he defended his own and Camerarius's scholarly and poetic productivity at the
school. Erasmus responded soothingly (though not always diplomatically) in Ep. 2446, dated
12 March 1531, and Ep. 2495, dated 17 May 1531 (both published in the *Epistolae floridae*,
Basel, September 1531). By the spring of 1531, as Camerarius hints, Eobanus had decided
against carrying on a public vendetta with Erasmus, all the more so as Pirckheimer had died a
few months earlier, on 22 December 1530.

    [76]Justus Menius (Jodocus Menig) was born at Fulda in 1499. He matriculated at Erfurt
in 1514, becoming B.A. in 1515. In 1519 he went to Wittenberg to continue his studies with
Luther and Melanchthon. He became vicar in Mühlberg near Erfurt in 1523, but lost this po-
sition in the spring of 1525 and returned to Erfurt. Before long he was named pastor at St.
Thomas's. After three difficult years in Erfurt, he moved to Gotha in 1528. He was appointed
pastor and superintendent at Eisenach in 1529, taking part in the Marburg colloquy that same
year. In 1556 he was pastor in Leipzig, where he died two years later.

    [77]Johann Frank of Burgtonna (ca. 1499–after 1568) enrolled at Erfurt in 1515, earning
the B.A. in 1517. In about 1521 he left Erfurt and became rector of a school in Gotha. The
name "Portunus" (taken from the ancient Roman deity who presided over harbors) was no
doubt meant to recall Frank's birthplace Burgtonna.

However, when he learned that Philip wanted a description of Calumny from him, he answered that he could not do other than to oblige him and would therefore accept this commission, even though the theme was alien to his character and temperament, he being a man who neither in jest nor in earnest or even for the sake of warning or admonishing was given to verbal attacks or rebukes.[74] That is how much Eobanus's mind-set and disposition recoiled from this whole business of finding fault with particular persons or of censuring and berating the vices of others. Many years later, when we lived in Nuremberg together, he did start thinking long and hard of defending himself and me, because someone from whom we hardly deserved such treatment appeared to be subjecting the two of us to shameful abuse. Since he refrained from carrying out his plan, however, I shall cloak it in silence, not only for our own sake, but also for the sake of those to whom this matter pertains.[75]

18 But to return to my subject: In this sodality Eobanus furthermore counted Justus Menius,[76] virtually unequalled in his devotion to the truth and the liberal arts and in his high sense of duty, as well as the man who was close to me like a brother, my housemate Johann Frank, whom we called "Portunus."[77] He was also good friends with Meckbach, who neither in build nor in temperament was all that much different from Eobanus[78]; likewise with Jakob Micyllus[79] and the Anton for whom Eobanus made up the surname "Musa," a man who afterwards rose to a position of honor in the church[80]; also with the then still young Valentin Paceus, whose piety, learn-

---

[78] Johann Meckbach (Meckenbach) of Spangenberg (b. 1495) enrolled at the University of Leipzig in 1514. In 1516 he matriculated at Erfurt, becoming B.A. in 1519 and M.A. in 1521 (together with Camerarius). He left Erfurt in 1528 to study medicine at Padua. After earning his M.D. he returned to Germany and became personal physician and privy councilor to Philip of Hesse at Kassel in 1532. He was professor of medicine at Marburg in 1534/35 and rector of the university in 1535. That same year he returned to Kassel as personal physician to the landgrave. He died in 1555.

[79] The Neo-Latin poet Jakob Micyllus (Molsheim, Moltzer) was born at Strasbourg in 1503. After matriculating at Erfurt in 1518 and studying with Eobanus Hessus, he continued his education in 1522/23 with Philip Melanchthon at Wittenberg. In 1524 he moved to Frankfurt am Main to become rector of the local Latin school. He was appointed professor of Greek at Heidelberg in 1533; the low salary, however, left him no choice but to return to Frankfurt in 1537 and resume his post as rector. From 1547 until his death in 1558 he was again professor of Greek in Heidelberg and, with the support of Melanchthon, worked to reform the university. Besides numerous textbooks, editions of the classics, commentaries, and translations into Latin, Micyllus produced much excellent verse, including a splendid epicedium on Eobanus's death. Most of his poetry was gathered up posthumously by his son Julius in *Sylvarum libri quinque* (1564).

[80] Anton Musa (West, Wesch) of Wiehe on the Unstrut matriculated at Erfurt in 1506 (B.A. 1507). From 1509 he studied at Leipzig. After his return to Erfurt he earned the M.A. in 1517. Musa became pastor in Erfurt in 1521, first at St. Moritz's and then at the Augustinian church. From 1524 he served as preacher in Jena, becoming pastor there in 1527 and superintendent in 1529. He resigned his post in 1536. The following year he became preacher and superintendent in Rochlitz. In the spring of 1544 he accepted a call to Merseburg, where he died in 1547.

cuius nunc etiam pietas, doctrina, eruditio celebris est, et D. Stibarus, quo neminem cognovi unquam flagrantiorem cupiditate discendi, cum innumerabilia ad perseverandum illi impedimenta obiicerentur, quique longius dignitate progressus voluntatem tamen erga studia et studiosos bonarum artium constantissime servat, et alii complures, quibus incensis optimarum artium studiis referta erat Erphordiana Academia: in hoc igitur coetu ille tum virtute, eruditione, facultate, scientia litterarum, dignitate excellens optimos autores linguae Latinae explicando operam navabat discere volentibus. 2 Alliciebat autem fama nominis Eobanici invitabatque permultos ut in Academiam Erphordianam vel discendi caussa migrarent vel ad visendum saltem Eobanum excurrerent. 3 Inter quos venit eo anno, quo post congressum celebrem illum Lipsicum M. Lutheri et Ioanni Eccii (qui autore illustrissimo Principe Georgio ad controversandum publice Lipsiam venerant) pestilentiae contagio Lipsiae infesta fuit: tum igitur ad nos venit acqualis et qui fuisset aliquando condiscipulus et contubernalis meus, Sebaldus Munsterus Noricus, qui postea, summos honores studiorum consecutus, iuris publici doctrinae praefuit VVitebergae.

C2ᵛ   4 Cumque pietate | et integritate et probitate, fide virtuteque excelleret, saepe nominis Eobanici memoriam renovare honorifica mentione et praedicare solebat, se unum omnium illum cognovisse cum eruditione litterarum praestantissimum, tum minime opinionis aliorum cupidum, tum vero ab omni fuco et simulatione remotissimum, et eum, qui neminem ab usu humanitatis suae excluderet.

19, 1 Sed Eobani quo tempore quasi decurrens spacium suum aetas vigebat et incitabatur studium, eo haec studia, bonarum, inquam, litterarum et humanitatis, malignius augebantur, horumque magistri atque doctores negligentius sub-

18, 3 Lutheri *Carpzov et Kreyssig*: Luteri *A*.

[81]Valentin Paceus (Hartung) was the first Lutheran preacher in Erfurt (since 1524). He moved to Lützen in 1544 and to Leipzig in 1547. There he took a doctorate in theology, lectured at the university, and preached at St. Nicholas's. In 1556 he returned to the Catholic fold and was named professor in Dillingen. As he was traveling to Lauingen in 1558, he was mistaken for a rich Jew and murdered.

[82]The nobleman Daniel Stiebar von Buttenheim was born in 1503 at Rabeneck, between Bamberg and Bayreuth. He matriculated at Erfurt in 1515, and in 1518 began a lifelong friendship with Camerarius. After studying in Wittenberg (1523) and Louvain, he spent several years at Würzburg. He resumed his studies in 1527 at Basel, from 1529 to 1530 at

ing, and scholarship are even now renowned,[81] and with the equally young Daniel Stiebar, who was the most enthusiastic student I have ever known, considering the innumerable obstacles to his perseverance that were thrown up in his path, and who, though he has since risen to become a prelate, has nevertheless remained well disposed toward the pursuit of learning and steadfastly continues to look after the students of the liberal arts[82]; and with a host of other fervent adherents of the humanities, with whom the University of Erfurt was crammed full at the time. It was in this band of comrades, then, that he, preeminent in virtue, erudition, ability, knowledge of literature, and stardom devoted his energies to explicating the best Latin authors to his students. And indeed, the glory of Eobanus's name was a magnet that attracted droves of people to the University of Erfurt, who either moved there to study or made the trip just to see Eobanus. Among the ones arriving in that year when Leipzig was stricken with an epidemic of plague (it followed that celebrated encounter between Martin Luther and Johann Eck, who had come to hold a public debate in Leipzig at the invitation of the illustrious Duke George[83]): well then, among those who came to us there was a youth my own age, a former fellow student and housemate of mine, Sebald Münster of Nuremberg, who subsequently, having earned the highest academic degrees, held the chair of civil law in Wittenberg.[84] And since he excelled in reverence and integrity and righteousness, in loyalty and virtue, he used to keep the memory of Eobanus's name alive by often speaking of him with the deepest respect. Indeed, he liked to say that he knew him not only as the single most outstanding literary scholar in the whole world but also as the least assuming person imaginable, a man totally free of affectation and pretense, who excluded no one from his circle of friends.

19 But just at the point when Eobanus's life, running its course, so to speak, had reached its prime, just when his zest for learning was in full flower, those studies – the study of good literature and culture, I mean – suddenly fell on hard times, in which the teachers and professors of the liberal arts received far too little help from those who had sole responsibility for such matters

---

Freiburg. In 1529 he became a canon in Würzburg. His bishop often sent him on diplomatic missions. Thus he attended the diets of Augsburg (1530) and Regensburg (1532), the Haguenau conference of 1540, and the diets of Regensburg (1541) and Nuremberg (1542). In 1552 he became provost of the Würzburg chapter. A moderate Catholic, he remained a steadfast friend and patron of the German humanists and poets, in particular the Protestants Camerarius and Petrus Lotichius. Stiebar suffered a stroke in 1552 and died three years later .

[83]The Leipzig Disputation between Luther and Johann Eck was held in June and July 1519 under the patronage of George the Bearded (1471-1539), duke of Saxony since 1500.

[84]Sebald Münster of Nuremberg matriculated at Leipzig in 1515, obtaining his B.A. in 1516, his M.A. in 1519. In the autumn of 1519 he rejoined his friend Camerarius in Erfurt. Thereafter he continued his studies in Wittenberg. In 1527 he earned a doctorate of laws and became professor at the university. He died of the plague in 1539.

levabantur ab iis quibus solis ea res tum in manibus erat. 2 Ac Maternus quidem, insignis illa tempestate Erphordiae theologus, nonnihil contulit ad culturam harum. 3 Sed ad quem Erphordiam me primum contuli, Georgius Paetus Vorhemius, vir is, de cuius pietate et praestantia si commemorare vellem quae utrique nostrum, Adame, nota sunt, iam novum argumentum oriretur et aliud scriptum texendum esset, ille vero tum quicquid potuit clam palamve suis et aliorum viribus, facultatibus, gratia, authoritate facere et moliri, in eo neque labori et studio pepercit neque invidiam fugit neque odium pertimuit, quo minus ea ageret, consuleret, reperiret, institueret quibus professio optimarum litterarum atque artium undique fulciretur atque sustentaretur. 4 Qui si diutius vitam conservare potuisset (dicam fortasse benevolentia erga illum copiosius, sed C3ʳ   vere me | dicturum esse existimo), et staret illa schola et dignitatem ac nomen retineret, quae quam ruinam fecerit, non possum sine maximo dolore cogitare.

5 Erat Crotus, cuius paulo ante feci mentionem, ab antiquo notus Eobano, vir doctus et egregius, sed cum ingenio vario tum mutabili sententia. 6 Is magistratu functus regendi Academiam Fuldam primum concessit et in Borussiam postea discessit. 7 Indeque reversus alienavit a se multorum studia, nescio qua de causa, vel nolo potius perscribere, ne, quem viventem colui, ei mortuo obtrectare videar. 8 Degebat tum, ut significavimus, in familia Augustiniana cognitione utriusque linguae instructus et varia ac multiplice doctrina praeditus Iohannes Langus, cui Eobanus fuit amicissimus. 9 Hic postea in confusione omnium solus sua diligentia, studio, industria et ecclesiasticam rem et scholasticam sustinuit Erphordiae, una cum Georgio Sturciade, usque ad annum fatalem, non modo ipsis, sed Germaniae, quo uterque sibi quidem neque praemature neque infeliciter, sed reipublicae intempestive et luctuose decessit.

[85]Maternus Pistorius (Pistoris) of Ingwiller in Alsace matriculated at Erfurt in 1488 (B.A. 1490, M.A. 1494). In ca. 1504 he became lector ordinarius in poetry and rhetoric. Eobanus praises him as such in *Laud.* 136-138 and 178-190. For a long time he was the leading humanist at Erfurt. Throughout his career he occupied prominent positions in the university (for example, dean in 1504/05, 1510/11, and 1518; rector in 1516 and 1527/28). In addition to his teaching and administrative duties, he continued his studies, becoming licentiate of theology in 1513 and doctor of theology in 1514. A good friend of Mutianus Rufus, he invited the latter to attend the graduation ceremony. However he had little or no contact with Eobanus Hessus and his circle; and during the tumultuous twenties he played only a minor role. As suffragan of the archbishop of Mainz for Thuringia, he was named bishop of Ascalon in January 1534; but he died on 5 September, before being consecrated.

[86]Georg Petz of Forchheim, more commonly known as Georg Forchheim, matriculated at Erfurt in 1507 as "Georgius Bitzbaudeler." He graduated B.A. in 1509, M.A. in 1515, and

then. There were exceptions, of course. Maternus, the distinguished Erfurt theologian in that era, contributed not a little to humanistic studies.[85] So did Georg Petz of Forchheim, the man to whom I turned first after arriving in Erfurt.[86] But if I wanted to mention everything about his piety and preeminence that the two of us, Adam, know from personal experience, I would get sidetracked into a new theme and be obliged to weave another composition. Without a doubt he did whatever he could in those days, maneuvering behind the scenes or out in the open, using his power, talent, influence, and authority, and urging others to do the same. In that battle he spared neither toil nor trouble, he neither flinched from ill will nor quailed before hatred, so long as he could accomplish, take thought for, devise, or set into motion whatever it took to shore up and sustain the teaching of the best literatures and arts. If he could have stayed alive longer (perhaps I am too generous in this estimation out of sheer goodwill towards him, but I do think I am speaking the truth), that school would still be standing today with its dignity and reputation intact. Now that it has gone to ruin, I cannot think back on this without the greatest distress.

Crotus, whom I mentioned a bit earlier,[87] was an old friend of Eobanus's, a learned and eminent man, but moody and fickle-minded. Having completed his rectorate at the university, he first left for Fulda and later moved to Prussia. But after returning from there, he began to alienate many people, why, I do not know, or rather, I do not want to detail, lest I seem to disparage in death one whom I respected in life. Also living in Erfurt at that time, as I indicated, was a member of the Augustinian Order, a man trained in both Latin and Greek and furnished with a broad and many-sided education, Johann Lang, with whom Eobanus was the best of friends.[88] It was he alone who afterwards, amidst the general confusion, devoted all his diligence, zeal, and industry to save the ecclesiastical and scholastic institutions of Erfurt from utter collapse, he, together with Georg Sturtz, right up to that year, so fateful not only for themselves, but also for Germany, when both of them died[89] – a death neither premature nor unhappy for themselves, to be sure, but untimely and grievous for their country.

---

bachelor of divinity in 1520. During the summer semester of 1518 he was named a member of the Collegium maius and hence also of the faculty council; and in 1520 he was elected taxator. Camerarius lived at Forchheim's house while at Erfurt. An enthusiastic follower of Luther, Forchheim studied at Wittenberg during the summer term of 1521. It is to him that Eobanus dedicated the Luther-elegies in May 1521. He died unexpectedly on 10 July 1522.

[87] See *Nar.* 17, 17, with fn. 71.

[88] See *Nar.* 17, 3, with fn. 57.

[89] Johann Lang and Georg Sturtz both died in 1548, the year when Emperor Charles V tried to end the religious schism by imposing the Augsburg Interim. Apart from some minor concessions to the Protestants, this formula amounted to a restoration of Catholic ritual and doctrine.

20, 1 Hic Georgius Sturciades singulari me amore, cum primum Erphordiam ex Italia reversus venisset, complexus fuit, ut a natura ipsa nos quasi copulari appareret, meque recepit in aedes suas, quas de soceri Eobani haeredibus emerat. 2 Et multis postea beneficiis auxit ornavitque iudicio suo, cum tantum tribueret tam iis, quae a me disputabantur, quam commenda-

C3ᵛ   tionibus et testimoniis, ut me non vereretur | saepe gravissimarum rerum autorem nominare et nihil unquam de altero petenti negaverit, neque, si quid a me affirmaretur, dubitando reddiderit incertum. 3 Cum hoc designatus fui et mox renunciatus decimus nonus, secundo loco, ut opinor, Magister Optimarum Artium, declarante iudicium de nobis eorum, qui suffragia tulerant, Eobano Hesso, qui tum luculentam habuit orationem, ut fert mos Academiarum. 4 In renunciatione Sturciades non affuit, revocatus in patriam iis negotiis quae in aliud tempus differri aut negligi non deberent neque possent. 5 Petiverat una hunc honorem Antonius Niger, laudatissimus iuvenis, cuius nunc splendor nominis et famae claritas multis nationibus innotuit. 6 Sed huic quorundam tum ieiuna malevolentia cum maxima ipsius gloria obstitit, neque quicquam causae reperiebatur quam quod bonarum artium et studiorum humanitatis avidior et in his colendis fuisset liberior. 7 Aliam igitur ingressus viam nos petitores antevertit et frementibus invidis consecutus id fuit quod hi negarant, aliquanto quidem, ut ita dicam, pomposius et splendidius quam ipsi conferre potuissent. 8 Hic annus fuit Christi Iesu M.D.XXI incipiens. 9 Iunxit autem amicitiam cum Eobano Sturciades, cum Erphordiam venisset, quam postea sanctissime et fidelissime conservavit atque coluit. 10 Sed tum in Italiam rediit et abduxit secum Euricium Cordum, qui adiutus a Sturciade autoritate publica ibidem Doctor Medicinae renunciatus fuit.

---

[90]In 1519.

[91]See *Nar.* 14, 7-8, with fn. 45.

[92]Of the 19 candidates for the M.A. in January 1521, only Antonius Niger did not pass. The top candidate was Georg Sturtz. Camerarius ranked fourth (not second, as he remembered).

[93]This oration is not extant. For another commencement speech, delivered in 1520, see *Epp. fam.*, pp. 248-252.

[94]Anton Spet, better known by his humanist name Niger (Melas, Mela), was born in Wrocław around the turn of the century. He matriculated at Erfurt in 1516 and graduated B.A. in 1518. From 1518 to 1521 he taught at the school of St. Mary's, where Euricius Cordus was rector. An impassioned humanist, he joined Eobanus Hessus in writing scathing epigrams against Edward Lee (June 1520). Accordingly, when a radically pro-Lutheran notice was posted on the door of the Collegium maius in August 1520, the suspicion immediately fell on

20 As soon as he returned from Italy to Erfurt,[90] this Georg Sturtz embraced me with such unusually warm love, that it seemed as if we were joined in friendship by nature herself, and welcomed me into his home, which he had purchased from the heirs of Eobanus's father-in-law.[91] Even in after years he showered many blessings upon me and honored me with his esteem. Indeed, he thought so highly of my publications as well as of the commendations and testimonials that came my way that he did not shy from often calling me an authority in the weightiest matters and never turned down a request from me or questioned anything that I had affirmed. Together with him I graduated as Master of the Finest Arts, ranking second, I believe, in a class of nineteen.[92] Eobanus Hessus announced the decision of those who had voted on us and then delivered a superb oration, as academic tradition requires.[93] Sturtz did not attend the graduation exercises, for he had been called back to his hometown on the kind of business that neither should nor can be postponed or neglected. Another who had applied for that degree along with us was Anton Niger, a most praiseworthy youth, whose splendid renown and brilliant fame are now celebrated in many countries.[94] But he was blocked, not only by the barren malevolence of a certain clique, but also by his own extraordinary reputation, apparently for no other reason than that he had been too eager for the liberal arts and humanistic studies and too unrestrained in cultivating them. Forced to take a different path, therefore, he stole a march on the rest of us candidates; for while the backbiters grumbled, he obtained the very thing that these men had denied him; and if I may say so, he got it with quite a bit more pageantry than they themselves could have provided. This occurred early in the year of Christ Jesus 1521. Now when Sturtz arrived in Erfurt he became close friends with Eobanus, a friendship he afterwards maintained and cherished with uttermost purity and faithfulness. But then he returned to Italy and took along Euricius Cordus, who with Sturtz's financial support was granted the degree of Doctor of Medicine by one of that country's universities. That same year I myself left Erfurt, now riven with dissension and riots and infected with an epidemic of plague.[95]

Niger. Though his involvement in this affair was never proven, the conservative professors turned him down for a promotion to M.A. in early 1521. Undeterred, he seems to have gone directly to Wittenberg and graduated there. Upon his return to Erfurt, the younger professors encouraged him to hold lectures despite the faculty's refusal to admit him. He continued until his expulsion in the summer of 1522. After stays in Wrocław, Vienna, Poznań, and Leipzig he was named professor of natural sciences at Marburg in 1533. In 1536 he graduated M.D. in Padua. The following year he was appointed town physician in Brunswick, where he continued to teach Greek and natural science. He died in 1555.

[95] In April, June, and July 1521, Lutheran mobs ransacked and destroyed the houses of the conservative canons and theologians in Erfurt. With the city split into bitter factions, the university in turmoil, and a plague ravaging Erfurt throughout the summer, many of the teachers and students – Camerarius included – left the city for good.

11 Eo anno et nos | Erphordiam reliquimus, iam dissidiis et tu-
multuatione quatefactam et pestilentiae lue infectam. 12 Rever-
sus autem ex Italia denuo Sturciades quem se erga Eobanum ges-
serit, de Eobanicis scriptis potest cognosci. 13 Is enim erat
Eobanus, qui merita aliorum non modo tegendo non obliterare,
sed praedicando etiam amplificare soleret. 14 Quamvis autem
hae res fortasse exiles et parvae esse videantur, tamen de Eobani et
Sturciadae usu cum caritatis singularis tum fidei, liberalitatis
memoriae exempla pulcerrima relicta esse statuo.

21, 1 Et si autem multis de caussis abhorret animus ab in-
dicatione fortunae Eobanicae, quae ingenio, doctrina, virtute,
studio illius revocanti forte ad humanae rem intelligentiae ratio-
nes indigna fuisse videatur, tamen postulat fides mea ut non
praetereatur silentio id, quod cum verum sit, tum apud pru-
dentes diminuere existimationem viri nequeat. 2 Ut enim alia
innumerabilia cum disputata sapienter tum gesta praeclare ad
paupeitatis gloriam et ignominiam divitiarum taccam, quid So
lonis, cui in proclivi esset principatu civitatis florentis opibus ac
viris potiri si vellet, elegia canat, videamus, de nostra quidem, si
placet, conversione. 3 Sic igitur ille:

Divitiis auget multos fortuna scelestos
    Atque bonos nulla commoditate levat.
Nos tamen haud ducemus opes virtute priores.
    Haec est certa. Illas sors regit instabilis.

4 Cum igitur Eobani eo ferme tempore admodum in an- |
gustum cogerentur copiae, ut ait Terentius, et publicus respectus
penitus illi subtraheretur, privati pauci (inter quos principem
locum tenebat Sturciades) sublevarent hominem doctum
probumque et innocentem et, quod erat caput, amicum, de-
liberantibus his de salute propemodum cum ipsius tum liberum,
placuit quaestuosae eum arti cuipiam operam dare, non iam
famae amplificandae caussa, sed ne fame laborare mox cogere-
tur. 5 Atque autores illi fuere amici ut medicinam disceret,
quoniam priores conatus forenses parum successissent. 6 Hoc
ille fretus potissimum ope et adiumentis a Sturciade cupidissime
amplexus fuit et statim libros comparavit et illas res studio maxi-
mo coepit cognoscere. 7 Et si autem ad factitandam artem pro-
gressus non fuit, hoc tamen studium quam diu vixit coluit et

20, 11 tumultuatione *Carpzov et Kreyssig*: tumultatione *A*.   21, 3 Illas *Carpzov et Kreyssig*:
Illos *A*.   21, 6 potissimum *Carpzov et Kreyssig*: potiss. *A*.

How Sturtz conducted himself toward Eobanus after coming back from Italy a second time, one can find out from Eobanus's writings. For Eobanus was not the man to consign his benefactors to oblivion by keeping their merits under wraps, but liked to exalt them by singing their praises. And even though these matters may perhaps seem paltry and insignificant, I nonetheless feel that the friendship between Eobanus and Sturtz has bequeathed to our memory the loveliest examples, not only of extraordinary affection, but also of loyalty and generosity.

21 Now even though my mind for many reasons shrinks from touching on Eobanus's misfortune, which to anyone who tries to account for it in terms of human reason must seem unworthy of his genius, learning, virtue, and zeal, still my sense of honesty demands that I not pass over in silence something which, true as it is, cannot detract from the man's reputation among prudent people. To say nothing of the countless other sage treatises and lustrous exempla demonstrating the glory of poverty and the shame of riches, let us observe what Solon sings in an elegy of his – Solon, who as archon of a wealthy and populous city could easily have enriched himself, had he wanted to. The translation, if you please, is my own. This, then, is what he tells us:

> Fortune blesses many scoundrels with abundance of money,
>   but to good men she never offers relief.
> We, however, will not consider riches superior to virtue.
>   Virtue abides. Fickle fate rules over wealth.

Well then, when Eobanus's resources at just about that time were, to use Terence's phrase, "reduced to dire straits" and the city's support for him was utterly withdrawn,[96] a few private individuals (among whom Sturtz occupied the first place) did everything they could to support this learned and upright and blameless man and, most importantly, this loyal friend of theirs. After careful deliberation about the welfare both of himself and his children, they agreed that he should apply himself to some lucrative profession, not in order to become more famous but to avoid being famished in the very near future. It was those friends, therefore, who suggested to him that he study medicine, since his earlier attempts at reading law had gotten nowhere.[97] Relying especially on Sturtz's help and financial backing, he avidly threw himself into this field of study, at once purchased the necessary books, and began to master this body of knowledge with the greatest eagerness. And though he admit-

---

[96] In early May 1525 the city council withdrew Eobanus's salary, ostensibly to facilitate a reorganization of the university. With a growing family to support, Eobanus now had to live on just 30 florins a year, paid to him by the university for teaching a one-hour class daily.

[97] Before switching to the study of medicine in the summer of 1523, Eobanus had taken a notion to resume his legal studies and become a lawyer. See Mutian. *Ep.* 617.

librorum de illa compositorum lectione admodum fuit delecta-
tus. **8** Tum igitur Eobanus, cum propemodum a solo Sturciade
retineretur Erphordiae, ibi haesit ut potuit, conflictatus cum
multis adversis, ad annum usque Iesu Christi 1526, quo, autore
et conciliatore Philippo Melanchthone, qui et amabat et admi-
rabatur et magnifaciebat et venerabatur Eobanum eximium in
modum, Norimbergam venit, ab illa civitate accersitus perquam
benigne. **9** In qua una cum illo ego et Michaelus Rotingus vix-
imus annis circiter septem et eas litteras atque artes quas
didiceramus docuimus, sine specie quidem dignitatis, sed cum
aliquo certe non vulgaris commoditatis fructu, id quod | ab
aliis iam statui et dici par fuerit, praesertim cum rationes
nostrae quasi gestae provinciae relatae sint et extent.

22, 1 Praeerant tum Noricis ludis omnes optimi et doc-
tissimi viri, sed duo duobus primis, Ioannes Chezimanus, natus
ad puerilem institutionem, qui illi civitati moriens ingens sui de-
siderium reliquit, et Sebaldus Heidena, qui, cum haec scribere-
mus, suo adhuc loco laudabiliter curabat. **2** Cum his uni-
versis Eobano et nobis iucundus consuetudinis usus inter-
cedebat. **3** Hoc tempore quo Norimbergae Eobanus mansit
multa quae ante edita fuerant recognovit et iterum edidit, multa
nova fecit carmina, quae omnia sunt in medio. **4** Attentius etiam
tum quam ante Graecos autores legere coepit, cumque ei inpri-
mis Theocriti bucolica arriderent, in illa convertenda Latine
incubuit. **5** Quem conatum omnibus ego rebus adiuvare stude-
bam. **6** Nam initio multa obiiciebantur illi, quibus impetus
animi retunderentur, ipse vero, si quid non celeriter procedebat,
haud consueverat urgere. **7** Nihil faciebat omnino anxie aut
solicite, sed tantum sequebatur ductum naturae et ingenii

C5ʳ

21, 9 Michaelus *Kreyssig*: Micaelus *A*.

[98]In early May 1526.

[99]The nephew of Veit Werler (see *Nar.* 11, 4, with fn. 33) and brother-in-law of Johann
Ketzmann, Michael Roting was born in Sulzfeld (Franconia) in 1494. He began his studies at
Ingolstadt, but switched to Leipzig in 1515 (B.A. 1518). Impressed by Luther at the Leipzig
Disputation in 1519, he matriculated at Wittenberg and became friends not only with Luther
himself, but also with Philip Melanchthon, Hieronymus Baumgartner, and Joachim Camera-
rius. From 1526 he taught rhetoric, dialectic, and theology at the Gymnasium of St. Aegidius
in Nuremberg. After Camerarius's departure Roting served as rector of the school (from 1535
to 1543). He died in 1588, at the ripe old age of 94.

[100]Johann Ketzmann, Michael Roting's brother-in-law, was born at Schwabach in 1487.
After obtaining his M.A. (in Ingolstadt?) he lived for some time in Cologne. In 1517 he was
appointed rector at the St. Lorenz school in Nuremberg, a position he held until his death in
1542. Eobanus addresses a lighthearted poem to him in *Sylv.* 9, 25.

tedly never advanced so far as to practise medicine, he nonetheless pursued these studies as long as he lived and greatly enjoyed reading books that dealt with that subject. Thus, held fast at Erfurt only by Sturtz and practically nothing else, Eobanus persevered as long as he could, all the while battling his many adversaries right up to the year of Jesus Christ 1526, when at the instigation and mediation of Philip Melanchthon, who loved and admired and extolled and revered Eobanus to a remarkable degree, he came to Nuremberg,[98] having been invited by that city on exceedingly generous terms. It was there that he and I and Michael Roting[99] lived together for some seven years and taught those literatures and arts in which we were experts. But while our position may have lacked prestige, we certainly brought forth some uncommonly agreeable fruit. But that is for others to judge and say, especially since the account of how we managed our province, so to speak, has been duly recorded and published.

22 The schools of Nuremberg were at that time headed exclusively by the very best and most learned of men, two of them in particular, each in a different school: Johann Ketzmann, a born teacher of boys, who at his death left a huge void in the city's heart,[100] and Sebald Heyden, who even as I write these words is still laudably performing his duties.[101] With all of them Eobanus and I were joined in a delightful friendship. During the time that Eobanus lived in Nuremberg he revised a good many of the works he had published earlier and brought them out again; he also wrote many new poems, which are all still in print. In addition, he now started reading the Greek authors more attentively than before; and since he was especially taken with Theocritus's bucolics, he set himself the task of translating them into Latin. This was a project I endeavored to facilitate with all the means at my disposal.[102] For initially he ran into many obstacles that blunted his determination to continue; in truth, when the going was slow, he was not one to keep plodding on. He was never in the least finicky or painstaking in any-

---

[101] Sebald Heyden of Bruck near Erlangen (1499-1561) received his elementary education in Nuremberg and then studied in Ingolstadt from 1513 to 1519. Upon his return to Nuremberg in 1519 he was appointed cantor at the school of the Hospital Church, becoming its rector in 1521. From 1525 until his death in 1561 he taught at the St. Sebald school. Heyden wrote numerous Protestant hymns, several of which remained popular into the eighteenth century. His reworking of the Marian antiphon "Salve regina" into a praise of Christ (1520) caused an uproar, to which he responded in *Adversus hypocritas calumniatores* (1524). He also made a name for himself through several textbooks on musical theory, in particular *Musicae, id est, artis canendi libri duo* (1537; second edition 1540). For some poems that Eobanus addressed to him see *Sylv.* 5, 36; 5, 47; and *Epp. fam.*, p. 230.

[102] Textual corruptions and other obstacles often made Eobanus despair of ever finishing the verse translation; but after three years of intermittent work he was finally able to publish it as *Theocriti Syracusani idyllia triginta sex* (Haguenau, 1531). The extant correspondence bears out Camerarius's recollection that Eobanus called on him time and again to help him with philological problems. When Eobanus's translation appeared in 1531, Camerarius supplied the accompanying Greek text.

incitationem. **8** Itaque abiecta semel non fere solebat resumere neque interrupta contexere. **9** Neque non animadverti a lectore attento hoc facile potest, quod continuo cursu aequabiliter defluant Eobanica omnia neque uspiam quasi ad considerationis solicitae obiices refringantur. **10** Itaque noster Milichius dicere solebat Eobanum solum omnium quos novisset simul facere versus et | scribere, cum alii prius commentando modo has, modo illas partes absolverent et ita tandem scriberent aliquid, alii prius scriberent et fingendo atque corrigendo demum facerent aliquid qualiumcunque versuum. **11** Quae cum ita se habere experirer, nonnihil negotii fiebat mihi, etiam calliditatis aliquid usurpandum erat, ne Eobanus voluntatem perseverandi in traductione Theocriti deponeret neve ardor animi illius restingueretur: ita enim profecto opus illud luculentissimum intercidisset, quod absolutum et celebrat ingenium atque facultatem Eobani et studiosis bonarum artium ad fructum eruditionis percipiendum propositum est. **12** In quo perficiendo et cohortationem et operam meam aliquid praestitisse laetor.

C5ᵛ

23, **1** Cum autem ita peractum sit illud prope septem annorum tempus quod consumsit Norimbergae Eobanus, ut me ille valde diligeret et ego eum, ut par erat, observarem, quasi perpetuo una nos futuros esse certum esset, ita in securitate quadam postea sensi fastidium tacite obrepsisse mihi eius boni quod haberem in manibus. **2** Ac nunc quoque intelligo in aetatis iuvenilis levitate vel fuisse sensum praesentis felicitatis meum hebetiorem vel hanc certe minoris me fecisse quam debuerim. **3** Itaque cum iam carendum esset consuetudine Eobani, tum magis cognovi quantum iucunditatis mihi esset ereptum, quam copiam oblatae commoditatis animadverteram, dum frui illa concedebatur. **4** Etsi autem non ea, qua par fuit, cupiditate vide- | or mihi persecutus esse occasiones familiaritatis et assidui usus amicitiae Eobani et multis in partibus fuisse negligentior, tamen quamdiu in illa urbe simul viximus, nihil ego sine illo in studiis conandum moliendumve aut edendum duxi, nihil ipse suscepit de quo non mecum communicaret, magis quod coniunctionis nostrae suavitate delectaretur quam quod opera ei nostra esset opus, et si ille quidem mihi tantum tribuebat quantum ipsius epistolae et alia scripta loquuntur. **5** Inter quae unus totus liber

C6ʳ

---

[103]Born at Freiburg im Breisgau in 1501, Jakob Milich matriculated there in 1514 (B.A. 1515, M.A. 1520). After graduating M.D. at Vienna in 1524 he settled in Wittenberg as practising physician and professor of philosophy (later of medicine). In 1536 Milich accompanied Melanchthon on a visit to the Palatinate, making a detour to Marburg to see Eobanus in September. He died at Wittenberg in 1559.

thing he did, but only followed the lead of nature and the impulse of his mind. In consequence he would hardly ever go back to something he had dropped or resume weaving a composition that had been cut short. And in fact this cannot fail to be readily apparent to an attentive reader – namely that all of Eobanus's verses flow evenly in unbroken course and are nowhere checked, so to speak, by the barriers of anxious fretfulness. That is why our good friend Milich[103] used to say that, of all the people he knew, Eobanus was the only one who could simultaneously create verses and write them down, whereas some poets first laboriously work out now this part, now that one and only then put something on paper, while others start off by scribbling lines and then through polishing and correcting finally produce some verses of indifferent quality. Since I knew from experience how matters stood with him, I had to go to a great deal of trouble and even resort to some tricks to make sure that Eobanus did not abandon his intention of sticking with the translation of Theocritus or let his enthusiasm flag, for otherwise that absolutely splendid work of his would surely have perished. Now that it is finished, however, it does honor to Eobanus's talent and skill and stands as a shining example for students of the liberal arts to bring their learning to fruition. That my encouragement and effort were in some measure responsible for its completion makes me happy indeed.

23 Now because that almost seven-year span of time that Eobanus spent in Nuremberg passed in such a way that he loved me greatly and I (as was only right) honored him as if we could count on staying together indefinitely, I was at length lulled into a certain complacency, so that I secretly felt welling up in me a satiety of that good which I had within my grasp.[104] And even now I realize that in the light-mindedness of my youthful age either my sense of present happiness was too dull or I certainly made less of it than I should have. And so, when I actually had to do without Eobanus's company, I realized far more acutely how much delightfulness had been snatched away from me and recognized the fullness of this proffered blessing far more keenly than I had ever done, while I still had a chance to enjoy it. But even though it seems to me that I did not take every possible chance to be in Eobanus's company and bask in his friendship as fervently and assiduously as I ought to have done and in many ways took him for granted, still for as long as we lived together in that city I never thought of taking up or laboring at or publishing any literary project without him, and he for his part never undertook anything without staying in constant touch with me, more because he enjoyed the pleasure of our fellowship than that he needed my assistance, even if he did give me as much credit as his letters and other writings contend. Among

---

[104] During the early thirties Camerarius started to distance himself somewhat from the improvident, hard-drinking poet, who at times seemed quite out of place among the sober-minded merchants and patricians of Nuremberg.

carminum mihi ab illo dicatus et relatus in Silvas eius ostendit et quantum me (utinam meo merito!) dilexerit et quam honorifice de me senserit et quanti fecerit necessitudinem nostram.

24, 1 Habebat autem complures alios, a quibus colebatur et cum quibus hilariter vivere et apud quos libenter esse consueverat. 2 Ex quibus unus vicinus ipsius Vilhelmus musicus assiduus comes erat Eobani, quotiescunque hoc agebat ut vel prodeambulando vel ad sodalitium se conferendo curis animum relaxaret et studiorum defatigationi repararet. 3 Thomae Venatorii consortium erat Eobano pergratum, nam et simplex in homine libertas huic probabatur et communitas studiorum placebat. 4 Thomas enim et ingenio acri erat et industria studii sui opera doctrinae edebat luculenta. 5 Ex caeteris qui doctrinae sacrae praeerant et venerabatur et diligebat maxime Vincilaum Lincum, cum propter pietatem et studium veritatis tum huma- |

C6ᵛ   nitatem atque candorem, quae in illo viro omnia erant eximia. 6 Vincentius autem Obsopaeus non diu postquam nos venissemus Norimbergam discessit in viciniam, ubi munificentia Marchionis Georgii, illustrissimi principis, et ipse ocium in studio litterarum traducendum nactus fuit. 7 Bilibaldo Pircamero valetudo obstabat, quo minus crebro ad se accerseret et invitaret Eobanum.

[105] See the fifth book of Eobanus's *Sylvarum libri VI* (1535; repr. in *Sylvarum libri IX,* 1539).

[106] Wilhelm Breitengraser (Breytengasser) was born at Nuremberg in ca. 1495. He matriculated at Leipzig in 1514, but never obtained an academic degree. Hence he returned to Nuremberg and became a schoolmaster at the monastery school of St. Aegidius in ca. 1519. A tippler like Eobanus, he was also a gifted composer. His polyphonic compositions (secular and sacred songs, a mass, organ music) enjoyed considerable popularity in Germany and abroad. When Breitengraser died in 1542, Thomas Venatorius wrote an epitaph for him.

[107] The humanist and theologian Thomas Venatorius (Jäger) was born at Nuremberg in 1490. After studying the arts, mathematics, and theology at various universities, he came back to Nuremberg in 1520 at the urging of his friend Willibald Pirckheimer. In 1523 he was appointed preacher at the Hospital Church and in the next few years became a leader of the Reformation in Nuremberg. From 1533 to 1547 he served as pastor of St. Jacob's. Besides theological and ethical writings (including *De virtute Christiana,* 1529), he composed Latin verse (among them a "Monodia" on Dürer's death in 1528 that was published together with Eobanus's epicedium), translated Aristophanes' *Plutus* (to which Eobanus contributed a liminary epigram, 1531), and edited the works of Archimedes in Greek and Latin (1544). He died at Nuremberg in 1551.

[108] Wenceslaus Linck of Colditz in Saxony (1483-1547) enrolled at Leipzig in 1498, but broke off his studies in 1501/02 to enter the order of Augustinian Eremites. In 1503 he was sent to Wittenberg. There he graduated B.A. in 1504, M.A. in 1506, and doctor of theology in 1511. After several years serving the order at Wittenberg and Munich, he was named preacher at Nuremberg in 1517. A close friend of Luther, he attended the Leipzig Disputation of 1519. In 1520 he was named vicar-general of the order, but resigned the position in 1523 to become preacher in Altenburg. From 1525 until his death in 1547 he preached in Nuremberg and published a series of biblical exegeses.

them, an entire book of poems that he dedicated to me and included in his
Sylvae demonstrates not just how fond he was of me (if only I deserved it!),
but also how much he respected me and how deeply he valued our
friendship.[105]

24 Of course he had quite a number of other friends too who were de-
voted to him and with whom he used to have a good time and whose
company he gladly kept. One of them was his neighbor Wilhelm, a musician
on whom Eobanus could always rely whenever he wanted to go for a walk or
needed some companionship to unwind from his work and relax the mind
from his exhausting studies.[106] Eobanus was also very glad to spend time with
Thomas Venatorius, for he approved of the man's straightforward and out-
spoken style and liked that they had so many interests in common.[107] And
indeed, Thomas was not only possessed of a keen intellect, but also labored
long and hard to publish splendid works of erudition. Among the other pas-
tors he especially revered and loved Wenceslaus Linck, as much for his piety
and devotion to the truth as for his humanity and kindness, which were all ex-
ceptional in that man.[108] Vincent Obsopoeus, by contrast, left Nuremberg
not long after we arrived there and went to a nearby town, where through the
munificence of that illustrious prince Margrave George he obtained the lei-
sure to devote himself to literary scholarship.[109] Willibald Pirckheimer's
health prevented him from often inviting Eobanus and having him over at
his house.[110]

[109]Vincent Opsopoeus (Heydnecker, Heidecker), the son of a Bavarian cook, taught for
a while in Salzburg before matriculating at Leipzig in April 1524. Later that year he moved to
Nuremberg, became friends with Willibald Pirckheimer, and began editing and translating
various Greek authors. Among his poetic works are a translation of books 2 and 9 of Homer's
Iliad (1527), which Eobanus criticized severely, a verse paraphrase of selected Psalms (1532),
and three books on the art of toasting (*De arte bibendi,* 1536). In 1526 Opsopoeus made fun
of Eobanus for writing a seven-foot hexameter. Ignoring Camerarius's call for restraint, Eoba-
nus struck back in the third of his *Elegiae tres.* From about 1528 until his death in 1539
Obsopoeus was rector of the Latin school in Ansbach.

[110]Willibald Pirckheimer, the last male descendant of a patrician family in Nuremberg,
was born at Eichstätt in 1470. A student of law and the humanities at Padua and Pavia, he re-
turned to Nuremberg in 1495 and was elected to the city council, a post he held from 1495 to
1502 and from 1505 to 1523. During the war between Maximilian I and the Swiss confed-
eration, Pirckheimer was captain of the contingent from Nuremberg. A skillful administrator
and diplomat, he often represented his native city at diets and conducted embassies to neigh-
boring states and princes, in particular the margraves of Brandenburg-Ansbach. It was his
erudition, however, that earned him fame throughout Europe. He edited and annotated many
of the ancient classics, translated works from Greek into Latin and from both classical lan-
guages into German, and wrote numerous literary works of his own, including an ironic praise
of podagra (1522) and a moving elegy on the death of Albrecht Dürer (1528). During the
Reuchlin-controversy, he vigorously defended the great humanist against the obscurantists.
As the Reformation took hold in Nuremberg and threatened to force the closure of the nun-
neries where his seven sisters and three daughters were living, Pirckheimer grew increasingly
hostile to Luther and his doctrines. He died on 22 December 1530. Eobanus never did become
friends with Pirckheimer – not because of the latter's fragile health, as Camerarius suggests, but

8 Hieronymus autem Baumgertnerus ex senatoribus, ut in studiis optimarum disciplinarum et artium educatus, quam humanitatem (quae erat summa) cum natura ei contulerat tum addiderat institutio, ea Eobanum complectebatur, omnium cura et respectu dignissimum et cui sublevatione et auxilio esset interdum opus, quod neque peritus gubernationis domesticae neque impendens ullam cogitationem rei familiari vel stabiliendae vel augendae neque sollicitus de patrimonio constituendo saepenumero plagam acciperet vel ab iis, quibus fidem temere habuerat, vel interdum incircumspecte cum cautis et attentis contrahendo negotia vel etiam debitis inconsiderate sese implicando. **9** Sed amicorum studio fiebat, ut publica liberalitate, quoties haerebat, explicaretur, quam ipsum saepe deinde magnifice praedicasse et nonnunquam in aliis desideravisse comperimus.

10 Dabat tum operam Noribergensi civitati Iohannes Mylius iurisconsultus, vir iusticia et prudentia nemini secundus, doctrina et virtute cultuque religionis multis prior. **11** Apud hunc saepe convenieba- | mus, et de illius sententia institutum sodalitium fuit. **12** In quo praecipui erant ipse Mylius, Michaelus Rotingus collega noster, Georgius Hopellus scriba primarius senatus et summi viri Lazari Spengeleri collega, ego. **13** In orbem autem convertebatur acceptio, quae erat potus ad vesperam cum bellariis. **14** Proponere autem materiam oportebat eum, cuius partes erant ut acciperet alios, de qua tum quaereretur et disputaretur. **15** De hac ubi verborum satis fecisse videbamur, tum reliquum tempus iocis et familiaribus collocutionibus atque interdum ludicris impendebatur, dum discederemus quisque ad

C7ʳ

24, 8 Baumgertnerus *Kreyssig*: Bamgertnerus *A*.

because the patrician-humanist wanted to keep the sometimes irresponsible Protestant poet at arms' length. When Eobanus proposed that they publish their epicedia for Dürer jointly, Pirckheimer seems to have rebuffed him brusquely; and when he dedicated the revised and augmented *Idyllia* to him in 1528, Pirckheimer greeted the gesture with silence.

[111] Hieronymus Baumgartner was born at Nuremberg in 1498. After five years of study at Ingolstadt and a semester at Leipzig in 1518, he matriculated at Wittenberg in the autumn of 1518 to study philosophy, mathematics, law, and ancient languages. Much taken with Luther and Melanchthon, Baumgartner helped introduce the Reformation in Nuremberg and co-founded the Gymnasium of St. Aegidius in 1526. During the following years he occupied influential posts in the city government and often represented Nuremberg at the diets (Speyer, 1529; Augsburg, 1530; Schmalkalden, 1536) and on diplomatic missions. He died in 1565.

[112] Johann Möller of Würzburg matriculated at Erfurt in 1502 (B.A. 1504, M.A. 1508). In the latter half of 1509 he edited three poems by Eobanus, printed in *Palladii de*

Speaking of the city councilors: Hieronymus Baumgartner, as a man educated in the best disciplines and arts, embraced Eobanus with the peerless humanity that nature had bestowed on him and his superb training had enhanced.[111] For he regarded Eobanus as one who, of all men, was the most worthy of attention and respect, but who occasionally needed a boost and a lift because, having no idea how to run a household and giving no thought to either maintaining or increasing his personal possessions and showing no concern with building up savings, he often got hurt, either by people he heedlessly trusted or at times by making imprudent deals with wary and frugal people or even by getting himself carelessly entangled in debts. But whenever he was stuck, his friends were able to prevail on the city council to bail him out. It was a generosity that he himself thereafter often praised to the skies and sometimes found lacking in others, as I have learned.

Working as a lawyer for the city of Nuremberg during those years, Johann Möller was a man second to none in justice and prudence, superior to many in learning, virtue, and religiosity.[112] We often gathered at his home, and it was at his suggestion that our fraternity was founded. Its most prominent members were Möller himself, our colleague Michael Roting, Georg Hoppel,[113] who was chief secretary of the city council and colleague of the councilman Lazarus Spengler,[114] and I. Each member in turn would invite the others to his house for an evening of drinks and dessert. Whoever had the task of playing host was also responsible for proposing a topic that was then examined and debated.[115] When we felt we had argued long enough about it, we would then spend the rest of the time trading jokes and conversing informally together and sometimes playing games until it was time for each of

---

insitione carmen. Παραινέσεις duae de famuli legibus. Πρόγνωσις in Venetos ... [Erfurt, Joh. Knappe the Elder, 1509?], sig. B2ʳ-B3ʳ. Eobanus renewed contact with him in 1519 by sending him a copy of Hodoeporicon along with a letter recalling their friendship; see Epp. 2, sig. B1ʳ-B2ᵛ. Having become a licentiate of law and a councilor in Bamberg, Möller moved to Nuremberg, where he was appointed municipal lawyer in 1526 and "Consulent" in 1527. He died in 1540.

[113]For Michael Roting see fn. 99 at Nar. 21, 9. Georg Hoppel (Höpel) served his native city as Registrator (1526-1528) and Kanzleischreiber (1528-1533). He was named secretary of the Council in 1533, but died on December 12 that same year. During Eobanus's stay in the city, he and Hoppel became close friends. It is to him that Eobanus dedicated the epicedium for the city treasurer Hieronymus Ebner (1532).

[114]Lazarus Spengler of Nuremberg (1479-1534) studied law at Leipzig from 1494 to 1497 before entering the civil service of his native city. In 1507 he was appointed secretary to the town council and in 1516 member of the Greater Council. A friend of Dürer, Pirckheimer, Staupitz, and Linck, Spengler took an active role in the Reformation of Nuremberg and the founding of the Gymnasium of St. Aegidius. He wrote numerous evangelical pamphlets and two hymns, one of which became very popular in Protestant churches.

[115]In Norica sive de ostentis libri duo (1532) Camerarius depicts one such disputation. Gathered in Möller's garden, Eobanus, Roting, and Möller debate the significance of the comets then appearing in the night sky.

se. **16** Prodeambulationes autem erant cum aliis vicinis locis tum ad unum in Silva Norica fonticulum, ad lapidem unum ferme urbe distantem, qui Eobani versibus non minus perenni aqua manabit quam Athenis quondam sempiternam in arce olea viriditatem tenere aut palma in Delo non exarescere potuit.

17 Hac fere ratione eos annos, quibus Norimbergae duravit coniunctio nostra, absumsimus, praebente illa civitate sedem et hospitium Musis Eobanicis perbenigne et comiter, ut, quamvis illius extent et pietatis praeclara opera et beneficentiae in alios larga munera, tamen vel hoc nomine, quae vim et atrocitatem grassationis et populationis et saevitiam hostium experiri tam immanem in modum debuerit, indignissima esse videatur. **18** De quo impedior dolore et lacrimis ne plura scribam.

C7ᵛ **19** Etiam hoc magis agendum | esse intelligo, ut, quoniam aetas nostra in hunc fatalium mutationum articulum incidit, ad ea quae acciderint ferenda potius nos paremus quam ut tristiciam eventuum reddere velimus acerbiorem querelis nostris, etsi profecto rabies saeculi huius et mundi furor, qui indies ingravescit, non potest non commovere indignationem vel moderatissimorum hominum. **20** Sed haec quamvis moerentes et animis conturbati omittamus et ad Eobani mentionem reducamus narrationem.

25, 1 Cum fere septennium confecisset Norimbergae, sollicitatus crebris litteris et magnis pollicitationibus Eobanus ab Erphordiensibus amicis illo reverti decrevit, quo retrahebatur desiderio puerilis et iuvenilis vitae et recordatione laudis quoque ac decoris, quod aetate constantiore in illa Academia gesserat. **2** Mores etiam civitatis illius admodum ei placebant. **3** Sed haud scio an nihil impulerit illum magis ad reversionem hanc quam Langi et Sturciadae semper expetita coniunctio, etsi Groningo maxime et ipso delectabatur. **4** Rediit igitur Erphordiam anno Iesu Christi M.D.XXXIII, quo postea aestas pestilens fuit, quam in vicino vico cum familia nos una cum secuta hieme transegimus. **5** Venit autem illo cum spe eiusmodi, cui eventus non respondit. **6** Et tamen factum est amicorum studio et cura et di-

---

25, 1 pollicitationibus *Carpzov et Kreyssig*: policitationibus *A*.

---

[116]Eobanus describes this natural spring in *Nor.* 601-633.

[117]In antiquity visitors to the Acropolis were shown an olive tree that was reputed to be the very one planted by Athena. On Delos they could still marvel at the same palm tree that Ulysses saw; cf. Hom. *Od.* 6, 162-163.

[118]Some of these charitable institutions are described in *Nor.* 915-1018.

us to go home. There were also walks to various nearby places, particularly to a small spring in the Nuremberg Forest, about a mile outside the city – a spring that in Eobanus's verse[116] will as little run dry as the olive tree of old could lose its greenery in the citadel of Athens or the palm tree could wither at Delos.[117]

On the whole, this is the way we spent those years of friendship in Nuremberg, while that town very kindly and courteously offered Eobanus's Muses a dwelling place and a home. Though the city's noble works of compassion and lavish gifts of charity to others are a matter of record,[118] nonetheless on this account alone it seems utterly undeserved that she has since had to suffer the violence and horror of devastation and plundering as well as the barbarity of her enemies to such a dreadful extent.[119] Sorrow and tears stop me from going on about this. Such a course of action appears to me all the more necessary now that the fateful changes sweeping this age of ours are at a critical juncture, so that we should be steeling ourselves to bear whatever may befall us rather than trying to make the sadness of these events more bitter with our laments, obvious though it may be that the madness of this generation and the frenzy of mankind, which is growing worse by the day, cannot but arouse the indignation of even the most restrained of men. But grief and dismay notwithstanding, let us quit this subject and turn back to the story of Eobanus's life.

25 When he had lived for some seven years in Nuremberg, Eobanus, tempted by numerous letters and grand promises from his friends in Erfurt, decided to return there. He felt drawn back in any case by nostalgia for his life as a teenager and young man and also by the recollection of the fame and prestige he had enjoyed at that university in a more tranquil period. Besides, he genuinely liked the way of life in that city. But I am inclined to think that nothing impelled him more to this return than the always longed-for reunion with Lang and Sturtz, even if he also took the greatest pleasure in Gröningen himself. He therefore returned to Erfurt in the year of Jesus Christ 1533.[120] Later that year there was a plague; so together with my household I myself passed the summer and following winter in a nearby village.[121] Eobanus, however, arrived in Erfurt with expectations that were not borne out by events. All the same, through the effort, care, and diligence of his friends he spent the

---

[119] As Camerarius was putting the finishing touches on this biographical essay, Nuremberg was embroiled in the Second Margrave's War. In May and June of 1552 Margrave Albrecht Alcibiades of Brandenburg-Kulmbach occupied a part of the city's territory, ravaged the countryside, and extorted huge "reparations." The following year he came back to wreak even more destruction. The terror did not cease until Albrecht was defeated by a coalition of princes and cities in June 1554.

[120] In early May of that year.

[121] During the plague that struck Nuremberg in the latter half of 1533 Camerarius and his family took refuge in the village of Eschenau, north of the city. He returned to Nuremberg in January 1534.

ligentia, ut satis commode ibi degeret annis fere quatuor et ut ad illam scholam collapsam non modo instaurandi viam mon-
C8r straret, sed rationem etiam inchoa- | ret, quam tamen sequi vel noluerunt vel non potuerunt ii, penes quos administratio esset scholae illius. 7 Docuit illic publice privatimque cum utilitate aliorum et sua laude multa. **8** Multa etiam scripsit et de Graecis versibus quosdam praeclare fecit Latinos.

26, 1 Post quadriennium invitatus clementissime a Philippo, illustrissimo Hessorum principe, Marpurgum commigravit, cum neque eum schola Erphordiana amplius liberaliter acciperet et anni ingravescerent et liberi crescerent aetate et numero et patria quoque dulcedine quadam sui insita omnibus ad sese revocaret occultis blanditiis civem suum. **2** Perfecerat autem Princeps Philippus (quod tu melius nosti, Adame, non minima pars rerum illarum, quam ego) ut omni genere doctrinae celebres et spectati Marpurgi congregarentur, quo in loco consecrato piis Musis munificentiaque sua stipendiis non spernendis constitutis honeste et non incommode vitam ducere possent in studiorum bonorum cultu et virtutis ac sapientiae doctrina. **3** Ibi Eobanus et reliquum aetatis breve tempus peregit et praeclara opera multa elaboravit ingenii bonitate et industria studii sui inque primis totam Homeri Iliada convertit in versus Latinos. **4** Opus autem egregium atque praeclarum autore et hortatore Philippo Melanchthone inchoare coeperat, ut ad Christianum ritum fastorum libros conscriberet, cuius vix paucos initii versus absolvit, et hanc decedens palmam reliquit in
C8v medio eruditis secuturae aetatis, quam | qui amico nostro Ioanni Stigelio praeripiat, persuasum mihi est futurum esse neminem, a

26, 3 studii *coni. Kreyssig*: ingenii *A*. **26, 4** inchoare *Carpzov et Kreyssig*: incoare *A*.

[122]Camerarius is referring to Eobanus's translation of Coluthus's *Rape of Helen,* published as *Coluthi Lycopolitae Thebani ... De raptu Helenes ac Iudicio Paridis poema* (Erfurt, 1534).

[123]Eobanus left Erfurt in late August, arriving in Marburg on 1 September 1536.

[124]Philip the Magnanimous was born at Marburg on 13 November 1504. When his father William II died in 1509, Philip became landgrave of Hesse. He was declared of age in 1518. In 1522 and 1523 he helped put down the uprising of Franz von Sickingen; in 1525 he crushed the rebellious peasants at Frankenhausen. Having introduced the Reformation to Hesse in 1526, he founded the first Protestant university at Marburg the following year. His desire to reconcile Lutherans and Zwinglians led him to organize the abortive Colloquy of Marburg (1529). In 1530 he signed the Augsburg Confession and in 1531 became one of the founders of the Schmalkald League. In a swift campaign conducted in 1534 he restored Duke

next four years or so in reasonable comfort. He not only showed how the school might be brought back to life after its collapse, but also initiated a plan of action; however, those who were responsible for the administration of the university either would not or could not follow his lead. In Erfurt he gave public and private instruction that was of much profit to others and a great credit to himself. He also wrote much and completed some excellent verse translations from Greek into Latin.[122]

26 After four years he moved to Marburg[123] at the gracious invitation of the illustrious Landgrave Philip of Hesse.[124] The University of Erfurt had stopped being so generous to him, he himself was getting on in years, his children were growing in age and number,[125] and his homeland too, through that special sweetness of hers that is inbred in all of us, exercised her mysterious charms to call her son back to herself. Now at the instigation of Prince Philip (and this is something that you, Adam, know better than I, since you play a prominent role at the university) famous and distinguished scholars in every branch of learning were brought together at Marburg. In that place consecrated to the pious Muses and at salaries that in their munificence are not to be despised they could live in style and comfort as they cultivated the humanities and taught virtue and wisdom. Here it was that Eobanus spent the brief time that still remained of his life and worked out many brilliant books by dint of his sound intellect and hard work and above all translated the entire *Iliad* of Homer into Latin verse.[126] At the instigation and with the encouragement of Philip Melanchthon he also embarked on the outstanding and splendid project of describing the Christian calendar, of which he barely completed a few opening verses.[127] It was a prize he left at his death for the learned men of the next generation to strive for. If our friend Johann Stigel[128]

Ulrich of Württemberg to the throne and thus dramatically expanded the territories ruled by Protestant princes. After his bigamy (1540) became known, he lost much of his influence. Defeated in the Schmalkald War (1547), he spent the next five years in prison. He returned to Hesse in 1552 and died at Kassel in 1567.

[125]By 1536 Eobanus had four surviving sons (Hieronymus, Julius, Heliodorus, and Callimachus) and one surviving daughter (Norica). Anastasius had died in 1532.

[126]The verse translation of Homer's *Iliad,* begun in Nuremberg and completed in 1537-1539, was first published at Basel in 1540.

[127]Of this project, which was to have done for the Christian calendar what Ovid did for the pagan one, only the six opening distichs are extant. See *Epp. 3,* sig. C1ʳ (repr. in Krause, *HEH,* vol. 2, p. 255, n. 2). Eobanus had conceived the project in Prussia; but fearing that it would require far more books than he had access to, he wrote the *Heroides* instead. See *Her. Chr.,* ded. 8, 1-2. By 20 March 1540, however, he could finally tell Johannes Dantiscus that he was now wholly engrossed in composing 12 books of "fasti Christiani" for his great friend.

[128]Johann Stigel of Gotha (1515-1562), one of Philip Melanchthon's closest friends, matriculated at Wittenberg in 1531. Intending to study law, he soon turned to classical languages, medicine, natural science, and astronomy. His Latin verse won him the admiration of Melanchthon, Luther, Sabinus, and Eobanus. At Melanchthon's recommendation, Stigel was

quo hi libri iam pridem expectantur, exituri propediem, ut speratur, in lucem, et nostris temporibus et autoris famae gloriam et claritatem conciliaturi sempiternam. 5 Sed nihil est quod in tota vita sua praestiterit maius aut melius quam quod Psalmos Davidicos religiose et erudite in Latinas elegias transtulit, primum quidem Erphordiae, sed denuo et maiore cum cura et assiduitate Marpurgi, ubi et praeclara argumenta quaternis versibus compraehensa praeposuit singulis Psalmis, ut prodierit tum vere sacrosanctum opus omnibus, ut dicitur, numeris absolutum. 6 Quo vir pietate insignis et casto pectore et religioso studio celebravit aeternum Deum et omnibus non prophanis neque vecordibus occasionem de rebus divinis cupide et ardenter commentandi praebuit, qui est ad Deum cultus summus et maximus ad homines fructus. 7 Hoc igitur opus et hic labor est, quo Eobanus sibi spem singularem gratiae ac benevolentiae divinae comparavit et admirationem sui ac caritatem reliquit posteris, quorum nemo est, nisi improbus et malus aut imperitus et barbarus, qui non illum hoc potissimum nomine amet et veneretur.

27, 1 Fuit autem non minus principi gratus praesens Eobanus, quam studio ille habuerat ut sibi hunc adiungeret. 2 Iocos et seria cum ipso miscere non dubitabat, inprimis de simplicitate et candore et studio veritatis | amans Eobanum, quod iudicium ipse posset facere, cum de eruditione doctrinae aliis affirmantibus crederet. 3 Magnopere delectabatur Eobanus latrunculorum ludo, quo ferunt saepe principem suaviter cum Eobano lusisse, cum iracundiam illius commoveret, circumventi et inclusi, dum in celeritate minus caute produceret illas calculorum copiolas. 4 Vere enim ludebat Eobanus: neque considerationi aliquid diligentiae impendebat neque tempus terere cogitando sustinebat. 5 Itaque nihil erat facilius quam, si quis calliditatis aliquid usurparet, insidiis eum vincere. 6 Tum igitur, cum cernebat se haerere, commoveri vehementer, sed ita ut simul cum amissa victoria illa perturbatio resideret vel potius abiret. 7 Sed a iocis ad seria redeamus.

D1ʳ

27, 2 posset A *(in erratis)*: posset A *(in textu)*.   27, 3 produceret A *(in erratis)*: producere A *(in textu)*.

---

appointed professor of poetry at Wittenberg in 1543. In 1547 he left Wittenberg to help found a Latin school at Jena; the next year he was appointed professor at the newly founded university. Many of his poems, which include versifications of the Psalms, Christian eclogues and fasti, as well as much occasional verse, were published posthumously in eight books of *Poemata* (1566-1569), rounded off with a ninth book in 1572.

does not win it for himself, then, I am convinced, no one will. I have been expecting these books from him for a long time now and am hopeful that they will soon see the light of day, to the everlasting glory and renown both of our age and of the author himself. But there is nothing Eobanus accomplished in all his life quite so great or quite so good as his paraphrase of the Psalms of David, which he rendered devoutly and eruditely into Latin elegiacs, first of all at Erfurt, to be sure, but thereafter with greater care and diligence at Marburg.[129] Here he also prefaced each of the Psalms with magnificent four-line summaries, so that this truly sacred work might now go forth finished, as they say, down to the last detail. In it this man of remarkable faith, chaste heart, and religious zeal celebrates the eternal God and gives all those who are not profane or demented an opportunity to ponder things divine with eagerness and fervor, which in the eyes of God is the highest form of worship and yields the greatest fruit in the hearts of men. This, then, is the task and this the labor by which Eobanus obtained for himself an extraordinary hope in the grace and benevolence of God and left behind at his death the regard and affection that later generations have borne him. For with the exception of the wicked and evil or ignorant and barbarous, there is no one who does not love and revere him especially on this account.

27 Now the enjoyment that the prince found in Eobanus's presence was just as great as the zeal with which he had labored to have Eobanus join him. He did not hesitate to have lighthearted or serious conversations with him, particularly since he loved Eobanus for his open nature and plain speech and devotion to the truth. Here, at least, he could form his own opinion, while in the case of scholarly erudition he had to rely on the word of others. Eobanus took an especial delight in chess. As a matter of fact, I am told that the prince often had a good time playing that game with Eobanus, seeing that he could provoke him to anger by hemming him in and cutting off every avenue of escape whenever Eobanus got in a rush and moved his pieces around recklessly. For Eobanus was a player in the true sense of the word: he never took the trouble to think ahead and could not stand wasting his time pondering the next move. As a result it was the easiest thing in the world to beat him; all you had to do was use a bit of cunning and set a trap. Well then, once he realized that he was caught, he would get tremendously upset, but in such a way that his vexation settled down or rather blew over as soon as victory was out of his reach. But let us leave the games behind and return to serious matters.

---

[129]This is the *Psalterium universum carmine elegiaco redditum atque explicatum* (Marburg, 1537) that Eobanus began in Nuremberg and largely completed in Erfurt by 1536. A new edition, augmented with versified arguments for each psalm, appeared at Schwäbisch Hall in 1538. Dedicated to Landgrave Philip, the work drew high praise from Luther and Melanchthon and went on to become a steady bestseller. By the end of the century there were over fifty reprints of it, often in combination with Eobanus's verse paraphrase of the book of Ecclesiastes.

28, 1 Erat Eobanus magnus osor superstitionum et veritatem cum propter naturae simplicitatem tum liberalitatem institutionis amabat. 2 Itaque venerabatur et colebat eos qui illis temporibus monachorum potentiae et barbariae opponere audebant confessionem et assertionem veritatis atque bonarum artium. 3 Cum autem his negotiis, quemadmodum fit, principum quoque studia admista essent (nam hoc omnibus temporibus observatum est, ecclesiae et reipublicae quasi fluctuationes aut commotas simul aut non longo intervallo sese mutuo consecutas esse), tum igitur principibus quoque eam rem curantibus, conventus interdum habiti et necessariae deliberationes susceptae fuerunt. 4 Cum autem princeps Cattorum |

D1ᵛ Philippus illo tempore operam diligentiae impenderet stabiliendae doctrinae religiosae singularem, conventum aliquoties harum rerum caussa fuit in oppido quod, in silvis Dyringiacis situm, propter crebras illis in locis aeris ac ferri fodinas et huius generis officinas "Chalcidem" solebat nominare Philippus Melanchthon. 5 Eo igitur, anno Christi M.D.XXXVII, cum celebre concilium indictum fuisset, Eobanus quoque se cum Hessiacis contulit. 6 Atque ibi Ioannem Stigelium, cuius paulo ante mentionem fecimus, tum admodum adolescentem, honesta familia gentis Duringiacae natum, primum familiariter cognovit et statim incredibili amore complexus neque obscure neque falso vaticinatus fuit quam ille facultatem Latini carminis consecuturus esset, eam nimirum, ut tanquam germana soboles laudem ac nomen, quod Eobanus sibi ingenio et industria ac studio peperisset, Stigelius quasi haereditatem legitimam ab illo relictam paulo post adiret atque cerneret. 7 Itaque iam tum Eobanus non aliter quam filii appellatione vocare Stigelium, iocari cum eo suavissime, complecti illum amantissime, materiam et argumenta interdum illi versuum faciendorum proponere, denique ita se gerere erga adolescentem, ut divinitus animum senis commoveri et favorem excitari et dirigi iudicium appareret. 8 Stigelius quidem quam non fefellerit praesensiones Eobanicas quodque veluti soboles ingenua paternum genus referens in

D2ʳ nomen quoque illius atque decus successerit, | scripta ipsius facile declarant, neque me plura de his in praesentia verba facere decet, vel ne amico viventi atque florenti assentati fuisse vel ne ad augendam hanc narrationem omnia undique collegisse videamur. 9 Hoc neque silentio est praetereundum neque alienum videri poterit, eam a Stigelio gratiam relatam fuisse amori Eoba-

---

28, 6 germana *scripsi*: Germana *A*.

28 Eobanus was a great hater of superstitions and loved the truth, as befitted his guileless nature and liberal education. That is why he revered and honored the men who in those days dared to oppose the power and barbarism of the monks by avowing and championing the truth and the humanities. Now when the princes also became involved in these affairs, as does happen (for it may be observed throughout history that the turbulences, so to speak, in church and state either arise simultaneously or follow each other at a brief interval): well then, when the princes also took a hand in that business, they held congresses every so often and participated in the necessary deliberations. Since Landgrave Philip of Hesse, however, was devoting an exceptional amount of energy to the establishment of religious doctrine, meetings were organized on several occasions to deal with these questions in Schmalkalden, a town situated in the forests of Thuringia.[130] (On account of the numerous copper and iron mines and metalworking shops in that area Philip Melanchthon was in the habit of calling it "Chalcis" or "Coppertown.") It was to that place, then, that Eobanus repaired with the other Hessians in the year of Christ 1537, after the famous congress had been announced. And it was there that he first became intimately acquainted with Johann Stigel, whom I mentioned a bit earlier.[131] Born of a respectable Thuringian family, he was still very much a young man at the time. Eobanus embraced him right from the start with unbelievable love and prophesied openly and correctly that Stigel would someday match his own skill in Latin poetry – indeed, that Stigel, like a true offspring of his, so to speak, would shortly inherit the fame and renown that he, Eobanus, had made for himself by dint of talent and industry and zeal, just as if he were leaving it to him in his will. And so he henceforth took to addressing Stigel only by the appellation "son," bantered most cheerfully with him, hugged him most lovingly, sometimes suggested themes and topics for him to write verses on, and in brief conducted himself in such a way toward the youth that it seemed as if God himself were stirring the older man's mind and rousing his goodwill and directing his judgment. How well Stigel lived up to Eobanus's expectations and indeed, like a freeborn son taking after his father, succeeded to his fame and glory, that his writings easily make clear. It is not fitting for me to say anything further about his poetry right now, lest I give the impression either of flattering a friend who is alive and flourishing or of bringing together everything under the sun, just to prolong my story. This, at least, must not be passed over in silence or could possibly seem out of place, namely that Stigel showed his gratitude for Eobanus's love by unstintingly paying homage to him and honoring him with the reverence due to

---

[130]The congress of Schmalkalden was held in February-March 1537. For this meeting Luther wrote the Schmalkald Articles, a cogent statement of his doctrines and faith.

[131]See *Nar.* 26, 4, with fn. 128.

ni ut impense eum ille observaret et reverentia debita patri prose-
queretur et omnibus officiis vivo studiosissime inserviret et
memoriam fato suo defuncti in terris posteritati elegantissimis
suis versibus commendaret, ornatam cum epitaphiis carmini-
bus, ut fieri consuevit, tum accurata mentione aliis in argu-
mentis, ubi locus esset occasioque sese offerret honorificae com-
memorationis de illo aut speciosae appellationis nominis Eoba-
nici. **10** De his igitur hactenus.

29, **1** Ac nunc deinceps ad tristissimam narrationem, ita re
poscente, procedat expositio, ut iis quae retulimus quasi colo-
phon addatur exitus ex hac vita et migratio in meliorem locum
Eobani, qui suo tempore miseras et afflictas multiplici clade ter-
ras reliquit, cum tamen adhuc rei aliquid quo ille delectaretur et
spei nonnihil quo sustentaretur esset reliquum.

2 Eobanus itaque in patriam reversus, cum omnibus iis in
locis in quibus fuerat memoriam praeclaram nominis sui re-
liquisset et quodam tamen, ut ita dicam, Homerico fato migra-
tionibus exagitatus fuisset, quatuor annis et in re meliore et spe
luculenta Marpurgi vixit, annoque il- | lo qui mortem antecessit
correptus fuit interdum podagricis et arthricis morbis. **3** Quibus
cum sentiret se tentari, initio tulit hunc casum molestius. **4** Sed
aegritudinem simul ac cruciatus die mitigante, desiit queri de hoc
malo ac incidit in diuturnum ac tabificum morbum, praeter
opinionem omnium, qui fere alios metuebant. **5** Propemodum
igitur anno toto magis languoribus quam aegrotatione confectus
tandem tertio Nonas Octobris, cum diu tacuisset, de improviso
voce emissa, se velle ad Dominum suum ascendere dixit. **6** Idque
iis qui aderant approbantibus, quod arbitrarentur in animo ipsi
esse congressum cum principe, et affirmantibus principi id gra-
tum fore, Eobanus nihil ad haec, sed paulo post placido fine
conclusit vitam in terris suam et in coelum, ut significarat, hinc
commigravit ad aeternum Deum Dominum suum, cui fideliter
servierat et cuius ministeria sedulo obierat ea gnavitate et solertia
quam ille idem ipsi fuerat largitus.

30, **1** Morte Eobani nunciata, affecti omnes tristitia fu-
erunt, sed princeps inprimis indoluisse huic fertur. **2** Qui
praebuit se permunificum erga relictam coniugem Eobani, foe-
minam lectissimam, et utriusque sexus liberos, quibus etiam
locum secum esse voluit, et munera aulica demandavit filiis, vir-

D2ᵛ

---

[132]During his last year Eobanus suffered not only from podagra, but also from fever,
coughing spells, and catarrh. He himself interpreted these symptoms as stemming from
phthisis.

a father and placing himself at his service with the utmost devotion while Eobanus was still alive and, after his passing, commending his memory to future generations of men in his most elegant verses and eulogizing him not just in the customary verse epitaphs, but also in the studied remarks he made in other contexts, whenever it was appropriate and a suitable occasion presented itself to make honorific mention of him or deferentially bring up Eobanus's name. Enough of this, therefore.

29 But now, because the facts demand it, I must go on to tell the saddest part of my story, so that to the events already recounted I may add, by way of a finish line so to speak, Eobanus's departure from this life and his migration to a better place, for he left the world in good time, when it was in a woeful state and plagued with a multitude of disasters, when nevertheless there was still something left for him to delight in and some measure of hope to keep his spirits high.

And so, having returned to his native land, having left behind a glorious memory of his name in all those places where he had stayed, and having been driven from place to place by an (if I may say so) Homeric fate, Eobanus lived four years at Marburg in rather more favorable circumstances and excellent hopes; but in the year that preceded his death he occasionally suffered bouts of podagra and arthritis. When he felt himself afflicted like that, he took it quite hard at first. However, as the disease and pain became more tolerable in time, he stopped complaining about this malady, but then fell into a chronic and wasting illness, contrary to the expectation of all his friends, who tended to fear other ailments.[132] Worn out after virtually a whole year, then, more from sheer exhaustion than illness, he at last, on the fifth of October,[133] after long remaining silent, unexpectedly regained his speech and declared that he wanted to go up to his Lord. When those who were present, believing that he had a mind to visit the prince, nodded their approval at this and affirmed that the prince would be glad to see him, Eobanus said nothing in reply, but shortly thereafter, in a peaceful death, concluded his life on earth and, as he had indicated, went up to heaven to live with the eternal God his Lord, whom he had served faithfully and whose ministry he had sedulously performed with all the diligence and skill that God himself had bestowed on him.

30 When Eobanus's death was announced, all were moved to sorrow, but the prince is said to have grieved over him more than anyone else. He showed himself exceedingly generous to Eobanus's widow, a most excellent woman, and to their children of both sexes and even desired to give them employment with him. To the sons he offered a position at his court; the daughters

---

[133] Here Camerarius is mistaken. Eobanus died during the night from the third to the fourth of October, most probably shortly after midnight. In the Marburg University Register the date is correctly given as "IIII Non. Oct." (4 October), 1540. Cf. *Nar.* 31, 2, with fn. 135; Krause, *HEH,* vol. 2, p. 259, with n. 2.

gines et matrem commendavit illustrissimae principi coniugi suae. 3 Itaque illi marito et patre amisso tamen sic postea vix-erunt ut orbitatis quidem et desiderii, sed nullo alio incommo-do | afficerentur. 4 Reliquerat autem Eobanus, ut hoc genus so-let, nihil fere suis nisi famam excellentem et nomen celebre et laudem ingenii, doctrinae, virtutis. 5 Quae indies ad victum et cultum huius vitae minus adiumenti afferre incipiebat haere-dibus, nunc etiam aliquando nocere depraehenditur.

31, 1 Hic est cursus quem nos cognovimus peregisse in terris Eobanum et quem exponendum esse descriptione nostra duximus. 2 Vixit autem annos LIII, menses VIII, dies XXVIII. 3 Statura corporis erat procera et robusta, pectus latum, facies aliquanto torvior, ut Albertus Durerus dicere soleret, si illum non nosset et imaginem expressam aspiceret, suspicaturum se illam esse bellatoris. 4 Et erat profecto animus in homine magnus et qui metuere nesciret, sed voluntas minime dimicatrix aut contentiosa. 5 Ipse neque in cibo neque potu delicatus aut lautitiarum appetens, neque scires quo maxime prae ceteris caperetur aut alliceretur. 6 Salsis tamen pisciculis ac acido olere delectabatur et in autumno iuglandes recentes incisas superfuso vino ita comedebat et mustum sic bibebat, ut inde aliquid vo-luptatis se percipere non dissimularet.

7 Signo quo utebatur erat olor per ramum lauri ascendens et attingens capite nubes. 8 Quod cum depictum fixisset super ianua aedicularum quas conductas Norimbergae incolebat, ad-didit elogium horum versuum duorum:

31, 2 menses VIII, dies *Carpzov et Kreyssig*: M. VIII. D. *A.*   31, 7 Signo *A*: Signum *Carpzov et Kreyssig.*

---

[134]The two eldest sons Hieronymus and Julius were given positions at the court. At the time of their father's death, Heliodorus was just eleven years old, Callimachus nine. By 1546 Heliodorus too was working for the landgrave. During Philip's expedition to the upper Danube (July to November 1546) he was a secretary in the war chancellery. See Franz Gund-lach, *Die hessischen Zentralbehörden von 1247 bis 1604,* Veröffentlichungen der Historischen Kommission für Hessen und Waldeck, no. 16, vol. 1 (Marburg, 1931), pp. 185-186. Around 1548 he went to the Netherlands and thence to Brazil, where he led a colorful life. See Helmut Andrä, "Heliodor Eoban Hesse, o co-fundador do Rio de Janeiro," *Revista de História* 35 (São Paulo, 1967): 357-376. Callimachus matriculated at Marburg in 1542 and later studied law. Of Eobanus's three daughters, only Norica was still alive in 1540. Cf. fn. 44 at *Nar.* 14, 7.

[135]In contrast to *Nar.* 29, 5, these indications suggest that Eobanus died on 3 October 1541. This date is also given by Wigand Lauze (p. 437).

[136]Albrecht Dürer of Nuremberg (1471-1528) apprenticed with his goldsmith-father Al-brecht and later with Michael Wolgemut in Nuremberg (1486-1490). In 1490-1494 he was a journeyman in Strasbourg, Colmar, and Basel. Married to Agnes Frey in 1494, he twice made journeys to Italy (1494-1495 and 1505-1506). In 1509 he acquired a stately house in Nurem-

and mother he commended to the care of his illustrious consort, the land-gravine.[134] Consequently, despite the loss of husband and father they were nonetheless able to live afterwards in such a way that they, to be sure, were afflicted by bereavement and mourning, but not by any other misfortune. Now Eobanus, as is typical for this kind of man, left his family with practically nothing but his outstanding renown and celebrated name and reputation for intellect, learning, and virtue. As time went on, this renown began to bring his heirs less and less tangible help for their sustenance and the necessities of life – nowadays it is even found to harm them on occasion.

31 This is the course that I know Eobanus completed on earth and that I thought worth tracing in my narrative. Now he lived fifty-three years, eight months, twenty-eight days.[135] His build was tall and robust, his chest broad, his face somewhat fierce, so that Albrecht Dürer[136] used to say: If he did not know him and had only his portrait to look at, he would have guessed it was that of a warrior. And assuredly, he was a man of great and fearless spirit, but of a disposition that was not in the least combative or quarrelsome. He was not fastidious, be it in food or in drink, nor did he have a craving for delicacies, and you could never tell what his favorite dishes were or what appealed to him above all else. Still, he did have a fancy for salted whitebait and sauerkraut, and in the autumn he would munch with such gusto on freshly cracked walnuts dipped in wine and would quaff his must with such relish that he did not hide the pleasure he derived from them.

The symbol he adopted was a swan ascending along a laurel branch and touching the clouds with its head.[137] After having this emblem painted, he fastened it above the door of the small rented house where he lived in Nuremberg and added the following two-line inscription:

---

berg and became a member of the Greater Council. From 1512 he was in the employ of Emperor Maximilian I. Following a visit to the Netherlands in 1520-1521 his health declined markedly. He died on 6 April 1528. During the two years they were together in Nuremberg, Dürer got to know Eobanus well and created several portraits of his friend, including the silverpoint now in the British Museum and the figure of St. Mark in "The Four Apostles." See: Bernhard Saran, "Eobanus Hesse, Melanchthon und Dürer: Unbefangene Fragen zu den 'Vier Aposteln,'" *Oberbayerisches Archiv* 105 (1980): 183-210. After Dürer's death Eobanus published an epicedium for him, along with a "Dream about Dürer" and some epitaphs (1528).

[137]The swan, which proverbially sings just before it dies, has long been an emblem of the lyric poet. See, for example, Hor. *Carm.* 2, 20, 1-16; 4, 2, 25; Eob. *Buc.* 3, 17; *Sylv.* 1, 5, 37; cf. *Buc.* 10, 31 (n.). Eobanus adopted the emblem for himself as early as 1508, probably at Mutianus's instigation. See *Buc.* 3, where he is the shepherd "Cygnus" (Swan). The most famous rendition of his emblem is in the splendid *Wappentafel* that Crotus Rubianus inserted in the university register at the end of his term as rector (1520/21). There the swan, standing on a field of gold and looking up at blue clouds, is depicted on an escutcheon at the center of the top row. Above the escutcheon is a gold crown, symbolic of Eobanus's stature as "the king of poets," and the letters "E. Hes." See Eckhard Bernstein, "Der Erfurter Humanistenkreis am Schnittpunkt von Humanismus und Reformation. Das Rektoratsblatt des Crotus Rubianus," in: *Pirckheimer-Jahrbuch* 12 (1997): 137-165.

D3ᵛ

Nubila scandentem lauri de stipite cygnum,
Hesso stemma suum libera Musa dedit.

9 In adversis, vel quicquid forte accideret quod molestiam afferret, pronunciare solebat nomen patientiae, quo se ad ferenda tristia confirmabat. **10** Nihil minus ferre poterat neque peius oderat quam obtrectationes aut criminationes aliorum, quas obortas quocunque loco aut tempore etiam iracunde refutabat et cohercebat. **11** Mendacium neque ipse dicebat et dicto graviter offendebatur. **12** Insidias calliditatis neque norat neque cavebat, itaque iniquissime patiebatur se ludibrio haberi et fidem atque simplicitatem suam malitiae deridendam exponi indignabatur. **13** Inter iocos hunc libenter exercebat, ut propositum versum aliqua parte sui mutari iuberet, veluti in hoc, "Vitam quae faciunt beatiorem," quid pro ultimo nomine numerose posset reponi, ut quaereret. **14** Ac memini saepe unam aut alteram horam talibus permutationibus inter epulas nos absumsisse. **15** Sed in his parvis exercitatiunculis immensa vis ingenii Eobanici innotescebat. **16** Versus etiam tum facere et ad faciendos alios invitare, statim et sine ullo animi cogitationisque adminiculo neque cura inveniendi quid diceretur adhibita. **17** In quo genere proferebantur ab ipso saepe complures versus numeris et verbis ita concinni ut nihil fieri posse videretur elegantius, sed sensus nullus exprimebatur. **18** Itaque memini aliquando quosdam qui sibi arrogarent aliquid facultatis poeticae deceptos fuis- | se, cum argumentum quoppiam explicatum esse putarent et quid rei significaretur quaererent. **19** Solebat et invertere in convivio voces, non enim poterat quiescere, et nihil illi nisi quod et laederet neminem et esset ingeniosum placebat et seria tamen tum non patiebatur admisceri et ostentatoribus ingenii, sive quis sapientiae tum disputationes explicare seu recitare aliquid scriptorum suorum seu quocunque modo doctrinae et eruditionis suae specimen edere conaretur, admodum irascebatur eorumque ineptias interdum repudiabat asperius. **20** Invertere igitur solebat voces Teutonicae inprimis linguae, quod erat factu ideo facilius, quia in hac omnia fere sunt primae originis vocabula unius syllabae. **21** Ad hanc usurpationem ita nos usu assuefeceramus, ut ignari negotii arbitrarentur externa lingua nos colloqui.

D4ʳ

31, 16 ullo *Carpzov et Kreyssig*: ulla *A*.

A swan ascending to the clouds along a sprig of the laurel:
    the free-spoken Muse has lent Hessus her personal crest.

In adversity, or whenever something or other happened that brought him distress, he used to utter the word "patience," whereby he fortified himself to bear his misfortunes. There was nothing he could stand less or hated worse than the disparagement or slandering of others. If ever he heard such slurs, no matter where or when they came up, he would angrily refute the allegations and put a stop to them. He himself never told a lie and was deeply offended if somebody told one to him. As for cunning tricks, he neither practised them nor was on the lookout for them, and so he took it very badly if he found himself made a laughingstock and became indignant at seeing his trusting and straightforward nature exposed to the derision of malicious people. For fun he liked getting us to produce variations on a verse that he proposed. In the phrase, "The things that make for a happy life," for example, he would ask what could be put in the place of the last word and still fit the meter. Indeed, I remember we often spent an hour or two over dinner dreaming up permutations like this. Yet it was in these little exercises that the immense power of Eobanus's talent shone forth. He would then also compose verses and invite others to do the same, all on the spur of the moment, without the benefit of reflection and thought and without taking care to come up with something to say. In this manner he often produced quite a number of verses, so beautiful in rhythm and language that nothing could possibly seem more elegant, yet which made no sense whatsoever. And so it happened on occasion, I remember, that certain individuals who claimed to possess some skill in poetry found themselves deceived, for they assumed he had been developing a specific theme and wondered out loud what he was driving at. At dinner parties he also used to say words backwards, for he was irrepressible and enjoyed every sort of game, provided it did not hurt anyone and was clever. However, he would not let anybody get serious then, and if some show-offs still tried to get him involved in disquisitions about wisdom or insisted on reading some of their writings out loud or in some other way tried to present a specimen of their learning and scholarship, he would fly into a rage and sometimes reject their trifles in pretty harsh terms. As I was saying just now, he liked to turn words around, especially German ones, which is easier to do in this language for the simple reason that virtually all the indigenous words are monosyllabic. We got so accustomed to this way of talking, that people who were not in on the game assumed we were speaking a foreign tongue.

32, 1 Haec habui, Adame, quae ducerem narranda esse de Eobano nostro, cui serius quidem quam tu voluisti et ego debui, sed fide et diligentia maxima hoc officium praestiti et quasi iusta funeris persolvi, cum profecto inter praecipua bona numerem amicitiae et familiaritatis usum et vinculum quocum Eobano Deus me coniunctum esse voluit. **2** Qui quidem breve curriculum vitae suae laudabiliter et feliciter confecit, etsi molestiis non caruit, praesertim rei familiaris, et hanc vitam in terris eo momento reliquit quo, quasi de convivio tempestive discedens, ita impendentem con- | fusionem et turbas, denique ea ad quae nostra producitur, declinando vitavit. **3** De quibus plura nunc scribenda et dolori perturbationique indulgendum esse non putavimus. **4** Eodem anno multi ingenio, dignitate, virtute, sapientia, doctrina praestantes viri diem suum obierunt, ut hunc studiis bonarum artium et excellentiae humanae fatalem fuisse credi posse videatur. **5** E quorum numero Guilielmum Budeum hoc loco nominasse satis habuimus.

6 Composuit autem, ut scis, Mycillus noster elegantissimum carmen de Eobano, quo ipso pertexuit historiolam quandam vitae fortunaeque et mortis illius. **7** Quod est in manibus omnium. **8** Nos etiam hoc loco apponere voluimus nostros versus quos conscripsimus quasi ad sepulcrum Eobani apponendos, id est, ἐπιταφίους.

33 HELIO EOBANO HESSO, VIRO OPTIMO, PRINCIPI POETARUM, AMICO SUAVISSIMO, IOACHIMUS CAMERARIUS PABEBERGENSIS F.

Hic situs est Hessus, patria tellure receptus
    Quo rediit domino se revocante soli.
Dum circum huc illucque vagus fert seque domumque
    Quaerit et Aonio praemia digna choro,
5   Nonnihil ille quidem reperit. Sed praemia Musis
    Huius nulla satis digna fuere viri.
Nec potuere dari, neque saecula nostra tulerunt
    Tantum, aetas Hessum nosset ut illa, boni.

D4ᵛ

D5ʳ

32, 1 quocum *scripsi*: quo cum *A*.

[138]Guillaume Budé of Paris (1468-1540) was the greatest of the French humanists.

32 This is everything I have, Adam, that I considered worthwhile to relate about our dear Eobanus. It is for him that I am performing this service and to him that I am paying, as it were, my last respects – later indeed than you wanted and later than I ought to have done, but with the utmost faithfulness and diligence, for I certainly reckon among the paramount blessings the enjoyment and bond of that intimate friendship in which God wanted me to be joined with Eobanus. The race of life, brief as it was, he completed laudably and successfully, even though it was not lacking in troubles, particularly as regards his personal finances. And just as if he were leaving a banquet at the right time, he departed this life on earth at the very moment when confusion and turmoil loomed. By turning aside, therefore, he managed to escape the chaos into which your life and mine have been extended. To write more about this now and wallow in grief and distress would not be appropriate, I feel. Many other men, preeminent in intellect, authority, virtue, wisdom, and learning, ended their days in that same year, so that one might well regard it as a fateful one for the study of the liberal arts and humanities. Among these luminaries I consider it enough at this point to mention Guillaume Budé.[138]

Now our good friend Micyllus, as you know, has composed a most elegant poem about Eobanus, in which he finished weaving a kind of narrative about his life and fortunes and death.[139] That work is in everybody's hands. I too at this point should like to append some verses of mine that I wrote as if to be placed at Eobanus's grave, that is to say, *sepulchral.*

33   FOR HELIUS EOBANUS HESSUS, THE BEST OF MEN,
THE PRINCE OF POETS, A MOST DELIGHTFUL
FRIEND, BY JOACHIM CAMERARIUS OF BAMBERG

Here lies Hessus, received back into the soil of the native
land to which he had returned at his lord's behest. As he
wandered about from place to place, searching for a home
and the guerdons worthy of the Aonian choir, he certainly
obtained not a few. But no guerdons were sufficiently wor-
thy of this man's Muse. They could not be bestowed, nor
did this century of ours offer a prize equal to the excellence

[139]Camerarius refers to Jakob Micyllus's *Epicedion Helii Eobani Hessi poetae*, a moving tribute to Eobanus that was first published in *Epicedia scripta a Iacobo Micyllo in mortem Eobani Hessi poetae et Simonis Grynaei* (Wittenberg, 1542) and was reprinted at the head of Johann Drach's edition of *Helii Eobani Hessi, poetae excellentiss. et amicorum ipsius, epistolarum familiarium libri XII* (Marburg, 1543), sig. *3ʳ–*7ᵛ. In Carpzov's edition of Camerarius's *Narratio* the poem appears on pp. 70-82; in Kreyssig's it stands on pp. 75-86.

Gloria sera venit meritis. Post fata superstes
10 Inque dies melior fama sepulta redit.
Et tamen ipse suae cognovit nomina laudis
  Audiit et tempus se celebrare suum.
Caepit et ingenii de fructu commoda vivus
  Virtutisque suae crescere vidit opus.
15 Sed maiora ferunt insignia scilicet anni,
  Viventis caedens quos abit ante decus.
Illi etiam eximiae famae praeconia, mundus,
  Hesso, donec erit, splendidiora ferent.
Hoc satis est. Hessi busto sepelitur in isto
20 Corpus; in aetheria spiritus arce manet.
Per terras bona fama volat, speciosaque laudis
  Nomina Pieria testificata manu.

D5ᵛ **34 ΗΛΙΩΙ ΕΩΒΑΝΩΙ ΕΣΣΩΙ, ΑΝΔΡΙ ΒΕΛΤΙΣΤΩΙ
ΚΑΙ ΠΟΙΗΤΗΙ ΕΜΜΕΛΕΣΤΑΤΩΙ**

Ἀστέρα Μουσάων, Χαρίτων ἔρνος, στόμα Φοίβου,
  Ποιητὴν λιγυρῶν ἡδυθρόον μέλεων,
Κήρυκ᾽ ἀθανάτου τε θεοῦ θνητῶν τε δικαίων,
  Ἔσσον Ἐωβανὸν τῇδε κέκευθε κόνει
5 Δεξαμένη πατρὶς αὖθις ἑοῖς κόλποισι θανόντα,
  Ἧι μετ᾽ ἐν ἐκ πολλῶν ναῖεν ἀναστάσεων.
Ἔνθα μαραινόμενός τε φθινώδεσιν ἠρέμα νούσοις
  Ἥσυχον ἐλλογίμου τέρμα λέλογχε βίου.
Ὄλβιος ὃς κλέος ἐσθλὸν ἐν ἀνθρώποισι λελοιπώς,
10 Κεῖθεν ἐς οὐρανίους εὐθὺ βέβηκε δόμους.
Ἐι δέ που ἐν τῇ γῇ πολυπλαγκτοσύνησι κέκμηκεν,
  Ἔσχ᾽ ἀφ᾽ Ὁμηρείου καὶ τόδε δῆτα τύχης.

**ἀπὸ Ἰωαχείμου Καμεραριάδου
μνημόσυνον σεβάσμιον**

it recognized in Hessus. To the deserving, glory always comes too late. Fame lives on after death; [10] day after day it rises more resplendent from the grave. Nevertheless he did receive recognition and heard his own times extol him. He not only lived to enjoy the fruits of his genius, but also saw his creative achievement grow. The passing years clearly do bring higher distinctions; however, he departed this life before he could receive the crowning glory. As long as the world exists, future ages will pay ever more splendid tributes to Hessus and his extraordinary fame. This is enough. Hessus's body lies buried in this tomb; [20] his spirit abides in the citadel of heaven. His renown flies throughout the whole wide world, as does the brilliant fame attested by the Muse's hand.

34 FOR HELIUS EOBANUS HESSUS, THE BEST OF MEN AND MOST MELODIOUS OF POETS

The star of the Muses, the scion of the Graces, the mouth-piece of Phoebus, the sweet-strained poet of tuneful melodies, the herald of immortal God and righteous mortals, Eobanus Hessus it is whom his native land covers in this grave. She took the dying man back to her bosom, where he now abides after being uprooted so often. And there, wasted by consuming diseases, he peacefully reached the end of his illustrious life. Happy the man who leaves behind a noble reputation among people [10] and thence steps directly into the heavenly homes. But if ever he grew weary of his many wanderings on earth, he undoubtedly owed that too to his Homeric fate.[140]

**By Joachim Camerarius
as a reverent memorial.**

---

[140]Cf. *Nar.* 29, 2 above. Also cf. *Nar.* 5, where Camerarius compares Eobanus's lot to Homer's and finds that the two poets have much in common.

DE RECESSU STUDENTUM EX ERPHORDIA
TEMPORE PESTILENCIAE

THE STUDENTS' DEPARTURE FROM ERFURT
DURING A TIME OF PLAGUE

Title page of *De recessu studentum ex Erphordia*
[Erfurt: Wolfgang Stürmer, 1506]
Staats- und Universitätsbibliothek, Bremen

DE RECESSU STUDENTUM EX ERPHORDIA

Introduction

In his chronicle of Frankenberg in Hesse, Wigand Gerstenberg reports:

> In the year of our Lord 1505 there was much dying in Erfurt on account of the plague. So the magisters left the city and scattered in all directions. Among them were four magisters who were native sons of Frankenberg. Three of them were full brothers. Their names were Magister Peter, Magister Johann, Magister Deynhard, known as the Emerichs. The fourth was Magister Ludwig Stippen [Christiani]. The last-named also brought two other magisters with him to Frankenberg. The one came from Melsungen, the other from Usingen. They were accompanied by Bachelors of Arts and a goodly number of other students, noblemen as well as commoners. And there they worked toward their degrees, studying and attending lectures, and spent their money with the citizens of Frankenberg. And after the dying was over they went back to Erfurt.[1]

Among the young scholars who left plague-stricken Erfurt in August 1505 and studied in Frankenberg until the early spring of 1506 was the precocious poet Eobanus Hessus. Still a teenager, he had been writing Latin verse for several years already, carefully preserving his best efforts but never daring to publish any of them. But as his erudition deepened and his genius grew more confident, the eighteen-year-old began testing his wings with ever more ambitious works. No sooner had he returned to Erfurt than he set himself to describe the experiences of the previous half-year.[2] The resulting narrative was published in September 1506 as *The Students' Departure from Erfurt during a Time of Plague* – almost simultaneously with a shorter poem recounting *The Battle Between the Students of Erfurt and a Mob of Sworn Scoundrels* that had taken just place.

The story how Eobanus came to publish *De recessu studentum* and *De pugna studentum* at virtually the same time can be reconstructed from internal evidence as well as from the extant letters in Mutianus Rufus's correspondence.

---

[1] See Wigand Gerstenberg, *Stadtchronik von Frankenberg*, ed. Hermann Diemar (Marburg, 1909), pp. 473-474.

[2] According to *Rec.* 215-217 the students and their teachers went back to Erfurt in the early spring. Since Eobanus saw Hutten in Erfurt around Easter, April 12 (see *Laud.* B 3, with fn. 87), the return journey must have taken place a week or two before.

[95]

On Sunday, the 9th of August 1506, a mob of artisans and laborers stormed the university district and attacked the students. Eobanus and his comrades, who had been carousing at a nearby tavern, immediately leaped into the fray. After a violent street battle, in which stones were hurled and swords wielded in earnest, the students beat the rioters back. When the townsmen returned the next day with reinforcements, they were arrested and jailed. Eobanus wasted no time hailing the victory in a heroic poem and circulating it among his friends. Encouraged by its reception, he thought of publishing the work "as a fitting memorial" to their triumph, but first wanted the advice of Mutianus Rufus, the Gotha canon whose wonderful humanity and erudition had already attracted a circle of like-minded scholars. In mid-August Eobanus sent him a stylish letter (no longer extant), reverently greeting Mutianus and asking for his opinion on the enclosed battle-poem.

Mutianus at once hailed the young man's talent. In an epigram, written around August 23 and preserved in *Ep.* 79 (Gillert), he briefly sums up *De pugna studentum*, enthusiastically praises the young warrior-poet, and promises him a bright future.[3] Thrilled with joy, Eobanus dashed off a rapturous poem of thanks (*Ep.* 417), to which Mutianus responded with further encouragement and sage advice on August 27 (*Ep.* 80). Now there was no reason for further diffidence. Without delay Eobanus took both works – *De recessu studentum* and *De pugna studentum* – to the printer. Already by October 1 Mutianus was able to compliment him on these first fruits (*Ep.* 45):

> Just recently I read [your poem about] the sudden outbreak of violence between the students and artisans. It's as if one is actually there, watching that attack – so vividly you depict the brawling and fighting that occurred! After a one-week interval I read how you and your fellow students had to flee in all directions and wander abroad. These travels into exile, if I may call it that, undertaken for fear of the plague, you deplore so convincingly that you come across as grieving from the bottom of your heart.

And in a contemporaneous letter, sent to Herbord von der Marthen (*Ep.* 47), he exults:

> Together with your letter I received three poems, one by the Carmelite bard,[4] two by the Hessian poet. I regard the latter so highly that you and the rest may justly call him a modern Pindar – so clearly is he the prince of lyric poets in

---

[3] The epigram was sent via Hermann Trebelius (see Mutian. *Ep.* 80). The exact composition date can be inferred from the epigram to Trebelius, *Ep.* 79, lines 19-20: the sun is said to be entering Virgo (on August 23 or 24). See Krause, "Beiträge," p. 45.

[4] Baptista Mantuanus, the Italian humanist who had entered the Carmelite order at age 16. The booklet referred to is probably Mantuanus's *Elegia contra amorem*, published in 1506 by Wolfgang Stürmer – the same printer who produced Eobanus's maiden works. See Von Hase, no. 96.

the German nation, so rich is he in themes and words, that, just as Horace deservedly regarded the ancient Pindar as absolutely inimitable on that account, I myself am so firmly of the same opinion that I proclaim the genius of this latter-day Pindar to be beyond all hazard.

De recessu studentum was published just once, with no indication of place, printer, or year [Erfurt: Wolfgang Stürmer, 1506]:

A (1506)

DE RECESSV STVDENTVM EX ERPHORDIA | tempore peſtilenciæ. Eobani Heſſi Francobergii | Carmen Heroicum Extemporaliter | Concinnatum | [*woodcut*]

Collation:	4°: a⁶, [$3 (a2 missigned a3) signed], 6 leaves
Contents:	a1ʳ title page; a1ᵛ-a6ʳ *De recessu studentum*; a6ʳ *Ad M. Laurentium Usingen Eob. H. F. Phaleutium endecasyllabum*; a6ᵛ woodcut; beneath it: *Ad candidum lectorem hexastichon*
Copy-text:	Bremen, Staats- und Universitätsbibliothek Call number: VI.3.b.13/4

The copy in Bremen [A¹] differs slightly from the three other known copies: [A²] Jena, UB (4° Bud. Op. et Ep. 50/3 Inc.); [A³] London, BL (Print Room); and [A⁴] New Haven, Yale University Library (Cr 12 H 469 R 4). Each of the latter three copies offers the correct signature on sig. a2ʳ. As noted in the critical apparatus, their text occasionally diverges slightly from that in the Bremen copy.

The Bibliothèque Nationale et Universitaire, Strasbourg, possesses a nineteenth-century handwritten facsimile (Cd 102401), the readings of which closely agree with A² and A⁴.

DE RECESSU STUDENTUM EX ERPHORDIA
TEMPORE PESTILENCIAE
Eobani Hessi Francobergii carmen heroicum
extemporaliter concinnatum

THE STUDENTS' DEPARTURE FROM ERFURT DURING A TIME OF PLAGUE
A heroic poem by Eobanus Hessus of Frankenberg that he composed extemporaneously

Tempus erat, iam laeta Ceres adoleverat arvis
Sole sub ardenti, lunata falce colonus
Venerat agrestis segetes incidere. Vites
Frondebant. Iam sylva leves porrexerat umbras.
5   Floruit omnis ager, campi sylvaeque patentes,
Et laeti arboreis cantum sparsere volucres
Frondibus argutum. Repetunt arbusta cicadae,
Et nova transpicuis arrident gramina rivis.
Laeta per integrum redierunt gaudia mundum;
10   Quicquid erat laetum fuit exultatque per orbem.
   Annus erat post quinque decem quoque saecula quintus
Postquam virginea Deus exiit aeditus alvo.
Tranquilla stetit infoelix Erphordia pace,
Tempore non illo foelix velut esse solebat,
15   Antea loetiferi quam vis infausta veneni
Sparsit in egregios flammantia taela Minervae
Cultores. Stygio pestis suffusa furore
Iamiam Nesseo totam madefecerat urbem
Sanguine. Mortiferas papulas effundit et atras
20   Viroso vomit ore faces et corpora diris
Inficit hulceribus virusque effundit in omnes
Vipereum. Nulli licuit sperare salutem
Cui semel affixa est lateri laetalis harundo.
Una lege ruunt cuncti, iuvenesque senesque –
25   Innocuam rabies adeo grassatur in urbem
Letiferae pestis. Danaos non tanta peremit
Impietas altae vastantes moenia Troiae,
Dum pater abductam repetit Chriseida Calchas.
Urbs luget, tetri sanie polluta veneni.
30   Ante suos obeunt nati nataeque parentes,
Et patris moriens spectat crudelia natus
Funera, nec propriam cognoscit filia matrem.

19 effundit *scripsi*: effudit *A*.   **21** effundit *scripsi*: effudit *A*.

It was that season: already the bountiful grain had ripened in the fields under a blazing sun; the rustic farmer had come with his crescent sickle to reap the harvest. The grapevines were in leaf. For some time now the trees had been casting gentle shade. Flowers bedecked the whole countryside, the fields no less than the far-spread woods, and the birds joyously warbled their shrill song in the leafy crowns. Once again the cicadas haunted the orchards, and fresh grass smiled at the limpid brooks. Throughout the whole world cheerful gladness returned; [10] everywhere on earth nature rejoiced and exulted.

It was the year fifteen hundred and five since God was born from a Virgin's womb. Though tranquil and at peace, Erfurt was filled with misery. At that time she was not happy as in days past, before the accursed violence of a death-dealing poison shot its fiery shafts at the eminent votaries of Minerva. A plague, drunk with Stygian fury, had now all but splattered the entire city with Nessus's blood.[1] Pouring out lethal pustules and [20] spewing forth pitch-black flames from its venomous mouth, it daubs bodies with hideous boils and drips its viperous poison on everyone. There is no hope of recovery once your side is pierced with the deadly arrow. Without distinction all the people perish, the young as well as the old – so savagely does the death-dealing pestilence rage against the blameless city. It is far more virulent here than when it killed the Greeks ravaging the walls of lofty Troy, while father Calchas demanded the release of the abducted Chryseis.[2] Defiled by the plague's horrible venom, the city is in mourning. [30] Sons and daughters die before their parents. Expiring, the son sees the cruel death of his father; the daughter no longer recognizes her own mother. As the la-

---

[1] Nessus was the centaur whose blood, poisoned by Hercules' arrow, was smeared on the hero's robe and eventually brought about his death.

[2] When Agamemnon refused to return Chryseis to her father Chryses (a priest of Apollo at Chryse), Apollo sent a plague on the Greeks before Troy. The seer Calchas then explained to the assembled Greeks that the plague would cease only after Agamemnon had released the girl. Cf. lines 166-169 below.

Exoritur miseranda lues, it rumor ad aedes
Palladis, et quosdam rabies haec inficit ex hiis
35   Quos miseri quondam ad studium misere parentes.
Inficit et tristi languencia corda veterno
Obtenebrat, ferit incautos, volat ocyor Euro.
Haec fera nunc illos, iaculo nunc percutit illos,
Nec metuit quemquam, quantumvis doctus ad arma
40   Pallados exurgat. Furit, aestuat, inficit, aufert
Corpora. Ut esuriens lupus inter ovilia plena
Imbelles obtruncat oves nec exit ab illis
Nec praeda absistit donec non traxerit omnes
Mortis ad exitium, fera non secus illa cruentis
45   Aestuat hulceribus.
                    Magnae domus alta Minervae
Moeret, et ingentes morientum sydera planctus
Accipiunt. Ipso sedet alti culmine Pallas
Tegminis et peplo faciem velata nephandas
Conqueritur coedes ac tristia fata suorum.

50   Sic cytharam posuit moestam crinitus Apollo,
Calliopeque fugit, nymphis comitata Latinis.
Conquerimur cuncti quos docta Erphordia quondam
Fovit et electos gremio suscepit aperto.
Vota precesque Deo ferimus iuvenesque senesque.
55   Aerea vasa sonant, sanctae qua Virginis aedes
Tres celebres Mariae tollunt ad sydera turres
Atque aliis quibus hec urbs est celeberrima templis.
Atria clauduntur, studiis aptissima quondam;
Clauduntur portae. Nigris capita alta cucullis
60   Velantur iuvenum. Superest spes nulla salutis.
   Iamque ubi desperata salus, ubi nulla precantes
Vota iuvant, ubi mors vitae dominatur et omnes
Lege ruunt parili nec erat mens certa morandi,
Effugimus. Dum quisque potest, dum vita superstes
65   Cuique sua est quos preteriit furor ille cruentus,
Effugimus. Iuvat ire procul patriosque penates
Visere et externas studiis renovarier urbes
Palladiis, multos quarum iam fama per annos
Delituit. Fugiunt una omnes mente magistri
70   Quisque suos repetuntque lares, unaque studentes
Quisque suum sequimur per daevia longa magistrum.

---

43 praeda *scripsi*: praedae *A*.

mentable epidemic rears its head, the rumor reaches the
sanctuary of Pallas.[3] Before long the mad fury infects some
of the ones whom their wretched parents sent in happier
days to study here. It infects them and benights their enfee-
bled minds in a dismal torpor; it strikes the unwary, it flies
swifter than the east wind. With its shafts it ruthlessly
pierces now these, now others. Fearing no one, no matter
how high [40] he may have risen in Pallas's ranks, the pesti-
lence rages and seethes, infects and carries off bodies. As a
hungry wolf in a full sheepfold tears the helpless sheep apart
and does not depart from them or leave off from his prey
until he has done them all to death, so the ferocious plague
seethes in the gory boils.

The lofty abode of mighty Minerva grieves, and the
stars hear the great laments of the dying. Brooding on the
very ridge of the high roof, Pallas veils her face with her robe
and bewails the abominable slaughter and grim fate of her
followers. [50] Similarly, long-haired Apollo has laid down
his joyless lyre, and Calliope flees with her train of Latin
nymphs. We chosen ones, whom scholarly Erfurt used to
cherish and take upon her open lap, we all lament aloud.
Young and old alike, we offer vows and prayers to God. The
bronze bells ring, not only where the holy church of the Vir-
gin Mary raises its three famed towers up to the stars, but
also in the other churches for which this city is justly cele-
brated. The lecture halls, formerly so well suited to studies,
are closed; the doors are locked. [60] The youths cover their
noble heads with black hoods. They give up all hope of
surviving.

And as we already despair of being saved, when vows
are of no avail to those who offer them, when death lords it
over life and all the people perish in the same manner and
the determination to brave it out begins to waver, we make
our escape. While each of us is still able to, while there is still
life in those of us whom that bloody fury has passed by, we
make our escape. We look forward to going far away and re-
turning to our hometowns and using our Palladian studies
to revive distant cities whose fame has been languishing
now for many years. With one accord, all the instructors
flee, [70] each going back to his own hometown; and with
one accord each of us students follows his teacher on the

---

[3]The University of Erfurt.

Quorum aliquos memorare libet. Quis proferet omnes?
Hos quorum pars ipse fui cantare magistros,

a3ʳ

Pierides Musae, liceat, Phoebique sorores,

75   Quae iuga Parnassi, quae Delphica rura tenetis.
    Tres pietate una insignes et laude magistros
Quos mea Musa iuvat cantabo et carmine laudes
Persolvam meritas. Quibus illi ad littora ventis
Venerunt, quibus et vaelis, quo turbine pulsi,

80   Iam satis expositum est. Igitur surgente tumultu
Dum sic quisque fugit, primum Ludovicus honestis
Editus ex atavis claraque propagine natus
Moelsingensis adest, Usingeniusque probatis
Moribus insignis Laurentius, et Ludovicus,

85   Artibus egregiis clarus, virtutis amator,
Quem puerum primis urbs Francobergia in annis
Misit ad ingenuas venandum Pallados artes,
Consuluere fugae. Turba comitante diserta
Quorundam effugimus iuvenum, loca nota petentes,

90   Inclyta qua laeto procul eminet Hessia cultu
Moelsingenque altas ad sydera porrigit arces,
Inclyta diviciis, opibus foecunda, puellis
Formosis ornata, viris celeberrima doctis.
    Illic mansuri fuimus, sic fata iubebant.

95   Sed secus est visum superis. Heu, tristia miscet
Quam subito Fortuna, bonis inimica, secundis!
Ad bene speratam vix iam pervenimus urbem,

a3ᵛ

Quom subito en vacuas spes vana recessit in auras
Quam properata diu peperit fuga. Namque sodalis

100 Unus erat iuvenes inter pulcherrimus omnes,
Nobilis ex atavis et sanguine clarus avorum,
Illustrans patrias virtute Lupambulus urbes,
Nota gente satus, genitor quem nobilis artes
Staffel ad ingenuas misit puerilibus annis.

---

76 magistros A^1 A^2 A^4 : magistri A^3.   91 altas A^1 A^2 A^4 : altos A^3.

---

[4]Ludwig Platz of Melsungen (d. 1547) matriculated at Erfurt in 1497, earning his B.A. in 1499, his M.A. in 1504, and a licentiate in theology in 1519. After 1506 he was regularly elected to various high offices in the university, for example, dean in 1513 and 1519/20, rector in 1520. In 1515 Eobanus dedicated *Hymnus paschalis* to him.

long byways. I should like to mention just a few of these
men here. Who could list them all? Allow me to praise the
magisters to whom I attached myself, O Pierian Muses and
sisters of Phoebus, you who dwell on the heights of Parnas-
sus and in Delphi's fields.

There are three magisters whom I wish to celebrate in
song. Famed as much for their piety as for their scholarship,
they take delight in my Muse, and I shall give them here the
praise they deserve. With what winds, on what ships they
came to these shores, by what violent storm they were
driven away, [80] that has already been related in sufficient
detail. So then, as the panic grew and we all fled for dear life,
these were the men who counseled us to escape. First of all
there was Ludwig of Melsungen, descended from distin-
guished ancestors and born into an illustrious family[4];
Lorenz of Usingen too, noted for his high moral standards,[5]
and Ludwig, famous for his exceptional learning, a lover of
virtue, whom the town of Frankenberg had sent here in his
youth to pursue the liberal arts of Pallas.[6] Accompanied by a
well-spoken band of other students, we fled, making for the
familiar countryside [90] where Hesse, renowned for its fer-
tile farmlands, is visible from afar and Melsungen raises its
lofty citadel up to the stars – a town celebrated for its riches,
productive of wealth, adorned with pretty girls, and ac-
claimed far and wide for its men of learning.

There we intended to stay; that was what fate decreed.
But heaven had other plans for us. Alas, how suddenly does
Fortune, the enemy of all virtuous people, turn success into
grief! Scarcely had we arrived in the city to which we had
been looking forward with such optimism, when – lo and
behold – the false hopes that our hasty flight had long since
engendered abruptly vanished into thin air. For [100] we
lost one of our comrades, the most handsome among
all the youths, of ancient lineage and noble blood: Wolf-
gang Staffel, who through the excellence of his character
added luster to the cities of his homeland, the scion of a
well-known family, whose his highborn father had sent in

---

[5]Lorenz Arnoldi of Usingen received the M.A. at Erfurt in 1504, together with Ludwig
Platz. Initially a strong voice for humanistic studies at Erfurt, he turned more conservative in
his later years and became a vociferous opponent of Luther. He died of the plague in the sum-
mer of 1521.

[6]Ludwig Christiani (Stippen) of Frankenberg. See Camerarius, *Nar.* 7, 1, with fn. 18.

105 Hunc fera Lernaeo rabies confusa veneno
     Corripit et iaculo incautum prosternit acuto.
     Ille cadit victus laetali vulnere, quondam
     Egregius iuvenis, clarus virtute paterna.
     Languida ad invisum componit membra grabatum.
110 Ac ubi vipereo viridi flos aggere morsu
     Desectatus obit nec adhuc marcescere fulgor
     Incepit solito nec iam candore refulget,
     Non secus infoelix lecto puer incubat aegro,
     Multa gemens. Longo solvit moestissima fletu
115 Lumina, luctificos fundens e pectore questus.
     Post longos tandem gemitus fatalia solvit
     Munera et excedens vita morientia claudit
     Lumina fallaces animamque exhalat in auras.
        Ah, puer infoelix, sic te Fata impia, sic te
120 Crudeles voluere deae iuvenilibus annis
     Ignotisque mori laribus. Non nobile stemma,
     Non generosa tibi stirps profuit. Urbe sepultus
     Externa recubas. Patrio non ossa sepulchro
     Componi licuit. Cuncti te flemus ademptum.
125 Heu, miserande puer, quantos tua fata dolores
     Intulerint genitori aegro miseraeque parenti!
     Quas lachrimas aut quanta tulit suspiria, quando
     Mors tua maternas primum pervenit ad aures!
     Talia non miserae dederas promissa parenti,
130 Quom tua candidulis complectens colla lacertis
     Extrema iam voce vale tibi dixit eunti.
     Quid tibi forma nitens, quid mollis profuit aetas?
     Mortuus ignota tu nunc requiescis in urna.
     Exequias tibi funebres persolvimus ipsi,
135 Spargimus et tumulum foliis superosque precamur
     Et tali impositum signamus carmine marmor:
     "Illustrans patrias virtute Lupambulus urbes,
     Hac iaceo tumulatus humo, qui peste peremptus
     Crudeli ante diem externis moriebar in oris.
140 Formosus fueram iuvenis multisque placebam.
     Nunc trahor in cineres. Non me mea forma iuvabat.
     Nobile quod fuerat corpus putrescit et aesca
     Vermibus est. Fallax haec praebet gaudia mundus.

a4ʳ

---

111 adhuc *scripsi*: aduc *A*.   **112** Incepit *A*¹ : Incoepit *A*² *A*³ *A*⁴.   **115** questus *scripsi*:
quoestus *A*.

boyish years to study the liberal arts.[7] Steeped in Lernaean venom, the plague attacked him with savage fury and struck him down with its keen shaft just when he least expected it. He collapsed, mortally wounded, an outstanding young man to the end, a credit to his excellent father, and laid down his weary limbs on the hated bed. [110] As when a flower on a verdant riverbank wilts after it has been cut by a viper's bite; its brilliant color has not yet begun to fade, but is also no longer resplendent with its customary beauty: so the unfortunate youth lay moaning aloud on his sick-bed. A stream of tears poured from his mournful eyes, while heart-rending laments welled from his breast. At last, after many a groan, he paid the debt of nature. Departing this life, he closed his dying eyes and breathed his last into the treacherous winds.

Ah, unfortunate lad! So that is what the ruthless Fates, that is what [120] those cruel goddesses had in store for you: to die in youthful years and in the house of a stranger! Your noble lineage, your highborn stock could not save you. Now you lie buried in a distant city. It was not granted to you to have your bones laid to rest in the family vault. We all lament your loss. Alas, piteous lad, what enormous grief did your fate cause your brokenhearted father and wretched mother! How bitterly she wept, how deeply she sighed, when the news of your death first reached her maternal ears! Those were not the promises you gave your poor mother [130] when she threw her white arms around your neck and said a last good-bye, as you were already leaving. What did your radiant good looks, what did your tender age avail you? Dead, you now rest in a faraway urn. We ourselves perform the funeral rites for you. We strew flower petals on the grave and send up a prayer to heaven and set the following inscription on the tombstone:

It is I, Wolfgang, who lie buried in this grave. Through the excellence of my character I added luster to the cities of my native land. Slain by the cruel plague, I died far from home, before my time. [140] I was a handsome youth, and many found me attractive. Now I am turned to ashes. My good looks did not avail me. My body, which was of noble blood, is moldering and has become food for worms. Those are the joys that this deceitful

[7]Wolfgang Staffel of Ballenstein (Posen) had matriculated at Erfurt in the autumn of 1504, together with Eobanus.

Hospita terra, vale. Tuque, o quicumque viator
145　Qui mea fata legis, saltem mihi dicito, quaeso:
　　'Spiritus aeterna super aethera pace quiescat.'"
　　　Ast ubi iam sperata salus rumorque quievit
　　Debachans totam qui iam commoverat urbem,
　　Ecce iterum curae surgunt quas protinus omnes
150　Evasisse rati fuimus. Namque aegra recumbit
　　Mortiferis mulier taelis infecta grabato
　　Fatali, tua chara parens, Ludovice. Sagittis
　　Tacta venenatis moritur vitamque per auras
　　Dispergit celeres. Tegitur sub marmore corpus
155　Sarcophago, et tales ducta exprimit orbita versus:
　　"Clauditur hoc tumulo, nullae virtute secunda,
　　Foeminei specimen, mulier, speciale pudoris.
　　Cuius in aetherea requiescat spiritus arce."
　　　Iamque fere totam rabies bachatur in urbem,
160　Atque adeo nec tutus erat quis. Denique restat
　　Consuluisse fugae. Placuit, nihil obstat, eundum est.
　　Heu, furibunda lues furiaque ferocior omni
　　Eumenidum, quid tam variis errare periclis
　　Caecropios cogis iuvenes per inhospita tesqua?
165　Nonne semel satis est te nos pepulisse? Quid ergo
　　Nos sequeris? Germana sumus, non Graeca iuventus!
　　Non ducis Argivi raptos defendimus ignes,
　　Non Troiam petimus, Xanti non vidimus undas,
　　Pervenit nullus nostras Agamemnon ad oras.
　170　Parce igitur sacros taelis flammantibus artus
　　Polluere et tetris iuvenilia corda venenis!
　　　Nil restat: via tentanda est. Discedimus omnes.
　　Effugiunt iuvenum turba comitante magistri
　　Una omnes, niveis ubi Francobergia muris
175　Cincta iacet, foveis circumvallata profundis,

---

169 Agamemnon *scripsi*: Agamennon *A*.

world has to offer. Hospitable earth, farewell. But you, passer-by, whoever you may be who are reading of my fate, say at least this prayer for me, I beg you: "May his soul rest above the sky in everlasting peace."

But when we were already fancying ourselves safe, when the rumors that had spread like wildfire and frightened the entire city were already quieting down, lo and behold, there the worries rose up again – the very ones that all of us [150] thought we had escaped long since. For a woman fell sick, infected by the fatal shafts, and lay down on her deathbed. It was your dear mother, Ludwig.[8] Pierced by the poisoned arrows, she died and scattered her life in the swift winds. Her body was buried in a stone coffin. The epigraph inscribed on its rim consisted of the following lines:

Buried in this grave is a lady who was second to none in virtue. She was the very embodiment of the modesty that so becomes a woman. May her spirit find rest in the citadel of heaven.

Before long the plague ran amuck through virtually the entire city, [160] to the point that no one was safe anymore. Finally, nothing remained for us but to consider fleeing again. The counsel pleased us. Nothing stood in the way; we had to leave. Alas, furious pestilence, more ferocious in your rage than any of the Furies, why do you force young people like us, followers of Athena, to wander in constant danger, through inhospitable wastelands? Isn't it enough that you have driven us away once already? Why then are you pursuing us? We're German lads, not Greeks! We are not trying to hold on to that captive girl whom the Argive leader loved with such passion – we are not making for Troy, we have not seen the waters of Xanthus, no Agamemnon has come to our shores.[9] [170] So stop desecrating the hallowed limbs with your fiery shafts and the young men's hearts with your horrible poisons!

There is no other way: we must try to escape. All of us depart. Accompanied by a band of young men, the magisters flee one and all to the place where Frankenberg lies, ringed with snow-white walls and encircled by a deep moat,

---

[8]Ludwig Platz of Melsungen. See fn. 4 at lines 81-83 above.

[9]Another allusion to the plague that Apollo sent on the Greek camp before Troy. Cf. lines 26-28 above, with fn. 2.

Urbs praeclara bonis opibus, celeberrima Musis,
Edera transpicuis quam preterlabitur undis
Clarus et obliquos ducit per saxa meatus.
Quem super arboreae iaciunt umbracula frondes.
180   Parte alia lacus est nitidis pellucidus undis,
Quem circum innumeris crescunt arbusta rosetis.
Parte eadem situs est collis redolentibus herbis
Consitus arboribusque nitens ornatus amenis.
Urbs igitur studiis fuit haec aptissima nostris,
185   Sic visum superis.
                   Ad dictam venimus urbem.
Ingredimur portas propria tum sponte patentes.
Excipiunt nos tota cohors iuvenesque senesque,
Et sua formosae spectantes vota puellae
Evenisse novis ornant sua tempora sertis.
190   Ipse etiam Aoniis Musis comitatus Apollo
Advenit, et longis feriunt concentibus auras.
   Hic igitur longo fatis foelicibus usi
Tempore mansuri proprias delegimus aedes

Iuxta Virginei splendentia culmina phani,
195   Qua meriti dudum Mariae solvuntur honores.
Et iam dissimiles Phoebi lux alma Dianae
Partitur cum nocte vices et preterit aestas.
Instat hyems redeuntque nives. Obducta pruinis,
Verna prius tristatur humus. Iacet obruta tellus
200   Frigore Hyperboreo, manantque latencia stricto
Flumina pacta gelu. Rediit iam flebile tempus.
   Instamus studiis. Longas fama exit ad oras.
Urbs viget. Augentur comites. Studiosa iuventus
Crescit et incumbit studiis noctesque diesque.
205   Illic Socraticae discuntur dogmata sectae,
Doctus Aristoteles illic perplexaque nodis
Multa sophismaticis. Non tantum Acadaemia sylvis
Laudis habet Graecis quondam celebrata Platonis
Quantum nostra novis urbs illustrata triumphis,
210   Aemula Cecropiae studiis melioribus urbi.

a city renowned for her goodly wealth, celebrated far and wide for her Muses. The Eder, famous in its own right, glides past the town with transparent waters as it winds its way through rocky cliffs. A canopy of leafy boughs shades it from the sun. [180] On the other side there is a lake, with shining pellucid waters. Orchards, girded with countless rose bushes, grow all around it. On the same side there lies a hill, thickly planted with fragrant herbs and gaily adorned with lovely trees.[10] This city, therefore, was perfectly suited to our studies; and so it seemed to the gods.

We reached the aforementioned city. As we are about to enter, the gates swing open by themselves. A large crowd of young and old has turned out to welcome us, and attractive girls, who are seeing their dreams come true, deck their heads with fresh garlands. [190] Even Apollo himself drops by, attended by the Aonian Muses, and their harmonious singing long strikes the sky.

Well then, since we intended to take advantage of our good fortune and stay here for quite some time, we selected a house of our own next to the resplendent roofs of the Church of Our Lady, where Mary has long been venerated with due honors.[11] And now Phoebus's kindly light is becoming shorter, while the nights of Diana are growing longer. The summer is over, winter is at hand, and snow is beginning to fall again. Covered with hoar, the earth mourns the loss of her vernal beauty. The ground lies buried [200] under hyperborean frost, and the streams run hidden under sheets of ice. The dismal time of year has now returned.

We apply ourselves to our studies. Our fame flies to distant shores. The city prospers. New comrades flock to us. The students increase in number and devote themselves to their work night and day. Here the teachings of the Socratic school, here the wisdom of Aristotle and the many knotty problems of the dialecticians are the subjects of study. Plato's Academy, formerly celebrated in the groves of Greece,[12] is not as famed as our town, now that these latest triumphs of ours have added luster to her name. [210] In the liberal arts she is the rival of Athens. Here is the spring

---

[10]The Goßberg outside Frankenberg is also described lovingly in *Buc.* 1, 116-117.

[11]Hermann Diemar, *Die Chroniken des Wigand Gerstenberg von Frankenberg* (Marburg, 1909), p. 474, n. 5, says that this building was probably the schoolhouse.

[12]Plato's Academy was located in a grove outside Athens.

Illic Castaliis fons est uberrimus undis,
Pieriusque latex illic et Delphica laurus,
Illic Aonius vertex, loca vatibus apta,
Namque placent Musis umbrosae tegmina sylvae.
215   Postquam autem studiis hyemem transaegimus illam,
Ver redit. Aestivos Phoebus iam colligit ignes,
Arboribusque novae redeunt cum germine frondes.
Paulatim tetros Erphordia docta furores
Post multas tandem caedes evasit et aestus.
220   Candida mox iterum ventis dare vaela paramus,
Assuetam fatis petituri hortantibus urbem.
    Urbs luget, commota novae formidine famae.
O quales gemitus nostri peperere recessus,
Quas lachrymas! Quales miserunt lumina fletus
225   Tristia, quae nostros abitus odere diemque
Invisum! Moestam multis comitantibus urbem
Linquimus, immodico confusi tempora Bacho.
Hinc tandem portum per daevia longa petitum
Contigimus, ubi nunc fatis melioribus usi
230   Vivimus et gremio fovet Erffordt clara receptos.

Τέλος

that bubbles over with Castalian waters, here the Pierian stream and the Delphic laurel, here the Aonian peak[13] – places suited to bards, for the Muses love the awning of a shady wood.

After we have spent that winter in assiduous study, however, springtime returns. Already the sun is gathering the heat of summer, and again new leaves are budding on the trees. Little by little scholarly Erfurt has at length emerged from the plague's horrible fury, but only after much dying and anguish. [220] Shortly thereafter we once more prepare to hoist our white sails to the winds, as fate urges us to head back to the familiar city.

Utterly shocked at the news, the town is in mourning. Oh, what sighs, what tears does our departure elicit! What torrents stream from unhappy eyes that hate to see the odious day of our parting! With a great escort we leave the saddened city, our heads all giddy from a surfeit of wine. From there, on long byways, we at last reach the yearned-for harbor, where we now enjoy a happier [230] life and illustrious Erfurt once again caresses us lovingly in her lap.

The End

---

[13] Mount Helicon, sacred to the Muses.

B 1   AD M. LAURENTIUM USINGEN
EOBANI HESSI FRANCOBERGII
PHALEUTIUM ENDECASYLLABUM

Heroo tragicos decet poetas
Pomposos pede condidisse versus;
Nescit grandisonos puer boatus.
Agrestes igitur libens Camoenas,
5   Laurenti, tenuis feras poetae
Qui nil magnificum canit precamur.
Dives mittat opes pecuniosas,
Argentum, lapides, Phalerna, Choas
Vestes. Carmina pauperes poetae
10   Mittunt, diviciis venustiora,
Quae non longa dies peraedet unquam
Nec rodent tineae nec ignis uret.
Vivent carmina dum poli manebunt.
Dives diviciis suis peribit.

a6ᵛ

B 2   AD CANDIDUM LECTOREM HEXASTICHON

Quisquis es, hos aequo spectans examine versus
Pendito. Nil puero livida verba nocent.
Zoile turpis, abi. Teneris humane faveto
Carminibus lector. Zoile turpis, abi.
5   Parce, puer, puero. Senior, puerilia come
Carmina nec nasum rhinocerotis habe.

B 2   1 aequo *manus correctoris in* A^1 A^2 A^4: aequa A^3.

B 1 TO MAGISTER LORENZ OF USINGEN.[14]
SOME PHALAECIAN HENDECASYLLABLES
BY EOBANUS HESSUS OF FRANKENBERG

For tragic poets it is fitting to compose stately lines in heroic verse; a youth must eschew such grandiloquent bellowing. Therefore, Lorenz, have the goodness, I beg you, to accept this simple poem, written by a plain-spoken poet who does not sing in exalted tones. The rich can send money, silver, gemstones, vintage wines, and garments of Coan silk.[15] In return, penniless poets offer songs [10] far lovelier than riches — poems that the long passage of time can never consume, nor moths gnaw, nor fire burn. Songs will live as long as the heavens last. The rich man will perish with his riches.

B 2 A HEXASTICH TO THE FAIR-MINDED READER

Whoever you are who read these verses, weigh them on balanced scales. Spiteful remarks cannot harm the young poet. Abominable Zoilus,[16] off with you! But you, kind reader, be well-disposed to these songs of youth. Abominable Zoilus, off with you! Adolescent, be forbearing with the adolescent. Older man, trim these unfledged poems and don't turn up your nose like a rhino.

[14]For Eobanus's instructor Lorenz Arnoldi of Usingen see fn. 5 at lines 83-84 above.

[15]"Coan" garments were made of the expensive silk first woven at Cos.

[16]The sophist Zoilus poked fun at Homer's errors and inconsistencies and so became a byword for a spiteful critic. See, for instance, Ov. *Rem.* 365-366. Like so many of his fellow humanists, Eobanus often rails at this bogeyman (or at Envy). See, for example, *Pug.* B 1; *Laud.* 392-394; 575-585; *Buc.* B 1, 8; *Nup.*, postscript; *Her. Chr.* B 1.

DE PUGNA STUDENTUM ERPHORDIENSIUM
CUM QUIBUSDAM CONIURATIS NEBULONIBUS

THE BATTLE BETWEEN THE STUDENTS OF ERFURT
AND A MOB OF SWORN SCOUNDRELS

Title page of *De pugna studentum Erphordiensium*
Erfurt: Wolfgang Stürmer, 1506
Staats- und Universitätsbibliothek, Bremen

DE PUGNA STUDENTUM ERPHORDIENSIUM

Introduction

This attractive poem vividly describes the street fight between town and gown that took place in Erfurt on Sunday, 9 August 1506. Eobanus wrote it in the first flush of victory and published it the following month. See the introduction to *De recessu studentum*, pp. 95-97 above.

Ever since Franz W. Kampschulte's *Die Universität Erfurt in ihrem Verhältnisse zu dem Humanismus und der Reformation*, vol. 1 (Trier, 1858), p. 67, the year when the street battle took place has always been given as 1505. This date is in fact erroneous. According to *De pugna studentum*, lines 7-8, the students were attacked on a Sunday; and according to lines 77-78 the immediately following day was sacred to St. Laurence, that is to say, August 10. Since the ninth and tenth of August fell on a Saturday and Sunday in 1505, but on a Sunday and Monday in 1506, the correct year is 1506.

The location of the riot can be pinpointed with the help of the woodcut printed on the work's title page. For in the Bremen and London copies, the building to the left in the background is labeled, each in a different contemporary hand, as "Porta celi" ("Porta caeli") – the Collegium Amplonianum that stood at what is now Michaelisstraße 44. It was torn down in 1758.[1]

De pugna studentum was reprinted at Erfurt in 1507. A new edition, with many notes on the poem's Latinity, was produced by Johann T. Kreyssig in: *Ioachimi Camerarii narratio de Helio Eobano Hesso. Accesserunt Christ. Theoph. Kuinoelii oratio de Helii Eobani Hessi in bonas literas meritis et Helii Eobani Hessi carmina, De pugna studentum Erphordiensium cum quibusdam coniuratis nebulonibus et in bonarum artium detractorem, iterum edita* (Meissen, 1843), pp. 61-71; reprinted, in facsimile, in: Dietrich Emme, *Martin Luthers Weg ins Kloster: Eine wissenschaftliche Untersuchung in Aufsätzen* (Regensburg, 1991), pp. 186-194.

Like Kreissig's, our text is based on the editio princeps (Erfurt: Wolfgang Stürmer, 1506):

---

[1] See Kleineidam, vol. 1, pp. 366-369.

A (1506)

DE PVNGNA STVDENTVM ERPHORDIENSIVM | cum quibuſdam coniuratis nebulonibus | Eobani Heſſi Francobergii | Carmen. | [*woodcut*]

Colophon, sig. a4ʳ: Expreſſum in alma Vniuerſitate Erphor- | dienſi typis
VVolfii Sturmer Anno | M.D.VI.

Collation:	4°: a⁴, [$3 signed], 4 leaves
Contents:	a1ʳ title page; a1ᵛ-a3ᵛ *De pugna studentum Erphordiensium*; a3ᵛ-a4ʳ *In bonarum artium detractorem invectivum*; a4ʳ colophon; a4ᵛ woodcut
Copy-text:	Bremen, Staats- und Universitätsbibliothek Call number: VI.3.b.13/3

I have also consulted the following copies: Cambridge (Mass.), Harvard University Library (GC5. Eo 164.506d); Jena, UB (4° Bud. Op. et Ep. 50/4 Inc.); London, BL (Print Room); and Gotha, Forschungs- und Landesbibliothek (Mon. typ. 1509 4° 13/2). The last-named copy is inscribed in Eobanus's hand with the words "Spalatino suo" (For his dear friend [Georg] Spalatin); it lacks sig. a4.

The editio princeps was reprinted the following year by Wolfgang Stürmer at Erfurt:

B (1507)

DE PVGNA STVDENTVM ERPHORDI | ENSIVM CVM QVIBVSDAM | coniuratis nebulōibus Eobani | Heſſi Francobegii Carmen | [*woodcut*]

Colophon, sig. A4ʳ: Expreſſum in alma Vniuerſitate | Erphordienſi Typis |
Vuolphii Sturmer | Anno. M.D.VII:

Collation:	4°: A⁴, [$3 signed], 4 leaves
Contents:	A1ʳ titlepage; A1ᵛ-A3ᵛ *De pugna studentum Erphordiensium*; A3ᵛ-A4ʳ *In bonarum artium detractorem invectivum*; A4ʳ colophon; A4ᵛ woodcut
Location:	Vienna, Österreichische Nationalbibliothek Call number: 71 H 5b

This reprint is not mentioned by Von Hase. I know of no other copies.

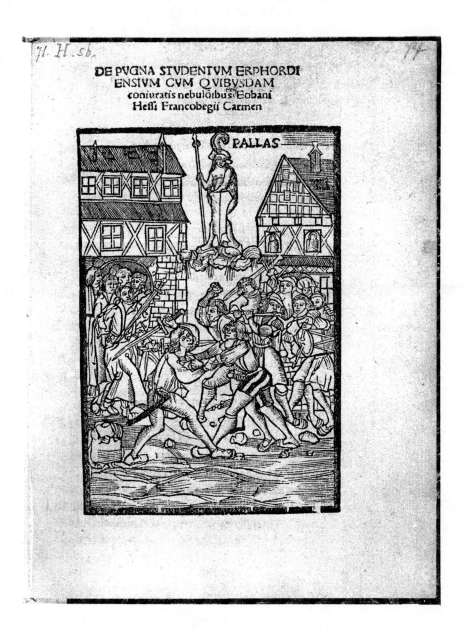

Title page of *De pugna studentum Erphordiensium*
Erfurt: Wolfgang Stürmer, 1507
Österreichische Nationalbibliothek, Vienna

DE PUGNA STUDENTUM ERPHORDIENSIUM
CUM QUIBUSDAM CONIURATIS NEBULONIBUS
Eobani Hessi Francobergii carmen

THE BATTLE BETWEEN THE STUDENTS OF ERFURT AND A MOB OF SWORN SCOUNDRELS

A poem by Eobanus Hessus of Frankenburg

DE PUGNA STUDENTUM ERPHORDIENSIUM
CUM QUIBUSDAM CONIURATIS NEBULONIBUS
EOBANI HESSI FRANCOBERGII CARMEN

Fervidus ardentes foecit iam Procyon aestus
    Et gravis ignivomo splenduit axe Canis,
Quom nova non solito tumuerunt bella tumultu,
    Bella Sophocleo commemoranda pede.
5   Ut meminisse iuvat! Quo nam victoria maior,
    Tanto plus belli commeminisse iuvat.
Iam rude festivos vulgus celebrabat honores;
    Sacra Panompheo lux erat illa Deo.
Bacho indulgebant consueto more studentes
10   Quos celebri fovet Erphordia docta sinu.
Suavia dulcisonae fundebant carmina voces,
    Qualia Syrenes vix cecinisse ferunt;
Illic argutos fudit cava tybia cantus,
    Quales Mysenus, Triton et ipse stupet,
15   Quom subito insani turbarunt tanta furores
    Gaudia. Tristitia gaudia nulla carent.
Sed non tristiciam, nullum sensere furorem
    Gaudia, laeticia post celebrata nova.
Ecce caterva ingens, subito cumulata furore,
20   Excitat irata Martia taela manu.

Rustica gens, rude vulgus, iners moechanica turba
    In nova iurato proelia Marte tument.
Arma omnes capiunt: enses hastasque verutas
    Taelaque plumbatos exiciosa globos.
25   Incaedunt formata acie, ceu Dorica contra
    Castra ferus celeres duceret Hector equos.
Tergora tensa boum crepitant, tuba ductilis auras
    Verberat et sonitu clangit ad astra gravi.
Iamque sacras venti divinae ad Palladis aedes,
30   Ingeminant duplici singula verba sono.
Fit clamor – puto Stentoreos nihil esse boatus –
    Quale tonat rapido Sicelis Aethna Iovi.

5 Ut *scripsi*: Et *AB*.   27 tuba *A*: turba *B*.

THE BATTLE BETWEEN THE STUDENTS OF ERFURT AND A MOB OF SWORN SCOUNDRELS. A POEM BY EOBANUS HESSUS OF FRANKENBERG

Torrid Procyon was already causing sweltering heat, the Dog Star gleamed oppressive in the fire-spewing sky,[1] when without warning a battle royal broke out – not your everyday brawl, but a battle that deserves to be commemorated in Sophoclean verse. What a joy to call it to mind! For the bigger the victory, the greater the delight in recalling the fray.

Just then the vulgar crowd was celebrating a festive holiday, that day being sacred to God, the author of prophecies.[2] According to time-honored custom the students [10] whom scholarly Erfurt caresses in her celebrated lap were indulging in wine. Their sweet-sounding voices were pouring out melodious songs, the likes of which even the Sirens, or so we're told, could scarcely have produced; a hollow flute was there too, pouring forth silvery tunes of a caliber that would have astonished Misenus and Triton himself,[3] when suddenly, out of the blue, a mad frenzy disrupted the joyous revelries. You just can't have joy without grief. But neither grief nor frenzy dampened the students' spirits. Afterwards they went right back to their revels with renewed hilarity.

Lo and behold, a huge mob that has worked itself up into a sudden frenzy [20] is raising the weapons of Mars with wrathful hand. Peasant folk, uncouth riffraff, an idle crowd of workmen are banding together to attack us anew in pitched battle. They all grab their weapons: swords and sharp pikes and – deadly missiles these! – leaden balls. They march forward in battle array, looking for all the world as if fierce Hector were leading swift chargers against the Greek camp. The stretched cowhides boom, the coiling trumpet lashes the air and blares its deepmouthed call to the stars. And now, having arrived at the sanctuary of our goddess Pallas, [30] they repeat every single word at twice the volume. The bellowing they make – Stentor's shouts, I think, are nothing by comparison – is like the thunderous roar with which Sicily's

---

[1] The rising of the star Procyon (Canis Minor) and the Dog Star (Sirius) heralds the dog days of July and August. Cf. *Laud.* 566-567.

[2] That is to say, it was a Sunday (9 August 1506).

[3] Aeneas's trumpeter Misenus was so confident of his skills that he challenged the sea-god Triton to a contest in blowing a conch shell. See Verg. *A.* 6, 162-174; Eob. *Buc.* 5, 53-54; *Nup.* 295 (as a type of the virtuoso musician).

Insuper et furiis nos et clamore lacessunt
   Et rabidis blactrant scandala multa genis.
35 Turpia verba vomunt, infamia nomina iactant,
   Qualia damnatos sacrilegosque decent,
  Qualia Tantaleos Ixioniosque furores
   Quaeque decent facinus, Sysiphe stulte, tuum,
  Quae deceant Prognesque virum Scyronaque saevum,
40   Qualia vix Caci facta decere putem.
  Hiis accensa, novos pubes studiosa furores
   Concipit et rapida surgit in arma manu.
  Exiliunt; enses manibus vibrantur acuti.
   Palladios iuvenes Martius urget amor.
45 Et furor audaces et laesae iniuria famae
   Foecit et immites iussit habere manus.
  Concurrunt miscentque manus, ensesque colorat
   Victrices iuvenum fusus ab hoste cruor.
  Culmine saxa volant, densis velut imbribus aether
50   Solvitur et multo verbere tangit humum.
  Pars tecta ascendunt, patulis pars taela fenestris
   Hostibus eiiciunt perniciosa suis.
  Diva suis vires Pallas cultoribus affert
   Et timidos flexo territat angue viros.
55 Delphicus hostiles arcus vibrabat Apollo,
   Torve quibus Python tu quoque victus obis.
  Vicimus inque fugam victos convertimus hostes,
   Quos timor impigros iussit habere pedes.
  Sic furiosa cohors didicit quid Pallados arma,
60   Quid possint molles in fera bella manus.
  Torva Medusei facies obiecta capilli
   Exuperat flammas, Mars furibunde, tuas.
  Sic fugiunt, fugisse quidem sic profuit illis,
   Tutior hostis enim victus ab hoste fuga est.
65 Inque fugam tamen hos pauci vertere studentes,
   Namque alios clausae detinuere fores.

a2ᵛ (at line 45)

---

36 damnatos *A*: damnatus *B*.   **40** putem *A*: putam *B*.   **56** Python *Kreyssig*: Phyton *AB*.
57 victos *A*: victus *B*.   **63** fugisse *A*: fuisse *B*.

Etna fills the whirling heavens. As if that isn't bad enough, they provoke us with furious shrieks and battle cries and jabber a host of insults with cheeks gone berserk. They spew out profanities, they call us bad names, names that are fitting for convicts and scoundrels, names that suit the violent madness of a Tantalus and an Ixion or the crime of foolish Sisyphus, names that would aptly describe Procne's husband and fell Sciron, [40] the sort of names, I should think, that are scarcely appropriate even for Cacus's misdeeds.[4]

Incensed by these taunts, the students fly into a terrible rage and straightway reach for their weapons. They jump into action, brandishing razor-sharp swords in their hands. Lust for the exploits of Mars impels the youthful devotees of Pallas. Fury and injured pride make them courageous and bid their hands be ruthless. Rushing forward, they join battle, and the blood shed by the enemy reddens the youths' victorious swords. Stones fly down from on high, much as a cloudburst [50] lashes the ground in a heavy downpour. Some climb up to the roof; others hurl missiles out of wide-open windows, to the detriment of their enemies. The goddess Pallas gives her votaries strength, and her writhing serpent strikes terror into the cowardly men.[5] Apollo of Delphi shakes his bow at the enemies, the very same bow with which he slew the savage Python,[6] among others.

The victory is ours! We've defeated our foes and put them to flight! Driven by fear, they run as fast as their feet can carry them. So the frenzied rabble has learned the hard way what the weapons of Pallas, [60] what tender hands can accomplish in ferocious combat. Medusa's dreadful, serpent-haired visage that we hold up in front of us has overpowered your flames, raging Mars. So they take to their heels, knowing full well that flight is their only salvation. For truly: a defeated enemy who runs away lives to fight another day. All the same, it took just a handful of students to put them to flight, for the closed doors held the others back.

---

[4]The Lydian king Tantalus betrayed the secrets of the gods. Ixion, king of the Thessalian Lapiths, tried to rape Juno. Sisyphus, a king of Corinth, was notorious for his trickery. Procne's husband, the Thracian king Tereus, raped his sister-in-law Philomela and then cut out her tongue to stop her from witnessing against him. Sciron was a notorious brigand killed by Theseus. Cacus was a giant killed by Hercules for stealing some of the cattle of Geryon.

[5]The snake was one of the attributes of Pallas Athena. Her aegis, moreover, was adorned with the snake-haired head of Medusa; cf. line 61.

[6]The Python was an enormous serpent killed by Apollo near Delphi.

Rustice sic celebres peperisti stulte triumphos,
Talia sperato Marte trophea refers!
Et iam clausa dies summo decessit Olympo
70   Et vehitur nivea casta Diana rota.
Pectora nec facilem coeperunt laesa quietem,
Victa nec optatus lumina somnus adit.
Ille dolet vulnus accepti flebilis ictus,
Hic queritur viduo tempora laesa thoro.
75   Pars medicos quaerunt, pars accersire videntur.
Alter habet, promptam postulat alter opem.
Sol redit Occeano, festa solennia luce
Chratifero redeunt concelebranda patri.
Conveniunt iterumque accensis mentibus omnes
80   Inveniunt varios, turba prophana, dolos.
Scilicet hesternae memores iurata diei
Bella parant animis asperiora pares.
Tantus habet fatui livor praecordia vulgi,
Invide sic dignum rustice nomen habes!
85   Nec mora, correptis incedunt protinus armis,
Una cohors numero multiplicata novo,
Quom levis incoeptum prohibens Fortuna laborem
Obstitit, ah, certas nescia ferre vices.
Namque novo rabidi preventi Marte latrones
90   Fortiter incoeptae poenituere viae.
Urbis enim domini fortes civilibus armis
Coepere insanos Marte favente viros.
Hinc meritas carcer poenas manet. Omnibus una
Digna domus tanto crimine carcer erat.
95   Sed iam speratum invidit Fortuna triumphum,
Promisit pueris quem dea glauca suis.
Venissent utinam quantumvis fortibus armis!
Illa dies ipsis exicialis erat.
Iam collecta aderant collectis viribus arma.
100   Nil nisi spaerati copia Martis abest.
Consuluit nostrae forsan Fortuna saluti,

---

93 meritas *AB*: meritos *Kreyssig.*   **97** fortibus *A*: furtibus *B*.

Stupid louts! So that is the glorious victory you've won for yourselves! Those are the spoils you bring back from the battle you were hankering for!

And now the day, drawing to a close, was leaving the heights of Olympus, [70] and chaste Diana was riding her snow-white chariot. The wounded hearts, however, cannot find tranquil repose, and longed-for sleep fails to steal over the eyes of the vanquished. This fellow whines about the painful stab he's received; that one bewails a head wound as he lies all alone in bed. Some of them are visiting a doctor; others appear to be sending for one. They are either getting or demanding prompt attention.

As the sun rises again from the ocean, the annual holy-day dawns when we honor the saint who bears the grid-iron.[7] The villains – sacrilegious scoundrels that they are – all come together again and with revenge on their minds [80] hatch sundry plots. Obviously they haven't forgotten yesterday's events! As determined as ever, they swear to fight even harder this time around. So deeply is malice ingrained in the hearts of the fatuous masses! Envious louts, you really do live up to your reputation!

Without delay, they snatch up their weapons and start marching forward, one single mob, whose numbers swell with every step. But then fickle Fortune placed herself in their way and kept them from carrying out their assault. Ah, how capriciously she changes course! As it turned out, the raging bandits ran into an unexpected battle that stopped them short [90] and gave them good reason to regret their undertaking. For a strong contingent of civil guards over-whelmed the madmen and took them into custody. Now they await their just deserts in jail. Indeed, prison is the one place they all deserve for so heinous a crime. To us, on the other hand, Fortune begrudged the hoped-for triumph that the bright-eyed goddess[8] was holding out to her youthful followers. If only they had come at us! No matter how well armed they might be, that day would surely have been disas-trous for them. We had already rallied our forces and stockpiled weapons. [100] All that was lacking was a chance to fight the battle we were spoiling for. But perhaps Fortune

---

[7] St. Laurence's feast day is August 10, which fell on a Monday in 1506. He was martyred by being roasted alive. Hence he was often depicted as bearing a gridiron.

[8] Pallas Athena.

Laus siquidem pugnae nostra futura fuit.
Hos ego cantatos palmae victricis honores
    Emerita cecini laude trophea ferens.
105 Hoc ego Palladia vobis Eobanus, honestis
    Obediens votis, struximus arte decus.
Palladii vobis iuvenes haec scripsimus, inquam,
    Vester ut aeterno nomine duret honor.

Τέλος

had our best interest at heart, since the glory from that me-
lee was bound to be ours anyway.

Now that I have celebrated the glorious renown that
this famous victory brought us, I offer this song of praise as
a fitting memorial. Yielding to honorable requests, I, Eoba-
nus, have erected this monument for you with Palladian art.
It is for you, I say, youthful votaries of Pallas, that I have
written these verses, so that your fame may endure forever.

The End

B 1　IN BONARUM ARTIUM DETRACTOREM INVECTIVUM

Zoile mordaci quid latras dente bilinguis,
　　Quid vomis e labris verba canina tuis?
Quid dentes acuis, balatro, latrator Anubis?
　　Quid laceras doctos, belua trunca, viros?
5　　I, miser, immundae sordes versato cloacae
　　Et procul a doctis siste, proterve, pedem!
Non decet obscoenas iactare in balsama sordes
　　Nec vitreo turpes tingier amne sues.
Non tibi Cecropiae loca sunt calcanda Minervae.
10　　Te decet ignavum foeda cloaca pecus!
Sola velut tacitis ululat sub nocte latebris
　　Noctua, pennigeras dum sopor ambit aves,
Sic quos praesentes non audes carpere, damnas
　　Absentes verbis, livide, saepe tuis.
15　　Improba lingua, sile. Tantos cohibeto furores,
　　Aut laceret rabidus labra proterva canis.
Et modo ni cesses dente oblatrare minaci
　　Et bona pestiferis rodere scripta modis,
Cornua torva tuae cervici impinget Apelles
20　　Et statuet Phrygii tempora trunca Midae.
Saeve tuos igitur latratus pone Molosse!
　　Mollia magnanimus rhaecia frangit aper.
Exaedat rapido volucris tua corda Promethei
　　Gutture, Caucaseis surripienda feris.
25　　I miser et fato vitam diffunde Licambes,
　　Causa etenim fati garrula lingua tui.

Laus Deo

a4^r

---

17 ni *A*: in *B*.　　19 tuae *Kreyssig*: tuo *AB*.　　25 Licambes *scripsi*: Licambis *AB*, Lycambae *Kreyssig*.

B 1 AN INVECTIVE AGAINST A DISPARAGER OF LIBERAL STUDIES

Double-tongued Zoilus,[9] why do you bark at us with snapping jaws? Why do you spit out snarling words from your lips? Why are you whetting your fangs, buffoon, you yapping Anubis?[10] Why are you tearing into learned men, you mutilated ogre? Go, wretch, and dump your filth into a stinking sewer! Stay far back from scholars, impudent oaf! It is not right for filthy swine to scatter their loathsome dung on balsam or to wallow in a crystal-clear stream. The places sacred to Athenian Minerva are off-limits to you. [10] Lazy brute, you belong in a foul sewer! Just as an owl in its quiet hiding-places hoots all alone through the night while sleep envelops the other winged birds, so you, spiteful dolt, keep carping at those behind their back whom you dare not criticize to their face. Insolent tongue, be silent! Restrain your mad fury, or else some rabid dog will mangle your impudent lips. But if you don't stop barking at us with menacing tooth and gnawing at fine books in that pernicious way of yours, then some Apelles[11] will fasten formidable horns onto your head [20] and fix the ass's ears of Phrygian Midas onto your temples. So stop your barking, savage mastiff! The dauntless boar can easily breach your flimsy nets. May Prometheus's bird devour your heart with its ravenous gullet, may the wild beasts of the Caucasus Mountains steal it away![12] Go, wretched Lycambes,[13] and gasp your last, for it is your garrulous tongue that will be the death of you.

Glory to God

[9]The sophist Zoilus poked fun at Homer's mistakes and so became a synonym for a captious critic. See fn. 16 at *Rec.* B 2, 3.

[10]The Egyptian god Anubis was represented as a dog or with a dog's head; cf. *Her. Chr.* 4, 74.

[11]Apelles was the most famous of the ancient Greek painters.

[12]While Prometheus was chained to the Caucasus for stealing fire from heaven, an eagle (or vulture) continually tore at his immortal liver. Eobanus, however, insinuates that it is Prometheus's heart that is devoured. He does so also in *Ama.* 32, 70-71 and *Her. Chr.* 18, 103-104.

[13]The Theban Lycambes refused to let his daughter marry Archilochus, whereupon the poet lampooned him so savagely that he and his daughter committed suicide.

DE LAUDIBUS ET PRAECONIIS
INCLITI ATQUE TOCIUS GERMANIAE CELEBRATISSIMI
GYMNASII LITTERATORII APUD ERPHORDIAM

A PANEGYRIC
EXTOLLING THE RENOWNED UNIVERSITY OF ERFURT,
THE MOST CELEBRATED IN ALL GERMANY

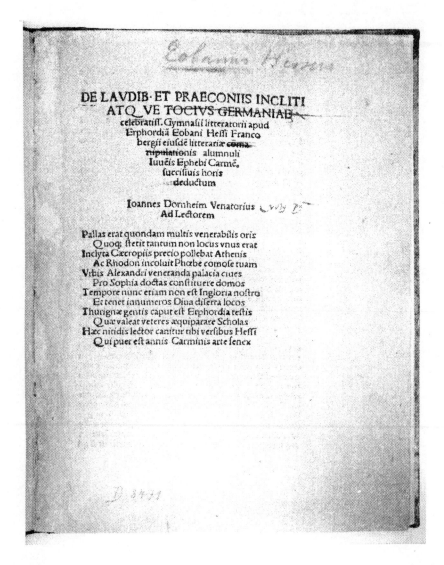

Title page of *De laudibus et praeconiis incliti gymnasii apud Erphordiam*
Erfurt: Wolfgang Stürmer, 1507
Universitätsbibliothek, Heidelberg

DE LAUDIBUS ET PRAECONIIS INCLITI GYMNASII APUD ERPHORDIAM

Introduction

With his B.A. in hand in the early autumn of 1506, Eobanus felt the time had come to express his gratitude by doing for the University of Erfurt what Hermann von dem Busche had done for Leipzig in his encomiastic *Lipsica* of ca. 1504.[1] As one might expect from an impoverished student, the grand gesture also had a more practical purpose: cultivating the patronage of Johann Bonemilch of Laasphe, the auxiliary bishop and professor of theology who had already been giving Eobanus a measure of support. The book evidently had its intended effect. Not long after its publication in the summer of 1507, Bonemilch appointed Eobanus headmaster of the chapter school of St. Severi and granted him free meals at his house.

From various pieces of evidence it is plain that Eobanus began working on the poem in October 1506, not long after he published *De recessu studentum* and *De pugna studentum*. The opening verses tell us that two winters have passed since Eobanus came to Erfurt (in 1504) and that the third harvest is now in full swing. The poet then points with pride to the *Sylvae* that he is hoping to publish shortly – the poetry collection that Mutianus Rufus first broaches in *Ep.* 45 (written on 1 October 1506) and urges him to put together as soon as possible.[2] And in lines 489-494 Eobanus proudly notes that he has now earned his B.A. and is working toward the M.A. Several borrow-

---

[1] For Hermann von dem Busche's *Lipsica* [Leipzig, 1504?] see: Joseph Neff, ed., *Helius Eobanus Hessus, Noriberga illustrata und andere Städtegedichte* (Berlin, 1896), pp. 73-91. Walther Ludwig suggests that Eobanus was also influenced by Georgius Sibutus's praise of Wittenberg, published as *Silvula in Albiorim illustratam* (Leipzig, [winter 1506/07]). See "Eobanus Hessus in Erfurt: Ein Beitrag zum Verhältnis von Humanismus und Protestantismus," *Mittellateinisches Jahrbuch* 33 (1998): 158-159; also see his article "Die Darstellung südwestdeutscher Städte in der lateinischen Literatur des 15. bis 17. Jahrhunderts," in: *Stadt und Repräsentation*, ed. Bernhard Kirchgässner and Hans-Peter Becht (Sigmaringen, 1995), pp. 52-55. While Eobanus does indeed allude to both city poems near the end of his own panegyric (lines 542-543), most of the poem had been written well before Sibutus's *Silvula* was published in the winter of 1506/07. (The date of publication of Sibutus's work can be deduced from the repeated allusions to the plague at Wittenberg during the summer and autumn and to the university's return from Herzberg on 9 December 1506.)

[2] Eobanus alludes to his planned *Sylvae* not only in lines 6-8, but also in line 280.

ings from Mutianus's earliest letters to Eobanus also point to autumn 1506 as the composition date. The phrase "Ausonis ora, vale" in line 68 derives from Mutianus's epigram to Eobanus in *Ep.* 79 (ca. August 23), while the words "totam / Encyclopaedian" in lines 102-103 may well have been suggested by *Ep.* 80 (August 27): "Est operae pretium tractare totam encyclopaediam." The expression "Margaritanae / Stirpis honos" in lines 151-152 has its counterpart in the same letter, where Mutianus praises Herbord as "Margaritanae domus ornamentum singulare." Like the poem itself, the dedicatory letter to Bishop Johann Bonemilch was also written in 1506. In *ded.* 7 Eobanus notes that he is still just a tyro, being not yet twenty years old. Since at that time he believed he was born in 1487 (see fn. 13 at Camerarius, *Nar.* 5, 15), it follows that he assumed he would turn twenty on 6 January 1507.

Though Eobanus composed the work not long after passing the B.A. examinations in late September 1506, he did not publish it until the next year. The reasons for this delay are unknown. That the book was revised and published in the summer of 1507 can be inferred partly from the date July 10 appended to the dedicatory letter and partly from Eobanus's reference at the end of the poem to the dog days of summer (lines 566-567). This inference is corroborated by a letter of ca. mid-1508, in which Eobanus tells Bishop Bonemilch that he completed the encomium of the university during the previous summer: "carmen hoc heroicum, quod de laudibus nostrae universitatis superiore aestate composui" (*Epp. fam.*, p. 10).

The booklet was published just once (Erfurt: Wolfgang Stürmer):

A (1507)

DE LAVDIB. ET PRAECONIIS INCLITI | ATQVE TOCIVS GERMANIAE | celebratiſſ. Gymnaſii litteratorii apud | Erphordiā Eobani Heſſi Franco | bergii eiuſdē litterariæ cōma | nipulationis alumnuli | Iuuēis Ephebi Carmē. | ſucciſiuis horis | deductum | Ioannes Dornheim Venatorius | Ad Lectorem | [*6 distichs*]

Colophon, sig. C5ᵛ: Formatum Typico Charactere Erphordie | apud Magiſtros Vuolphii | Sturmer diligentia | Anno Chriſti | M.D.VII.

Collation: 4°: A⁶, B⁴, C⁶, [$3 (– B3) signed], 16 leaves

Contents: A1ʳ title page; A1ᵛ-A2ʳ dedicatory letter; A2ʳ-C3ᵛ panegyric poem; C4ʳ-C5ᵛ concluding epigrams; C5ᵛ colophon; C6 blank

Copy-text: Heidelberg, Universitätsbibliothek
                 Call number: D 8471

I have also consulted the copy in Jena, UB (4° Bud. Op. et Ep. 50/8). A copy formerly in the Sächsische Landesbibliothek, Dresden, was lost in 1945.

The definitive history of the University of Erfurt is Erich Kleineidam's *Universitas studii Erffordensis*, Erfurter Theologische Studien 14, 22, 42, and 47 (Leipzig, 1981-1992), 4 vols.

DE LAUDIBUS ET PRAECONIIS
INCLITI ATQUE TOCIUS GERMANIAE CELEBRATISSIMI
GYMNASII LITTERATORII APUD ERPHORDIAM
Eobani Hessi Francobergii,
eiusdem litterariae commanipulationis alumnuli,
iuvenis ephebi, carmen succisivis
horis deductum

IOANNES DORNHEIM VENATORIUS
AD LECTOREM

Pallas erat quondam multis venerabilis oris,
    Quoque stetit tantum non locus unus erat.
Inclyta Caecropiis precio pollebat Athenis
    Ac Rhodon incoluit, Phoebe comose, tuam.
5   Urbis Alexandri veneranda palacia cives
    Pro Sophia, doctas, constituere, domos.
Tempore nunc etiam non est ingloria nostro
    Et tenet innumeros diva diserta locos.
Thurignae gentis caput est Erphordia testis,
10   Quae valeat veteres aequiparare scholas.
Haec nitidis, lector, canitur tibi versibus Hessi,
    Qui puer est annis, carminis arte senex.

A PANEGYRIC
EXTOLLING THE RENOWNED UNIVERSITY OF ERFURT, THE MOST CELEBRATED IN ALL GERMANY
A poem written in his spare time
by Eobanus Hessus of Frankenberg,
an adolescent currently studying at that same
institution of higher learning

JOHANN JÄGER OF DORNHEIM[1]
TO THE READER

In ancient times Pallas was venerated in many countries and had temples in more than just one place. The famous goddess was especially worshiped in Cecropian Athens, but she also dwelt in Rhodes, sacred to long-haired Phoebus.[2] The citizens of Alexandria built august palaces – houses of learning – in honor of Wisdom.[3] Even now, in our own day, the well-spoken goddess is not lacking in fame; indeed, she dwells in countless places. Erfurt, the capital of Thuringia, can bear witness to that, [10] for she is the equal of the ancient schools. All this, reader, is described for you in the polished verses of Hessus, who is a youth in years, a graybeard in the art of song.

---

[1] For Johann Jäger (Johannes Crotus Rubianus) see fn. 71 at Camerarius, *Nar.* 17, 17.

[2] Rhodes is sacred to Phoebus because of its Colossus, an enormous statue of the sun-god Helios (Phoebus Apollo). Cf. *Laud.* 81; *Her. Chr.* 19, 85-86.

[3] Under the Ptolemies, Alexandria became home to the famed library, Museum, and university. Cf. *Laud.* 95-96, with fn. 20.

REVERENDISSIMO IN CHRISTO PATRI AC DOMI-
NO, D. IOANNI LASPHE, EPISCOPO ECCLESIAE
SYDONIENSIS, SACRAE PAGINAE PROFESSORI
EXIMIO, ARCHIPRESULIS MOGUNTINI IN PON-
TIFICALIBUS VICARIO, DOMINO SUO COLENDIS-
SIMO, EOBANUS HESSUS FRANCOBERGIUS S. D. P.

Plutarchus Cheronensis philosophus insignis, prestantis-
sime Presul, in eo libro quem Apophthegmatum Graeci
dicunt scriptum reliquit Artaxerxen illum fratrem Cyri Iu-
nioris cognomento Memorem, quom adeuntibus se non
modo benignum, verum et liberalem et admodum iucun-
dum exhibuisset, tum (quod summae et excellentissimae
humanitatis indicium quis ambiget?) legitimae uxori regii
currus aulea undique tolleret, quo adeuntibus se in itinere
aditus pateret, iussisse, paupere autem homine ac rudi, cui
nihil aliud esset, malum ingentis magnitudinis ei offerente,
iucunde subridensque, quippe qui non rei quae dabatur vel
inopia vel usu, sed alacri dantis voluntate gratiam metiretur,
suscepisse. 2 Existimabat enim ille eum qui benigne parva
prompteque acciperet non regali minus humanoque mu-
nere fungi quam si magna elargiretur.

3 Huius ego quoque sententia ductus, tenuia haec et pu-
erilia munuscula, quae inter lasciviencium Musarum coetus
nuper, dum ab ocio litterario severioris disciplinae recreandi
atque quasi Laethaeo flumine conspersi refovendi animuli
mei gratia paulisper diverterem, raptim et extemporaliter in
arctum collegi, tuo nomini dedicare volui, existimans ea, ubi
te eis patronum praefoecissem, ab invidentium rabularum
venenosis et efferatis morsibus facile fore defensata. 4 Es
enim tu plane huiusmodi vir qui cum omni antiquitate de
universae virtutis laude contendis ita ut nihil ad decus tibi,
nihil ad gloriam defuerit. 5 Nam quom sapiencia praecipue
in rebus gerendis plerosque mortalium ita exuperes ut nihil
prorsus mea sentencia ad splendidissimae tuae prudenciae
cumulum accesserit, tum doctrina atque humanitate (quae
multum in presule commendabilis) nulli secundus glorio-

---

1 Apophthegmatum *scripsi*: Apophtegmatum *A*.   3 existimans *scripsi*: exstimans *A*.

---

[4]Johann Bonemilch of Laasphe in Hesse matriculated at Erfurt in 1462, graduating B.A.
in 1465, M.A. in 1469, and doctor of theology in 1487. An energetic, well-liked, and generous
colleague, he was named professor of philosophy in 1482 and of theology in 1487 and was

TO THE MOST REVEREND FATHER AND LORD IN CHRIST, HIS EXCELLLENCY JOHANN OF LAASPHE,[4] BISHOP OF SIDON, DISTINGUISHED PROFESSOR OF BIBLICAL STUDIES, SUFFRAGAN OF THE ARCHBISHOP OF MAINZ, HIS MOST HONORED LORD, EOBANUS HESSUS OF FRANKENBERG SENDS MANY GREETINGS.

In the book that goes by the Greek title *Apothegms,* preeminent Bishop, the noted philosopher Plutarch of Chaeronea records the following anecdote about Artaxerxes,[5] the brother of Cyrus the Younger. This Artaxerxes, surnamed Mnemon, used to show himself not only kind to supplicants, but also magnanimous and altogether congenial. Indeed (and who can fail to recognize this as a mark of the highest and most excellent humanity?) he went so far as to bid his queen consort raise the curtains on each side of the royal carriage to make it easier for people to approach him en route. One day a poor laborer, who had nothing else to offer, presented him with an enormously large apple. The king accepted the gift with a cheerful smile, measuring the favor not by its rarity or the service it rendered, but by the ready goodwill of the giver. For it was his opinion that he who graciously and readily accepts small presents fulfills his duty as king and human being no less than he who freely bestows large ones.

That sentiment being my guiding light also, I wanted to dedicate this small gift, slight and juvenile though it is, to your honored name. Not long ago, when I was taking a break from my academic studies,[6] I threw the work together hurriedly and extemporaneously amidst the frolicking band of the Muses in order to refresh and revive that dear little soul of mine, besprinkled, in a manner of speaking, with the waters of Lethe.[7] By naming you as patron of this poem, however, I am confident that it will easily be made immune from the venomous and savage bites of jealous pettifoggers. For you are obviously a man of the sort who measures up to all antiquity in every laudable virtue, to such an extent that nothing is wanting in your fame, nothing in your glory. In sound judgment, particularly on administrative matters, you so surpass the vast majority of people that your dazzling wisdom, in my opinion, has reached the pinnacle of perfection. You are, furthermore, unexcelled in your learning and culture – a truly commendable virtue in a bishop. Accord-

---

elected to numerous influential positions at the university, for example dean in 1478/79 and 1492, rector in 1485/86, 1495/96, and 1503/04. In 1484 he became parish priest at St. Michael's. Consecrated titular bishop of Sidon and suffragan to the archbishop of Mainz in 1498, he ordained Martin Luther as priest in the spring of 1507. Bonemilch resigned his position as *vicarius in pontificalibus* in 1508 and died in 1510.

[5]Artaxerxes II Mnemon, king of Persia from 404 to 359 BC.

[6]In October 1506, after finishing his B.A. examinations in late September.

[7]The waters of the river Lethe in the underworld were said to induce forgetfulness of the past. Cf. Otto 943; Häussler, pp. 25, 74, 177, and 275.

sum tuae dignitatis ac magnificenciae statum cunctis saeculis admirabilem reddis, nomen ad posteros transmittis nunquam intermoriturum. 6 Bonarum litterarum studia amas ut qui maxime rectissimarum artium studiosos quosque mira humanitate prosequeris. 7 Taceo quantis meritis me politioris litteraturae tyrunculum nondum quadrilustrem iam dudum accumulaveris atque ita tibi (quamvis nullis meis meritis) devinxeris ut si quid | ingenii in me, si quid concinnitatis unquam posteritati etiam commendabile esse videatur, id tibi totum me debere cognoscam.

A2ʳ

8 Ne igitur ingratitudinis vicio (quod quantum sit apud maiores nostros detestatum nemo est qui ignoret) accusandus esse videar et ut olim innumeris tuis erga me beneficiis ex aliqua, licet exigua parte respondeam, breves hasce et extemporales ineptias ad te quasi rectissimorum studiorum antistitem et patronum transmittere volui. 9 Quas, ubi a curis ecclesiasticis quibus tu frequenter obrueris ad quietioris vitae tranquillitatem secesseris, legas precor. 10 Invenies enim inter alia florentissimi nostri studii Erphordiensis preconia, tuae quoque professionis laudes non mediocres. 11 Ego interim, ubi tu hiis oblectatus fueris, ad maiora indies tibi dedicanda vel non invitus accingar. 12 Vale, Presul humanissime atque unicum nostrae tenuitatis refugium.

13 Ex caenobio nostro litterario, sexto Idus Iulias.

9 tu *scripsi*: tum *A*.

ingly, because you are making the prestige of your lofty rank and eminence an object of admiration for all time to come, you are handing down to posterity a name that will never perish. The humanities are so dear to your heart that you honor every true devotee of the noblest arts with extraordinary kindness. I shall say nothing about the generous benefits which you have long heaped on me, the not yet twenty-year-old novice in belles-lettres,[8] and by which you (through no merit of mine, to be sure) have laid me so deeply under obligation to you that – if I have any natural ability to speak of, if posterity should ever deem my poetic style worthy of praise – I must acknowledge I owe this all to you.

Therefore, so as not to appear guilty of ingratitude (and we all know how thoroughly our forefathers detested that vice) and to repay you at long last in some, albeit small way for the innumerable kindnesses you have shown me, I wanted to hand these brief, extemporaneous trifles over to you, the high priest and patron, so to speak, of humanistic studies. When you have a chance to withdraw from the ecclesiastical affairs with which you are so frequently overwhelmed and get to enjoy the leisure of a rather more tranquil life, then, I beseech you, read these verses of mine. For among other things, you will find here a panegyric of the marvelously flourishing studies at our university in Erfurt as well as no mean praise of your own profession. If you should happen to take pleasure in the present poem, I shall gladly gird myself to complete another, constantly-growing book that is to be dedicated to you.[9] Farewell, most considerate of bishops, the one and only refuge of my poverty.

From my academic cloister, July 10.[10]

---

[8]For much of his life Eobanus believed that he was born in 1487. See fn. 13 at Camerarius, *Nar.* 5, 15. By that reckoning he would not turn twenty until 6 January 1507.

[9]In 1508, after Bonemilch withdrew the privilege of free board at the episcopal residence, Eobanus appealed to the bishop to reconsider his decision, all the more so as he was about to dedicate a large book ("grande volumen") to him; see *Epp. fam.*, p. 11. The project he has in mind is not the *Bucolicon* (Krause, *HEH,* vol. 1, pp. 57 and 74-77), but rather a collection of occasional poetry entitled *Sylvae* after the miscellanies of Statius, Polizianio, and Baptista Mantuanus. On 1 October 1506 Mutianus Rufus had urged Eobanus to publish such a volume. Around the same time Mutianus was enlisting the help of Herbord von der Marthen to have it printed. See Mutian. *Ep.* 45 and 46; Eob. *Laud.*, lines 5-8 and 280. Cf. also *Ama.* B 1, 2 (where he promises to publish several books of them shortly); *Nup.* 13-14; and *Her. Chr.* 24, 115-118. The term *Sylvae* originally meant "pieces of unfinished material," i.e., impromptu pieces. Eobanus uses it in that sense in his *Sylvae duae* of 1514. In *De laudibus* he prefers to interpret it as "Forests." See lines 5-8 and 280 below.

[10]The "academic cloister" is one of the university dormitories, in which all students at Erfurt were required to live. The date "July 10" refers to the year 1507, when Eobanus sent the book to the printer. Like most of the panegyric itself, the dedicatory letter was in fact written in mid-autumn 1506. See the introduction.

DEO OPTIMO MAXIMO AUSPICE

Tercia ferventes messis iam colligit aestus,
Altera fugit hyems postquam me magna recoeptum
Hospicio vidit materno Erphordia, postquam
Nulla meae dignas coepit resonantia grates
Carmina Calliopes. Quamvis diversa per urbem
Hanc eciam molli cantavimus illita succo
Carmina, mox lucem florentibus indita sylvis
Perpetuam visura. Sed haec promissio vana est
Nec firmata satis. Si Flaccus viveret, aiet,
"Parturient montes, partum ridebimus."
Illinc
Labor ab incoepto. Meritorum ne tamen ulli
Arguar ingratus, flamma propiore canenti,
Phoebe, fave, qui regna tenes in montibus arcis
Ethereae. Sed enim dignus mihi vindice nodus
Incidit hinc.
"Elegi molles, discedite," dixi.
A2v Non levis hic turpes faciet lascivia motus.
Littera non dominae missam feret ulla salutem.
Non risus, non verba canam proclivia turpem
In Venerem. Res maiores maiore canemus
Pectine. Gericolam mens est extollere ad astra
Pallada. Nec veteres ideo mirabor Athenas,
Non Academiaci studium vulgare Platonis,
Quippe nec Ausoniae quodquam memorabile gentis,
Gymnasium Germanus enim nunc possidet orbis.
Quicquid habet Latium studii melioris et artes
Sola potest Italas aequare Erphordia – tantum
Barbara Teutonicus posuit cognomina, tantum
Arma inter crevere artes, sic numen utrumque
Armigerae nobis favet artiferaeque Minervae,

17 ulla *scripsi*: illa *A.*

[11]As two winters are said to have elapsed since Eobanus arrived in Erfurt in 1504 and he is now in his third harvest-season at Erfurt, the year thus paraphrased is 1506.

[12]Eobanus is referring to the poetry collection *Sylvae* ("forests") that Mutianus Rufus, in a letter of 1 October 1506, had urged him to publish. See fn. 9 at *Laud.,* ded. 11. For unknown reasons the projected volume never materialized. It was not until 1535 that Eobanus finally brought out six books of *Sylvae,* augmented with three more books in 1539.

UNDER THE FAVOR OF GOD, THE BEST
AND GREATEST

The third harvest is already gathering the torrid heat of summer, the second winter has passed since exalted Erfurt welcomed me to her maternal bosom.[11] All the same, she has yet to receive from my Muse a song resounding with the thanks she deserves. It is true that I have composed many different poems in this city also. Daubed with youthful sap, they will soon become part of a blossoming forest and see the light of day forever.[12] But this remains an empty promise, one that has not been fully kept. If Horace were alive, he'd say, [10] "The mountains will go into labor, and we'll laugh at the offspring."

But I am straying from my theme. Lest someone accuse me of being ungrateful for any of her boons, smile on me as I sing, bring your flame closer, O Phoebus, you who hold sway over the heights of heaven. But the fact of the matter is that I am confronted here with "a knot that truly requires a deliverer."[13]

"Amorous elegies, get out of my sight," I exclaimed. I'll have no shallow wantonness here making lascivious gestures, no billets-doux sending greetings to some mistress. Don't expect me to tell jokes or write poems that incite readers to lechery. My theme is a more exalted one, and I want to sing it in a more exalted [20] tone. It is the Pallas who dwells by the Gera that I have a mind to praise to the skies. Hence you won't find me marveling at ancient Athens and Plato's uncommon Academy or, for that matter, at any of the remarkable Italian schools, for Germany now boasts a university of its own. Everything that Italy has to offer in the way of humanistic studies and the arts, Erfurt can match by herself – so far have we Germans gone to shed the by-name "barbarian," so far have the arts advanced amidst the clash of arms, so graciously has the twofold power of Minerva, god-

---

[13]That is, the appeal to Apollo (here identified with Christ) is justified because the poet is confronted with a knot worthy of so mighty a deliverer. Eobanus alludes to Hor. *Ars* 191-192, which counsels the dramatist to avoid the *deus ex machina* unless such a deliverer is absolutely necessary to untie the knot (denouement). Eobanus alludes to the same passage in lines 376-377 below.

30   Tot Germana vigent celebrata per oppida passim
       Gymnasia! Hinc artes crescunt crescentibus annis
       Ingenuae. Nostras Cicero migravit ad oras.
       Hinc vereor multum doleas, Rhomane, dolebat
       Audito Cicerone velut vir Graeculus olim,
35   Ausonias veritus secum transferret ad urbes
       Eloquium ex Graecis. Sed cum Cicerone Maronem
       Nos tibi deripimus, Latium venerabile, quamvis
       Tu minus invideas forsan. Iam noster ubique
       Notior Erydano Gera est, non flumine maior,
40   Qui prope fluctivomis oriens e montibus ad nos
       Labitur et rivis nostram deductus in urbem
       Influit innumeris. Alias tamen illa canemus,
       Quom nova nascetur nostris Erphordia Musis.
       Tum laudes urbisque situm, iam Pallada solam
45   Scribimus hac ipsa celebrem.
                        Quid denique longas
       Volvor in ambages? Vos o quibus ardua primum
       Scandere tam sancti licuit suggesta theatri,
       Quo primas meruit victrix Erphordia palmas
       Teutonicas inter tot claras artibus urbes,
50   Vos, inquam, placide qui tantae molis habenas
       Flectitis, insignesque viri celebresque, favete,
       Este meis faciles concentibus. Ut quibus ipse
       Carminibus vestras nequeo describere laudes,
       Ipsi ignoscatis. Si quid peccare videntur,
55   Parcite peccatis. Vos vestraque scribimus, aequum est.
       Quid loquar? Anne etiam sancti mea verba senatus
       Egregias olim venient fortassis ad aures?
       Dicite, magnates populi, dic, sancte senatus,
       Quem vos carminibus nostris debetis honorem?
60   Quod cano novistis titulis succedere vestris
       Gymnasium. Res vestra agitur! Notissima cunctis
       Sit licet et maior tot iam fugientibus annis
       Gloria perpetuis veniat mansura diebus,
       Attamen et nostra crescet crescente Minerva.

A3[r]

[14]While in Rhodes, the young Cicero delivered a speech in Greek before an audience that included the famed rhetor Apollonius Molon. Everyone except Apollonius was thrilled at his performance. Asked why he looked so glum, Apollonius replied that Cicero's brilliance heralded the end of Greece's monopoly on culture and eloquence. Through Cicero, he said, these glories would now belong also to the Romans. See Plutarch, *Cicero* 4, 5-7; Erasmus, *Ep.* 45, lines 77-81.

dess of war and culture, favored us, [30] so numerous are the renowned universities that flourish everywhere in the cities of Germany! This is the reason why the liberal arts have been advancing here with the advancing years. Cicero has moved to our shores. And that, I'm afraid, is bound to upset the Romans greatly, just as it disturbed that Greekling long ago to hear Cicero speak, for he feared that Cicero would take Eloquence from Greece and bring her back with him to the towns of Italy.[14] But along with Cicero we're also snatching Vergil away from you, venerable Latium, although you perhaps won't be quite so jealous. Our Gera, while no greater in size, is already more famous throughout the world than the River Po – the Gera, [40] which, rising in the water-spewing mountains nearby, tumbles down towards us and, fed by innumerable brooks, finally flows into our city. But those things I plan to extol elsewhere, when a new Erfurt is born in my verse.[15] That will be the place to sing the city's praises and the lay of the land. Here I want to focus on the abode of Pallas itself, a celebrated place in its own right.

Why on earth am I rambling on and on? O you, who were privileged to mount the initially hard-to-reach stage of this blessed theater where Erfurt triumphantly carries off the palm among the many German cities that are famed in the arts, [50] O you, I say, who calmly hold the reins of this great institution, you eminent and celebrated men, lend me your support, be indulgent to my song. Forgive me, if I fail to praise your merits highly enough in my verse. Bear with me, if you catch me making mistakes. Since I'm extolling you and your achievements, that seems only fair. What am I about to say? Will my words perhaps also reach the illustrious ears of the venerable councilors someday? Speak, you who are great among the people, speak, venerable city council: How much honor do you owe to my songs? [60] Surely you are aware that my praise of the university redounds to your credit? Your own honor is at stake! And though your glory is already world-famous, though it has been growing for so many years already and will remain intact to the end of time, nevertheless it will mature even as my

---

[15] Eobanus intends to complement his panegyric of the university with an encomium of Erfurt, along the lines of Hermann von dem Busche's praise of Leipzig (ca. 1504). See the introduction, with fn. 1; cf. lines 542-543 below.

65 Quae bona sunt, faciles reddunt meliora Camenae;
Sint meliora, etiam versu haec facit optima vates.
　　Caedite, quas mea Musa prius summovit, Athaenae.
Ausonis ora, vale. Nil succensebitis et vos,
Urbes Teutonicae, si vos Erphordia forsan
70 Vicerit in nostro studiis me iudice versu.
Caedite, dissimiles. Sic stat sentencia. Certum est.
Hic soror intonsi nata est pulcherrima Phoebi,
Geraque mutato fertur nunc nomine Triton,
Ut reor, hunc etenim iuxta Iove nata perhennem
75 Delegit sedem Pallas.
　　　　　　　　Quae structa decenter
Urbe iacet media, sumptu non infima certe,
Si modo quo coepta est etiam finita fuisset.
Tum neque pyramides iactet mihi barbara Memphis,
Nec mihi narrabis Carium, Mausole, sepulchrum.
80 Sed neque mirifici mihi sunt miracula sumptus
Scribenda aut Rhodii moles operosa Colossi.
At domus interior varios depicta colores
Exprimit et vivas nullo discrimine formas.
Si quis ab antiquis ad nos huc migret Athaenis,
85 Non minus hic patrios mirabitur advena vultus
Quam Tyriam ductor quondam Troianus in urbem,
Susceptus patriae interitus et proelia terrae
Inspiciens quae tum paries depictus habebat,
Obstupuit quibus externas ea casibus urbes
90 Et tam longinquos petiisset fama penates.

　　O domus, o foelix magnae penetrale Minervae!
Regia tu sanctae vincis Capitolia Rhomae.
Caedite, Rhomulei veteres, quos multa beatos
Copia librorum potuit foecisse, beatum
95 Si quem res faciunt. Caedat Ptholomaeia libris
Bibliothaeca suis totum vulgata per orbem.
Quicquid habent Graii, quicquid novere Latini,
Quicquid ab Hebraeis concaessit vatibus, hic est.

---

[16]Apollo's sister Pallas Athena is said to have been born on the banks of the Triton in Boeotia. Hence she is sometimes called "Tritonian," as in lines 407 and 442 below.

[17]The original university building, later called the "Collegium maius," stood next to St. Michael's. Donated to the university by Heinrich of Gotha, the structure was renovated by the city in the early 1390's. See Kleineidam, vol. 1, pp. 18-19.

[18]The Mausoleum at Halicarnassus was one of the Seven Wonders of the ancient world. It was built in the fourth century BC as a tomb for King Mausolus. For the Colossos of Rhodes, mentioned in the next sentence, cf. *Laud.*, lim. 4 above, with fn. 2.

artistry matures. The gracious Muses make all good things better. As for things already superior, the poet makes them supremely good through his verse.

Step aside, Athens. My Muse has already put you in your place. Good-bye to you, Italy. You too, cities of Germany, don't be angry with me if, in my judgment and my verse, Erfurt should perchance [70] surpass you in learning. Step aside, second-rate towns. That is the decision I've reached. My mind is made up. Here the most beautiful sister of unshorn Phoebus was born, and the Triton River, I imagine, has now changed its name to Gera; for truly it is on the banks of the Gera that Jove's daughter Pallas has chosen to take up her lasting dwelling place.[16]

The handsome building stands in the middle of the city. It would certainly have been far more sumptuous, had it been completed according to the original plans.[17] Then barbarous Memphis would not vaunt her pyramids to me, nor would you, Mausolus, brag to me about your tomb in Caria.[18] [80] But there is no eighth wonder of the world for me to describe, no massive ornate structure like the Colossus of Rhodes. The inside of the building, however, is adorned with all kinds of paintings that, without exception, are true to life. If one of the ancient Athenians could come to visit us, the stranger would be no less astounded at seeing the likenesses of his ancestors here than that Trojan leader of old who, having entered the Tyrian town, gazed speechless on the destruction and the battles of his homeland that were depicted on the walls there and wondered by what circumstances that tale might have reached foreign cities [90] and such distant abodes.[19]

O temple, O happy shrine of mighty Minerva! You surpass the magnificent Capitol in holy Rome. Step aside, ancient Romans, you who were blessed with great libraries – if possessions can ever make anyone blessed. Step back, Ptolemaic Library, as famed as you are all over the world for your wealth of books.[20] Everything the Greeks have to offer, everything the Romans know, everything that the Hebrew

---

[19] Awaiting the arrival of Queen Dido in the temple to Juno at Carthage, Aeneas marvels at the scenes of the Trojan War that were depicted on the frieze. See Verg. *A.* 1, 443-493. Carthage is called "the Tyrian town" because it was a colony of Tyre.

[20] The famed Alexandrian Library was founded by Ptolemy I Soter and expanded by Ptolemy II Philadelphus early in the third century BC. Cf. *Laud.*, lim. 5-6.

Esto grammaticus, rhetor, dyalecticus idem,
100 Musicus, et rerum caedat tibi mensio, spectes
Sydera et immensae describas climata terrae,
Hic tamen invenies quod te iuvet. Hec tibi totam
Encyclopaedian libraria proferet, omne
Doctrinae genus. Hic multo studiosa labore
105 Turba frequens iuvenum studiis insudat honestis.
Non secus ac viridis circum vineta Timoli
Inter odoriferas Hyblaei nectaris herbas
Poplite Aristeae volucres inventa capaci
Mella trahunt; vario fervent strepitantibus alis
110 Murmure florigeri vallesque rubique virentes,
Mirrha, thymum, casiae, cythisi, narcissus, amomum,
Cynnama Coriciumque crocum thymbraeque calentes:
Non aliter iuvenum circum subsellia fervet
Gymnica continui series immensa laboris.
115   Illic viva viget Latiae facundia linguae.
Graeca prius, post facta Latina, novissima nostra est.
Hic est cum docto magnus Cicerone Pericles
Et plures alii quos laudat Graeca vetustas,
Quos Rhomana refert. Orantem audiveris horum
120 Ad populum quemquam, iacientem fulgura dices.
Presul ad has prior accedis dignissime partes,
Barbara cui titulos peperit Sydonia, cuius
Hessia habet cunas, Lasphe vulgata parentes.
Parva licet, meritis tamen illis aucta refulget,
125 Hessiacas inter nulli non dignior urbes.
Teque Iodoce tuum decus Isennache manebit,
Inclyte divinae preco virtutis et inter
Eloquio celebres velut inter sydera Phoebus.
Inde Sebastianus, virtutis amator honestae,

A4ᵛ

---

103 omne *scripsi*: omnis *A*.   **124** illis *scripsi*: illus *A*.

---

[21]Eobanus lists the seven liberal arts taught at Erfurt: grammar, rhetoric, dialectic, music, mathematics-geometry, astronomy, and geography. Cf. *Idyl.* 16, 38-45, referring to Nuremberg.

[22]The main university library was housed in the Collegium maius (since 1407). The university also possessed the extraordinarily rich collection bequeathed by the physician Amplonius Rating of Bercka (Rheinberg) in 1412 and hence known as the "Amploniana." That collection belonged to the Collegium Amplonianum (Porta celi).

[23]The mythical hero Aristaeus taught the art of beekeeping.

bards have left us: it is all here. If you wish to study grammar, rhetoric, dialectic, [100] or music or have an interest in geometry, if you'd like to observe the stars or map the regions of the vast earth,[21] here you'll find everything you need. This library will offer you the entire circle of knowledge, every branch of learning.[22] Here the students gather in large numbers, laboring and sweating at their honorable studies. Just as Aristaeus's insects[23] fly round about the vineyards of verdant Tmolus, amidst herbs fragrant with Hyblaean nectar, and carry the honey they've gathered on their capacious thighs, their wings whirring with manifold [110] murmurs; meanwhile the flowery valleys and green brambles, the myrrh, thyme, marjoram, clover, narcissuses, balsam, cinnamon, Corycian saffron, and fiery savory all hum with activity: so the school benches hum with the youths' endless round of assiduous studies.

Here lively oratory in the Latin language continues to thrive. Invented by the Greeks, afterwards practised by the Romans, eloquence has now at last become our own. Here one can find the great Pericles along with the learned Cicero and many others besides who enjoyed renown in ancient Greece and Rome. If you heard any of these orators speak [120] to the people, you'd say he was hurling thunderbolts. In this sphere, worthiest of bishops, it is you who set the pace – you to whom foreign Sidon has lent her title, whose cradle stands in Hesse, and whose parents live in the well-known town of Laasphe.[24] Small though it is, it nonetheless shines forth through the honor you have bestowed upon it, so that it now ranks among the most meritorious cities of Hesse. You too have made a lasting name for yourself, Jodocus of Eisenach, illustrious preacher of God's saving power, as resplendent among the celebrated orators as Phoebus is among the stars.[25] That may be said also of Se-

[24] Eobanus's patron Johann Bonemilch of Laasphe was titular bishop of Sidon. On his life see fn. 4 at *Laud.*, ded.

[25] Jodocus Trutfetter of Eisenach (1460-1519) matriculated at Erfurt in 1476, earning his B.A. in 1478, his M.A. in 1484. Though a bachelor (1488) and licentiate of theology (1493), he remained in the philosophical faculty, partly because he had no prospect of becoming professor of theology at Erfurt, partly because he could not afford the costly promotion. However, after serving in various administrative posts (for instance, dean in 1493/94 and 1499/1500, rector of the university in 1501, dean of the Collegium Marianum later that year), he was finally able to graduate doctor of theology in 1504. He was the author of several widely-used textbooks: *Breviarium dialecticum* (1500), *Summule totius logice* (1501), *Summa in totam physicen* (1514), and *Summa philosophiae naturalis* (1517), the latter two graced with an epigram

130 Doctor Cyriaco multum praefectus ovili,
     Atque alii quorum resonat facundia Christi
     Dogmata, divinae legis precepta, Moysi
     Quae Deus in summo commisit vertice Choreb.
     Innumeri, quibus est non tonsa corona, valentes
135 Eloquio celebri, nostris accedere possunt
     Carminibus. Sat erit paucos dixisse. Mereris
     Ferre prior palmas parte hac, Materne, priores,
     Orator vatesque simul, Pistorie, tuque,
     Bartholomee, mei non ultima cura laboris
140 Et decus et nostrae specimen, laus, fama palestrae,
     Vivida cui multum debet Dialectica, cuius
     Ingenio, Chrysippe, tui laus caedit acervi.
     Per te floret honor studii, per te utraque multis
     Quae latuit natura patet. Te grata iuventus,
145 Grata senecta colit, stupet, admiratur, amatque.
          Tene mei sileant versus, Hereborde diserte,
     Tam genere insignis quam Pallade, floribus aevi
     Innocui qui ludis adhuc crescentibus? O qui
     Bis denos mecum iam vix adolescis in annos
150 Et iuvenis criticos audes ridere forenses,
     Pene aetate puer, studiis vir, Margaritanae

A5^r

by Eobanus. In 1507 Trutvetter accepted a call to teach theology at Wittenberg. He was promptly elected rector of the university for the winter semester 1507/08 and dean of the theological faculty from 1508 to 1510. Offered a professorship of theology in Erfurt, he returned in 1510.

[26]Sebastian Weimann (Wyman, Wynman) of Oschatz matriculated at Leipzig in 1468, earning a B.A. in 1472. From 1479 he studied at Erfurt, where he became M.A. in 1482 and doctor of theology in 1490. He was elected rector of the university in 1493. That same year he was named preacher at St. Mary's. According to Eobanus's indication, he also preached in the cloister of St. Cyriacus, next to St. Andreas's. In 1505 he was appointed professor of theology at Erfurt. He died in 1510.

[27]For Maternus Pistorius (Pistoris) of Ingwiller (Alsace) see Camerarius, *Nar.* 19, 2, with fn. 85.

[28]Bartholomew Arnoldi of Usingen matriculated at Erfurt in 1484, receiving the B.A. in 1486, the M.A. in 1491. Soon thereafter he began publishing a series of textbooks, the most famous of which was his *Parvulus philosophie naturalis* (1499). After twenty years of distinguished service, he resigned his professorship in 1512 and entered the Augustinian monastery in Erfurt. Promoted to doctor of theology in 1514, he accepted a professorship in theology in 1519. Until 1521 he served as preacher in the Augustinian church; but after he turned against the Lutheran Reformation, he was replaced by Johann Lang. Thereafter he preached at St. Mary's. In 1525/26 he moved to Würzburg, where he died in 1532.

bastian, an admirer of decency and virtue, [130] who often preaches at the cloister of Saint Cyriacus.[26] The same is true for the other churchmen, whose eloquence resounds with Christ's teachings and the commandments of the divine law that God gave to Moses on the peak of Mount Horeb. As for those whose crown is not tonsured, I could add to my song innumerable men who are famed for their powers of speech. It will be enough to mention a few of them. In that eminent company, you, Maternus Pistorius, deserve to carry off the palm, both as orator and as poet.[27] You too deserve this distinction, Bartholomew, not the least of those who figure in this work, [140] you ornament and glory, luminary and star of our school.[28] Vigorous Dialectic is much indebted to you; indeed, the honor of Chrysippus's "heap" falls to your intellect.[29] Thanks to you, the sciences now enjoy the highest respect; thanks to you, physics and metaphysics have yielded their secrets to many students. Filled with gratitude, both young and old revere, idolize, admire, and love you.

Are my verses going to pass you by in silence, eloquent Herbord?[30] You are as illustrious by your ancestry as by your wisdom, even though you are still sporting in the budding flower of innocent youth – O you, who together with me have just barely reached your twenties[31] [150] and as a young man already have the courage to poke fun at loud-mouthed critics. In age little more than a lad, in learning a

[29]Chrysippus, the Stoic philosopher and dialectician of the third century BC, was credited with developing the chain syllogism or *sorites* (fallacy of the heap). This fallacy is traditionally illustrated by the following example. A single grain of wheat does not make a heap. Add another grain, and you still have no heap. If you continue this process, one grain at a time, you will never have a heap.

[30]Herbord von der Marthen and Löwenburg (ca. 1480-1529) matriculated at Erfurt in 1496, graduating B.A. in 1500, M.A. in 1504, and bachelor of civil and canon law in early 1508. During these years he became good friends with Mutianus Rufus, in the late summer of 1506 also with Eobanus Hessus (cf. *Laud.* B 5; *Buc.* B 6). From late 1508 to 1511 he taught at the monastery of Georgenthal. That is why Eobanus introduces him as Phileremus ("Lover of solitude") in *Buc.* 4; see also *Sylv. duae* 1, 189-190, where Eobanus asks if "Phileremus" is still at the monastery. After earning a licentiate and a doctorate in civil and canon law (1512), Herbord was named professor at the university. In 1514 he became syndic of Erfurt. Following his rectorate in 1515/16 he was arrested for treason; but breaking his oath, he fled the city in early 1517 and entered the service of the archbishop of Mainz. Subsequently he was councilor at the court of Maximilian I, later also of Charles V.

[31]In 1506/07 Herbord was in fact in his mid-20's. As for Eobanus, he believed he turned 20 on 6 January 1507. Cf. *Laud.*, ded. 7, with fn. 8.

Stirpis honos: te prole parens insignis uterque.
　　Quo feror? Immensum pelagus tranare volebam.
　　Dum vix incipio, languentes brachia nervos
155　Contraxere, abeunt vires pugnantibus undis.
　　Eloquio tot habet celebres Erphordia linguas
　　Quot tua Rhoma tulit te iudice, Naso, puellas.
　　　Nec minus hic sancti Phoebo solvuntur honores.
　　Hic tripodas Clarii veneramur Apollinis, hic est
160　Aonius vertex, hic est Peneia Daphne,
　　Pierides castae, sunt hic Parnassides umbrae.
　　Hic sacra Teutonici celebrant Heliconia vates.
　　Hic faciles gelidis Musae spaciantur in umbris
　　Cumque suis placide nectunt sed casta poetis
165　Brachia et albentes praecingunt flore capillos

A5ᵛ

　　Innumero et socias ducunt sub fronde choreas
　　Arborea, Phoebo cytharam pulsante canoram.
　　　Dum video stupeoque procul properancia spectans
　　Gaudia et accedens herebam ad limina furtim.
170　Ac veluti Vestae sacratas virginis aedes
　　Spectet et ingressus petat immundissima Phryne,
　　Quod sacra virgineae prohibet reverentia vittae,
　　Quaeve triumphantem lassato podice cunnum
　　Praetulit et foedum mutata veste lupanar
175　Preposuisse thoro fertur lasciva potenti,
　　Sic ego divinae cupidus (licet inscius) artis
　　Non potui sancti tetigisse palacia regni.
　　Ecce sed egressus sacras Pistorius aedes
　　Affuit et cupidum manibus Maternus amicis
180　Duxit ad ignotae secreta cubilia sylvae
　　Et, "Quid has," dixit, "trepidas, Eobane, puellas?
　　Quem metuis? Tuus hic amor est, tuus ignis in illis.
　　Neu mihi finge metus! Sic, sic Laeander adibat

---

[32]The tripods used by the Pythian priestess at Delphi here stand for the oracles of Apollo. Claros in Ionia was another place sacred to him; cf. lines 254 and 302 below.

[33]Mount Helicon.

[34]Daphne, the nymph loved by Apollo, was changed by him into a laurel. See Ov. *Met.* 1, 452-567.

grown man, ornament of the Von der Marthen family: with a son like you, both parents are ennobled.

Where am I drifting off to? I wanted to swim across the boundless sea. But no sooner have I started than the muscles of my arms grow weak and my strength leaves me in the choppy waves. For the fact is that Erfurt has as many silver-tongued orators as ancient Rome (in Ovid's opinion) had girls.

No less impressive are the divine honors that are paid here to Phoebus. Here we venerate the tripods of Apollo, lord of Claros[32]; here stands [160] the Aonian mount[33]; here dwells Peneus's daughter Daphne[34]; here one can find the chaste Muses and the shady groves of Parnassus. Here the bards of Germany observe the Heliconian rites. Here the gracious Muses walk about in the cool shade and link their arms gently, but chastely with their poets and wreathe their ash-blonde hair with countless flowers and lead their part-ners in a dance beneath the leafy canopy of trees as Phoebus plays on his sonorous lyre.

While I watched from afar, gazing dumb-struck at the dancing revelers, I furtively drew nearer. Upon reaching the threshold, however, I felt myself rooted to the spot. [170] As when some sleazy whore[35] looks at the hallowed temple of the virgin Vesta but is kept from entering by holy reverence for the virgin's fillet, or that lecherous lady who, having worn out the anus, thrust her cunt forward in triumph and, after changing clothes, is said to have preferred the shameful brothel to her imperial couch[36]: so I, though lusting (if un-consciously) for the divine artistry before me, could not bring myself to enter the palace of that sacred realm. But look, there was Maternus Pistorius himself coming out of the sanctuary and leading me, eager as I was, with friendly hand [180] toward the couches hidden away in a grove, of whose existence I had been unaware. "Why," he said, "are you trembling at these virgins, Eobanus? What are you afraid of? They are the very ones you love. It is for them that you're burning. Don't put on that frightened act with me! This is precisely how Leander of Abydos swam to Sestos,

[35] Literally "Phryne," an Athenian courtesan who became a byword for prostitute.

[36] Eobanus is thinking of Valeria Messalina (ca. AD 22-48), the notoriously libidinous third wife of Emperor Claudius. See Juv. 6, 115-132. The phrase "in triumph" alludes to the anecdote told in Plin. *Nat.* 10, 172, according to which she slept with a record number of 25 men in a single night.

Seston Abidenus, Phrygiam sic Tyndaris urbem,
185   Colchis ad Oemonias sic venit Phasias urbes.
Et tibi sancta deae capita inclinare videntur
Adventumque tuum nutu placuisse fateri.
Aude animo, tantis iuvenis dilecte puellis.
Nil tibi non promitte. Puer, maiora videbis
190   Praemia promissis."
                              Ego protinus illa loqutum
Dum stupeo, summo titubat lingua palato,
Quid frustra conata loqui. Mirabile dictu,
Nescio quem sensi circum stupefacta furorem
Tempora dispergi, veluti Ganimedis ab urna
195   Nectareos latices se quis per somnia credat
Potare et fictis cupiat magis haustibus uti.
Seu furor aethereo talis mihi venit Olympo,
Gratus erat, sive Elysiis deductus ab hortis.
Numen erat certe. Nec flammam rebar Iuli
200   Caelitus immissam sic absumpsisse capillos.
Pectore divinos calido precoepimus aestus.
Lubrica per vaenas errabat flamma calentes,
Tam rapido accensae candebant igne medullae.
Ossa furor penetrat.
                              "Non est quae lambere possit
205   Flamma comas pueri." Rudis haec ignorat asellus,
Bos negat, insultat caper improbus. "Ite," ait, "ite,
Quaecumque hunc stulte sentitis turba furorem."
    Ibimus, o Musae! Totum peragrabimus orbem,
Ibimus Ethiopas ultra Tanaimque nivalem.
210   Ibimus et priscos vatum queremus honores.
Moecenas si vivat adhuc sub sydere quisquam
Ignivomo, forsan salvabimur. Ivit ad umbras,
Deliquit terras. O divum cura, poetae,
Dicite, securos quae vos nunc terra tenebit?
215   Quis locus in terris ubi non latrator Anubis
Terreat admissas, torva crudelior Hydra,
Pierides? Quid restat adhuc, divine poeta?
Consule, Catholicos qui servas, Christe, poetas.

A6[r]

A6[v]

---

[37]Leander swam the Hellespont in order to see his beloved Hero in Sestos. Tyndareus's daughter is Helen of Troy. The Colchian princess Medea helped Jason obtain the Golden Fleece and returned to Thessaly as his bride. Cf. *Ama.* 35, 39-40.

how Tyndareus's daughter ran off to Troy, how Medea of Colchis eloped to the towns of Thessaly.[37] As you can see, the goddesses are already bending their holy heads toward you and nodding their pleasure at your coming. Take heart, young man, for you are dear to these mighty virgins. You have everything to look forward to. In fact, my lad, you will see greater [190] rewards than you ever dared hope for."

At these words I was utterly dumfounded. My tongue clove to the roof of my mouth, stuttering, unable to speak. In this stupefied state – a marvel to tell – I felt a strange frenzy spreading round about my temples. It was like a dream where one is sipping nectar from Ganymede's pitcher and has no other desire than to keep drinking those illusory draughts. Whether this kind of frenzy came to me from heavenly Olympus or was sent from the gardens of Elysium, it gladdened my heart! A godlike power, I was sure, had come over me. I was thinking that the heaven-sent flame [200] singeing my hair was not the one that had licked Iulus's locks.[38] And then the divine ardor began to scorch my breast. As the darting flame roamed through the burning veins, the marrow caught fire and grew red-hot. The frenzy ran up and down my bones.

"There's no such thing as a flame that can lick a lad's hair!" The ignorant ass knows nothing about this, the ox denies it, the randy goat jeers at it. "Get out of here," he taunts. "Off with you poets, if you're so stupid as to experience a frenzy like that!"

Let's be off, Muses! We'll wander the length and breadth of the earth; we'll go beyond the Ethiopians and the snowy Don. [210] We're going to go in search of the honors that used to be accorded to poets. If some Maecenas should still be alive under the fire-spewing sun, we may yet be saved. But he has gone down to the shades; he has left the earth. O darlings of the gods, you poets, tell me: Is there still a country somewhere that will keep you safe and sound? Is there a place on earth where Anubis, more cruel than the pitiless Hydra, does not terrify the Pierian Maidens with his barking?[39] What lies in store for you, divine poets? Look after us, Christ, for you watch over us Catholic poets. We'll

[38] See Verg. *A.* 2, 682-684, describing a good omen that happened to Aeneas's son Iulus during the final hours of Troy.

[39] Cf. *Pug.* B 1, 3, with fn. 10.

Ibimus et cythara tristes tentabimus umbras,
220   Elysiis Moecenatem deducere campis
Si faveant. Et Threicio fumantia vati
Tartara caesserunt; quaesitam reddidit Orcus
Eurydicen. Quem tu dubitabis vincere, vates?
Vincite victores. Victi licet, este poetae.
225   Spicula Nessaeo sunt vestra infecta veneno.
    Ah, satis offensa, furor, excandescis honesta.
Ad concoepta redi, sed lenior. Ecce furentem
Calliope spectans, "Quibus ignibus ureris!" inquit.
"Terque quater foelix, quando te mollior aetas
230   Nunc fovet et castos venari vidit amores.
Meque meas, certum est, ardes, Eobane, sorores.
Et nobis dilecte, vale. Foeliciter arde."
    Hiis mea Calliope succendit pectora dictis
Et plus ardentes ignes coniecit in ignes.
235   Quid memorem antiquos quos fabula narrat amantes?
Quos non torsit amor, sed inanis perdidit error.
Me certe, me versat amor, nec pallida demens
Guttura praestringam laqueo nec tristia ferro
Pectora perfodiam. Caedat Venus improba. Castum
240   Castus amor vatem decet. O qui sacra prophanas
Musica et Aonio Paphium pro fonte lupanar
Incolis, i, turpi sacra solve, Cratine, Priapo.
Desine virginei decus incestare pudoris.
Calliopen castus celebrat, non Thaida vates.
245   Liquerat interea meditantem talia virgo
Ductrix Thespiadum sacrasque evasit ad aras.
Progredior. Furor audacem faciebat et ultro
Dispulit obiectos preceps insania postes.
Venimus ad sacras vitrei Permessidos undas,
250   Hic ubi mutato mediam perlabitur urbem
Nomine Gera, novos hedera frondente racemos
Effundens viridique tegens victricia lauro

B1ʳ

---

[40]Orpheus went down to Hades to bring his wife Eurydice back to life.

[41]The centaur Nessus was killed by Hercules' envenomed arrow. His poisonous blood, smeared on a robe, eventually brought about the hero's own death.

[42]Paphos on the island of Cyprus was sacred to Venus. The "Aonian spring" is the Hippocrene on Mount Helicon, sacred to the Muses.

[43]Cratinus was one of the greatest poets of Old Attic Comedy. Cf. Hor. S. 1, 4, 1-5.

[44]A celebrated Athenian courtesan, Thais became a byword for sexual profligacy.

[45]The Permessus River, rising on Mount Helicon, was sacred to the Muses.

go, and with our lyre we'll try to rouse the sympathy of the grim shades [220], to see if they'll let us bring Maecenas back with us from the Elysian Fields. Murky Tartarus also gave in to the Thracian bard; the underworld offered him his Eurydice back, after he had gone down to find her.[40] Why do you poets doubt that you can be victorious? Conquer the conquerors. Even if you are conquered, be the poet. You have arrows tipped with Nessus's poisonous blood![41]

Ah, frenzy, you have now waxed indignant enough in your righteous anger. Return to your theme, but more calmly. Look, Calliope has been observing you while you raved. "How ardently you burn!" she exclaims. "O many, many times happy, because tender youth [230] still animates you and sees you in pursuit of chaste love. You are in love with me and my sisters, Eobanus, that's for sure. We love you too. Fare well, then, and be happy in your love."

With these words Calliope set my breast on fire. Casting flames on the flames, she made them blaze even hotter. Need I speak of those ancient lovers who are the stuff of legend? What tormented them was not love at all; and what destroyed them was the merest delusion. Certainly, I too am in the throes of love; but I am not so mad as to put a noose around my pallid neck or plunge a dagger into my broken heart. Step aside, shameless Venus. [240] Chaste love behooves a chaste poet. And you, who profane the holy mysteries of the Muses and live in a Paphian brothel instead of by the Aonian spring[42] – you Cratinus,[43] go ahead and perform the rites of your obscene god Priapus. But stop defiling the honor of virgin modesty. Chaste bards sing the praises of Calliope, not Thais.[44]

While I was pondering these things, the virgin queen of the Thespian Maidens left me and went up to her sacred altars. I strode forward. Frenzy emboldened me, and of its own accord sudden ecstasy broke down the remaining barriers. So I reached the holy waters of the glassy Permessus[45] – [250] here where it flows through the midst of our city under the different name Gera, showering us with ivy leaves full of fresh berries and covering the victorious heads with garlands of green laurel.[46] "Nymphs," I cried, "make known

---

[46] In antiquity the poet's wreath was made of ivy (sacred to Bacchus) or laurel (sacred to Apollo).

Tempora. "Phoebeos," dixi, "mihi pandite, nymphae,
Cultores Clariumque mihi monstrate liquorem."
255   Finieram mediaque deas in voce reliqui.
Ecce sed a laeva vario sedilia cultu
Apparent ornata sacrique ex ordine vates
Sedebant. Aliqua ex illis pro corpore vatum
Nomina servabant tantum. Sic proxima Phoebo
260   Inscriptum sedes monstrabile carmen habebat:
"Haec prius insignis coluit subsellia Rufus,
Qui nunc finitimae fulgentia maenia Gothae
Incolit et placidos vitae tranquillior annos
Exigit, insani ridens ludibria vulgi,
265   Consilio Atrides, animo non victus Achilles,
Iudicio Minos, Numa relligione probatus."
Sed quid ego haec refero? Popularis temnit amorem
Laudis, odit fastus secum contentus inanes.
Quid nebulis, quid, Rufe sacer, versaris in umbris?
270   Qur tua Calliope campos non intrat apricos?
Quid faciles tam sepe iubes concerpere versus
Et quasi divino conspersos rore? Quid hoc est?
Versibus immodicos quidam venantur honores
Illepidis. Tu, ne qua tibi popularis ad aurem
275   Aura sonet blandis turbans tranquilla susurris
Ocia, divini abscondis monumenta favoris,
Tanquam Teutonicis faveas male laudibus. O qui
Montibus Hessiacis prognatus prodis in auras,
Dormis adhuc. Ego te tam longa sepe sepultum
280   Nocte querar. Nostris resonabunt omnia sylvis.
Quando rudes dicent mihi pastoralia Musae
Carmina, te ficto sublatum funere Daphnim
Cantabo. Sed vivis adhuc. Sed vive, precamur.
Vive aliis longumque vide foeliciter aevum.

B1ᵛ

---

[47]Claros in Ionia was sacred to Apollo. Cf. *Laud.* 159 and 302.

[48]For Konrad Mutianus Rufus see Camerarius, *Nar.* 12, 12 – 13, 10, with fn. 36. In prais-ing Mutianus's "counsel" and "courage," Eobanus plays on the name Konrad (= "kühn-Rat," "bold-counsel"). Cf. *Idyl.* 2 and 4, where Eobanus calls him "Thrasybulus" (= "kühn-Rat").

[49]Eobanus politely urges his mentor to start publishing his verses. He makes the same ap-peal in "Ad Mutianum Rufum elegia" and in *Buc.* 6.

to me the followers of Phoebus. Point out to me the limpid water of Claros."[47]

With these words I turned away from the goddesses. But look, to my left there appeared a row of chairs, emblazoned with various adornments. They were occupied by venerable poets. A few of the seats were empty and bore only the bard's name. The one that stood next to Phoebus's, for example, [260] was inscribed with the following memorable verses: "This chair was formerly occupied by the distinguished Rufus who now dwells within the gleaming walls of nearby Gotha and spends the quiet years of his life in serene tranquillity, laughing off the insults of the madding crowd, esteemed as an Agamemnon in counsel, an invincible Achilles in courage, a Minos in judgment, a Numa in piety."[48]

But why do I mention this? He scorns all desire to win the approbation of the masses. Content with himself, he hates false pride. Why do you insist, sublime Rufus, on passing your days in mists and shadows? [270] Why does your Calliope not step out onto the sunlit fields?[49] Why do you so often command us to tear up your skilful verses, even though they are besprinkled, as it were, with heavenly dew? What is the point? Some people chase after extravagant praise by writing witless verse. You, lest the breath of popular favor reach your ears and trouble your tranquil leisure with its seductive whispers – you suppress divinely inspired writings, as if you were ill-disposed toward the fame of us Germans. O you, born in the mountains of Hesse! You rise up to the skies, yet are still asleep. I shall often lament that you still lie buried in such a long [280] night. This will all resound in my *Forests.*[50] When the rustic Muses stir me to pastoral song, I am going to celebrate you as Daphnis, imagined as taken from us by death.[51] But you are still alive. Go on living, we beg you. Live for others and enjoy a long and happy life.

[50] In the *Sylvae,* a planned collection of his occasional verse. See fn. 9 above, at *Laud.*, ded. 11; and *Laud.* 5-8, with fn. 12.

[51] According to an ancient interpretation widely accepted in the Renaissance, Vergil's fifth eclogue celebrates the deification of Julius Caesar, represented as the shepherd Daphnis. Cf. Eob. *Adnot.,* sig. K4ʳ-K4ᵛ; *Idyl.* 6, argument. Though quite aware that eulogizing a friend not yet deceased is ticklish business, Eobanus promises that he will nevertheless follow Vergil's example and write an apotheosis of Mutianus.

285   Dum queror, ecce aderat plectris Enricus eburnis
        Insignis, cui magnanimi vulgata leonis
        Nomina iamdudum aeternum peperere decorem,
        Et, "Quid," ait, "quereris? Quas moesto pectore curas
        Volvis tristiciam lachrimis confessus obortis?"
290   Sic ait et cytharam curas lenire movendo

B2r   Aggressus consedit humi, spargentibus umbram
        Arboribus facilem. Tum divae nuda puellae
        Brachia iactabant, flavus subrisit Apollo.
        Mirabar, magis ardentes in pectora flammas
295   Accipiens, veluti stipulas iam lenior ignis
        Appositas flammis rursum crepitantibus urit.
        In terram attentis stabam defixus ocellis
        Fronde sub umbrosa. Mox et vicina trahentem
        Inter Ioannem stupidas loca vidimus aures
300   Chordarum sonitu, castae cui cura Dianae
        Candida ab hirsutis foecit cognomina sylvis.
        Qui Clarii sylvas nunc Venatorius intrat
        Ruris et aeternae venatur nomina laudis,
        Castus ut Hyppolitus Phaedra tutatus ab omni,
305   Dum colit Aonii nemoris sanctissima tempe
        Et Musas castis fruitur complexibus inter.
        Cui facilis primos Elegeia debet honores.
            Hunc ego ut aspexi, lachrimis ita fabar obortis
        (Nam lachrimas faciebat amor): "Tune ille prioris
310   Sortis, Ioannes, nostrae comes? Hic mihi tandem
        Optatus venis! O tecum foelicibus arvis
        Qui fruar! Interea, quando vacat, optime vates,
        Dic quibus huc fatis venisti."
                                    "Venimus," inquit,
        "Huc puer a patriis fatis foelicibus oris.
315   Ne queras, Eobane, ultra. Cognovit uterque

---

298 et *scripsi*: ut *A*.

---

[52]Heinrich Leonis (Leo) of Bercka (Rheinberg) matriculated at Erfurt in 1486, receiving
his B.A. in 1488 and his M.A. in 1491. Humanistically minded, he began teaching mathe-
matics and astronomy at Erfurt in 1500. In 1503 he became dean of the prestigious Collegium
Amplonianum (Porta celi). Leonis was often elected to prominent administrative positions in
the university, serving, for example, as collector in 1501, dean of the philosophical faculty in
1500/01, 1505, 1512/13, and 1523, and rector of the university in 1516/17. He died in 1543.

As I was lamenting like this, lo and behold, there stood Heinrich, the poet who has so distinguished himself with his ivory plectrum and whose famous last name, taken from the great-hearted lion, has long since given him eternal glory.[52] "Why are you lamenting?" he asked. "What's troubling you and making your heart ache? The tears welling from your eyes tell me that you're distressed." [290] These were his words. To soothe my cares, he sat down on the ground and began to play his lyre in the pleasant shade of the trees. Then the divine Maidens threw their naked arms about and golden Apollo smiled. To my amazement I felt the flames in my breast blazing hotter, just as a fire that has already died down leaps once more into crackling flames as soon as someone flings straw on it. There I stood, staring down at the ground, eyes alert under the shady boughs. Before long I noticed Johann Jäger in the vicinity.[53] He too was listening entranced [300] to the sound of the strings. It is his zeal for the chaste [huntress] Diana, scrambling through thorny brambles, that has given him his illustrious surnames. This Hunter is now entering the woods of Claros[54] and hunting for a name that will be praised forever. Chaste like Hippolytus,[55] he will be safe from every Phaedra, so long as he dwells in the most holy vale of the Aonian grove and enjoys chaste love in the arms of the Muses. To him gracious Elegy owes her foremost successes.

As soon as I saw him, the tears welled up (for love brought tears to my eyes) and I spoke these words: "Is it you, [310] Johann, the comrade who has stuck by me through thick and thin? So you've come back at last![56] I've sorely missed you. Oh, how I'm going to enjoy being with you in this blessed land! Meanwhile, if you have a moment, best of poets, do tell me: By what stroke of luck did you come here?"

"It was my good fortune," he answered, "to leave my homeland and come here as a lad.[57] But stop asking me any

---

[53] Johann Jäger of Dornheim, better known by his later name Crotus Rubianus ("Archer of Dornheim"). In the following lines Eobanus plays on these names (Jäger = Venatorius or "Hunter"; Rubianus = "of Dornheim," "of Thorn-home"). See Camerarius, *Nar.* 17, 17, with fn. 71.

[54] Claros in Ionia was sacred to Apollo. Cf. *Laud.* 159 and 254.

[55] Because he spurned the advances of his stepmother Phaedra, Hippolytus became a byword for chastity. See Otto 810; Häussler, pp. 105 and 171; Erasmus, *Adag.* 3, 6, 65.

[56] Crotus returned to Erfurt in the spring of 1506, after spending the winter semester studying in Cologne.

[57] He matriculated at Erfurt in 1498, at age 18.

Nostrorum res alterius vitaeque labores.
Notior insano Pilades non vixit Oresti,
Pyrithoo Theseus, forti Patroclus Achilli,
Quam tibi ego, mihi tu. Nec enim locus ille requirit
320 Commoda preteritae casus et taedia vitae.
Quisquis amat Musas, causas non curat inanes."
    Dixit et oppositas pueros monstrabat inertes
Ludere propter aquas, qui iam florentibus annis
Sacrorum meritis ineunt consortia vatum.
325   Foelix gymnasium, foelix Erphordia, tantis
Aucta bonis! Alias superas tu laudibus urbes.
Illos hic vates presenti numine Phoebus
Tutatur nobis quos mystica Musa recenset –
O neque Thersites inter vulganda loquaces! –
330 Innumerosque alios hic Musica sacra professos.
Hic magnos Phoebaea sonant suggesta poetas;
Publica Castalii manant hic flumina fontis.
    Ne nimium quod amem videar laudare (licet non
Laudari nimium queat!), hinc ad caetera pergam.
335 Pergite, Pierides, nec solum vestraque vosque
Dicite. Divinae superat laus Theologiae,
Perpetuo signanda cedro fortique adamante,
Ne cataclysmeae mergatur fluctibus undae,
Si quando in terras rursum Deus egerit olim
340 Iratus Tethymque vagam Neraeaque regna.

Pergite, Pierides, nec solum vestraque vosque
Dicite. Divinae superat laus Theologiae,
Perpetuam nostra sedem quae legit in urbe.
O super humanae quam possit inertia mentis
345 Aut capere aut fragilis facundia promere linguae,
Relligionis opus, divina scientia! Quantis
Laudibus efferri studuit te, Erphordia, quando
Tot tibi magnifica statuit virtute triumphos!
Sive Hebraea prius sive hanc Caldaea vetustas
350 Graecave reppererit seu manet origine forsan
Ex alia totumque fere lustraverit orbem,

---

343 quae *scripsi*: que *A*.

more questions, Eobanus. Each of us knows everything about the events and hardships of the other's life. Pylades was not as well known to the mad Orestes, Theseus to Pirithous, Patroclus to the valiant Achilles,[58] as I am familiar to you, you to me. Besides, this place doesn't ask [320] whether you've lived a life of ease or of hardship. Anyone who loves the Muses is unconcerned with trifling matters like that."

When he had finished speaking, he pointed to the lads on the opposite bank, who were composing songs at their leisure. So great is their merit, that already in the flower of their youth they enter the company of sacred bards.

Fortunate university, fortunate Erfurt, blessed with such marvelous advantages! In excellence you surpass the other cities. Here Phoebus with ever-present deity watches over those bards whom the Muse enumerates to us in secret – a roll call that must not be divulged to people as loquacious as Thersites! – [330] as well as the countless others who publicly teach the holy rites of the Muses. Here the podiums dedicated to Phoebus resound with great poets; here Castalia's streams flow out to the public.

Lest I seem to praise too highly what I love myself (though it can never be praised too highly!), I shall go on to other things. On, then, Pierian Maids, and do not praise just your own work and your followers. It remains for us to sing the praises of divine Theology, to be inscribed in lasting cedarwood and stout adamant so they can survive a cataclysmic deluge, should God ever be so angered again as to send [340] roaming Tethys and the realms of Nereus to cover the earth. On, then, Pierian Maids, and do not praise just your own work and your followers. It remains for us to sing the praises of divine Theology, who has chosen our city as her permanent dwelling place. Oh, too sublime for the indolence of the human spirit to grasp or the eloquence of a frail tongue to express – the work of faith, the science of God! With what great achievements does she endeavor to exalt you, Erfurt! How often do her splendid successes give you cause for celebration! Whether Hebrew or Chaldean [350] or Greek antiquity first discovered her or whether she perhaps sprang from some other source and thence tra-

[58]The three pairs of exemplary friends occur together also in Ov. *Pont.* 2, 3, 41-45. The friendship between Orestes and Pylades was proverbial; see Otto 1307; Häussler, pp. 114 and 196. So was that between Pirithous and Theseus; see Otto 1779; Häussler, pp. 20, 65, 80, and 289.

Huc tamen optatum veniens invenit asylum
Quaesitamque diu residens nunc possidet urbem
Cultoresque habet innumeros. Quis credere posset?
355 Hic Augustino non ulla parte minores,
Quos probet Ambrosius laudetque Hieronimus et quos
Gregorius sacer admirans commendet habentur.
Quis numerare queat? Quis singula theosophorum
Nomina commemoret? Stultum est comprehendere paucis
360 Plurima velle, nec in tumulum cogetur Olimpus
Exiguum. Satis est parvum traxisse parergon,
Dum sua pictorem superant incoepta. Nec audet
Parrhasio certare rudis nec pingere botros
Zeusinos, quales stupeat vel Chous Apelles.
365   Ast ego dum Liciam vigili sequor arte Chymeram,

Venor avem. Celeres fugiunt tenuissima cervi
Rhetia. Dum coeptae meditor praeconia laudis,
Vis abit ingenii. Laudis describimus umbram,
Cuius iam laudes superabant. Theologiae
370 Sed tamen ex rerum laus cognitione patescit
Cuique satis, quae laudari sed iure merentur.
Eximium est quod laudari nequit amplius. Ergo,
Musa, laborantes aliis expande lacertos
Iamque fere melius portus habitura guberna
375 Vaela, precor. Vatum requies, caelestis Apollo,
Nodus inest operi qui dignus vindice, nodus
Herculea solvendus ope. Discaede, prophane,
Caede. Manu tangis mysteria sacra prophana.
Et semel insontes satis est laesisse Camaenas.
380 Neu Triviam occulto mireris fonte Dianam –
In nova consuetam mutabis corpora formam!
Ibis eris, quo nil sub sole malignius unquam

---

⁵⁹Parrhasius was a famed Greek painter of the early fourth century BC. Zeuxis of Heraclea in Lucania (end of the fifth century BC) could paint so realistically that his grapes were said to have deceived the birds. See Plin. *Nat.* 35, 65-66.

⁶⁰Acclaimed as the greatest of all Greek painters, Apelles of Colophon (fourth century BC) is sometimes called Coan because of his celebrated Aphrodite Anadyomene on the island of Cos.

⁶¹The Chimera – a monster in Lycia with a lion's head, a goat's body, and a serpent's tail – here stands for a wild fancy, as in *Ama.* 24, 5. Chasing after a bird is a proverbial expression for going after something difficult or impossible to attain. Cf. Pers. 3, 61; Erasmus, *Adag.* 3, 3, 44.

⁶²Cf. lines 13-15 above, with fn. 13. To the earlier association with Horace's dramatic knot Eobanus now adds an allusion to the proverbial "knot of Hercules" – a complicated knot supposedly invented by Hercules. Cf. Otto 803 and 1233; Häussler, p. 238 and pp. 64, 76, 112-113, 193, 241, 281; Erasmus, *Adag.* 1, 9, 48.

versed virtually the entire world, Theology nevertheless came here and found the sanctuary she had prayed for. In this city, for which she searched so long, she has now established her residence and rejoices in countless votaries. Who could have believed it? They are regarded here as in no wise inferior to Augustine – the kind of theologian Ambrose would applaud, Jerome would praise, and Saint Gregory would commend with admiration. Who is able to count them all? Who could possibly enumerate every single one of these theologians? It would be folly [360] to try to squeeze so many names into a few lines. Mount Olympus cannot be crammed into a molehill either. It is enough to sketch a modest outline until the subject overwhelms the painter's abilities. A raw beginner dare not compete with Parrhasius or paint Zeuxis's grapes,[59] so true to life that even Apelles of Cos[60] was astonished at them.

But in pursuing the Lycian Chimera with vigilant guile, I find myself chasing after a bird.[61] Swift stags break through nets that are too thin. Even as I am thinking how best to finish the laudation I started, my strength of mind fails me. I have described only the shadow of merit; the true merits remain to be shown. [370] No matter: Theology's merit is plain enough to anyone who knows about her genuinely praiseworthy accomplishments. Anything that is beyond praise is obviously extraordinary. Therefore, Muse, stretch out your flailing arms to other shores. Or better yet, direct your sails to port, I beseech you. Repose of poets, heavenly Apollo, my work contains "a knot that truly requires a deliverer," a knot that can be untied only with Hercules' help.[62] Stand clear, you who are unsanctified. Stay back. You are laying profane hands on sacred mysteries. It's enough that you have hurt the blameless Muses once before already. [380] Don't think that you can admire Triform Diana bathing in her hidden spring – she will metamorphose you and give you a different body![63] You'll turn into an ibis,[64] for there has never been anything quite so spiteful

[63] After Actaeon surprised Diana at her bath, the goddess changed him into a stag and had him killed by his own hounds; see Ov. *Met.* 3, 173-252. Eobanus uses the story as a warning to the uninitiated who blunder into a sacred realm. Diana was revered as the moon-goddess Cynthia in heaven, as Diana on earth, and as Proserpina in Hades. Hence she was called "Trivia" (Triform) and worshiped at places where three roads meet.

[64] In the vitriolic poem *Ibis* Ovid assails his bitterest enemy. To be turned into an ibis, then, is to become the object of a lampoon. Eobanus refers to Ovid's *Ibis* explicitly in line 392 below.

Aut fuit aut venturum alios durabit in annos.
Vulgus ab arcanis labor est arcere prophanum,
385   Cui preter sua nulla placent. Trivialia norint
Grammata, in Aonias latrant iam denique Musas
Vulgares rabulae. Sed adunco stertere naso
Nos iuvat. O longum divae miseranda Poesis
Condicio, quae tot pateris convicia! Qur non
390   Spicula Lernaeo tingis Nessaea veneno
Saevaque Achillaeo laedis praecordia ferro?
Ibis adest. Qur, Naso, iaces? Requiescis, Homere?
Zoilus atroci validum sub pectore virus
Colligit, Elysiis iterum revocatus ab umbris.
395   Surge, sacer vatum triplex defensor Apollo,
Qui teretem summo mundum metiris ab orbe.
Surge, iuva (tua cura sumus), venerabile numen,
Perde malignantes animas. Satis, imo superque
Salva triumphanti sua stat victoria Phoebo.
400   Quo vehor? An quo tu veheris, furor? Ergo prophanum
Vulgus abesse iubes. Laedi mysteria non vis.
Tutatur nostras satis hec sentencia partes.
Sed ne longa aures offendant taedia dextras,
Rursus ad incaeptae vehimur molimina causae.
405   Ergo triumphales meruisti, Erphordia, palmas
Quod tua per cunctas vulgata est gloria gentes,
Quam tibi iamdudum cumulat Tritonia Pallas.
Ausonis ora probat, Rhodanus te laudat et Ister,
Saeva ubi fraternum sparsit Maedaea cruorem,
410   Et quae porrectas ultra gens incolit oras.
Artibus ingenuis polles ut floribus aestas,

B4ʳ (margin, by line 391)

---

397 numen *scripsi*: nomen *A*.

[65]Hercules envenomed his arrows with the poison of the Hydra and then used one of them to kill the centaur Nessus. Cf. *Rec.* 18-19 and *Laud.* 225.

[66]The sophist Zoilus made fun of Homer's errors and so became synonymous with a malignant critic. See fn. 16 at *Rec.* B 2, 3.

[67]Eobanus refers to the Christian Trinity. Cf. lines 13-14 and 375 above; *Laud.* B 4, 2 below; *Ama.* 35, 113-114; *Buc.* 10, 41; 10, 93.

under the sun as you, nor will there ever be in all the years to come. We must labor to keep the uninitiated crowd away from our secrets. They only like what they are familiar with, nothing else. Once they have learned their grammar in school, these run-of-the-mill tub-thumpers think they have earned the right to snarl at the Aonian Muses. But we'll gladly snore through it all, with our noses turned up. Oh, the lamentable plight of divine Poetry! How long have you suffered already! How many insults have you had to swallow! Why don't you [390] dip your arrows in the poisonous blood of the Lernaean Hydra, as Hercules did when he shot Nessus?[65] Why don't you pierce their savage breast with Achilles' steel? Ibis has come to life again. Are you going to take that lying down, Ovid? Why are you napping, Homer? Zoilus has come back from the Elysian shades, his ruthless heart filled with potent venom.[66] Rise up, threefold Apollo, holy protector of poets, O you who from highest heaven measure the smooth round of the world.[67] Rise up and help us, venerable deity – we are your darlings! Destroy those wicked spirits. Phoebus can count on being triumphant; his victory is sufficiently, no, unshakeably secure.

[400] Where am I wandering off to? Or rather, where are you wandering off to, poetic frenzy? Ah yes, you're commanding the unhallowed mob to stand clear. You don't want them to lay hands on our mysteries. That resolution alone is sufficient to protect our side from harm. But so as not to vex sympathetic ears with long digressions, let us return to the great theme that we embarked on.

Well then, Erfurt, you have deserved to win the palm of victory, because the glory that Tritonian Pallas[68] has long been heaping on you is known among all the peoples on earth. Italy thinks highly of you, the Rhône praises you, so does the lower Danube where savage Medea scattered the bloody pieces of her brother's body,[69] [410] and so do the people who inhabit the lands further east. You are as rich in

---

[68]Pallas is called "Tritonian" because she was born on the banks of the Triton; cf. lines 72-75 above.

[69]After helping Jason win the Golden Fleece in Colchis, Medea delayed their pursuers near the mouth of the Danube by killing her brother Absyrtus, dismembering his body, and scattering the pieces.

Alitibus ceu sylva virens, ut piscibus aequor.
Teutonicae quamvis passim celebrentur Athenae,
Iura prior cunctis mortalibus aequa ministras
415 Inter tot celebres Germani nominis urbes.
Nec mihi iuridicos veteres Rhomana vetustas
Praetulerit vel Sulpicios Nervasque probatos
Atque alios quorum cura studioque tenaci
Salva triumphantes meruit respublica fasces.
420 Graecia docta, vale. Nec te iactaveris ultra.
Hic celebres magno certant Solone Licurgi,
Tam studio insignes Latii fervente vigoris
Consilio quam proficui iurisque periti.
Urbs nimium foelix, foelix respublica, cuius
425 Ocia Caesareis civilia legibus aequant
Paceque commissas placida moderantur habenas
Publica cura fori quibus est commissa regendi.
Pax viget, urbs tranquilla manet, respublica floret,
Crescunt divitiae, socios concordia cives
430 Unit, et observat divum reverentia cultus.
Caedit adulterium; terret lex Iulia moechos.
Furta, doli, fraudesque abeunt turpesque rapinae,
Incestus et stupra iacent. Meliora iuventus
Ad studia et mores crescit formata pudicos.
435 Absunt insidiae, caedes, convicia, fastus.
Virtus per plateas niveo redimita cucullo
Inclyta, Iusticiae comes incorrupta, vagatur.
Nullus deprimitur contra legesque piumque.
Ensiferi recto florent sub iudice fasces.
440 Dii populum faciles et maenia tuta tuentur.
Hiis nostram donis cumulavit Iuppiter urbem,
Quando tot insignes fovet hic Tritonia Pallas
Eloquio Marcos, facundo iure Catones,
Nasicas quoque et Antipatros celebresque Sabinos,
445 Cecilios, Crassos, Alphenos, et Labeones.
Utque aliquos saltem memorem, ne turpia forsan
Texere dicamur fictis mendacia rebus,
Primus ad Henningum, bifida ut quem iura monarcham
Observent, referendus honor. Qui, sicut habundans

B4^v

C1^r

---

438 Nullus *scripsi*: Mullus *A*.

noble arts as the summer in flowers, as the verdant forest in birds, as the sea in fish. Although there are many celebrated university towns all over Germany, you are far ahead of the other famed German cities in codifying laws that are fair to all people. Now don't let Roman antiquity tell me she prefers her ancient jurists to ours – even if they are as well-reputed as Sulpicius and Nerva and the others whose zeal and unflagging devotion saved the Republic and made her worthy of her triumphant consuls. [420] Good-bye, scholarly Greece. You won't be bragging anymore either. Here we have renowned Lycurguses who rival the great Solon, men as remarkable for their ardent devotion to vigorous Latinity as they are wise in counsel and expert in law.

O lucky, more than lucky city! Lucky community, whose political stability is grounded in its code of civil law and whose government handles the reins entrusted to it to maintain law and order! Peace flourishes, the city remains tranquil, the commonwealth prospers, riches multiply, concord unites the citizens in partnership, [430] piety reveres God and his saints. Adultery has ceased; the Julian law[70] deters would-be adulterers. The disgraceful crimes of theft, swindling, fraud, and robbery have disappeared; incest and fornication are unheard of. Here young people grow up well-disposed to the liberal arts and chaste morals. Treachery and murder, quarreling and contumely are absent. Wearing a snow-white hood, illustrious Virtue strolls through the streets as the incorruptible companion of Justice. No one is oppressed contrary to law or fairness. The sword-bearing judiciary flourishes under impartial judges. [440] Favorable gods and impregnable walls keep the population safe from attack.

These are the gifts that Jupiter has showered on our city, seeing that Tritonian Pallas cherishes so many distinguished jurists here. In oratory they are a match for Cicero, in eloquent pleading they are the likes of Cato and Nasica and Antipater, the equals of the famed Sabinus, Caecilius, Crassus, Alfenus, and Labeo. To mention at least a few of them by name, lest perhaps I be accused of making this up and shamelessly weaving a web of lies: The first place of honor must be given to Henning, for both branches of law regard

[70] Augustus's law on adultery.

450   Fons scatet et rivos producit, fonte perhenni
        Spargit in aeternos causarum saemina rivos.
        Cuius ad Istricolas nuper facundia Dacos
        Venit et externas virtus legalior urbes.
        Hinc, Byrmuste, venis, sed non leviore canendus
455   Pectine, iusticiae servator, iuris honesti
        Cultor, Ioannes, cui se debere fatentur
        Iura viro tantum iusta trutinata bilance,
        Andino quantum vati divina Poesis,
        Aeacides quantum sublimi debet Homero.
460   Te quoque florentis commendat gratia linguae,
        Quam Cicero probet et vulgi Latialis ad aurem
        Deferat invitus. Nec deteriore ferendus
        Laude, micans supra falcati syderis astrum,
        Cultor honestatae virtutis, Margaritanae
465   Stirpis honos legumque decus, Martinus, et inter
        Causarum iurisque minas strepitusque forenses
        Mite patrocinium iustis.
                                "Quid denique longas
        Ambages sequeris?" monuit Patareus Apollo.
        "Ebria quos adeo scrutatur Musa meatus?"
470   Quamvis perpetuo labantur flumina cursu
        Et requiem finemque velint, redduntur eisdem
        Principiis notosque iterum volvuntur ad ortus.
        Sic ego, propositi metam dum spero laboris,
        Labor in ambages semperque reducor ad ortus
475   Principiumque rei. Sed nunc properate, Camenae.
        Maior gymnasii laus est referenda prioris.
        Pene quidem portus fessa properante carina

C1ᵛ

---

[71]The legal scholar Henning Göde of Werben near Havelberg (ca. 1450-1521) matriculated at Erfurt in 1464, graduating B.A. in 1466, M.A. in 1474, and doctor of civil and canon law in 1489. In addition to his teaching duties at the university he frequently held high administrative positions: for example, taxator in 1477, 1479/80, and 1483, dean of the philosophical faculty in 1480/81), rector in 1486/87 and 1489/90, and vice-chancelor from 1501 to 1502. A shrewd negotiator, he was much sought after by Erfurt and other cities as well as by princes and lords to represent them, particularly at imperial and regional diets. His legal handbooks were published posthumously in numerous editions. Forced to flee the city during the riots of 1509, he moved to Wittenberg where he taught law until his death. Later Eobanus wrote an epigram in his praise as well as an epitaph for him. For the former see *Sylv.* 8, 23; for the latter see *Epp. 1.*, sig. T1ʳ.

[72]Johann Biermost of Erfurt matriculated at the university in 1474. After earning his B.A. in 1480, his M.A. in 1484, and the degree of bachelor of law in 1491, he served as dean of the philosophical faculty in 1491, as taxator in 1492, rector in 1492/93, and collector in 1493/94.

him as their monarch.[71] Just as an overflowing [450] spring gushes out of the ground and gives rise to brooks, so he from his perennial fountain pours out the seeds of legal cases in unending streams. The Transylvanians dwelling on the banks of the Danube recently witnessed his eloquence; foreign cities have seen his abilities as a legal scholar. Johann Biermost is next in line.[72] As guardian of justice and student of law par excellence, however, he deserves no less praise in my song. Having weighed the case on balanced scales, Jurisprudence acknowledges that she is as deeply indebted to this man as divine Poetry is indebted to the bard of Andes[73] or Achilles to the sublime Homer. [460] He too possesses that graceful brilliance of speech that Cicero could applaud and gladly commend to the ears of the Roman people. Equally worthy of praise is another jurist who shines more brightly than the sickle-shaped star in the heavens: Martin von der Marthen, a wooer of honorable virtue, the glory of his family and the ornament of jurisprudence, the kind defender of the righteous amidst menacing lawsuits and wrangling lawyers.[74]

"Are you going to go on rambling forever and ever?" admonished Apollo, lord of Patara. "Where will your drunken Muse be wandering off to next?" [470] Even though the rivers flow in never-ending streams and would be glad to rest at their destination, they always return to the same sources and keep going back to the fountainheads they know so well. Likewise I keep going on and on, even as I look forward to finishing the work as planned, and am constantly drawn back to the source and wellspring of my theme. But let's get on with it now, Muses. Let's praise this premier university of ours to the stars! True, we were about to rush this weary vessel of ours into harbor, and here I am heading out

---

He obtained a doctorate in canon and civil law in 1494 and was thereupon appointed professor of secular law at Erfurt and counselor and chancelor to Frederick the Wise. Like Göde he was forced to leave Erfurt during the riots of 1509. He died in 1512.

[73]The Roman poet Vergil, who was born in the village of Andes near Mantua.

[74]Martin von der Marthen was the cousin of Gerlach von der Marthen, vicegerent of the archbishop of Mainz (see fn. 36 at *Buc.* 4, 29). He earned his M.A. at Erfurt in 1487, a bachelor's degree in laws in 1491, a licentiate in canon and civil law in 1495, and a doctorate in laws in 1497. Thereafter he was professor of law in Erfurt. He was elected rector for the winter semester 1496/97 and for an entire year in 1521-1522. From 1534 to 1549 he was vice-chancelor of the university. He died in 1552. Eobanus's praise notwithstanding, Martin von der Marthen was an old-style conservative, hostile to the humanists, later also to the Reformation. Mutianus Rufus called him a barbaric jurist who cared only about making a fortune.

Contigimus, spaciosum iterum delabor in aequor,
Sed facile et cursu multo breviore natandum.
480   Tam celebris totumque licet vulgata per orbem
Gymnasii vigeat cantati gloria famae,
Attamen hic nostris magis est vulganda Camaenis
Et merito dignae referenda est gratia matri
Quae me nutrivit puerum nutrice Minerva
485 Lacte salutari quod marmore manat eburno,
Barbara Christicolam qua servat Pallada Syna,
Costis ad angelici quae nunc Catharina sepulchri
Saxa suo coelis sponso sociata quiescit.
Quae iuveni cultu venienti paupere portus
490 Hospiciumque mihi dedit opportuna petitum
Insuper et meritis cumulavit pluribus, ultro
Prebuit immeritae titulos et stemmata fronti
Promisitque olim superis maiora daturam
Auspicibus melioris ad haec insignia palmae.
495   Alma inopum nutrix, Erphordia, mater egentum,
Pauperibus domus, hospitium venerabile fessis,
Exulibus portus, studii florentis asylum,
Erudit ignavos, rigidos polit, ornat inertes
Moribus, ingenio, studiis, virtutibus, explet
500 Divitiis inopes. Quot sunt quibus indiga primum
Vita fuit, quibus et chari cecidere parentes
Ante diem, quibus acceptos invidit honores
Insanum torvo minitans Rhamnusia vultu,
Quos nunc divitiis melior fortuna beavit
505 Innumeris, quoniam tot iam labentibus annis
Gymnica Gericolae statuerunt castra Minervae.
    Scis, neque teste opus, ad quales profectus honores,
Presul Ioannes, perveneris, optime, postquam
Te Pater omnipotens melioribus induit annis.
510 Pauper eras primoque puer derelictus in aevo.
Non tibi subsidium chari potuere parentes
Addere, non opibus iuvenilis inertia vitae

C2ʳ

---

[75]St. Catherine of Alexandria, patroness of philosophers and scholars, is the Christian answer to Pallas Athena. After defeating fifty pagans in a learned disputation, she was martyred by Emperor Maxentius and decapitated. Her body was carried by angels to Mount Sinai. It was there that Justinian I founded the celebrated cloister named after her. Oil and milk were said to flow from her tomb. In *Her. Chr.* 4 Eobanus offers a poetic treatment of the most famous part of her legend (also alluded to in line 488 below), her mystic marriage to Christ.

[76]Now that he has earned his B.A. (October 1506), Eobanus is studying toward his M.A. (1509).

to open sea again. But this time the voyage will be plain sailing and much shorter too.

[480] Although the glorious renown of our distinguished and celebrated university is in full flower all over the world, nevertheless it is incumbent upon my Muses to make her even more famous and to give her the thanks that a mother worthy of the name deserves. A boy at Minerva's breasts, I drank from her the salutary milk that flows out of the ivory marble where faraway Mount Sinai keeps our Christian Pallas: Catherine, the daughter of Costus, whose body now rests in the crypt where the angels bore it, but whose soul is united with her bridegroom in heaven.[75] When I came here, an ill-dressed youth looking for refuge [490] and shelter, she not only took me in kindly, but also overwhelmed me with all kinds of favors. On top of that, she granted my undeserving brow titles and garlands and promised to add to these someday, God willing, the even higher distinction of an advanced degree.[76]

Bountiful nurse of the poor, mother of the indigent, home for the destitute, venerable hospice for the weary, haven for exiles, asylum for flourishing studies, Erfurt educates the lazy, polishes the churlish, adorns the uncouth with manners, character, learning, and virtue, and sates [500] the needy with riches. How great is the number of those who grew up in poverty, who lost their dear parents at an early age, who inherited rank and privilege only to have these gifts taken away by the scowling, outrageously menacing goddess of Rhamnus,[77] but whom a better fortune has since blessed with innumerable riches because, year after year, they have been coming to enlist in the scholarly ranks of the Minerva who dwells by the Gera.

You know this at first hand, most excellent Bishop Johann,[78] having yourself attained to such remarkable honors after the Father Almighty invested you with manhood. [510] In adolescence you were penniless and left to fend for yourself. Your dear parents could not offer you their help;

---

[77]The goddess worshiped at Rhamnus is Nemesis; see Erasmus, *Adag.* 2, 6, 38. Though she is properly the goddess of retribution, Renaissance authors often identify her with Fortuna. See, for example, Erasmus, *Adag.* 2, 6, 38, *ASD* 2, 4, p. 49, lines 724-730; *Moria, ASD* 4, 3, p. 176, lines 861-862; Eob. *Her. Chr.* 8, 7-8.

[78]Johann Bonemilch of Laasphe. For his life see fn. 4 at *Laud.,* ded.

Tempora sustentare ullis aut divite cultu.
Nunc tua sors Croeso similis, nunc portus et aura
515 Pauperibus qui pauper eras. Erphordia sic te
Divitiis plenum foecit de paupere, magnum
De parvo, de vulgari servoque potentem.
Prima rudimentis crevit iuvenilibus aetas
Ad tua foelicis tempus deducta senectae
520 Faustiter, acceptos qua nunc insignis honores
Doctoralis habes palmae sacrataque presul
Pontificis geris arma Dei. Praelate sacerdos,
Multis Catholicam meritis Ecclesian ornas.
Candida caelicolis statuis delubra; statutis
525 Perpetuis fieri ter ternas cantibus odas
Instituis. Rigido Costis dominata tyranno
Hoc tibi succedit titulo. Scis, dive Michael,
Cuius ad ensiferae celeberrima virginis aedes
Templa frequentantur, magnae qua structa Minervae
530 Atria praelucent sublimibus alta fenestris.
　　Scis, inquam, venerande pater, quae praemia, quales
Sublimata bonis Erphordia pendat honores.
Palladiae, scis, tota cohors collecta coronae.
Scitis et externae quantis virtutibus urbes
535 Urbs nostra emineat. Quamvis Germania multis
Gymnasiis passim vigeat laudata probatis,
Hoc uno cunctis praefertur gentibus. Illi
Austriacae studium quamvis insigne Viennae
Caedit, Agrippinaeque decus, laus nobilis, urbis,
540 Friburgique vigor. Rhenana Moguntia caedat,
Quaeque Palatini sceptrum sedemque Philippi
Urbs tenet, et Musis Lips amplificata Latinis
Caedat, et Albioris studio vulgata recenti.
Caedat Sarmaticae celebris Cracovia gentis
545 Metropolis, studiis satis imo superque probatae
Ingenuis. At non victus levitate locoque
Aeris innocui, virtutem venditis auro.

C2ᵛ

C3ʳ

---

538 Viennae *scripsi*: Vienne *A*.　　**544** Cracovia *scripsi*: Crocavia *A*.

---

[79]In 1500 he funded a chapel in St. Michael's dedicated to St. Catherine of Alexandria.

[80]The main university buildings were all located close to St. Michael's. Dedicated to learning, they are a temple to Minerva (Pallas Athena), the virgin goddess of wisdom and the arts.

they were not able to support the leisure time of your youthful life with money or rich attire. Now you are as rich as Croesus; now you, though formerly needy yourself, are a harbor and breeze to the needy. So thoroughly did Erfurt transform you from a poverty-stricken lad to a man of substance, from a lowly churl to an eminent bishop, and from an ordinary servant to a powerful lord! You have enjoyed good fortune from the first school days of your boyhood to the time of your happy old age, [520] in which you now have the signal honor of a doctoral degree and as suffragan bishop bear the consecrated arms of God. Exalted prelate, you adorn the Catholic Church with your numerous merits. You erected a beautiful chapel to the inhabitants of heaven; and after it was built, you endowed it with thrice three Masses, to be sung perpetually. That is how the daughter of Costus, who mastered the merciless tyrant, redounds to your glory.[79] Of this, Saint Michael is well aware. His famous church, always much frequented, stands next to the buildings dedicated to the sword-bearing virgin.[80] It is there that the lofty halls built for mighty Minerva [530] shine forth through their towering windows.

As I was saying, reverend Father, you know the kind of rewards and honors that sublime Erfurt grants to the worthy. The whole circle of scholars, every follower of Pallas knows it. Foreign cities, too, recognize the outstanding qualities that have made our city preeminent. For although Germany earns high praise for the many fine universities scattered throughout her realm, she is universally esteemed on account of this one alone. The University of Vienna in Austria, distinguished though it is, yields to ours. This holds true also for Cologne's pride and joy [540] and for Freiburg's heart and soul. Rhenish Mainz should give place to us; so should the capital city and residence of Count Palatine Philip.[81] Extolled by the Latin Muses, Leipzig too must step aside, and so must Wittenberg, celebrated though she was in a recent work.[82] Let famed Cracow, the capital of Poland, make way, no matter how superb her reputation in the liberal arts. But none of you universities sells your goods cheaply, for a mere song. You sell your excellence in

[81] Heidelberg, the seat of Count Palatine Philip II (1448-1508).

[82] Hermann von dem Busche extolled Leipzig in his poem *Lipsica* (ca. 1504). Cf. Eob. *Laud.* 42-43, with fn. 15. Georgius Sibutus did the same for Wittenberg in his *Silvula in Albiorim illustratam,* printed in the winter of 1506/07.

Magnos erigitis, locupletes divitiores
Redditis; at rarus post plurima taedia pauper
550   Ad decus optati tandem consurgit honoris,
Et iuvenes longa spe defraudatis egentes.
Ast inopum nutrix, Erphordia, mater egentum,
Pauperibus domus, hospicium venerabile fessis,
Omnibus aequa pares cunctis impendit honores –
555   Equa bonis, inquam, pravis metuenda noverca.
Erudit ignavos, rigidos polit, ornat inertes.
Huc age, digne puer, primis te confer ab annis!
Hic vir eris. Patrios repetes cum laude penates
Eximia. Si pauper, eris de paupere dives,
560   Deque rudi doctus, multa virtute politus.
Huc, iuvenes, properate citi, quos cura parentum
Deserit, hic certum namque invenietis asylum.
Et iam deficiunt lassatae membra carinae.
Hic teneat proiecta petitos anchora portus.
565   Hic requiem sperare licet. Discedite, Musae.

Tempus adest. Fervens caelo iam Procyon ardet
Et minitat tristes furibunda Canicula morbos.
Ite, puellari succingite tempora lauro.
Iamdudum talem, Musae, meruistis honorem.
570   Ipse ego fagineo cingam languentia ramo
Tempora et impexos taxo florente capillos –
Talia enim tali debentur serta poetae –
Rursus et impurum Gerae spumantis ad amnem
Precipitata novae ructabo carmina laudis.
575   Ite bonis avibus, neu vos latrator Anubis
Terreat incautas morsuque offendat iniquo.
Tu quoque qui quondam mihi Zoilus esse solebas,
Desine. Parce, precor, iuveniles rodere versus.
Vellem, Livor edax, siquidem non lecta tulisses

---

[83]The Dog Star (Sirius, Canicula) was believed to bring on the unwholesome heat of the
dog days of July and August. Cf. Verg. *A.* 10, 273-274; Eob. *Pug.* 1-2 (referring to August 9);
Her. Chr. 18, 42. The reference to the dog days suggests that Eobanus put the finishing touches
to his poem in the summer of 1507.

return for gold. You exalt the high and mighty, you make the wealthy richer; but only rarely does a penniless student, after much vexation, [550] rise at last to the cherished distinction of an academic degree. More often than not, you cheat indigent youths out of long-held hopes. Erfurt, by contrast, nurse of the poor, mother of the indigent, home for the destitute, venerable hospice for the weary, is fair-minded to all and awards honors to everyone in equal measure. She is fair-minded, I say, to the virtuous; to the crooked she is a frightful stepmother. She educates the lazy, polishes the churlish, adorns the uncouth. Come on, worthy lad, get over here as soon as you are old enough! Here you will become a man. You will return home covered with glory. If you are poor, you will be changed from a pauper to a rich man [560], from an ignoramus to a learned and accomplished scholar. Quick, youths, hurry to us if your parents can no longer take care of you. For here you can count on finding refuge.

And now the timbers of my sea-weary vessel are giving out. Throw out the anchor here and let the craft ride in the port we were making for. Here we can look forward to peace and quiet. Say your good-byes, Muses. It's time. Already Procyon is glowing red-hot in the sky and the mad Dog Star is threatening dreadful diseases.[83] Go and crown your brows with sprigs of maidenly laurel.[84] For quite some time now, Muses, you've deserved an honor like this. [570] As for me, I'll wreathe my languid forehead with beech sprays[85] and bind my unkempt hair with flowering yew – for that is the sort of wreath that suits a poet like me – and then I'll sit by the muddy water of the foaming Gera again and, off the top of my head, spout new songs of praise.

I wish you good luck as you go out into the world. Don't let Anubis terrify you with his barking, but don't get so careless either as to let him inflict a nasty bite. You too, who were my Zoilus[86] the last time around, hold off! Stop carping at these youthful verses, please. How I wish, gnaw-

---

[84] The laurel is "maidenly" because it is associated with the virginal Daphne, who was turned into a laurel tree by Apollo. Cf. *Buc.* 6, 54.

[85] The beech stood for humble poetry, particularly pastoral, because it is mentioned in the opening line of Vergil's first eclogue. The image that Eobanus projects here and in the following lines, then, is that of a rustic poet with no aspirations to elegance.

[86] Zoilus stands for a vicious critic. See fn. 16 at *Rec.* B 2, 3.

580   Aequa mente prius vel iam despecta, sceleste,
       Nunquam legisses. Non, si te ruperis? Ergo
       Quid iacis in sacras demens convicia Musas?
       Quid volucres coelo tentas convellere nubes,
       Ex adamante favos deducere, lumen ab undis?
585   Parce! Liget fidos stabilis concordia fratres.
       At vos, o quicumque viri, quicumque Magistri
       Doctoresque pii quorum mihi nomen honorque
       Carmen erant, faciles nostris estote Camaenis
       Subrudibusque modis. Viciis ignoscite, si qua
590   Non bene tornato cecini difformia versu.

Finis

ing Envy, that you could be [580] unprejudiced against
something you haven't even read yet, or that you wouldn't
bother to read a work for which, scoundrel, you've already
expressed your contempt. Not until you burst? Then why
are you madly hurling insults against the holy Muses? Why
are you trying to rend the fleeting clouds in the sky, draw
honey out of steel, light from the sea? Just stop! Lasting
friendship binds us faithful brothers together. You, on the
other hand, everyone of you men, everyone of you noble-
minded instructors and professors whose fame and glory
were the subject of my song, go easy on my Muses and their
rather clumsy rhythms. Excuse the shortcomings, if ever
[590] I've expressed myself poorly in some misshapen verse.

The End

C4^r   **B 1   AD ERPHORDIAM ELEGI CONCLUDENTES**

Nunc melior toto vives, Erphordia, mundo
   Venturaeque stupor posteritatis eris.
Donec firma levi pendebit in aere tellus,
   Cynthia dum niveis Luna vehetur equis,
5   Debita caelestes donec movet orbita sphaeras,
   Dum retinet caelum sydera, gramen humus,
Non tua sub terras veniet, non ibit ad umbras
   Clarior ad superas laus referenda domos.
Tu potes in cineres verti tenuesque favillas;
10   In mea nil fatum carmina iuris habet.
Clara prius Danais ceciderunt Pergama flammis,
   Vivit adhuc celebres Ilias inter avos.
Non minus antiquae periisset gloria Thebes,
   Ni celebris toto Thebais orbe foret.
15   Sic tibi perpetuis veniet mansura diebus
   Gloria, laus, splendor, fama, perhennis honor.
Has tibi pro meritis grates laudesque rependo.
   Qualis erit Musis gratia, quaeso, meis?

B 2   SUSQUE DEQUE FERENDUM

Palladiae cecini titulumque decusque coronae.
   Numen habet Pallas, numen inane tamen.
Tu mihi persolves dignas, Erphordia, grates,
   Namque nihil vacuis gratibus indigeo.

B 2   3 grates *scripsi*: crates *A*.

B 1   A CONCLUDING ELEGY TO ERFURT

Now you will live forever throughout the world, Erfurt, and be a marvel to the generations to come. As long as the solid earth remains suspended in thin air, as long as Cynthian Luna rides her snow-white steeds, as long as the heavenly spheres move in their appointed paths, as long as the sky continues to have stars, the soil grass, your fame will not go down to the underworld or descend to the shades, but will be carried ever more brilliant up to the mansions on high. You can be reduced to rubble and fine ashes. [10] Over these verses of mine fate has no power at all. The famed citadel of Troy has long since fallen to the fires kindled by the Greeks, but the *Iliad* lives on to the present day, along with the celebrated ancestors. Likewise the fame of ancient Thebes would now be wholly extinguished, were the *Thebaid* not known the world over. In the same way you will garner perennial glory, praise, splendor, fame, and honor that will endure to the end of time. In return for the blessings you have bestowed on me I offer you this poem of gratitude and praise. What kind of thanks, I wonder, can my Muses expect?

B 2   TAKE IT OR LEAVE IT

Now I have extolled the fame and glory of our Palladian university. Pallas has power, to be sure; but her power lacks substance. You, Erfurt, will repay me according to my deserts, for I don't need empty thanks.

C4ᵛ   **B 3   IN EOBANUM HESSUM VIVACISSIMI**
INGENII ADOLESCENTEM ULRICHI
HUTTENI ELEGIA

Si qua tenet nunquam morituros gloria vates
Et trepidos fugiunt carmina nostra rogos
Famaque stat putres ubi terra recondidit artus
(Nam fovet Aonios quid nisi fama viros?),
5   Semper eris vivus postque ultima fata superstes,
O iuvenis, patriae spesque decusque tuae,
Primus ad ignotam qui duxti Pallada terram
Et reparas Hessis nomina longa tuis,
Cuius honoratam meruit facundia laurum
10   Quique vafros tenero vincis in ore senes.
Ergo tulit merito foelicia pondera mater,
Quae enixa est utero pignora tanta suo.
Plaudat et ad gratos ponat nova munera divos,
Ingenii dotes si sapit illa tui.
15   Et non vulgares partus et numina laudet,
Quae dederint votis vela secunda suis.
Sive canas grandes, heroica munera, versus
Gestaque terribili praelia quaeque manu,
Sive cothurnatus curvis videare theatris
20   Et recites veterum tristia fata ducum,
C5ʳ   Aut tua cum tensis modulere poemata nervis,
Excultum facili pumice pergit opus.
Est tibi cum facili fluidissima vaena lepore.
Manat ab ingenio copia viva tuo.
25   Quicquid aves scriptis venturos scire nepotes,
Hoc potes ornatis exoluisse modis.

---

11 Ergo *Böcking*: Eego *A.*   **16** Quae *Böcking*: Que *A.*   **21** tua *scripsi*: sua *A.*   **26** ex-
oluisse *A*: excoluisse *Böcking.*

[87]This epigram and the next must have been written around Easter (12 April) 1506, dur-
ing the few days that Hutten spent in Erfurt on his way from Cologne to the new University
of Frankfurt an der Oder (opened on 26 April 1506).

The Franconian knight and humanist Ulrich von Hutten was born at the castle of Ste-
ckelberg near Fulda in 1488. A frail and sickly youth, he received his early schooling in the
Benedictine monastery of Fulda in 1499-1503. Thereafter he studied at Erfurt (1503?-1505),
where he was mentored by Crotus Rubianus. Declining to return to the monastery, he ma-
triculated instead at Mainz (summer semester 1505), Cologne (winter semester 1505/06), and
Frankfurt an der Oder (1506-1508). Here he passed the B.A. examination on 14 September

**B 3   ON EOBANUS HESSUS, A MOST
HIGH-SPIRITED YOUTH. AN ELEGY
BY ULRICH VON HUTTEN[87]**

If Fame can grant poets immortality, if our songs escape the
flaming pyre and our name endures after the earth has cov-
ered our decomposed remains (for what does Fame cherish
if not the Aonian bards?), then you will live forever and sur-
vive your dying day, young man, hope and ornament of
your fatherland. For you are the first to bring Pallas to that
unfamiliar country and are reviving the ancient renown of
your fellow Hessians. Your eloquence deserves to be hon-
ored with a laurel wreath, [10] for already in your youth you
speak better than cunning old men. Your mother, therefore,
carried a truly blessed burden, seeing that she gave birth to
so great a son. She ought to be clapping her hands and mak-
ing new thank offerings to the gods, if she has any ap-
preciation of your mental gifts. She should be praising both
her exceptional offspring and the heavenly powers who gave
her prayers smooth sailing.

Whether you are singing of heroic deeds in epic verse
and of terrible hand-to-hand battles, or strut buskined on
the theater's curving stage [20] and recite the doleful fate of
ancient leaders, or accompany your lyrics on well-tuned
strings, your work is always polished with fine pumice.[88]
Besides an easy wit, you possess a most fluid poetic vein.
You have all the resources of language at your fingertips.
Whatever you wish to pass on to future generations in your
writings, you are able to carry out in richly embellished po-

---

1506. After stays at Leipzig, Greifswald, Rostock, and Vienna, he studied at Pavia and Bologna
in 1512-1514 and then returned to Germany. In 1515-1517 he resumed his law studies in Ita-
ly. While in Bologna he wrote a poetic letter to Emperor Maximilian, in which the personified
Italia appeals to the emperor to rescue Italy from her foreign oppressors. Eobanus published it
in 1516 along with his own strongly patriotic *Responsio Maximiliani*. Upon Hutten's return to
Germany, Maximilian crowned him poet laureate in Augsburg (12 July 1517). Thereafter he
emerged as a passionate champion of humanistic, religious, and political reform in Germany,
writing an (anonymous) sequel to the *Epistolae obscurorum virorum* (1517), satiric dialogues in
Latin and German, as well as nationalistic songs and attacks on the papacy. Allying himself
with the firebrand knight Franz von Sickingen, he enthusiastically embraced Luther's cause,
but fled to Switzerland in November 1522. His health broken, repudiated by Erasmus, he died
an exile in late August 1523. Eobanus wrote an admiring funeral poem for him in dialogue
form, first published in the *Epicedia* of 1531.

[88] By Easter 1506 Eobanus had written many poems, but not yet published any. *De recessu
studentum* may have been in progress already; *De pugna studentum* still lay some months ahead.

Quae natura dedit studiosae conseris arti,
　　Nec maculant versus barbara verba tuos.
Talis erat Phrygios qui condidit urbe penates,
30　　Et male Sarmatica Naso sepultus humo,
Cuius et ornavit Nemesis laudata libellos,
　　Quique dedit varium Bilbilitanus opus.
Talis adhuc iuvenis cum sis primisque sub annis,
　　Ventura est facto gloria quanta viro!
35　Vive memor nostri qui te delegimus unum,
　　Sitque comes scriptis semper Apollo tuis.

B 4　EOBANI GRACIARUM ACTIO EXTEMPORALIS

Ergo vale longum superis, Huttene, secundis.
　　Catholicus menti spiret Apollo tuae.
Pergis abhinc. Tua te expectat Francfordia vatem.
　　Dimidium nostri te fugiente fugit.
5 ·　Aemule Nasoni, viridi signande corona
　　Et titulo multis nobiliore, vale.

C5ᵛ　**B 5　HEREBORDI MARGARITI LEOBURGII
AD SUUM EOBANUM HEXASTICHON**

Hesse puer, meritis vetulos victure poetas,
　　Quam facili sacrum pollice tangis ebur!
Ergo per immensum stabit tua gloria mundum,
　　Si sacra, ut perhibent, carmina morte carent.
5　Vive diu. Vita longaevum Nestora vincas,
　　Versibus Oceani caedet harena tuis.

34 Ventura *Böcking*: Venturo *A.*

[89]The poets referred to are: Vergil, the singer of the *Aeneid*; Ovid, who during the last years of his life lived in exile in Tomis on the Black Sea; Tibullus, who wrote love poetry to his mistress Nemesis; and Martial, a native of Bilbilis in Spain.

etry. You combine your innate gifts with laboriously ac-
quired art. No barbarous words ever spoil *your* verses! You
are as classical as that epic poet who set up the gods of Troy
in the city of Rome, [30] as classical as Ovid, who was trag-
ically buried in Sarmatian soil, and as that lyricist who sang
the praises of Nemesis and as that epigrammatist from Bil-
bilis who left us that varied oeuvre of his.[89] Because you are
already such an accomplished artist as a youth, though you
are only in the springtime of life, how great will your glory
be once you reach manhood! Good luck, and do remember
me as one who picked you to be his sole friend. May Apollo
always be your companion in everything you write.

B 4   EOBANUS'S THANKS, WRITTEN EXTEMPORE

Good-bye and good luck to you also, Hutten. May the
Catholic Apollo inspire you. You are about to leave us. Your
Frankfurt is expecting you, her poet.[90] As you depart, half
my soul departs with you. Rival of Ovid, you deserve to be
distinguished with a verdant wreath and a much nobler
title.[91] Farewell.

B 5   A HEXASTICH BY HERBORD VON DER MARTHEN AND LÖWENBURG[92] TO HIS FRIEND EOBANUS

Hessian lad, who in achievements are destined to surpass the
ancient poets, how deftly you touch the sacred lyre with your
thumb! Your glory, therefore, will abide in all the boundless
world, if (as they say) sacred poems are deathless. Enjoy a
long life. May you live longer than Nestor, may your verses
be more numerous than the grains of sand in the ocean.

---

[90] Hutten left for Frankfurt an der Oder in mid-April 1506.

[91] Hutten too is worthy of being crowned with the laurel wreath and of being called "poeta
laureatus" – a title more noble than "knight."

[92] For Herbord von der Marthen und Löwenburg see fn. 30 at *Laud.* 146.

B 6   IOANNIS CHRISTIANI FRANCOBERGII DYSTICHON

Una eadem nobis patria est, Eobane, duobus,
     Unus amor. Duo sunt corpora, mens eadem.

Patrii sperate nepotes.

B 6   A DISTICH BY JOHANN CHRISTIANI OF FRANKENBERG[93]

The two of us share one and the same homeland, Eobanus, and one and the same love. We are two bodies, one single soul.

Take heart, fellow countrymen.

---

[93] Johann Christiani of Frankenberg matriculated at Erfurt in 1504. He obtained his B.A. in 1506 and his M.A. in 1509, in each case together with Eobanus.

DE AMANTIUM INFOELICITATE, CONTRA VENEREM, DE CUPIDINIS IMPOTENTIA

ON THE WRETCHEDNESS OF LOVERS, AGAINST VENUS, ON THE MAD FURY OF CUPID

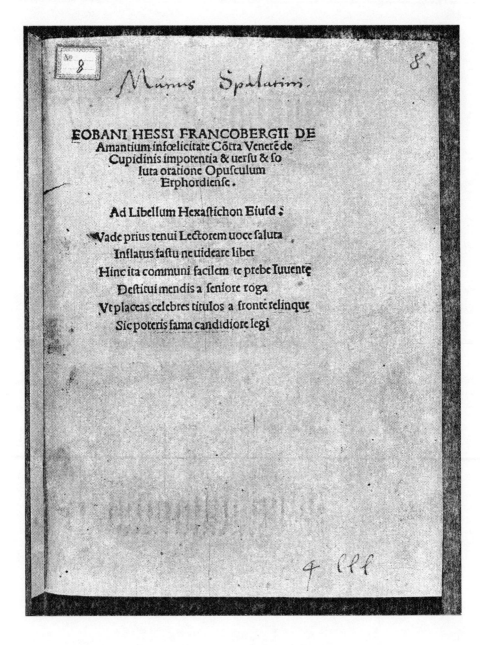

EOBANI HESSI FRANCOBERGII DE
Amantium infœlicitate Côtra Venerê de
Cupidinis impotentia & uersu & so
luta oratione Opusculum
Erphordiense.

Ad Libellum Hexastichon Eiusd:

Vade prius tenui Lectorem uoce saluta
Inflatus fastu ne uideare liber
Hinc ita communi facilem te prebe Iuuentę
Destitui mendis a seniore roga
Vt placeas celebres titulos a fronte relinque
Sic poteris fama candidiore legi

Title page of *De amantium infoelicitate*
Erfurt: Johann Knappe the Elder, 1508
Universitätsbibliothek, Munich

Eobani Hessi Francobergij de

Amantiū infœlicitate contra Venerem de
Cupidinis impotentia & versu & so/
luta oratione Opuscu/
lum.

AD LIBELLVM Hexast. Eiusdē.

Vade prius tenui Lectorem voce saluta

Inflatus fastu ne videare liber

Hinc ita communi facilem te prebe Iuuentæ

Destitui mendis a seniore roga

Vt placeas celebres titulos a fronte relinque

Sic poteris fama candidiore legi.

Title page of *De amantium infoelicitate*
Wittenberg: Johann Grunenberg, 1515
Universitätsbibliothek, Munich

DE AMANTIUM INFOELICITATE

Introduction

As he explains in the dedicatory letter to his friend Peter (Petrejus) Eberbach, Eobanus wrote this prosimetric satire while enjoying a brief holiday from his "terribly wearisome" teaching duties at the chapter school of St. Severi in the late spring of 1508. The work tackles a subject all too familiar to the young author himself: the overwhelming power of passionate love. A friend of his, Fronto Fundinus by name, has fallen head over heels in love with a local beauty. Only after he has squandered all his money on her does he learn that the girl is a prostitute. Mad with passion and shame, the heartbroken gallant pines away all alone in the woods. Eobanus happens to run into him on one of his walks in the country, learns what has happened, and cures him with the Muses' aid.

Since Eobanus characterizes "Fronto Fundinus" as an old friend of his (*Ama.* 4, 3), the question arises whether he (like the shepherds in the *Bucolicon*) might not be modeled on one of Eobanus's acquaintances at Erfurt. As a matter of fact, the text does offer several clues regarding his identity. He is evidently a well-to-do young man, humanistically educated, poetically gifted, a fellow student and close friend of Eobanus's for many years already. Moreover, he has fallen for the bewitching, but flighty Fulvia. These clues point to the book's dedicatee Petrejus Eberbach, a student at Erfurt since 1497. The identification is corroborated in *Sylv.* 2, 22, 5-6, sent to Petrejus in ca. late 1515. In that epigram Eobanus wonders where Petrejus is hiding out these days. Might he have fallen under Fulvia's spell again and abandoned the Latin Muses? ("Anne iterum veteri te Fulvia fune retraxit, / Oblitum Romae Pieridumque chori?")

Petrejus Eberbach was born in ca. 1480 at Rothenburg ob der Tauber. One of the two sons of the Erfurt professor of medicine Georg Eberbach, he matriculated at Erfurt in 1497, receiving his B.A. in 1502 and his M.A. in February 1508. Later he earned a bachelor's degree in law at Basel (1512) and a licentiate in law at Heidelberg (1529). He died in 1531/32. Friends lauded his wit and erudition; but aside from some lyric poems and letters to Mutianus, Hutten, Reuchlin, and Eobanus he published no major works under his own name. He must have been involved in the writing of several humanistic pamphlets, however. The anonymous satire on drunkenness *De generibus ebriosorum* (Erfurt, 1516), to which Eobanus and other Erfurt humanists contributed, may be largely attributed to him. For his friendship with Eobanus see also Camerarius, *Nar.* 17, 10-11, and Eob. *Buc.* 5 (where he is "Floridus").

Composed during the Pentecost holidays in early June 1508, the work seems to have gone to the printery later that month. In *Ama.* 22, 6 Eobanus alludes to an epitaph for Konrad Celtis that he composed at a dinner party in Mutianus Rufus's house on 10 August 1508; see Mutian. *Ep.* 78; Krause, *HEH*, vol. 1, p. 70. The allusion is inserted so awkwardly, however, that it must have been added at the last minute, either just before Eobanus delivered the manuscript or while the printing was already in progress.

The book appeared twice. The editio princeps was published in Erfurt by Johann Knappe the Elder:

A (1508)

EOBANI HESSI FRANCOBERGII DE | Amantium infœlicitate Cōtra Venerē de | Cupidinis impotentia & uerſu & ſo | luta oratione Opuſculum | Erphordienſe. | Ad Libellum Hexaſtichon Eiuſd. | [*3 distichs*]

Colophon, sig. C6ʳ:	TRANSFORMATVM EST HOC OPVS	Impenſis Eobani Anno poſt cōmunis Chriſti	anorum dei natalē DDDVIII. Erphor	die ad Diui Seueri. In Edib. Ioan	nis Knap nouicii ſed uix ue=	tuſtiorib. Poſthabendi	In Latinis Cal.	cogtaphi [*sic*]	[*printer's device*]
Collation:	4°: A-C⁶, [$3 signed], 18 leaves
Contents:	A1ʳ title page; A1ᵛ blank; A2ʳ-A2ᵛ dedicatory letter to Peter Eberbach; A3ʳ Eberbach's response; A3ᵛ two epigrams; A4ʳ-C3ʳ *De amantium infoelicitate*; C3ʳ Eobanus Hessus to the reader; C3ʳ-C5ᵛ dialogue between Calliope and Hessus; C5ᵛ Eobanus Hessus to the reader; concluding epigram; C6ʳ colophon; C6ᵛ blank
Copy-text:	Munich, Universitätsbibliothek Call number: 4° P. Lat. rec. 911/8

The copy once belonged to Eobanus's friend Georg Spalatin, for the title page bears the handwritten inscription "Munus Spalatini." I have also consulted the two other known copies: Münster, UB (Coll. Erh. 329) and Strasbourg, BNU (R 104214).

The work was reprinted in Wittenberg by Johann Grunenberg:

B (1515)

[*Fraktur:*] Eobani Heffi Francobergij de | [*roman:*] Amantiū infœlicitate contra Venerem de | Cupidinis impotentia & verfu & fo- | luta oratione Opufcu- | lum. | AD LIBELLVM Hexaft. Eiufdē. | [*3 distichs*]

Colophon, sig. C6ʳ: Wittenburgi in ædib. Ioan: Grunenbergi. | Anno dñi.
                M.D.XV. | Apud | Auguftinianos.

Collation: 4°: A-C⁶, [$3 signed], 18 leaves

Contents: A1ʳ title page; A1ᵛ two epigrams; A2ʳ-C4ʳ *De amantium infoelicitate*; C4ʳ Eobanus Hessus to the reader; C4ʳ-C6ʳ dialogue between Calliope and Hessus; C6ʳ concluding epigram and colophon; C6ᵛ blank

Copy-text: Munich, Universitätsbibliothek
                 Call number: 4° P. Lat. rec. 911/6

This reprint is not mentioned in Maria Großmann, *Wittenberger Drucke 1502 bis 1517: Ein bibliographischer Beitrag zur Geschichte des Humanismus in Deutschland* (Vienna, 1971). I know of no other copies.

Eobani Hessi Francobergii
DE AMANTIUM INFOELICITATE,
CONTRA VENEREM, DE CUPIDINIS IMPOTENTIA
et versu et soluta oratione opusculum Erphordiense

AD LIBELLUM HEXASTICHON EIUSDEM

Vade. Prius tenui lectorem voce saluta,
Inflatus fastu ne videare, liber.
Hinc ita communi facilem te prebe iuventae.
Destitui mendis a seniore roga.
5   Ut placeas, celebres titulos a fronte relinque.
Sic poteris fama candidiore legi.

Tit. Erphordiense *A: om. B.*

Eobanus Hessus of Frankenberg
ON THE WRETCHEDNESS OF LOVERS,
AGAINST VENUS, ON THE UNBRIDLED FURY OF CUPID
A little work in verse and prose, written at Erfurt

TO THE BOOK. A HEXASTICH BY THE SAME AUTHOR

Away you go, book! First, be modest when greeting your readers,
    lest they think you're puffed up with conceit.
Second, be open and friendly to all the young people.
    Ask the older ones to correct your mistakes.
5   To find favor, keep your brow free of high-sounding titles.
    Then your fame will grow brighter day after day.

EOBANUS HESSUS FRANCOBERGIUS MAGISTRO PETRO EBERBACHO ERPHORDIANO, IUVENI ET DOCTRINA MIRIFICA ET MORUM SANCTITATE COMMENDABILI, SUO AMICISSIMO S. D. P.

Pulchrum est et preclarum, Petre suavissime, in submissioribus negociis ita esse ociosos ut occupatissimi videamur. 2 Necessarium enim puto bonis quibusque literarum studiosis, iusta sapientissimi Senecae preceptum, ne semper in actu sint, sed interdum animum a morosis meditationibus (quales Musicae palestrae investi tyrones in meretoriis prelectionibus experimur fere quottidie) absolvant et per liberioris ocii oportunitatem quasi in seipsis revirescant, dum intermissam requiem ad graciosissimas Musarum conversationes traduxerint et ea demum egerint in ocio quae criticos istos et curiosos censores ad negocia provocare vel invitos consueverunt.

3 Illud ad hoc referimus. 4 Quom superioribus diebus a molestissimis ludi literatorii laboribus pro tempore vacarem, ociosus esse volui ut viderer occupatissimus. 5 Conscripsi libellum de amantium infoelicitate et Cupidinis impotentia versu et oratione soluta sub formam dialogi coactum, nulla alia causa inductus quam ut literato ocio mentis hebetudinem et animi languorem devitarem et ingenium ab inviso negotio suspensum novo scribendi genere, quasi e tenebris sub dio paulisper expaciatus, oblectarer. 6 Nam ocium sine literis plerumque aut turpe est aut ignavum. 7 Quorum utrumque Minervalis exercitii palestritae cuique tanquam presentissimum venenum fugiendum censeo.

8 Libellum ipsum qualemcumque, licet nulla vetustae, hoc est rectae Latinitatis elegantia aut splendore conditum, statim et a principio tibi, mi Petre, dedicavimus, non quod eo te scriptionis genere adeo oblectatum acceperimus ut Xenocrati philosopho apud formosam Phrynen continenter recubanti Nasonem poetam in Corynnae amplexibus mori expetentem preferas. 9 Sed nos interim delicati iuvenes

Ded. A: *om.* B.

---

[1]For Petrejus Eberbach's life see the introduction.

[2]During the Pentecost holiday in early June 1508.

[3]Eobanus's claim to be the first to mix verse and prose does not, of course, mean that he invented the genre, but only that he introduced it to German literature. Later he would make

EOBANUS HESSUS OF FRANKENBERG SENDS MANY GREET-INGS TO HIS DEAREST FRIEND PETER EBERBACH OF ERFURT, M.A., A YOUNG MAN WHO IS NOT ONLY MARVELOUSLY LEARNED, BUT ALSO PRAISEWORTHY FOR HIS MORAL PURITY.[1]

It is a fine and splendid thing, dear Peter, to be so leisurely engaged in trifling matters that we actually appear to be hard at work. Indeed, following the precept of the consummately wise Seneca, I believe it is essential for all good students of literature not to be always in harness. Now and then, in fact, we really do have to take a break from the kind of morose fretting that I – naked tyro on the wrestling-mat of the Muses – experience almost daily when teaching classes to earn a living. By making the most of our spare time, we can, so to speak, rejuvenate ourselves in spirit. And if we use these intermittent periods of relaxation to bring about the most charming intimacy with the Muses, we shall end up spending our idle hours accomplishing the very things that provoke those critics and faultfinders to do their business, whether they like it or not.

Let me explain what prompted this train of thought. During the past few days, when I had some time off from my terribly wearisome labors as a schoolmaster,[2] I wanted to enjoy my vacation in such a way that I would appear to be hard at work. So I wrote a little book about the wretchedness of lovers and the unbridled fury of Cupid, in verse and prose, structured in the form of a dialogue, for no other reason than to put my leisure to some literary use, avoid dullness of mind and idleness of spirit, and, relieved of that hateful schoolwork, amuse my talent with a new genre of writing[3] – just as if I had gotten out of a gloomy prison for a little while and were strolling about in the open air. For assuredly, leisure without letters is mostly either disgraceful or downright lazy. Anyone who goes to the mat to exercise himself in the arts of Minerva should, I think, avoid these two extremes like the plague.

Though the present booklet, whatever its worth, cannot lay claim to the elegance or brilliance of ancient, that is to say, true Latinity, I immediately and right from the start wanted to dedicate it to you, my dear Peter. Of course I'm quite aware that this sort of writing doesn't appeal to you overly much – at least not to the extent that you'd prefer the poet Ovid, who desired to die in the arms of Corinna, over the philosopher Xenocrates, who lay continently beside the beautiful Phryne. For the time being, however, we squeamish

---

similar claims about pastoral poetry and the Christian heroic epistle. Formally, the work stands in the tradition of Menippean satire. Petronius's *Satyricon*, Seneca's *Apocolocyntosis*, and Boethius's *Philosophiae consolatio* belong to the genre; so, for example, does Alan of Lille's *De planctu Naturae*. See further W. Scott Blanchard, *Scholars' Bedlam: Menippean Satire in the Renaissance* (Lewisburg, 1995), especially pp. 11-45.

Sophoclem senem a rebus | Venereis abstinentem imitabimur et tanquam emasculati Musarum sacerdotes Venerem in hortis Epicuri lascivientem deridebimus.

10 Quamvis certe non defuturos augurer qui hunc nostrum et si pium laborem tanquam prophanum a literatorum omnium consortio reiicere conabuntur. 11 Et dicet quispiam: "'Tractant fabrilia fabri.' Impudicus impudice scribit Eobanus." 12 De hoc nos erudito lectori iudicium relinquimus. 13 Is mea sententia non est impudicus qui impudicitiae crimen totis viribus detestatur et dissuadet, siquidem contra impudicum amorem hunc libellum elucubravimus, quem sub tui preclari nominis praesidio tutum in publicum aedidimus aeditumque futurae posteritati transmittentes immortalitati consecravimus. 14 Vale.

15 Ex edibus nostris Erphordiae, ad solsticium aestivale anno M.D.VIII.

---

15 Erphordiae *scripsi:* Erphordie *A.*

young fellows will follow old Sophocles' example and renounce all things erotic; and like emasculated priests of the Muses, we'll make fun of Venus as she frolics in the gardens of Epicurus.

All the same, I can practically guarantee that there will no lack of those who will brand this work of mine as obscene, however pious it is in actual fact, and will try to have it thrown out of the community of all cultured people. Somebody or other will even claim: "'Artisans handle artisan's tools.' The immoralist Eobanus promotes immorality." This is a matter that I'll leave for the learned reader to decide. If you ask me, a man can hardly be called immoral if he abhors the crime of immorality with every fiber of his being and vehemently argues against it. Let me remind the reader that this little book was written specifically to *counter* immoral love. In the knowledge, then, that it will be safe under the protection of your illustrious name, I now bring it before the public, hand it down to future generations, and consecrate it to imperishable fame. Farewell.

From my lodgings in Erfurt, at the summer solstice, 1508.[4]

---

[4]In 1508 Eobanus lived at the "Engelshaus" (Angel's house). This house was a dormitory, most likely one belonging to the Collegium Amplonianum (Porta celi), for at Erfurt all students were required to live in one of the university's residence halls or bursae. See Kleineidam, vol. 1, p. 365. Cf. *Ama.* B 1, 4 and B 3, 4 below. Petrejus Eberbach may well have lived in this bursa himself before he received the M.A. Cf. *Ama.* 4, 3 and 28, 1, where Fronto Fundinus (Petrejus himself) is said to be a former housemate of Eobanus's.

Since Petrejus's response is dated June 15 and *De amantium infoelicitate* was written in early June, the present letter must in fact have been written shortly before mid-June, just like *Ama.* B 1 (June 13) and *Ama.* B 3 (June 11). The phrase "at the summer solstice" probably indicates the time when Eobanus finished the book and sent it to the printer.

A3ʳ   **A 1**   **PETRUS EBERBACHUS, ARTIUM DOCTOR, EOBA-
NO HESSO, CANDIDISSIMO VATI, SUBSCRIPTORI
SUO RARO, SALUTEM ET FOELICITATEM.**

Est ut ais. 2 Et P. Scipionem eum, qui primum Aphricanus
appellatus est, dicere solitum scripsit Cato, pulchrum sane
et praeclarum, nunquam nos minus ociosos quam cum
ociosi. 3 Dum enim manuaria opera rei familiaris ergo obi-
mus, dum alter elementarii ludi, alter publici myropolii
negocia administramus, expoliendo ingenuis studiis animo
operam dare non possumus. 4 Quocirca nisi ad ociosum
tempus id operae reiiciamus, actum erit de studiis nostris et
evanescet virtus omnis. 5 Proinde foelices censeo quibus
hoc a diis immortalibus datum est, ut dum nihil agunt ali-
quid agant et quae nepotes admiraturi sunt praeclara moli-
antur facinora, ut tibi nuper contigit, qui in scholasticorum
laborum intermissione id operis architectatus es, quod du-
bio procul et delectabit et instituet qui nunc sunt litterarum
adsertores quique post aliis erunt in annis. 6 Quid enim iu-
cundius quam pedestri orationi mixti numeri? 7 Quid item
salubrius quam in libidinem proclivi adulescentiae ad
amplexandam virtutem, ad declinandam impudiciciam
hortamenta subministrare, qualia in tuo libro affatim extu-
berant? 8 Tantum itaque abest ut vereri debeas ne qui futuri
sint laboris tui subsannatores ut et candidissimam famam et
gratiam non vulgarem etiamnum tibi polliceri queas.
9 Quam eandem ago multo maximam quod nos in limi-
naris paginae frontispitio gestat liber et nominatim mihi
consecratus prodit in propatulum, relaturus olim quo ad
eius rei oportunitas concedetur et facultas. 10 Interea tem-
poris, quod facis, amiciciae nostrae nexum inenodabilem
custodito et vale faustiter.
    11 Ex Laterano, XVII. K. Quintil. anno DDD.VIII.

A 1 *A: om. B.*   **8** tui *scripsi* (*sic etiam manus vetus in exemplari Argent.*): rui *A.*

A 1   PETER EBERBACH, M.A., SENDS GREETINGS AND BEST WISHES TO THE UNUSUALLY GOOD-NATURED POET EOBANUS HESSUS, AN EXTRAORDINARY SUPPORTER OF HIS.

You're quite right. Publius Scipio too, the first who went by the name "Africanus," was fond of saying, as Cato tells us, that "we are never less at leisure than when we are at leisure" – a fine and splendid remark, indeed. For while the two of us are busy plying a trade to make a living, the one working in a grammar school, the other in a public pharmacy,[5] we find it impossible to devote ourselves to cultivating our mind with liberal studies. In consequence, if we didn't save such work for a time of leisure, our studies would be done for and whatever excellence we might have attained would vanish without a trace. Accordingly I regard those people as fortunate to whom the immortal gods have given the gift of keeping busy, even when they aren't busy, and of producing brilliant works that future generations will look up to with admiration. And that is precisely what you have succeeded in doing just now, during a break in your pedagogical labors. You have devised a work that, without any doubt whatsoever, will delight and profit all champions of good letters, not only those who are alive today, but also those in the years to come. What, indeed, can be more charming than a work that combines prose and verse? Likewise, what can be more salutary than exhorting young people, who are naturally inclined to wantonness, to embrace virtue and eschew lewdness? For it is with exhortations like these that your book is filled to overflowing. You need have no fear, therefore, that people will poke fun at your work. On the contrary: Even now you can count on both resplendent fame and extraordinary gratitude. I myself want to thank you from the bottom of my heart for putting my name on the very first page and sending out your book into the world expressly dedicated to me. Someday I hope to repay you for this kindness of yours, insofar as opportunity and ability permit. In the meantime, do keep up the inseverable bonds of our friendship! Farewell and good luck.

From the Lateran, 15 June 1508.

---

[5]After obtaining his M.A. in February 1508, Petrejus worked in the pharmacy that his mother operated in the "Lateran," the Eberbach family house. In his spare time he studied law.

A3ᵛ

A 2   AD LECTORES RELIGIOSOS, PALLIATOS ET SEVEROS CRITICOS EOBANUS

Si legitis vestri foelices carmina Galli
   Davidis, nihil hinc vos prohibere potest.
Scribimus et pueris et virgine digna Diana,
   Quae legat et tetricus difficilisque Cato.

A 3   V. I.

Aurea cui mens est cupidis inimica puellis
   Et sine Cyprigenae crimine vita placet,
Qui volet hymbriferae contemnere frigora noctis
   Nec dominae surdas sollicitare fores,
5   Hinc legat auxilium duraeque remedia sortis.
   Doctus in hoc Hessus codice foecit opem.

P. D.

A 2   **EOBANUS TO THE DEVOUT READERS, LITERATI,
AND STERN CRITICS**

If priests can happily read the songs of their David,
   you have no reason at all to shy away from this book.[6]
What I have written is suitable for boys and the virgin Diana.
   Even a Cato could read it, glum and morose though he is.

A 3   **CONTRIBUTED BY THAT EMINENT MAN PETER**

If you've resolved to turn your back on promiscuous girlfriends
   and know that a life of venery is not what you want,
if you don't fancy spending cold, rainy nights serenading
   the stone-deaf door of that mistress of yours,
5   here you'll find helpful remedies against that ill fortune.
   In this book the learned Hessus offers a cure.

[6]Though its subject is passionate love, Eobanus's book is as chaste as the Psalms of David.

EOBANI HESSI DE AMANTIUM INFOELICITATE, CONTRA VENEREM, DE CUPIDINIS IMPOTEN- TIA ET VERSU ET ORATIONE SOLUTA OPUS- CULUM ERPHORDIENSE

1, 1 Deambulanti mihi nuper inter saliceta, plurima cum fontium tum viridantis loci amaenitate conspicua, quibus non longe situs e regione imminebat lucus robustissimarum arborum proceritate densus, umbrositate etiam late se extendentium ramorum commendabilis, cum ad fontem, quem inibi ex patulae fagi radicibus limpide scaturientem pro consuetudine sacrum habebam, mei colligendi gratia citatiore aliquantulum gressu quasi festinabundus descenderem iamque apud summum emanantis rivuli, nescio quid cogitationis mente volvens, aliquandiu substitissem, apparuit iuvenis quidam satis decoro sed lacero vestitus amictu, capillo flavo sed inordinato, capite nudo, vultu pallido et iugi erumpentium lachrimarum discursu squallido, aspectu alioqui et oculorum acie satis venerabili. **2** Qui in sedili quod fonti proximum erat discumbens, miserabiles eiulatus ex imo pectore crebra suspiria ducens edidit. **3** Stupebam visu et quasi numine quodam lucano attonitus herebam ad vestigium. **4** Mirabar mecum, non tam efflictim quam qui maxime inopinatae visionis spectaculo perculsus mirum in modum, et accedens tandem audatior recollectis aliquantisper viribus moestum et plorabundum iuvenem hiisce verbis habunde salutans reverenter alloquebar:

2, 1 "Et quis tu, infoelix adulescens, et unde solus in has tenebricosas valles et cuius rei necessitate compulsus miser accessisti? **2** Quid tristaris? Quare ita moestus es? Quid tam querulo planctu has silentes umbras inquietanter incessis? **3** Satius tibi fuisset, importune adulescens, qui infoelicitatem tuam in solitudine gemens eo maiorem durioremque reddis quo ab hominibus es secretior, si a mortalium coetu nullibi declinasses, convictus nanque hominum curas et tristicias levat, miseris sola- | tium prebet. **4** Solitudo moeroris mater est. **5** Et ut scriptum reliquit poaetarum ingeniosissimus:

> Loca sola nocent: loca sola caveto.
> Quo fugis? In populo tutior esse potes.

Tit. Erphordiense *A: om. B.* **1, 1** Deambulanti *B:* Eambulanti *A.* citatiore *A:* citatiorem *B.* iamque *A:* cumque *B.* **1, 3** quodam *scripsi:* quoddam *AB.* **1, 4** mirum in modum *scripsi:* mirumimmodum *AB.*

ON THE WRETCHEDNESS OF LOVERS, AGAINST VENUS, ON THE UNBRIDLED FURY OF CUPID. A LITTLE WORK IN VERSE AND PROSE, WRITTEN AT ERFURT BY EOBANUS HESSUS

1 Not long ago I went for a walk among the willows that have always attracted me because of the remarkable beauty of the place, with its natural springs and its greenery. Close by, immediately across from them, rises a grove where mighty trees grow thick and tall and far-reaching branches cast pleasant shadows. Intending to take a breather there, next to the spring that bubbles up clear and fresh between the roots of a spreading beech and that I'm accustomed to hold sacred, I walked down a little faster than usual, almost in a hurry. I had been standing beside the fountainhead of a purling brook for some time already, lost in thought, when I caught sight of a young man dressed in quite elegant but tattered clothes, his hair blond but unkempt, his head bare, his face wan and smeared with the tears that burst forth in an ever-flowing stream, his demeanor and penetrating eyes nonetheless commanding a great deal of respect. Reclining on a bench that stood right next to the spring, he let out piteous wails, constantly punctuated with deep groans. I was dumfounded at the sight and, as if thunderstruck by some sylvan deity,[7] remained rooted to the spot. It was not so much a matter of my being driven to distraction, however, as being overwhelmed to an amazing degree by the spectacle of this wholly unexpected apparition. After a little while, accordingly, I regained my composure. Growing bolder, I approached the mournful, sobbing youth, greeted him profusely, and addressed him respectfully in these words:

2 "Well, who are you, unhappy young man, and what brings you here, all alone, into these shady valleys? What kind of distress impels you, poor fellow? Why are you grieving? What makes you so mournful? Why are you incessantly rending these silent shadows with such querulous laments? By bemoaning your unhappiness in solitude, unsociable youth, you make it worse and harder to bear – all the more so, the further you keep away from people. You would be better off if you didn't turn your back on society! Companionship relieves cares and sorrows; it offers consolation to those in grief. Solitude is the mother of sadness. And as that most ingenious of poets once wrote:

> Lonely places are harmful: avoid lonely places.
> Where are you fleeing? In a crowd you'll be safer by far.

---

[7]According to ancient popular belief, sylvan deities like Pan or the fauns could induce "panic" fear or drive people to distraction. Cf. Ov. *Ep.* 4, 49-50; Erasmus, *Adag.* 3, 7, 3.

6 Paratius est apud homines quam apud arbores moestitu-
dinis remedium. 7 Tu vero, adulescens, quando tempus
nobis suppetit, quando ad medii diei consuetudinem qui-
escunt animalia nec volucres quidem ipsae meridianae
taciturnitati vel minimo alarum strepitu obmurmurant,
quare huc et unde adveneris mihi securiter edicito."

3, 1 Sic effatus conticui et ex opposito fontis inter nos
mediantis latere sessum capiebam, cupidus quid ille respon-
deret arrectis auribus accepturus. 2 Ille vero perinde ut erat
subtristis suspirans plenum lachrimis vultum erexit et ex ad-
verso hebetes in me oculos coniiciens, "Tu vero," inquit,
"expectatissime Eobane, oportune mihi in tantis calamita-
tibus posito et commodum advenisti. 3 Iamdudum enim
huiusmodi quempiam qui saltem aliquid mihi quantulum-
cumque solatii afferret expectabam. 4 Quem unum te
ex omnibus electissimum esse nihil dubito. 5 Multos iam
annos vetus mihi tecum necessitudo est, nisi mente tibi for-
tasse per tantillum, quod abfui, temporis exciderim."

4, 1 Hiis ille finem loquendi faciebat. 2 Tenebar iam
totus incredibili desiderio cognoscendi hominis ubi nomi-
nari me ab incognito audiebam. 3 Et acutiore obtutu moesti
iuvenis vultum contemplatus, aliquandiu coepi agnoscere
veterem amicum et eum quidem Frontonem Fundinum,
quondam contubernalem meum, poeticum iuvenem.
4 Quem ubi eum esse non dubitabam, coepi profundius ex-
clamare:

5, 1 "Dii boni, dii nemorum sylvarumque magistri,
quid novitatis hic accipio? 2 O Fortuna, quam mirabili mor-
talium res arbitrio dispensas, volvis et revolvis! 3 Nunquam
te aequam experiuntur miseri. 4 Bonis plerumque in-
vides, malos erigis. 5 Rotae semper in omnes partes volubili
insistis. 6 Caeca tamen es atque adeo impotentiam tuam
ubivis locorum exerces. 7 Itane tu bonum et innocentem iu-
venem ex foelici infoelicissimum, ex divite pauperem tuis
ludibriis reddidisti? 8 Sed agedum, charissime Fundine, quis
te huc deorum compulit? Bonusne an cacodaemonum pessi-
mus? 9 Quis miseriae tuae finis? 10 Quid ita lacer | distorto
capillo vultum quondam formae beneficio incomparabilem
tam largo lachrimarum profluvio madidum, udum, atque
adeo deformem reddis?"

A5^r

You're more likely to obtain solace from grief among people than among trees. But since we have plenty of time on our hands, young man, since the animals are taking their siesta and not even the birds themselves are breaking the noon-time silence with the slightest flapping of wings, tell me why you're here and where you've come from. You can trust me."

3 After addressing him like this I fell silent and took a seat on the other side of the spring that flowed between us and waited eagerly, with my ears pricked up, to see how he would respond. At this, looking pretty dejected, he let out a deep sigh. Then, raising his tearful face and casting dull glances at me from the opposite side, he cried: "I'm so glad you came, Eobanus! You've certainly arrived at a perfect time for me, given the terrible misfortune I'm in. As a matter of fact, I've long been waiting for somebody like you to offer me at least a shred of consolation. Don't doubt for a minute that of all my friends you're the one dearest to me! We've been old comrades for many years already. Or have you perhaps forgotten me in the short time that I've been gone?"

4 With this he stopped talking. I was already seized with overwhelming desire to get to know the man, when I heard my name mentioned by this complete stranger. But as I looked more closely at the disconsolate youth's face, I gradually began to recognize him as my old friend – in fact, as Fronto Fundinus, a former housemate of mine, a poetically gifted young man.[8] As soon as I was sure it was he, I burst out in loud exclamations:

5 "Good heavens! Gods of the groves and lords of the forests, what is this news I'm hearing! O Fortune, by what freakish whims do you control the affairs of us mortals, whirling and roiling everything around! Never yet have poor wretches found you to be evenhanded. Mostly you're just jealous of good people, lifting up the bad ones instead. You stand on a wheel that is perpetually turning, in every sense of the word. All the same, you're blind. Or rather, you exercise your fury anywhere you please. Didn't you just now in your capriciousness change this good and blameless youth from a happy fellow to a most unhappy one, from a wealthy man to a pauper? But go on, my dear Fundinus! What god brought you to this pass? A good one or the worst of the evil demons? What's going to come of all your misery? Why are you so tattered? Why is your hair so disheveled? And your face, which used to be incomparably handsome – why do you drench it and soak it and totally disfigure it with such a copious outpouring of tears?"

---

[8]He may be identified as the book's dedicatee Petrejus Eberbach. See the introduction. Though Petrejus's love affair was doubtless real enough, we should be careful not to take Eobanus's caricature as reflecting the actual course of events in all particulars. The scandalous detail that Fulvia was a prostitute, for example, is evidently taken over from Aeneas Silvius's "Amoris illiciti medela." See n. *Ama.* 11, 12 – 12, 4.

6, 1 Vix eo loquendo progressus eram, cum ille plura dicturum preveniens medium sermonem interrupit et, "Noli," inquit, "Eobane, Fortunam longius accusare! 2 Surdo fabulam canis. 3 Caecam dixisti. Surda etiam est, non audit imo. 4 Ut iam audiat, non tamen exaudit miserorum innocentiam. 5 Illa me iamdudum in mille pericula et vitae et corporis redactum nondum vel minima sperati fruitione consolatur."

6 "Quid igitur speras?" inquam ego. "Cuius rei fruitione consolari desideras?"

7 Tum ille aliquantopere altius ingemiscens, "Quoniam ita fert occasio," respondit, "mi Eobane, multum certe consolationis adeptus videor. 8 Et profecto non fallor – talis enim qualem te nunc experiri cupio mihi ab ineunte aetate semper extitisti – si te meae infoelicitatis arcana non caelavero. 9 Audi igitur et diligenter audi, miserabilem amici fortunam accipies." 10 Atque haec dicens totus in lachrimas effluebat, singultientem animam crebris planctibus percutiens.

7, 1 Extorsit mihi quoque punctim lachrimas lugubris amici habitus. 2 Cuius tandem lachrymis oppido commotus, ipse quoque plorabundus sic inquiebam: "Fundine, nisi consolatione egeres, ego te tanquam amiciciae nostrae prevaricatorem apud te ipsum accusarem, qui tam diu tuos acerbissimos affectus mihi occultare voluisti. 3 Perge igitur et eloquere audacter, nihil amicum caeles."

4 At ille, "Inhonesta," inquit, "res est quam enarrare coram te constitui."

5 Cui ego, "Inhonesta non secus quam honesta cum amico sunt communicanda."

6 Hic ille composito aliquantisper animi turbine, "Eobane," inquit, "si diis placuisset, iamdudum morte vitam meam occupari optassem atque hac una via laboris mei requiem adeptus fuissem. 7 Mors miseris quam vita est iucundior. 8 Ita in extremum redactus sum! 9 Heu me miserum, quo deveni? In quas syrtes incidi? Quis me hinc deorum eripiet? 10 Perditus sum! In amorem sed infortunatum, sed immitem, sed infoelicissimum miser incidi."

11 Mox ego: "Huiusmodi quippiam ex tam turbulento vultu suspicabar. 12 Sed perge, obsecro. Quo nam incidisti?"

6, 5 vitae et *A*: vite *B*.   7, 10 immitem *B*: immittem *A*.

6 I had scarcely gotten this far in my speech when he, cutting off further questions, broke in: "Stop accusing Fortune, Eobanus! You're singing to deaf ears anyway. You called her blind just now. She's also deaf; or rather, she won't listen. And even if she did listen, she doesn't care a fig if the people she's made wretched are blameless or not. She's plunged me into so many dangers for life and limb already that I've lost count. Yet she has never once offered to cheer me up by letting me enjoy even a little of what I've been hoping for."

"What are you hoping for, then?" I asked. "What do you long to enjoy before you can be cheered up?"

He sighed rather more deeply at this and replied: "Since chance has brought us together, my dear Eobanus, it would seem that I've indeed found a great source of consolation. I certainly won't make a mistake if I go ahead and tell you the secret story of my unhappiness, for ever since boyhood you've been the sort of confidant that I'd like you to be for me now. Hear me out, therefore, and pay close attention as you learn more about your friend's misfortune." Even as he spoke these words, he completely dissolved in tears, again and again piercing his sobs with loud laments.

7 My friend's mournful appearance also stabbed me to the heart and wrung tears from me. After some time, profoundly moved by his weeping, I too spoke with a tear-choked voice: "Fundinus, if you weren't so much in need of consolation, I'd accuse you to your face of violating the sacred trust of our friendship, because you've wanted to keep your bitterest feelings hidden from me for so long. Go on, then, and feel free to tell me what is on your mind. Don't conceal anything from your friend."

But he objected, "The story I've resolved to tell you is not an honorable one."

"The dishonorable," I rejoined, "should be shared with one's friend no less than the honorable."

Hereupon the turmoil in his breast calmed down for a while. "Eobanus," he said, "if it had pleased the gods, I would have long since prayed for death – the only way for me to find relief from my suffering. To a heartbroken man, death is a lot more agreeable than life. That's how desperate I am! Alas, alas! What's to become of poor me? On what shoals have I run aground? What god will come to my rescue? I'm lost! Miserable wretch that I am, I've fallen in love – unfortunate, unrequited, most unhappy love!"

"I suspected something like that from your troubled look," I answered. "But go on, please. How did you end up in this mess?"

8, 1 Tum ille, "Clavo," inquit, "Cupidinis transfixus sum. 2 Animus meus mecum non est, | verum apud fores amatae heret perdius et pernox. 3 Dii boni, quantum Amoris est imperium! 4 Sentio poaetas nihil errasse qui omnipotentem dixerunt Amorem. 5 Certe verum est: 'Regnat et in superos ius habet ille deos.' 6 'Improbe Amor, quid non mortalia pectora cogis!' 7 Multos iam dies per haec invia lustra, per hos densissimos vepres infoelix erro, lacer et informis. 8 Totos dies hac atque illac errabundus querelis continuis et ululatibus incessanter discurro recurroque non intermissa requie. 9 Noctes insomnes ago. 10 Et si aliquando (quod mihi rarissime usu venit) defessos ex nimia lachrymarum effusione oculos somnus contexerit,

9   Occurrunt variae quasi somnia vana figurae
       Perturbantque animum incutiuntque metum.
    Inter serpentes, apros, avidosque leones
       Iactor et esuros cerno per ossa canes.
5   Aucupor in viridi mendaces cespite somnos;
       Dum careo veris gaudia falsa iuvant.
    Seu lateat Phoebus seu terris altior extet,
       Hec mihi luce dolor, hec mihi nocte venit.

10, 1 "Inde ubi evigilo, 'nunc huc, nunc illuc et utroque sine ordine curro,' pallidus, macer, et ieiunus sylvestribus tantum cibis, arbutis, nucibus, locustis, et simplicis undae haustu contentus. 2 Eo usque me redegit Amoris impacientia. 3 O foelix, quisquis talia non pateris! 4 Certe gravissimus morborum est amor, et eo gravior quo minus optato frui conceditur. 5 Quod ego mortalium infoelicissimus habunde nunc experior, cui neque spei quippiam amplius neque refugii superest. 6 Quid faciam miser? Quo me divertam? Quid consilii sumam? 7 Quippe cum omnia denegentur, mortis occasio denegari michi certe non potest. 8 Infoelicissimorum amantium numero adscribar. 9 Pyramus gladio se interemit, eodem Thysbe. 10 Phyllis laqueo vitam perdidit. Dido super ensem Troianum animam profudit. Sappho se in Leucada praecipitem dedit. 11 Quid mirum si illi ita et innumeri alii miserabiliter perierunt! 12 Certe maius est Amoris quam vitae imperium."

11, 1 Non potui non commoveri ad lachrymas haec audiens. 2 Et tandem, "Novi," inquam," quae sint Cupidinis

---

10, 5 quippiam *A*: quispiam *B*.

8 Hereupon he said: "I've been pierced with Cupid's spike. My soul is no longer with me. Instead, it haunts the doors of the beloved day and night. Good heavens, how great is the power of Love! I recognize that poets are in no way deluded when they call Love omnipotent. It's true beyond all doubt: 'Even the gods on high are subject to his whims.' 'Cruel Love, to what lengths do you force the human heart!' Day after day I've been wandering through these pathless woods, through these tangled brambles, miserable, tattered, and disfigured. For days on end I've been roaming aimlessly hither and yon, constantly lamenting, incessantly wailing, without a respite or pause. The nights I spend sleepless. And if from time to time – something I've only rarely given in to – sleep envelops my eyes, worn out as they are with the profuse flow of tears,

9   All kinds of nightmarish shapes rise up to confront me
       and trouble my soul and inspire me with dread.
    I toss and turn among snakes, wild boars, and ravenous lions;
       in my mind's eye, hounds are set to gnaw at my bones.
5   On the greensward I lie in wait for dreams that show my beloved;
       while true joys fail me, counterfeit pleasures enchant.
    Whether Phoebus is hidden or stands high in the heavens,
       she grieves me by day, she accosts me by night.

10 "Then, when I wake up, 'I run back and forth, at random, in every direction.' Pallid, gaunt, and hungry, I eat only such food as the forest has to offer, arbute berries, nuts, and locusts, and content myself with a drink of plain water. That's the state to which Love's fury has reduced me. Oh, you're lucky not to suffer like this! Love is surely the most grievous of diseases, all the harder to bear, the less one has the chance to enjoy what one longs for. Most wretched of men that I am, I'm now finding this out by hard experience, for I have no hope left at all, no refuge. What am I poor fellow to do? Where should I turn to? What should I decide? Of course, if all else fails, nobody can stop me from finding a way to die, that's for sure. Then I'll be reckoned among the most unfortunate of lovers. Pyramus committed suicide with his sword; so did Thisbe. Phyllis hanged herself. Dido breathed her last over the Trojan sword. Sappho threw herself from the cliff of Leucas.[9] It's no wonder that they and countless others perished miserably like this! Clearly, Love has greater power than life."

11 When I heard him say these things, I could not help but be moved to tears. At long last I answered: "I know all about Cupid's power! Not just once

---

[9]The tragic story of Pyramus and Thisbe is told in Ov. *Met.* 4, 55-166. Phyllis hanged herself after waiting in vain for her lover Demophoon to return; see Ov. *Ep.* 2. Dido committed suicide with Aeneas's sword; see Verg. *A.* 4, 663-665 and Ov. *Ep.* 7, 181-196. And Sappho, in despair at losing her lover Phaon, leaped off the promontory of Leucas; see Ov. *Ep.* 15.

vires, qui non semel, sed sepissime perduxit amantes ad obitus miserabiles. 3 Quibus te Amoris pedicis illaqueatum ita sentio | ut neque regredi possis neque lachrymas ullo pacto inhibere. 4 Quare huic malo quantum licet occurrendum est. 5 Commovit me non mediocriter, ut de aliis taceam, hoc quod ultimo de infoelici amoris exitu recensuisti, infoelicissimorum amantium numero te adscribi velle affirmans. 6 O inconsultam dementiam! 7 Tune, carissime Fundine, ita mente omnino alienatus es ut mori ex amoris impatientia mavelis quam vivere et animam simul et corpus in precipitium dare quam salvari et esse cum foelicibus? 8 Noli, obsecro, ita delirare! 9 Stultissimum est ex unius corpusculi cupiditate preciosissimum humani corporis animam negligere. 10 An ignoras te, si mortem ipse tibi consciseres, perpetuas apud inferni Plutonis familiam poenas daturum? 11 Linque istas enormes et phanaticas cogitaciones! Ad te ipsum redi et mihi te interroganti pro sententia responde. 12 Valde enim dubito virginemne an coniugatam ames."

12, 1 "Neutram illarum," inquit ille.

2 At ego, "Viduam igitur?"

3 "Nec eam quidem," respondit.

4 Cui ego, "Prostitutamne tam efflictim quispiam deperierit?"

5 "Ita eam comperi," refert ille.

6 Et quo nam pacto hoc evenisset quom scissitarer, ille iterum effuse lachrymans inquit: "Nostin Fulviam, illam civem utriusque nostrum, corporis formositate Veneri ipsi equiparandam, animi etiam dotibus spectabilem, eloquentem, callidam, doctam ad decipiendas animas, bonae etiam et integerrimae famae sed pauperculam?"

7 "Novi," inquam.

8 Tum ille ulterius ita: "Hanc ubi effusis continentiae habenis supra humanae affectionis modum adamarem, putans vicissim me amari, in qua re cum mihi vehementer applauderem, consumpsi et prodigaliter ad arbitrium dominae expendi quicquid ex paternis mihi bonis suppetebat. 9 Illa mihi quottidie petulantius efferebatur, quottidie ornatior incedebat. 10 Nunc enim pectine compta et distincta gemmis coma, nunc calamistro crispati et involuti auro crines oculos meos insaciabili ardore alliciebant, nunc pendentes a collo margaritae. 11 Nunc fasciis artatum pectus

---

11, 8 delirare *A*: delirari *B*.

but exceedingly often he's brought lovers to a miserable end. I sense that you are so hopelessly caught in the snares of Love that you can neither go back nor in any way restrain your tears. That leaves us with only one way out: we have got to come to grips with this disease, as far as possible. To say nothing about the rest, I am deeply troubled by what you were telling me about the ultimate outcome of unhappy love and by your assertion that you want to be reckoned among the most unfortunate of lovers. Oh, the crazy lunacy! Have you, my dear Fundinus, gone so utterly mad that you would prefer to die for the frenzy of love rather than go on living, or that you would cast body and soul into perdition rather than be saved and remain with those who are happy? Stop raving like this, I beseech you! It is the height of folly, out of lustful desire for a single wench to neglect what is most precious in the human body – our soul. Don't you know that if you commit suicide you will suffer everlasting punishment in the Devil's household? Drop these preposterous and frenzied thoughts! Return to your senses and answer my questions, as you see fit. For example, I'm completely in the dark as to whether the girl you love is unmarried or married."

12 "Neither one," he replied.

"Is she a widow, then?" I asked.

"Not that either."

"Is it possible that somebody could be so smitten with a prostitute?"

"I didn't find out until later," he stammered.

When I inquired how that might have come about, he said, crying disconsolately again: "Do you know Fulvia, the girl who lives in our town? In bodily beauty she's a match for Venus herself. She's intellectually gifted too, articulate, crafty, expert at duping people. As for a good and unblemished reputation, however, she's as poor as they come."

"Yes, I know her," I answered.

Then he went on: "She's the one I've fallen in love with, letting my passion go unbridled, far beyond the limits of ordinary affection, for I was sure she returned my love. But even as I vigorously congratulated myself on this success, I squandered all my patrimony – everything I could lay my hands on – and spent it prodigally at my mistress's whim. From day to day she grew more high-handed and insolent toward me; from day to day she would walk around more ostentatiously adorned. Sometimes it was the way she did up her hair with a comb and set it off with precious stones that would attract my eyes with insatiable ardor; sometimes it was the way she curled her locks with tongs and bound them up with a gold clasp; at other times it was her pearl necklace. Sometimes she'd wear a tight bra to push up her swelling breasts,

tumentes exprimens mamillas, quas plerumque subtilissimis
et perspicuis sudariolis quasi aranearum taelis contexerat, ut
quod appeti volebat id occultari velle videretur, nunc un-
guentis, nunc cerussa purpurissoque | ac aliis fucis affecta et
linita facies imprudentem me et incautum in amoris laby-
rinthum inextricabilem adeo deduxit, imo (ut verius loquar)
seduxit, ut exire hinc vel nulla arte, nulla etiam alarum per-
nicitate liceat. 12 O utinam vel saltem aliquid remedii mihi
afferre posset Iuppiter immortalis!"

13, 1 Tum ego, "Quod," inquam, "tibi verbum excidit
Iovem immortalem, huic tantillo malo mederi posse diffidis.
2 Qualis haec est insipientia? 3 Ita caecus est omnis amans
ut deorum etiam potestatem unius animae voluntati post-
ponere nihil dubitet."

14, 1 "Preterea," inquit ille, "ubi iam sepius mihi sui
copiam foecisset, ex quo me foelicem esse putabam et ego
pauper factus, non haberem unde perniciosum amorem
pascerem. 2 Immanissimo dolore affectus et quasi furioso
percitus oestro, quottidie me ubicunque occasione oblata
puellae oculis obiiciens per amicae viciniam debachabar,
aedes circuibam, conabar et videri et haberi non modo ele-
gantior, verumetiam praestantior ac dignior. 3 Illa vero
crudelis magno et elato animo, rigido vultu, torvis oculis,
inimica fronte me respiciens se amantem me neglexit tan-
quam pecudem. 4 Clamore insuper ac maledictis quoties
pristinae consuetudinis vestigium insequi conabar, tan-
quam indignum qui se tangeret repulit. 5 Ego hoc in-
telligens, diffamatum me apud amicam putans, accessi
talibus eam verbis ultro compellans:

6 "'Eya, unicum meae iuventutis refugium, electum mei
cordis habitaculum, mea lux! Animi propter te languentis
unicum solatium, mea hera, mea imperatrix! 7 Quis tam sae-
vus inter nos et tam iniquus mediator extitit? Quis voluit
mihi te eripere? 8 Gaude et revivisce, meum suavium! 9 Tuus
totus sum. Nulla pellice – quod falso tibi suggessisse quem-
piam cacodaemonum cacozelum suspicor – tuum amorem
offendi aut unquam offensurus sum, quo ad vita utrique
nostrum concedetur. 10 Redi nunc mecum in gratiam, mea
suavitas, meum delicium! 11 Noli tam miserabiliter cruciare
te plus quam oculos suos amantem. 12 Age, iterum iun-

14, 1 quo me *A*: quo *B*.

though she generally covered them with see-through lace as delicate as a spider's web, so she would appear to be concealing what in fact she wanted me to desire. Sometimes she'd anoint her face with cold creams and make up her cheeks with ceruse, rouge, and other cosmetics. With these charms, naive fool that I was, she induced me, or rather (to be honest with you) seduced me to enter so deeply into the inextricable labyrinth of love that I found it impossible to escape from it, either by guile or on swift wings.[10] Oh, if only immortal Jupiter could offer me some kind of cure!"

13 At this I exclaimed: "Though you let the words 'immortal Jove' slip out, you really don't expect him to cure you of this petty disease of yours. What kind of nonsense is this? But then every lover is so blind that he doesn't hesitate for a moment to regard even the gods' power as inferior to the will of the one angel he worships."

14 "On top of that," he went on, "after she had already let me enjoy her quite often, which made me feel happy even as it was turning me into a pauper, I no longer had the wherewithal to feed my ruinous passion. Afflicted with horrible grief and stirred up, as it were, by a maddening gadfly, I spent every day hoping to catch the girl's attention, whenever I had a chance. I raved around my sweetheart's neighborhood, continually circling her house while trying hard to look like a dandy and putting on terribly aristocratic and dignified airs. The cruel girl, however, looked down on me with overweening pride, a stern expression, glaring eyes, a hostile mien, and took no more notice of me, her lover, than of a beast. Not only that, but whenever I yelled and cursed at her in my attempts to resume my intimacies with her, she would push me away as if I weren't worthy of touching her. Once I realized this, I imagined that somebody must have slandered me to my girlfriend. Hence I confronted her and spoke to her as follows:

"'Hey, sole refuge of my youth, chosen dwelling place of my heart, my light! One and only solace of my soul that's pining away for you, my fair lady, my empress! Who is the savage and spiteful person that has driven a wedge between us? Who has been wanting to snatch you away from me? Be glad and cheer up, my darling! I'm yours, heart and soul. Believe me, there's no other woman in my life – some caricature of a devil, I imagine, must have put that notion into your head. I have never cheated on you, nor will I ever cheat on your love as long as we two are alive. Now let's kiss and make up, my dearest, my angel! Don't inflict such hellish torments on one who loves you more

---

[10]Unlike Daedalus, who escaped from the Labyrinth in Crete by fashioning wings for himself and his son Icarus, the lover has no way of extricating himself.

gamus nobis communes delicias, solitis nos amplexibus dulciter oblectemur.'

15, 1 "Hiis et pluribus aliis verbis tam longis quam flebilibus nihil profeci. | 2 Operam omnem perdidi. 3 Illa vero, ut me totum suis laqueis irretitum intellexit, magis superbivit tanquam imperiosa domina in abiectae sortis commune mancipium atque talibus me aliquando verbis increpabat:

4 "'Abi hinc in malam rem, cunnilinge, et quotquot volueris tibi pellices in mei invidiam compara! 5 Ego te non amo nec amavi unquam tui quippiam preter tuberis marsupii largam aperitionem. 6 Hac ubi privatus es, vade procul, gloriose amator! 7 Scio enim quantum gloriaberis te a me amari. 8 Iamdudum mihi tributarius fuisti ut alios inde te mihi multo chariores inter delicias et voluptatis officia reservarem. 9 Nihil est quapropter amplexus nostros deinceps sperare debeas, quos hactenus non ut amicae, sed ut insidiantis inimicae sacros habuisti.'

16, 1 "Hiis ego conviciis et opprobriis contemptum me et decoeptum videns – heu, nimis sero! – pedem invitus retuli. 2 Tabescebam prae dolore, nescius quid facerem quidve primum aggrederer. 3 Res patefacta erat omnibus, nec enim tantum dolorem dissimulare potui, quin amicis id suo iure contendentibus rem omnem ut erat ex ordine recenserem. 4 Deridebant me non nulli tanquam insanum et dementem, utpote qui communi et mercennariae Veneris sacerdoti tantum amoris impenderim. 5 At ego communem ignorabam. 6 Nunc tandem cum maximo et corporis mei et illustris famae detrimento expertus sum. 7 Et adhuc sub Amoris dominio versor, sub Cupidinis imperio impatientissimam militiam ago, ut cernis, ut vides. 8 Heu me miserum! Utinam deorum aliquis mihi vitam eriperet!"

9 Hec ubi dixisset, dextro cubito vultum excipiens, discurrentes ex oculis lachrimas more profluvii cuiusdam pluvialis a summo vertice cadentis profusissime emittebat.

17, 1 Trahebat me ad misericordiam flebilis amici status, cogitabamque quo nam modo aegrotantem animum ad seipsum revocarem. 2 Lunatoque mox utroque poplite utraque manu utramque fontis ripam apprehendens, os ad vivi laticis exitum applicans, summis labris summum fontis ad satietatem ebibi, hausto deinde concava manu quantum

16, 2 prae *scripsi:* pre *A,* p̃ *B.*

than his own eyes. Come on, let's have some fun together again. Let's enjoy each other's embraces, the way we used to.'

15 "With these and many other words, as long-winded as they were plaintive, I got nowhere with her. It was an utter waste of time. However, when the girl saw how thoroughly I was caught in her snares, she grew even haughtier, like an imperious lady at a common slave of the lowest degree, and finally screamed at me:

"'Get the hell out of here, you cunt-licker! Keep as many mistresses as you like, just to spite me, and see if I care! I don't give a damn about you. The only thing I ever liked about you is the way you kept your bulging purse wide open. Now that you're broke, you can shove off, you braggart lover! See, I know exactly how you went around bragging that I'd fallen for you. You've been giving me expensive presents for a long time now, and what for? So I could keep other men around who are far dearer to me and much better lovers too! There's no reason in the world to expect snuggles from me anymore. Sure, you've always adored sex with me – not as if I were your friend, but a tricky enemy.'

16 "Seeing myself scorned with insults and taunts like these and finding myself deceived – alas, far too late! – I returned home, dragging my feet. I was pining away with grief, not knowing what to do or what my next step should be. The incident became the talk of the town, for I was unable to keep so great a heartache to myself. Indeed, when my friends insisted they had a right to hear it from my own lips, I told them the whole story from beginning to end. Quite a few of them made fun of me, calling me insane and raving mad, given that I had fallen head over heels in love with a whore, a hired priestess of Venus. But I never knew she was a whore. Only then did I finally learn the truth, to the greatest detriment of my body as well as my good name. And even now I live under the rule of Love – serving in Cupid's army and performing the most intolerable duties, as you can see and hear for yourself. Alas, poor me! If only one of the gods would snuff out my life!"

When he had finished, he laid his face on his right elbow and let the tears stream from his eyes like some torrent tumbling down a mountainside after a downpour.

17 My friend's lamentable condition moved me to pity, and so I tried to think of a way to restore his lovesick soul to itself. Before long I went down on my knees, grasped both sides of the spring with each hand, and brought my mouth to the source of the bubbling water. With lips just barely touching the surface of the fountain, I drank to my heart's content. Then I scooped up as

aquae unius palmae circumflexu continere potui sudorem
vultus abluebam. 3 Et ut idem ipse faceret rogitabam, scom-
mate verbum prosequtus: "Agedum, Fundi- | ne, aquam
sume ut amoris incendium extinguas. 4 Ego enim contra
flammarum impetus quam aquam vidi nihil efficatius."

18, 1 Hic ille, licet extremo moerore confectus, semota
paululum frontis caligine tenuiter subridens, "Cavillaris,"
inquit, "ut soles, Eobane. 2 Iucundus certe es, tua nanque
consuetudine dum foelix adhuc inter mortales agerem nihil
mihi fuit iucundius."

3 "Quasi autem nunc inter mortuos agas," inquam ego.

4 Tum ille: "Anne is tibi videtur infoelix et a mortalium
commertio destitutus et quasi demortuus, qui sub arbitrio
superbae mulieris constitutus perpetuis cruciatur affectibus,
qui sui omnino impos, ignito Cupidinis currui alligatus,
omnem secum miseriam trahit? 5 Meo iuditio satius est
agere animam quam invitum aura vitali vesci. 6 Is autem
omnino invitus inter mortales agit qui misere amat, qui op-
tato nequit frui, cui et foelicitati ita interdictum est ut ne
sperare quidem foelicem eventum audeat. 7 Nihil est eo mi-
serabilius qui ita vivit ut mortem optare videatur. 8 Profecto
ita despecti amantes vivimus – si modo quispiam ita, ut ego,
amavit unquam. 9 Vivit et semper moritur qui amat."

19, 1 Hic ego medium sermonem interrumpens, "Ac-
quiesce," inquam, "hiis, Fundine, nec te tam infoelicem
existimes ut restitui tibi non possis. 2 Nemo in hoc mundo
adeo infoelix esse potest, quin foelix iterum si velit fieri pos-
sit. 3 Omnes miseri sumus, quotquot vivimus. 4 Con-
solatione egemus diversi diversimode. 5 Sperare tamen, non
desperare iubemur. 6 Etenim sperandum est vivis. Non est
spes ulla sepultis. 7 Sperare debes, ne (quod turpissimum est)
in desperationem cadas. 8 Contemnere te contemnentem
assuesce. 9 Nihil stultius est quam eos amare qui in nostram
perniciem vigilant. 10 Et quis sapiens inimico suo faveat?
11 Haec tibi quam amas inimica est et multos insuper tibi
inimicos peperit. 12 Animam tuam in precipitium aegit, in
laqueos coniecit, in puteum Acherontis detrudere etiam
voluit. 13 Et tu huic faves! 14 Corporis tui vires enervavit, in-
genium minuit, memoriam destruxit, mentem alienavit,
animum suspendit, miserabili teipsum vulnere affecit. 15 Ex

much water as I could hold in the hollow of one hand and used it to wash the sweat off my face. After repeatedly urging him to do likewise, I added jokingly: "Come on, Fundinus, have a drink of water to put out the fire of love. For against raging flames I personally see nothing more effective than water."

18 Though he was crushed by deepest sorrow, the gloom clouding his brow lifted just a little at this. Smiling wanly he answered: "You're jesting as usual, Eobanus. You're fun to be with, that's for sure. Indeed, when I was still living happily among human beings, I found nothing more delightful than your company."

"As if you're living among the dead now!" I retorted.

"Don't you think," he replied, "that a man may be rightly called unhappy, cut off from human society, and hence as good as dead if he's subject to the whims of a scornful woman and tormented by unremitting passions – if he's completely out of his mind, if he's chained to Cupid's fiery chariot[11] and forced to drag all his misery along? In my judgment, it is better to give up the ghost than to go on drawing the breath of life against one's will. But a man lives totally against his will among his fellows when he's desperately in love, when he can't enjoy what he longs for and is so down on his luck that he doesn't even dare hope for a happy outcome. There is nothing more wretched than living in the hope of dying. Without question that is the kind of despicable life we lovers live – assuming there has ever been one who has loved as deeply as I do. You're always living and dying when you're in love."

19 As he said this, I couldn't help but cut in: "Resign yourself to your lot, Fundinus, and don't think you're so unfortunate that you can't be restored to yourself. Nobody in this world can be so unhappy that he can't become happy again if he wants to. Sooner or later we all get our hearts broken. Everybody needs consolation, each in his own way. Still, we're enjoined to keep on hoping, not to give in to despair. And indeed as long as there's life, there ought to be hope. Only the dead are beyond hope. You ought to keep your hopes up, so you won't make the truly disgusting mistake of falling into despair. Get used to the idea of despising someone who despises you. Nothing can be more foolish than to be in love with people who are on the lookout for a chance to ruin us. Besides, what rational person would side with his own enemy? That woman you're so infatuated with, she's your enemy and has made you a lot of enemies to boot. She has thrown your soul down from on high, cast it into bonds, and even wanted to plunge it into the pit of hell. And you go right on adoring her! She has enervated your physical strength, impaired your intellect, ruined your memory, deprived you of sanity, kept your hopes dangling, broken your heart. She has changed you from a rich man to a

---

[11] That is, as one of the captives in Cupid's triumphal procession.

B2ʳ

divite pauperem, ex sano aegrum, ex animoso et laeto tristem, ex prudente insanum te, et – quod precipue detestari debes – ex homine bestiam | fecit. 16 Et tu huic faves! 17 Nescis quid facias, miser. 18 Nulla maior stulticia est quam nescire quid facias. 19 Erras, incaute. Non vides quorsum per hoc scopulosum iter ambulans tandem deventurus sis. 20 Nemo magis errat quam qui errorem suum non cognoscit. 21 Refer pedem, dum potes, ab imminenti interitu! Cohibe, imprudens, vestigium! 22 Sapiens viator quo vadat agricolas iuxta viam rus colentes consulit. 23 Tu vero cum multos recti itineris duces habeas deviare mavis et per abrupta montium cum labore solus fatigari, quam cum multis per amaenum et iucundum iter ad foelicem campum pervenire. 24 Tu per abrupta vadis ad interitum, cum per planum ingressus pateat ad aeternam requiem.

20, 1 "Sed quid in amfractibus et velatis sentenciis remoram nobisipsis facimus, cum amoris incommoda et mala ad oculos aperte et quasi in tabella depicta habeamus? 2 Chymeram poetae fingunt habere virgineum caput, caprinum ventrem, caudam serpentinam. 3 Huic amorem prisci illi literarum antistites similem dixerunt, et meo iudicio recte quidem et sapientissime. 4 Caput virgineum habet, hoc est iucundum et delectabile initium. 5 Foelices nobis videmur ubi amare incipimus. 6 Ubi amari nos ex aliqua, licet exigua parte intelligimus, eo nihil optabilius nobis esse ducimus. 7 Libenter hoc iugum patimur dum suave adhuc et toleratu non nimis difficile. 8 Nobis applaudimus; omnia stulte, nihil sapienter agimus, dum nobis sapientes videmur. 9 Ita iuvenes perverso sumus iudicio. 10 Ubi amare incipimus, insanire discimus. 11 Atque ita maior pars perdiscimus, ut dediscere tam commune cuiuscumque et sexus et aetatis vitium nunquam vel cum maxima difficultate vix possimus.

21, 1 "Tum nobis pulchra res videtur amor, qui tum virginea pulchrum caput arte figurat. 2 Ubi vero ad medium devenerimus, caprinum, hoc est immundum, sordidum, olidumque tanquam pecus offendimus. 3 Quid enim sordidius, quid foedius quam continuo et sine intermissione inter voluptates muliebres, inanes ac molles illecebras, impudicos meretricum amplexus tam deformes quam turpes vitam bestialem ducere? 4 Et profecto mea sententia nihil peius, nihil etiam homini turpius quam cum bestiis vitam

19, 24 per planum *A*: planum *B*.

pauper, from a man bursting with health to one who is pining away, from a spirited, happy youth to a lovelorn wretch, from a prudent person to a madman, and – what you ought to loathe most of all – from a human being to a beast. And you go right on adoring her! You don't know what you're doing, poor chap. It is the height of folly not to know what you're doing. You've gone astray without even knowing it. You don't see where this rocky road is going to take you in the end. No one goes further astray than the man who doesn't realize that he's strayed. Step back from the brink of death, while you still can! Stop, imprudent fellow, before it's too late! A seasoned traveler asks for directions from the peasants who till the land along his way. You, to be sure, have many people who point you in the right direction; and yet you prefer to wander off the road all by yourself and wear yourself out with great travail on steep mountain paths rather than walk with the crowds on a charming and delightful road to reach the land of bliss. You clamber over sheer cliffs to your death, when there is a road over level ground that will take you straight into eternal peace.

20 "But why beat around the bush with dark conceits, when we have a clear picture of love's troubles and woes right before our eyes, in the form of an emblem, so to speak? The poets tell us that the Chimera has the head of a maiden, the body of a goat, and the tail of a serpent. In this monster those ancient high priests of literature saw the very image of passionate love – quite rightly too, in my judgment, and most wisely. It has a girl's head, that is to say, it looks comely and delightful at first. We imagine we're happy when we fall in love. When we notice that our love is requited, be it ever so slightly, we think we're in the seventh heaven. We gladly bear this yoke, as long as it's still pleasant and not too hard to put up with. We congratulate ourselves; we do everything foolishly and nothing wisely, though we fancy ourselves wise. That's how wrong-headed we young people are. The minute we fall in love, we learn to go crazy. It's a lesson most of us learn only too well, which is why this vice is endemic in every sex and age group and why unlearning it proves either impossible or at best extremely difficult for us.

21 "At this stage, love still seems to us a thing of beauty; at this stage, it still artfully presents the beautiful head of a maiden. But once we get down to the middle, we run into what might be called the goat's body, that is, the dirty, filthy, and so to speak bestially stinking part. For what can be more filthy and disgusting than to surround oneself continually and incessantly with the pleasures of women, to give in to false and flabby allurements, to have intercourse with prostitutes, whose unchaste embraces are as degrading as they are shameful, and in this way to lead a swinish life? There is no doubt about it in my mind: the worst and most disgraceful thing a man can do is to

habere communem. | **5** In hoc homo ceteris animantibus praestat ut rationem, non libidinem vitae ducem habeat. **6** In amoris vero medio libido vitae regimen occupat.

22, 1 "Expertum habemus eos qui nunquam Veneris officium exercuerunt, de quibus non immerito dici potest tanquam de innocentibus olim pueris, 'Hii sunt qui cum mulieribus non sunt coinquinati,' formosos esse, fortes, magnanimos, ingeniosos, ac boni odoris spiritum habere, quales olim nostrates Germanorum pueros fuisse legimus, quibus ante vicesimum annum mulieribus quoquo modo copulari nefas erat. **2** Nunc vero ante decimum, nedum vicesimum aetatis annum et sciunt, faciunt, et loquntur turpia. **3** Ita Germanica virtus exolevit, quae nos omnibus olim nationibus longe praetulit. **4** Exolevit, inquam, Germanica virtus, 'quandoquidem luxus nos tenet Italicus.' **5** Longe enim aliam quam nunc est Germaniam priscis fuisse temporibus cum plures alii tum precipue Cornelius Tacitus testis est nostrarum antiquitatum refertissimus. **6** Scripsit post eum Conradus Celtis nostras, poeta laureatus, homo uti in omni scientiarum genere eruditissimus ita Germanicae vetustatis inquisitor diligentissimus (cuius manes nuper apud sodalitatem Latinae fraternitatis versibus extemporaliter deductis et venerati sumus reverenter et pro communi studiosorum iactura deploravimus): **7**

> Mos erat uxori castum servasse cubile,
> > Ut framea et sonipes constitit ante fores.
> Tunc firmus iuvenis robustam corpore prolem
> > Sustulit et matris pastus ab uberibus.
> 5 Arborei foetus et, agrestia munera, caules
> > Et rapum teneris faucibus esca fuit.
> Pars hominum glandes, placidas pars maxima fagos,
> > Et Cererem festa non nisi lance dabant.

22, 1 annum mulieribus *B*: annum muliebribus *A*.

[12] The Roman historian Cornelius Tacitus gives an ethnographical account of the Germanic tribes in his *Germania* (*De origine et situ Germanorum*), written in AD 98.

[13] The "archhumanist" Konrad Celtis of Wipfeld near Schweinfurt (b. 1459) earned his B.A. at Cologne in 1479 and his M.A. at Heidelberg in 1485. Crowned poet laureate by Frederick III in Nuremberg in 1487, he spent the next two years in Italy and then studied math-

live like a beast. Man is superior to the other living beings in that he can let himself be guided by his reason, not his libido. But in the middle part of passionate love sexual desire takes control of our lives.

22 "Those who have never performed the act of Venus – the ones of whom it may be rightly said, as of the virtuous youths long ago, "It is they who have not defiled themselves with women" – those we have found by experience to be handsome, strong, brave, talented, and possessed of sweet-smelling breath. They are like those ancient countrymen of ours, those Germanic youths of whom we read that they considered it unnatural to associate with women in any way until they were at least twenty years old. But nowadays they know, perform, and utter indecencies before they're ten, let alone twenty years of age. That shows you how much Germanic manliness has gone out of fashion, though once upon a time it exalted us far above all other nations. Germanic manliness, I say, has gone out of fashion, 'inasmuch as Italian luxury holds us in thrall.' Indeed, that the Germany of old was far different from the one we know today can be gleaned from quite a few writers, above all Cornelius Tacitus, the author who gives us the most detailed look at the way our ancestors lived.[12] He was followed by our countryman, the poet laureate Konrad Celtis, a scholar accomplished in every field of knowledge and a most diligent investigator of our Germanic past.[13] (Just the other day I paid tribute to his shade in extemporaneous verse at a gathering of our Latin fraternity and respectfully mourned his loss in the name of all men of learning.[14]) But let me quote a few lines from him:

> According to their custom, the wife kept the bed undefiled;
>   spear and horse stood at the ready outside.
> The sturdy young man fathered offspring of robust build,
>   all of them nursed at their mother's breasts.
> 5   Fruit plucked from trees and such garden produce as cabbage
>   and turnips served younger throats as their food.
> Some adults ate acorns, but most preferred savory beechnuts,
>   and bread was served only at festive repasts.

---

ematics and astronomy at Cracow. In 1491 he was appointed professor of rhetoric and poetics at Ingolstadt, in 1497 at Vienna. He was an indefatigable promoter of humanism in the German-speaking regions, founding literary sodalities in Heidelberg and Vienna. Among his works are four books of love-poetry entitled *Amores* (1502) as well as posthumously published *Odes* and *Epodes*. A passionate student of German history, he edited the *Germania* of Tacitus (1500), the works of the tenth-century nun Hrotsvit von Gandersheim (1501), and the medieval epic *Ligurinus* (1507). He died in Vienna on 4 February 1508.

[14]During a dinner party at Mutianus Rufus's house on 10 August 1508 Eobanus and others composed epitaphs for Konrad Celtis. See Mutian. *Ep.* 78.

8 Et plura alia in eodem carmine secundi libri Amorum, ad quod studiosum lectorem remittimus. **9** Sed linquamus | aliena, prosequamur nostra.

23, 1 "Contra vero hii, qui in quottidiana Venere foelicitatem ponunt et nunquam ab impudicis amplexibus recedunt, deformes sunt, debiles et corpore et animo, pallidi et exangues, male foetentem odorem habentes, qualem Lemnii olim habuisse dicuntur. **2** Anne videntur tibi sordida haec? **3** Certe bonis quibusque sordidissima caudam serpentis habet. **4** Etenim omnis amor impudicus infoelici fine concluditur. **5** Tunc serpentinum, hoc est venenatum, saevum, impium amorem experimur, ubi conscientia pungimur, ubi sera nimis poenitentia ducimur. **6** Tunc more draconis reflexus cauda nos pungit et vitam plerumque adimit.

24, 1 "Haec multis exemplorum argumentis confirmare non est opus, cum ex omni antiquitate tanquam ex speculo quodam sereniore atque pellucido quam infoelices et miseri sint qui amant quodammodo reluceat. **2** Exemplis plena est omnis vetustas, quae etiam nobis ad Chymerae similitudinem praemonstravit amorem, utinam ex nulla parte dissimilem! **3** Sed Chymeram imaginamur; amorem habemus ad oculos et experimur quottidie. **4** Sed tu cum Chymera amorem recte compara. **5** Et ita ut Chymera in rei veritate nihil est (modo non intelligas montem Lyciae), ita nulla sint apud te miserrimi amoris vestigia. **6**

> Excute concoeptas e casto pectore flammas,
> Si potes, infoelix.

25, 1 "Pone, quaeso, ante oculos et recto examine amoris incommoda perpendito. **2** Marsilius Ficinus inter quinque studiosorum hostes monstri loco enumerat Venereum coitum. **3** Eo nihil est literarum studiosis perniciosius, praesertim si vires excesserit. **4** Subito nanque exhaurit spiritus, praesertim subtiliores, cerebrumque debilitat, labefactat stomachum atque precordia, quo malo ingenio nihil adversius esse potest. **5** Hippocrates quoque, medicorum optimus, officium Veneris comitiali morbo simile esse dixit, mentem enim, quae sacra est, concutit. **6** Quare non iniuria prisci theologi, hoc est poaetae, Musas atque Minervam virgines esse voluerunt. **7** Huic sententiae

---

25, 5 quae *scripsi*: que *AB.*

And so forth in the same poem of the second book of his *Amores*, to which I refer the studious reader. But let's leave other men's writings and continue with our own.

23 "Those, by contrast, who pin all their happiness on having intercourse every day and never shy away from unchaste embraces, they are disfigured, enfeebled in body and mind. They look ashen and bloodless and smell as bad as the men of Lemnos are said to have done in ancient times. Don't you find such things degrading? Certainly, all decent people will agree that an utterly debasing affair has a serpent's tail. And indeed, unchaste love invariably comes to an unhappy end. Only then do we recognize that erotic love is serpentine, that is, venomous, cruel, impious. Only then are we stung by conscience; only then, but far too late, do we start feeling remorse. In this final stage, we are stung, so to speak, with a stroke of the dragon's tail, and as often as not it costs us our life.

24 "There's no need to prove this with many arguments and examples since we can see reflected in all antiquity, as if in some clear and unclouded mirror, how disconsolate and wretched people are when they're in love. All of ancient history is full of such examples; after all, it also warned us about passionate love by way of the Chimera emblem. If only the likeness were not so striking in every respect! And yet the Chimera is only a figment of the imagination; passionate love is something we see before our eyes and experience for ourselves every day. But go ahead and compare passionate love rigorously with the Chimera. As the Chimera is in reality nothing but a wild fancy (provided you're not thinking of the mountain in Lycia), so there ought to be no trace in you of that most miserable kind of love.

> Rid your chaste heart of the flames that are smoldering there,
> if you still can, unhappy youth!

25 "Picture, if you will, the troubles of passionate love and weigh them carefully in balanced scales. Marsilio Ficino includes coitus among the five enemies or monsters that scholars have to contend with.[15] There is indeed nothing more ruinous to serious students of literature than love-making, particularly if it exceeds our strength. As a matter of fact, it exhausts the spirits in no time at all, especially the more subtle ones; it addles the brain and weakens the stomach and chest. No other disease is so harmful to your intelligence as this one. Hippocrates too, that best of doctors, compared the act of Venus to epilepsy because it impairs the mind, which is sacred. Hence the ancient theologians, that is to say, the poets, had good reason to maintain that the

---

[15] In his book *De vita*, first published in 1489, the Italian humanist and philosopher Marsilio Ficino (1433-1499) teaches intellectuals how to keep in good health.

Platonicum illud quadrat: 'Cum Venus Musis minitaretur nisi sacra Venerea colerent se contra illas suum filium armaturam, responderunt Musae: "Marti, | o Venus, Marti talia minitare! Tuus inter nos Cupido non volat."' 8 Nec immerito scripsit Baptista Mantuanus:

Pierides castae, castae Libetrides undae,
    Castalides aiunt virgine matre satas.

26, 1 "Sed quid tu adeo obstinatus haeres in diobolari scorto, quae se quaestus gratia nulli non prostituit, quae corpus suum publicavit ut Deo furetur animas? 2 Formae bono decoeptus es. 3 At

Forma bonum fragile est, quantumque accedit
    ad annos,
Fit minor et spatio carpitur illa suo.

4 Et tu iusta lyrici Davidis praeceptum oculos tuos a vanitate nondum avertisti. 5 Crocodili lachrimis decoeptus es, qui sub pietatis specie allectos ad se homines devorat. 6 Ita te decoepit foedissimum animal, quod licet pietatis imaginem foris mentiatur, intus aconita nutrit et Nessaeum sanguinem. 7

Sicut enim viridi tectus latet anguis in herba,
    Sic blanda faciles in meretrice doli.

27, 1 "Audistin Syrenes dulce cantantes blanda dulcedine soporatos et allectos ad se nautas in mari submersisse? 2 Quarum ut astutiam devitemus sapientissimum Ulyssem imitemur, qui a Troia revertens cum in eas incidisset a Circe prius admonitus aures caera obstruxit et exiciali dulcedini

---

[16]Libethra was a spring on Mount Helicon, sacred to the Muses. The Castalian nymphs (traditionally identified with the Muses) are the guardians of the sacred spring on Mount Parnassus. Mantuanus's commentator Sebastian Murrho explains how they came to be "born of a maid." Apollo, he says, was intent on raping the nymph Castalia when he saw her wandering on the mountainside. As she fled from him, she slipped and tumbled down a cliff. Thereupon she was changed into the Castalian spring. See Baptista Mantuanus, *Contra poetas impudice loquentes*, ed. Mariano Madrid Castro, in *HL* 45 (1996): 122.

[17]Crocodiles were believed to shed false tears in order to attract their victims.

[18]The centaur Nessus was killed by Hercules' envenomed arrow. His poisonous blood, smeared on a robe, eventually brought about the hero's own death.

Muses and Minerva are virgins. Plato's well-known remark accords with this view: 'When Venus told the Muses to celebrate the rites of love lest she arm her son against them, the Muses rejoined: "Oh, come on, Venus! Make threats like that against Mars, if you please. We won't let your Cupid fly in our midst."' And Baptista Mantuanus was quite justified in writing:

> Chaste are the Muses, and chaste is the fountain Libethra.
> The Castalian nymphs, they say, were born of a maid.[16]

26 "But why on earth do you cling so obstinately to a two-penny whore that earns her living by prostituting herself to every man who comes along and sells her body to steal souls from God? You have been deceived by the blessing of beauty. Just remember,

> Beauty's a fragile good. The more we advance in age, the
> smaller it becomes, for the passing years eat it away.

In spite of the teaching of the psalmist David, however, you still haven't turned your eyes from vanity. You have been tricked by the tears of a crocodile that attracts people to itself by appearing affectionate and then devours them.[17] That is exactly how that disgusting beast has deceived you. Though outwardly she may put on a great show of affection, inwardly she nurses wolfsbane and Nessus's poisonous blood.[18]

> For just as a snake lies hid in the grass of the greensward,
> so deft tricks lurk in a blandishing whore.

27 "Haven't you heard how the sweet-sounding Sirens used to sing wondrously melodious songs to lull sailors to sleep, lure them nearby, and drown them in the sea? To avoid their cunning, we should imitate that wisest of men Ulysses, who came upon them on his way back from Troy.[19] Fore-warned by Circe, however, he barred the way for their fatal charms by stop-

---

[19]Cf. Hom. *Od.* 12, 39-54 and 166-200, which Eobanus at the time knew only indirectly. According to a standard ancient and medieval interpretation, the Sirens were the embodiment of carnal temptation. Odysseus, on the other hand, was seen as a Stoic hero of wisdom and fortitude, unmoved by the siren songs of the world. See Hor. *Ep.* 1, 2, 17-18; Hugo Rahner, *Griechische Mythen in christlicher Deutung* (Zürich, 1957), pp. 424-430; *Symbole der Kirche: Die Ekklesiologie der Väter* (Salzburg, 1964), pp. 260-266; and, for example, Brant, *NS* 66, 133-136; 108, 69-93. Eobanus moralizes the story also in *Her. Chr.* 15, 177-184 and *Sylv.* 6, 6, 31-42.

viam preclusit seque ad puppim alligari foecit, ne si carminis
(quod Homerus in duodecimo Odysseae refert) dulcedinem
sequtus mortis inveniret amariciem. 3 Has nos surda aure
transire oportet, ut inquit divus Hieronimus, ut exicium de-
vitemus. 4 Omnes enim meretrices Syrenes sunt, quarum
amore nihil bono iuveni detestabilius. 5 Si vero omnino no-
bis temperare non poterimus, melius est amare probam et
continentem virginem quae et in amore respondeat et caste
amet quam ita grave cum nefandissimo scorto habere com-
mertium. 6

> Pelle pharetrati cum matre Cupidinis arcum
> Atque Dionaeo subtrahe colla iugo.

28, 1 "Solebas olim, dum sub uno contubernio fami-
liariter conversaremur, poaetas omnes studiose perquirere
et optimos quosque scriptores vel digitis tuis tibi notiores
efficere. 2 'Et nondum amoris incommoda intelligis,' dixit
olim Typhernus noster:

B4ʳ

29   Non amor est aliud quam tristis et aegra voluptas,
       Nil nisi cura placens, nil nisi dulce malum.
    Gaudia si spectes, ea sunt in amore pusilla
       Et quam dulcedo maior amaricies.
5   Sunt in eo lachrimae, sunt et sine fine querelae,
       Iurgia, suspicio, continuusque timor.
    Diminuit famam, studiis melioribus obstat,
       Exiguo magnas tempore perdit opes.

30, 1 Et quae sequuntur in hunc modum non parum multa.
2 Sed tu, ut mihi videre videor, ad turpia paranda optimis
disciplinis usus es abususque hiis rebus quibus gloria quaeri-
tur, utique praeter spem et votum ignominiosus effectus es.
3 Hoc tibi Musarum profuit dulce atque adeo sanctum so-
dalitium? 4 Ubi nunc magnanimi pectoris ille pristinus
vigor? Ubi vis ingenii tam vivacis quam acutissimi? Ubi

27, 3 devitemus *B*: daevitemus *A*.

[20]Ulysses, Eobanus suggests, lashes himself to the mast *and* stops his own ears with wax
in order to escape the fatal lure of the Sirens' song. This concept, of course, runs counter to
Homer, *Od.* 12, but is a medieval and Renaissance commonplace. It goes back to the ancient
Stoic interpretation that made Ulysses into the exemplary wise man, while the Sirens repre-
sent the world's seductive pleasures. For if it is true, as proverbial wisdom has it, that the wise do
not wantonly expose themselves to temptation and instead stop their ears to all siren songs
(Sen. *Ep.* 31, 2; Otto 213 and 1657; Häussler, pp. 117 and 213), it follows that Ulysses,

ping his ears with wax and having himself lashed to the ship.[20] As Homer re-
lates in the twelfth book of *The Odyssey*, yielding to the sweetness of their
singing would have meant tasting the bitterness of death. We too, according
to Saint Jerome, should turn a deaf ear to the Sirens if we are to avoid eternal
death. Each and every whore is a Siren; and nothing is more abominable than
for a virtuous youth to fall in love with one of them. If, on the other hand, you
are totally unable to restrain yourself, it is far better to marry a modest and
continent maiden, one who returns your affection and loves you chastely,
than to have such pernicious intercourse with that unspeakably wicked
harlot.

> Reject Cupid with his bow and arrows, along with his mother,
>   and wrench your neck out of Venus's yoke.

28 "In days past, when you and I were still housemates together, you
used to study all the poets in great detail, so you would know each and every
one of the finest writers better than the back of your own hand. 'But you still
don't understand the troubles of passionate love,' our Tifernate[21] once said:

29   Love is nothing but a gloomy and anxious pleasure,
            just a delightful care, just an agreeable grief.
        If you look for the joys of love, you'll find they are tiny,
            with the bitter outweighing the sweet.
5   In love there are tears, there are also laments without number,
            quarreling, mistrust, and unending alarm.
        It diminishes fame, encumbers liberal studies,
            and in a moment squanders a fortune away.

30 And so forth in this manner, at considerable length. But you, it would
seem to me, have used the finest education for ignoble ends and abused the
very things by which glory is won. To be quite frank with you, even though
we had the highest hopes and expectations for you, you have utterly disgraced
yourself. Is that the benefit that the delightful and altogether holy fellowship
with the Muses has brought you? Where now is that boldness of mind, that

---

as the exemplar of wisdom, must himself have stopped his ears against the deadly songs. See
Hier. *In Hieremiam* 3, 1, *CCSL* 74, p. 119; St. Basil, *Ad adolescentes* 4, as translated by Leonardo
Bruni: "auresque claudendae [sunt], non secus atque ipsi ferunt Ulyssem ad Sirenum cantus";
Eob. *Nup.* 301; *Her. Chr.* 15, 183-184. See further Harry Vredeveld: "'Deaf as Ulysses to the
Siren's Song': The Story of a Forgotten Topos," *Renaissance Quarterly* 54 (2001): 846-882.
    [21]Gregorio Tifernate (Tifernas) was born in 1413/14 near Cortona. After studying in
Città di Castello and Perugia and spending several years in Greece, he taught Greek and med-
icine in Italy and France. Among his pupils were Giovanni Pontano and Baptista Mantuanus
(who praises him as "Umber" in *Ecl.* 4). During the papacy of Nicholas V, Tifernate concen-
trated on translating the Greek classics, among them works by Aristotle, Theophrastus, Dion
Chrysostom, and Strabo. He died in ca. 1464. His poetic works were published posthumously
in *Gregorii Tipherni poetae clariss. opuscula* (Venice, 1498).

cytharae cantus? 5 Age tandem teipsum consolare, ad Apol-
linem convertere, Musas invoca, cytharae nervos extende,
modulare quippiam, ne omnino te extinctum amici pute-
mus."

31, 1 Haec ubi dixissem, dicto citius e manibus mihi
quam gestabam chelin eripiens suis eam brachiis coaptare
coepit atque ita leniter errantibus inter chordas digitis flebili
quidem harmonia in hunc modum coepit conqueri:

B4ᵛ

32   "Heu, funesta feri taela Cupidinis!
      Heu, quantum miseros cogit Amor pati!
         Saevo saevior angue
            Cum nato Venus impio.
5   O foelix, miseris quisquis amoribus
      Liber taela dei ridet et integer
         Vita, pace beatus,
            Dulci vivit in ocio.
      Nondum saeva meis diva doloribus
10   Imponis requiem, sed magis aestuas.
         Heu, quantum miserandi
            Quicumque hoc tolerant iugum!
      Quem tandem lachrimis, diva, dabis modum?
      Sic me fata mori, sic superi iubent.
15   Sic, sic fata precabor,
            Et dulce est miseris mori.
      Quis tantam rabiem flere satis queat?
      Plorantes lachrimae deficient genas,
         Saevum quisquis Amorem
20   Fletu vincere nititur.
      Auratae patior vulnus harundinis,
      Qua me fixit Amor saevus et improbus,
         Per quem pectora multis
            Languent victa doloribus.
25   Vos me Pieriae plangite virgines.

B5ʳ   Vates vester eram, sanus et integer,
         Quem nunc proxima dirae
            Morti fata iubent mori.

old vigor of yours? Where is the force of your intellect, once as lively as it was keen? Where is the music of your lute? Come, console yourself at long last, turn to Apollo, call upon the Muses, tune the strings of the lute, play anything you want, so that we friends of yours won't think you're completely snuffed out."

31 I had no sooner spoken these words, than – faster than I can say – he snatched the lute I was carrying out of my hands and began to cradle it in his arms. And as his fingers ran lightly over the strings in a heartrendingly plaintive melody, he began to sing the following lament:

32   "Alas for the deadly shafts of ruthless Cupid!
      Alas for the pain that Love inflicts on the hapless!
         Crueler than a cruel snake
          are Venus and her wicked son.
5   Oh, happy the man who, free from the pangs of love,
      laughs at the god's arrows and, living an upright
         life, blessed with serenity,
          enjoys his tranquil leisure.
      Savage goddess, you still have not granted me
10   relief from my anguish, but rage ever more wildly.
         Alas, how pitiable are they
          who have to endure that yoke!
      When, goddess, will you finally put an end to my tears?
      Only when fate, only when the gods tell me to die.
15   That's what I'll beg of fate,
         for death is sweet to the wretched.
      Who could weep enough for so wild a passion?
      Tears would soon fail the grieving eyes
         if you struggled to overcome
20   savage Love with your weeping.
      I suffer from the wound that the fierce, wicked
      god of love inflicted with his golden arrow.[22]
         His shaft overpowers my heart,
          breaking it with endless grief.
25   Mourn for me, you Pierian Maidens! I used to be
      your poet when I was still sound in mind and limb.
         Now fate, the cousin of fell
          Death, is telling me to die.

---

[22] According to Ov. *Met.* 1, 470-471, Cupid has two kinds of arrow. The one made of lead repels love, while the golden one induces it.

O quaecumque nemus numina floridum
30   Servatis, satyri, Panes, Oreades,
  Moestum dicite carmen,
   Cantent flebile tybiae.
Fontes, Naiades, linquite vitreos.
Huc siccis pedibus currite, vos precor,
35   Solantes pereuntem
   Inter taela Cupidinis.
At tu, saeva Venus, tuque, ferox puer,
Quid rides? Quid adhuc non minuis faces?
  Nostro laeta dolore
40   Dempto fine superbies?
Quid restat? Miserum quis manet exitus?
Quis finem lachrimis ponet inanibus?
  Quis me vulnere salvum
   Priscis reddet honoribus?
45   Quin fatis animam precipitem dabo?
Inter densa iuvat lustra quiescere.
  Nymphae corpus humatum
   Servabunt venerabiles.
Sed tu, cura mei maxima pectoris,
50   O crudelis adhuc, talia despicis.
  Moestum spernis amantem,
   O immitis et aspera!
Et nunc stant patulae frondibus arbores,
Verni tota viret gratia temporis,
55   Et me sola gementem
   Inter lustra vident ferae.
Nunc mecum volucres flebile cantilant,
Arrident nitidis gramina fontibus,
  Et nunc omnia rident;
60   Solus tristia conqueror.
Seu Phoebus lateat sive reluceat,
Heu, quantis maceror corda doloribus!
  Et sperata recedit
   Mors vitae miserabili.
65   Insani cuperem turbinis impetu
Ad deserta vehi divitis Indiae,
  Qua foelicia Ganges

B5ᵛ

---

58 fontibus *A*: frontibus *B*.   **65** cuperem *A*: caperem *B*.

All you deities who watch over the flowery
30   grove, you satyrs, fauns, and oreads, sing
      a dirge for me to the doleful
        accompaniment of your flutes.
Leave your glassy fountains, you naiads.
Run hither on dry feet, I beseech you.
35   Console me, for I'm perishing
        amid the arrows of Cupid.
But you, savage Venus, and you, fierce boy, why are you
laughing? Why have you still not assuaged my flames?
      Exulting in my heartache,
40   will you always be haughty?
What's in store? What fate awaits me poor fellow?
Will anyone ever put an end to my futile tears?
      Who will heal my wound and give me
        back the honors of yore?
45   Why don't I give up the ghost, just like that?
I'd love to rest among the dense haunts of beasts.
      The venerable nymphs will watch
        the grave where my body lies buried.
But you, the biggest care of my heart, as relentless
50   as ever, you still look down on this anguish of mine.
      You disdain your mournful lover,
        O harsh and merciless girl!
And now the spreading trees are in leaf;
the loveliness of spring is all in blossom.
55   But in the lonesome woods
        the wild beasts watch as I groan.
Now the birds are singing a doleful song with me;
now the grasses smile at the shimmering springs.
      As nature smiles, I all alone
60   beweep my outcast state.
Whether Phoebus is hidden or shines by day,
alas, how great a grief torments my heart!
      And still the death I pine for
        yields to this sorry life.
65   How I wish that the force of a raging whirlwind
could carry me to the deserts of wealthy India,
      where the Ganges waters the fertile

Dulcis prata rigat soli,
Qua vicina videt sydera Caucasus,
70   Qua saevam volucrem perpetuo miser
     Pascit corde Prometheus,
       Sed me longe beatior.
Heu, quae me miserum dilanient ferae?
Fortes este, lupi! Quin mea frangitis
75   Saevi colla dracones?
       Sic fortasse quievero.
Nondum, saeva Venus, flebilibus modis
Lenis mota faces. Flete, poaeticae
     Musae! Vos superavit
80   Tanta prole potens Venus.
Nunc vos, o lyrici, dulce decus, modi,
Post nostros cineres este superstites,
     Ut me saera peremptum
     Fatis saecula lugeant."

33, 1 Hec modulatus conticuit finemque querendi foecit. **2** Cytharam simul mihi cum eburno pectine restituit. **3** Cumque relaxatis aliquantulum nervis ad lyrici accentus altitudinem extensis elegiacum tenorem inducerem, animadvertens ille, "Scio," inquit, "Eobane, quid pares. **4** Non est opus flebilibus elegis! **5** Satis superque deploravimus infoelicitatem nostram. **6** Insanus amor nullo carmine extingui potest, etiam si Orpheus ille Thrax (qui primas post Mercurium Trismegistum antiquae theologiae partes obtinet) ab inferis revocaretur. **7** Qui etiam etsi montes, sylvas, flumina, et animalia cantus dulcedine flexisse dicatur, amoris incendium vitare nequaquam potuit. **8** Nec tu certe, quod meum est infortunium, hoc tam perniciosi fati genus arcere poteris. **9** Satis est me semel periisse. **10** Tu desperatum consolari desine. **11**

Iam mea flagrantes penetrarunt viscera flammae,
Saevus in ardenti pectore fervet amor."

33, 7 Qui *B*: Cui *A*.   33, 11 mea *A*: me *B*.

fields of that lovely land,
or where the Caucasus looks up to the nearby stars,
70 where wretched Prometheus forever feeds the
savage bird with his heart,[23]
but is much luckier than I.
Alas, what kind of beasts will tear poor me to pieces?
Be strong, wolves! Why don't you break my neck,
75 fierce dragons? Only then,
perhaps, will I find rest.
My doleful song, savage Venus, has still not moved you;
you still have not soothed my flames. Weep, Muses
of poetry! You've been defeated
80 by Venus, ruling her mighty son.
Now, you lyrical measures, O my glory and delight,
Go on living long after I have turned to ashes,
so distant ages may grieve
that fate has ended my life."

33 After singing these words, he put an end to his lament and fell silent. At the same time he handed the lute back to me, together with the ivory plectrum. But when he noticed that I was slackening the strings a bit – they were still tuned to the high pitch required for lyrical intonation – and was lowering their pitch to the elegiac register, he exclaimed: "I know what you have in mind, Eobanus. There's no need for tearful elegies! I've already bewailed my unhappiness more than enough. Mad love can't be quenched with any song, not even if that Thracian Orpheus (who occupies first place in ancient theology, right behind Mercury Trismegistus[24]) could return from the underworld. Even though he's supposed to have moved mountains, trees, rivers, and wild beasts with the sweetness of his song, he himself failed to keep clear of love's fire. You too, that's for sure, will not be able to ward off this misfortune of mine, this kind of ruinous fate. I have died once already, and that is enough. Stop trying to console a desperate man.

Already the blazing flames have penetrated my vitals;
cruel love seethes inside my passionate heart."

---

[23]Cf. *Pug.* B 1, 23-24, with fn. 12.

[24]Hermes (Mercury) Trismegistus is the Greek name for the Egyptian god Thot. All mystical, alchemical, and astrological doctrines reputedly go back to him.

34, 1 "Cum ergo versibus adhuc," inquam, "frequenter uteris, tui ordinis nondum omnino oblitus, Ovidianus certe es, qui dum in Foro Rhomano apud prophanum iudicium constitutus causas vulgares ageret, rabularum clamoribus extemporaliter, tanquam sacerdos apud tabernariorum operarios, carminibus obstrepebat, ita ut post longum a Caesare Augusto in exilium missus in Tristibus scribere non dubitarit: | 2

B6ᵛ

> Sponte sua carmen numeros veniebat ad aptos.
> Quicquid conabar dicere, versus erat.

3 Sed haec gratia paucis admodum et vix paucissimis in creatione divinitus infunditur. 4 In quo laudis genere, dii boni, quantum excellere semper studui, preclarius esse ducens pauperem apud Musas immortalitati me consecrasse quam multas divicias absque preclari nominis gloria posteris reliquisse. 5 Sed quid a pomposo Cupidinis theatro ad poaeticas fores divertimur? Ad quas utinam tu quoque tuto mecum diverti posses! 6 Sed age tamen, mi Fundine, frena reluctantem animum, digredere mecum paulo liberius, accedamus propius. 7 Istic enim Castalius fons lenissimo susurro per amaena Musici prati lilileta labitur. 8 Cui si te totum immerseris, non dubito quin omnem flammarum impetum vel certe multam partem extinxeris."

9 Hec dicens precedebam, alioqui nutabundum iuvenem respiciens. 10 Quem cum manu apprehensum aequo iam mecum vestigio incedentem aspexissem, lyra simul increpui:

35   "Heu dolor, insano quae vis, quod numen Amori!
>   Par superum volucri quis velit esse deo?
>   Regnat et hiis totum sub legibus occupat orbem
>   Cunctaque vel solus regna gubernat Amor.
5   Prorsus dira lues et inextinguibilis ardor,
>   Vulnera, dii, quantis viribus ista facit!
>   Nulla est in toto pestis truculentior orbe
>   Quam levis, ex omni parte timendus Amor.
>   Dulce malum Venus est et delectabile virus.
10   Incautos iuvenes precipitanter agit.
>   Intrat et occulto serpit per viscera lapsu
>   Et clausis tandem sensibus haeret amor.

34, 1 ergo *scripsi*: ego *AB*.   tabernariorum *scripsi*: tabernorum *AB*.

34 "Well, well!" I replied. "Since you're obviously still peppering your speeches with verse and have by no means forgotten your calling, you're definitely following in the footsteps of Ovid. When hearing run-of-the-mill cases as a judge of common pleas in the Forum Romanum, he, like a priest among workmen, used to outshout the pettifoggers with his extemporaneous verses. Indeed, long after he had been sent into exile by Caesar Augustus he did not hesitate to write in his *Tristia*:

> Song came to me unbidden, ready-made in suitable meters;
> everything I tried to say came out as verse.

But this is a talent granted to just a few people. Even fewer are divinely inspired like that when they create poetry. Good Lord, how I myself have always striven to excel on this path to renown! For to live as a pauper with the Muses while consecrating myself to immortality seems to me far more splendid than to leave great piles of money to my descendants, but never achieving a brilliant reputation. But why are we wandering away from Cupid's pompous stage and opening the door to poetry? If only you too could safely wander over there with me! Now come on, my dear Fundinus. It's high time you curbed your unruly spirit. Let your guard down a little and come along with me. Let's walk side by side. I'll take you down to that Castalian spring over there. See how it runs with a barely audible whisper, through gorgeous lily beds in the Muses' own meadow. If you'd immerse yourself completely in it, I have no doubt that you'd extinguish all the flames of passion, or at least the greater part of them."

As I spoke these words, I went ahead, all the while looking over my shoulder at the youth, who by now was visibly wavering. At that point I took him by the hand. And when I noticed that he was now keeping pace with me, I sang the following words to the lute:

35   "Ah the pain! How great is the might of maddening Love!
      What deity can claim to be a match for that winged god?
   Cupid rules the whole world. He subjects it to those laws of his
      and reigns by himself over every kingdom on earth.
5   A truly monstrous disease, an unquenchable fire – with
      what vigor, ye gods, does Love inflict wounds!
   In all the world there's not a plague so ferocious as
      fickle Love. He's to be feared in every respect!
   Venus is a sweet distress and an enjoyable poison.
10   Unwary youths fall for her every time.
   Once love has entered, it creeps through our innards unnoticed
      and ends up holding all our senses in thrall.

C1^r

Sed feriunt pueros hec non nisi taela volentes.
  Quisquis amat, voluit stultus amare prius.
15 Quis furor est? Quae tanta animas daementia vexat
  Ut tam saeva velint vulnera sponte pati?
  Ad Seston iuvenem quis iussit amare natantem?
  Iura voluntates sunt in amore piae.
  Quis Helenen, ardere ferum quis iussit Achillem?
20 Tanta quis Iliacum misit in arma Parin?
  Pyrame, fatales quis te tulit error in umbras?
  Cur prius alba tuo sanguine mora rubent?
  Pendula quis miserum funus tibi Phylli coegit?
  Cur secat impatiens regia Dido latus?
25 Quis patrium Scyllae furari iussit honorem?
  Ah, certe voluit preter amare nihil.
  Pallida cur plumas induta Semiramis albet?
  Cur liquidam sitiens Biblida potat aper?
  Fraena pati miserae voluerunt talia mentes.
30 Deme voluntatem, non erit ullus amor.
  Quid nisi velle fuit, donec Tyrinthius heros
  Observat nutus, Oechali nympha, tuos?
  Arma vir et clavam posuit pellemque leonis.
  Debile robusto pollice nevit opus.
35 Omnia vicisti, te callida vicit Iole.
  Vade, triumphantis praemia, victor, habe!
  Quid nisi velle fuit, raptum Chyronis ab antro

C1^v

  Aeaciden longa delituisse toga?
  Phasias Argivam conscendit Iasonis Argo,

---

17 Seston *scripsi*: Sestos *AB*.   **32** Oechali *scripsi*: Oebali *AB*.   **36** triumphantis *A*: trium-
phantes *B*.

---

[25]Leander swam the Hellespont to see his beloved Hero in Sestos. See Ov. *Ep.* 18.

[26]Helen fell in love with Paris and then ran off with him to Troy; see Ov. *Ep.* 16-17.
Achilles' love for Briseis is vividly depicted in Ov. *Ep.* 3. Cf. Eob. *Her. Chr.* 22, 15.

[27]After the supposed death of his lover Thisbe, Pyramus committed suicide under a mul-
berry tree. At this the mulberries – formerly white – turned a blood-red color. See Ov. *Met.* 4,
51-52 and 125-127; Serv. *Ecl.* 6, 22.

[28]Phyllis hanged herself after waiting in vain for her lover Demophoon to return; see Ov.
Ep. 2. Dido committed suicide after Aeneas left her; see Verg. *A.* 4, 663-665 and Ov. *Ep.* 7,
181-196.

[29]To prove her love for Minos, Scylla betrayed her father, King Nisus, by cutting off the
red lock on which his life depended. See Ov. *Met.* 8, 6-151.

[30]Semiramis was turned into a dove – the bird of Venus – after her death. See Ov. *Met.*
4, 47-48.

But only willing youths are struck by these arrows. Every
   lover starts out by foolishly wanting to love.
15   What kind of madness is this? What makes people so crazy that
   they endure such savage wounds of their own free will?
Who told the youth that swam to Sestos he had to fall in love?[25]
   When you're in love, tender affections are your commands.
Who told Helen and fierce Achilles to burn with such passion?[26]
20   Who sent Trojan Paris to start such a horrible war?
What delusion carried Pyramus off to the shades of the dead?
   Why are mulberries, formerly white, now red with his blood?[27]
Who forced Phyllis into her wretched death by hanging?
   Why did Queen Dido in desperation fall on the sword?[28]
25   Who ordered Scylla to steal a lock of her father's hair?[29]
   Ah, beyond any doubt, nothing but yearning for love!
Why is pale Semiramis decked out in white feathers?[30]
   Why does a wild boar quench his thirst in Byblis's spring?[31]
To submit to love's bridle, that's what the poor devils longed for.
30   Take away the desire, and passionate love is no more.
What else but desire made the hero of Tiryns put himself
   at the beck and call of the Oechalian nymph?[32]
Laying down his weapons – the club and the lion's skin – the
   man spun feeble strands with his stalwart thumb.
35   All-conquering Hercules, you were conquered by crafty Iole.
   Triumph all you want, conqueror: here's your reward!
What else but desire made Achilles hide in a girl's robe
   after being forced to leave Chiron's cave?[33]
Medea boarded Jason's Argive ship Argo, and why? Only

[31] Byblis fell in love with her brother Caunus and was turned into a spring. See Ov. *Met.* 9, 454-665.

[32] After Hercules ("the hero of Tiryns") had killed Iphitus, Apollo agreed to purify him only on condition that he be sold as a slave and the proceeds given to Iphitus's father Eurytus. Omphale, queen of Lydia, bought him and set him to labors of all kinds, including women's work, and dressed him in women's clothes. See Prop. 3, 11, 17-20; Ov. *Ep.* 9, 53-80; *Fast.* 2, 305-326; Eob. *Sylv.* 4, 6, 29-32. But according to a well-known medieval and Renaissance variant of this story, it is the "Oechalian nymph" Iole, daughter of king Eurytus of Oechalia, who humiliates Hercules by making him spin wool while dressed in women's clothes. See Paul G. Schmidt, "*Hercules indutus vestibus Ioles*", in: *From Wolfram and Petrarch to Goethe and Grass: Studies in Literature in Honour of Leonard Forster*, ed. D.H. Green et al. (Baden-Baden, 1982), pp. 103-107; Eob. *Her. Chr.* 9, 115; *Venus* 1, 55-58.

[33] Achilles was still a boy when his mother Thetis learned that he would die at Troy. She tried to foil fate by taking him away from his tutor, the centaur Chiron, dressing him in girl's clothes, and raising him among the maidens of Lycomedes' court in Scyros. There he fell in love with the princess Deidamia (see line 73 below).

40   Impia cum Graias vellet inire faces.
     Tot mala perpessi, mala tot voluere. Sed intrat
       Principio tanquam non metuendus amor.
     Gaudet amans primum, quia non intelligit ignes,
       Incautos laqueum non videt ante pedes.
45   Rhetia non cernit, puteum non cernit abyssi
       Quam super infoelix precipitatur amans.
     Vadit ad interitum, crudeli colla tyranno
       Subiicit et forti libera colla iugo.
     Laese Cupidinea nimium nimiumque sagitta,
50   Pendis apud Paphias longa tributa fores.
     Heu, ubi nunc iuvenile decus? Quo gloria formae,
       Quo vigor effluxit pectoris ille tui?
     Quid palles, miserande puer? Quid inania luges
       Gaudia, quae vitae sunt aconita tuae?
55   Liber eras, memini, prius et sine legibus ibas,
       Quas tibi nunc tacita fraude paravit Amor.
     Quid langues, decoepte puer? Quid inhospita lustras
       Avia? Nil sylvae vulnera tanta iuvant.
     Acrior in sylvis amor est, quia sepe per umbras
60   Cum pharetra didicit callidus ire puer.
     Excute flagrantes accensi pectoris aestus,
       Subtrahe mordaci colla subacta iugo.
     Disce, puer, quid agas, quem taela Cupidinis arcent.
       Sanari cupias vulnera, sanus eris.
65   Principium est certae sanari velle salutis.
       Semper qui medicum despicit, aeger erit.
     Apparet pueris Venus insanabilis error;
       Vir negat hoc volucrem virus habere deum.
     Liquit Didonem, licet incessanter amatam,
70   Per quem cum patria, Turne subacte, iaces.
     Flevit Ulysseae properantia vaela carinae
       Grandis in Ionio cognita nympha mari.
     Liquit et Aeacides dilectam Deidamiam,
       Cum peteret Phrygios Graecia tota lares.

C2ʳ

---

68 deum *scripsi*: deam *AB*.

[34]The sorceress Medea helped Jason obtain the Golden Fleece and then returned with him to Thessaly to become his bride. Cf. *Laud.* 185.

40   because the wicked girl wanted to marry a Greek.[34]
        Every woe they suffered came from their own free will. But
           initially love never comes on like a thing to be feared.
        At first the lover rejoices. That's because he doesn't feel the
           flames or see the snare in front of his imprudent feet.
45   He doesn't notice the nets, he doesn't notice the bottomless pit
           into which the hapless lover tumbles head over heels.
        Rushing to his doom, he bows his neck to the cruel tyrant,
           he submits his freeborn neck to the unyielding yoke.
        Wounded deeply, all too deeply by Cupid's arrow,
50   you have long placed tributes at Venus's door.
        Alas, where is your youthful charm now? Where did your noble
           beauty go to, where that mental vigor of yours?
        What made you so wan, pitiable fellow? Why do you bewail those
           empty joys that have all but poisoned your life?
55   You used to be free, I recall. You went wherever you wanted,
           unbound by the laws that Love has foisted on you.
        What made you sick, deceived fellow? Why do you wander in the
           lonely wilds? Forests can't staunch wounds of this kind.
        Love is more intense in the woods. After all, it's in the shade
60   that the wily boy often goes to practise his shot.
        Drive the blazing fire out of your passionate vitals,
           wrench your prostrate neck out of the biting yoke.
        Watch what you're doing, lad! Cupid's shafts still transfix you.
           If you want those wounds to be cured, then you'll be fine.
65   The first step to sound health is a strong wish for healing.
           Keep despising the doctor, and you're bound to get sick.
        To young people, passionate love seems an incurable madness.
           Grown men deny that the winged god has poison like that.
        Though he kept on adoring Dido, the hero who vanquished
70   Turnus and his homeland nevertheless left his lover behind.[35]
        Ulysses sailed away in a hurry, while the mighty nymph, so
           well-known in the Ionian Sea, wept bitter tears over him.[36]
        And don't forget Achilles! He left his beloved Deidamia
           when all of Greece was making for Troy.[37]

[35] Pursuing his quest to found a new city in Italy, Aeneas abandoned Dido at Carthage and went on to defeat Turnus, the king of the Rutuli.

[36] Calypso, the daughter of Atlas, received Odysseus as a guest on the island of Ogygia. Having borne him a son, she was understandably loath to see him leave.

[37] Achilles grew up among the maidens of Lycomedes' court in Scyros and fell in love with the king's daughter Deidamia (see lines 37-38 above). However, after he was discovered by Odysseus and other Greek envoys, he willingly went with them to Troy.

75   Hos non mollis amor, non hos secura voluptas
        Movit, et in plumis deliciosa Venus.
     Non lachrimae, non mille preces, non mille querelae
        Hos a virtutis destituere via.
     Ocia magnanimus tam dulcia sprevit Achilles.
80   Dii superi, quanta vectus ad astra cheli!
     Coge reluctantes in vincla tenacia flammas
        Teque doce totis viribus esse virum.
     Pluma levis facili passim reflectitur aura;
        Pervolat audaces missa sagitta Notos.
85   Tu quoque ne rapido caedas impune furori,
        Verum age nunc vires experiare tuas.
     Protinus invisae mitescent tempore flammae,
        Omnis ab aelato pectore caedet amor.
     Exige quam valeas, animum cognosce potentem.
90   Vince repugnantes, mens animosa, faces.
     Et quid in hac adeo niveum contage pudorem,
        Quid bona tam putri polluis alba luto?
     Quid moeres? Quid fata gemis cognata? Quid optas,
        Quod fieri nulla conditione potes?
95   Stulte, quid in blanda tabes meretrice? Quid haeres
        In sola formae luxuriantis ope?
     Quae rubet exterius vultum depicta cerussa,
        Interius foedam tota mephytin olet.
     Sic aliquis puro sitiens aconita sub auro
100   Non videt et poenas exiciumque bibit.
     Tam brevis hoc prodest, hoc est tantilla voluptas,
        Ut habeas quod te perdat et excruciet.
     Quid quod amas, largum quae cunctis vendit amorem?
        Quid tu communem solus amare potes?
105   Pellegis antiquos, vatum scrutator, amantes.
        Iudice te peius nullus amavit amans.
     Dum potes et phas est, flammas extingue nocentes
        Teque tuis Musis redde. Beatus eris.
     Longa Dionaeae veniant tibi taedia vitae.
110   Sit pudor in tantum degenerasse nefas!
     Te moveant saltem divae, laus nostra, Camoenae,
        Quae nitidum casti lumen amoris habent.

C2ᵛ

---

112 Quae *B*: Que *A*.

75   Now those were real men! No tender love, no safe pleasures could
           hold them back, no delicious sex in soft feather beds.
      No tears, no amount of begging, no amount of laments were
           able to make them stray from manhood's true path.
      The great-hearted Achilles spurned to take his sweet ease, and
80   good Lord, look what a lyre praised him to the skies![38]
      Keep your recalcitrant passion on a tight leash. You've got to
           prove your manhood with all the strength that you have.
      A light feather is wafted hither and yon with the breeze; but an
           arrow shot from the bow flies through the stormiest winds.
85   You too, don't yield to the raging fury without a fight. Just
           trust me: now's the time to put your strength to the test.
      As soon as you do, the hateful flames will start to die down and
           all that love will slink out of your high-minded breast.
      Prove your mettle, find out what stuff you are made of.
90   Bold spirit that you are, extinguish those refractory flames.
      Why stain your snow-white honor with this sleazy contagion?
           Why defile your bright talent with such moldering muck?
      Why lament? Why bemoan a fate you've brought on yourself?
           Why long to be someone you cannot possibly be?
95   Fool, why pine for a seductive whore? Why cling to the only
           thing she has going for her – her voluptuous shape?
      Outside, her face is made up with rouge and painted with ceruse.
           Inside, rotten to the core, she smells like the plague.
      So a thirsty man, not seeing the aconite lurking in the pure
100   gold, drinks punishment and death unbeknown to himself.
      That's what this fleeting, puny pleasure is good for: it gives you
           a fine way to ruin your health and torture your heart.
      Besides, the girl you adore sells her love unstintingly to all who
           will pay. How can you keep a whore's love just for yourself?
105   As a student of poetry, you're familiar with all the old lovers.
           In your judgment, no lover was ever as hapless as you.
      While you still can and may, extinguish those noxious flames and
           restore yourself to the Muses. Then you'll be happy again.
      Your life in the service of Venus ought to have turned your
110   stomach long ago. Shame on you for so disgracing yourself!
      Just let your heart be touched by the godly Muses. Our pride and
           joy, they possess the shining light of chaste love.

---

[38] In *The Iliad* of Homer.

C3^r

        Te moveat saltem summus, dux noster, Apollo,
          Cuius in aeternum praedominatur amor.
115 Vade, nec ulterius tam turpibus urere flammis.
          Ad vitam mortis de ditione redi.
        Nunc ita sors tecum! Nullo discrimine laesus,
          Consilio posses non eguisse meo."

36   Pendula quid lyricae lassatis plectra Camoenae?
          Sit satis hec vestro fabula dicta choro.
        Rumpite Phoebeae languentia fila sorores.
          Vestra venenosus numina ridet Amor.
5   Haec tibi, quisquis amas, cecini. Tu denique palles!
          Priscus adhuc calido pectore fumat amor.

36, 4 venenosus *A*: venenosos *B*.

Just let your heart be touched by our highest leader Apollo.[39]
 His love reigns supreme for all time to come.
115 Go and burn no more with so disgraceful a passion.
 Return to the living; leave the dominion of death.
Now then, may fortune be with you! Blindly wounded by Love,
 you cannot do without the counsel I give."

36 Why are you, lyrical Muses, wearing out the wavering plectrum?
 It's time for your choir to put an end to this tale.
Tear out the weakened strings, you sisters of Phoebus.[40]
 Venomous Cupid laughs your power to scorn.
5 I have sung this for each of you, lovers. You're pale yet!
 The old love still burns in the smoldering breast.

---

[39] That is, "Christus Apollo." Cf. *Laud.* 13 (n.).
[40] Like Apollo, the Muses are the offspring of Zeus. Cf. *Rec.* 74.

B 1 EOBANUS HESSUS FRANCOBERGIUS LECTORI-
BUS S.

Libuit hic addere ludicra quaedam, ut varietate quoque tam
diversa quam iucunda etsi in parvo opusculo lectu digni
videremur. 2 Vos haec pauca sed qualiacumque absque fi-
gurato naso pellegite, Sylvarum Erphordiensium libros
(toties promissos) ex officina nostra literatoria prope diem
accepturi. 3 Valete, candidi lectores, et Eobanum vestri stu-
diosum mutua reverentia prosequimini.

4 Ex aedibus Erphordiensis Mercurii, ad Idus Iunias
anni M.D.VIII.

B 2

Maxima Pieridum tristatum viderat Hessum
    Et subito tales aedidit ore sonos:

Calliope
Hesse, quid est solito quo tristior esse videris?
    Quidve, precor, quod te laeserit esse potest?

Hessus
5   Virgo, decus vatum, nostri te causa doloris
    Non latet. Hic vati consule, diva, tuo.

C3^v   *Calliope*
Ah, nimis incautus, nimis imprudenter aberras.
    Dulce tibi dextra garrit in aure Venus.

Hessus
Effuge, victe pudor! Nunc libera lingua loquatur,
10   Libera vox animi: vincula cogit Amor.

B 1   2 literatoria *A*: literaria *B*.   3-4 et Eobanum – anni *A*: *om. B.*

[41]Eobanus alludes to the poetry collection *Sylvae* that he had been planning since October
1506. See fn. 9 at *Laud.*, ded. 11. It was not until 1535, however, that he finally brought out
six books of *Sylvae*, augmented with three more books in 1539.

[42]In less poetic terms: the "Engelshaus" (Angel's house). Cf. *Ama.*, ded. 15 above, with fn.
4; B 3, 4 below; and *Epp. fam.*, p. 11, at the end of a letter to Bishop Bonemilch of Laasphe
(1508): "Ex aedibus Angelicis." As the winged messenger of heaven, Mercury was often asso-
ciated with the angel Gabriel.

B 1   EOBANUS HESSUS OF FRANKENBERG GREETS THE READERS.

I thought I would add some lighter poems here to make this opuscule of mine, small as it is, seem worth your while also on account of the diverse and pleasurable variety it offers. So do peruse the next couple of poems, such as they are, but without turning up your nose at them. The books of *Sylvae* that I have written here in Erfurt (and have promised you so often) should be leaving my literary workshop and reaching you any day now.[41] Farewell, kind readers, and treat your devoted Eobanus with the same respect he feels for you.

From the house of Mercury[42] in Erfurt, 13 June 1508.

B 2

Noticing Hessus mope,[43] the chief of the Pierian Maidens
addressed him as follows without further ado:

Calliope
What's bothering you, Hessus? Why are you sulking around so?
Tell me, please! What can it be that's making you hurt?

Hessus
5   Virgin, pride of poets, you know very well why I'm grieving.
Goddess, do give your poet some counsel on this.

Calliope
Ah, you really did go astray, you rash and imprudent fellow!
It was Venus who gabbled sweet nothings in your right ear!

Hessus
Flee, vanquished shame! Now I'll give free rein to my tongue
10   and the voice of my heart: Love has flung me in bonds.

[43]During his student years at Erfurt, Eobanus fell in love with a girl he calls "Flavia" (Blonde). See *Sylv. duae* 2, 31-37, where he alludes to the present dialogue with the Muse; *Buc.* 9, 1-2, where "Sylvius" is Eobanus and "flavae puellae" evidently refers to Flavia. In *Sylv.* 1, 6, 17-18, written in Prussia, he swears that he still loves her. He mentions her again in *Nup.* 12, written in February 1512. Krause, *HEH*, vol. 1, p. 140, suggests that "Flavia" may well be Katharina Später, to whom Eobanus proposed a month or two after his return to Erfurt in late July 1514 (see Mutian. *Ep.* 427) and whom he married at year's end. Cf. Camerarius, *Nar.* 14, 7.

Calliope

Vincula cogit Amor pueris stultaeque iuventae.
Pierio vatum spiritus igne calet.

Hessus

Spiritus igne calet vatum quoque nobilis isto.
Omnipotens nulli parcere novit Amor.

Calliope

15   Polluit intactam Cypris lasciva poaesim,
Egregias mentes degenerare docet.

Hessus

Egregias mentes Venus instruit, expolit, ornat
Et iuvat et morum nos docet omne genus.

Calliope

Quisquis amat, tacito secum consumitur aestu.
20   Nil facit et requiem nescit ineptus amans.

Hessus

Tabet ineptus amans, pueros Venus odit ineptos.
Quid sit amor quisquis noverit, aptus amat.

Calliope

Stulte puer, quid amas? Quid poma fugacia captas,
C4ʳ   Tantale? Vanescens tam cito languet amor.

Hessus

25   Quem non cogit Amor, quem non Venus aurea laedit?
Laesus in aversa virgine Phoebus erat.

Calliope

Mentitur varios error gentilis amores.
Falsa deum Christi numina vincit amor.

Hessus

Iuppiter Europam, Minoida Bachus, aquum rex
30   Phorcida, Mars Venerem, Pallada frater amat.

---

[44]The Lydian king Tantalus was punished in Hades by having fruit and water close at hand, yet forever out of his reach.

[45]The story of Apollo and Daphne is told in Ov. *Met.* 1, 452-567.

Calliope

Love flings only youths in bonds, only foolish young people.
  Poetic souls are fired with love for the Muse.

Hessus

The poets' noble soul can also be fired with passionate loving.
  Almighty Love can't bring himself to give quarter, alas.

Calliope

15   That wanton Cyprian defiles poetry, which ought to be spotless.
  First-rate minds she teaches to wallow in mud.

Hessus

Venus instructs, polishes, adorns, and helps first-rate talents;
  she also teaches them behavior of every kind.

Calliope

When you're in love, you exhaust yourself in unspoken passion.
20   The silly lover can't do a thing and hasn't a minute of peace.

Hessus

Silly lovers pine away. Venus detests silly fellows like that.
  If people knew what love is, they'd love with good sense.

Calliope

Foolish lad, why are you in love? Why do you grasp at elusive
  fruits, you Tantalus?[44] That's how fast fleeting love wanes.

Hessus

25   Is there anyone whom Love doesn't constrain, whom beautiful Venus
  doesn't hurt? A coy maiden even broke Phoebus's heart.[45]

Calliope

Pagan delusion invented love affairs of every description.
  Christ's love has conquered the gods' mythical might.

Hessus

Jupiter was in love with Europa, Bacchus with Ariadne, the sea-king
30   with Medusa, Mars with Venus, a brother with Pallas, no less.[46]

---

[46] Jupiter changed himself into a bull in order to ravish Europa. Bacchus fell in love with Minos's daughter Ariadne and placed her crown among the stars. Neptune (Poseidon) had an affair with the Gorgon Medusa, a daughter of Phorcus. Mars was caught sleeping with Venus. And Vulcan (Hephaestus) fell in love with his half-sister Pallas Athena and tried to rape her when she refused to marry him.

Calliope

Quid mirum potuit demens errare vetustas?
    Plena malis, expers luminis illa fuit.

Hessus

Incubat ille etiam Christi cultoribus error,
    Dum Paphias sentit tonsa corona faces.

Calliope

35   Quid quod ais, vates, Christi num sacra prophanas?
    Vita sacerdotes non violata decet.

Hessus

Sacra prophanat Amor, sacras Venus occupat aras.
    Haec etiam tetricus furta cucullus amat.

Calliope

Heu scelus! O, nostri quanta est patientia Christi,
40   Crimina qui miti lumine tanta videt!

C4ᵛ

Hessus

Languet inexpleta compressa libidine virtus,
    Et meretrix totas una gubernat opes.

Calliope

Caede! Pias verbis offendis talibus aures.
    Verba decet vatem non nisi casta loqui.

Hessus

45   Caede! Quid ulterius nostro non parcis amori,
    Alea cum tantos luserit ista viros?

Calliope

Parcimus et veniam largimur opemque ferendam
    Duximus. Errorem novimus, Hesse, tuum.

Hessus

Vulnere gaudet amans, medicantes despicit artes
50   Et cupit hiis aeger febribus esse diu.

Calliope

Is it any wonder that those silly ancients could be so badly
  mistaken? Blinded by sin, they lacked the true light.

Hessus

Even those who serve Christ harbor this madness, the minute
  their tonsured heads feel the torches of Love.

Calliope

35 What are you saying there, bard? Aren't you profaning the holy
  religion of Christ? Priests ought to keep themselves pure.

Hessus

Cupid defiles our religion; Venus occupies the sanctified altars.
  Even the glum-looking cowl loves stolen pleasures like these.

Calliope

Oh, the crime! Oh, how great is the forbearance of Christ, who
40 looks upon such deadly sins with a merciful eye!

Hessus

Virtue flags when it's crushed with insatiable lewdness,
  and one single whore controls all the wealth.

Calliope

Stop it! With such words you offend the ears of the pious.
  It behooves a bard to speak nothing but virtuous words.

Hessus

45 Stop it! Why don't you show some forbearance with *my* love,
  seeing that this fate befalls the most eminent men?

Calliope

We'll gladly forbear and forgive you; we've offered such help as
  you need. Hessus, we know exactly how you have erred!

Hessus

The lover rejoices in his wound. He scorns all the healing
50 arts; he loves his fever and wants to stay sick.

Calliope
Vana tuam quoties armat sententia mentem!
Quam facile causas invenit omnis amans!

Hessus
Uror, et indomitae serpunt per viscera flammae.
Causa prior menti non venit ulla meae.

Calliope
55   Supprime flammantes accensi pectoris aestus.
Quid nocet ingenio mobilis umbra tuo?

Hessus
C5ʳ   Prosunt ingenio Veneris commertia, verum
Ingenium nulla proficit arte magis.

Calliope
Sacra canunt veri, Veneris non furta, poaetae.
60   Quod prohibent vates, turpiter illud amas.

Hessus
Lydia Vergilium, te Cynthia, magne Properti,
Ussit Nasonem pulchra Corynna suum.

Calliope
Quos rapuit lasciva Venus, puer, expue vates.
Quod redolet Christi numina carmen ama.

Hessus
65   Delia Rhomani commovit plectra Tibulli,
Et tua, Galle sacer, cura Lycoris erat.

Calliope
Concinit illustres noster Baptista puellas,
Nulla tamen Paphia carmina sorde linit.

---

51 quoties *scripsi*: toties *AB*.   **56** Quid *A*: Qui *B*.

[47]The love poem *Lydia* was traditionally attributed to Vergil.
[48]The reference is to Vergil's friend, the poet C. Cornelius Gallus. Cf. Verg. *Ecl.* 10, 22.

Calliope

How often you arm your mind with specious opinions!
    How quick is every lover to find an excuse!

Hessus

I'm burning with passion; the unquenchable ardor is creeping
    through my entrails. Making excuses never entered my head.

Calliope

55   Put out the fire that flames up in your passionate vitals.
    Why let a shifting shadow do harm to your mind?

Hessus

Dealing with Venus is good for the mind. I can't think of
    any other art that avails poetic talent as much.

Calliope

True poets sing holy themes, not the stolen pleasures of Venus.
60   What the bards proscribe, that's what you shamefully love.

Hessus

Lydia inflamed Vergil,[47] Cynthia the great poet Propertius.
    The beautiful Corinna set her lover Ovid on fire.

Calliope

Lad, spit out the bards who were carried away by lewd Venus.
    Songs redolent of Christ's power are what you should love.

Hessus

65   Delia inspired the songs of the Roman Tibullus. And your true
    love, venerable Gallus, was Lycoris, wasn't she now?[48]

Calliope

Our Baptista sings the praises of illustrious maids.[49] Still,
    none of his poems are besmirched with illicit amours.

---

[49] Giovanni Battista Spagnolo of Mantua (1447-1516), better known as Baptista Mantuanus, wrote a series of narrative poems called *Parthenicae* on famous Christian virgins, including three books on the Virgin Mary (1481) and another three on St. Catherine of Alexandria (1489). Eobanus thought very highly of him, as did many of his Christian contemporaries. See *Buc.* 3, 17-27, with notes.

Hessus

Galla quid est illi? "Semel insanivimus omnes,"
70   Quando ait, insanus nunquid et ille fuit?

Calliope

Poenituit post tanta sacer discrimina vates,
Tecta cucullata lumina fronte gerens.

Hessus

Magne vale Baptista, Dei divine sacerdos.
C5ᵛ   Nos humili vates conditione sumus.

Calliope

75   Tuque vale, miserande puer. Tibi dexter Apollo!
O nimis infoelix et miser omnis amans!

Hessus

Sic ait aufugiens. Toto michi pectore flammae
Coesserunt calidae, coessit ineptus amor.

B 3   EOBANUS HESSUS FRANCOBERGIUS LECTORI-
BUS S.

Pauca haec ad exercitium ingenii conducere posse putantes
inter importunas scholastici ludi occupationes succisivis
horis et deduximus partim et coegimus, ut coram cernitis,
optimi litterarum iudices, pulchrum etiam et praeclarum
fore arbitratus, si nostrum hoc laudatissimum et in Germa-
nia princeps gymnasium Erphordiense in utroque Latinae
scriptionis genere pro ingenii mei viribus, si non mirifice,
qualitercumque tamen illustrarem. 2 Quod eo facilius me
facturum confidite, quo ad legendum vos premetium hoc
de pleno spicilegio contextum propensiores intellexero.
3 Valete.

    4 Ex edibus deorum nuncii Erphesfordiae, tertio Idus
Iunii anno DDD.VIII.

---

75 Apollo *B*: Appollo *A*.
    B 3   *A*: *om. B*.   4 Erphesfordiae *scripsi*: Erphesfordie *A*.

---

    [50]After the shepherd Faustus (whom Eobanus identifies with Mantuanus himself) has told
Fortunatus about his passionate love for Galla, Fortunatus comments, "semel insanivimus
omnes" (Mant. *Ecl.* 1, 118). This saying quickly became proverbial. Cf. Eob. *Buc.* 1, 34-35 (n.).

Hessus

So what is Galla to him? Since he said, "We've all been
70   crazy once," wasn't he once crazy himself?[50]

Calliope

After weathering such great storms, the holy poet repented.
That's why he covers his eyes and head with a cowl.[51]

Hessus

Farewell, great Baptista, divine priest of God! Compared
with you, the rest of us poets don't measure up.

Calliope

75   Farewell to you too, pitiable lad. May Apollo show you his
favor! Oh, how unhappy and wretched are people in love!

Hessus

These were her words as she vanished. The hot ardor left me;
the giddy passion wholly abandoned my breast.

**B 3   EOBANUS HESSUS OF FRANKENBERG GREETS THE
READERS.**

My primary purpose in writing this little work was to exercise my mind while
I was enjoying a break from the relentless demands of my teaching job. That
is the reason why I wrote it partly in prose, partly in verse, just as you see it be-
fore you, most excellent literary critics. But I also thought it would be a fine
and splendid thing if I should manage to add, if not a wondrous, then at least
some degree of luster to this university of ours at Erfurt, the most renowned
and distinguished in all of Germany, and to do this to the best of my abilities
in both types of Latin composition. Rest assured that this will be all the easier
for me, the more I find you inclined to read these first fruits, gleaned from the
full harvest. Farewell.

From the house of the messenger of the gods,[52] Erfurt, 11 June 1508.

[51] In a cycle of ten moral-allegorical eclogues, largely written during his youth and hence
entitled *Adulescentia* (1498), Mantuanus introduces the themes of licit and illicit love in *Ecl.*
1-4 and then tells how one of the shepherds, seeing a vision of the Virgin Mary, turns his back
on passionate love and enters a Carmelite monastery (*Ecl.* 7). Like other contemporaries,
Eobanus interpreted these eclogues to refer allegorically to the poet himself.

[52] That is, the "Engelshaus" (Angel's house). Cf. *Ama.*, ded. 15 above, with fn. 4.

B 4   UT LIBELLUS EXEAT

Vade, liber, nec vana time convicia, nam te
   Duringa nullus livor in urbe manet.
Te manet et populi favor et reverentia vulgi.
   I, placida cunctis excipiere manu.
5   Et legit et nostros Erphordia clara libellos
   Laudat. Ut huic placeas, caetera sperne, liber.

B 4   SOME PARTING WORDS TO THE BOOK

Off you go, book! Don't be afraid of fatuous insults. No one
   in this Thuringian city will regard you with spite.
They'll all love you; you'll be the toast of the town. Go.
   They can't wait to lay hands on you – nicely, of course!
5 Illustrious Erfurt is reading, even praising my poems. Just try to
   please her, my book. You can thumb your nose at the rest.

BUCOLICON

A BUCOLIC POEM

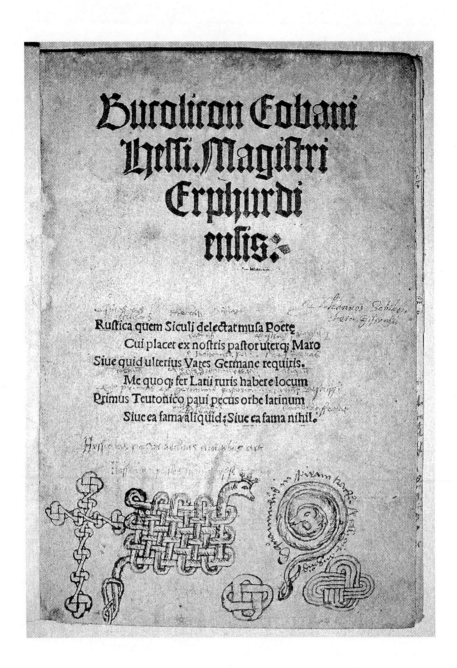

Title page of *Bucolicon*
Erfurt: Johann Knappe the Elder, 1509
Collection and photo B. N. U. Strasbourg

BUCOLICON

Introduction

In the liminary epigram to his *Bucolicon* Eobanus boasts that he is the first German to write an entire cycle of pastoral eclogues and pays homage to three masters of the genre: Theocritus (of whose idylls he knew the first seven in Martino Filetico's translation), Vergil, and the contemporary Italian humanist Baptista Mantuanus, famed in his day as the "Christian Vergil."

The three poets to whom Eobanus pays tribute may be taken to stand for three distinct versions of pastoral, as understood in the later Middle Ages and the Renaissance. The first and – to the Christian mind – lowest level is literal pastoral, exemplified in Theocritus's idylls. Here the herdsman is a shepherd pure and simple, an emblem of the natural man. On the allegorical level, as represented by Vergil's bucolics, the shepherd is a mask for the poet himself, his friends, patrons, and rivals. On the deepest level, however, the eclogue gains a tropological dimension and confronts us with questions of good and evil. This is the level exemplified by Baptista Mantuanus's incredibly popular *Adulescentia*, first published in 1498.

Each of these models comes to the fore in the *Bucolicon*. In imitation of Theocritus, Eobanus has his shepherds talk about everyday events or (as in eclogue 7) debate the merits of their flocks. But literal pastoral is nearly everywhere overshadowed by veiled allusions to the author and his circle of friends and rivals. On this allegorical level Eobanus recounts how Ludwig Christiani prodded him in the summer of 1504 to leave his native Hesse and attend the University of Erfurt. He describes university life, praises his friends Mutianus Rufus, Georg Spalatin, Justus Jonas, and Crotus Rubianus, among others, and mourns the death of Landgrave William II of Hesse. In other eclogues he satirizes the disastrous political and social conditions in Erfurt, lampoons the rival poet Riccardo Sbruglio, and expresses his disappointment at not receiving the laurel crown that lesser lights had so readily obtained. But the *Bucolicon* is also a moral-religious work, whose underlying theme is the story of Eobanus's inner growth. In the first eclogue he is a callow, if precocious youth, piping songs of innocence in his native Hesse. But no sooner has he reached Erfurt than he metamorphoses into a lusty swain and desperately falls in love (*Buc.* 3). In the latter half of the book

Eobanus comes of age. Now a mature twenty-one-year-old, he embraces Mu-
tianus's ideal of tranquillity (*Buc.* 6), satirizes passionate love as folly (*Buc.* 7),
and eschews it as "inutilis error" (*Buc.* 9). Thus Eobanus's pastoral cycle,
which like Vergil's bucolics starts off with the theme of displacement, fit-
tingly concludes with a Mantuanesque praise of love divine, as exemplified
by the Virgin Mary, goddess and guiding light of all good shepherds.

See further: Harry Vredeveld, "Pastoral Inverted: Baptista Mantuanus'
Satiric Eclogues and their Influence on the *Bucolicon* and *Bucolicorum Idyllia*
of Eobanus Hessus," *Daphnis* 14 (1985): 461-496; "A Neo-Latin Satire on
Love-Madness: The Third Eclogue of Eobanus Hessus' *Bucolicon* of 1509,"
Daphnis 14 (1985): 673-719; and "The *Bucolicon* of Eobanus Hessus: Three
Versions of Pastoral," *Acta Conventus Neo-Latini Guelpherbytani*, ed. Stella P.
Revard et al. (Binghamton, N.Y., 1988), pp. 375-382. For a discussion of the
pastoral tradition from antiquity to the Renaissance see Thomas K. Hub-
bard, *The Pipes of Pan: Intertextuality and Literary Filiation in the Pastoral
Tradition from Theocritus to Milton* (Ann Arbor, 1998). For an overview of
European and German Neo-Latin pastoral poetry see W. Leonard Grant,
Neo-Latin Literature and the Pastoral (Chapel Hill, 1965) and Lothar Mundt,
ed., *Simon Lemnius, Bucolica: Fünf Eklogen* (Tübingen, 1996), pp. 9-52.

Eobanus seems to have thought of writing an eclogue as early as the au-
tumn of 1506, for at *Laud.* 281-283 he imagines himself composing a
pastoral apotheosis of Mutianus Rufus, in imitation of Vergil's deification of
Daphnis in eclogue 5. It was not until 1508, however, that he began working
on his bucolics in earnest. Additions and revisions continued almost up to
the moment of publication in late September the following year.

The book appeared just once in the original version (Erfurt: Johann
Knappe the Elder, 1509). Eobanus revised the work extensively in the *Idyllia*
of 1528 (*B*) and 1539 (*O*), transforming the first ten eclogues into twelve
Theocritean idylls, eliminating the concluding eclogue in praise of the Virgin
Mary, and adding five new poems.

An edition of the *Idyllia* (according to the text of *O*) is planned for vol-
ume 4. The critical apparatus in the present volume, accordingly, includes
only such variant readings from the *Idyllia* as are needed to establish a text of
the *Bucolicon*.

A (1509)

[*Fraktur:*] Bucolicon Eobani | Heſſi. Magiſtri | Erphurdi | enſis. | [*roman:*
3 *distichs*]

Colophon, sig H5ʳ: HOC BVCOLICON PRIMVS PER | tranſformatos
                    characteres diuulgauit | Ioannes Canappus Erphur | diæ
                    ad celebrē feriā di | ui dęmonis Mi | chael'. M. | D.IX.

Collation: 4°: A⁶, B-D⁴, E⁶, F-G⁴, H⁶, [$3 signed], 38 leaves

Contents: A1ʳ title page; A1ᵛ blank; A2ʳ-A2ᵛ dedicatory letter; A3ʳ-G4ʳ text of the eclogues; G4ᵛ *Aequo iudicio lectori*, followed by: *In omnibus bene, nullis male facere divinum est, non humanum. Quid verius? Satis hoc tanquam Palladis aegide, si quaedam hic moramenta (ut fit in hoc scribendi genere) suspiciantur, tutari potuit nostra innocentia. Attamen (ut ingenue fatear), erudite lector, quae hic vel ungue vel obelisco notata offendes, non tam librario quam nobis adscribito. Quae tamen omnia suis locis verae lectioni restituta nostra diligentia fatebere. Vale.* Then follows a list of errata. H1ʳ *Teste conscientia* and four distichs, followed by: *Duce innocentia*; H1ʳ-H2ʳ poem of introduction to Johann Englender; H2ʳ-H2ᵛ three epigrams by Eobanus Hessus; H2ᵛ-H4ᵛ testimonials by Eobanus's friends; H4ᵛ-H5ʳ concluding poem by Eobanus Hessus; H5ʳ colophon; H5ᵛ and H6 blank

Copy-text: Strasbourg, Bibliothèque Nationale et Universitaire
Call number: R 104198

I have also consulted the two other known copies: Braunschweig, Stadtbibliothek (I 19/689); and Gotha, Forschungs- und Landesbibliothek (Mon. typ. 1509. 4° 13).

B (1528)

[*red:*] HELII EO= | BANI HESSI, BVCOLICORVM | IDYLLIA XII. NVPER | [*black:*] *anno demum decimooctauo* | *à prima æditione reco* | *gnita, ac dimi* | *dia plus* | *parte uel aucta, uel* | *concisa, atq; in ordinem ali=* | *um redacta.* | His acceſſere ex recenti æditione | *Idyllia Quinque.* | [*red:*] AVTHOR DE SEIPSO. | [*black: 3 distichs*]

Colophon, sig. G7ʳ: HAGANOAE IOHANNES SECE= | *rius excudebat.*
Anno. M.D.XXVIII. | *Menſe Auguſto.* | [*printer's device*]

Collation: 8°: A-G⁸, [$5 signed], 56 leaves

Location: Marburg (Lahn), Universitätsbibliothek
Call number: XVI C 372ᵍ/Ang. 2

This edition will be described more fully in volume 4.

O (1539)

OPERVM | HELII EOBA | NI HESSI FARRAGINES DVAE, NV | *per ab*
eodem qua fieri potuit diligentia contractæ, et | *in hanc, quam uides formam*
coactæ, quibus | *etiam non parum multa acceßerunt* | *nunc primum et nata &* |
ædita. | *Catalogum operum ipforum uerfa pa=* | *gella oftendet.* | *Acceßit*
unicuiq; farragini fuus etiam index, explicās | *quid in fingulis libris contineatur,*
& ad | *quos potißimum autor scribat.* | HALAE SVEVORVM | ANNO
XXXIX. | [*without indication of printer (Peter Braubach)*]

Collation: 8°: A⁸, a-z⁸, ²A-V⁸, ³A-Q⁸, [$5 signed], 480 leaves
Location: Wolfenbüttel, Herzog August Bibliothek
                        Call number: 143 Poetica

The book is divided into a "prior farrago" and a "posterior farrago." The
idylls, entitled *Bucolicorum idyllia XVII* in this redaction, are printed in the
first farrago, on sig. a2ʳ-g7ʳ. The *Operum farragines duae* will be described
more fully in volume 2 of this edition, introduction to *Sylvae duae.* See also
my *Helius Eobanus Hessus, Dichtungen: Lateinisch und Deutsch*, vol. 3 (Bern,
1990), pp. 569-571.

BUCOLICON
Eobani Hessi, Magistri Erphurdiensis

Rustica quem Siculi delectat Musa poetae,
    Cui placet ex nostris pastor uterque Maro,
Sive quid ulterius, vates Germane, requiris,
    Me quoque fer Latii ruris habere locum.
5   Primus Teutonico pavi pecus orbe Latinum,
    Sive ea fama aliquid, sive ea fama nihil.

A BUCOLIC POEM
by the Erfurt Magister Eobanus Hessus

If the rustic Muse of the Sicilian poet[1] delights you, if you, my fellow countrymen, take pleasure in the bucolics of the two Vergils,[2] or if any of you German bards are hankering for something else, put up with me as I too take my place in the Latin countryside. I am the first to pasture a Latin flock on German soil, whether that counts for something or not.[3]

---

[1]Theocritus of Syracuse (ca. 300–ca. 260 BC). Eobanus knew the first seven of his *Idylls* in the verse translation by Martino Filetico (ca. 1430–ca. 1490).

[2]The "two Vergils" are the Roman poet Vergil (70-19 BC) and the Italian poet Baptista Mantuanus (1447-1516). The latter was celebrated in his day as the "modern" or "Christian Vergil." He was especially famous for his *Adulescentia* (1498), a cycle of ten pastorals. Cf. Eob. *Buc.* 3, 17-27, with notes.

[3]Though by no means the first German to try his hand at the eclogue, Eobanus could rightly claim to be the first to write a whole "flock" of them.

A2ʳ

AD CLARISSIMUM VIRUM IOANNEM ENGLENDRUM DOCTOREM, DECURIAE CANCELLARIORUM HASSIAE PREFECTUM SUMMUM, EOBANI HESSI BUCOLICORUM DEDICATIO

Cum sol aestiva iam lampade finderet arvum
    Et calidus multo lumine Cancer erat,
Has ego vicinis collegi in montibus agnas
    Quos cum Turingo belliger Hessus habet.
5   Cunque coaegissem gelida pecus omne sub umbra,
    Iam nimia plenus messe calebat ager.
"Ibitis Hessiacam – servet vos Iuppiter – urbem.
    Illic vos," dixi, "qui tueatur erit.
Ibitis obliquo princeps ubi Cassela Fulda
10   Fluctuat in partes dissociata duas."
Accipe Doctor oves prestans Englendre bimestres,
    Munera si vatis sunt spetiosa tui.
Accipe, spes patriae, legum venerande triumvir,
    Quae tibi de proprio lacte colustra damus.
15   Par fuit ut tali condonareris honore,
    Qui patriae clarus vivis honore meae.
Par fuit illa meae pecudes in septa redirent
    In quibus haec primum grex mihi lecta fuit.
Scilicet Hessiacae debent mea carmina terrae,
20   Infanti puero quae mihi mater erat.
Primus honor patriae, primus mea iure tulisti
    Carmina et hoc primus munere dignus eras.

A2ᵛ
Nam quo se potius iactet mea patria quam te?
    Cui, rogo, plus debet quam tibi nostra chelis?
25   Alter ut es nostris Moecenas natus in oris,
    Virtutis debes praemia ferre tuae.
Teste Deo nescit virtus manifesta negari,
    Quae patet ut proprio lucifer igne deus.

---

[4]Johann Englender (Engelländer), who had earned a doctorate in civil and canon law, was head of the chancellery of Landgrave William II at Kassel, having succeeded Mutianus Rufus's brother Dr. Johann Muth in that position in 1505. From about 1511 to early 1514 Englender was chancellor in Mainz. He died at Nuremberg in 1517. Eobanus introduced himself to this potential patron in the autumn of 1508, at the urging of Mutianus Rufus. See *Buc.* B 2, with fn. 101.

TO THAT MOST CELEBRATED GENTLEMAN, DOCTOR JOHANN ENGLENDER,[4] HEAD OF THE CHANCELLERY OF HESSE, DEDICATORY LETTER OF EOBANUS HESSUS'S BUCOLICS

When the sun was already cracking open the fields with its summery torch and the hot Crab shone brightly in the sky,[5] I brought these lambs together in the nearby mountains that the warlike Hessians share with the Thuringians.[6] And after I had herded the whole flock in the cool shade, the farms were already humming with the harvest and stood full of rich sheaves of grain. "May Jupiter watch over you," I said, "for you're going to go to the capital of Hesse. There you'll find someone to protect you. You're going to go to the place where the capital city Kassel, [10] split in two by the winding Fulda, rises on rolling hills."

Excellent Doctor Englender, take charge of these two-months-old sheep,[7] if this gift from your bard appeals to you. Hope of our native land, venerable triumvir of our legal system, accept the beestings that I am giving you from my own milk. It is fitting that you be honored in this fashion, for you have attained honor and renown in my homeland. It is fitting that my sheep should return to the same folds where I first began to gather this flock. My poems, after all, are profoundly indebted to the land of Hesse [20] that was my mother during my earliest youth.

First ornament of my fatherland, you are the first dedicatee of these poems of mine, and rightly so, for you are the first who is worthy of this favor. Indeed, in whom does my fatherland glory more than you? To whom, I ask, does my lyre owe more than you? And inasmuch as you are another Maecenas – a home-grown one at that – you deserve to receive the rewards for your magnanimity.[8] No one invoking God as his witness can deny conspicuous virtue, particularly when it shines forth with its own fire, just like the sun-god.

[5] Because the sun enters the Crab at the summer solstice, this constellation is associated with the heat of midsummer. Cf. Ov. *Met.* 10, 126-127; Eob. *Her. Chr.* 5, 15; 6, 35.

[6] He has now collected the eclogues written during the past two years at Erfurt.

[7] The sheep (eclogues) are still young, having been born only recently.

[8] Eobanus compares Englender to Gaius Maecenas (about 70-8 BC), the Roman statesman who patronized such literary giants as Vergil and Horace, and goes on to suggest that Landgrave William II of Hesse is another Caesar Augustus. He does so also in *Buc.* B 2, 31-32.

Macte igitur, priscos tecum revocabimus annos,
30   Quale sub antiquo Caesare tempus erat.
Tu nostras fautor tantum defende Camaenas,
     Te canet aeterna nostra Thalia cheli.
Interea celebri capras numerabis in aula,
     Donec armenti copia grandis erit.
35 Sic alacrem tecum formosa Halerina iuventam
     Expleat, optata prole beata parens.
Addere non parvis maiora studebimus istis,
     Munera non sordent si tibi nostra. Vale.

Hail to you, therefore! Together we'll bring back the days of yore – [30] an age such as existed during the reign of ancient Caesar. Just protect and support my Muses; then my Thalia will sing your praises in eternal song. In the meantime you will count my goats at the renowned court until the herd grows enormously large. So may the lovely Halerina spend a vigorous youth by your side and become a mother blessed with the offspring you wished for![9] I for my part will try to add greater works to these not insignificant ones, provided that you find these gifts of mine not wholly unworthy of you. Farewell.

---

[9]Englender's wife, née Haler, is praised extravagantly in *Buc.* B 2, 39-44.

BUCOLICORUM EOBANI HESSI AEGLOGA PRIMA

Paniscus, Camillus

Pan. Alma sinum vario turgentem germine Mater
Ore renidenti pandit paritura, Camille.
Vernat humus, frondent sylvae, viridantia rident
Pascua. Nunc etiam salientibus undique rivis
5 Gramina luxuriant, quando omnibus omnia terris
Sponte sua veniunt. Patria tu solus in umbra
Ocia non ullam ducis referentia laudem,
Ut caper aut hircus pingui castratus in arvo.
Laetus adhuc et flore virens vix puberis aevi,
10 Montibus et sylvis quibus Hessia dives abundat
Digna cothurnatae modularis carmina Musae.
Et te summa licet mirentur culmina sacrum
Cantantem sine teste melos, hic foenore nullo
Ludis et heu sterilem quondam experiere Camaenam,
15 Pascua cum sero patriae placuisse dolebis.
Desertas inter pecudes inconditaque arva
Tam dulces annos, tam florida tempora perdis!
Nos alios fines melioraque rura tenemus
Pastores quos fertilibus Turingia pratis
20 Pascit. Fortunate puer, si talibus arvis,
Si tali liceat mecum considere terra
Et dites habitare casas et plena videre

Ubera quae totos replent mulctralia soles!
O tibi quam nostrae resonabunt dulcia sylvae
25 Omnia! Non isto quicquam iucundius aevo.
　　Cam. O Panisce, tuae quanta est facundia Musae!
Inter Apollineas laurus exercite, nondum
Talis eras quando hinc laudatam egressus in oram.
Vix puer undenas poteras numerare capellas.

---

*Buc.*1 *Cf. Idyllion 1 in BO.*　　**1** *Nomen pastoris in margine* Pan. *om. A.*　　Alma *BO:* Lma *A.*
14 experiere *A (in erratis) BO:* experire *A (in textu).*　　**20** *In margine add. A nomen pastoris* Ca.,
sed del. in erratis.　　**27** Apollineas *scripsi:* Appollineas *A.*

[10]Like Vergil's first bucolic, this eclogue deals with the theme of uprooting: how Eobanus
came to leave Frankenberg, Hesse, and enroll at the University of Erfurt in the autumn of
1504. Paniscus ("Little Pan") stands for Eobanus's teacher Ludwig Christiani of Frankenberg,

THE FIRST ECLOGUE OF EOBANUS HESSUS'S BUCOLICS[10]

Paniscus, Camillus

Paniscus. Our bountiful Mother is opening up her bosom, swelling with all kinds of buds. Her face beaming, she's about to give birth, Camillus. The ground is turning green, the woods are in leaf, the verdant pastures are smiling. Now, with the brooks tumbling again everywhere, the grass too is growing lush. In fact, all things all over the world are coming back of their own accord. Only you are still living a life of lease in the shade of your homeland, without making a name for yourself, just like a castrated goat or buck on a fattening pasture.[11] Still rejoicing in the flower of your teen-aged youth, [10] amidst the mountains and forests in which wealthy Hesse abounds, you pipe songs worthy of the buskined Muse.[12] But even if the highest peaks admire you as you sing a sacred tune to yourself, your playing here brings you no profit at all. Alas, one of these days you'll wake up to find that your Muse has grown sterile and will regret too late that you were so attached to the pastures of your homeland. Surrounded by solitary sheep and unplowed fields, you're wasting your finest years, the very bloom of your youth! We herdsmen inhabit another country with better fields – Thuringia gives us a good living on her fertile meadows. [20] Happy young poet, if only you would come with me and settle on fields like that, in such a blessed land, and live in prosperous huts and see full udders that keep brimming the milk pails day in, day out! Oh, how sweetly would our forests echo all your songs! In this day and age there is nothing quite so delightful.

Camillus. O Paniscus, how marvelous is the eloquence of your Muse! Trained among Apollo's laurels, you weren't such a brilliant poet back then when you departed hence for the land you now praise so highly. As a lad you were barely

---

who matriculated at Erfurt in 1501 and became M.A. in 1505. See Camerarius, *Nar.* 7, 1, with fn. 18; Eob. *Rec.* 84-87; *Idyl.* 1, argument. Paniscus reappears as Eobanus's mentor in *Buc.* 8, 65-97. Camillus ("Adolescent") is Eobanus himself.

[11] Though Camillus is an active poet-singer with a fertile mind, he has not yet published any of his work.

[12] Greek and Roman actors of tragedies wore buskins – high boots with a very thick sole. Hence "buskined" figuratively means, "concerned with lofty themes."

30 Saepe ego (nam memini) cum fors compelleret agnos,
"Coge tuos," dixi, neque tu discernere posses.
Discrevi. Tu flens munuscula pauca dedisti –
Caseolos, floccos, plumas, coclearia, fundas.
    Pan. Nemo vir evadit qui non puer. Attamen omnes,
35 Ut reor, in primis pueriliter aegimus annis.
Atque utinam crescente aevo sapientia saltem
Crescat et ingrediens veniat cum laude senectus!
    Cam. Non mihi iam pastor tantum, Panisce, videris
Qui canat in triviis passim, sed qualibus aiunt
40 Orphea carminibus fatum deflesse nefandum
Euridices. Qualis Thamiras, Amphion, Apollo,
Qualis erat qui magnanimum victrice leonem
Confecit funda, talem te nostra tulerunt
Saecula. Nate bonis avibus, tibi numina rident.
45   *Pan.* Tu quoque, dumosis licet in convallibus erres
Et lacer heu sola totis sub rupe diebus,
Carmina per duras longe resonantia cautes
Concinis, aeterna dignus quem fronde coronent
Pierides. Nec enim credebam in vepribus istis
50 Orphea vel Thamiram vel clarum Amphiona cantu
Vel qui magnanimum (quisquis fuit ille) leonem
Stravit inexperta quemquam potuisse Camaena
Dicere. Vix nostri pastores tale loquuntur.
    Cam. Haec ego nescio quo didici referente magistro,
55 Cum puer hunc olim vix possem ferre bacillum.
Cernis, adhuc memori sunt haec mihi scripta papyro.
Verum age, quando breves exaltatissimus umbras
Sol facit et valles et frigida lustra capellae
Pascentesque tenent loca sublucentia thauri,
60 Dic age, quam vobis foelicia pascua, quae vos
Tam doctos regio pastores educat, unde
Et quare patrios tandem remearis ad agros.
Dic age. Iam lectas omnis grex ruminat herbas.
    Pan. Et placet, auditu dulce est et amabile dictu.

A4ʳ

---

51 fuit *A (in erratis)*: om. *A (in textu)*.

[13]When still a young shepherd, David killed a lion and a bear; see 1 Samuel (Vulg. *1. Reg.*) 17, 34-37. The biblical story is silent about the sling in connection with the wild beasts, but does mention it immediately afterwards (1 Samuel 17, 40-50) as the weapon used to kill Goliath.

able to count eleven goats. [30] Often (for I remember it
well), when chance drove our lambs together, I'd say to you,
"Round up your animals." But you couldn't tell yours from
mine, so I would do it for you. You would start crying and
give me little gifts – small cheeses, tufts of wool, feathers,
spoons, slings.

Paniscus. No one grows into manhood who wasn't a boy
first. But I imagine we've all acted childishly while growing
up. If only wisdom increased with increasing years and we
could enter on old age with our reputation intact!

Camillus. Now you no longer strike me as the average
shepherd that sings at every crossroads, Paniscus, but rather
as an Orpheus who, we're told, [40] lamented the tragic fate
of Eurydice in songs no less moving than yours. A second
Thamyras, Amphion, Apollo, a match for him who slew the
great-hearted lion with his victorious sling[13] – that is what
our own century has produced in you. You must have been
born under a happy star, for the gods are smiling upon you.

Paniscus. Though you roam about in brambly valleys,
though your skin, alas, is torn as you sit piping all day long
beneath a solitary cliff, you too sing songs that echo from
afar over the hard crags, you too deserve to be crowned by
the Muses with an evergreen garland.[14] I certainly didn't
expect to encounter a poet in these briers [50] who, despite
his inexperience, would manage to mention Orpheus or
Thamyras or the famed singer Amphion or allude to the man
(whoever he was) who brought down the great-hearted lion.
Where I come from, the shepherds hardly ever talk like that.

Camillus. Those names I learned long ago from some
teacher, I forget who, when I was still so small that I was
barely able to carry this staff. See, I still have it written down
in my notebook. But come now, since the noonday sun is
casting short shadows, since the goats are keeping to the val-
leys and cool woods and the grazing bulls to the shady spots,
[60] do tell me: what about those happy pastures that you
spoke of? What region produces such learned shepherds as
you? From where and for what reason have you finally re-
turned to your native land? Come, tell me. By now the
whole herd is chewing the cud it has gathered.

Paniscus. I'll be glad to comply, for it is a delight to hear
and a pleasure to tell. But first let's move into the cool

---

[14]That is, with the laurel crown symbolic of poetic immortality. Cf. *Buc.* 8 below.

65   Quin prius huic ambo gelidae succedimus umbrae,
    Ne calor aestivus sitientia labra retardet.
       Cam. En etiam hiis dulces saliunt radicibus undae.
    Hic sacri latices, hic vivida vaena scaturit,
    Hic duo florali sedilia cespite vernant.
70   Hic mihi grata quies. Alia tu parte sedeto.
    Hiis tamen incoepto divertimur. Incipe, vates.
       Pan. Proxima montanis Turingia terminat Hessis

    Imperium, dives regio florentibus arvis,
    Laeta iugis nemorum, sed multo laetior agro.
75   Illic flava Ceres, Rhodiensibus aemula pratis,
    Foelices pingui campos obducit arista,
    Et gravidae plenis turgent in collibus uvae.
    Sunt etiam gregibus sua pascua dum viret annus
    Mille per abruptos montes, et summa capellae
80   Transcendunt iuga, mille boves in vallibus herbas
    Non ullo carpunt foetas serpente. Videres
    Gramineum innumeras pratum tondere bidentes.
    Iamque aliquis summo speculans a vertice pastor
    Certantes in valle stupet, plena omnia Musis.
85   Ille deos laudat, miseros hic deflet amores,
    Et cava multiplici resonant obstacula cantu.
    Mammosae Veneres illic et Phillides errant,
    Sylvani satyrique leves faunique salaces,
    Sylvestres nymphae, Dryades, mollesque Napeae.
90   *Cam.* Hem, quid mammosa faciunt in Phillide fauni?
    Absint nequitiae nostris ab ovilibus omnes!
       Pan. Macte, puer, tali dulcem visure senectam
    Ingenio, si firmus eris. Nunc coepta sequemur.
    Urbs vetus in media est regione, Erphurdia nostris
95   Dicta, potens, opulenta, ingens, quam (credere durum est)
    Non facile unius tibi terminet orbita visus.
    Illa vorat duri quicquid peperere labores.

    Seu pera seu pileolo seu forte galero

[15]In this Arcadian world, reminiscent of the golden age, there are no snakes in the grass. Cf. Verg. *Ecl.* 4, 22-25; Calp. *Ecl.* 1, 37-42; Hor. *Carm.* 1, 17, 5-12; *Epod.* 16, 51-52; Eob. *Buc.* 4, 31-33; 6, 23-25; 9, 98-104; 11, 84. The idyll is disturbed in the later eclogues. See *Buc.* 4, 6-26 (in the late spring of 1509, during the so-called "Mad Year" in Erfurt) and *Buc.* 9, 29-35 (after the death of Landgrave William II on 11 July 1509).

[16]Walther Ludwig suggests that this shepherd is the famed humanist Mutianus Rufus, who lived in nearby Gotha. See his "Eobanus Hessus in Erfurt: Ein Beitrag zum Verhältnis von

shade over here, both of us, so the summer heat won't parch our lips and hinder our singing.

Camillus. Look! There's sweet water here too, tumbling through the roots. Here is a sacred spring, a rill of bubbling water gushing forth. And here are two fine places to sit in the flowering greensward. [70] I'll take my ease in this spot. You can sit on the other side. But with this talk we are turning away from our topic. Go ahead, poet.

Paniscus. Not far from here, the dominion of the mountain-dwelling Hessians is bounded by Thuringia. It is a land rich in flourishing farms, abounding in mountain ridges and woods, but far more abounding in arable land. There, striving to equal the fields of Rhodes, golden Ceres covers the fecund acres with plump ears of grain, and heavy grapes swell on the laden hillsides. The herds have their pastures too, as long as the year greens on a thousand steep hills. Goats [80] clamber over the highest ridges, and cattle without number graze placidly in the valleys, for the grass is not teeming with snakes.[15] Countless sheep may be seen cropping the grassy pasture. And now some shepherd[16] keeping watch on a hilltop marvels at the pipers who compete with each other in the valley below. The whole countryside is full of singers. One extols the gods, another beweeps his unrequited love, and the mountain vales resound with the manifold songs. Bosomy Venuses and Phyllises stray about there, sylvans too and wanton satyrs and lascivious fauns as well as the nymphs of the woods: dryads and voluptuous dell nymphs.

Camillus. [90] Hem, what are those fauns up to with the bosomy Phyllis? Let all depravity stay far away from our sheepfolds!

Paniscus. Bravo, lad, for such an attitude! If you stick to it, you're sure to enjoy a sweet old age. Now let's get back to our topic. In the center of the region there is an ancient city we call Erfurt, powerful, affluent, and so huge that, believe it or not, you can't easily take it all in with a single glance. The town devours everything that hard labor can produce. If you need a bag, a felt cap or perhaps a wide-brimmed hat

Humanismus und Protestantismus," *Mittellateinisches Jahrbuch* 33 (1998): 159. Cf. Eob. *Buc.* 2, 100-101, with fn. 24. On Mutianus's life see Camerarius, *Nar.* 12, 12–13, 10, with fn. 36. In the summer of 1504 Mutianus was not yet in contact with the Erfurt humanists; but Eobanus evidently writes these lines from the perspective of ca. 1508.

Seu manicis opus est, donat pro munere merces.
100   Illa etiam, si forte velis, pro vellere nummos
Porrigit et rem re mutat. Vorat omnia, reddit
Omnia: pro tribulis spinas, pro verbere plagas.
Ergo age, dum viridi succo tua pullulat aetas,
Collige si qua tenes parvi congesta peculi.
105   Foelices mecum campos et pinguia rura
Quaere. Nocent pecori vepres et tristis achantus.
     Cam. Hessia, dives agris densisque uberrima sylvis,
Finitimas (ne praefer!) opes ita vincit ut agnum
Imbellem furibunda audax in praelia thaurus,
110   Ut fluvio parvum superat vagus Aedera Nemphim –
Aedera qui veteri non est minus aurifer Hermo.
Hic fluviis alacres praeterlabentibus herbae
Alludunt. Cernis quam consita littora, quam sit
Pingue solum. Viret omnis ager. Stant gramina circum
115   Stagna, lacus, fontes, puteos, rivosque virentes.
Aspice summa procul frondentis culmina Gosi.
Quam nitet et ver aspectu testatur amaenum!
Hos agros, has delitias, haec pascua linquam?
Sed linquam. Dulces curae, loca nota, valete.
120   Tu vero infoelix mecum laudata videbis
Rura pecus. Laetos fines, i, perge videndum,
O cui non licuit patrios errare per agros
Amplius et quondam consuetas carpere frondes.
     Pan. Sol ruit interea. Vocat ad mulctralia vesper.
125   Sume pedum, compelle gregem, numeraque capellas,
Ne quis forte absens in vepribus haereat hircus.

A5ᵛ

AEGLOGA SECUNDA

Carmina cum primum mihi pastoralia divae
Pierides canerent et me florente iuventa
Iuppiter indueret, tum sic Eobanus in umbra

---

99 *In margine add. A* Pa., *sed del. in erratis.*
  Buc. 2. *Cf. Idyllion 2 in BO.*

[17]The "small animals" refer allegorically to the poems Eobanus has composed thus far.

or some gloves, it will provide you these wares upon payment. [100] Or, if that is what you wanted perhaps, it will also offer you money for wool or will barter one thing for another. The town devours everything and pays back all things in kind: thorns for thistles, a thrashing for a whipping. Come on, while you're in the bud of youth and your sap is still green, gather up whatever you've been able to acquire in the way of small animals[17] and come with me to those blessed fields and fertile farms. Briers and the spiny acanthus are harmful to livestock.

Camillus. Hesse, rich in farms and covered with dense forests, outclasses the neighboring states (don't put them ahead!) just as a bull outstrips the peaceful lamb when he recklessly charges into furious battle, [110] just as the meandering Eder surpasses the tiny Nemphe with the force of its current – the Eder that is no less gold-bearing than the Hermus of old. Here the nimble grass sports with the streams that glide past. You can see for yourself how overgrown the banks are, how fertile the soil is. Every field is green. There is grass all around the ponds, lakes, springs, wells, and verdant brooks. Look at the crest of the tree-covered Goßberg over there.[18] How radiant it is! By its very appearance it testifies to the beauty of springtime. How can you expect me to leave these fields behind, these delights, these pastures? But I'll leave them nevertheless. Good-bye, favorite haunts of mine, places I know so well! [120] But you, poor flock, you'll be going with me to see that wonderful country. Let's go and visit those blessed meadows. Alas, I can't let you roam the fields of our homeland anymore and let you nibble the leaves that you've gotten used to.

Paniscus. The sun has begun to set in the meantime. Evening calls us back to the milk pails. Take your crook, round up the flock, and count the goats, lest some missing buck be caught in the briers.

THE SECOND ECLOGUE

When the divine Muses first inspired me to pastoral song and Jupiter endowed me with blooming youth, then I, Eobanus, being a shepherd already, leaned back in the

[18]The Goßberg is a hill to the north of Frankenberg, on the other side of the Eder. Cf. *Rec.* 182-183.

Proclivis charo cecini, iam pastor, amico.
5   Vallis erat curvo paulum secreta recessu,
Clausa iugis, vitreo manans laetissima rivo.
Stat domus in medio divi veneranda Georgi,
Tecta vetusta, ipsis requies gratissima Musis.
Hac olim domini sacrae qui praefuit aedi
10   Cum servaret oves puer in convalle Pudicus,
Quod tum floreret iuvenis, quod mollibus annis
Ferventi dulces sequeretur pectore Musas,
Ad rivum salientis aquae cum sepe veniret,
Ludere fragranti sic est auditus in herba:
15   "Musae, noster amor, dulces mea gaudia Musae,
Pro Iove quae Christum canitis, quae rura beati
Syderis Aeoum longe proiecta sub orbem
Servatis, fatali ubi saevus ab arbore serpens
Pastorem vetitum iussit decerpere pomum,
20   Ite, novos, Musae, flores legite, ite, Camaenae.

A6r   "Vos ego per sylvas, valles, iuga, culmina, montes,
Lustra, rubos, vepres, fluvios, vada, saxa, latebras,
Rura, casas, villas, agros, nemora, antra, cavernas,
Stagna, lacus, rupes, scopulos, mare, tesqua, salebras,
25   Vos ego per pluvias, ventos, nymbosque repentes,
Frigora dura, nives, glaciem, gelicidia, brumas,
Hirsutasque hyemes, laedentesque arva pruinas,
Vos ego per tenebras sequerer noctesque profundas,
Musae, noster amor, dulces mea gaudia Musae.
30   O utinam volucres faceret mihi Daedalus alas!
Aoniam, Cyrrham, Parnassum, Helicona, Cytheron,
Culmina Christicolis etiam venerata poetis,
Prepetibus pennis ad vos ego sepe venirem.

[19]Just as *Buc.* 1 is reminiscent of Vergil's first eclogue, so *Buc.* 2 echoes Vergil's second. After a brief narrative introduction, both Vergil's and Eobanus's poems offer a shepherd's monologue – a passionate declaration of love. But while Vergil's Corydon is head over heels in love with the handsome lad Alexis, Pudicus exults in his chaste love for the Christian Muses.

Pudicus ("Chaste") is Eobanus's friend Georg Burckhardt (1484-1545), better known as Spalatinus after his native Spalt, southwest of Nuremberg. Spalatin matriculated at Erfurt in 1498, obtaining his B.A. the following year. In October 1502 he enrolled at Wittenberg (M.A. in early 1503). Having returned to Erfurt in 1504, he continued his legal studies during the winter semester and joined the circle of humanists around Mutianus Rufus. At the latter's recommendation, he was appointed librarian and teacher of novices at Georgenthal in 1505. He was ordained priest in July 1508. Two months later he was appointed tutor to John Frederick of Saxony, nephew of Elector Frederick the Wise. In 1516 the Elector made him his pri-

shade to sing the following words to the friend I loved dearly.[19]

There is an enchanting valley, somewhat off the beaten track in its winding seclusion, surrounded by mountain ridges and watered by a glittering brook. In its midst stands an old house consecrated to Saint George,[20] a resting place that the Muses themselves find most welcome. [10] It was in this valley that the lad Pudicus used to watch over the sheep of the lord who was in charge of the holy sanctuary. And because he was then in the flush and flower of life, because in his tender years he followed the sweet Muses with ardent heart and often came to the tumbling brook, he once was heard singing thus in the redolent greensward:

"Muses, my dearest love, sweet Muses, my greatest joy – you who sing of Christ instead of Jove, you who dwell in the land that lies under a blessed star far away in the East where the fell serpent bade the shepherd pluck the forbidden fruit from the baneful tree – [20] go, Muses, gather fresh flowers, go, you Camenae.

"I'd follow you through forests, valleys, ridges, peaks, mountains, thickets, brambles, briers, rivers, fords, rocks, lairs, fields, huts, farmhouses, plowlands, woods, grottos, caverns, ponds, lakes, crags, reefs, seas, deserts, rocky roads, I'd follow you through rainstorms, whirlwinds, and sudden downpours, hard frosts, snow, ice, hail, cold snaps and shaggy winters and field-scarring rime, I'd follow you through gloom and pitch-black nights, Muses, my dearest love, sweet Muses, my greatest joy. [30] Oh, how I wish Daedalus could fashion fleet wings for me! Aonia, Cyrrha, Parnassus, Helicon, Cithaeron – peaks revered by us Christian poets too – I'd fly to you again and again on soaring wings.

---

vate secretary. He eventually became the prince's confidant, confessor, and court preacher. A vigorous supporter of Luther, Spalatin often mediated between him and Frederick the Wise and did much to help the cause of reformation, both in the university and in the church. After the Elector's death in 1525, Spalatin became pastor in Altenburg and actively conducted church visitations. In 1528 he was appointed superintendent of the Altenburg district; later he served as advisor to the Elector of Saxony at the diet of Augsburg (1530) and at various religious colloquies. See also Camerarius, *Nar.* 17, 7.

The present eclogue must have been composed in the summer of 1508, not long after Spalatin's taking holy orders and before his departure from Georgenthal in the autumn of that year.

[20]The monastery of Georgenthal ("George's dale"), south of Gotha, where Spalatin worked from 1505 to the autumn of 1508.

"Ite, novos, Musae, flores legite, ite, Camaenae.
35   "Carmina sacrorum sunt immortalia vatum,
Immortalis honor. Pereunt aes, purpura, gemmae
Quas nigris avidus tollit mercator ab Indis,
Nomina quarum olidis sunt cognita dactilothecis.
Iaspida me docuit mater viridemque smaragdon
40   Quaeque gerunt collo suspensa corallia nymphae.
Omnia pretereunt; nescitis fata, Camaenae.
Vos mea cum dulci captatis pectora flamma,
Despitio quicquid curae est mortalibus usquam –
Nec mirum, vobis presentibus omnia sordent,
45   Musae, noster amor, dulces mea gaudia Musae.
      "Luxuriant Zephyro flores, nova gramina rivis,
Vitali pluvia Cereris sata, fontibus horti,
Littoribus salices, procera paludibus alnus,
Graminibus vaccae, lascivae fronde capellae.
50   Gaudet apis cythiso, sed dulci plus apiastro.
Vos mea cura deae, Musae, mea sola voluptas,
Vita, salus, requies, divae, vos omnia, Musae.
"Ite, novos, Musae, flores legite, ite, Camaenae.
"Non ita mellitae sapiunt mihi dulce placentae,
55   Non pyra, non cerasum, non grati segmina porri,
Non oleata Ceres et nuper cocta polenta,
Non sic hesterno perfusum lacte moretum,
Quam vestrum mihi dulce decus, quam vos mihi gratae,
Musae, noster amor, dulces mea gaudia Musae.
60   "Sum puer, et viridi succo mea pullulat aetas
Ut nova quae veteri turget de palmite vitis.
Et mihi forma decens. Nuper, cum pectine crines
Comeret hos niveo, dixit mihi sedula mater:
'Accipe et in speculo te contemplare, Pudice.
65   Vicinum forma superas, ni fallar, Adonim.'
'Vestrum, quicquid id est,' dixi, 'mea gaudia, Musae.
Hoc decus, iste vigor, vobis mea pullulat aetas.'
"Ite, novos, Musae, flores legite, ite, Camaenae.
"Integer ut putri turgescit surculus agro,
70   Sicut senta rosae subter spineta rubentes,
Sic inter pueros et mille Pudicus agrestes
Vester erit. Vos acceptum referetis honorem

A6ᵛ (margin, left of line 46)

B1ʳ (margin, left of line 70)

---

36 gemmae *BO*: gemme *A*.   *Post* 69 *add. A in ima pagina* Musae, noster amor, dulces mea gaudia Musae, *sed del. in erratis.*

"Go, Muses, gather fresh flowers, go, you Camenae.

"The songs of the holy bards are immortal, an everlasting glory. Other treasures pass away – money, purple, the jewels that the covetous merchant brings back from the swarthy Indians, the gems that bear names familiar to fragrant ring caskets. Mother told me about the jasper and the green emerald [40] and the corals that girls wear as a necklace. All these things pass away; only you, Camenae, are deathless. When you captivate my breast with sweet ardor, I scorn everything that people normally hold dear – and no wonder, for in your presence everything else seems shabby, Muses, my dearest love, sweet Muses, my greatest joy.

"Flowers thrive in warm breezes, fresh grass next to brooks, grain crops in life-giving rain, gardens near springs, willows on riverbanks, towering alders in marshes, cows on grass, randy goats on leaves. [50] Bees are fond of clover, but even more of sweet-smelling balm. You goddesses are my true love; you Muses are my one delight, my life, my health, my repose. You are everything to me, divine Muses.

"Go, Muses, gather fresh flowers, go, you Camenae.

"To me no honeyed muffins can ever taste so sweet, no pears, no cherries, no, not even the chopped leeks that I like so much, no bread sprinkled with oil or barley fresh from the stove, no dish of herbs drenched with one-day-old milk, as your beauty is sweet to me, as you are dear to me, Muses, my dearest love, sweet Muses, my greatest joy.

[60] "I'm just a lad. Still bursting with youth, with my sap running green, I feel like a new bud swelling on the old vine shoot. And I am good-looking too. The other day, as she was combing out my hair with a snow-white comb, my sedulous mother told me: 'Hold this mirror and look at yourself, Pudicus. Unless I'm mistaken, you're much handsomer than our neighbor Adonis.'[21] 'For what it's worth,' I cried, 'this belongs to you, Muses, my greatest joy. My good looks, my energy, my youth, they all sprout for you.'

"Go, Muses, gather fresh flowers, go, you Camenae.

"As a vigorous seedling spreads its roots in loamy soil, [70] as red roses bloom among thorns, so Pudicus will always be yours, even among a thousand farm boys. You'll be

---

[21]The name "Adonis" recalls the beautiful youth with whom Venus fell in love. He is mentioned again in *Buc.* 3, 142; 5, 32; and 7, 41. Euricius Cordus uses the name in *Ecl.* 1 for Landgrave Philip of Hesse.

Hunc mihi: stabit enim nivei flos ille pudoris
Qui nunc fertilibus vobis protuberat annis,
75 Musae, noster amor, dulces mea gaudia Musae.
   "Dicite, quae potior, quae maior in orbe cupido,
Musica qui sacra velatis tempora lauro,
Quam Musas colere et Musarum amplexibus uti,
Vivere apud Musas, doctis se tradere Musis?
80 Ite procul, veneres et inanis gaudia formae,
Forma, genus, tituli, fastus, laus, gloria, sanguis!
Me iuvat in viridi requietum gramine doctam
Ducere segnitiem, tactis ubi laeta lapillis
Unda sonat tacitaeque labans admurmurat aurae
85 Lataque fructificans extendit brachia lotos
Aut ramosa levem dilatat populus umbram.
   "Ite, novos, Musae, flores legite, ite, Camaenae,
Samsucos, hederas, amaranthon, smilaca, nardos,
Lilia verna, thimum, colocasia, balsama, stacten,
90 Et crocon, et calthas, violas laetumque nepenthe.
Cingite victuros milleno flore poaetas,
Inter quos utinam quota pars ego nomen haberem!
Valle sub hac viridi canerem te, dive Georgi,
Qui Musas inter sanctas in monte quiescis
B1ᵛ 95 Sydereo vultuque vides hec pascua laeto.
   "Carmina morte carent vatum. Gaudete, capellae.
Rodite frondosas fagos. Sperate, capellae.
Cras ego, si vivam, liquido vos fonte lavabo
Culmine sub viridi solis qui prospicit ortum,
100 Largiter emanans, ubi parvo condita colle
Eminet et celebrem reditu Gotha possidet agrum.
I, caper. Ite, meae, mecum gaudete, capellae."
   Sic bonus ille puer cecinit. Cum proxima forsan
Pastor Tranquillus subter coryleta latebat,
105 Omnia concepit, namque illo doctior alter
Non erat, et suaves incidit in arbore versus.

---

²²Spalatin was ordained priest in July 1508. See Irmgard Höss, *Georg Spalatin, 1484-1545* (Weimar, 1956), pp. 35-36.
   ²³The cherrylike fruit of the lotus or nettle tree was said to induce a state of dreamy contentment and indolence. The poplar tree, sacred to Hercules, was associated with the "active life" in pursuit of virtue; cf. *Buc.* 11, 23, with fn. 96.
   ²⁴Spalatin's and Eobanus's mentor Mutianus Rufus lived in the town of Gotha, not far from Erfurt. Cf. *Buc.* 1, 83-84 above, with fn. 16.

grateful to me for this honor I'm rendering you: that flower of snow-white chastity that has been blooming for you in my fertile years, it will stand intact for you,[22] Muses, my dearest love, sweet Muses, my greatest joy.

"Tell me, poets, you who wreathe your Muse-inspired brows with the sacred laurel, is there a nobler, more consuming desire in all the world than cultivating the Muses and enjoying the Muses' embraces, living with the Muses, devoting oneself to the learned Muses? [80] Get out of my sight, meaningless delights and charms of physical beauty, good looks, ancestry, titles, haughtiness, fame, glory, noble blood! What I enjoy is taking my ease on the green grass studying literature – especially when a brook babbles joyfully nearby as it runs over pebbles and whispers softly to the quiet breeze and a fruit-bearing lotus extends its spreading arms or a many-branched poplar casts nimble shadows.[23]

"Go, Muses, gather fresh flowers, go, you Camenae. Pick sweet marjoram, ivy, amaranth, smilax, nard, spring lilies, thyme, Egyptian lilies, balsam, myrrh, [90] also saffron and marigolds, violets and exhilarating nepenthe. Crown the ever-living poets with a thousand flowers each. If only I had some small renown in their circle! Then in this green valley I'd sing a song of praise to you, Saint George, who rest among the holy Muses on the heavenly mount and look upon these pastures with a cheerful face.

"The bards' songs are deathless. Rejoice, goats. Nibble at the leafy beeches. Take heart, my goats. Tomorrow, as sure as I'm alive, I'm going to dip you in the clear water of a spring – the one beneath the tree-crowned height that faces the rising sun. [100] The place is known far and wide, for that is where Gotha, built on a small hill, rises up and possesses a farm celebrated for its yield.[24] Go, billy! Let's get moving, goats, and rejoice with me."

So sang that excellent lad. The shepherd Tranquillus chanced to be nearby.[25] Hidden in a hazel thicket, he committed the whole song to memory, for he was second to none in learning, and carved those sweet-sounding lines on

---

[25]Tranquillus ("Tranquil") is Mutianus Rufus, whose motto was "beata tranquillitas" (blessed tranquillity). See Camerarius, *Nar.* 12, 18; cf. Eob. *Buc.* 6, 70. Tranquillus reappears as the umpire in a singing contest between Floridus (Petrejus Eberbach) and Vernus (Justus Jonas) in *Buc.* 5. Euricius Cordus uses the name Tranquillus for Mutianus Rufus in the tenth eclogue of his *Bucolicon* (1514), but changes it to Amyntas in the 1518-edition (*Ecl.* 5).

Extat adhuc pregnans in cortice littera. Foelix
Cresce arbor; viridi crescetis in arbore, versus.
Atque olim spectans aliquis vos, "Crescite," dicet,
110   "Crescite et in vestri titulum supereste poetae."

AEGLOGA TERTIA

Cignus, Philaegon, Narcissus

Cygn. Hic ubi Gerha vagus nutantes alluit herbas
Et virides umbrant alni quae littora circum
Crebra repercussis resonat mugitibus echo,
Hic ubi foelices ditant sata pinguia pagos
5   Villarumque casas et pastoralia tecta,
Hic mihi parta quies maneat. Quid rere, Philaegon?
Num tibi et hac mecum placeat considere terra,
Inter inurbanas matresque rudesque puellas,
Et dulces curas et inertem ducere vitam?
10   *Phil.* Cygne, nihil tecum prohibet requiescere, quando
Unus amor, studium commune ambobus, et uno
Numine coniunctos facit esse Salutifer orbis,
Numine quo vatum flammantia pectora noster
In sublime rapit coeli terraeque Poaetes,
15   Numine quo raptus sublimis Tityrus olim
Ardua rurali pulsabat sydera canna,
Numine quo foelix geminum produxit olorem
Mantua, qui Ocneis ubi Mintius errat in agris.
Ille deos veteres, Christum hic, cecinere potentes
20   Spiritibus dubiamque tulere in carmina palmam.

B2ʳ (margin, at line 8)

---

109 vos *A (in erratis) BO*: nos *A (in textu)*.
   Buc. 3. *Cf. Idyllia 3 et 7 in BO.*   **1** *Nomen pastoris in margine* Cygn. *BO: om. A.*
Hic *BO*: Ic *A*.

---

[26]This eclogue may well have been written in the summer of 1508, not long after *De in-foelicitate amantium*, with which it shares not a few similarities in theme and phrasing. Cygnus ("Swan") is, of course, Eobanus Hessus himself; cf. Camerarius, *Nar.* 31, 7-8, with notes. Philaegon ("One who loves goats") is probably Crotus Rubianus. For his life see fn. 71 at Camerarius, *Nar.* 17, 17.

[27]Cygnus-Eobanus has left his native Hesse and is now living by the Gera in Erfurt (that is, he is studying at the university). His emphasis on rich harvests (lines 4-5), love (lines 8-9), and leisure (line 9) indicates that to his (as yet naive) way of thinking he has indeed arrived in the promised land that Paniscus had described to him in *Buc.* 1.

a tree. The words, now swollen, may still be seen in the bark.
Grow, blessed tree; grow along with the verdant tree, you
verses. And someday, when a passer-by reads you, he'll ex-
claim: "Keep growing, [110] keep growing, to the unending
fame of your poet!"

THE THIRD ECLOGUE[26]

Cygnus, Philaegon, Narcissus

Cygnus. Here where the meandering Gera laps the swaying
grass and green alders shade the banks that keep resounding
with the repeated echoes of lowing, here where plentiful
harvests enrich the fortunate region, the farm cottages no
less than the shepherds' huts, here I want to go on enjoying
the leisure I've found.[27] What do you think, Philaegon?
Wouldn't you like to settle down with me in this land,
among rustic matrons and unsophisticated girls, and pursue
the sweet cares of love and live a life of ease?
    Philaegon. [10] Cygnus, nothing stops me from taking
a break with you. After all, the two of us share a single love,
one and the same passion. The Savior of the world, indeed,
has joined us together through one single force – the divine
force with which our Father, creator of heaven and earth,
carries the bards' flaming hearts to the skies; the divine force
that enraptured the sublime Tityrus long ago when he
struck the lofty stars with his oaten flute[28]; the force that al-
lowed happy Mantua to bring forth those twin swans, there
where the Mincio winds through Ocnus's fields.[29] The one
sang of the ancient gods, the other of Christ; but both of
them are mighty poets, [20] divinely inspired. So well are
they matched in song, that each of them bore off the palm.

---

[28]Vergil was traditionally included among the poets inspired by the Holy Spirit, espe-
cially on the strength of his fourth, "Messianic" eclogue. He is called "Tityrus," because the
shepherd Tityrus in Vergil's first bucolic was identified with Vergil himself. See Serv. *Ecl.* 1,
1; and, for example, Mart. 8, 56, 8; Calp. *Ecl.* 4, 62-64; 4, 160-163; Eob. *Buc.* 6, 11.
    [29]The "twin swans" are Vergil and Baptista Mantuanus. Cf. *Buc.*, lim. 2, with fn. 2; *Sylv.*
1, 5, 37-38. For the swan as a metaphor for the poet see fn. 137 at Camerarius, *Nar.* 31, 7. The
metaphor is especially appropriate in the case of the two poets of Mantua, for the Mincio,
which flows by that city, was famed for its swans. See, for instance, Verg. *Ecl.* 9, 27-29; *G.* 2,
198-199; Andrel. *Ecl.* 6, 39-40. "Ocnus's fields" are the fields of Mantua, a city founded by
Ocnus.

    Cygn. Ut lentas corylos damnosa securibus ilex,
    Quantum humiles superat cornus ramosa genistas,
    Tam meus in versu praecedit Tityrus illum
    Qui Faustum gelida cecinit resupinus in umbra.
25   Ah, male quorundam trivialis iudicat error!
    Magnus uterque tamen. Sed maiestate verendus
    Ille prior. Summum faciunt haec saecula Faustum.
    Phil. Tu breviore tamen quamvis gradiare cothurno
    Et tua non aequet Mantoos Musa poaetas,
30   Hic tamen efferris adeoque beatiter audes
    Antiquos revocare modos et carmina pastor
    Rhomula Teutonicas passim cantare per oras.
    Sed quid "inurbanas matresque rudesque puellas"
    Commemoras, incaute puer? Quid talibus ergo
35   Illecebris pares? Non debent talia vates.
    Sit procul a Musis Venus et puer ille Cupido,
    Quem semper volucres aiunt portare sagittas.
    Est alacer, passim pueros volat inter amantes
    Et ferit incautos et dulcia vulnera nutrit.
40   Et tantum pueros, nam qui sapit odit amores.
    Foelix rure suo et parvo contentus agello,
    Non ulla laesus Venere, hic si pauper egebit,
    Dummodo succedat pecus et lac quottidianum,
    Laetus erit pomisque famem solabitur aegram,
45   Arbuta sylvestresque nuces edet. Illius oci
    Dulcis amor, secura quies, aeterna voluptas!
    O igitur mihi chara soror vel frigida mater
    Instruat ardentemque focum tenuemque popinam
    Et panes et olus lac et cocleare ministret!
50   Ipse ego lactantes agnas et ovilia secter,
    Foelix pace bona et tranquillo tutus in antro.
    Cygn. Aut lapis est aut truncus iners qui nescit Amorem.
    Nemo terdecimum quin arserit attigit annum.
    Dic ubi legisti mutatis corpora formis

B2ᵛ

---

[30]Faustus is Baptista Mantuanus, whose first eclogue begins with that name. For the same reason Vergil is often called Tityrus; see fn. 28 above.

Cygnus. Just as that menace to axes, the holm oak, rises high above bending hazels, just as the many-branched cornel tree overtops the lowly broom, so does my Tityrus surpass the other poet in verse – the Faustus who sings reclining in the cool shade.[30] Ah, the prevailing judgment, espoused by certain critics, is sadly mistaken! Obviously they are both great men. But the former has a majesty about him that is more awe-inspiring. Our own century regards Faustus as its finest poet.

Philaegon. Though you are a lesser light and your Muse does not equal the poets of Mantua,[31] [30] you nevertheless earn high praise in this country for daring to bring back ancient verse forms – quite successfully, I might add – and as a shepherd to sing Latin songs in German lands everywhere. But why did you mention "rustic matrons and unsophisticated girls" just now, imprudent lad? Why on earth do you give in to such allurements? Bards should not be talking like that. Let Venus and that son of hers keep far away from the Muses! For Cupid, they say, carries winged arrows wherever he goes. He is nimble too. Wherever there are young fellows ready to fall in love, he is sure to be fluttering among them. He strikes the unwary and fosters their sweet wounds. [40] But only young lads get caught like that, for the wise hate such amours. Happy the man who, living on a farm of his own and content with a small plot of land, remains untouched by passionate love. Be he ever so poor, as long as he has his herd and his daily milk, he'll be merry at heart and assuage the pangs of hunger with fruit; he'll eat arbute berries and nuts from the forest. Oh, the sweet yearning for that life of leisure, the untroubled peace, the unending delight! If only my dear sister or my aged mother were still tending the blazing hearth and the simple kitchen and serving bread and vegetables and milk by the spoonful! [50] I myself would look after the suckling lambs and the sheepfolds, happy in my undisturbed peace and safe in my quiet grotto.

Cygnus. Anyone who doesn't know Love is either a stone or an inert tree trunk. You simply can't turn thirteen without getting burned. Tell me now, where did you read that "all living beings, no matter what their form or their

---

[31] The same expression of humility is found in *Buc.* 6, 1-3, where Eobanus acknowledges his inferiority to Vergil. Instead of the phrase "Though you are a lesser light," the Latin literally says: "Though you walk on a humbler buskin." For this expression cf. *Buc.* 1, 11, with fn. 12.

55   Diversum genus in furias ignemque ruisse.
      Dic ubi nec nostri generis nec sanguinis infans
      Aeditur, et gratos tecum linquemus amores.
B3ʳ   *Phil.* Dicere quid sit Amor, quam fortis et impiger ales,
      Non aliquis nostris in papilionibus audet.
60   Hinc tamen errantes prius, hinc age, Cygne, capellas,
      Ne vicina intrent fractis sata sepibus. Ito.
      Lascivum pecus est hircus, lasciva capella.
             Cygn. Vos sata, vos cythisum, vos gramina laeta, capellae,
      O felix pecus, et florentes carpitis herbas.
65   Me me, qui primis custos sum vester ab annis,
      Pulchra infinito Foenilia torquet amore,
      Quamvis illa meos miserata fidelior ignes
      Saepius has mecum vobis pascentibus alnos
      Viderit. O dulces salvete perhenniter herbae,
70   In quibus illa sedens delapsa in gramina palla
      Explicuit flavasque comas teretesque papillas.
      Dicite, foelices, ubi nunc mea cura, capellae?
      An duro coniuncta viro, iam nubilis aevi,
      Scilicet interclusa meos lugebit amores?
75   Hei mihi, quam perii! Quam sum mutatus ab illo
      Alite quem pharetram dixit gestare Philaegon!
             Phil. Cygne, quid est, donec pecus hinc a sepibus arces,
      Quod quereris? Totis resonat querimonia sylvis.
             Cygn. Perfidus ille hircus potum descendit ad amnem,
80   Quem procul haec molli tangit via pendula clivo.
      Ipse pecus revocatum ad cognita flumina veni.
      Ecce sed horrendum visu, miserabile dictu,
B3ᵛ   Sub rupe aerea fagi viridantis in umbra
      Ad fontem longos noster Narcissus amores
85   Deflebat misero planctu, quibus ille Rubinam

---

56 sanguinis *A (in erratis) BO*: sanguis *A (in textu).*   **70** gramina *B*: gramine *AO.*

species, rush madly into that fire"? Tell me, where is it men-
tioned that "that boy is not of our kin, not of our flesh and
blood"? Then, and only then, will I follow your lead and
abandon the pleasures of love.[32]

Philaegon. To describe what Love really is, how power-
ful and tireless the winged boy is, that is something which
nobody in *our* huts dares undertake. [60] But first, Cygnus,
drive the roving goats away from here or they'll break
through the fence and get into the neighboring grainfield.
Get going. That billy is a mischievous beast, and so is the
nanny.

Cygnus. You nibble at the grain, the clover, the luxuri-
ant grass, O you goats, you fortunate beasts, and crop the
flowering herbs. But I, who have been your herder since
childhood, I'm tormented with undying love for the beau-
tiful Foenilia. She was truly devoted to me, often taking pity
on my blazing passion as we lay together under these alders.
You were there yourselves, grazing about. Hail to you for-
ever, lovely meadow! [70] That is where she sat as her cloak
slipped down in the grass; that is where she undid her flaxen
locks and her well-rounded breasts. Tell me, fortunate
goats, where is my sweetheart now? Did she get married to
some hard-hearted man? She's ripe for marriage. But if she's
shut in, will she still grieve for my love? Alas, how I am pin-
ing away! How I've been transformed by that winged boy
who Philaegon says carries a quiver!

Philaegon. What is the matter, Cygnus? What were you
complaining about over there, while you were driving the
goats away from the fences? The whole wood echoes with
your laments.

Cygnus. That shifty billy went to get a drink from the
stream, [80] a fair distance down this gently sloping path on
the hillside. When I reached the river we know so well, I was
about to call the beast back. But lo and behold, a fearful
sight, pitiful to relate! There, beneath an airy cliff, in the
shade of a verdant beech, beside a spring, there was our Nar-
cissus miserably weeping and wailing for his enduring love.

---

[32]Cygnus, the champion of Vergil's primacy over Mantuanus (lines 21-27), now turns
into a defender of Amor as well. His argument is drawn (not coincidentally) from Vergil,
though he clearly does take the master's words out of context. Lines 52-53 and 56-57 allude
to Verg. *Ecl.* 8, 39-45; lines 54-55 point to Verg. *G.* 3, 242-244. However, Cygnus ignores the
import of these passages: the grievous consequences of passionate love as "error" (*Ecl.* 8, 41)
and the reduction of eros to the level of the beasts in the *Georgica* passage.

Fastibus ardentem misere despexerit et nunc
Quam male despectos in se converterit ignes.
Dum rogo moeroris causam, nihil ille, sed amens
Centenam loquitur repetita voce Rubinam.
90 Hinc mea spes, mea lux subiit mihi. Me quoque tali
Fixit Amor iaculo. Nec tu me laeta videbis
Amplius arguto meditari carmina plectro.
Ni saciatus amor meus hos mihi finiat ignes,
Ni dabitur quod amo, letam sperare senectam
95 Non erit. Insano, satis est, servimus Amori.
　　Phil. Ambo aetate pares, pueri, studioque canendi,
Quo vos fata vocant? Quid te, Narcisse, Rubina,
Quid te, Cygne, levis blando Foenilia vultu
Mortis ad exitium vivum trahit? Ergone tandem
100 Una homini cunctos concludit foemina sensus?
Quin potius notum mecum descendis ad amnem.
Et iam sol medium coeli transcendit et axem
Fert medio temone. Gregem ducemus aquatum.
　　Cygn. Ite, meae pecudes, liquidum potabitis amnem.
105 Me coquet interea sitis altera, qualis in unda
Non queat extingui si totum Nerea potem.
Eheu, quam fortes urunt mea pectora flammae!
　　Phil. Cygne, viden? Sedet, ecce sedet Narcissus in umbra!
O salve, Narcisse. Quid haec tam sola frequentas
110 Abdita convictusque fugis commertia nostri?
　　Narc. Donec eram foelix, nec me formosior alter
Pastor erat nec qui mecum contendere vellet
Cantando. Mea sepe hylares connubia nymphae
Optabant. Ego formosas malesanus amantes
115 Sprevi, Faustinam, Catulam, nigramque Fidillam,
Atque alias. Quas una inter formosa Rubina
Tota in me, veluti post fortem verna iuvencum
Vacca, ferebatur, totos insana per agros
Errabat, clamans Narcissum, et nomine tantum
120 Quo potuit longum consolabatur amorem.
Non illam duri poterant prohibere parentes,
Non commissa gregis custodia, sola per omnes
Quin sylvas sequeretur. Et hac me sepe sub umbra
Cum vidisset, ego in nemora et saxa aspera fugi,

B4ʳ

90 subiit *BO*: subyt *A*.　　**96** canendi *A (in erratis) BO*: cavendi *A (in textu)*.

He's filled with remorse for the arrogant way he spurned the passionately loving Rubina, now that she's turned the tables on him. When I asked him for the cause of his sorrow, he offered no reply, except to repeat the name "Rubina" like crazy, a hundred times at least. [90] That reminded me of my own darling, the light of my life. I too was pierced in the same way by Love's arrow. Never again will you see me practising a happy song to a bright-sounding tune. If my love isn't sated and my fire isn't quenched, if I can't have the girl I love, I see no hope for a happy old age. Enough said: we are slaves of madding Love.

Philaegon. Both of you lads, equal in age and equally enthusiastic in singing, where is fate calling you to? Why are you, Narcissus, letting Rubina, why are you, Cygnus, letting the fickle Foenilia charm you with her good looks and drag you down into a living death? Is it true, then, [100] that a woman can totally bewitch a man's senses? But why don't you go down with me to the stream we both know so well. By now the sun has climbed to the mid-point of the sky and drives his chariot with level pole. Let's lead the flock to water.

Cygnus. Forward, my beasts! You'll get to drink from the clear river. Meanwhile, I'll be parched with a different thirst, the kind that can't be slaked with water, even if I drank the whole ocean. Alas, how hot are the flames that scorch my breast!

Philaegon. Cygnus, do you see that? Look over there – it's Narcissus sitting in the shade! Well hello, Narcissus. Why are you haunting these lonely, [110] out-of-the-way places and shunning the camaraderie of our fellowship?

Narcissus. When I was still happy, no shepherd could match my good looks or wanted to challenge me to a singing-match. Lighthearted girls would often desire me as their husband. Fool that I was, I turned those beautiful charmers down – Faustina, Catula, the dusky Fidilla, among others. But one of them, the fair Rubina, like a cow in heat lusting after a husky bull, was completely carried away by me. Mad with ardor, she roamed through the whole countryside shouting "Narcissus," and with the mere mention of this name – [120] for that was all she could do – she solaced her enduring love. Neither her strict parents nor the flock entrusted to her care could stop her from chasing me by herself, no matter where I went in the forests. But whenever she spotted me here in the shade, I would run

125 Et quamvis cuperem, tamen illa ut peius amaret
      Frivola crudeli foeci praeludia flammae.
      Heu heu, qui nimium formae confidit inani
      Et se posse miser nunquam non credit amari!
      Pene sed indigno mulier consumpta furore,
130 Semianimis cum se iam desperaret amari,
      Ad patrias iterum pecudes aversa recessit.
      Occului tacitum nondum confessus amorem,
B4ᵛ   Et tamen illa mihi visa est res dulcis. Ut essem
      Formosus, didici vultum componere, crinem
135 Comere, sed plenum non intellexerat ignem
      Mens mea. Iamque magis cupiebam semper amare.
      Dulce videbatur si quis me pastor amantem
      Diceret. Interea totum Venus ignea, totum
      Exurunt corpus flammae. Tum denique vulnus
140 Fassus, opem petii superos pulchramque Rubinam.
      O mulierum ipsis levior constantia ventis!
      Interea illa suos in Adonim transtulit ignes –
      Illum qui toties nobis furatus et haedos
      Et teretes calamos, timet haec in rura venire.
145   *Cygn.* Infoelix puer, o sortem, Narcisse, dolendam!
      Rhetia quae tendis miser incidis. Atque ita forsan
      Iusserit alma Venus, fastum quae vindicat omnem.
      Quam velles dominae, liceat, servire puellae!
      Quisquis amat, quamvis sit rex, famulatur. Et illud
150 Ut scirem docuit mea me Foenilia verum.
          Narc. Ipse Palepaphia percussus harundine, solus
      Per sylvas et rura queror. Mea sepe videntes
      Fleverunt Dryades et inertes vulnera nymphae.
      Ut magnos ipsae pecudes videre dolores,
155 Gramina non carpunt nec dulcia flumina potant.
      Saepius haec mecum tamen, "O formosa Rubina,
      Quo fugis?" exclamo. "Mea flamma, revertere! Non est
C1ʳ   Quem fugias, miserere sed impatienter amantis.
      Huc ades, o mea lux. Quem tantum nuper amasti,
160 Te vocat ille tuus Narcissus. Scilicet illum

146 Atque *O*: An *AB*.   **151** Palepaphia *BO*: Palepephia *A*.

away into the woods and the rugged rocks. And though I
desired her too, still, to make her even more madly in love, I
cruelly went ahead with this trifling foreplay of mine. Woe,
woe to the wretch who puts too much faith in superficial
beauty and thinks that girls will never stop adoring him!
When the woman, however, had nearly worn herself out
with unrequited passion and, [130] just barely alive by now,
despaired of ever being loved in return, she had a change of
heart and went back to her father's herds again. For a while I
kept my amorous feelings to myself, telling no one about
them. Even so, being in love seemed to me something
utterly sweet. To appear handsome, I learned to compose
my features and comb my hair. What I had not realized yet,
however, was the full force of the ardor within me. In fact, all
I wanted now was to be in love forever. It was music to my
ears if some shepherd called me a lovebird. Meanwhile fiery
Venus had set my whole body, every last part of it, ablaze
with the flames of passion. Then, and only then [140] did I
bare my lacerated heart, praying to heaven and the fair
Rubina to help me. Oh, the constancy of women, more
fickle than the wind itself! In the meantime she had shifted
her love to Adonis – the very one who has stolen kids and
smooth reed pipes from us so often that he's afraid to show
his face in this country.

Cygnus. Unhappy lad! What a deplorable fate, Narcis-
sus! You're caught in the net that you stretched out yourself,
poor fellow. But perhaps kindly Venus commanded it to
happen this way, for she punishes all pride. How you longed
for a chance to be enslaved to that lass and make her your
mistress! Everybody who is in love – even a king, for that
matter – is no more than a serf. [150] My Foenilia taught
me the truth of that too.

Narcissus. Pierced by Love's arrow, I wander around all
alone, lamenting in field and forest. At the sight of my
wounds, the dryads and nymphs often stopped in their
tracks to weep for me. As soon as the flocks saw the depth of
my sorrow, they refused to crop the grass or drink the river's
sweet water. Many times, however, I cry out to myself: "O
fair Rubina, where have you gone? My darling, come back!
There's no reason to flee from me. Instead, take pity on the
man who is so madly in love with you. Come here, my
sweetheart. The one you loved so much just now, [160] that
Narcissus of yours, it's he who is calling you. Surely you

Nunc fugis? An miserum potius spe fallis inani?"
Dum queror, impediunt lachrimae. Proh lumen et auras,
Quid mihi cum superis? Iuvat ire et perdere vitam.
Tormentum grave durus amor, Venus acre venenum.

165 Hic ego vos inter placida iam morte quiescam,
Lanigerae pecudes. Vos ad mea funera, moestae,
Nec salices, caprae, nec, oves, captate myricas.
Vos mea, pastores, meritae date membra quieti
Floreque signatam cognomine spargite terram

170 Et deflete meos ignes, aevoque futuro
Si quis amator erit male, quod legat addite carmen:
"Cum miser indigno Narcissus amore periret,
Exemplo ne quis contendat amare reliquit."

AEGLOGA QUARTA

Argus, Phileremus

Arg. Montibus hiis mecum quondam, Philereme, solebas
Pascere oves alternaque decantare vicissim
Carmina et urgentes calamo depellere curas.
Quae nunc arva tenent, quod te nemus? Aut ubi tandem
5 Usque adeo solus tecum, Philereme, recedis?
    Phil. O Arge, infaustos quid adhuc non deseris agros?
Noxia quid pecori non linquis pascua, quando
C1ᵛ Hic steriles tribuli, lolium, zizania, lappae,
Carduus, et spinae surgunt, ubi nulla beatos

***Buc.* 4.** *Cf. Idyllion 5 in BO.*   **1** Montibus *BO*: Ontibus *A.*

[33]The argument in the 1539-edition informs us that the dialogue is set in Thuringia, somewhere between Erfurt, Eisenach, and Georgenthal. Since the Hörselberg is said to be visible to the west (lines 77-80 below), the location may be imagined more exactly as halfway between Eisenach and Georgenthal.

The speakers are identified in the marginal notes to *Idyl.* 5 in the 1539-edition. Argus is Eobanus himself. The name, which also occurs in Petrarch, *Ecl.* 2 and Bocc. *Ecl.* 3, 4, and 6, is intended to recall the ever-vigilant, many-eyed guardian of Io; see Ov. *Met.* 1, 625-627. As for Phileremus ("Lover of solitude"), he is Herbord von der Marthen, the friend who is first praised in *Laud.* 146-152 (where see fn. 30). See also *Epp. 4,* sig. F1ᵛ-F2ᵛ (dated 25 May 1508), in praise of Herbord, Gerlach, and Wolfgang von der Marthen; *Sylv. duae* 1, 189-190; and *Sylv.* 2, 6.

On one level the poem is a tribute to Herbord von der Marthen, who left Erfurt in the autumn of 1508 to succeed Georg Spalatin as teacher in Georgenthal. Fundamentally, how-

aren't running away from him? Or rather, are you deceiving the poor wretch with empty hope?"

As I lament, tears choke my voice. Alas, sunlight and breezes, what have I to do with the living? It will do me good to go and lose my life. Pitiless love is a grievous torment, Venus a bitter poison. Here I'll rest among you in peaceful death, you woolly beasts. At my funeral don't snatch at the willow shoots, mournful goats, or at the tamarisks, sheep. You herdsmen, lay my limbs to the rest they deserve. To mark the grave, bestrew it with the flowers that bear my name, [170] and shed tears for my passion. And if in some future age a lover should feel distressed, add this epitaph for him to read:

> When the hapless Narcissus pined for love unrequited,
> he taught this lesson: that love must not be withstood.

THE FOURTH ECLOGUE[33]

Argus, Phileremus

Argus. Once upon a time you used to pasture the sheep with me in these mountains, Phileremus. We used to take turns singing songs to each other and playing the flute to rid ourselves of pressing cares. Which fields, which forests hold you now? Where in the world have you withdrawn to, Phileremus? Why are you keeping so much to yourself these days?

Phileremus. Oh, Argus, why haven't you abandoned these ill-starred fields yet? Why don't you leave these pastures that are so harmful to the livestock? Look, the only things that will grow here are barren caltrops, darnel, weeds,

---

ever, it is a satire on the disastrous political, social, and economic conditions in Erfurt in mid-1509. The citizens of Erfurt, already hard hit by economic and social crisis, cuts in pay, and heavy taxes, were finally told at the end of May 1509 how desperately the city was mired in debt. Blaming the disaster on the plutocrats who dominated the city council, the townspeople revolted and took control. The troubles did not end until the spring of 1510, when a new city council was sworn in. On the so-called "Mad Year" in Erfurt's history see Theodor Neubauer, *Das tolle Jahr von Erfurt,* ed. Martin Waehler (Weimar, 1948); R.W. Scribner, "Civic Unity and the Reformation in Erfurt," *Past and Present* 66 (1975): 30-38.

Internal evidence, then, points to a composition date in the late spring or early summer of 1509.

10 Otia pastores faciunt, sed semper egentes
Spe rapiunt facili suspensaque vota morantur?
Pascua serpentes habitant, umbrosa lacertae.
Heu, fuge, vicinae ne dum successeris umbrae
Forte pedem tenerum calcata remordeat anguis.

15   *Arg.* Vera refers, nec ego dicam mendatia. Quando
Hesterna saturas mulgerem luce capellas
Sub viridi quercu, longum, mirabile dictu,
Hac virga colubrum subter radice latentem,
Ora exertantem, et summa me fauce petentem

20 Effugi et largo mulctrum cum lacte profudi.
    Phil. Credo equidem, nec quae memoras mihi mira videntur,
Quando etiam haec vulpes lateant per ovilia perque
Incustoditas serpat nepa livida caulas.
Est pecudum commissa lupis custodia. Cernis,

25 Limina cede tepent, sparguntur sanguine postes
Innocuo. Nihil est custode voratius ipso.
Me tenet umbrifero vallis secreta recessu
Ad quartum vestra lapidem, quam servat, ab urbe,
Qui pater Armeni colit enthea signa Georgi.

30 Hic ego propter aquas viridi requietus in antro
Saepe leves capio somnos. Secura vagantur
Per sylvas armenta; nihil locus insidiarum
Ille habet. Haec vita est nostro iucundior aevo.
    Arg. Ocia quandoquidem laudas, Philereme, fatebor:

35 Ipse ego silvestresque casas et agrestia tecta
Praetulero urbanis opibus vitaeque forensi.
Et me chara parens viridi connixa sub umbra
Aedidit et molles circum Floralia cunas
Dona tulit teneraque sedens lactavit in herba,

40 Gemmeus Hessiacos ubi percutit Aedera montes.
Nunc tenet infoelix Erphurdia, cuius, ut inquis,
Tot mala destituunt quondam bona pascua, cuius

C2ʳ

---

[34]The Arcadian landscape of *Buc.* 1, 72-89, which Cygnus-Eobanus was still praising in
Buc. 3, has turned into a nightmare.

[35]The reference is to the "Löwenburg," the Von der Marthen estate outside Erfurt.

[36]Herbord's father, the Erfurt patrician and jurist Gerlach von der Marthen (1465-1515),
served as vicegerent of the archbishop of Mainz from 1499 to 1504. He was a member of the
Order of St. George, a crusading order that had been revived by Maximilian in 1494. Cf. *Epp.*
4, sig. F5ᵛ (1508). Driven from Erfurt in 1504, he retired to his mansion outside Erfurt.

burs, thistles, and thorns. Here there is no [10] leisure to make the shepherds happy. Quite the opposite! Always in poverty, they are cheated of easy hopes as their wishes remain unfulfilled. The meadows are crawling with adders, the shadows with lizards. Ah, flee while you can! You could easily step on a snake in the nearby shade and get yourself a nasty bite in the foot.[34]

Argus. You speak the truth, and I won't equivocate either. Yesterday I was milking the goats after they had eaten their fill. There I was, sitting under a green oak, when – strange to say – a long snake lurking in the roots thrust out its head and lunged at me with its fangs bared. With the help of this stick of mine I managed to escape it, [20] but spilled all the milk in the milk pail.

Phileremus. I truly believe you. In fact, your story doesn't strike me as amazing at all, seeing that foxes lurk in the very sheepfolds here and deadly scorpions creep through the untended cotes. The task of guarding the flock has been entrusted to wolves. Just look about you! The gates reek with gore; the jambs are spattered with innocent blood. In this place nothing is so ravenous as the herdsman himself. As for me, I'm living in a valley tucked away in a shady nook, at the fourth milestone from your town.[35] My father, who follows the holy banners of George the Armenian, resides in that very dale.[36] [30] There, taking my ease in a verdant grotto by the water, I often take a refreshing nap. Meanwhile the cattle roam unafraid through the woods, for that place is free of all pitfalls. It is the most pleasant life imaginable in this day and age.

Argus. Since you praise the life of leisure, Phileremus, I'll confess that I myself would have preferred forest huts and farmhouses to the opulence of the city and the hurly-burly of the marketplace. My dear mother not only bore me in the green shade, she also placed the gifts of Flora around my soft cradle and nursed me as she sat in the tender grass,[37] [40] there where the sparkling Eder breaches the mountains of Hesse. Now I'm stuck in Erfurt, that unhappy town. It used to have lots of good pastures; but, as you say, they've long since turned nightmarishly bad. Wolves and snakes

[37] In *Nar.* 5, 7 Camerarius takes these lines literally. However, Eobanus is simply saying that he too is from the country, having been born in the village of Halgehausen near Frankenberg on the Eder.

Et lupus et serpens et amantes saxa lacertae
Plenaque ventrosus graditur per ovilia bufo.
45   *Phil.* O certe infoelix Erphurdia, perdita postquam
Ah male servatos respublica luget honores!
        Arg. Dum loquimur, tuus in nostram furit ecce iuvencam
Thaurus et a nostro cornuta fronte repulsus
Aestuat ut dulci satiari possit amore.
50   Cernis ut ecce iterum concurrunt duriter ictis
Frontibus. O faveas nostro, Pan maxime, thauro!
O montana Pales, celebrem largire triumphum!
Mulctram, diva Pales, capies, Pan magne, coronam.
Vicisti, bone thaure! Tua est victoria! Frontem
55   Ergo feres querna redimitam fronde. Placere
Sic potes et niveae coniunctior esse iuvencae.
Quid tibi de nostro thauro, Philereme, videtur?
C2ᵛ   *Phil.* Pinguis – et hoc mirum! – tuus haec per inania thaurus
Pascua devicit macrum pecus, ergo corona
60   Dignus. At ille pedum meus inter cornua durum
Sentiet, ut forti discat concurrere. Tandem
Tu quoque fers meritam, nequissime thaure, coronam.
I nunc et pugna pro pulchra, stulte, iuvenca!
        Arg. Ah, miserum pecus! Insano dum servis amori,
65   Et Venerem et pugnam perdis. Fers verbera tantum.
        Phil. Sol coquit arentes campos et corpora fuscat.
Umbra iuvat. Gelidae quid non succedimus umbrae?
        Arg. Gratior hic locus est, tilias ubi frigida laeves
Aura agit et summa Zephirus sub rupe remugit.
70   Dum tamen hoc ambo viridi consedimus antro,
Lude aliquid, Philereme. Levant et mutua curas
Carmina. Dispositis ego respondebo Camaenis.
        Phil. Magna canam, non quae sapiant trivialiter, Arge,
Non quae quisque sua moduletur harundine pastor.
75   *Arg.* Incipe, namque tibi foelix aspirat Apollo
Assurgitque tuae vicinia tota Camaenae.
        Phil. Aspicis aereo sublatum vertice montem,
Qua levis occidui deflectitur aura Favoni.
Horrisonum Latio vicinus nomine dicit
80   Qui Nessum bibit undosum. Quam scilicet urbem

---

75 Apollo *BO*: Appollo *A.*   76 vicinia *A (in erratis) BO*: vicina *A (in textu).*

and stone-loving lizards and potbellied toads wander freely here through the crowded sheepfolds.

Phileremus. Ah, unhappy Erfurt indeed, ever since the bankrupt town has been mourning the loss of its honor!

Argus. While we're talking, your bullock has been madly courting my heifer. Butted away by my own bull, he's spoiling for a fight so he can sate his sweet ardor. [50] Look how they're charging each other again and knocking their heads together hard. O mighty Pan, smile on my bull! O mountain-dwelling Palēs, grant him a famous triumph! You'll get a pail of milk, divine Palēs and you, great Pan, a garland. You are the winner, brave bull! The victory is yours! In recognition, you're going to be crowned with an oak wreath. That way you can please the snow-white heifer and be even closer to her. What do you think of my bull, Phileremus?

Phileremus. Your sleek bull – and that's a miracle, given the barren meadows around here! – has decisively beaten my scraggy beast. Therefore he's entitled to his wreath. [60] But that animal of mine will get to feel the hard crook between his horns, so he'll learn to charge at a powerful rival. There, you worthless bull! Now you too bear the crown you deserve. Get moving, fool, and fight for the beautiful heifer!

Argus. Ah, hapless beast! By following your maddening lust, you've lost both love and battle. All you get is a beating.

Phileremus. The sun is baking the parched fields and tanning our bodies. The shade looks appealing. Why don't we move into the cool shadow?

Argus. This is a nicer place, here where the cool breeze stirs the smooth lindens and the zephyr moos beneath the towering cliff. [70] But now that we've both sat down in this verdant grotto, play something, Phileremus. We'll take turns singing – an excellent way to relieve our worries. When you're done, I'll respond with verses of my own.

Phileremus. I'm about to tackle a great theme – nothing hackneyed, Argus, not the sort of thing your average shepherd sings on his panpipe.

Argus. Go ahead, for Apollo breathes his favor upon you, and when you sing, the whole neighborhood gives you a standing ovation.

Phileremus. You see the mountain that rises up over there, its airy summit deflecting the light breeze of the west wind. The townsfolk nearby, [80] who drink the water of the swelling Nesse, call it by the name "Horrid-sounding

Isidis a veteri cultu dixere liburnam.
Istic ante duas messes cum saepe venirem,

C3ʳ Ignarus nemorum, vidi discurrere larvas
Per nemora et montes, tanquam nocturna vagantes
85 Terriculamenta et pueros terrere paventes
Quas lamias dicunt. Quibus est exemptile lumen.
Quas vigiles aiunt extra sua limina lynces,
Esse domi talpas – animal mirabile certe!
    Arg. O Philereme, istis quis sat maledicere larvis,
90 Quis lamias poterit satis execrare nocentes,
Lyncea qui passim vertunt per rura, per urbes
Lumina, per plateas, per conciliabula quaeque,
Per fora, per thermas, ganeas, delubra, diaetas?
Omnia scrutantur, pensant, rimantur ad unguem.
95 Livor, edax animal, comitatur. Videris, illi
Milvinos oculos emissiceosque putares.
    Phil. Non tamen urbanas larvas lamiasque forenses
Me vidisse puto. Verum cum saepe reversus
Ad montem pecudes inter sub rupe iacerem,
100 Obscuram vidi picea fuligine flammam
Surgere et a summo delapsum vertice sulphur.
Tum vero aereas ingens ploratus ad auras
Tollitur et miseris clamoribus intonat aether.
Obstupui retroque boves a monte coegi.

---

101 sulphur *A (in erratis) BO*: fulgur *A (in textu).*

[38]The Hörselberg in Thuringia, east of Eisenach, was popularly believed to be the site of hell and purgatory. Here the damned suffer; here the devil and his army of demons and witches make their home. See Heinrich Weigel, *Der Sagenkreis der Hörselberge* (Bucha bei Jena, 2001).

[39]Eobanus explains the name Eisenach as deriving from "Isis-Nachen" or "Barque of Isis." (The town's name, incidentally, has never been satisfactorily explained, but may well go back to Celtic times.) Tacitus, *Germania* 9, mentions a cult of Isis among the Suebi, adding that her symbol there is a barque. For the reputed connection of the name Eisenach to the goddess Isis cf. Mutian. *Ep.* 79 (ca. 23 August 1506), poem to Hermann Trebelius, lines 1-9; and, for example, Trebelius, *Epigr.*, sig. B5ᵛ, in a poem of late summer 1506: "Isidis urbem" (city of Isis); sig. D2ᵛ, in a poem to Eobanus written in the early summer of 1508, referring to the forests around Eisenach: "Antea linigerae tota dicata deae" (formerly wholly consecrated to the linen-clad goddess [Isis]).

[40]Literally, "Offspring of Helios [Apollo]." A sidenote in the 1539-edition identifies him as the Neo-Latin poet Hermann Trebelius (Surwynt) of Eisenach. Heliades makes another appearance in *Buc.* 8, as a poet newly crowned with the laurel wreath, perhaps also in *Buc.* 10, as "Mannus."

Born around 1475, Trebelius matriculated at Erfurt in 1500, studying Greek privately with Nikolaus Marschalk. Two years later he and his teacher moved to the newly-founded University of Wittenberg, where they continued their studies, taught classes themselves, and man-

Mountain."[38] As for the town itself, it must once have been called "Isis-Nachen" or "Barque of Isis" because people used to worship that goddess here in ancient times.[39] Anyway, two harvests ago I used to come to the mountain quite often. Not yet familiar with the forests there, I was amazed to see demons running up and down the woods and mountains, roaming about like the bogies of the night and the vampires that are supposed to frighten children out of their wits. They have eyes that can be taken right out of their sockets. Out of doors they're said to be as watchful as lynxes. At home, though, they're as blind as a mole – a marvelous creature, for sure!

Argus. Oh, Phileremus, who can ever revile those demons enough? [90] Who can ever curse those wicked vampires to the extent they deserve? They cast their lynx eyes on everything – fields, cities, streets, all the meeting places, markets, bath houses, cookshops, churches, homes. Nothing escapes their scrutiny, their meddling, their relentless prying. Envy, that gnawing beast, is their constant companion. If you could see it, you'd think it had the eyes of a kite or a spy.

Phileremus. All the same, I don't think I saw city demons and market vampires. In fact, I often went back to the mountain. Once, lying among the herd at the foot of a cliff, [100] I saw a flame shooting up, dark with pitch-black soot, and sulfur raining down from the summit. At this a horrendous wailing rose high into the air, and the heavens rang with piteous laments. Stupefied, I drove the cattle back from the mountain. But look, no sooner had I reached the valley than I ran into Heliades,[40] who was looking for a lost

---

aged a printing business. When a plague broke out in late June and forced the university to close in early July, Trebelius returned to Eisenach, taking his printing equipment along. But the plague, which was raging in Eisenach too, soon took the life of Trebelius's son Elias. In August 1506 he spent some time in Erfurt and Gotha. After leaving his printing equipment with Wolfgang Stürmer (who used it in 1506-1507) and becoming friends with Eobanus, Trebelius went back to Eisenach as a teacher. However, finding himself bitterly attacked from the pulpit (cf. lines 107-111 below), he was forced to leave town in 1508. In June of that year he was crowned poet laureate at Wittenberg. By early August he was in Gotha, visiting Mutianus and Eobanus (see Mutian. *Ep.* 78) and thence went to Frankfurt an der Oder. While studying law, he published two collections of verse (1509) and taught poetry and rhetoric. Eobanus renewed his friendship with him in the summer semester of 1513, when he himself was studying law at Frankfurt an der Oder. In *Sylv.* 1, 9 we see him inviting himself to Trebelius's house for dinner. By 1514 Trebelius was professor of civil law at the university. He seems to have died a few years later.

105   Ecce sed amissam quaerens in valle iuvencam
      Affuit Heliades. Qui mox ut constitit inquit:
      "Heu, fuge terribiles lucos, loca foeta venenis

C3ᵛ

      Tartareis! Nigri, fama est, hic ianua Ditis
      Panditur, hic Furiae tristes Acheronta recludunt.
110   Coge pecus, ne, si virosi graminis herbam
      Attigerit, pingui macrum tibi fiat in arvo."
      Haec ubi, quaesitum sylvam pecus ivit in altam.
        Arg. Nos etiam multos dites lamiasque per urbem
      Vidimus humanas fracta stipe mandere carnes.
115   *Phil.* Dum fugio, raptis mecum sine lege modoque
      Rebus, in effossum cecidit mihi subula fontem.
        Arg. Frigida nox properat, thauros includere pastos
      Tempus et errantes inducere ovilibus agnas.

AEGLOGA QUINTA

Floridus, Vernus, Tranquillus iudex

Pastores viridi duo convenere sub ulmo,
Floridus et Vernus, pictas ubi plurima ripas
Alluit et dulces labens facit unda susurros.
Una aetas ambobus erat, formosus uterque,
5   Carmine uterque potens. Et tum certare parati
    Sederunt studio intenti calamosque ligabant,
    Tranquillus senior cum forte supervenit. Illum
    Ut pueri videre, prior sic Floridus inquit:
      Flor. Huc ades, o Tranquille. Pecus iam dormit in umbra.
10   Huc ades et nostri iudex certaminis esto.

---

106 constitit *A (in erratis) BO*: constiti *A (in textu)*.
   Buc. 5. *Cf. Idyllion 4 in BO.*   **1** Pastores *BO*: Astores *A*.

---

[41]Tranquillus, whose wisdom is praised in *Buc.* 2, 103-106 and again in line 11 below,
is Eobanus's mentor Mutianus Rufus. For his life see Camerarius, *Nar.* 12, 12–13, 10, with
fn. 36. In the argument prefixed to *Idyl.* 4 in the 1539-edition Eobanus confirms this identi-
fication and also unmasks the other shepherds. Floridus ("In the flower of youth") is Petrejus
Eberbach, the friend to whom he dedicated *De infoelicitate amantium* in June 1508; for his life
see the introduction to that work. The shepherd Vernus ("In the springtime of life") is Justus
Jonas of Nordhausen (1493-1555). Justus returns the compliment in *Buc.* B 9.
    At the time this eclogue was written (probably in the summer of 1508) Justus Jonas was
a precocious fifteen-year-old, who had earned the B.A. in 1507 and would obtain his M.A. in

heifer. He stopped at once and shouted: "Woe, run from these terrible woods, these places teeming with hellish poisons! Here, they say, black Pluto opens the gate to hell; here the grim Furies lay bare the underworld. [110] Round up the cattle lest they touch a blade of that fetid grass and become lean on the fattening pasture." After these words he went off into the deep forest to search for his heifer.

Argus. I've seen plenty of plutocrats and vampires in the city too, who will devour human flesh for a pittance.

Phileremus. In my rush to get away, I gathered up my belongings haphazardly and at random, but accidentally dropped my awl in the well that had been dug there.

Argus. Cool night is hurrying near. It's time to stable the sated bulls and lead the roving lambs to the sheepfolds.

THE FIFTH ECLOGUE

Floridus, Vernus, the umpire Tranquillus[41]

Two shepherds, Floridus and Vernus, met under a green elm tree where many a wave washes the painted banks and creates sweet whispers as it glides along. The two were equal in age, handsome lads both, both skilled in song. And there they sat, intent on their pastime, ready to vie with each other, and were busy fastening the reeds together when the older Tranquillus happened to come by. As soon as the lads saw him, Floridus called out to him as follows:

Floridus. Come over here, Tranquillus! Your herd is already dozing in the shade. [10] Come here and be the

---

early 1510. From 1511 he studied law in Wittenberg, earning a legal baccalaureate in 1515. Upon his return to Erfurt he continued his studies. In 1518 he became licentiate of civil and canon law and was appointed professor at the university. Inspired by Eobanus, he visited Erasmus at Louvain in the spring of 1519. Thereafter, at Erasmus's urging, he began to study theology and Greek. In April 1521 he accompanied Luther to the diet of Worms. Later that year he was appointed professor of canon law in Wittenberg; but after earning a doctorate in divinity (14 October 1521) he transferred to the theological faculty. He soon became an indefatigable champion of the Reformation, helping organize the evangelical church, translating many of Luther's and Melanchthon's Latin works into German, and chronicling the reformer's life and death.

A contemporary manuscript note in the Strasbourg copy of the *Bucolicon* gives a different explanation for the names Vernus and Floridus. Vernus, we read there, is Eobanus himself. Floridus is said to be a fellow countryman ("conterraneus meus"), identified only by the initials "I. H."

Et tua per nostras resonat sapientia sylvas.

 Tran. Audaces pueri, plus quam pueriliter ausi

C4ʳ Alternis certare modis, audatia laus est

In puero, si non temeraria. Dicite quales

15 Victor opes referet? Quae pignora ponitis ergo?

Ipse ego, quandoquidem mihi stant ad flumina thauri,

Iudex vester ero et meritos largibor honores.

 Vern. Hunc tibi lunatum pro pignore ponimus arcum,

Floride, quem duro teneri de stipite pomi

20 Foecimus hiis manibus tornoque polivimus acri,

Distinctum venis bubulis viscoque tenaci.

Aspice deductum circum duo cornua funem.

Quam bonus! Herculeis gravius ferit ille sagittis.

Hoc ego quot tulerim non est numerare volucres –

25 Cornices, corvos, cuculos, turdos, et anates.

Saepe etiam lepores coepi capreasque fugaces.

Dextro Phillirides cornu caelatus, ut ille

Spicula cum pharetra puero praemonstrat Achilli.

Gnosius ex alio serpentem interficit Alcon,

30 Ut puer illesus docto sua taela parenti

Gratus et ex medio veluti Phlegethonte reportat.

Sepius hunc nobis invidit stultus Adonis.

 Flor. Iudice Tranquillo mecum si munere certes,

Vicimus. En ista quae pendet fistula pinu,

35 Ut reor, illa tuum pretio supereminet arcum,

Non calamis compacta tribus rudibusve cicutis,

Non cera connexa levi, quibus impius olim

C4ᵛ Pan deus agrestes docuit resonare poetas,

Sed teres ex viridi buxo tornata monaulos.

40 Quam tamen ipse vola nequeas concludere, quamvis

Longa tibi digitum pater internodia foecit.

Hanc ego muneribus venalem grandibus emi.

Vellera bina dedi raptamque a matre capellam.

Hac ubi personui scopulo vocalis ab alto,

45 Floruit omne nemus, fragrabant lilia, flores

---

40 ipse *BO*: ipsa *A*.

[42]The centaur Chiron, son of Saturn and Philyra, was Achilles' tutor.

 [43]Hercules' comrade Alcon was a master archer. Once, when a snake coiled itself around his sleeping son, he shot the beast without injuring the boy. See Serv. *Ecl.* 5, 11.

umpire of our singing-match. Everyone in our forests knows of your wisdom.

Tranquillus. Daring lads, you've dared beyond your years to sing against each other in alternating verse. Daring is a virtue in a lad, so long as it does not become reckless. Very well, then: Tell me, what prize is the winner to take? What stakes are you willing to name? Since my bulls are just standing there on the riverbank, I'll be your umpire and award the prize you deserve.

Vernus. As my stake I pledge you this crescent-shaped bow, Floridus. I made it with my own hands from the hard bole of a young fruit tree, [20] then smoothed it on a sharp-cutting lathe and strung it with ox-gut and sticky glue. Just look at the cord that is wound around the two ends. What a fine piece of work! That bow will hit its target harder than Hercules' arrows. I couldn't begin to count the number of birds I've bagged with it – crows, ravens, cuckoos, thrushes, and ducks. Often I've even used it to shoot hares and fleet-footed roe deer. Embossed on the right end is Phi-lyra's son,[42] busy showing the boy Achilles how to use a bow and arrow. At the other end there's Alcon of Crete, who has just killed the serpent.[43] [30] Grateful to his skilled father for saving him unharmed, the boy is carrying the arrows back. Doesn't he look as if he's just gone through hell? Like the fool he is, Adonis has often begrudged me that bow.[44]

Floridus. If you're trying to impress the umpire Tranquillus by praising your stake over mine, then I'm the clear winner. Look at that flute hanging over there in the pine tree! I'm sure it's worth far more than your bow. It's not made of three reeds or a set of hemlock stalks joined with light wax – not the crude sort of pipe on which the wicked god Pan once taught country poets to make music, but a recorder of pale-green boxwood, smoothly turned on a lathe. [40] And yet you couldn't hold it in the palm of your hand, no matter how long the fingers are that you inherited from your father. I paid a good price for it when it was offered for sale: two fleeces and a kid snatched away from its mother. When I played my best tunes on it, atop a high rock, the whole forest blossomed, the lilies smelled sweetly, the genial

---

[44]Adonis is a handsome lad (*Buc.* 2, 65), who steals hearts as well as possessions (*Buc.* 3, 142-144; 7, 41).

Fundebat genialis humus, gravis aura quievit,
Spirabant Zephiri, mollisque Favonius ibat,
Applaudens leni circum mea tempora flatu.
Illa tuo nunquid caelata fidelius arcu?
50   Cernis ut hic fugiat victorem Marsia Phoebum.
Daemens qui divos vocat in certamina! Cernis
Auriculas Phrigio per tempora surgere regi.
Hic etiam excoeptum Misenum in littore Triton
Obruit. Arrident circum cava littora nymphae.
55   Illam, Verne, tamen tecum deponimus. Ergo
Quis prior incipiat tibi sit, Tranquille, relictum.
    Tran. Ludite iam, pueri. Satis est pro pignore dictum.
Ludite ut incipiant motare cacumina sylvae
Blandaque formosae saliant ad carmina nymphae.
60   Incipe, Verne, prior: tua carmine dignior aetas.
    Vern. Dicite, Pierides, certantes dicite Musae.
Quis fuit ante cahos et prima exordia mundi?
Quis mare, quis terras, quis lucida sydera foecit?
Unus in aeternum qui contrahit omnia regnum.
65   Gratia, Pierides, vobis sit gratia, Musae.
    Flor. Currite, Thespiades, faciles properate Camaenae.
Virginis intactae castum referemus amorem
Christophorae, sed quae genialis nescia lecti
Aedidit arcano conceptum semine natum.
70   Plaudite, Thespiades, faciles gaudete Camaenae.
    Vern. Dicite, Pierides, certantes dicite Musae.
Quis movet hanc molem? Tantum quis terminat orbem?
Quis rutilum fissis iaculatur nubibus ignem?
Unus ab aeterna mundi ratione creator.
75   Gratia, Pierides, vobis sit gratia, Musae.
    Flor. Currite, Thespiades, faciles properate Camaenae.
Vidit et incaluit, non vidit et acrius arsit.
Nobilis in solo flagravit nomine Virgo,
Ut calet a Zephiro pingui flos pulcher in horto.
80   Plaudite, Thespiades, faciles gaudete Camaenae.

D1ʳ

---

67 intactae *BO*: intacte *A*.

[45]The satyr Marsyas challenged Apollo to a contest in flute-playing. But the god defeated him and flayed him alive for his presumption. See Ov. *Met.* 6, 382-391; *Fast.* 6, 703-708; cf. Eob. *Buc.* 6, 97; *Her. Chr.*, ded. 10, 2.

[46]After Apollo won a musical contest over Pan, the Phrygian king Midas criticized the judgment. As punishment Apollo gave him ass's ears. See Ov. *Met.* 11, 146-179.

earth brought forth an abundance of flowers, the wind gusts
subsided, zephyrs blew, and a gentle breeze from the west
applauded softly as it circled my forehead. Isn't the carving
on it truer to life than the one on your bow? [50] Here you
see how Marsyas flees from the victorious Phoebus.[45] Only a
fool would challenge the gods to a contest! Look at the ass's
ears growing on the head of the Phrygian king.[46] And here's
Triton too. He has just caught Misenus on the shore and is
drowning him, as the nymphs on the hollowed-out beaches
watch with a smile.[47] All the same, Vernus, I'm going to
stake it with you. Well then, as to who should start first,
that, Tranquillus, is for you to decide.

   Tranquillus. Get playing now, lads. Enough has been
said about the stakes. Play, so the trees start swaying their
crowns and lovely nymphs dance to the charming songs.
[60] Since you're the younger one, Vernus, it seems fair that
you should lead off.

   Vernus. Sing, Pierian Maidens, sing, competitive
Muses. Who existed before the primeval Chaos and the cre-
ation of the world? Who made the sea, the lands, and the
shining stars? He alone, who brought all things together
into one eternal realm. Thanks, Pierian Maidens, thanks be
to you, Muses.

   Floridus. Run, Thespian Maidens, hasten, gracious Ca-
menae. Let us sing the chaste love of the untouched Virgin,
Mother of Christ. A stranger to the marriage bed, she none-
theless bore a Son conceived from mysterious seed. [70]
Applaud, Thespian Maidens, rejoice, gracious Camenae.

   Vernus. Sing, Pierian Maidens, sing, competitive
Muses. Who moves this great structure? Who keeps the vast
world within bounds? Who throws the fiery lightning that
cleaves the clouds? He alone, who created the world in ac-
cordance with everlasting reason. Thanks, Pierian Maidens,
thanks be to you, Muses.

   Floridus. Run, Thespian Maidens, hasten, gracious Ca-
menae. She saw and grew hot, saw nothing and burned even
hotter. The noble Virgin warmed at the mere mention of his
name, as a beautiful flower in a fertile garden is warmed by
the zephyr. [80] Applaud, Thespian Maidens, rejoice, gra-
cious Camenae.

---

[47] Aeneas's trumpeter Misenus was blowing a conch shell and overconfidently challenged
the gods to a contest. Triton caught him, however, and drowned him in the sea. See Verg. *A.*
6, 171-174; cf. Eob. *Pug.* 14.

Vern. Dicite, Pierides, certantes dicite Musae.
Quis prohibet ventos? Quis rauca tonitrua torquet?
Quis nebulam spargit? Quis nubes densat in arctum?
Unus qui solus rerum discrimina pandit.
85 Gratia, Pierides, vobis sit gratia, Musae.
   Flor. Currite, Thespiades, faciles properate Camaenae.
Dum flores in serta legit, dum sola per agros
Errat, ab Eoa perflavit Spiritus aura.
Quando afflata, novum concoepit Virgo tumorem.
90 Plaudite, Thespiades, faciles gaudete Camaenae.
  · *Vern.* Dicite, Pierides, certantes dicite Musae.
Quis facit has segetes? Quis campum pingit arista?
Quis foecundat agros? Quis sylvam frondibus ornat?
Unus qui propria nescit virtute secundum.
95 Gracia, Pierides, vobis sit gratia, Musae.
   Flor. Currite, Thespiades, faciles properate Camaenae.
Interea dulci tumuit gestamine venter;
Aedidit in terris similem caelestibus ipsis.
Virgineum meruit Genitrix servare pudorem.
100 Plaudite, Thespiades, faciles gaudete Camaenae.
   Vern. Dicite, Pierides, certantes dicite Musae.
Quis veteres faunos, satyros quis trusit ad umbras?
Quis Phoebum et Bacchum? Quis numina cuncta deorum?
Unus qui solus Deus est, qui cuncta gubernat.
105 Gratia, Pierides, vobis sit gratia, Musae.
   Flor. Currite, Thespiades, faciles properate Camaenae.
O pia caelesti Virgo praelata coronae,
Huc ades et nostrum foecunda floribus arvum.
Fistula sic divam nunquam te nostra silebit.
110 Plaudite, Thespiades, faciles gaudete Camaenae.
   Tran. Sit satis. Inclinata dies requiescere suadet.
Claudite vocales, pueri, iam claudite cannas.
Vicit uterque; ipsi vestrum vicistis utrumque.
Vos faciunt et forma pares et carmen et aetas.
115 Arcus, Verne, tibi, tibi fistula, Floride, caedat,
Ut prius, et vestros concordes pascite thauros.

D1ᵛ (left margin, line 88)
D2ʳ (left margin, line 113)

---

97 tumuit *A (in erratis) BO*: timuit *A (in textu).*   **114** carmen *A (in erratis) BO*: carmine *A (in textu).*

Vernus. Sing, Pierian Maidens, sing, competitive Muses. Who keeps the winds in check? Who hurls the crashing thunderbolts? Who spreads the fog? Who gathers up the clouds? He alone, who laid out the bounds of all things. Thanks, Pierian Maidens, thanks be to you, Muses.

Floridus. Run, Thespian Maidens, hasten, gracious Camenae. While she was picking flowers for a chaplet, while she was strolling alone through the fields, the Spirit breathed upon her in the east wind. After the Breath had come upon her, the Virgin wondrously conceived and became big with child. [90] Applaud, Thespian Maidens, rejoice, gracious Camenae.

Vernus. Sing, Pierian Maidens, sing, competitive Muses. Who produces these crops? Who emblazons the plain with wheat? Who makes the fields fertile? Who adorns the forest with leaves? He alone, who has no equal in power. Thanks, Pierian Maidens, thanks be to you, Muses.

Floridus. Run, Thespian Maidens, hasten, gracious Camenae. Meanwhile her womb swelled up with its dear burden; it brought into the world One who was like the celestial beings themselves. His Mother was worthy of keeping her maidenhood. [100] Applaud, Thespian Maidens, rejoice, gracious Camenae.

Vernus. Sing, Pierian Maidens, sing, competitive Muses. Who thrust the ancient fauns and satyrs down to the shades? Who drove Phoebus and Bacchus and all those heathen gods down to hell?[48] He alone, the one true God who rules the universe. Thanks, Pierian Maidens, thanks be to you, Muses.

Floridus. Run, Thespian Maidens, hasten, gracious Camenae. O gentle Virgin, exalted with a heavenly crown, come hither and make our meadow fecund with flowers. Then my flute will never cease to praise you as goddess. [110] Applaud, Thespian Maidens, rejoice, gracious Camenae.

Tranquillus. Let that be enough. The close of day is urging us to rest. Stop singing and piping now, lads. Each one of you has won; each of you has defeated the other. You two are a perfect match in beauty and singing and youth. Let the bow fall to you, Vernus, the flute to you, Floridus, just as it was before. Now go in amity to pasture your bullocks.

---

[48]The old demons, who had introduced superstitions and false cults into the world, were thrust down into hell after Christ's birth. For this traditional belief cf. *Her. Chr.* 9, 83-92, with note.

AEGLOGA SEXTA, AD RUFUM

Ludimus Ocnaeo si quid spectabile versu,
Quam longo Andinas imitabimur intervallo
Pierides! Modo sit sylvas intrare patenteis,
Iuglandes si grande, nuces captare colurnas
5   Non vetet, arbusta atque humiles cantare myricas.
Nunc tamen audaces nimium nimiumque Camaenas,
Primus ego in patrios agros et Teutona ducam
Pascua. Nunc etiam nostrae sua carmina sylvae
Incipient resonare.
                              Ausis ignoscite, Musae
10   Ausonides! Nec tu, quo se mea rustica tantum
Iactat Musa tuo quantum te, Tityre, Varo,
Non tu difficiles mihi dedignabere montes
Et valles habitare sacras lucosque silentes,
Rufe, per Aonios colles notissime. Qui nunc
15   Cictiaco dulcem trutinas examine vitam,
Ingredere et mecum sylvis assuesce iugosis.
En tibi detectum frondet nemus, omnia pleno
Fundit aperta sinu tellus, tibi germinat arbos
Omnis. Odoratos nunc primum lilia montes
20   Incipiunt habitare novo vernantia luxu.
Nunc gelidi fontes manant et rupibus altis,
Frigida milleno labuntur flumina lapsu
Per virides ripas et amaena silentia. Postquam
Te nostri accipiunt saltus, fugit omnibus omnis
25   Graminibus serpens, fragrant suavissima tempe,
Quale apibus dicunt Siculam stipantibus Hyblen.
Sub pedibus lascivit humus, tua scilicet ipsae
Excipiunt laetis vestigia motibus herbae.

D2ᵛ

***Buc.* 6**. *Cf. Idyllion 8 in BO*.   **1** Ludimus *Gillert*: Udimus *A*.   **5** vetet *B*: veter *AO*.
6 nimium *scripsi*: minium *A*.   **7** in *A (in erratis)*: inter *A (in textu)*.   **20** novo *A (in*
erratis) BO: nova *A (in textu)*.   **22** flumina *A (in erratis) BO*: fulmina *A (in textu)*.

---

[49]This eclogue, tellingly placed at the center of the *Bucolicon*, represents the heart of
Eobanus's pastoral ideal: Mutianus Rufus's dream of "blessed tranquillity" and leisure for hu-
manistic learning, a life of wisdom untrammeled by passion or the vulgar crowd. Cf. *Laud.*
263-264; *Epic.* 4, 191-192, referring to Mutianus Rufus; Camerarius, *Nar.* 12, 18. For Mu-
tianus's life see Camerarius, *Nar.* 12, 12–13, 10, with fn. 36.

As early as *Laud.* 280-284 Eobanus had expressed a desire to immortalize his friend and
mentor in pastoral song, just as Vergil (in the traditional view) had eulogized Julius Caesar as
Daphnis in *Ecl.* 5. To be sure, Mutianus was still very much alive; but since he refused to pub-
lish any of his writings, he was dead to the outside world. Eobanus's pastoral, accordingly, has

THE SIXTH ECLOGUE, TO RUFUS[49]

If the bucolic verses that I write for my amusement have any
value, at what a great distance do I follow my model, Vergil's
pastoral Muse![50] At least allow me to enter those spacious
woods. And if the grandeur of that place doesn't forbid it,
give me leave to reach for walnuts and hazelnuts and to sing
of hedgerows and humble tamarisks. All the same, I'm now
the first to bring the audacious, no, reckless Muses to my
homeland and onto the pastures of Germany.[51] Now our
forests too will start to resound with songs of their own.

Forgive the audacity, Muses [10] of Italy! You too, in
whom my rustic Muse glories just as much as Vergil did in
his friend Varus[52] – you won't disdain to dwell with me
in the strenuous mountains and sacred vales and silent
groves, O Rufus, renowned on Mount Helicon's slopes.
You, who now weigh your delightful life in the Stoic bal-
ance, come with me and get used to living in the hills and
woods. Look, the bare forest is putting on its verdure for
you. The earth has opened up and is pouring forth every-
thing she has from her full bosom. All the trees are in bud
for you. Only now are the spring lilies [20] beginning to
flourish as never before in the odorous hills. Now the
springs run with cool water, and from the high cliffs icy
streams tumble down in a thousand rills, along overgrown
banks and through the lovely silence. Ever since our glades
have welcomed you, the snakes have all fled from the pas-
tures everywhere. The valleys are redolent of sweet-scented
flowers, just like Mount Hybla in Sicily, which they say is
swarming with bees. The ground frolics under your feet.
And as you walk on it, the grass joyfully bends and springs

---

a dual purpose. On the one hand, it is intended to broadcast Mutianus's fame in the republic
of letters; on the other, it tries to persuade him to share his poetry with a wider audience. Since
the theme as well as the phrasing are reminiscent of "Ad Mutianum Rufum elegia," which was
probably written in the spring of 1508, we may place the present eclogue at about the same
time. For the theme see also *Her. Chr.*, ded. 4, 5.

[50]The poem starts off with an expression of modesty and humility: Trailing far behind the
pastoralist Vergil, Eobanus will content himself with culling verses and motifs from the mas-
ter's eclogues; cf. *Buc.* 3, 28-29. For the display of modesty see Curtius, *ELLMA*, pp. 83-85.

[51]Even though Eobanus is no match for Vergil, he can nonetheless be proud of being Ger-
many's first pastoralist. For this claim cf. *Buc.*, lim. 5 (n.).

[52]Varus, the patron whom Vergil praises in *Ecl.* 6, may perhaps be identified as the juris-
consult P. Alfenus Varus, consul suffect in 39 BC.

Aspice quam niteat toto formosior anno
30 Phoebus et insolito mundum splendore serenet.
Hoc erat, hoc adeo nostros quod saepe per agros
Optabam, hoc mecum nemora omnia et ipsa petebant
Saxa salebrosas subter squalentia rupes.
Saepe graves pratis dum pasco virentibus agnas,
35 Quem canerem assiduo resonantem carmine Rufum
Quaerebant socii, cum sic ego forte canebam:
    "Dum nemora et sylvae stabunt, dum flumina current,
Dum mare, dum tellus, dum ventus et aura manebunt,
Rufe, meis et si rudibus dicere Camaenis.
40 Ipsa tuas etiam laudes armenta feraeque
Sylvestres avidique lupi sevique leones,
Tigrides et lynces et in ipsis partubus ursae
Auribus accipient stupidis. Dumque omnis ad auras
Carmina nostra canet pastor, te montibus altis
45 Aereae rupes et concava saxa sonabunt.

D3ʳ

O tantum ne turpe feras haec sordida circum
Rura, boves inter, florum redolentia regna
Incolere et dulcem captare sub arbore somnum
Umbrifera vivoque sitim restinguere fonte
50 Et cantu mulcere auras. Hic subter opacas
Quercus fagineumque nemus pinusque decoras
Et virides ulmos pulchram sine nomine vitam
Ducere et urbanum poteris vitare tribunal.
Hic ubi virgineae laurus et frigida surgit
55 Saeminibus lactuca piis, ubi tonsile buxum
Et nativa humiles faciunt topiaria corni,
Lecta corona tibi est, castos quae plurima crines
Contegat. En divae dicunt bona verba Camaenae:
'Vernantes in flore tegi patiare capillos.'
60 Quem tibi non ullae Veneres meditantur honorem.
Nulla Dryas, neque Naiades, non mollis Oraeas,
Nulla tibi assistet Phillis, non ulla Lycoris.
Et tibi mollitie nihil est invisius ista.
Non ita fraxineae invisae serpentibus umbrae,
65 Non sic agna lupos, non sic fugit aera talpa,
Quam tu quicquid habet perfectae incommoda vitae.
Quicquid Acidalio generosam caumate mentem

---

32 ipsa *A (in erratis) BO*: ipse *A (in textu)*.   36 socii *BO*: sotii *A*.   49 restinguere *BO*: re-
stringere *A*.

back. Look how Phoebus shines more beautifully now than at any other time of the year [30] and brightens the world with uncommon splendor. This is the very thing I have so often prayed to see on our fields. This is what all the woods have been yearning for too, as have the rugged rocks at the foot of craggy cliffs. Often, as I pastured the gravid ewes on the verdant meadows, my comrades wanted to know more about the Rufus whose name resounded in my assiduous song, particularly when I happened to sing something like this:

"As long as groves and forests stand, as long as rivers run, as long as sea and land exist, as long as winds and breezes blow, so long, Rufus, will I praise you in my songs, however artless they may be. [40] The very cattle will listen with spellbound ears as I sing your praises; so will the beasts of the forest, the ravenous wolves, savage lions, tigers, lynxes, and she-bears – even while bringing forth young! And as long as every shepherd sings my songs to the breezes, the sheer cliffs and hollow rocks in the high mountains will echo with your name. Oh, don't think it beneath you to live in the homely countryside, amidst the cattle, to dwell in the fragrant realm of flowers, to take a pleasant snooze under a shade tree, to slake your thirst at a bubbling spring [50] and caress the air with your singing. Here, under shady oaks and beeches and handsome pines and leafy elms, you could lead an honorable life, out of the public eye, and steer clear of urban politics. Here, where maidenly laurels grow and cold lettuce sprouts its salutary seeds, where clipped boxwoods and cornel shrubs form natural topiaries, a splendid garland awaits you, woven to cover your chaste hair. Lo, the divine Muses are uttering words of good omen: 'Allow us to wreathe your locks with spring blossoms.' [60] This is not an honor devised by some Venus. No voluptuous dryad, naiad, or oread, no Phyllis or Lycoris will be standing beside you. For to you there is nothing more odious than wantonness like that. Not so anxiously do snakes avoid the shade of the ash tree, not so eagerly do lambs flee the wolf, moles the air above, as you stay clear of every obstacle to a perfect life. Anything that infects a noble spirit with the heat of lust and extinguishes the desire for higher things you

Inficit extinguitque animos maiora volentes,
Tu fugis ut pulchris aconita latentia gemmis.
70   "O vitae tranquilla quies et summa beatae!
Sic mihi preteritos olim Deus exuat annos,
Talem sera dies videat me, seu mihi longos
Invideant mea fata dies seu frigidus annis
Ante diem presso moriatur corpore sanguis.
75 Non mihi post cineres potioris cura sepulchri,
Dummodo corporea iam functus mole feratur
Spiritus ante Deos. Caedat caro putris in escam
Vermibus, aut volucres pascat sublime volantes
Cura eadem. Stultus, qui foeda cadavera in auro
80 Collocat et vanis infundit balsama membris
Daemens et frustra miseros amplectitur artus.
Qui faciunt simulachra virum defunctaque servant
Corpora, dii superi, quam delyrare videntur!
Ergo vel ignotus moriar, vel si qua poaetis
85 Gloria debetur dulcis post aedita vitae
Tempora, sub quacumque licet tellure quiescam.
    "Tu modo, seu magno testaris iubila Christo
Nocturnis inhians sacris cytharamque novenis
Percurris fidibus resonantem carmina regis
90 Vatis Iessei, seu divite bibliothaeca
Confusus, libros mille inter, solis ad ortum
Leniter afflantem tua pectora suscipis Eurum,
Tu modo – namque olim tibi nostra fidelius ibunt
Carmina liberiusque canam tua nomina, Rufe –
95 Ad rus et montana veni. Maiora volebam
Pangere, ni pastorem humilis decuisset harundo
Et rudis averso cecinisset Apolline faunus."

D3ᵛ

D4ʳ

---

71 Deus *A (in erratis) BO*: deos *A (in textu).*   **88** inhians *A (in erratis) BO*: inhiant *A (in textu).*   **96** ni *BO*: in *A.*

[53] As a canon at St. Mary's, Mutianus regularly attended mass and participated in the singing of the Psalms.

shun as if it were aconite, lurking in beautiful goblets encrusted with gems.

[70] "Oh, the tranquil and sublime peace of a blessed life! May I be living like that when God someday strips me of the years past! That is the sort of man I should like to be on my dying day, whether fate begrudges me a long life or whether I reach the years where the body is burdened before its time and the blood runs cold. I don't care for an elaborate tomb after my death, as long as my soul, relieved at last of its corporeal mass, is borne aloft before God. Let the putrid flesh be food for worms, for all I care, or let it become carrion for the birds that soar on high. What folly to lay out hideous corpses in state, all tricked out with gold! [80] What insanity to embalm lifeless bodies and embrace the wretched limbs, to no avail! By the gods above, how raving mad are those who make images of men and so preserve the bodies of the dead! Therefore, whether I die as an unknown or as a celebrated poet – if indeed poets deserve some glory after they depart this sweet life – I shall rest in peace, no matter where I am buried.

"Now you, whether you are making a joyful noise to the mighty Christ as you longingly await the nocturnal Sacrament and run your fingers over the nine-stringed lyre and sing the Psalms of the poet-king [90] David,[53] or whether you are standing in your rich library at sunrise, troubled amidst a thousand books as you feel the east wind gently breathing upon your chest[54] – for someday I'll sing songs that portray you more faithfully and praise you more freely, Rufus – do come to the fields and mountains! I would have liked to compose something more exalted in your honor, were not the humble reed pipe proper to a shepherd and were I not mindful of that rude faun whose song so angered Apollo."[55]

---

[54] Since the rising sun symbolizes the risen Lord and the heavenly Jerusalem, the faithful often said their prayers while facing east.

[55] In telling himself to stay within pastoral bounds, the poet is reminded of Marsyas who, having challenged Apollo to a musical competition, was flayed alive for his presumption. Cf. *Buc.* 5, 50, with fn. 45. Marsyas was in fact a satyr, not a faun; but the terms were practically synonymous. Cf. Ov. *Met.* 6, 392-393.

AEGLOGA SEPTIMA

Cautus, Caldus

Caut. Tercius immenso rediit iam Lucifer orbi,
Altera nox abiit postquam mihi perditus istis
Quaeritur in sylvis aries, ubi plurima densant
Umbrosum virgulta nemus. Dic, optime Calde,
5   Nunquid aberrantem vidisti? Nam neque quicquam
Notius hoc uno. Niger est, caret aure sinistra,
Cornua pene oculos tangunt redeuntia torvos,
Quorum ope sepe lupis idem occursare solebat.
    Cald. Ah, pecus infoelix! Non te tua cornua tutum,
10   Non torvi foecere oculi. Tibi vera fatebor,
Caute, decus nemorum. Vix post ientacula mane,
Dum volucrum varia scrutabar in arbore nidos,
Excoeptum pecus ipse lupus iam dente comedit
Sanguineo, frendens in me. Nisi forte fuissem
15   A cane defensus, mea mordicus ora petisset.
Ne doleas quod fata iubent, quod ferre necesse est.
    Caut. Hei mihi, nunc primum evenit quod sepe verebar!
Hei, miserande aries! Quod eras audatior aequo,
Nunc peris et meritas persolvis sanguine poenas.
20   Inter oves puduit viridem te pascere terram.
Tu cythisum tiliasque leves dulcemque cyperon,
Stulte, sequebare et semper mihi solus abibas.
Ergo nunc rapidi rodunt tua viscera corvi.
Qui nimis est audax, sepe infoeliciter audet.
25   *Cald.* Est ut ais. Pecoris verum obliviscere adempti.
Qua potes, hanc alia iacturam sorte repende
Et mecum viridi laetus succede salicto,

D4ᵛ

Buc. 7 Cf. Idyllia 9 et 10 in BO.   1 Tercius *scripsi*: Ercius A, Tertius BO.   5 neque A *(in erratis)*: queque A *(in textu).*

THE SEVENTH ECLOGUE[56]

Cautus, Caldus

Cautus. For the third time already morning has dawned on
the wide world, two nights have come and gone since I
started looking for the ram that ran off on me in these
woods. The underbrush is so dense in this shady forest that
you can't find anything. Tell me, excellent Caldus, you
didn't see him wandering off someplace, did you? He's
pretty notorious around here, as you know. He's black all
over, his left ear is missing, and his horns, with which he of-
ten liked to charge wolves, curve back so far that they nearly
touch his glowering eyes.

Caldus. Ah, hapless beast! Neither your horns [10] nor
your glowering eyes sufficed to keep *you* out of harm's way.
I'll tell you the truth, Cautus, pride and joy of the wood-
lands. Just after breakfast this morning, when I was
searching out birds' nests in various trees, a wolf was already
devouring the beast he'd caught. Gore dripping from his
jaws, he was gnashing his teeth at me. If my dog hadn't been
there to defend me, he'd have gone right for my face and
mangled it. Don't lament a loss that fate has ordained, that
you have to endure.

Cautus. Alas, what I often feared has now finally hap-
pened! Ah, wretched ram! Because you were overly reckless,
you're dead now. You paid the penalty with your blood, as
you deserved. [20] Grazing among the sheep in the grass-
land was beneath your dignity. Instead, fool, you went
looking for clover and easily digestible linden leaves and
sweet galingale. You were always disappearing on me, all by
yourself. Well, now the fierce ravens are tearing at your guts!
He who is recklessly bold is bold at his peril.

Caldus. You're quite right. Just forget about that dead
ram of yours. As best you can, make up for this loss in some
other way. Enjoy yourself and come with me into the shade
of the green willows over here where the bullock-born in-

---

[56] Absent any hints from Eobanus himself, the shepherds Cautus ("Cautious," "Prudent")
and Caldus ("Hot," "Passionate") cannot be identified. For the name Cautus cf. n. *Ama.* 12,
11 ("incautum"). The theme of unrequited passionate love, shared with *De infoelicitate aman-
tium* (June 1508) and *Buc.* 3, suggests that this eclogue was written in mid-1508. An allusion
to *Buc.* 2 (mid-summer 1508) in line 166 points in the same direction.

Hic ubi thaurigenae stipant nova mella volucres
Et circum pleno stridunt examine flores.
30   *Caut.* Aspice, per superos, multo res digna cachinno.
Quam saliunt petulanter oves in tramite plano!
    Cald. Quam rudis es, nec dum diuturno exercitus usu!
Naturas ovium nescis, cautissime pastor.
Vicina ruber est cortex delapsus ab ulmo,
35 Causa novi saltus. Nam talia cuncta verentur
Et neque vere rosas neque rubra papavera mandunt.
    Caut. Tale quid in nostris etiam Deus ipse capellis
Ridiculum natura dedit. Nam vincula cruri
Foeceris ex scirpo vel vimine sive genista
40 Sive alio quocumque, per omnes claudicat agros.
Quod cum vidisset sceleratus risit Adonis.
    Cald. Hoc leve naturae specimen mirabilis aiunt,
Id grave. Populeis si sueta canalia virgis
Corticibus demptis spargas, tum frondibus albis
45 Intentae meditantur oves gliscente colorem
In coitu niveum. Quae tunc concoeperit, albam
Aedit ovem. Sic se magnus didicisse Philaegon
Dixit et in parvo monstrabat codice scriptum.
    Caut. Sic etiam ex alba niger hircus sepe capella
50 Diversam generat prolem variique coloris.
Idque ego, dum capio teneri incrementa peculi,
Non semel expertus longo sum doctus ab usu.
    Cald. Eheu, Caute, pedem mihi spina offensa momordit!
Aspicis ut soleam cono diffindit acuto.
55 Affer opem misero! Spinam extrahe dente tenaci,
Si potes, et maneat ne pars in carne videto.

E1ʳ (margin, beside line 47)

---

29 stridunt *B*: stridant *A*, strident *O*.

[57]According to an old belief, the putrefying blood of a slain bullock can bring forth bees. See, for example, Verg. *G.* 4, lines 281-314 and 548-558; Ov. *Met.* 15, 364-367; Plin. *Nat.* 11, 70.

sects[57] are packing their new-made honey away and whirring in a great swarm around the blossoms.

Cautus. [30] Look over there, by gad! Isn't that the funniest thing you ever saw? The sheep are jumping around like mad on the level path!

Caldus. What a greenhorn you are, not yet trained by daily experience! You haven't a clue what makes sheep tick, do you, most cautious of goatherds! Some of the ruddy bark has fallen off the nearby elm tree – the cause of those freakish jumps you saw. They are really scared of anything red. That's the reason they won't munch roses or red poppies in springtime.

Cautus. God himself – their instinct, if you will – has given my goats a ridiculous quirk just like that. For if you made a bracelet of bulrush or wicker or broom [40] or anything else and put it on their legs, they'd limp all over the place. When Adonis saw that, he burst out laughing, miscreant that he is.

Caldus. Now that is what you might call a lightweight example of nature's wonders. Here is a heavyweight one. If you peel the bark from poplar rods and place them in the accustomed watering troughs, the sheep will stare at the white twigs. If they happen to be breeding just then, they'll have the snowy color in mind. Any lamb conceived at that moment will be born white. The great Philaegon[58] told me this when he found out about it and showed me the passage in a small book.

Cautus. Likewise, a black buck mated with a white goat often [50] produces kids of different or variegated color. I've seen that more than once with my own eyes when obtaining offspring from the young livestock – well-versed as I am through long experience.

Caldus. Ouch, Cautus, I've stepped on a thorn! How it hurts! You see how the sharp spike has gone right through the sole. Help me out of this misery! Extract the thorn with your clenched teeth, if you can, and be sure not to leave a splinter stuck in the flesh.

[58] Philaegon is the learned goatherd (Crotus Rubianus) whom we met earlier in *Buc.* 3. He reappears as a moral authority in line 166 below.

Caut. Tam pauxilla doles, o virgine mollior omni!
Magnanimum decet esse virum nec caedere parvis.
Sed tamen haec omnem peracuta novacula callum
60 Quae secet attentanda mihi est. En sanguine vulnus
Profluit. Educto nunc liber acumine surge.
   Cald. Ergo tibi salvae maneant in rure capellae,
Pignora chara domi, sperataque messis in agro!
Effugi miserum te salvatore dolorem.
65 *Caut.* Quam levis humanos etiam dolor occupat artus!
Nunc age confer oves foecundis, Calde, capellis.
Quod prius effectum voluisti, perge fateri.
   Cald. Hic neque certandi locus est, neque talia tecum,
Caute, volo. Decet esse bonos pacem inter amicos,
70 Ni iucunda magis quam sint mordatia dicta.
Si placet ergo, iocos, non seria saeva canemus.
   Caut. Incipe, Calde, placet, coelo dum Procyon ardet,
Dum iuvat umbra pecus, dum flumina grata capellis.
Hic melius rivi preterlabentis ad undam
75 Sub viridi platano molli requiescimus herba.
Incipe, ut inspirent nobis divina Camoenae.
   Cald. Caprarum grex atque ovium mihi mixtus amatur.
Sed tamen ante pilos caprarum lana bidentum
Nobilis. Et plures accommoda nunquid ad usus?
80 *Caut.* Et mihi sunt ovibus mixtae per pascua caprae.
Grex tamen hirta placet, tantoque est gratior illa
Quanto fertilius lana lac est comedenti.
   Cald. Lana homines vestit. Lanam cum divite pauper
Gestat emitque libens et murice tingit et ostro.
85 Frigora propellit, corpus tutatur ab aestu.
   Caut. Lac homines nutrit. Tanto est nutritio maius
Vestitu quam vita neci foelicior atrae.
Caseolos, butyrum lac dat, duo maxima dona.
   Cald. Non equidem inficior. Sed habent etiam ubera plena
90 Lactis oves, seroque ad mulctram vespere ductae
Omnia distentis complent mulctralia mammis.

E1ᵛ

---

65 *Nomen pastoris in margine* Caut. *addidi: om. A.*   **68** *Nomen pastoris in margine* Cald. *ad-*
didi: om. A.   **69** Caute *scripsi:* Calde *A.*

Cautus. It's just a pinprick that is making you cry out in pain. You're as touchy as a girl! A brave man shouldn't give in to a scratch like that. Well, it can't be helped; [60] I'll have to try to cut the whole callus with this supersharp razor of mine. Look, the wound is beginning to bleed. There! The thorn is out. Now you can get up again unhindered.

Caldus. May your goats thrive in the meadow, your dear children at home, and the hoped-for harvest in the field! You've saved me much agony.

Cautus. How even a little pain can take hold of a man's body! Now go ahead, Caldus, compare your sheep with my fertile goats. Carry on with your observations on the subject.

Caldus. This isn't a very good spot for a singing-match. Besides, I don't want to vie with you, Cautus. There ought to be peace between good friends, [70] unless the words passing between them are rather more witty than caustic. So if you agree, we'll sing in jest, not in vehement earnest.

Cautus. Agreed, Caldus! Lead off, while Procyon blazes in the sky, while the sheep are enjoying the shade, while the streams appeal to the goats. Over there is a better place to sing. Let's rest by the water of the running brook, in the soft grass under the green plane tree. Begin, so the Muses can inspire us with songs divine.

Caldus. I like a mixed flock, made up of goats and sheep. Nevertheless, sheepwool is superior to goathair. And doesn't wool lend itself to many more uses?

Cautus. [80] I too let my sheep graze with the goats on the meadows. Nevertheless, I prefer the shaggy flock – all the more so as milk is far more nutritious than wool.

Caldus. Wool provides people with clothing. Rich and poor wear wool; they gladly purchase it and dye it with purple and crimson. It wards off the cold and protects the body from heat.

Cautus. Milk gives people nutrition. Nourishment is more important than clothing to the same extent as life brings more joy than black death. Milk gives us cheese and butter, two of the finest gifts you could ask for.

Caldus. Sure, I won't deny it. But sheep also have udders full [90] of milk. And led back to the milk pails at sundown, they fill all of them with their distended teats.

Caut. Sola capella die plusquam ter quinque bidentes
Lactis agit pastuque domum compulsa reportat,
Bisque omnes una mulgentur luce capellae.
95   *Cald.* Ha ha, mentiri nescis, cautissime Caute!
Ridiculum quod ais, plus tu rideberis ergo.
Perge, precor. Faciles etiam risere Camoenae.
        Caut. Capra polos adiit. Solo est spectabile cornu
Sydus Amalthaeum. Docto si credis Iarbae,
100   Iuppiter Oleniae suxit deus ubera caprae.
        Cald. Lucida Phryxaeum pecus inter sydera fulget.
Cui fulvum rutilo vellus distinguitur auro.
Sic ego me puero didici, vix namque recordor.
        Caut. Nec rurale sonant nec sunt trivialia, quae nunc
105   Verba iocos inter surgunt. Vix talia pauci
Urbani sapiunt et nescio quale Lycaeum.
        Cald. Ergo rudes merito pueri syringa canemus,
Naiada quam canna texit Venus alma palustri,
Ut nostros etiam nemus omne intelligat ignes.
110   En venit et nobis Canace venit obvia! Cernis
Ut niveae molli sinuentur flamine vestes
Albentesque fluant post lactea terga capilli,
Ut virga in manibus varias discriminat agnas,
Quas nunc illa domum poto compellit ab amne.
115   O salve, facies mihi dilectissima! Salve,
Nympharum decus, ante omnes formosa puellas!
Iamdudum cupio tecum mihi mutua dentur
Colloquia. Heu, quanto miserum me conficis aestu!
Nulla mihi requies sine te datur, omnia curis
120   Plena. Dies votis totos consumimus istis.
Longa quiescendas turbant insomnia noctes.
Huc ades et nostros, Canace formosa, dolores

---

[59]In the summer, sheep and goats were normally milked early in the morning and again after sundown. Caldus's laughter is directed at the claim that goats give fifteen times more milk than sheep.

[60]Iarbas, who reappears in *Buc.* 8, is Crotus Rubianus (or, less likely, Eobanus's fellow student Johann Christiani of Frankenberg). See fn. 66 at *Buc.* 8.

[61]Amalthea's goat (or, in another version, the goat Amalthea) suckled the young Jupiter on Mount Ida in Crete. After one of the goat's horns was accidentally broken off, it was placed among the stars, along with the goat herself (Capella). See Ov. *Fast.* 5, 111-128. The epithet "Olenian" comes from an identification, common in the Roman poets, of the star Capella with Aege, the daughter of Olenos.

E2^r

E2^v

Cautus. A single goat, driven home from the pasture, produces more milk per day than fifteen ewes, and all the nannies are milked twice a day.

Caldus. Ha, ha! You're no good at lying, are you, most cautious Cautus![59] The more you raise a laugh, the more you'll get laughed at. But go on, please. The gracious Muses laughed too.

Cautus. A goat rose up to the heavens. With her single horn, Amalthea's star is a sight to behold. According to the learned Iarbas,[60] [100] the god Jupiter sucked the teats of that Olenian goat.[61]

Caldus. Phrixus's ram also shines among the bright stars.[62] Its yellow fleece is set off with ruddy gold. I learned that as a boy; indeed, I just barely remember.

Cautus. The words that popped up just now amidst the jokes don't sound a bit rustic or everyday. Few if any townsmen or academics are familiar with allusions like that.

Caldus. Well then, rustic lads that we are, we'll just play on the syrinx – the naiad whom kindly Venus covered with marsh reeds[63] – so the whole forest can also hear about my flame. [110] Look, she's coming, Canace is coming our way! See how her snow-white dress is billowing out in the gentle breeze and her flaxen hair is streaming down her milky back. With a switch in her hand, she's culling the mottled lambs and driving them back home, now that they've drunk their fill in the river.

Hail, my dearest beauty! Hail, enthralling nymph, comeliest of all maidens! I have long been eager for a chance to talk with you. Alas, how my raging love for you is wearing me out with grief! Without you, I can find no rest. My whole life [120] is filled with cares. I spend entire days yearning for you. Lengthy dreams disturb the nights when I should be resting. Come here, lovely Canace, and see how I

---

[62] Phrixus and his sister Helle escaped from Colchis on a ram with a golden fleece. This ram later became the constellation Aries.

[63] The naiad Syrinx rejected Pan's love and was changed into reed by her sisters (not by Venus, as Eobanus has it, except indirectly, as a result of Pan's passion). The god then used the reed to fashion a syrinx (panpipe). See Ov. *Met.* 1, 689-712. Despite his show of shifting from the "urbane" to the rustic, Caldus continues to play urbane tricks with words. To him, "syrinx" is an oaten flute *and* the naiad herself. For this kind of mythological metonymy see Eob. *Buc.* 9, 60, where "Cynirae puellam" means the maiden Myrrha and hence myrrh; *Idyl.* 1, 37, where "Daphne" means laurel; and *Idyl.* 17, 143, where "Lycios agrestes" (Lycian peasants) are frogs.

Aspice! Tum requies nobis erit una sub umbra
Faginea, ad fontem latices ubi dulcia vivi
125 Murmura per frondes faciunt tremulumque susurrant.
Hic tibi castaneae sumentur et allia mecum
Et pyra quae fortes vicinis montibus Hessi
Mittunt. Illa tuo servamus prandia ventri.
Huc ades, o Canace! Miseri cape munus amantis:
130 Hunc leporem turdosque duos castamque palumbem,
Munera quae lustris tibi sum venatus in altis.

    Uror ut in stipulas ignis proiectus agrestes
Sole sub autumni. Sic me dolor ille fatigat
Qui mea nescio qua transegit corda sagitta.
135 O si respiciat Canace mea vulnera sero,
Ut quondam cum prima malum Venus egit in artus,
Dulcisona laetos modularer harundine versus
Inter oves, cantu sylvae et nemus omne sonarent.

    Heu, crudelis Amor, quantum mortalia mutas
140 Pectora! Nulla tibi par est sub sole potestas.
Sic me, sic posito vitae melioris honore
Cogis et ante diem facis hanc languere iuventam,
Florida ceu subitis flaccescunt arva pruinis.

    Hoc tamen omne tibi patimur sine nomine vulnus,
145 O Canace, maiora pati tormenta parati
Te propter. Tu sola mei medicina furoris.
E3ʳ   Huc olim properans fido dabis oscula amanti,
Qualia Luna suo quondam dedit Endimioni,
Qualibus Oenone Pariden complexa lacertis
150 Servantem pecudes Phrygiae sub vallibus Idae.
Huc olim properans tu nos complexa iuvabis.
Flate, leves Zephyri, spira, venerande Favoni.
Ferte meam Canacen, ad nos huc ferte puellam.

    Lingua stupet, rubor in vultum concaessit anhelus,
155 Membra tremunt, saliunt praecordia, namque propinquat
Quae mea corda sui clausit sub pectoris antro.
Quo fugiam? Quo non abeam? Potiusne manebo
An fugiam? Quid, Caute, loquar? Pudor obstat amori.

suffer! Then we two can rest together in the shade of a beech tree, next to the spring where rippling water murmurs sweetly through the leaves and burbles in tremulous whispers. Here you'll enjoy chestnuts and garlic with me, also the pears that the hardy Hessians send us from the nearby mountains. I've saved up this meal for your belly. Come here, Canace! Accept this gift from your hapless lover: [130] a hare, a brace of thrushes, and a chaste ringdove, presents I hunted for you deep in the forests.

I am all ablaze like stubble in the fields, set on fire under the autumn sun. For that is how this anguish of mine has been consuming me since it transfixed my heart with some unseen arrow. Oh, if Canace could look upon my wounds someday, then, like that time long ago when Venus first afflicted me with this ailment, I would again play joyful tunes on the sweet-sounding flute, amidst the sheep, and all the woods and groves would resound with my singing.

Woe, cruel Love, how profoundly you transform the human [140] heart! Nothing under the sun can match you in power. You have robbed me of the best season of life – this is how you overwhelm me and cause my youth to languish before its time, just as flowering fields wither during a cold snap.

Nevertheless I'm going to go on suffering this unspeakable wound, all for you, O Canace, and am prepared to suffer even greater torments for your sake. You're the only one who can cure my passion. Someday you'll rush up to me, your faithful lover, and shower me with kisses just like the ones that Luna once gave to her sweetheart Endymion, just like those that Oenone gave when she clasped Paris in her arms [150] while he was still herding sheep in the valleys of Phrygian Ida. Someday you'll hasten to me and enchant me in your embrace. Blow, gentle zephyrs, breathe, venerable west wind. Waft Canace hither, waft my darling to me.

My tongue stammers, blood is flushing to my cheeks, my limbs are trembling, my chest is pounding, for she's approaching – the one who keeps my heart enclosed within her breast. Where should I run to? Where should I turn to? Would it be better to stay, or should I make a run for it? What should I tell her, Cautus? Bashfulness is a great hindrance to love.

Caut. Ergo Caldus eras, calido dum servis Amori,
160 Vix tu de gregibus mecum cantare volebas.
Mirabar quid namque modos et nostra perosus
Carmina deserta solus sub rupe iaceres,
Moestior et solito barbam squalentior usu.
Scilicet, "ergo rudes pueri syringa canemus."
165 Non ita! Nos alio iuvenes ardore fruemur,
Quem meus hec olim cecinit per rura Phylaegon,
Exosus Veneremque deam natumque potentem.
Stulte, quid instabilis tabes in imagine formae?
Ut rosa mane rubens quae vespere tacta recumbit,
170 Quam cito bulla perit, tam flos cadit ille iuventae.
Desipit omnis amans moriturque in corpore vivo.
Caprarum docuit pastor, sic ille monebat.
Cald. Ut nequit extingui Neraeis fluctibus Aethna,
Sic gravis ille ardor qui me mihi sustulit omnes
175 Contemnit monitus. Nescit Venus impia flecti.
Heu, quibus immergor curis, quibus ignibus uror!
Caut. Interea Oceano pluvias sol attrahit undas.
Et Libs et Boreas luctantur et humidus Auster.
Tempestas oritur! Pastu discedere tempus.

AEGLOGA OCTAVA

Iarbas, Poliphemus, Heliades

Iarb. Surgit ab Oceano Titan venerabile sydus.
Mane fit, et pulsa reserantur pascua nocte.
Colludunt teretes per frigida gramina guttae.
Omne pecus passim patulis immittitur arvis,
5 Et matutinae cantant ad mulctra puellae.

---

177 pluvias *BO*: pluvius *A*.
  Buc. 8. *Cf. Idyllion 12 in BO.*   1 Surgit *BO*: Urgit *A*.

[64]Ardent love of God and the saints.
[65]In *Buc.* 3. Cf. line 47 above, with fn. 58.
[66]This eclogue describes Eobanus's short-lived hopes of being crowned poet laureate in the summer of 1508, not long after his friend Hermann Trebelius was laureated by Frederick the Wise of Saxony. Internal evidence shows that the poem itself was written some seven or eight months later, in February or March of 1509.
  The argument prefixed to the poem in the 1539-edition confirms that Heliades ("Offspring of Helios [Apollo]") is the humanist poet Hermann Trebelius. For his life see fn. 40 at

E3ᵛ

Cautus. Obviously your name fits you to a tee, Caldus,
scalded as you are in the service of Love! So that's [160] why
you could barely bring yourself to sing with me about the
herds! I was wondering why you kept avoiding our music-
making and singing, preferring instead to lie down by your-
self beneath a lonely cliff. A sad sight you've been too, with
your beard even more unkempt than normal. Sure, "rustic
lads that we are, we'll just play on the syrinx." No, we won't!
We young men will enjoy a different kind of ardor,[64] the
kind that my dear Philaegon used to sing about all over this
country.[65] He detested the goddess Venus and her powerful
son. Fool, why do you pine for a pretty face? Beauty doesn't
last. As a rose blows red in the morning and wilts at the touch
of evening, [170] as quickly as a bubble bursts, so falls the
bloom of youth. Every lover is demented and dies a living
death. That was the goatherd's message, that was his counsel.

Caldus. Just as you can't extinguish Etna with the
ocean's water, so the raging fire that is driving me mad defies
all warnings. Pitiless Venus doesn't know how to relent. Ah,
how I'm overwhelmed with cares, how I'm ablaze with the
fires of love!

Cautus. In the meantime the sun has been building up
rain clouds over the ocean. The southwester and the north
are fighting it out with the humid south wind. A storm is
brewing! It's time to start leaving the pasture.

THE EIGHTH ECLOGUE[66]

Iarbas, Polyphemus, Heliades

Iarbas. The venerable star Titan is rising from the ocean.
Day is breaking; and with darkness in full flight, the pas-
tures stand revealed. Beads of dew sport with each other in
the cold grass. Everywhere all the herds are being let out
into the open fields. The maids are up too, singing by their

Buc. 4, 106. Polyphemus ("Prolific singer"), the shepherd who fails to receive the laurel crown,
is Eobanus Hessus himself. The argument goes on to identify Iarbas as Crotus Rubianus
(cf. fn. 26 at *Buc.* 3; and fn. 71 at Camerarius, *Nar.* 17, 17). The glossator of the Strasbourg
copy, however, suggests that Iarbas is Eobanus's countryman and fellow student Johann Chris-
tiani of Frankenberg (see *Laud.* B 6, with fn. 93).

Solus adhuc dulci stertis, Polipheme, sub antro
Ut somnolenti glires vitulique marini.
Non tibi mille avium voces potuere soporem
Tam longum excutere aut durum vox agricolarum.

10   Sed vigila! Iam sol extat plus quattuor ulnis
Altus ab Oceano et terras supereminet omnes,
Et vacuae clausis balant in ovilibus agnae.

       Poli. Improbe, quam dulci somno me excludis, Iarba!
Non hoc me levius memini dormire semestri.

15   Sed tamen, heu, miserae pecudes, iam montibus altis,

E4ʳ   Ut video, sparsum iubar omnem illuminat orbem.
Nulla tamen nostrum lucis pars venit ad antrum.
Tam clauso post hac nolim requiescere lecto.

       Iarb. Ut primum radiis Phoebus patefoecerit orbem,

20   Evigilo et plumis caput extraho dulcibus. Ergo
Lanigeris campos ovibus, dumeta capellis
Orto sole damus. Gaudent in rore iuvenci.

       Poli. Plenius haec alio repetemus tempore, quando
Nunc animum potiora movent, res digna relatu,

25   Quae mihi praeteritam turbarunt somnia noctem.
Dii superi, quam certa fides! Oracula credas.
Sic viva praesens elusit imagine Morpheus.

       Iarb. Dic igitur, dic formiferam, Polipheme, quietem,
Quas facies, quae mira novis simulachra figuris

30   Videris. Interea pecus haec viridaria circum
Pascetur, decimam dum sol ascendit in horam,
Et nos hanc subter corylum recubabimus, unde
Possimus velut e tumulo pecus omne videre.
Pascite gramen, oves, frondes nudate, capellae,

35   Donec monstriferae referantur somnia noctis.

       Poli. Tempus erat, sacros nox caeca reduxerat ignes,
Quo gravidos iam prima quies obnubilat artus,
Cum sylvae pecudesque tacent volucresque canorae
Totaque Tartareo circumdata numine tellus

40   In requiem conversa silet. Me somnus habebat

E4ᵛ   Altior et clauso requievi dulciter antro.
Propter aquas super herbosis errare videbar
Aggeribus frondesque manu resecare capellis
Laetus et arguta modulari dultia canna

---

32 hanc *BO*: hunc *A*.

milk pails. You're the only one still snoring, Polyphemus, deep in your agreeable grotto, as sleepy as the dormice and sea calves. Neither the countless birdsongs nor the shouts of the hardy peasants have been able to rouse you out of that long sleep of yours. [10] But wake up! The sun is already four ells above the ocean and stands high above the earth, and the hungry lambs are bleating in the closed sheepfolds.

Polyphemus. You cad, Iarbas! What a delightful sleep you've just ruined! I can't remember sleeping this well in the past half-year. All the same, I feel bad for the poor sheep. Already the sun's beams are striking the mountaintops, as I see, and illuminating the whole world. Yet not one bit of this light reached down to my grotto. I don't ever want to rest in a cocoon like that again.

Iarbas. As soon as the sun's rays unveil the world, [20] I wake up and stick my head out of the comfortable blanket. That way I can be sure the woolly sheep are out in the fields and the goats in the thickets by sunrise. The bullocks love the dewy grass.

Polyphemus. We'll have to discuss that at length some other time. Right now my mind is preoccupied with more important things, something worth recounting – namely the dream that troubled my sleep last night. Ye gods, how real it all seemed! You'd think it was an oracle. Only Morpheus himself could have put on so vivid a show.

Iarbas. Go ahead, then, and tell me about the phantasmagoric dream you had, Polyphemus. What surreal forms and shapes, what marvelous images [30] did you see? Meantime the flock will crop the meadow around us, until the sun rises to the tenth hour, and we'll take our ease under this hazel tree. From here, as from a hilltop, we can keep an eye on the whole flock. Crop the grass, sheep; strip the leafy boughs, goats, while the dreams of wonderworking night are being recounted.

Polyphemus. It was the time when blind night has brought back the sacred stars, when sleep first beclouds the heavy limbs, when woods and flocks and songbirds are stilled and the whole earth, enshrouded in Tartarean darkness, [40] has gone to rest and is silent. I was fast asleep, resting comfortably in the enfolding grotto. It seemed to me that I was walking along the water's edge on a grassy riverbank, happily lopping foliage for my goats and playing sweet tunes on the melodious panpipe, while fiery Leo

45   Carmina, dum calidi coelo fremit ira Leonis,
       Cum mihi, nescio quo succenso pectus amore
       Musarum Phoeboque sacrae Permessidos undae,
       Culmine ab aereo summoque a vertice Musae
       Desuper ostentant lauri de fronde coronam
50   Conspicuam ductrixque chori regina verendi
       Tale procul summa cecinit mihi carmen ab arce:
          "Qui nunc graminea pecudes in valle coerces,
       Digne ovium custos, hiis digne virentibus arvis
       Quae secat allabens Gerhae vicinior Unster,
55   Huc propera, servata tuae fer praemia fronti,
       Praemia perpetuis tecum victura diebus.
       Huc propera, lauru vates ornande vetusta,
       Cinge comas hedera, viridi tege tempora bacca.
       En ultro porrecta tibi, Polipheme, corona est."
60   "Accipe," cum dixisset, ego in sublime ferebar
       Vi rapida solitoque magis velotior, ac si
       Umbra levis vel pluma forem, pernitior Euro.
       Iamque adeo prope limen eram venerabilis antri
       Unde prius nostras carmen descendit ad aures,
65   Cum mihi forte venit cursu Paniscus anhelo
       Obvius et multis circumvenientibus ipsum
       Qui comitabantur. Passis mea colla lacertis
       Complexus, "Quo," dixit, "abis? Iuvenilibus ergo
       Fraena cupidinibus non ponis, et illa sequutus
70   Mollia Musarum ludibria, quaeris honorem
       Qui tibi proripiat sero maiora petenti
       Praemia? Namque leves pueri florentibus annis
       Quando Musarum coepere insignia forsan,
       Despiciunt quicumque canunt sine fronde poaetas –
75   Tanquam donatae faciant bona carmina lauri! –
       Et pecus et sylvas et oves et ovilia damnant.
       Laudantur, mirantur, et omnia scire putantur,
       Cum pulchro faciles vernant in flore capilli.
       In sublime tument et coelum vertice pulsant.
80   Non inter pueros, non amplius inter agrestes

E5ʳ

---

[67] Since the sun enters the sign of Leo on about July 23, it is now mid-summer.
[68] The source of the river Permessus on Mount Helicon.
[69] Calliope, as at *Laud.* 246 and *Ama.* B 2, 1.

roared with anger in the sky.[67] Suddenly, I felt my heart
burn with a hard-to-describe passion for the Muses and Per-
messis's fountain,[68] sacred to Phoebus. From a peak high up
in the air, from the very summit, the Muses showed me a re-
markable crown of laurel sprigs. [50] The leader and queen
of that august choir[69] then sang me the following song from
her distant perch on the mountaintop:

"You who now tend the flock in this grassy valley, wor-
thy herder of sheep, worthy of these verdant meadows that
the gently flowing Unstrut and the nearby Gera traverse,
hasten hither, accept the guerdon reserved for your brow, a
guerdon that will live with you until the end of time. Hasten
hither, bard, for you deserve to be adorned with the ancient
laurel. Wreathe your locks with ivy; garland your brow with
green bays. Look, Polyphemus, we are offering you this
crown of our own accord. [60] Take it."

After she had said this, I was carried aloft with violent
force, far more swiftly than I'm used to, as if I were a light
shadow or feather, much faster than the east wind. And al-
ready I was getting quite close to the threshold of the
venerable grotto from where the song had earlier come
down to my ears, when Paniscus[70] happened to cross my
path in breathless haste. He was surrounded by a great many
companions. Throwing his arms round my neck, he
exclaimed:

"Where do you think you're going? Can't you keep that
juvenile ambition of yours in check? Don't you realize, then,
that in going after those [70] easy playthings of the Muses
you are in fact seeking an honor that will rob you of the
chance to pursue more significant prizes later on? For when
light-minded lads happen to win the Muses' insignia while
they're still in the flower of youth, they look down on all po-
ets who sing without bays – as if poems only bear the cachet
of excellence after one is awarded the laurel! Soon they re-
nounce the cattle and the woods, the sheep and the
sheepfolds. They are praised, admired, and looked up to as
all-knowing, though their sleek hair is still decked with
lovely spring blossoms. And so, swelling with pride, they
touch the sky with their heads. [80] They don't spend time
among the farm hands or peasants any more. No, they run

---

[70] Paniscus is Ludwig Christiani of Frankenberg – the same man who in *Buc.* 1 extolled
the rich pastures of Erfurt and persuaded Camillus-Eobanus to move there.

Versantur. Quaerunt urbes, primatibus herent,
Praeclaros titulos faciunt; seque omnibus ipsi
Cum iam praetulerint, pudor est descendere et inter
Pastores versari et famam ambire minorem.
85   Praeterea multos invisa coegit egestas
Pascere oves iterum dominisque subesse superbis,
Ferre iugum grave, servitio sibi quaerere victum.
Ergo age, siste gradum. Iuvenili obstare furori
Est opus et melius vitam trutinare futuram.
90   Nos te purpureo donabimus ante galero
Qui pueris datur emeritis iam munere primo,
Quorum aetas bis undenos compleverit annos.
Sub dominis pastoribus hic tum prima probatae
Vitae signa refert et libertatis honorem.
95   Hunc super impositae lauri meliore virescent
Germine."
           Tantum effatus erat, cum tu mihi somnum,
Horrendum clamans, orto iam sole fugabas.
Haec sunt per longam quae vidi somnia noctem.
    Iarb. Mira refers et quae videantur claudere quaedam
100   Quae non vulgaris tractet mysteria pastor.
Ecce sed Aonia redimitus tempora lauro
Advenit Heliades. Tibi quid, Polipheme, videtur?
Nunquid Apollineis hic est numerandus in hortis?
    Heli. Salvete aeternum, socii, festivaque mecum
105   Carmina laetitiamque novam celebrate faventes.
Nunc calamos inflate leves, dum vestra poaetam
Rura novum meruere. Sonent rura omnia cantu.
    Poli. Quis te, digne puer, tanto dignatus honore
Extulit et sacra cinxit tibi fronde capillos?
110   Dic age dic. Aliquis superumne an pastor agrestis?
    Heli. Dum lustra amissum quaero per inhospita thaurum,
Monte sub obscuro ramis ubi plurima sacras
Arbor obumbrat aquas, raptum super ardua montis
Divae Pierides vatem foecere, quod olim

E5^v appears in the left margin at line 91.

103 Apollineis *scripsi*: Appollineis *A*.

[71]After receiving his "first distinction" (the B.A.) in October 1506, Eobanus earned the M.A. in February 1509. The cap granted to Masters of Arts at their graduation symbolized academic freedom and the attainment of a life of virtue. Cf. Erasmus, *Adag.* 2, 1, 27, *LB* 2, col. 416 E-F; Eob. *Her. Chr.*, ded. 19, 1.

off to the cities, attach themselves to some nobleman, acquire grandiose titles. And when they manage to exalt themselves above all others, they find it shameful and demeaning to live among the shepherds and strive for a humbler fame. Moreover many of them end up in such abject poverty that they are forced to go back and pasture the sheep and serve haughty masters, to bear a heavy yoke and make a living for themselves in bondage. Now then, go no further. You must resist this youthful madness of yours and aim for a more balanced life in the future. [90] For the time being I am going to bestow on you the purple cap that is granted to lads who have already earned their first distinction[71] and are twenty-two years of age.[72] Among the chief shepherds it counts for a premier badge of honor, signifying a life of virtue and liberty. If it is overtopped with laurels later, the bays will turn a nobler green."

That is as far as he got when you roused me out of my sleep with your fearsome shouts, well after sunrise. And those are the visions I saw in the long night that has passed.

Iarbas. You tell an amazing story! I would imagine it contains some hidden meanings [100] that your average shepherd doesn't discuss. But look, there's Heliades, his brow crowned with the poet's bays. What do you think, Polyphemus? Does this fellow belong in the Apollonian pleasance?[73]

Heliades. Hail for ever, comrades! Sing paeans of joy to help me celebrate the happy news. Now blow on the light reeds until your fields are worthy of the new poet. Let the whole countryside ring with song.

Polyphemus. Who, my worthy lad, deemed you worthy of so great an honor? Who exalted you like this and placed a crown of sacred leaves on your hair? [110] Do tell me, please. Was it one of the gods or a shepherd you met in the fields?

Heliades. While looking for a lost bullock in the inhospitable thickets, at the foot of a dark mountain where many a tree shades the sacred spring with its branches, I was carried aloft to the heights of the mountain. There the divine Muses made me a bard. The same thing happened long ago

---

[72] Eobanus in fact turned 21 on 6 January 1509; but at the time he believed he was already 22. See fn. 13 at Camerarius, *Nar.* 5, 15; also see Eob. *Buc.* 9, 9-10, referring to Eobanus in the summer of 1509 as a 22-year-old.

[73] That is, among the poets inspired by Apollo.

115   Contigit Ascraeo servanti armenta sub antro.

      Vidi presentes afflatus numine Musas

        Iarb. Praesentem vidisse puto te daemona, namque
      Quid sunt Pierides nisi delyramina Musae?

        Poli. Vana deas olim commenta est fabula Musas,

120   Quas tamen in versus alio traducimus usu,
      Quando unum triplici colimus sub numine numen.

        Heli. Sed tu, purpureo frontem signate galero,
      Nunquid ad hanc etiam aspiras, Polipheme, coronam?

        Poli. Nescio, sed tamen hiis alias de rebus agemus.

125   Non culter facit esse coquum, monachumve cucullus,
      Nec laurus vatem. Sua quemque professio monstrat.

        Iarb. Sit satis hoc. Vestrum me iudice praestat uterque.
      Sed tamen esse bonum res est divina poetam
      Atque adeo nostris non enarrabile pagis.

130   Ite, valete. Suas iam pascite quisque capellas.

AEGLOGA NONA

Iucundus, Silvius

Iucu. Nunquid adhuc, Sylvi, flavae te cura puellae
Detinet? An dulces liquisti fortiter ignes?
Quos tamen ante duas potuisti linquere messes –

Buc. **9** *Cf. Idyllion 6 in BO.*   **1** Nunquid *BO*: Unquid *A*.

[74]Hesiod was tending his flock near Ascra in Boeotia, at the foot of Mount Helicon, when the Muses made him a poet. See Hes. *Th.* 22-34; cf. Ov. *Ars* 1, 27-28; *Fast.* 6, 13-14.

[75]The argument to this eclogue in the 1539-edition explains that the deceased shepherd Iolas is William II (1468-1509), landgrave of Lower Hesse since 1493 and of Upper Hesse since 1500. An energetic ruler, who strove to consolidate and expand his territories, keep the roads safe from brigands, and reform the monasteries, William contracted syphilis in 1506 and spent his final years battling the ravages of the disease. Eobanus declines to identify the other two shepherds. Sylvius ("Woodsman") is easily recognized as Eobanus himself, partly because of the allusion to his sweetheart Flavia, partly because of the age reference in lines 9-10, which repeats the reference in *Buc.* 8, 92. This identification is confirmed by a contemporary gloss in the Strasbourg copy. As for Iucundus ("Delightful"), the glossator of the Strasbourg copy

to a herdsman tending the cattle beneath the grotto at As-
cra.[74] Inspired by their divine power, I saw the Muses in
person.

Iarbas. You saw the devil in person, I think. For what
else are the Pierian Muses but mere illusions?

Polyphemus. The myth about the Muses' being god-
desses was dreamed up a long time ago. [120] We
nonetheless introduce them into our verse, albeit to a dif-
ferent end, seeing that we serve the one God in three divine
Persons.

Heliades. But you, Polyphemus, now that you've re-
ceived the distinction of the purple cap, don't you aspire to
be crowned with the laurel too?

Polyphemus. I don't know. But we'll deal with that ques-
tion some other time. The knife doesn't make the cook, nor
the cowl the monk, nor the laurel the bard. What matters is
how well you master your calling.

Iarbas. Let that suffice. In my judgment each of you has
proven his worth. All the same, to be a good poet is some-
thing divine, far beyond the power of us countryfolk to
describe. [130] Be on your way, good-bye. Let each of us
now feed his own goats.

THE NINTH ECLOGUE[75]

Iucundus, Sylvius

Iucundus. Are you still infatuated with that blonde lass,[76]
Sylvius? Or have you been man enough to renounce the
sweet fires of love? But those you could have renounced two
harvests ago – if France could give up her Rhône and Ger-

---

suggests that he is Crotus Rubianus. For his life see fn. 71 at Camerarius, *Nar.* 17, 17; cf. the
introductory note to *Buc.* 3 (p. 467 below).

The eclogue must have been written within a few weeks of William's death on 11 July
1509. As Eobanus notes in the 1539-edition, the chief model is Verg. *Ecl.* 5, traditionally
interpreted as a eulogy for Julius Caesar in the guise of the shepherd Daphnis. Like Vergil's
fifth eclogue, in which the lament for Daphnis is followed by his apotheosis, the present
eclogue is essentially two-partite. The first part (lines 20-63) is a lament for Iolas; the second
(lines 69-118) praises his wife Galatea (Anna von Mecklenburg) and their two children
Elisabeth and Philip.

[76]Eobanus's sweetheart in Erfurt was a girl whom he called Flavia ("Blonde"). See fn. 43
at *Ama.* B 2.

Gallia si Rhodanum potuit, Germania Rhenum!
5 Aut qua nam langues compressus mole laborum
Quidve doles? Tuus hic moeror lugubria signat.
Sylv. O Iucunde, nihil turpes in fortia flammae
Pectora iuris habent. Iamdudum abscessimus istis

E6ᵛ

Delyramentis puerilibus. Et mea tandem
10 Aetas undecimum postquam bis venit ad annum,
Displicet omnis amor mulierum et inutilis error.
Est alius qui corda dolor premit altaque curis
Pectora corrodit mordacibus. Heu, ubi cantus
Festivique iacent calami? Nunc omnia moerent,
15 Laeta prius. Nunc omnis ager sylvaeque patentes
Tristantur, fracto montes plangore resultant.
Iucu. Qui fletus! Quae sunt fata haec tam tristia, Sylvi?
Dic, precor, interea calidus dum caessat arator
Et pecus illustri dum ruminat omne sub umbra.
20 *Sylv.* Flete, meae Musae, tristes lugete Camaenae.
Nobilis ante diem fato concessit Iolas.
Dicite fatales, crudelia numina, Parcae,
Ausurae violare deos, quid tale coegit
Perpetrare nephas? Iuvenis cum funus adempti
25 Lanificae videre procul sub rupe sorores,
Fleverunt viresque suas odere, paratae
Fila humili reparare manu, ni fata negarent
Ulla relabentes animas in corpora reddi.
Somnus ut extinctum rapuit Laethaeus Iolam,
30 Ferrea nox omneis visa est descendere in agros.
Et lupus et miles praedator ovilia lustrans
Debacchatur, agens effuso sanguine praedam.
Non passim velut ante boves per tuta vagantur

F1ʳ

Pascua. Clauduntur stabuli, custode tuentur
35 Limina. Certantes lacerant magalia venti.
Cernis ut obscuro turbatus flumine Fulda
Labitur, increpitans saxa indignantia motu.
Hunc iuxta, quando licuit, consuevit Iolas
Pascere oves. Illi quoque cum pastoribus ipsis

---

[77] For the age reference cf. *Buc.* 8, 92, with fn. 72.

[78] A year before William died, his ambitious second wife Anna von Mecklenburg pressured him into revoking his announced plan of entrusting the regency of Hesse to a council of noblemen and, contrary to custom, had him appoint her as regent. Immediately after the landgrave's death the nobles banded together to resist her claims. The power struggle fostered

many her Rhine! You really aren't yourself at all. Are you weighed down with some other trouble? What is distressing you? Your doleful looks are expressive of sorrow.

Sylvius. O Iucundus, the shameful fires of love can have no claim on a manly heart. I have long since abandoned those puerile delusions. Ever since I [10] turned twenty-two,[77] I find all desire for women disgusting, a baneful frenzy. No, there is another grief that burdens my soul and gnaws at the depths of my heart with biting cares. Alas, where have all the songs and lively melodies gone? Everything that was happy before is now in full mourning. Now all the fields and spacious woods are filled with sadness, and the hills echo the sounds of broken laments.

Iucundus. What a flood of tears! What tragedy has brought about all this sorrow, Sylvius? Tell me, I beg you, while the sweltering plowman is taking his ease and while the entire herd is chewing the cud in the dense shade.

Sylvius. [20] Weep, my Muses, weep, unhappy Camenae! The celebrated Iolas has succumbed to fate before his time. Tell me, cruel goddesses of fate, you Parcae who would venture to assail the gods, what made you perpetrate so heinous a crime? When those wool-spinning Sisters, watching at some distance beneath a cliff, espied the funeral procession of the youth they had killed, they shed bitter tears and cursed their own power. They were even prepared to mend the thread of his life with humble hand, had Fate not prohibited souls from ever slipping back and rejoining the body.

As soon as Lethean sleep carried off the dead Iolas, [30] iron night seemed to descend on all the fields. Wolves and marauding soldiers scour the sheepfolds. Running amuck, they spill blood and drive away booty. No longer do the cattle roam at large on safe pastures. The stables are barred; guards stand watch by the doors.[78] Brawling winds batter the shepherds' huts. Look how the Fulda seethes in turbid torrents and crashes headlong into the indignant rocks.[79] It was by this river that Iolas, while he still could, was accustomed to pasture his sheep. Subject to him, along with its

---

lawlessness and brought back the robber barons whom William had kept in check during much of his reign.

[79]The shepherds are imagined as speaking beside the Fulda River, not far from Kassel where the landgraves of Hesse resided since the thirteenth century.

40 Paruit omne nemus quod vitreus Aedera passim
    Fulda, Lanus, Rhenusque vident Moenusque biformis.
    Illum omnis novit mundus, nam sepe superbos
    Vicerat agresti iuvenes certamine. Ab illo
    Languet Rhenani castrata potentia Nisi.
45 Illum omnes timuere ferae furesque dolosi.
    Illius ad vocem Poeni stupuere leones,
    E sylvis fugere lupi. Non tempore nostro
    Alter erat pastor sublimi maior Iola.
        Nunc iacet heu tantum decus. Et iam fortior aetas
50 Te tulit, infoelix puer. Ergone pessima fata
    Invidere tibi? Iam fortibus utilis annis
    Longius et multas potuisti vivere messes.
    Fleverunt te sylvarumque deae collesque fragosi,
    Et cava flumineo sonuerunt littora planctu.
55 Tam dilectus eras, flevit te quicquid ubique est.
        Nunc te defunctum tumulo damus, hic ubi tardis
    Flexibus apricos pulcher Lanus alluit agros.
    Spargite odoratos, tumulo date, spargite flores.
    Narcissos, violas, et purpureos hyacinthos,
60 Balsama Coriciumque crocum Cyniraeque puellam
    Spargite et in viridi iuxta sic scribite fago:
    "Gloria sylvarum situs est hic pastor Iolas
    Quo non alter erat foelicior omnibus arvis."
        Iucu. Iam neque amore doles pressus nec mole laborum.
65 Non aliud quodcumque gemis, sed recta doloris
    Causa tui, tali magnus deflendus Iolas
    Namque fuit calamo. Non sic extinctus Iolas
    Extinctus mihi, sed potius superesse videtur.
        Sylv. Cum fleret niveis coniunx complexa lacertis
70 Corpus inane viri, coniunx pulcherrima dixit:
    "Urite subiectam flammis! Comitabor Iolam
    Mortua ad Elysium. Iacet, heu iacet ille pudoris

F1ᵛ

---

45 ferae *BO*: fere *A*.   60 Cyniraeque *scripsi*: Cynaraeque *A*.

[80]The Main River is formed by the confluence of the White and Red Main.

[81]William's campaign against Count Palatine Philip II (1448-1508) during the War of the Landshut Succession in 1504 netted him prestige and some territorial gains. Eobanus alludes to these exploits also in *Buc.* B 2, 28-30; *Hod.* 199-201; *Wirt.* 39-42.

[82]William was buried in the St. Elisabeth's Church in Marburg.

[83]Cinyras's daughter Myrrha was transformed into a myrrh tree. Here she stands for myrrh itself. For this kind of metonymy cf. *Buc.* 7, 107-108, with fn. 63.

shepherds, [40] was also the whole forest that the glittering
Eder, the Fulda, Lahn, Rhine, and the two-formed Main[80]
see stretching out along their shores. The entire world knew
him, for he had often defeated arrogant youths in rustic
conflict. It was he who laid low the once-potent might of
the Rhenish Nisus.[81] All the wild beasts and crafty thieves
feared him. At his voice, Punic lions stopped dead in their
tracks, wolves fled from the woods. In our day and age no
shepherd could match the lofty Iolas.

Now that magnificent treasure, alas, has passed away.
You had already reached manhood, [50] unhappy lad, when
you were taken from us. Did fate, then, in its unfathomable
wickedness begrudge you to us? Already a vigorous man, ca-
pable of doing your part, you could easily have lived longer
– many more harvests in fact. The goddesses of the woods
wept for you, as did the rugged hills, and the hollow banks
rang with the rivers' laments. You were so well loved that all
nature bewailed you.

Now that you have died, we are burying you here where
the lovely Lahn meanders in lazy loops through the sun-
kissed hills.[82] Strew fragrant flowers on the ground, place
them on the grave. Strew narcissuses, violets, and purple hy-
acinths, [60] balsam and Corycian saffron and Cinyras's
daughter.[83] Scatter them on the grave, and on a verdant
beech tree next to it carve the following words:

Here lies the glory of our woods, the shepherd Iolas.
In the whole country none was more blessed than he.

Iucundus. No longer is it the pangs of love or the burden
of cares that is breaking your heart. You're not lamenting
some trivial matter anymore. The cause of your heartbreak
is just, for the great Iolas deserved to be mourned in tones
such as these. Eulogized like this, the deceased Iolas no
longer seems deceased to me, but rather to be still alive.

Sylvius. When his wife[84] wept for him and threw her
snowy arms round [70] her husband's lifeless body, that fair-
est of consorts exclaimed: "Cast me onto the pyre too,
cremate me! Let me die, so I can accompany Iolas to Ely-

---

[84]Anna von Mecklenburg (1485-1525). William married her on 20 October 1500, five
months after the death of his first wife Jolanta.

Egregius nostri violator, amatus Iolas."
Sic ait et nivea proiecit fronte coronam,
75   Illa puellarum pulcherrima ruricolarum,
Quam, Galathea, parens septem compressa trioni
Oceano peperit. Formosior omnibus illa est.
     Iucu. Dignus erat qui nympharum frueretur Iolas
Connubio. Nunc ille brevi requiescit in urna.
80   Illa domo vidua perturbatos hymenaeos
Plorat et, heu, niveos lacerat formosa capillos,
Digna deum thalamis, defuncto digna marito.
     Sylv. Nobis ille tamen moriens duo pignora liquit,
Spem generis, puerumque marem teneramque puellam.
85   Aspice quam patrios referunt ad ovilia vultus,
Formosum ille patrem, formosam filia matrem.
     Iucu. Vivite et in patriam, pueri, coalescite sortem.
Tu nobis, tu vive, puer. Clarissime sanguis,
Ultime nate patris, tu magni tuta parentis
90   Pascua restitues. O misse patentibus astris,
Tecum nata salus nostris promittitur arvis.
Indolis egregiae et virtutis certa futurae
Signa in te, vultuque iubes sperare sereno
Optima quaeque, puer, nec enim sine numine quodam
95   Illa nitet facies, Phoebeae lampadis instar.
Claude oculos. Quis tam radios feret ignipotentes?
Sed neque claude. Aperi potius, da gaudia mundo.
Protinus effugient fures ab ovilibus omnes
Raptoresque lupique truces et frigidus anguis
100 Atque colorati squalentia colla dracones,
Scorpius et tetri serpens quaecunque veneni.
Si quis erit forsan nostra basiliscus harena,
Occidet, et parvus sed dente nocivior aspis.
Omnia securos praestabunt pabula foetus.
105 Spargite humum, nymphae, preciosis floribus, in qua
Foecerit ille puer niveae vestigia plantae.
Vos quoque, pastores genialia tecta periti
Thure vaporato circumlustrate quotannis

---

83 ille *BO*: illa *A*.   **105** preciosis *BO*: praeciosis *A*.

[85]The ancient Galatea was the daughter of the sea god Nereus. The modern Galatea is the daughter of the northern Ocean, because her birthplace Mecklenburg lies by the Baltic.

sium. Dead, ah, dead is that eminent ravisher of my maidenhood, the beloved Iolas." As she spoke these words, she took the crown from her snow-white brow and flung it to the ground – she, Galatea, most beautiful of country girls, daughter of the northern Ocean.[85] She is lovelier than all others.

Iucundus. Iolas was worthy of enjoying marriage with a nymph. Now he rests in a small urn. [80] She, in her widowed home, grieves for the broken bonds of her marriage and – oh, the pity of it! – tears her snowy hair. The lovely lady is worthy of wedlock with the gods, worthy of her late husband.

Sylvius. At his death, however, he left us two children, the hope of his house: a manly son as well as a tender daughter.[86] Look how they remind the sheepfolds of their parents' features! *He* takes after his handsome father, *she* after her beautiful mother.

Iucundus. Live and grow strong together, children, for the sake of your homeland. You, lad, live for us. Most illustrious offspring, last-born son of your father, you are the one who will make the pastures of your mighty father safe again. [90] O you, sent by the luminous stars, your presence gives our country the promise of deliverance! You have given us sure signs of an excellent disposition and future manliness, and with your radiant looks, boy, you bid us hope for the best in every way. Indeed, that face of yours has a kind of divine aura about it, for it shines as bright as Phoebus's torch. Close your eyes. Who can bear such fiery rays? But wait, don't close them. Keep them open instead and give the world joy. Forthwith all thieves and robbers will flee from the sheepfolds, savage wolves too and cold-blooded snakes [100] and spangled reptiles with scaly backs, scorpions and venomous serpents of every kind. Should a basilisk happen to be on our soil, he will die, and so will the small but sharp-fanged adder. Then the lambs will be safe on our pastures everywhere. Nymphs, strew precious flowers on the ground in which that boy will leave the imprints of his snow-white feet. You too, experienced shepherds, go to the house where he was born and purify it each year with

[86]The children are: Elisabeth (1502-1557), who married Duke John of Saxony in 1515 and became one of the most influential women rulers of the Reformation period; and Philip (1504-1567), the later landgrave. For Philip's life see fn. 124 at Camerarius, *Nar.* 26, 1.

F2ᵛ   Et carmen facite et laetantes dicite carmen:
        110   "Salve, semidei proles insignis Iolae,
                   Nympharum genus, a magno velut aethere missus,
                   Et nos et pecudes et rus defende paternum."
                       Sylv. Ergo beata illa est foelici pondere mater,
                   Quae subiecta videns inter dumeta capellas
        115   Altivagas errare ab summi culmine montis
                   Tam clarum viridi est enixa sub arbore foetum.
                       Iucu. Foelix ille etiam puer est qui talia suxit
                   Ubera quae magnis faciant suspiria divis.
                   Et nunc Oceano propior sol. Plura canemus
        120   Olim cum puerum matremque videbimus ipsam.

AEGLOGA DECIMA

Fastus, Mannus

Fast. Qui sylvas et rura colunt, qui culmina et agros
Pastores habitant, qui sunt a flumine Rheni
Ad Scythicum Tanaim, qui sunt vel ab Alpibus usque
Ad mare Balthiacum, qui vel didicere cicutis
5   Vel quodcumque levi diffundere carmen avena,
Multiforem buxum aut dulcem sufflare monaulon,
Pignoribus positis et si pro munere vitae

Buc. 10. *Cf. Idyllion 11 in BO.*   1 Qui *scripsi:* Ui *A.*

[87]In other words: Anna bore Philip in Marburg, while continuing to watch over her peo-
ple from her lofty castle.

[88]In this eclogue Eobanus lampoons the controversial Dalmatian poet Riccardo Sbruglio
(ca. 1480–after 1525). Born at Cividale di Friuli near Udine, Sbruglio lived in Venice and
Constance. After Emperor Maximilian recommended him to Frederick the Wise in early
1507, Sbruglio obtained a teaching position at Wittenberg in the spring. His panegyric verses
on the Elector (Leipzig, 1507) and his "extemporaneous poem" in praise of rector Christoph
Scheuerl (n. pl., 1507?) won him admirers, among them Georg Spalatin. But others, in-
cluding Mutianus Rufus, Hermann von dem Busche, and Ulrich von Hutten, thought little of
his talents. Forced to leave Wittenberg under a cloud of scandal, Sbruglio enrolled at Frank-
furt an der Oder in the spring of 1513 – at the very time Eobanus took up studies there
himself. In 1516 he was at the University of Cologne, in 1517 at Freiburg and Ingolstadt. By
1518 he was the emperor's poet and historiographer in Augsburg. When Maximilian died in
1519, Sbruglio continued to move from place to place, never able to secure lasting em-
ployment. Erasmus met him at Cologne in November 1520 and made him a speaker in the

fuming frankincense. Make up a birthday song for him and joyfully sing these verses: [110] "Hail, remarkable son of the demigod Iolas, offspring of nymphs! As one sent down, so to speak, from mighty heaven above, protect us and the sheep and the land of your father."

Sylvius. Blessed therefore is that mother who bore such a fortunate child. As she looked down from the hilltop and watched the high-climbing goats straying among the thickets below, she gave birth to her illustrious baby under a green shade tree.[87]

Iucundus. Happy too is that boy who sucked from such breasts as would elicit sighs from the great gods themselves. But the sun is now quite near to the ocean. We'll sing more [120] later, when we visit the boy and his mother.

THE TENTH ECLOGUE[88]

Fastus, Mannus

Fastus. You who live in the woods and the country, you shepherds who make your home in the hills and meadows that stretch from the waters of the Rhine to the Scythian Don or from the Alps all the way to the Baltic Sea, you who have learned to play some trivial tune on hemlock stalks or the light reed pipe or to blow on the many-holed boxwood flute or the sweet-sounding recorder, you who name your stakes and compete in singing-matches as if your life de-

---

colloquy "Convivium poeticum" of 1523. We last hear of Sbruglio at Salzburg in 1524 and in Hungary during the spring of 1525.

What prompted Eobanus to hurl this lampoon at Sbruglio is not known. Perhaps the Dalmatian had insulted his national pride with some dismissive remarks about the quality of German Neo-Latin poetry in general.

While the argument to the poem in the 1539-edition explicitly identifies Fastus ("Arrogance") as Sbruglio, Mannus is said to be either Eobanus himself or "some other German poet." The reference in lines 54-54 to Mannus's boldness and exceptional physical strength clearly fits Eobanus (cf. Camerarius, *Nar.* 8, 1-3). The name "Mannus," however, recalls Eobanus's friend Hermann Trebelius, who was crowned poet laureate at Wittenberg in June 1508 and thereafter moved to Frankfurt an der Oder (see fn. 40 at *Buc.* 4, 106 and fn. 66 at *Buc.* 8). Eobanus names him "Mannus" (short for "Hermannus") in a poem addressed to him in August 1506; see Trebelius, *Epigr.*, sig. F1ᵛ. In any case, the name has a decidedly patriotic ring, for according to Tac. *Ger.* 2, Mannus was the ancestor of all Germans.

Some unmistakable allusions to the papal interdict against Venice on 27 April 1509 and the French victory over the Venetians at Agnadello on 14 May 1509 place the poem in the late spring of 1509. See fn. 91 at lines 127-139 below.

Certantes, ego tam supero quam cedrus achantum,
Quam rosa septivagum superat Pestana ligustrum,
10 Nam neque prestantes tam barbara rura poaetas
Educunt. Ergo nostrates plaudite Musae.

Nemo audet mecum cantu contendere pastor.
    Mann. Advena, longinquas ad nos compulse per oras
Pauperie monstrante viam, pannosus et exul
15 Venisti – quis nescit? – in haec tam laeta recoeptus
Pascua. Grex postquam nostris collectior errat
Montibus et nivei cessit tibi copia lactis,
Postquam vix libros didicisti inflare colurnos
Confusumque brevi murmur blaterare cicuta,
20 Tolleris et fastu turges immanius ipso,
Tanquam nemo tibi par sit nec se tibi quisquam
Audeat ex nostris componere – stulte poaeta,
Qui tua cum nostris delyramenta Camoenis,
Ut tenebras cum luce, nihil conferre vereris.
25 Hos inter nemorum saltus, haec culmina circum,
Lenifluos amnes iuxta fontesque beatos
Floribus et multis circum fragrantibus herbis,
Haec propter dumeta canis tua carmina solus
Inter tot summa pastores laude canentes,
30 Ut quae, dum volucrum sit despectissima, certet
Vincere cantando morientes noctua cygnos,
Ut mille attagines, ut ducentas philomoenas
Aut calamita tenax aut sordida rana Seriphi
Increpet et sonitu certet superare palustri.
35 Plaudebunt ergo vestrates, Faste, Camoenae,
Quod te lucifugum superare in carmine vatem

Vernantes pueri primo iam pubere possunt.
Vade per infaustas iterum in tua pascua rupes.
Inter olorinos quid ineptis, noctua, cantus?
40   *Fast.* Si tibi tam facilis Venus est in carmine, si te
Tam celebri triplex anima perflavit Apollo,
Manne, sub hac mecum si non requieveris umbra
Hic quae sparsa patet plus quinis latior ulnis,
Non eris Aoniae quicquam de sorte coronae.
45   *Mann.* Faste, sub hac tecum quid si requiescimus umbra?

pended on it: I outdo you as the cedar outtops the acanthus, as Paestum's rose outclasses the hedge-roaming privet, [10] for this downright barbaric country produces no first-rate poets. Applaud me, therefore, Muses of my homeland. There is not a shepherd here who dares to match me song for song.

Mannus. Stranger, driven to us through far-off lands while poverty pointed the way, we all know how you came here – as a ragamuffin and exile! That is how we welcomed you to these flourishing pastures. But now that your flock has grown large ranging our hills and you have plenty of snowy milk coming your way, now that you've barely learned to blow on a hazelbark flute and eke out some garbled tune on a short hemlock stalk, [20] you assume an air of superiority and swell up tremendously with pride, as if you had no equal around here or as if none of my countrymen would dare to pit himself against you – you stupid poet, who aren't a bit afraid to set your blather against our Muses, like night against day. In these forest glades, around these hilltops, beside these gently-flowing streams, these springs rimmed with a profusion of fragrant herbs and flowers, hard by these thickets: here you sing your songs all alone, amidst so many shepherds renowned for their singing. [30] It's as if some owl, though the most despicable of birds, were striving to outsing dying swans, as if some obstinate tree frog or one of the squalid frogs of Seriphos were doing its utmost to drown out a thousand heath cocks or two hundred nightingales with its croaking and swamp noise. So the Muses of your homeland, Fastus, will indeed be applauding you ... seeing that our lads can outsing a skulking bard like you any day, even if they're just in the first bloom of youth. Go back over barren crags to your own pastures. Why do you hoot nonsense, you night owl, in the middle of swan songs?

Fastus. [40] If Venus is really so gracious to you in verse, if threefold Apollo[89] has really breathed his celebrated spirit upon you, Mannus, and you still refuse to take your ease with me here, in this shady spot stretching more than five ells across, then you'll never amount to anything in the circle of poets.

Mannus. What's the point, Fastus, if I were to take my ease in the shade here with you?

---

[89]The Christian Trinity, as in *Laud.* 395 (where see fn. 67).

Fast. Experiar quid nam potes, improbe, qualia iactes
Carmina, qui tantum potuisti spernere vatem.
Huc igitur concede. Tenent loca tuta capellae,
Sepibus et densis clausae stant vepribus agnae.
50　Certemus! Causam certandi, Manne, dedisti.
Non tibi cum puero certandum impubere, verum
Congrua cui molles aetas iam terminet annos,
Cui nativa genas iam vestiat umbra viriles.
Nec facile hanc nobis barbam tractaveris, audax
55　Sis licet et nulli pastorum robore caedas.
　　Mann. Est aliquid magno barbam tractare prophetae!
Dicere sed volui – lapsa est mihi lingua – "poetae."
　　Fast. Errat sponte sua quoties vult improba lingua.
Non sum adeo ignarus! Tibi scommate rideor isto.
60　　*Mann.* Quis ridere queat rugosi tubera nasi
Labraque continuo scabros nudantia dentes?
Sic fugat intrantes canis hic sata proxima thauros.
　　Fast. Verba probant animum. Ni vanus et improbus esses,
Crimina difficilis naturae nulla notares.
65　Non facies hominem, sed mens formosa venustat.
　　Mann. Invidia est, facie quae te facit esse canina.
Faste, quid obliquos in me convertis ocellos?
Ut cum zelotypus rivalem thaurus abhorret,
Indicat iram oculis et plagam fronte minatur.
70　　*Fast.* Quis tam mordaces feret aequa mente cavillos?
　　Mann. Omnia fert sapiens. Ni stultus et inscius esses,
Mordentem simili posses ridere cavillo.
Allatrata canis rellatrat, morsa remordet.
　　Fast. Scimus, et hoc versu non multum distat ab illo:
75　Concava carminibus vallis percussa remugit.
　　Mann. Verum nemo negat, sed in idem consonat illud:
Omnia procerae respondent iubila sylvae.

F4ʳ

Fastus. I want to find out what you're good for and what kind of poems you're bragging about, you whippersnapper, who see fit to scorn a great poet like me. So come over here. The goats are safe where they are, and the lambs are hemmed in with hedges and thick briers. [50] Let's have a singing-match! Just remember, Mannus, you're the one who picked this quarrel. And you won't be fighting it out with some beardless lad either, but rather with an adult who has left the years of childhood behind him and whose manly cheeks already sport genuine whiskers. Nor will you find it so easy to tug at my beard, though you're as brash as any and yield to none of the shepherds in strength.

Mannus. It's something all right, to tug at the beard of a great prophet! But pardon that slip of the tongue. I meant to say "poet."

Fastus. Your insolent tongue slips on its own, whenever it wants to. I'm not that ignorant! You were poking fun at me with that sneering remark.

Mannus. [60] Who could poke fun at the protuberance of your wrinkly nose and at the lips that constantly bare your scabrous teeth? That's exactly how this dog chases the bullocks away when they enter the neighboring wheatfields.

Fastus. Words attest the soul. If you weren't vain and insolent at heart, you wouldn't call attention to the defects that nature has saddled me with. What makes a man handsome is not his face, but his beautiful mind.

Mannus. It's envy, pure and simple, that has made you look like a dog. Why are you darting sidelong glances at me, Fastus? You act like a jealous bull recoiling from his rival. Anger flashing from his eyes, he threatens to butt with his forehead.

Fastus. [70] Who can endure such cutting taunts with composure?

Mannus. A wise man bears all things with equanimity. If you weren't a dolt and a numskull, you'd be poking fun at the taunter and repaying my insults in kind. Bark at a bitch, and she'll bark right back. A bitten one will snap back.

Fastus. I know that. And this verse isn't all that much different: Strike a hollow valley with songs and it will bellow them back.

Mannus. Yes, no one denies that. But this line has much the same import: The towering woods answer all our jubilant cries.

Fast. Liniger et sacra dum clamat in aede sacerdos,
Sub tota variae resonant testudine voces.

80   *Mann.* Garrula limosa dum rana palude coaxat,
Vociferae magnis reboant clangoribus undae.

Fast. Si bona cantaris, reddunt bona carmina sylvae.
Si mala per valles clamas, mala redditur echo.

Mann. Verum, qui bonus est loquitur bene. Si bonus esses,

85   Non velles conferre bonis mala carmina, Faste.

Fast. Si bonus es, fronti testem prescribe tabellam,

F4ᵛ   Ut qui te videat qui sis cognoscere possit.

Mann. Mille refert secum recti mens conscia testes.
Nescis adhuc, titulo virtus non indiget ullo.

90   *Fast.* Hora fugit. Cupidae nectis ludibria menti
Callidus et multo praecludis seria ludo.
Coepta sequi decuit. Nihil hac ambage movemur.
Si bonus es, si te verus perflavit Apollo,
Profer inaudaces pulchra in certamina Musas.

95   *Mann.* Ut maiora bonam redimat per vulnera famam,
Saucius invisam restaurat athleta palestram.
Victus es. Interea ne plus vincare caveto.

Fast. Antea cessabit plenas mulgere capellas
Caseolos pastor venum laturus in urbem,

100   Antea mellis apes fugient lita, salsa capellae,
Quam tibi tantillo tradam certamine palmam,
Quod neque luctator, salius, pugilve cruentus,
Sed pulchro dociles claudent examine Musae.

Mann. Urbica quis docuit nostrum certamina Fastum?

105   *Fast.* Cum primum mater mea me duxisset in urbem,
Vidi saltantes, luctantes, belligerantes,
Currentes, lapidem torquentes. Tempore ab illo
Nemo mihi saltu toto est prestantior agro.

Fastus. And when a linen-clad priest declaims in a church, the whole vault resounds with various voices.

Mannus. [80] When a chattering frog croaks in a muddy swamp, the reverberant waves return the favor with gusto.

Fastus. If you sing well, the woods will reward you with good songs. If you sing poorly in the valleys, the echo will repay you with poor ones.

Mannus. Quite right. The good man speaks well. If you were a good person, Fastus, you wouldn't compare bad songs with good ones.

Fastus. If you're that good yourself, put a testimonial sign on your forehead, so the people who see you will know what a fine fellow you are.

Mannus. A clear conscience is worth a thousand witnesses. Just in case you don't know this: Virtue has no need of a placard.

Fastus. [90] Time flies. You're just whetting my appetite, cunningly stringing me along with a sham fight while avoiding the real thing with all your shadowboxing. Let's get on with it. Beating around the bush like this doesn't impress me a bit. If you're really that good, if the true Apollo[90] has inspired you, then march out those cowardly Muses of yours and let them fight in honorable battle.

Mannus. To redeem his good name with even more grievous wounds, a reeling prizefighter returns to the ring he hates. You're a beaten man. Meanwhile, watch out you don't get beaten to pulp.

Fastus. Sooner will a shepherd stop milking the full goats when he wants to sell cheese in the city, [100] sooner will bees shy away from honeycombs, goats from salty fodder, before I'll concede the palm to you after such a trifling fight. This match won't be decided by some wrestler, jumper, or bloodied boxer, but by the Muses, who know beauty when they see it.

Mannus. Who was it that taught our Fastus these city sports?

Fastus. When my mother first took me into town, I saw jumpers, wrestlers, fencers, runners, stone throwers. Since that day, nobody in the whole countryside has been able to beat me at jumping.

---

[90]That is to say, Christ. Cf. *Laud.* 395, with fn. 67.

Mann. Pastorem curare greges, armenta tueri,
110 Arma palestriten, nautam tractare rudentes,
Sutorem crepidas, sua quemque agere ocia oportet.

G1ʳ Florales, i, Faste, tuum pecus intrat in hortos.
I, revoca! Dominus – non est puer – illius horti
Incautum occidet, certum est, ubi venerit hircum.
115 *Fast.* Hircus adest. Vicina boves viridaria pascunt.
Si vir es et duris animum qui obsistere rebus
Possit habes, versu mecum certabis agresti.
Mann. Qui tecum certare volet, quo iudice, Faste?
Fast. Debita iuditio stabit victoria recto.
120 *Mann.* Sepe solet vinci, temere qui provocat hostem.
Recta lacessito semper victoria caessit.
Ut lupus imbellem timet insatiabilis agnum,
Ut leporem canis, ut captum Iovis aliger anguem,
Teque tuasque minas metuo. Sed, amice, monendum,
125 Quando immane tumes. Quid, si te ruperis? Olim
Rupta perit dum rana bovi par esse laborat,
Et nunc Adriacae dum sufflant viscera ranae
Et sinuosa vago dispendunt brachia ponto,
Non contenta undis animalia pessima. Verum
130 Dum terras habitant et candida lilia turbant,
Grande ex vicina cecidit Iovis arbore fulmen
Disiecitque feras patriasque retrusit ad undas,
Grandia mox aquilae quassantes lilia ranas,
Quas non omne prius coepit mare, rursus in unam
135 Antiquamque coegerunt remeare paludem.
Nunc miserae proprio pascuntur sanguine ranae,
G1ᵛ Turgida flaccescunt, nunc pinguia viscera marcent.
Ut breviter dicam, quando voluere Gigantes

---

[91]Because Fastus hails from Dalmatia on the Adriatic and is thus associated with Maximilian's enemy Venice, Eobanus now applies the fable of the frog and ox to the Venetians, who (as Julius II stated in his bull of excommunication and interdict against Venice on 27 April 1509) had become "so puffed up with pride as to molest her neighbours and invade their territories." See John J. Norwich, *Venice: The Greatness and the Fall* (London, 1981), p. 141. The fable is likewise applied to the Venetians in Mutian. *Ep.* 160 (late spring? 1509); cf. also Mutian. *Epp.* 158 and 159; Eob. *Buc.* B 4 and 5; and *Nup.* 35-37.

After the decisive French victory at Agnadello on 14 May 1509, Venice lost virtually all her mainland possessions to the signatories of the Treaty of Cambrai – the Papacy ("oak"), France ("lilies," "fleurs-de-lis"), and the Holy Roman Empire ("eagles").

Mannus. A herdsman ought to tend his flocks and watch over his cattle; [110] a soldier should stick to his guns, a sailor to his ropes, a cobbler to his last. Everybody ought to do what he's good at. – Get up, Fastus! That beast of yours is sneaking into the flower beds. Go, get him back! If the owner of this garden comes by – he's no lad, you know – you may be sure he'll kill the improvident billy.

Fastus. There, the billy is back. The cows are grazing in the adjoining field. If you're a real man and have the pluck to stand up to a tough duel, you'll fight it out with me in rustic verse.

Mannus. Supposing someone wanted to vie with you, Fastus, who'd be the umpire?

Fastus. The winner will be duly determined by the Court of Good Taste.

Mannus. [120] He who recklessly provokes his opponent to battle often ends up the loser. By rights, the victory has always fallen to the one who was wronged. As the insatiable wolf fears the unwarlike lamb, as the hound fears the hare, as Jupiter's eagle fears the snake he has captured, that is how I fear you and your threats. But I must warn you, my friend, because you're frightfully puffed up. What if you burst? Once upon a time there was a frog that tried to be as big as an ox and died in the attempt. And now it's the frogs of the Adriatic that are puffing themselves up.[91] Not content to stay in their native swamp, the disgusting brutes are spreading out their crooked arms from the restless sea. But [130] when they started living on the dry land and disturbing the white lilies, a great thunderbolt fell from Jove's oak tree nearby[92] and scattered the aggressive beasts and thrust them back into the water, where they belong. It didn't take long for the eagles to pounce on them there. Brandishing great fleurs-de-lis, they forced the frogs, for whom the whole sea had been too small before, to return to one single ancient swamp. Now the miserable frogs feed on their own blood. Their once bloated and potbellied bodies have shriveled up and grown flabby. In short, when the lit-

---

[92]The Strasbourg copy of the *Bucolicon* glosses "Iovis" with "papae," that is, Pope Julius II. A member of the Della Rovere family, Julius II carried an oak tree in his coat-of-arms. The "thunderbolt" that fell from this tree is the bull that Julius issued on 27 April 1509, proclaiming a solemn excommunication and interdict against Venice and authorizing other states to do whatever harm they could wreak on the Venetian empire.

Esse breves ranae, coeperunt esse cicadae.
140 Discite, pastores, menti dare fraena superbae.
Altius erectum gravius cadit. Omne superbum
Invisum superis, pietas gratissima coelo.
Aspicis annosas convelli turbine pinus,
Flexilis ut nullos ventos horrescit harundo.
145 Fulmina non humiles tangunt crepitantia valles;
Semper summa petunt et coelo proxima turbant.
Tu quoque ne supra mortalem, Faste, feraris,
Ne grave post tristem doleas cecidisse ruinam.
Si bonus es, patiare parem. Tam nemo beatus,
150 Quem nemo aequiparet. Non dat Deus omnia soli.
Hereat ista tuae potior sententia menti.
    Fast. Sepe sub immundo lucentes pulvere gemmae,
Sepe latet fulvum duris sub cotibus aurum.
Nunc primum experior quales haec rura poaetas,
155 Hei mihi, quos vates genuit tam barbara tellus.
Sydera cuncta prius coelo casura putabam,
Nerea passurum flammas, quam talia possint
Carmina cantari vestris – dii, qualia! – sylvis.
Invideo vobis Musas, o rura, Latinas,
160 Barbara! Iam nullo tecum contendere vellem
Carmine. Sic iterum patrias inglorius urbes
Aspiciam. Ite, meae, mecum fugite, ite, capellae.
Ite per umbrosos sub iniquo sydere colles.
Non libate undas, frondes non carpite donec
165 O dulces mecum patriae venietis ad agros.
Barbara rura, pares non possum ferre, valete.
    Mann. Iam poteris tumidas imitari, livide, ranas!
Aedite ranarum de saemine, vade per aestum,
Per iuga, per valles, per mille pericula solus.
170 Obvia nuda silex obducat pascua, saevus
In media vicina siti sol flumina siccet,
Saeviat omne tibi stellati numen Olimpi,
Ut causa invideas nobis meliore Latinas
Pierides. I, Bardiaco signande cucullo.

G2ʳ

---

141 erectum *BO*: erectam *A*.

tle frogs wanted to be Giants,[93] they ended up as cicadas.
[140] Let this be a lesson to you, shepherds, to curb your
overweening pride. The higher the tower, the heavier its fall.
All pride is an abomination to God, but brotherly love is
well pleasing to heaven. You see how old pine trees are up-
rooted by a whirlwind, while the pliant reed shrugs off all
storms. Crashing thunderbolts don't touch the low valleys;
they always strike the summits and disturb the skyscraping
peaks. The same goes for you, Fastus. Don't set yourself
above the rest of mankind, lest you come a cropper and dis-
cover to your grief how hard you have fallen. If you're a good
poet, acknowledge that you've met your match. Nobody is
so fortunate [150] that he is utterly peerless. God does not
shower all his gifts on one single person. You had best keep
that maxim engraved on your mind.

Fastus. Ofttimes sparkling gems lie concealed in filth
and dust; ofttimes the yellow gold lies hidden under solid
rock. Only now do I find out by experience what fine poets
this country produces – alas, what great bards this barbaric
land has brought forth! I'd have thought it more likely that
the stars would all tumble down from the sky, that the sea
would catch fire, than that I'd hear such gorgeous songs in
these forests of yours. Gods, what beautiful singing! I envy
you your Latin Muses, O barbarous fields! [160] Now I've
lost all desire to vie with you in song. All right then, I'll have
to return to the cities of my homeland a humiliated man.
Go, my goats, hurry up. Go! We're heading back together.
With the sun beating down on us, take to the shady hills.
Don't touch the water, don't nibble at the leaves until you
and I reach the oh so sweet fields of home. I can't stand
equals. Barbaric country, farewell.

Mannus. Now you can copy those puffed-up frogs, you
jealous misfit! Son of a frog, go back where you came from –
through the heat of day, over hill and dale, all alone in
countless dangers. [170] May bare rock cover the pastures
along your path, may the pitiless sun dry up the nearby
streams in the midst of a drought, may every deity in the
starry heavens vent his rage against you, so you can be-
grudge us our Latin Muses with even better cause. Go, hide
your face in the Illyrian hood of your people.

---

[93]The Giants of ancient myth wanted to storms the heavens, but were destroyed by Ju-
piter's thunderbolts. See Ov. *Met.* 1, 151-155.

AEGLOGA ULTIMA

Hactenus errantes nostris in montibus agnas
Diximus audaci calamo. Mihi prima canenti
"Alma sinum vario pandebat germine Mater."
Tum "cecinere meae mihi pastoralia Musae."
5　　Postquam, "Gera vagus nutantes alluit herbas."
Successit: "Mecum quondam, Philereme, solebas
Pascere oves"; "viridi duo convenere sub ulmo."
Tum "lusi Ocnaeo quiddam spectabile versu."
"Tercius" ut vero "rediit iam Lucifer orbi,"
10　　Diximus: "Oceano Titan venerabile sydus";
"Nulla fuit, Sylvi, flavae tibi cura puellae."
G2ᵛ　　Postquam, "Rura colunt, sylvas, et culmina, et agros."
　　Hoc Musae decimum clauserunt ordine carmen.
Ultima difficiles in rus deducite nymphae
15　　Carmina et urbanum sub dio claudite ludum.
Ludite, Pierides – non quas vicisse novenas
Cantando memorant, gentilia numina, picas,
Sed quae divinam spiratis ab aethere mentem,
Caelestes animae, sanctorum numina vatum.
20　　Ludite, virgineae mentes, deducite carmen
Virginis in laudes, vestrae quae prima coronae
Cum mater fieret peperit cum flore pudoris.
　　Sic ubi populea cecinissem laetus in umbra,
Purior aereis radiis resplenduit aether,
25　　Sol stetit, et superi patuerunt limina mundi.
Quis calor hic subitus? Quae mentem incendia raptant?
O Virgo (sentimus enim nova numina!), Virgo,
Spes miserum, quae sceptra tenes altissima rerum,
Illa es, non fallor, noster quam Floridus olim
30　　Dixit ab Aeoo tumefactam viscera vento,
Quam clauso nuper recubantem pictus in horto
Monstravit paries, flores in fonte lavantem

Buc. 11. *A*: *om. BO.*　　　1 Hactenus *scripsi*: Actenus *A.*

[94]The final eclogue – a pastoral praise of the Virgin Mary – opens with a series of incipits from the preceding eclogues. Hence it must have been completed during the summer of 1509, perhaps in time for the Assumption of Our Lady on August 15. Cf. lines 67-88 below and *Buc.* B 6, 1.

[95]The Muses defeated the nine daughters of Pierus in a singing contest and then turned them into chattering magpies. See Ov. *Met.* 5, 294-678.

THE LAST ECLOGUE

Thus far in my adventurous song I have told you about the lambs that range the hills of our country.[94] In my first poem the "bountiful Mother opened up her bosom, swelling with all kinds of buds." Then "the Muses inspired me to pastoral song." After that came, "The meandering Gera laps the swaying grass." There followed: "You used to pasture the sheep with me in these hills, Phileremus," and "Two met under a green elm tree." Then I sang "bucolic verses of some value." But when "for the third time already morning dawned on the world," [10] I said: "The venerable star Titan is rising from the ocean"; "You're no longer infatuated with that blonde lass, Sylvius"; and then: "You who live in the woods and the country, the hills and meadows."

In this order the Muses ended the tenth poem. Now, austere nymphs, perform your last song here in the countryside and conclude this urbane show of yours under the open sky. Put on a last show, Pierian Maidens – not those heathen deities who are supposed to have defeated nine magpies in a singing-match,[95] but you, celestial souls, who breathe divine inspiration on us from on high, you Muses of the holy bards. [20] Sing, chaste spirits, compose a song in praise of the Virgin who, the first in your circle, became a mother and bore a child, yet kept her chastity's flower.

As I was happily singing like this in the shade of a poplar,[96] the air grew brighter, the sky gleamed with ethereal brilliance, the sun stood still, and the gates of heaven swung open. What sudden fire is this? What flame is enrapturing my mind? O Virgin (for I sense your numinous power!), Virgin, hope of the wretched, you who hold the supreme scepter in all creation, you are the one, I'm sure, whom my dear Floridus once [30] described as pregnant by the East Wind.[97] You are the one I saw not long ago in a mural that showed you reclining in an enclosed garden and sprinkling

---

[96]Eobanus's reference to the poplar tree is intended to remind us, via Mant. *Ecl.* 7, 88, of the famous story of Hercules at the crossroads. For in Mantuan's seventh eclogue the lovesick Pollux falls asleep under "Hercules' tree" (the poplar) and then has a dream in which the Virgin shows him the two roads of life: the paths of earthly and celestial love. Pollux thereupon chooses the arduous road that leads to heaven. In this final eclogue Eobanus shows us that he too has turned his back on passionate love and is setting his sights on love divine.

[97]See *Buc.* 5, 88.

Signifero. Tune illa Dei castissima Mater,
Quam veteres typico cecinerunt carmine vates?
35 Illa ipsa es, nec enim nostris te nescit in arvis,
Quicquid agit, nullae ignorant tua nomina sylvae.
Nota mari terraque pates, Dea prima dearum –
Non veterum quas gentiles heroidas aiunt,
Nam quis mortales tecum conferre puellas
40 Audeat? O magni lux presentissima mundi,
Pulchra nimis, formosa nimis, dilecta Tonanti,
Lilia quae vincis puro vernantia vultu
Mixta rosis, niveae similis spetiosa columbae,
Corpora cui nullae surgunt per eburnea mendae,
45 Tu nobis, tu prima Deum mortalibus aegris
Ostendens, res mira, ipso deducis Olimpo
Et paris immensum parva ad praesaepia Christum,
Frigora cum toti starent durissima mundo.
Quem duo nascentem proprio iumenta cubili
50 Cognovere Deum, nobis, pia Virgo, benignum
Effice. Natus agro populum non spernit agrestem.
Flecte pios oculos ad nos vultumque serenum.
Aspice sub misera lachrymarum valle iacentes.
     Virgo, decus coeli, terrae spes, terror abyssi,
55 Stella maris, medio quam clamat nauta profundo
Ut ventos nymbosque leves et naufraga serves
Membra ratis miserae! Sicco te rure colonus
Invocat ut ruptis largos des nubibus ymbres
Et plenis sterilem foecundes messibus agrum.
60 Orat et ardentes supplex procumbit ad aras.
Te vocat obscuro damnatus carcere, namque
Te nullum didicit magis exorabile numen.
Te gravidae matres ut foetae pondera ventris
Tunc cum tempus erit ponant foeliciter orant.
65 Rustica te celebrat, te plebs urbana frequenti
Et tua festivo extollit cerimonia ritu.
     Si qua tuas vulgo redeunt solennia ad aras,
Festo sacra die fiunt, opera omnia cessant.
Navita non illa sulcat mare luce, nec ullas
70 Dispensat mercator opes, non rura viator
Metitur, non verba gravis clamosa magister
Proiicit in triviis. Non tunc fumantia thauri

G3ʳ

G3ᵛ

flowers with water from a sealed fountain. Aren't you that most chaste Mother of God, whom the prophets of old predicted in typological song? You are indeed! There is not a soul in our fields who does not know you, no matter what his occupation; there is not a forest ignorant of your name. Renowned on sea and land, you manifest yourself as the Most High Goddess of goddesses – not the ancient ones whom the heathens called heroines, for who would venture to compare you with mortal girls? [40] O everpresent light of the wide world, beautiful beyond words, lovely beyond compare, dear to the Thunderer's heart, you who in purity of face surpass spring lilies mingled with roses, who are as fair as a snow-white dove and whose ivory body is entirely without blemish: you were the first to show God to us sin-sick mortals and – a miracle! – brought him down from Olympus itself. And when the whole world was in the clutches of wintry frost you bore the immense Christ beside the little manger. Make him, whom the two beasts of burden [50] recognized as God when he was born in their stable, O holy Virgin, make him well-disposed toward us. Country-born himself, he does not despise country people. Bend your merciful gaze and your cheerful countenance towards us. Look upon us who lie prostrate in this miserable vale of tears.

O Virgin, glory of heaven, hope of the earth, terror of the abyss! O star of the sea to whom the sailor appeals in mid-ocean that you may dispel the winds and the storm clouds and save his battered vessel from shipwreck! On dry land, the farmer calls on you to burst the clouds and grant abundant showers and implores you to make his barren land yield a bountiful harvest. [60] For this he prays, humbly falling to his knees before your blazing altar. The condemned man petitions you in the darkness of his cell, for he knows of no divinity more easily entreated than you. Expectant mothers pray to you that in due time they may be happily delivered of the child they carry in their womb. Countryfolk honor you, townsfolk praise you, and with joyous hearts they all throng to your sacred rites.

Whenever an annual feast returns to your altars, the holyday is given over to worship. All work stops. On that day no sailor furrows the sea, [70] no merchant sells any wares, no wayfarer traverses the fields, no earnest master scolds his pupils in school. Then the oxen do not groan at their work,

Terga gemunt. Vacuus stivam suspendit arator.
Garrulus herentes non curat vinitor uvas,
75 Dura nec oppressos explorant praela racemos.
Confluit et totum divam te vulgus adorat,
Imberbes pueri, iuvenes, et turba senilis.
Quo possunt cultu matrem venerantur Iesu
Et cumulant donis altaria. Serta puellae
80 Innuptae floresque ferunt, ova candida matres
Annosae caeraque ardentes paupere lychnos.
Tam veneranda dies ubi toti illuxerit orbi
Et sacra divinus tulerit libamina mystes,
Tuta salutares pascunt armenta per herbas,
85 Fronde coronantur pueri. Tum liber in arvis
Cantilat et dulci pastor non dormit in umbra.
G4ʳ Iamque aliquis summo tales de culmine voces
Incipit, et cantu rupes percussa remugit:
"O Dea, quae pecudes, quae rura et pascua servas,
90 Numine sub cuius series longissima rerum
Militat, aurato cuius diademate crines
Ornatos aiunt bissenas pingere stellas
(O non Gnosiacae similis fortuna coronae!),
Pande serenatae pulcherrima lumina frontis,
95 Aspice nos. Tua turba sumus. Tibi noster in arvis
Est labor; omne tuum pecus est sub lumine mundi.
Diva, pecus defende tuum, ne Martius hostis,
Ne lupus insidias lacero componat ovili.
Pelle dolos omneis. Fures averte malignos
100 A stabulis. Da tuta greges in pascua duci,
Da laetas segetes, da, vitae digna beatae,
Da facilem victum, Virgo. Da, si qua precantes
Vota iuvant, vitae functos presentis honore
Caelestem facili patriam contingere cursu,
105 O decus, o miseri requies dulcissima mundi."
Hos ego pastores cecini dum lentus in umbra
Carmina rurali meditor iuvenilia plectro.
Surgite, Pierides. Satis est in rure moratum.
Nox ruit, et gelidae veniunt in gramina guttae.
110 Iam, ne prolixas tellus riget humida vestes,
Ite, boves, pueri, stabulis includite pastos.

Τέλος

[98]Ariadne, daughter of King Minos of Cnossos in Crete, had a gem-studded golden
crown that was placed among the stars after her death.

their backs asteaming. The idle farmer hangs up his plow for the day. The garrulous vinedresser does not prune the clinging vines, nor does the unfeeling wine-press put the crushed grapes to the test. All the people flock together and venerate you as their goddess: beardless lads, youths, and old people. Each in his own way, they revere the mother of Jesus and heap the altars with gifts. [80] Unmarried girls bring garlands and flowers; aged mothers carry white eggs and burning tapers of inexpensive wax. When that truly venerable day has dawned on the whole wide world and the priest of God has offered the holy sacrifice, then the herds safely graze on the salutary grass and boys crown their hair with leaves. Then too the shepherd does not sleep in the refreshing shade, but freely sings his songs in the fields. And now someone chants the following words on the hilltop, and struck by his singing, the cliff echoes them back:

"O Goddess, you who watch over the flocks, the fields, and the pastures, [90] you under whose dominion all creation serves, you whose hair, they say, is adorned with a diadem of gold and embellished with twelve stars (oh, how unlike the fortunes of Ariadne's crown![98]), do open those incomparably beautiful eyes of yours. Look upon us with unclouded mien. We are your people. Our labor in the fields belongs to you; every flock under the sun is yours. Holy Lady, protect your flock, lest an enemy soldier, lest a wolf lie in ambush and ravage the sheepfold. Drive all treachery away. Keep wicked thieves [100] away from the stables. Grant that the herds be led to safe pastures, grant abundant crops, grant ready sustenance, O Virgin worthy of a blissful life. And if ever you hear our prayers, grant that those who have led an upright life may enjoy an easy journey to the heavenly fatherland, O glory, O sweetest solace of this wretched world."

These are the bucolics that I sang while taking my ease in the shade and practising the songs of youth in a rustic strain. Arise, Pierian Maidens. You have spent enough time in the country. Night is falling, and cold droplets are sprinkling the grass. [110] Now, so the damp ground won't soak your overalls, lads, go and shut the full-fed cows in their stables.

The End

H1ʳ   **B 1**   **TESTE CONSCIENTIA**

Nunc age, qui quondam mea carpere scripta solebas,
    Liber in haec odii proiice quicquid habes.
En tibi censurae campum prebemus apertum.
    Utere concesso, perfida lingua, tibi.
5   Nunc ego, Livor edax, turba numerabor in illa
    Quam tu vipereo rodere dente soles.
Quod tulit Andinus vates, quod magnus Homerus,
    Zoile, per superos da mihi, quaeso, pati.

DUCE INNOCENTIA

B 2   **EOBANI HESSI PRIMUM APUD ENGLENDRUM**
          FAMILIARITATIS ARGUMENTUM

Cum tua per multas, vir praestantissime, terras
    Fama sit illustres nobilis inter avos,
Cum tua non uno virtus precone feratur
    Et superent laudes hic et ubique tuae,
5   Dignus es heroo cantari carmine, dignus
    Quem celebret blanda noster Apollo cheli.
Laudabat, memini, nobis tua nomina Rufus,
    Qui colit affinis moenia celsa Gothae.
Quinetiam tua vulgares praeconia linguae
10   Non intermissa sedulitate canunt –
Tam catus et comis, tam diceris esse benignus,
H1ᵛ   Tam tua non ullo gloria teste caret.
Et si vera fides populari traditur aurae,
    Saecula te celebrant doctius ista nihil.
15   Primus in augusta Guilielmi principis aula,
    Consilio servas Hessica sceptra tuo,
Et merito, quia tu bifidi laus maxima iuris,
    Quem locet in primo curia tanta thoro.
Nobilis aeternum tibi prestitit Anglia nomen,

B 1 – B 11   *A: om. BO.*

[99]Vergil, born in the village of Andes near Mantua.
[100]For the sophist Zoilus, who poked fun at Homer's errors, see fn. 16 at *Rec.* B 2, 3.

B 1   **LET CONSCIENCE BE MY WITNESS.**

Come on now, you – yes you, who once made it a habit to
carp at my writings – feel free to throw all your hatred at this
book. Look, I'm giving you a field day criticizing my verse.
Here's your chance, backbiters – you have my permission.
Now I'll be reckoned among those whom you, gnawing
Envy, love to tear into with those viperous teeth of yours.
What the bard of Andes,[99] what the great Homer once suf-
fered, that, by the gods, is what I'd like you, Zoilus,[100] to
inflict on me now.

LET INNOCENCE BE MY GUIDE.

B 2   **A FIRST TOKEN OF EOBANUS HESSUS'S
FRIENDSHIP WITH ENGLENDER**[101]

Since you, most eminent sir, are famed in many countries
as one who has distinguished himself in a family of illus-
trious ancestors, since not a few proclaim your merits and
here and everywhere people praise your achievements to the
skies, you are worthy of being lauded in heroic song, worthy
of being extolled by my patron Apollo on his enchanting
lyre. Rufus, who lives within the lofty walls of neighboring
Gotha, spoke highly of you, I remember. As a matter of fact,
the common people too [10] sing your praises with unflag-
ging zeal – such is your reputation for shrewdness, kindness,
and generosity, such is the esteem in which everyone holds
you. And if there is any truth to public opinion, our own
age celebrates you as its most learned scholar. As chief sec-
retary at the august court of Prince William, you protect the
state of Hesse with your counsel, and rightly so, seeing that
you, the head of so important a chancellery, are the greatest
glory of two-branched law.[102] Renowned England has given

---

[101]In an "Ecloga pastoralis" of 15 October [1508] Mutianus Rufus urged Eobanus to
seek the patronage of Johann Englender (d. 1517), head of the chancellery of Landgrave
William II at Kassel. See Mutian. *Ep.* 149 (misdated by Gillert). Eobanus thereupon com-
posed the present poem in praise of Englender and his wife. The latter was so delighted with
Eobanus's compliments that her husband copied the poem out in his own hand and sent it
with a covering letter to Mutianus Rufus. See Mutian. *Ep.* 119, dated 17 January [1509]. En-
couraged by the favorable reception, Eobanus thereupon dedicated the *Bucolicon* to Englender
in the summer of 1509. For Englender's life see fn. 4 at *Buc.*, ded.

[102]That is, of civil and canon law.

20   Englendrum Latio barbara lingua dedit.
        Adde quod insignem tot te virtutibus aiunt,
            Quot praestare ipsos vix puto posse deos.
        Doctor, honos patriae, doctorum gloria, qualem
            Ingenii candor te facit iste tui.
25   Quam bene sub tanto clarescis principe, cuius
            Nobile miratur maximus orbis opus!
        Ortus et occasus Guilielmi nomen adorant;
            Nostra Palatinae regna fatentur opes.
        Scit ferus innumero transmissus milite Rhenus
30   Quam valeat forti regulus iste manu.
        Ergo sub hoc, magno veluti sub Caesare quondam
            Moecenas, vitam transigis innocuam.
        Suspicis ingenuas studiis melioribus arteis.
            Diceris et magno cum Cicerone loqui.
35   Clarior est studiis virtus coniuncta probatis;
            Efficit insignes lingua Latina viros.
H2ʳ   Docte vir, in tantum cum sis provectus honorem,
            Non poteris fama candidiore frui.
        Insigni praestare etiam te coniuge dicunt,
40   Cui daret Iliacus mystica poma Paris,
        Vincere quae Venerem Phrygia potuisset in Ida,
            Tradere cui speculum regia Iuno velit,
        Cui matronalis Lucretia casta pudoris
            Praemia, vel Sexto iudice, prima ferat.
45   Doctus et humanus divesque et coniuge foelix
            Cum sis, dicendus iure beatus eris.
        Ergo nec immerito princeps te tantus honorat,
            Dignus qui tanta praeficerere domo.
        Scripsimus ista tuae commoti nomine laudis,
50   Quae faciunt divos nomina sola. Vale.

---

[103]In 1504, during the War of the Landshut succession, Landgrave William II of Hesse attacked Count Palatine Philip II (1448-1508). Cf. *Buc.* 9, 43-44. For William II see fn. 75 at *Buc.* 9.

[104]Cf. fn. 8 at *Buc.*, ded.

you her eternal name; [20] her barbarous tongue has en-
riched Latin with the word "Englender." On top of all that,
they say you are distinguished by so many virtues that even
the gods, I daresay, could scarcely outdo you on that score.
Doctor of Laws, pride of your fatherland, ornament of
scholarship: it is your brilliance of mind that has made you
what you are today. How brightly you shine under that
powerful prince of yours, whose noble statecraft the whole
world admires! East and west pay homage to William's
name; the Palatinate acknowledges our rule. The Rhine,
which ferried countless soldiers across its untamed waters,
has seen for itself [30] how much this landgrave can accom-
plish with his resolute hand.[103]

Under this ruler, therefore, like Maecenas[104] long ago
under the great Caesar [Augustus], you lead a blameless life.
You honor the liberal arts with your scholarly studies. It is
even said of you that you are as eloquent as the great Cicero
himself. Virtue, when allied with commendable studies, be-
comes the brighter for it; the Latin language forms men of
distinction. Learned sir, because you have risen to such an
exalted position, the fame you enjoy could not possibly be
more brilliant. They also say that you are blessed with a re-
markable wife, [40] a beauty to whom Paris of Troy would
have offered the mystical apple,[105] who would have defeated
Venus on Phrygian Ida, to whom Queen Juno would have
wanted to hand over her mirror, and to whom chaste Lu-
cretia would have awarded the first prize for matronly
modesty – even with Sextus as umpire.[106] Since you are
learned and cultured and wealthy and happily married, you
may be fairly called a blessed man. There is ample reason,
then, why your mighty prince honors you as he does, for
you are worthy of overseeing his eminent house. I write
these lines under the spell of your dazzling renown. [50]
Such fame alone creates gods. Farewell.

[105]The golden apple that Paris of Troy offered to Venus as a prize for winning a beauty
contest with Juno and Pallas on Mount Ida. The story is told, for example, in Ov. *Ep.* 16; Hyg.
Fab. 92; cf. Eob. *Venus* 1, 72-74. The apple is "mystical" because the story was interpreted al-
legorically, with Pallas representing the contemplative, Juno the active, and Venus the
voluptuous life. For the epithet cf. *Her. Chr.* 2, 38; 10, 35; 16, 294; *Nor.* 909 (the gifts of the
three magi are "mystica").

[106]Lucretia was the wife of L. Tarquinius Collatinus. She committed suicide after being
raped by Sextus Tarquinius.

B 3 EIUSDEM IN MORTE GUILIELMI HESSORUM REGULI

Exue bellipotens festivos Hessia cultus,
    Taedigeno moestum pulvere sparge caput.
Et iacet et superos princeps Guilielmus adivit,
    Lux patriae, belli gloria, fama togae.
5   Nam quid ferales et februa moesta cupressi?
    Ecce deos cogunt impia fata mori.

H2ᵛ

B 4 EOBANI HESSI SCRUPUS IN VENETOS

Cum quateret coelum sperantes sydera ranas,
    Armiger et flores pro Iove fulmen erant.
Adria suscepit Rhodanum Rhenumque Tybrimque,
    Et minor est ranis quam fuit ante suis.
5   Non opus Oedipodas scrupis adhibere tricatis.
    Forsitan ex Venetis qui sciat unus erit.

B 5 EIUSDEM IN EOSDEM ΠΑΡΑΒΟΛΗ

Consuluere Iovem volucres ranaeque, petentes
    Per Styga vinceret utra cohortum.
"Quin vincetis, aves," deus inquit, et annuit illis
    Nescio quomodo pollice presso.
5   "Vincetis, ranae," deus inquit, et annuit illis
    Nescio quomodo pollice verso.
Iuppiter aequus erat digitis, non ore. Sed aequum
    Rana Iovem superata fatetur.

B 5   *Tit.* ΠΑΡΑΒΟΛΗ *scripsi*: παραβολε A.

[107]William II, landgrave of Hesse, died on 11 July 1509. For his life see fn. 75 at *Buc.* 9.
[108]This epigram and the next are contemporaneous with *Buc.* 10 (late spring 1509). For the historical background see *Buc.* 10, 127-139 with fn. 91.
[109]As Jupiter once hurled thunderbolts at the Giants who attempted to storm the heavens (cf. *Buc.* 10, 138-139), so the eagle (the Holy Roman Empire) and the lilies (France) now scatter the Adriatic frogs (Venice) with heaven's help. The glossator of the Strasbourg copy, who dutifully identifies the eagle and frogs, also explains that "heaven" ("coelum") in line 1 means the pope (Julius II). The "stars" ("sydera"), he says, indicate the city of Rome.

B 3   THE SAME POET ON THE DEATH OF WILLIAM, LANDGRAVE OF HESSE[107]

Valiant Hesse, cast off your festive adornments; sprinkle your mournful head with the ash of funeral torches. Prince William lies dead. He has gone to the gods above – he, the star of his fatherland, the glory of war, the ornament of peace. Why these feral cypresses and somber exequies, you ask? Look, ruthless fate compels even the gods to die.

B 4   A HARD NUT FOR THE VENETIANS, BY EOBANUS HESSUS[108]

When heaven cast down the frogs that were reaching for the stars, the eagle and the lilies served as Jupiter's thunderbolt.[109] The Adriatic received the Rhône and the Rhine and the Tiber[110] and now has less space for its frogs than before. No need to bring in an Oedipus[111] to crack this hard nut! Perhaps one of the Venetians will manage to figure it out.

B 5   A PARABLE FOR THE SAME PEOPLE BY THE SAME POET

The eagles and the frogs came to Jupiter for advice, asking him to swear by the Styx which of their two cohorts would be victorious. "Why, of course you eagles will win," said the god, as he nodded to them and somehow or other gave them thumbs up. "You frogs will win," said the god, as he nodded to them and somehow or other gave them thumbs down. Jupiter spoke fair with his thumbs, not his mouth. But in defeat, the frogs acknowledged Jupiter's fairness.

[110] The three rivers stand for the allies in the League of Cambrai: France, the Holy Roman Empire, and Rome.

[111] Oedipus, who solved the riddle of the Sphinx, was a proverbial solver of enigmas.

Quorundam amicorum testimonia

B 6   HEREBORDUS MARGARITUS IURISPERITUS

Enthea cum Mariae requiem pia turba canebat
Findebatque Canis sitientes undique campos
Falceque deposita festa ocia messor agebat,
Hessus in agresti monstravit carmina taela

H3ʳ   5   Et numeravit oves bonus armentarius omneis.
Quam dives pecoris! Meritoria septa redundant,
Et precium referent caulae, nisi sordet ephebis
Rustica merx, ceu scabricies et olentia ceno
Esopa. Nil subter saliens coryleta capellas.

10   Iubila pastorum sancto meditata furore
Lene susurrantes, pueri, percurrite visu.
Barbara sublimis sileat compago cathedrae.
Grande operae pretium Latio grege pascua reddent.

B 7   SALILLUM CROTI RUBIANI

Ludere sylvestri si quis non novit avena
Pascere nec simum colle virente gregem,
Fatidico comitem iuveni se prebeat Hesso
Et pecus herboso gramine doctus alet.

5   Hessus ad ignaros venit praeceptor agrestes;
Plurima ab hoc Latium pascua carmen habent.
Primus ab Aonia deduxit rupe capellas
In patriam, tanto pascua digna gregi.
Quae Padus aut magno cantatus Mintius ore

10   Audiit et Siculo terra superba sene,
Audit ab hoc eadem pecorosis Hessia campis,
Hessia, quae cornu divite spargit opes,
Hessia, quae toties stupet hunc superesse Camenis,

B 6   1 Enthea *scripsi*: Nthea *A*.   13 operae *scripsi*: opere *A*.
B 7   1 Ludere *scripsi*: Udere *A*.

[112] For Herbord von der Marthen see fn. 30 at *Laud.* 146.
[113] The Assumption of Our Lady is celebrated on August 15.

Testimonials from a Few Friends

B 6   THE LAWYER HERBORD VON DER MARTHEN[112]

When the holy priests, their hearts filled with God, were
singing the Requiem for Mary,[113] when the Dog Star was ev-
erywhere cracking the parched fields, and the reaper, having
put down his sickle, was merrily enjoying his free time, Hes-
sus showed off the songs he had woven on the rustic loom
and, like the good herdsman he is, counted up all his sheep.
How rich is he in livestock! His profitable paddocks are
filled to overflowing, and his folds will yield rich rewards, so
long as the young people don't turn up their noses at the
country wares as they would at scabies and goats' grease,
reeking of filth. Here you won't find any randy bucks cov-
ering the nannies in the hazel thickets. [10] These pastoral
songs were composed in a sacred frenzy. Look them over,
lads, softly whispering the words to yourselves. Let the
schoolmaster's barbarous lectern fall silent. These pastures
with their Latin flock will be well worth your while.

B 7   A LITTLE SALTSHAKER, BY CROTUS RUBIANUS[114]

If there is anyone among you who doesn't know how to play
the oaten flute or pasture the snub-nosed flock on a green
hillside, let him follow Hessus around and listen closely to
that oracular youth, and he too will soon be an expert at
feeding the herd in a grassy meadow. Hessus has come to
teach the ignorant rustics; a great many pastures possess a
Latin poem by him. He is the first to lead the goats from
Helicon's peak to his native land,[115] pastures fit for such a
distinguished flock. What the Po or the Mincio heard sung
by a mighty voice, [10] what Sicily heard her pride and joy
sing in bygone days,[116] that is what Hesse now hears from
him on her fields rich in herds – Hesse, that pours out her
riches from a horn of plenty, Hesse, that marvels each time

[114]For Crotus Rubianus see fn. 71 at Camerarius, *Nar.* 17, 17; introductory note to Eob.
Buc. 3 (p. 467 below).

[115]For Eobanus's claim to primacy in this field cf. *Buc.*, lim. 5 (n.).

[116]Eobanus's bucolics are worthy of being read in the homeland of pastoral poetry: along
the Po and Mincio rivers in northern Italy (Vergil's birthplace) and on the island of Sicily (the
birthplace of Theocritus).

　　　Carmine cum longo clauserit ille dies.
15　Discite, pastores, pecudes sanare per artem.

　　　Discite. Foelicis gloria ruris adest,
　　Hessus agros novit, pecudes, dumeta, rubosque,
　　　Vellera, caseolos, larda, salita, serum.
　　Scit sanare pecus turpesque avertere morbos.
20　　Hinc febre exangui nulla capella cadit.
　　Denique, quae veteres ovium scivere magistri,
　　　Hessus habet memori pectore cuncta suo.
　　Surgite, pastores. Rutilat lux alma diei,
　　　Et querulae sylvis iam modulantur aves.
25　Surgite. Perspicui lachrymantur gramine rores.
　　　Surgite. Iam stabulis liberat Hessus oves.

B 8　IDEM AD CELEBERRIMUM DOCTOREM ENGLENDRUM, PROTHOGRAPHUM HESSIAE

　　Cur movet Englendrus laeto nova gaudia vultu?
　　　A fato nam se quo tueatur habet.
　　Curia quod nunquam potuit praestare ducalis
　　　Aut quae tot stupidos lingua diserta facit
5　Nec domus ad votum fulvo saciata metallo
　　　Aebria nec mollis murice fila togae,
　　Hoc dedit audaci sylvestris Musa susurro,
　　　Et pastor patiens paupere veste nives.
　　Ergo semper eris, semper tua fama manebit,
10　　Dum nivei pecoris Hessia dives erit.
　　Tempora dum crescent tacito labentia cursu,
　　　Ille tuus magno foenore crescet honor.

B 9　IUDOCUS IONAS

　　Livor, ad exortam te protinus erige famam,
　　　Quam potes, et flammis perge nocere tuis!
　　Nomen habet nullis periturum mortibus Hessus,
　　　Uri famicremae qui nequit igne facis.

---

18 salita *scripsi*: sallida *A*.
　B 8　**1** Cur *scripsi*: Ur *A*.
　B 9　**1** Livor *Kawerau*: Ivor *A*.

at his mastery in poetry when he ends the day with a lengthy song. Shepherds, learn from him how to cure the livestock with professional skill. Learn from him. The pride of this happy country is here to teach you. Hessus knows his fields, cattle, thickets, and briers, his fleeces, cheeses, lard, pickles, and whey. He knows how to cure the flock and prevent loathsome diseases. [20] Henceforth no goat will fall victim to enfeebling fever. In short, everything the ancient shepherds knew, Hessus has stored in his memory. Get up, shepherds. The kindly light of day is reddening, and already the songbirds are warbling in the woods. Get up. Pellucid dewdrops are hanging like tears in the grass. Get up. Already Hessus is releasing the sheep from their pens.

B 8   THE SAME POET TO THE WORLD-RENOWNED DOCTOR ENGLENDER, CHANCELLOR OF HESSE[117]

What is making Englender so happy? Why is he wearing that big smile on his face? Easy. He has found a way to cheat death. What the chancellery of the landgrave could never accomplish nor the eloquent tongue that leaves so many speechless nor the house plastered with all the yellow metal one could want nor the soft toga's threads drenched with purple, that the pastoral Muse has granted with her bold whispers, indeed, a shepherd suffering from wintry cold in his poor clothes. So you're going to be immortal! Your fame will always live, [10] for as long as Hesse remains rich in snowy sheep. And as long as the passing ages keep on advancing with silent pace, that honor of yours will keep on growing with compound interest.

B 9   JUDOCUS JONAS[118]

Envy, don't waste any time jumping all over this star that has just now risen above the horizon. Attack him with everything you've got and keep blasting him with your flames! Hessus has earned an immortal name that cannot be burned in the fire of your fame-cremating torch. Your merciless

---

[117]For Dr. Johann Englender see fn. 4 at *Buc.*, ded.
[118]On Judocus (Justus) Jonas see fn. 41 at *Buc.* 5.

5   Cruda manet frustra genuinum flamma poetam.
           Te nihil in tantum iuris habere puta.
       Est habilis, doctus, facilis, communis, amicus.
           Est probus et fastu turgidiore vacat.
       Prisca greges aetas spissos satis amplaque rura
10   Ferre putabat opes ubere quasque manu.
       De grege dum novit sic noster commoda vates,
           Non haec, sed scripto de grege nomen habet.
       Imbre iuvantur agri botrosaque vinea sole;
           Noster Apollineas adiuvat Hessus opes.
15   Prodit agreste canens Germanus origine vates,
           Abstulit hic nostri nomina prima soli.
       At si Teutonicus scripsit quis ovile poeta,
           Res tamen et versus non meliore stilo.
       Quintus hic est, credo, pavone ex Pythagoraeo;
20   Meonidis venam carmine nosse licet.
       Teutonis ora suo nunc vate superbiat Hesso,
           Dissimulare suum ni velit illa decus.

H4ᵛ   **B 10 IOANNES PISTOR PHILOSOPHUS**

       Si deus Oleniam potuit suxisse capellam,
           Scribere tam sacrum tu potes, Hesse, pecus.
       Pastores, armenta, greges, vaccasque Latinas
           Germani primus ducis ad arva soli.
5   Debet oves, thauros, capras, et ovilia tota
           Teutonicus vates hinc, Eobane, tibi.

22 velit *Kawerau*: venit *A*.
  B 10   **1** Si *scripsi*: I *A*.   **6** Eobane *scripsi*: Eobani *A*.

[119]For this claim cf. *Buc.*, lim. 5 (n.).

[120]Jonas alludes to Pers. 6, 10-11, where Persius mocks the Roman poet Q. Ennius, who dreamed that he was the reincarnation of Homer by way of a peacock: "… Enni, postquam destertuit esse / Maeonides Quintus pavone ex Pythagoreo." (The peacock is "Pythagorean," because Pythagoras taught the doctrine of transmigration of souls.) However, according to an ancient, if erroneous interpretation of Persius's verse, "Quintus" is not the proper name Quintus Ennius, but the ordinal number "fifth." In this view, the series of reincarnations was imagined as follows: Pythagoras, peacock, Euphorbus, Homer, Ennius. Thus, to be the fifth in this series is to be a reincarnation of Homer. Cf. Eob. *Sylv.* 4, 8, 15: "An quintus ex pavone prodis …?" (Are you the fifth incarnation of the peacock?).

flame can go on waiting for a true poet, but to no purpose. Don't think you have any power over such a great bard. He is skillful, learned, affable, obliging, friendly. He is a man of integrity, not at all swollen with conceit.

Antiquity prided itself on its close-packed herds and abundance of pastureland [10] and believed it held every kind of wealth in its ample hands. Since our bard is just as well versed in the shepherd's art as those ancients, he has earned fame (though not the proceeds) from the herd he has written about. Rain is good for the crops, sun for the grape-bearing vine; our Hessus supports the troops of Apollo. He is the first German-born poet to come out with pastoral songs.[119] In so doing, he has won a first-rate reputation on our soil. Even if another German poet wrote bucolics earlier, his subject matter and style could scarcely have been as good as Hessus's. He is, I'm convinced, "the fifth incarnation of the Pythagorean peacock," [20] for his poetry evinces Homer's poetic vein.[120] Now Germany can plume herself on her own bard Hessus – unless she intends to put her light under a bushel!

B 10   THE PHILOSOPHER JOHANN PISTOR[121]

If a god could suck the goat Amalthea,[122] then surely you, Hessus, may write about a beast so hallowed. You are the first to introduce Latin shepherds, herds, flocks, and cows to Germany's pastures.[123] Henceforth, Eobanus, German bards will owe their sheep, bulls, goats, and the whole sheepfold to you.

---

[121]Johann Pistoris of Kirchberg, a friend of Eobanus Hessus and Crotus Rubianus, matriculated at Erfurt in the spring of 1503, becoming B.A. in 1504 and M.A. in 1507. By 1512 he was bachelor of theology and began lecturing at the university.

[122]See fn. 61 at *Buc.* 7, 98-100.

[123]Cf. *Buc.*, lim. 5 (n.).

B 11 EOBANI HESSI VELUTI CORONIDIS ADIECTIO

Vade salutatum vulgus, liber. Ite, capellae.
    Pascua iam vobis liberiora patent.
Ire licet. Nemo vos iam cohibebit ut olim,
    Ledere vicinos cum voluistis agros.
5   Ite per immensum, quando libet, ite per orbem,
    Et si non tellus sufficit, astra patent.
Non sat habet coelum spatii, descendite ad umbras.
    Est eciam Stygio grata capella Iovi.
Sed ne vos coelo fulmen, Styge vexet Erinnis,
10   Terra domus vobis tucior esse potest.
Illic si quid erit raptorum forte luporum,
    Sumite personam, dissimulate pecus.
Non canis officiet vobis quia cornua habetis;
    At leo tam simplex non volet esse pecus.
15   Si corvi crocitent contra, contemnite, nam vos
    Iam pridem fatuas non timuistis aves.
Forte videbimini nimium gestire severis.
    "Nos quoque qui pavit," dicite, "laetus erat."
Fallor, an est aliquis scabie qui dicet olentes?
20   Ah, nihil ex omni parte placere potest.
Ite bono auspitio. Totus mirabitur orbis
    Hessiacum Latio pascere rure pecus.
Si tamen Ocnaeas dabitur spectare iuvencas,
    Caedite. Sunt illo pascua sancta loco.
25   Este verecundae. Sic vos et gloria maior
    Et non exigua laude manebit honos.
I, pecus, i, quondam sylvestris cura poaetae.
    Te precor, in vulgo, qua potes arte, place.

H5ʳ

---

1 Vade *scripsi*: Ade *A*.

B 11   A POSTSCRIPT BY EOBANUS HESSUS, AS A KIND OF FINISHING TOUCH

Away you go, book, and greet the people for me. Go on, goats. You're free now to head for greener pastures. I'm letting you go. Now nobody will pen you in as before, when you were still intent on raiding the neighbors' fields. Go out into the wide world, as much as you like. Go on, and if the earth is too small for you, you can always reach for the stars. If the sky doesn't have enough room for you, go down to the shades. The she-goat is also dear to Jupiter of the Styx.[124] However, just so you're not harried by lightning up in the sky or by one of the Furies down in the underworld, [10] stay home on earth, where it's safe. If you should happen to run into prowling wolves here, put on a mask.[125] Don't let them know you are goats. No dog will block your path, because you have horns. The lion, on the other hand, won't want to devour so simple-minded a beast. If the ravens start croaking at you, pay them no heed. You learned long ago not to be afraid of those idiotic birds. Stern critics, perhaps, will find you too boisterous. Tell them: "The one who pastured us was just as exuberant." Am I hearing this right? Is there someone who says you reek of scabies? [20] Oh well, you can't please them all. Good luck to you, as you depart. The whole world will marvel that Hessian goats are grazing on Italy's turf. If, however, you should have the good fortune to see the heifers of Mantua, give place.[126] The pastures in that region are holy. Be unpretentious. Then you'll enjoy greater distinction and no little honor and fame. Go now, my flock, once the concern of your sylvan poet. Just do me this favor: ingratiate yourself with the public, as artfully as you possibly can.

---

[124]Cf. fn. 61 at *Buc.* 7, 98-100.

[125]The eclogues can protect themselves against malicious critics by hiding behind the mask of allegory.

[126]Eobanus urges his book to revere the two great pastoralists of Mantua: Vergil and Baptista Mantuanus. Cf. *Buc.*, lim. 2, with fn. 2.

SUPPLEMENTARY NOTES

Notes to Joachim Camerarius's
DE H. EOBANO HESSO NARRATIO

1, 1   **Recordanti mihi** For this opening cf. Cic. *de Orat.* 1, 1: "Cogitanti mihi saepenumero et memoria vetera repetenti ...." Both Cicero and Camerarius go on to recall the days of old from the perspective of present-day disaster.

1, 2   **Ut autem – affliguntur, ita** The image is taken from Cic. *Catil.* 1, 31: "Ut saepe homines aegri morbo gravi, cum aestu febrique iactantur, si aquam gelidam biberunt, primo relevari videntur, deinde multo gravius vehementiusque adflictantur, sic ...."
    iucunditatem illam – extinctum esse The memory of past happiness heightens the misery of the present. For the thought see, for example, Pl. *Rud.* 1321; Boeth. *Consol.* 2, 4, 2: "in omni adversitate fortunae infelicissimum est genus infortunii fuisse felicem"; Maxim. 1, 291: "dura satis miseris memoratio prisca bonorum."
    tantam contentionem Cf. *Nar.* 3, 5-8.
    ante oculos – sunt Verg. *A.* 11, 311.

1, 9   **licentiam** Camerarius sounds the same theme in his biography of Philip Melanchthon and elsewhere. See Friedrich Stählin, *Humanismus und Reformation im bürgerlichen Raum* (Leipzig, 1936), pp. 69-70.

1, 11   **Non ratio – verecundia** Cic. *ad Brut.* 1, 10, 3. The translation is by D. R. Shackleton Bailey (Loeb Classical Library).

1, 13   **floribus – apri** Cf. Verg. *Ecl.* 2, 58-59.

2, 1   **nos etiam – gessimus** Cf. Verg. *A.* 2, 89-90.

2, 2   **florentem – ingenio** Cf. Cic. *Fam.* 2, 13, 2: "hominem florentem aetate, opibus, honoribus, ingenio."
    eruditionis atque doctrinae Cf. Cic. *Off.* 1, 119: "eruditione atque doctrina ... ornati"; *Tusc.* 2, 11, 27: "eruditionem liberalem et doctrinam"; Camerarius, *Nar.* 31, 19: "doctrinae et eruditionis suae specimen." Also cf. *Nar.* 2, 4 (n.).
    studiorum similitudine Cic. *Fam.* 3, 10, 9.
    usu ... familiaritatis Cic. *Fam.* 13, 52, 1.

2, 4   **ferebar in oculis** Cic. *Har.* 48; *Phil.* 6, 11; *Q. fr.* 3, 1, 9.
    doctrinae eruditionem This patristic phrase also occurs in *Nar.* 17, 10 and *Nar.* 27, 2. Cf. *Nar.* 2, 2 (n.): "eruditionis atque doctrinae."

2, 8   **Τὸ δὲ – βιάζεσθαι** Cf. Simonides, Fragment 76 (Bergk) and Plato, *R.* 2, 365 c.

3, 3   **mediocris considerationis** August. *Contra Fortunatum Manichaeum* 22: "potest autem unusquisque nostrum mediocri consideratione invenire verum esse, quod dico."

3, 5   **aemulationes** For the plural form see Liv. 28, 40, 10; Vulg. *2. Cor.* 12, 20; *Gal.* 5, 20.

3, 8   **Ἀγαθὴ – βροτοῖσι** Hes. *Op.* 24.

3, 11   **et consiliis et consolatione** Cf. Cic. *Att.* 2, 18, 4: "nec ... consilium nec consolatio"; 9, 6, 5; 11, 25, 1.

4, 1   **te non fugit – literas soleret** For Eobanus's habits of composition cf. *Nar.* 7, 9 and 22, 7-10; Eob. *Her. Chr.*, ded. 3, 2.
    quicquid in buccam venisset A proverbial expression. See Otto 273; Häussler, pp. 53, 70, 161, and 263; Erasmus, *Adag.* 1, 5, 72.

[385]

τὸ ἐπιὸν Plato, *Phdr.* 264 b.

4, 2   **recordatione ... delectatus** Cic. *Fin.* 1, 17: "sapientes bona praeterita grata recordatione renovata delectant."

4, 3   **reconciliationem gratiae** Cic. *Har.* 51; *Rab. Post.* 32; *Att.* 9, 7A, 1.

4, 10   **descriptio et elaboratio** Cf. *Nar.* 17, 18, where "describi" is likewise immediately followed by "elaborationem."

5, 1   **ordiar de tuis indicationibus** In an undated letter (1544?) preserved in *Epp.* 3, sig. E6ᵛ-E7ʳ, Adam Krafft responds as follows to Camerarius's request for information about Eobanus's origins: "Quod ad optimum virum et poetam Eobanum Hessum attinet, valde probo te unum ex multis esse qui memor sit Eobani. Ego quicquid de incunabulis illius meo studio cognoscere potero, ex iis quos illa nosse credibile est, ad te diligenter perscribam." On 1 June 1544 Krafft was able to provide the desired information. See *Epp.* 3, sig. E7ʳ: "Anxie diuque pervestigavi haec quae mitto paucula de optimi vatis Eobani nostri crepundiis et infantia, quae tu pro tua copia non sines esse paucula, sed amplificabis et illustrabis pro dignitate .... Bene vale et perge consecrare memoriam Eobani."

5, 2   **Cattorum** Cf. *Her. Chr.* 24, 53 (n.).

5, 7   **Herodotus** See *Vita Herodotea* γ', in: *Homeri opera*, vol. 5, ed. Thomas W. Allen (Oxford, 1978), p. 194.

5, 8   **patria Homeri ignoratur** Gel. 3, 11, 6 offers a list of the places where Homer might have been born.

5, 11   **in parte aucta aut luculenta re** Kreyssig compares Ter. *Hau.* 798: "in lauta et bene aucta parte." However, all the mss. here read: "in lauta et bene acta parte" – a crux first emended by Bentley to: "in lauta esse et bene aucta re."

5, 16   **Firmico** See Firm. Mat. 6, 30, 23. Like Philip Melanchthon and many other humanists, Camerarius was a firm believer in astrology.

6, 5   **cum ageret – quartum** Krause, *HEH*, vol. 1, p. 16, takes this phrase to mean "at age 14," in 1502. But since Camerarius tells us that Eobanus came to Horle's school in the same year it was opened (1501) and adds later on (*Nar.* 7, 1) that Eobanus remained there for three years ("triennium"), we must interpret the phrase in the more literal, classical sense as "in his fourteenth year" – that is, at age 13, in 1501. (Krause, in fact, does so on p. 15, when he writes that Eobanus stayed in Gemünden "bis zu seinem 14. Jahre").

6, 6   **tradidit – faciendorum** Cf. *Her. Chr.* 24, 97-100.

6, 7   **Ego sum – tenebris** Vulg. *Joann.* 8, 12.

6, 9   **Deus et natura** Cf. Ov. *Met.* 1, 21.

6, 11   **ire per altum** = Lucr. 3, 1030; Verg. *A.* 3, 374; 4, 310.

7, 1   **quasi ad – profectus fuit** Cf. Cic. *Off.* 3, 6: "tamquam ad mercaturam bonarum artium sis profectus."

7, 4   **non tam – animi** Cf. Cic. *de Orat.* 2, 178: "impetu quodam animi ... magis quam iudicio aut consilio"; *Inv.* 2, 17: "impetu quodam animi potius quam cogitatione."

7, 5   **amantissimus ... studiosorum** Plin. *Ep.* 6, 6, 3.

7, 8   **imitationem Ovidianam** For the stylistic quirk represented by this phrase cf. also, for example, *Nar.* 8, 2: "Eobanico corpore"; 15, 8: "congressus Erasmici."

9, 2   **poculorum certamina** For these drinking contests see Konrad Celtis, *De origine, situ, moribus, et institutis Norimbergae* 11; [Eberbach], *Ebriet.*, pp. 140-141.

9, 7   **communem cladem – hominum** Drunkenness was the German national vice. Cf., for example, Walther 10284; 10284a; [Eberbach], *Ebriet.*, pp. 134-136; Eob. *Sylv.* 2, 2, 9-14.

9, 17   **ab axe Boreo** Cf. Ov. *Tr.* 4, 8, 41: "sub axe Boreo." The people who lived in northern Germany and along the Baltic coast were notorious beer-guzzlers. See

[Eberbach], *Ebriet.*, pp. 139-142.

9, 18   **in Platonis Convivio** See Plato, *Smp.* 213 e–214 a.

11, 8   **incunabula doctrinae suae** Cf. Cic. *de Orat.* 1, 23: "incunabulis nostrae ... doctrinae."

12, 1   **volentibus audire** For the sense "students" cf. *Nar.* 18, 1: "discere volentibus."

12, 6   **reliquit – suae** Cf. Cic. *Brut.* 2; *Rab. Perd.* 14; *Ver.* 4, 127; Camerarius, *Nar.* 22, 1: "sui desiderium reliquit."

12, 10   **epigrammatis** Cordus wrote 13 books of epigrams in all, collected in his *Opera poetica omnia* [Frankfurt am Main? 1550?], fol. 99ᵛ-286ʳ.

12, 11   **Cordum – matris suae** This explanation tallies with the one in Cordus's epigram "De seipso" (*Epigrammata* 2, 46), in: *Opera poetica omnia* [Frankfurt am Main? 1550?], fol. 122ʳ: "Autumnale velut sero sub tempore cordum, / Ultimus effoetae sic ego natus eram. / Conveniens igitur Cordi cognomen habebo. / Dii faciant illo post mea fata vocer." More immediately, however, "Cordus" is a latinization of the father's name "Cord" (= "Kurt," "Kunz"). See Gisela Möncke, "Der hessische Humanist Euricius Cordus und die Erstausgabe seines *Bucolicon* von 1514," *Daphnis* 14 (1985): 90-95.

12, 12   **Euricium** Cordus's first name was "Heinrich," abbreviated in Hessian dialect to "Ritze" and latinized as "Enricus" or "Ricius." Mutianus then added the Greek "eu" (good) as a prefix to "Ricius." See Cordus, *Epigr.*, p. 102 (*Contra Thiloninum defensio* 37, 1-2): "Legerat ut Rici versus, 'Euricius esto,' / Rufus ait, 'studii est syllaba prima tui.'"

12, 17   **incitare currentes** For this proverbial expression see Otto 486; Häussler, pp. 72, 151, 235, and 267; Erasmus, *Adag.* 3, 8, 32.

13, 2   **liberalibus – delectabatur** Cf. Sen. *Dial.* 2, 16, 4: "iocis temperatis delectamur."

13, 8   **frui aliorum stultitia** Cf. Erasmus, *Adag.* 2, 3, 39, quoting Plin. *Nat.* 18, 31: "optimum ... est ... aliena insania frui."

14, 1   **quemque ipse – nominat** See *Sylv.* 1, 2, 119, written in the winter of 1509/10: "At tu, Rufe, meae formator primae iuventae." This verse was dropped from the revised version that Eobanus published in 1514 in his *Sylvae duae.*
    Hesse – eris The verse occurs in a poem of ca. 23 August 1506, in which Mutianus Rufus congratulates the young Eobanus on his *De pugna studentum.* See Mutian. *Ep.* 79, line 26. Also see Eobanus's joyous letter of thanks, Mutian. *Ep.* 417, lines 36-37 (late August? 1506, but misdated in Gillert). Eobanus proudly quoted the line in the letter to Posterity that concludes his *Heroidum Christianarum epistolae.* See *Her. Chr.* 24, 104, with Mutianus Rufus's response in *Ep.* 416 (mid-August 1514). Eobanus reminds his mentor of the compliment also in a letter of April 1516 (Mutian. *Ep.* 556).
    sacri gloria fontis Mantuan. *Epigr.*, fol. 117ᵛ.

14, 8   **senecta aetate amarior** Cf. Cic. *Att.* 14, 21, 3: "amariorem ... me senectus facit."

14, 10   **fer patris imperium** = *Dicta Catonis* 4, 6, 2: "fer patris imperium, cum verbis exit in iram."

14, 12   **rebus ... ad victum ... necessariae** Cic. *Parad.* 27.

15, 13   **non quod iniquior – ipsi sibi** Cf. Erasmus, *Ep.* 2446, lines 130-132: "Eobanus in se habet quo sese nobilitet, ut nostra praedicatione vix alii minus sit opus."

17, 2   **illum ... accipiebat ... prolixe** Cf. Ter. *Eu.* 1082: "accipit homo [hominem *mss.*] nemo melius prorsus neque prolixius."

17, 10   **eruditione doctrinae** For the phrase see n. *Nar.* 2, 4.

17, 13   **in quadam – epistola** This letter was written at Stuttgart on 26 October 1514. It was first edited by Otto Clemen, "Briefe aus der Reformationszeit," *Zeitschrift für Kirchengeschichte* 31 (1910): 84-86. In the letter Reuchlin compliments Eobanus on his *Heroides Christianae* and declares that the name "Hessus" should henceforth be understood as a token of his regal majesty: "Ephesiis enim 'Hessen' idem quod 'rex' Latinus dicitur Callimacho poeta Cyrenaeo teste, qui Iovem non sorte lectum esse regem deorum asserit, sed operibus manuum, in hymno ad Iovem hoc utens carmine, 'οὔ σε θεῶν ἐσσῆνα πάλοι θέσαν, ἔργα δὲ χειρῶν,' ubi Hessena summum regem designat. Inter enim aetatis tuae Christianos poetas ipse rex es, qui scribendis versibus quodam potentatis et ingenii dominis eminentiore plus caeteris metro imperas et syllabas quasque ad regulam regis." Eobanus thanks Reuchlin in a letter of 6 January 1515. See *Illustrium virorum epistolae* (Haguenau, 1519), sig. y2ʳ-y4ʳ, reprinted in: Hutten, *Opera*, vol. 1, pp. 453-455.

    ἐσσῆνα This is the form found in Call. *Aet.* 1, 1, 23 (instead of "ἐσσῆνα").
    versum ... Callimachi See Call. *Jov.* 65.

17, 15-16 **Nullo – elegia quadam** Eobanus broaches the same topic in the dedicatory letter to his Luther-elegies of 18 May 1521. It is this booklet that contains the elegy "In Hieronymum Emserum Lutheromastiga invectiva." See *Habes hic, lector, in evangelici Doctoris Martini Lutheri laudem defensionemque elegias* (Erfurt, 1521), sig. C3ᵛ-C5ᵛ.

17, 15   **dentato** Cf. Pl. *Ps.* 1040: "dentatum virum"; Ov. *Tr.* 2, 563: "non ego mordaci destrinxi carmine quemquam."

17, 18   **describi ... elaborationem** Cf. *Nar.* 4, 10: "descriptio et elaboratio."

17, 19   **praeterea nihil** Camerarius seems to have forgotten about *Buc.* 10, lampooning the Dalmatian poet Riccardo Sbruglio, and *In poetam Sarmatam invectiva*, directed at an unnamed Polish poet (Johannes Dantiscus).

18, 1   **discere volentibus** For the sense "students" cf. *Nar.* 12, 1: "volentibus audire."

19, 2   **harum** Burkard and Kühlmann tacitly emend this form to "horum [sc. studiorum bonarum litterarum]." Cf. Nar. 19, 1. The change in gender, however, indicates that Camerarius is now thinking primarily of the "bonae litterae."

19, 9   **sibi quidem – luctuose** Cf. Cic. *Marc.* 25: "'Satis diu vel naturae vixi vel gloriae.' Satis, si ita vis, fortasse naturae, addam etiam, si placet, gloriae: at, quod maximum est, patriae certe parum."

21, 3   **Divitiis – instabilis** The verses that Camerarius here translates (= Solon, Fragment 15, Bergk) are quoted, for example, in Plutarch, *Solon* 3, 2.

21, 4   **Terentius** Ter. *Hau.* 669.
    famae ... fame For this play on words cf. Cic. *Att.* 1, 16, 5: "quos fames magis quam fama commoverit"; Eob. *In Ed. Leeum*, sig. A3ᵛ: "An te sic avidum faciunt ieiunia famae / Ut nisi contingas emoriare fame?"; *Epp. fam.*, p. 207 (letter of 5 October 1538): "famae studens, vix famem a me meisque depello."

21, 9   **rationes ... relatae sint** Cf. Cic. *Pis.* 61: "rationes ad aerarium continuo ... detuli"; *Fam.* 5, 20, 1: "in rationibus ... referendis." The phrase does not refer to some unidentified account by Camerarius, as is sometimes asserted, but to their record of literary and scholarly publications at Nuremberg.

22, 1   **sui desiderium reliquit** For the expression see n. *Nar.* 12, 6.

22, 7-10 **Nihil – versuum** For Eobanus's habits of composition cf. also Camerarius's comments in *Nar.* 4, 1 and 7, 9; Eob. *Her. Chr.*, ded. 3, 2.

23, 1-3 **Cum autem – concedebatur** Cf. Pl. *Capt.* 142-143, paraphrased by Camerarius in a rueful letter to Eobanus, written on 15 May 1533, shortly after the latter's departure for Erfurt (*Epp. 2*, sig. E3ʳ): "probatur ... etiam hac in re id, quod ille apud Plautum ait, tum demum intelligere homines sua bona, cum quae in manibus habuerunt, ea amiserint."

24, 16   **non minus – potuit** Cf. Cic. *Leg.* 1, 2: "... nisi forte Athenae tuae sempiternam in arce oleam tenere potuerunt, aut, quod Homericus Ulixes Deli se proceram et teneram palmam vidisse dixit, hodie monstrant eandem"; Plin. 16, 240: "nec non palma Deli ab eiusdem dei aetate conspicitur .... Athenis quoque olea durare traditur in certamine edita a Minerva."

24, 19   **aetas nostra – incidit** Cf. Cic. *Orat.* 39: "quorum aetas cum in eorum tempora quos nominavi incidisset"; *Fam.* 5, 15, 3: "in ea tempora nostra aetas incidit, ut, cum maxime florere nos oporteret, tum vivere etiam puderet."

26, 1   **patria – civem suum** Cf. Ov. *Pont.* 1, 3, 35-36.

26, 3   **ingenii bonitate** Cic. *Off.* 3, 14.

26, 5   **opus – absolutum** Cf. Plin. *Ep.* 9, 38: "librum omnibus numeris absolutum."

26, 6   **vir pietate insignis** Verg. *A.* 1, 10.

26, 7   **Hoc – labor est** An allusion to Verg. *A.* 6, 129: "hoc opus, hic labor est."

27, 2   **Iocos – miscere** Cf. Plin. *Ep.* 2, 13, 5: "cum hoc seria cum hoc iocos miscui."
      eruditione doctrinae See n. *Nar.* 2, 4.

28, 6   **haereditatem ... adiret atque cerneret** For this legal phrase cf. Plin. *Ep.* 10, 75, 2: "hereditatem suam adirem cerneremque."

28, 8   **scripta ipsius ... declarant** Cic. *Fin.* 4, 78.

28, 9   **epitaphiis carminibus** An epitaph by Stigel in four elegiac distichs was printed in *Epp. fam.*, p. 298.

29, 1   **colophon addatur** For this proverbial expression see Erasmus, *Adag.* 2, 3, 45. Cf. Otto 410; Häussler, pp. 12 and 99.

29, 2   **quodam tamen – exagitatus fuisset** Cf. *Nar.* 34, 11-12.
      arthricis This form of the adjective (for the classical "arthriticis") is taken directly from the Greek.

29, 6   **vitam in terris** *Nar.* 32, 2 (n.).

30, 2   **virgines** To our knowledge, the only daughter still alive in 1540 was Norica.
      In a letter of 10 May 1525 (*Epp. fam.*, p. 110) Eobanus writes that he and his wife now have three children and are expecting their fourth. Eobanus's first and second children were Hieronymus (b. 1519/20) and Julius (b. 1520/21). The third and fourth children must have been daughters, for in a letter of 4 June 1525 (*Epp. fam.*, p. 118) Eobanus reports that "the queen bore another princess eight days ago" ("Regina ante octiduum aliam reginulam peperit"). These daughters seem to have died in childhood, for in a letter of 8 March 1532 (*Epp. fam.*, p. 136) Eobanus laments that he now has "only one princess" ("reginulam enim duntaxat unam habeo"). The surviving "princess" is Norica, mentioned several times in Eobanus's correspondence during the 1530's.
      Norica's date of birth is not known. Krause, *HEH*, vol. 2, p. 105, n. 1, identifies her as Eobanus's fourth child, born in Erfurt in late May 1525 and named "Norica" because of the impending move to Nuremberg. See Eobanus's letters of 7 May (*Epp. fam.*, p. 117), 10 May (*Epp. fam.*, p. 110), and 4 June 1525 (*Epp. fam.*, p. 118). However, since the possibility of Eobanus's moving to Nuremberg did not arise until August of 1525 and the plans were not finalized until October of that year, the name "Norica" does not fit a girl born in Erfurt. Norica must have been born during Eobanus's stay in Nuremberg, sometime before 8 March 1532. See *Epp. Fam.*, p. 136, quoted above. (Her brother Callimachus, incidentally, was born a couple of days before 4 April 1531.) At any rate, in the early autumn of 1532 Eobanus confided to his friend Johann Meckbach that Katharina is now refusing to have any more babies – not because she is too old, but because she has had enough. See *Epp. fam.*, p. 66.

31, 8   **Nubila – dedit** The distich is also quoted in the Marburg University Register for 1538; see Krause, *HEH*, vol. 2, p. 229. As Krause notes in vol. 1, p. 44, it may well have been Mutianus Rufus who first assigned the swan-emblem to Eobanus. Cf. Mutian. *Ep.* 231. In his house Mutianus displayed a set of his friends' emblems, including Spalatin's, Crotus's, Eobanus's, and Cordus's. See

Euricius Cordus, *Nocturnae periclitationis Hessiaticorum fontium nymphis sacrum expiatorium poema* (Erfurt, 1515; here quoted according to his *Opera poetica omnia* [Frankfurt am Main? 1550?], fol. 81ʳ⁻ᵛ): "Pictus habet paries multorum insignia vatum, / [5 lines] / Praecipue condens caput inter nubila cygnus, / Hesseni merito tradita signa viro."

In *Sylv.* 7, 17, 9-12 Eobanus explains the emblem as follows: "quia fama viret nunquam moritura poetis, / Hic viridem laurum sub pede calcat olor. / Haec mihi florentes tribuerunt stemmata Musae: / Gloria nobilior non aliunde venit." An earlier version of the distich, dating from about 1521, is quoted in *Epp. 3*, sig. C8ʳ: "Cygne, quid audaci nimium petis alta volatu? / In stagnis poteras delituisse tuis."

libera Musa *Sylv.* 1, 7, 25: "Libera Musa animos a carmine sumit …."

31, 13   **Vitam – beatiorem** This hendecasyllable is taken from Mart. 10, 47, 1.

31, 19   **invertere in convivio voces** There are several examples of this game in the letters that follow Camerarius's *Narratio*. See sig. F8ʳ: "Pulpa tibi dabitur teneri de carnibus idrut [*turdi*], / Pectora et accedent loripedis sitana [*anatis*]"; and sig. I4ᵛ: "Cuius in hoc versu pudet aedere facta puellae, / Vis verum nomen dicere, dic, 'Arabrab' [*Barbara*]."

doctrinae et eruditionis For the phrase cf. *Nar.* 2, 2 (n.).

32, 2   **breve curriculum vitae** Cf. Cic. *Ac.* 1, 44: "brevia curricula vitae"; also cf. *Rab. Perd.* 30: "exiguum nobis vitae curriculum natura circumscripsit"; *Arch.* 28: "exiguo vitae curriculo."

hanc vitam – vitavit For the thought cf. Cic. *de Orat.* 3, 8; Tac. *Ag.* 44, 5: "… ita festinatae mortis grave solacium tulit evasisse postremum illud tempus, quo Domitianus … continuo et velut uno ictu rem publicam exhausit."

hanc vitam in terris Verg. *G.* 2, 538; cf. Camerarius, *Nar.* 29, 6.

quasi de convivio – discedens The image of death as a departure from the banquet of life occurs also in Lucr. 3, 938; 3, 959-960; Cic. *Tusc.* 5, 118; Hor. *S.* 1, 1, 117-121; Plutarch, *Moralia* 120 b (*Consolatio ad Apollonium* 34).

33 and 34 Meter: Elegiac distich.

33, 1   **Hic situs est** See n. *Buc.* 9, 62.

patria tellure = Ov. *Tr.* 1, 5, 83; V. Fl. 5, 233.

tellure receptus = Luc. 8, 510; cf. Ov. *Fast.* 1, 235.

33, 4   **praemia digna** = Verg. *A.* 1, 605; Ov. *Ars* 2, 702; *Fast.* 1, 678; et al.

33, 7   **saecula – tulerunt** Ov. *Tr.* 4, 10, 125.

33, 9   **Gloria – venit** = Mart. 1, 25, 8.

Post fata superstes = First line of an epitaph by Eobanus Hessus, contained in a letter to Camerarius (*Epp. 1*, sig. F6ʳ): "Si vitam redimit virtus post fata superstes"; and in another letter to Camerarius (*Epp. 1*, sig. K5ᵛ): "Si virtus spectanda foret post fata superstes." Cf. Eob. *Laud.* B 3, 5 (n.).

33, 10   **fama sepulta** = Ov. *Ep.* 7, 92; cf. *Pont.* 1, 5, 85.

33, 14   **Virtutis … opus** Verg. *A.* 10, 469; Luc. 9, 381; Stat. *Theb.* 8, 421.

crescere … opus = Prop. 3, 1, 34.

33, 17   **famae praeconia** Ov. *Ep.* 17, 207; Stat. *Theb.* 2, 176.

33, 19   **Hoc satis est** = Ov. *Am.* 3, 2, 84; Mart. 7, 99, 8.

33, 20   **Corpus – manet** ≈ Walahfrid Strabo, *Carm.* 42, 8 (ed. Ernst Dümmler, in: *MGH, Poetae Latini aevi Carolini*, vol. 2): "Cuius in aetheria spiritus arce manet"; cf. Eob. *Rec.* 158 (n.).

33, 21   **Per terras … fama** Ov. *Am.* 3, 6, 90.

bona fama Lucr. 6, 13; Pl. *Mos.* 228; Hor. *S.* 1, 2, 61; Ov. *Fast.* 4, 156.

fama volat Verg. *A.* 3, 121; 7, 392; 8, 554.

33, 21-22 **speciosaque … Nomina** Ov. *Met.* 7, 69.

34, 1-4   Ἀστέρα – κόνει These lines are modeled on *Anthol. Pal.* 7, 6, 1-4, an epitaph for Homer. Camerarius also associates Eobanus with Homer in lines 11-12 below; cf. *Nar.* 29, 2 above.

34, 1   Ἀστέρα Μουσάων *Anthol. Pal.* 7, 1, 8: "Μουσάων ἀστέρα καὶ Χαρίτων," referring to Homer.

Notes to

DE RECESSU STUDENTUM

Meter: Hexameter.

1-3   **Tempus – incidere** Cf. Mant. *Ecl.* 1, 63-64: "Tempus erat curva segetes incidere falce / et late albebant flaventibus hordea culmis." For lines 2-3 cf. also Hes. *Op.* 387 (trans. Niccolò delle Valle): "maturam incidere messem / Rursus et incipiunt dentata falce coloni"; Busch. *Lips.* 39: "durus cum falce colonus / Coeperit in gravidam messem destringere dentes"; Trebelius, *Epigr.*, sig. B6ʳ, describing a plague during the summer of 1506: "Incidit segetes lunata falce colonus." For the opening cf. Eob. *Pug.* 1-2 (n.). As in *De pugna studentum*, the month described is August. Cf. *Das Bakkalarenregister der Artistenfakultät der Universität Erfurt 1392-1521*, ed. Rainer C. Schwinges and Klaus Wriedt (Jena, 1995), p. 283: in 1505 the B.A. examinations had to be advanced by a month because of the plague, the results being announced ca. St. Bartholomew's day (August 24).

1   **Tempus erat, iam** This construction, with its ellipsis of "quo" or "cum," recurs in Eobanus's poetry. See *Buc.* 8, 36; *Nup.* 169; *Her. Chr.* 7, 45; 11, 79; 12, 123; *Hod.* 65; *Idyl.* 10, 1; *Wirt.* 186; and *Sylv.* 9, 1, 3. For "tempus erat" at the hexameter opening see, for example, Verg. *A.* 2, 268; Ov. *Met.* 6, 587; Eob. *Nup.* 333.

2   **Sole sub ardenti** = Catul. 64, 354; Verg. *Ecl.* 2, 13; Eob. *Idyl.* 10, 56; 17, 4; cf. *Buc.* 7, 133; *Her. Chr.* 23, 44.

2-3   **falce ... incidere** Verg. *Ecl.* 3, 11.

2   **falce colonus** = Mart. 6, 73, 1.

4   **leves ... umbras** = *Idyl.* 10, 2; cf. *Buc.* 2, 86 (n.).

5   **Floruit omnis ager** Cf. Verg. *G.* 2, 6; Eob. *Buc.* 1, 114 and *Ruf.* 6: "viret omnis ager"; *Buc.* 5, 45.

         omnis ager ... sylvaeque patentes *Buc.* 9, 15.

         omnis ager = Verg. *Ecl.* 3, 56; *A.* 4, 525; cf. Ov. *Fast.* 2, 660.

         sylvaeque patentes = Bocc. *Ecl.* 9, 13; cf. Eob. *Buc.* 6, 3 (with note at lines 3-5); *Nor.* 275.

6-7   **arboreis ... Frondibus** Ov. *Am.* 3, 5, 7-8; *Met.* 1, 632; 4, 637; Eob. *Rec.* 179; *Laud.* 166-167.

7   **arbusta cicadae** = Verg. *G.* 3, 328; *Copa* 27; cf. Verg. *Ecl.* 2, 13.

8   **nova ... gramina rivis** *Buc.* 2, 46; cf. Verg. *Ecl.* 10, 29: "... gramina rivis."

10   **Quicquid erat** = Tib. 2, 3, 14; Hor. *Ep.* 1, 15, 38.

11-60   **Annus – salutis** Descriptions of the plague recur in ancient and later literature. See Jürgen Grimm, *Die literarische Darstellung der Pest in der Antike und in der Romania* (Munich, 1965); Thucydides 2, 47-52; Lucr. 6, 1090-1286; Verg. *G.* 3, 478-566; Ov. *Met.* 7, 517-613; Luc. 6, 80-117; Sen. *Oed.* 37-201; Sil. 14, 580-617; Mant. *Calam.* 1, pp. 24-25. Eobanus offers another, much briefer description in *Her. Chr.* 22, 51-60.

12   **virginea ... alvo** = *Her. Chr.* 1, 153; cf. Hrotsv. *Maria* 219 (at this metrical position): "virgineo ... alvo."

13	**Tranquilla ... pace** Lucr. 1, 31; 2, 1093; 6, 78.
	infoelix Erphordia *Buc.* 4, 41; 4, 45.
14	**esse solebat** = Ov. *Met.* 11, 422; 13, 441; *Pont.* 3, 3, 13.
15	**Antea ... quam** For the idiom and the scansion of "antea" (it is to be read as a dactyl) see, for example, Ven. Fort. *Carm.* 2, 9, 38; 4, 25, 14; Locher, *Stult.*, fol. 106ʳ: "Antea quam festis reseratur porta diebus / Ecclesiae, populis uncta taberna sonat. / Ille bibit stomacho ieiuno, devorat alter, / Antea quam templi limina sacra videt."
	loetiferi ... veneni Cf. Mant. *Calam.* 1, p. 24, of the plague: "mortifero ... veneno." For the image of plague as poison cf. lines 20-21, 29, 153, and 171 below.
	vis ... veneni Juvenc. 1, 547: "... vis tetra veneni."
16	**flammantia taela** Cf. line 170 below. The image of the plague-arrows, which also occurs in lines 23, 37-38, 106, and 151-153, goes back to Hom. *Il.* 1, 42-53 and 1, 380-384, where the arrows are shot by Apollo. Eobanus alludes to the Homeric scene in lines 26-28 and 166-169 below; but since the god is to him the guardian of scholars (cf. *Rec.* 50; *Pug.* 55-56), he cannot represent Apollo as an archer here.
16-17	**Minervae Cultores** Cf. *Pug.* 53.
17	**Stygio – furore** Cf. line 105 below.
18-19	**Nesseo ... Sanguine** Ov. *Met.* 9, 153; cf. Eob. *Laud.* 225 (n.).
18	**totam ... urbem** = Verg. *A.* 2, 611; 4, 300; 8, 716; Eob. *Her. Chr.* 12, 47; 21, 93.
18-19	**madefecerat ... Sanguine** Ov. *Met.* 12, 301.
19-20	**atras ... faces** Luc. 2, 301.
20	**vomit ore** Verg. *G.* 3, 516; *A.* 10, 349; Ov. *Met.* 4, 729; 5, 353; *Pont.* 2, 10, 24.
21-22	**virus ... Vipereum** Mart. 7, 12, 7.
22	**sperare salutem** = Verg. *A.* 1, 451; 2, 354; *Ciris* 322; Ov. *Tr.* 3, 5, 43; et al.; Eob. *Her. Chr.* 6, 53.
23	**affixa est lateri** = Verg. *A.* 9, 579.
	lateri – harundo = Verg. *A.* 4, 73.
24	**Una – cuncti** Cf. lines 62-63 below.
	lege ruunt = Ov. *Met.* 2, 204.
	iuvenesque senesque = Ov. *Met.* 8, 526; *Epic. Drusi* 203; Mart. 1, 3, 5; et al.; Eob. *Rec.* 54 and 187.
26-28	**Danaos – Calchas** Cf. Hom. *Il.* 1, 8-456; Ov. *Rem.* 467-474.
27	**altae ... moenia Troiae** Cf. Verg. *A.* 1, 7. For "altae Troiae" see Hor. *Carm.* 4, 6, 3; Prop. 2, 8, 10; Ov. *Met.* 13, 197. For the tag "moenia Troiae" see, for example, Verg. *A.* 5, 811; 9, 144; 11, 288; Eob. *Nup.* 118 and 173.
28	**Chriseida** For the accusative form see Ov. *Rem.* 469.
29	**Urbs luget** = Line 222 below.
	tetri ... veneni Lucr. 4, 685; Prop. 2, 24, 27.
	sanie – veneni = Luc. 6, 457; cf. line 171 below.
31-32	**crudelia – Funera** ≈ Mant. *1. Parthen.* 3, 573-574: "crudelia nati / funera"; cf. Stat. *Theb.* 5, 218-219; Eob. *Her. Chr.* 22, 17 (n.).
32	**filia matrem** = Ov. *Fast.* 4, 485; Eob. *Buc.* 9, 86.
33-34	**aedes Palladis** For this paraphrase of "university" cf. *Rec.* 45; *Pug.* 29; *Laud.* 91; 178; 506; 529-530; *Idyl.* 17, 109: "Palladis arces"; *Epic.* 1, 65: "Palladiam ... domum."
37	**ferit incautos** *Buc.* 3, 39 (of Cupid).
	volat ocyor Euro = Stat. *Theb.* 6, 521. The stormy southeast wind was proverbial for rapidity. See Otto 1867; Eob. *Buc.* 8, 62.
41-44	**Ut esuriens – exitium** For the image cf. Vulg. *Act.* 20, 29; Verg. *A.* 9, 339-341 and Sil. 2, 683-688 (of a lion in the sheepfold).

41 **esuriens lupus** Pl. *Capt.* 912; *St.* 605.
    ovilia plena Verg. *A.* 9, 339; Eob. *Buc.* 4, 44.

42 **Imbelles ... oves** Cf. *Buc.* 1, 108-109 (n.).
    exit ab illis = *Her. Chr.* 10, 67.

43 **Nec – absistit** Cf. Verg. *A.* 1, 192; Ov. *Met.* 11, 531.

43-44 **traxerit – exitium** Cf. *Buc.* 3, 99. For "mortis exitium" see Apul. *Met.* 5, 27.

45 **Magnae – Minervae** Cf. *Rec.* 33-34 (n.). For "magnae Minervae" at this
    metrical position see V. Fl. 5, 504; Eob. *Laud.* 91 and 529.
    domus alta = Lucr. 2, 1110; Verg. *G.* 2, 461; *A.* 10, 101; et al.; Eob. *Her. Chr.* 1,
    19.

46 **ingentes ... planctus** = Stat. *Silv.* 3, 5, 53.

48-49 **nephandas ... coedes** Sil. 10, 585.

49 **tristia – suorum** = Luc. 9, 735.
    tristia fata *Laud.* B 3, 20 (n.).

50 **crinitus Apollo** = Enn. *scen.* 31; Verg. *A.* 9, 638; cf. Eob. *Her. Chr.* A 3, 14; also
    cf. *Laud.* 72 (n.).

51 **nymphis** The Muses. Cf., for example, Verg. *Ecl.* 7, 21, where Servius explains:
    "ipsae sunt nymphae quae et Musae"; Isid. *Orig.* 8, 11, 96; Eob. *Laud.* 253;
    Buc. 11, 14.

52-53 **quos – Fovit** Cf. *Rec.* 230; *Pug.* 10 (n.); *Her. Chr.* 24, 107-108.

52 **docta Erphordia** *Rec.* 218; *Pug.* 10; *Hod.* 34-35; cf. *Nup.* 267 (349; *Sylv.* 1, 1,
    31), of the university town Cracow: "Cracovia docta."

54 **Vota precesque** = Verg. *A.* 11, 158; Eob. *Vict.* 311: "Vota precesque ferunt ...."
    preces ... ferimus Verg. *A.* 8, 60.
    iuvenesque senesque = Line 24 above (n.).

55 **Aerea vasa** Cf. Konrad Celtis, *De origine, situ, moribus, et institutis Norimbergae*
    8: "vasis aeneis, quas campanas vocant."
    Virginis aedes = *Laud.* 170 (the temple of Vesta); 528 (of Minerva).

56 **tollunt ad sydera** ≈ Ov. *Met.* 1, 731; 6, 368; et al.

58 **studiis aptissima** Line 184 below.

59 **Nigris ... cucullis** *Her. Chr.* 15, 1.
    capita alta = Verg. *A.* 1, 189; 3, 678; 9, 678.

60 **spes – salutis** = Claud. *In Eutr.* 2, 276; Eob. *Psalt.* 16, 1; cf. Ov. *Fast.* 4, 538; *Tr.*
    1, 2, 33; Eob. *Her. Chr.* 12, 63 (n.).

61 **ubi – salus** Cf. line 147 below.

62 **Vota iuvant** = *Buc.* 11, 103.

62-63 **omnes – parili** Cf. line 24 above (n.).

64 **dum vita superstes** = Mant. *5. Parthen.*, fol. 123ᵛ; Brant, *Var. carm.*, sig. F1ᵛ
    (*Texte* 121, 5); Celtis, *Ludus* 108; cf. Luc. 8, 28; Eob. *Her. Chr.* 12, 25; 17, 273.

65 **furor ... cruentus** Sen. *Her. O.* 233.

66-67 **Iuvat – Visere** Cf. Verg. *A.* 2, 27-28.

66 **Iuvat ire** *Buc.* 3, 163 (n.).
    patriosque penates = Verg. *A.* 2, 717; Hor. *S.* 2, 5, 4; Eob. *Her. Chr.* 10, 11; cf.
    Ov. *Ep.* 3, 67; Luc. 1, 353; Eob. *Laud.* 558 (n.); *Her. Chr.* 10, 117 (n.).

67 **et externas ... urbes** = *Laud.* 453; cf. lines 122-123 below; *Laud.* 89; 534.
    renovarier Eobanus uses the archaic passive form in an active sense. He does so
    also in *Pug.* B 1, 8 ("tingier").

68 **multos ... per annos** = Ov. *Am.* 3, 1, 1; Sil. 14, 84; Eob. *Her. Chr.* 10, 79.

71 **per daevia longa** = Line 228 below.

74 **Pierides Musae** = Hes. *Op.* 1 (trans. Niccolò delle Valle); cf. Col. 10, 40; Eob.
    Buc. 5, 61 (refrain); 8, 118; *Idyl.* 15, 1-2.
    Phoebi ... sorores As the offspring of Zeus, the Muses were Apollo's sisters. Cf.
    Ama. 36, 3: "Phoebeae ... sorores"; *Venus* 2, 74, where they are called "progenies

Iovis."
75   **iuga Parnassi** Verg. *Ecl.* 10, 11.
    Delphica rura Cf. Ov. *Met.* 1, 515.
    rura tenetis ≈ Ov. *Met.* 3, 2; Eob. *Buc.* 1, 18.
76   **pietate ... insignes** Verg. *A.* 1, 10; 6, 403; Eob. *Luth.* 2, 30: "Insignes meritis et pietate viri."
77   **carmine laudes** = Verg. *A.* 8, 287; Ov. *Pont.* 4, 10, 71; cf. Eob. *Laud.* 574.
77-78   **laudes ... meritas** [Tib.] 3, 7, 3; Sen. *Her. F.* 829.
78   **littora ventis** ≈ Claud. *in Rufin.* 2, 527.
82   **Editus – natus** Cf. line 101 below.
    Editus ex atavis Cf. Hor. *Carm.* 1, 1, 1.
85   **virtutis amator** = Luc. 9, 562; cf. Eob. *Laud.* 129.
86-87   **primis ... in annis Misit** Cf. Verg. *A.* 2, 87.
86   **primis ... in annis** = Ov. *Ars* 1, 181; *Met.* 8, 313; cf. Eob. *Buc.* 1, 35; *Laud.* 557 (n.); *Buc.* 3, 65 (n.); *Her.*, ded. 31.
87   **ingenuas ... artes** = Ov. *Am.* 3, 8, 1; *Ars* 2, 121; *Tr.* 1, 9, 45; *Pont.* 2, 9, 47; Eob. *Buc.* B 2, 33; cf. *Rec.* 103-104; *Laud.* 31-32; 411 (n.); 545-546 (n.); *Her. Chr.* 10, 28.
    Pallados artes ≈ Prop. 3, 20, 7.
88   **Consuluere fugae** ≈ Line 161 below.
    Turba comitante = Ov. *Met.* 6, 594; Stat. *Ach.* 1, 27; Eob. *Rec.* 173.
89   **loca nota** = Ov. *Met.* 7, 353; Eob. *Buc.* 1, 119; *Her.* 1, 3, 69.
90   **procul eminet** = Stat. *Silv.* 2, 2, 83.
    Hessia cultu ≈ *Buc.* B 3, 1.
92-93   **puellis Formosis** Line 188 below (n.).
93   **viris ... doctis** Ov. *Tr.* 2, 419; 3, 14, 1; Mart. 7, 47, 1; et al.; Eob. *Pug.* B 1, 4; *Buc.* B 2, 37.
94   **sic fata iubebant** ≈ *Her. Chr.* 5, 155; cf. Ov. *Met.* 15, 584. For "fata iubebant" cf. also Eob. *Ama.* 32, 14; 32, 28; *Buc.* 7, 16.
95   **visum superis** = Verg. *A.* 3, 2; cf. *A.* 2, 428; Ov. *Met.* 1, 366.
95-96   **tristia miscet ... secundis** Cf. Ov. *Fast.* 6, 463.
96   **Quam subito** = Lucr. 2, 147; Ov. *Rem.* 650; Eob. *Her. Chr.* 4, 95.
97   **bene speratam** ≈ *Her. Chr.* 8, 11; cf. *Her. Chr.* 15, 133; *Max.* 133: "spera bene"; *Idyl.* 17, 198: "Nec sperare potest bene, quisquis turpiter egit."
98   **Quom – auras** Cf. *Her. Chr.* 4, 171; 12, 271 (n.); *Ebn.* 9: "Quam subito in tenues spes illa evanuit auras."
    Quom subito = Verg. *A.* 1, 509; 1, 535; 3, 590; Eob. *Pug.* 15; *Nup.* 174; *Vict.* 425.
    vacuas ... in auras = Ov. *Tr.* 1, 5, 11.
    spes vana Ov. *Met.* 14, 364; V. Fl. 7, 539.
    recessit in auras = Verg. *A.* 2, 791; cf. Eob. *Her. Chr.* 4, 171 (n.).
100-101   **iuvenes – atavis** Cf. Verg. *A.* 7, 55-56; also cf. *A.* 4, 141.
101   **Nobilis ex atavis** = Bebel, "Epitaphium [doctoris Galtheri de Vernia]," *Carm.*, sig. p6ʳ; Eob. *Nup.* 63; 101. Cf. line 82 above.
    sanguine ... avorum Stat. *Theb.* 3, 349; Sil. 4, 720.
    sanguine clarus = Verg. *A.* 1, 550; cf. Eob. *Nob.* 41; *Her.*, ded. 15: "... sanguine clarus."
102   **Illustrans – urbes** = Line 137 below.
    patrias ... urbes = Verg. *A.* 11, 793; Eob. *Her. Chr.* 5, 23; cf. *Buc.* 10, 161 (n.).
    Lupambulus This form – a literal translation of the name "Wolfgang" – occurs also in the colophon of several books published in 1501-1503 by the Erfurt printer Wolfgang Schenck. See Von Hase, pp. 3-5, nos. 29, 31, 33, 34, 35, and 42.

103-104 artes ... ingenuas Line 87 above (n.).
104 **puerilibus annis** = Ov. *Ep.* 5, 157; *Met.* 2, 55; *Fast.* 6, 417; Eob. *Her. Chr.* 1, 155; 10, 143; *Wirt.* 28.
105 **Lernaeo – veneno** Cf. line 17 above; *Laud.* 390. For "Lernaeo veneno" see Ov. *Ep.* 9, 115; *Met.* 9, 130.
106 **iaculo ... acuto** = Verg. *A.* 11, 574; cf. Ov. *Met.* 10, 130; *Fast.* 2, 187.
107 **laetali vulnere** = Verg. *A.* 9, 580; Luc. 6, 723.
108 **Egregius iuvenis** Verg. *A.* 5, 361; 6, 861; 12, 275.
  virtute paterna = Stat. *Silv.* 4, 4, 75; Sil. 10, 277; Eob. *Idyl.* 13, 114.
109 **Languida – grabatum** Cf. *Epic.* 2, 35.
  Languida ... membra = Lucr. 6, 1268; *Culex* 207; cf. Lucr. 5, 887; Ov. *Ep.* 21, 156 and 228; *Pont.* 3, 3, 8.
  invisum ... grabatum Cf. Ov. *Met.* 7, 572 (during a plague): "invisi ... lecti."
  componit membra Verg. *G.* 4, 438.
110-113 **Ac ubi – aegro** For the simile cf. Verg. *A.* 11, 68-71.
110 **viridi ... aggere** = Stat. *Theb.* 6, 929.
114-115 **Multa – Lumina** Cf. Verg. *A.* 1, 465. For "multa gemens" see also Verg. *G.* 3, 226; *A.* 4, 395; 5, 869; 12, 886. For "longo fletu" see Verg. *A.* 3, 344-345.
115 **fundens – questus** Cf. Verg. *A.* 5, 780. The tag "pectore questus" occurs also in Verg. *A.* 4, 553; Luc. 1, 247; V. Fl. 4, 117.
116-117 **fatalia – Munera** = *Her. Chr.* 4, 33-34.
117 **excedens vita** Cic. *Phil.* 2, 12.
117-118 **morientia – auras** Cf. Ov. *Met.* 6, 246-247. For "animam exhalat" see also Verg. *A.* 2, 562; Ov. *Met.* 7, 861.
  morientia ... Lumina Verg. *A.* 10, 463; Ov. *Met.* 9, 391.
118 **fallaces ... auras** Verg. *A.* 5, 850; Hor. *Carm.* 1, 5, 11-12.
  animam ... exhalat in auras Mant. *Calam.* 1, p. 25; cf. Eob. *Her. Chr.* 13, 23 (n.).
119 **Ah, puer infoelix** = Mant. *Ecl.* 2, 81; cf. Ov. *Fast.* 6, 146; Eob. *Buc.* 3, 145 (n.).
  Fata impia = Brant, *Var. carm.*, sig. a7^t (*Texte* 195, 324); cf. Sen. *Oed.* 1046; Eob. *Buc.* B 3, 6 (n.).
120 **iuvenilibus annis** = Ov. *Fast.* 5, 273; Stat. *Theb.* 1, 486.
121-122 **Non – profuit** Cf. line 132 below; *Epic.* 2, 21-22; 7, 55-56.
122-123 **Urbe ... Externa** Line 67 above (n.).
123 **Patrio ... sepulchro** = Hor. *S.* 2, 3, 196; Luc. 2, 732; cf. Verg. *A.* 10, 558.
123-124 **ossa – Componi** Cf. Ov. *Met.* 4, 157. For "ossa componi" cf. Prop. 2, 24, 35; V. Fl. 7, 207-208.
123 **ossa sepulchro** = Prop. 3, 1, 37.
125 **Heu – puer** = Verg. *A.* 6, 882; cf. Eob. *Ama.* 35, 53 (n.).
126 **miseraeque parenti** ≈ Ov. *Ep.* 6, 159; cf. line 129 below (n.).
127 **Quas lachrimas** = Line 224 below.
128 **maternas ... aures** Verg. *G.* 4, 349.
  pervenit ad aures = Verg. *A.* 2, 81; Ov. *Ars* 2, 449; *Met.* 5, 256; et al.; Eob. *Max.* 39.
129 **non – parenti** ≈ Verg. *A.* 11, 152; cf. *A.* 11, 45-46; 11, 152.
  miserae ... parenti = Stat. *Theb.* 9, 357 and 725; cf. Ov. *Fast.* 4, 579; line 126 above (n.).
130-131 **Quom – eunti** Cf. *Her. Chr.* 9, 45-46; 21, 157-158.
130 **complectens – lacertis** Cf. Ov. *Met.* 1, 734; Eob. *Buc.* 7, 149; 8, 67-68. For the tag "colla lacertis" see Ov. *Am.* 1, 4, 35; *Ep.* 8, 93; *Ars* 2, 457; et al.; Eob. *Nup.* 80.
131 **Extrema ... voce vale** Cf. *Her. Chr.* 9, 46; Verg. *A.* 4, 621; *Culex* 384.
132 **Quid tibi – aetas** Cf. lines 121-122 above.

Quid tibi ... profuit = Stat. *Silv.* 2, 5, 1.
forma ... mollis ... aetas Cf. Sen. *Tro.* 1144-1145: "formae decus, / ... mollis aetas"; Ov. *Ars* 1, 10: "aetas mollis"; Eob. *Laud.* 229: "mollior aetas."
forma nitens = Vegius, *Aen.* 274: "Nate, ubi forma nitens ...?"
quid ... profuit aetas Mart. 7, 96, 5.

133   **nunc – urna** *Buc.* 9, 79 (n.); cf. Ov. *Am.* 3, 9, 67; *Met.* 4, 166; Eob., epitaph for Konrad Celtis (1508), quoted in Mutian. *Ep.* 78: "Hac humili doctus requiescit Celtis in urna"; *Her. Chr.* 4, 249.

134-146 **Exequias – quiescat** Cf. *Buc.* 9, 56-63 (with notes).

135   **Spargimus – foliis** Cf. Verg. *Ecl.* 5, 40.
superosque precamur ≈ Verg. *A.* 5, 529.

136   **impositum – marmor** Cf. Mant. *1. Parthen.* 3, 946: "... et tali signarunt carmine marmor" (followed by an epitaph); Ov. *Ep.* 7, 194; *Met.* 2, 326; *Med.* 8; Eob. *Her. Chr.* 4, 250; *Epic.* 1, 110; 7, 99-100; 9, 116-117; *Ebn.* 175-176. For "carmen" in the sense "epitaph" see also Ov. *Ep.* 2, 146; 7, 194; *Met.* 14, 442; *Fast.* 3, 547; Eob. *Buc.* 3, 171; *Her. Chr.* 7, 154.

137   **Illustrans – urbes** = Line 102 above.

138   **Hac ... tumulatus humo** Cf. *Anthol. Lat.* 631, 10: "... hac tumulavit humo."

138-139 **peste – Crudeli** Alcuin. *Carm.* 3, 32, 9: "... crudeli peste peremptus"; cf. Catul. 64, 76.

139   **ante diem ... moriebar** *Buc.* 6, 74.
ante diem = Verg. *A.* 4, 620 and 697; Ov. *Met.* 1, 148; 6, 675; Eob. *Buc.* 7, 142; 9, 21; cf. *Laud.* 502 (n.); *Her. Chr.* 11, 53.
externis ... in oris Luc. 1, 515; cf. Verg. *A.* 7, 270; Ov. *Met.* 9, 19; Eob. *Her. Chr.* 22, 23.

141   **Nunc – cineres** = Bebel, "Epitaphium Barbarae," *Carm.*, sig. p5ʳ: "Nunc trahor in cineres. Hospita terra, vale" (cf. line 144 below!).
cineres As in line 133 ("in urna") Eobanus here hints at cremation (although the word "cineres" itself points only to the state of the dead body, cremated or not). In the next few verses, however, he abandons the antique posturing and – the better to drive home the *memento mori* theme – indicates that the corpse is moldering in a grave, food for worms.

142   **Nobile ... corpus** Luc. 4, 809; 8, 756.

142-143 **putrescit – est** Cf. *Buc.* 6, 77-78.
aesca Vermibus Paul. Nol. *Carm.* 31, 574: "[peccator] erit vermibus esca suis"; Alan. *Parab.* 6, *PL* 210, col. 594 A: "Esto memor quod pulvis eris, quod vermibus esca, / In gelida putris quando iacebis humo"; Walther 4667: "Cur caro letatur, que vermibus esca paratur?"; 4679; 7489a; 8037; 8332; et al. Cf. also, for example, Vulg. *Job* 21, 26; *Eccli.* 7, 19; 19, 3.

143   **Fallax – mundus** Cf. *Her. Chr.* 9, 119-120.

144   **Hospita terra, vale** = *Anthol. Lat.* 667, 4; Bebel, "Epitaphium Barbarae," *Carm.*, sig. p5ʳ (see note to line 141 above), and "Epitaphium Catharinae," sig. r6ᵛ. Cf. Tib. 2, 5, 42 and Ov. *Pont.* 4, 9, 105: "hospita terra"; *Met.* 13, 948: "terra, vale"; Eob. *Her. Chr.* 23, 120.
viator The passerby is often addressed in ancient epitaphs. See Richmond Lattimore, *Themes in Greek and Latin Epitaphs* (Urbana, 1962), pp. 230-237 and 328-329.

145   **dicito** With a short final syllable; cf. *Pug.* B 1, 5; B 1, 15.

146   **aeterna ... pace** Verg. *A.* 4, 99; 12, 504.
super aethera Verg. *A.* 1, 379; Ov. *Fast.* 3, 347; Luc. 1, 678.
pace quiescat ≈ Verg. *A.* 1, 249.

147   **ubi – salus** Cf. line 61 above.

147-148 **rumorque ... Debachans** Cf. line 159 below (n.).

149   Ecce iterum = Verg. *A.* 4, 576; V. Fl. 4, 302; Stat. *Theb.* 6, 802; et al.; cf. Eob.
           Buc. 4, 50.
           protinus omnes = Verg. *A.* 9, 149; Stat. *Theb.* 3, 44; et al.
152   tua chara parens Verg. *A.* 9, 84; cf. Eob. *Buc.* 4, 37; *Her. Chr.* 10, 133.
152-153   Sagittis ... venenatis Hor. *Carm.* 1, 22, 3.
153-154   vitamque – Dispergit Cf. Verg. *A.* 10, 819-820; 11, 617.
           per auras ... celeres Verg. *A.* 4, 226; 4, 270; 4, 357 (all with a transferred epithet
           referring to the messenger's speed).
154   marmore corpus = Man. 5, 612; Paul. Nol. *Carm.* 18, 93.
156   Clauditur hoc tumulo Cf. *Hymn.* B 2, 3: "Clausus in hoc tumulo"; also cf. *Her.
           Chr.* 4, 251.
           virtute secunda = *Nor.* 128; cf. *Buc.* 5, 94 (n.); *Nup.* 41 (n.).
157   Foeminei ... pudoris *Her. Chr.* 2, 45.
158   Cuius – arce Cf. Ennod. *Carm.* 2, 95, 7: "Spiritus aetheria congaudet lucidus
           arce"; Camerarius, *Nar.* 33, 20 (n.).
           aetherea ... arce = *Hod.* B 7, 31; cf. *Culex* 42; Ov. *Tr.* 4, 3, 5; 5, 3, 19; Eob. *Laud.*
           13-14; *Vict.* 333.
159   Iamque – urbem Cf. Verg. *A.* 4, 666; *Ciris* 167: "... infelix virgo tota bacchatur
           in urbe"; Eob. *Rec.* 147-148; *Her. Chr.* 12, 193.
           Iamque fere = Verg. *A.* 3, 135; 5, 327; et al.; Eob. *Laud.* 374.
160   Denique restat = Verg. *A.* 2, 70; 12, 793.
161   Consuluisse fugae ≈ Line 88 above.
           eundum est = Ov. *Ars* 3, 747; Juv. 3, 316.
164   per inhospita tesqua = Jacobus Magdalius Gaudensis, dedicatory poem in
           Erarium aureum poetarum ([Cologne], 1501), sig. A2ʳ; elegy in *Stichologia
           Gaudensis...*, *Naumachia ecclesiastica* ([Cologne], 1503), sig. I 6ʳ; cf. Hor. *Ep.* 1,
           14, 19.
165   semel satis est Verg. *A.* 6, 487; 9, 140; Eob. *Laud.* 379; *Ama.* 33, 9; *Her. Chr.*
           15, 86 (n.).
           Quid ergo = Lucr. 6, 1080; Hor. *S.* 2, 3, 89.
166   Graeca iuventus ≈ Ov. *Ep.* 12, 203.
168   Troiam petimus Verg. *A.* 10, 378.
           Xanti ... undas = Ov. *Met.* 9, 646.
170   taelis flammantibus See line 16 above (n.).
171   Polluere – venenis Cf. line 29 above (n.).
           iuvenilia corda Stat. *Silv.* 5, 3, 191.
           corda venenis = Juvenc. 2, 719; Boeth. *Consol.* 4, m. 2, 6.
172   via tentanda est *Her. Chr.* 17, 267 (n.).
173   turba comitante = Line 88 above (n.).
175   foveis Instead of "fossis."
           circumvallata profundis ≈ Sil. 12, 355.
176   Urbs – opibus Cf. *Sylv. duae* 1, 127.
177   Edera – undis Cf. *Buc.* 4, 40: "Gemmeus ... Aedera"; 9, 40: "vitreus Aedera";
           Her. Chr. 24, 56.
           quam – undis ≈ Stat. *Theb.* 1, 271.
178   obliquos For the epithet cf. Hor. *Carm.* 2, 3, 11; Ov. *Ep.* 6, 87; *Met.* 9, 18; Eob.
           Buc., ded. 9.
179   arboreae ... frondes Lines 6-7 above (n.).
           umbracula frondes = Paul. Petr. 4, 569: "praebebant ... umbracula frondes."
180   Parte alia = Verg. *A.* 1, 474; 8, 433; et al.
           nitidis ... undis = Ov. *Met.* 3, 407.
181   Quem circum = Verg. *A.* 9, 440; *Culex* 397.
           crescunt arbusta Lucr. 1, 351.

182	**redolentibus herbis** = Mantuan. *Ecl.* 3, 185.
184	**studiis ... aptissima** Line 58 above.
185	**Sic visum superis** ≈ Ov. *Met.* 1, 366.
186	**sponte patentes** *Her. Chr.* 1, 178.
187	**tota cohors** = Verg. *A.* 11, 500; Eob. *Laud.* 533; cf. *Her. Chr.* 16, 203.
	iuvenesque senesque = Line 24 above (n.).
188	**formosae ... puellae** = Ov. *Am.* 1, 6, 63; 2, 15, 1; 2, 15, 17; 2, 19, 37 (all singular); cf. lines 92-93 above.
189	**novis ... sertis** Ov. *Met.* 2, 867-868.
	ornant sua tempora Ov. *Met.* 6, 163.
	tempora sertis = Ov. *Tr.* 5, 3, 3; Sen. *Oed.* 430; Stat. *Silv.* 5, 3, 112.
190	**Aoniis Musis** *Laud.* 386; cf. Ov. *Fast.* 4, 245.
	Musis comitatus = Ov. *Ars* 2, 279.
	comitatus Apollo = Sil. 9, 290.
191	**feriunt ... auras** Cf. Verg. *A.* 5, 140; Eob. *Her. Chr.* 4, 213.
	concentibus auras = Andrel. *Eleg.* 1, sig. b2ᵛ.
192	**fatis foelicibus** = *Laud.* 314; *Epp. 4*, sig. F3ʳ (1508): "... fatis felicibus auctus." For "fatis usi" see line 229 below (n.).
194	**culmina phani** = Ven. Fort. *Mart.* 1, 280.
195	**meriti ... honores** Stat. *Theb.* 6, 619; 12, 819.
	solvuntur honores = *Laud.* 158.
196	**lux alma** = Verg. *A.* 3, 311; Ov. *Met.* 15, 664; Eob. *Buc.* B 7, 23; *Nup.* 207.
197	**Partitur – vices** = Sedul. 1, 255.
	preterit aestas = Verg. *G.* 2, 322.
198	**Instat hyems** = Bocc. *Ecl.* 15, 2; cf. Eob. *Hod.* 71.
199	**obruta tellus** Ov. *Met.* 7, 355.
200	**Frigore Hyperboreo** *Sylv.* 8, 20, 25.
203	**Studiosa iuventus** = Brant, *Texte* 172, 1; cf. Eob. *Pug.* 41 (n.).
204	**incumbit studiis** = Claud. *Cons. Mall. Theod.* 65.
	noctesque diesque = Verg. *A.* 6, 556; Hor. *S.* 1, 1, 76; Eob. *Her. Chr.* 17, 257.
207	**Acadaemia sylvis** Cf. Hor. *Ep.* 2, 2, 45.
208	**Laudis habet** = Ov. *Ep.* 15, 30: "Nec plus Alcaeus ... / Laudis habet."
209	**illustrata triumphis** = *Tum.* 7, 139.
210	**Aemula Cecropiae ... urbi** *Laus Pis.* 90: "Quin etiam facilis Romano profluit ore / Graecia, Cecropiaeque sonat gravis aemulus urbi." Cf. Eob. *Laud.*, lim. 3 (n.).
	studiis melioribus = Mant. *1. Parthen.* 2, 68: "Opprime succensum studiis melioribus ignem"; *Lud. Morb.*, fol. 221ᵛ; Tifernate, *Carm.*, sig. A8ʳ (quoted in Eob. *Ama.* 29, 7); Eob. *Buc.* B 2, 33; cf. *Laud.* 25; 433-434.
211-214	**Illic – sylvae** Cf. *Laud.* 159-167 (in Erfurt).
211	**Castaliis ... undis** ≈ Claud. *VI. Cons. Hon.* 27.
	uberrimus undis = Ov. *Tr.* 4, 10, 3.
212	**Pierius ... latex** *Culex* 18.
	Delphica laurus = Lucr. 6, 154.
213	**Aonius vertex** Verg. *G.* 3, 11; Eob. *Laud.* 160.
214	**placent – sylvae** Cf. Hor. *Ep.* 2, 2, 77-78; Eob. *Ruf.* 49-56; *Nor.* 625-628.
	umbrosae ... sylvae = Prop. 1, 20, 7; cf. Ov. *Met.* 1, 693.
	tegmina sylvae Cf. Verg. *Ecl.* 1, 1.
216	**aestivos ignes** Cf. *Laud.* 1; *Nup.* 340; *Her. Chr.* 11, 169; 17, 147. For "aestivos ignes" see Prop. 3, 20, 11.
	colligit ignes = Verg. *G.* 1, 427; V. Fl. 2, 354; Juv. 13, 146.
217	**Arboribus ... redeunt ... frondes** Ov. *Fast.* 3, 237; cf. Hor. *Carm.* 4, 7, 1-2.
	novae ... frondes Ov. *Fast.* 3, 138.

218   **Erphordia docta** Line 52 above (n.).

220   **Candida ... vaela** Catul. 64, 235; Prop. 1, 17, 26; Ov. *Ars* 2, 6; *Fast.* 5, 162; Eob. *Her. Chr.* 17, 162.

         ventis dare vaela = Verg. *A.* 4, 546; cf. Eob. *Her. Chr.* 21, 143 (n.); 22, 139.

222   **Urbs luget** = Line 29 above.

         novae ... famae Ov. *Ep.* 19, 108.

224   **Quas lachrymas** = Line 127 above.

         lumina fletus = Catul. 64, 242; Stat. *Theb.* 9, 601; *Silv.* 5, 1, 32; Eob. *Her. Chr.* 21, 35.

225-226   **diem ... Invisum** Sen. *Her. F.* 824.

226   **Moestam ... urbem** = Verg. *A.* 11, 26 and 147.

         multis – urbem Cf. Verg. *A.* 3, 346; Ov. *Met.* 13, 631; *Fast.* 3, 865; Prud. *Perist.* 11, 27: "... multis comitantibus ibat."

227   **tempora Bacho** = Tib. 1, 2, 3.

228-230   **Hinc – receptos** Cf. *Hod.* 525-527: "In patrios tandem salvi pervenimus agros, / Qua cum vate suo reduces Erphurdia Musas / Nunc etiam dulci gremio fovet."

228-229   **portum ... Contigimus** Sil. 2, 11; cf. Ov. *Rem.* 812.

228   **portum ... petitum** *Sylv.* 2, 5, 3: "...necdum portum tenuisse petitum."

         per daevia longa = Line 71 above.

229   **fatis melioribus usi** Verg. *A.* 6, 546; cf. Eob. *Rec.* 192; *Her. Chr.* 9, 166 (n.).

230   **gremio – receptos** Cf. *Rec.* 52-53 (n.).

         gremio fovet Verg. *A.* 1, 718; cf. *A.* 1, 692; Eob. *Idyl.* 16, 17: "gremio fotum."

         Erffordt clara Cf. *Ama.* B 4, 5.

B 1

Meter: Hendecasyllable.

1-3   **Heroo – boatus** Cf. Sedul. 1, 17-18: "Cum sua gentiles studeant figmenta poetae / Grandisonis pompare modis tragicoque boatu"; Locher, *Stult.*, fol. 94ᵛ: "Verbaque rhetorico ... prolata boatu."

4-6   **Agrestes – precamur** Cf. *Theoc.*, ded., sig. A2ʳ: "Accipe, nec tenuis spernas, Ebnere, poetae / Quae tibi de fundo paupere dona damus."

8-9   **Choas Vestes** Prop. 1, 2, 2; 2, 1, 6; 4, 5, 56-57; Tib. 2, 4, 29-30.

9-13   **Carmina – manebunt** For the commonplace that poetry is immortal see, for example, Hor. *Carm.* 3, 30, 1-9; Ov. *Am.* 3, 9, 28-32; *Met.* 15, 871-872; *Anthol. Lat.* 415, 9: "Carmina sola carent fato mortemque repellunt"; Eob. *Laud.* B 3, 2; B 5, 4; *Buc.* 2, 35-41; 2, 96; B 9, 3-4; *Nob.* 331-334; *Epp. fam.*, p. 216: "Cum aliae pereant annis ab edacibus artes, / Sola manet semper nescia Musa mori." For the related thought that poetry confers immortality on those it celebrates see *Laud.* 61-64 (n.).

9   **pauperes poetae** = *Sylv.* 7, 15, 5.

11   **Quae non longa dies** Cf. Verg. *A.* 5, 783.

         peraedet With a long second syllable, as in *Pug.* B 1, 23 ("Exaedat").

12   **Nec rodent tineae** Cf. Vulg. *Matt.* 6, 19; *Luc.* 12, 33.

14   **Dives – peribit** Cf. Vulg. *Prov.* 11, 28; *Jer.* 9, 23.

B 2

Meter: Elegiac distich.

1   **Quisquis es** = Verg. *A.* 1, 387; 2, 148; 4, 577; 6, 388; Ov. *Met.* 1, 679; et al.;
           Eob. *Her. Chr.* 4, 3; 4, 97; 13, 103; 24, 143.
           aequo ... examine Suet. *Ves.* 25; cf. Verg. *A.* 12, 725.
3-4   **Zoile – abi** For the epanalepsis, so popular in medieval verse, cf. *Pug.* 5-6; *Her.*
           Chr. A 1, 5-6; Ov. *Am.* 1, 9, 1-2.
5-6   **puerilia ... Carmina** Stat. *Ach.* 1, 240.
6   **nasum – habe** ≈ Mart. 1, 3, 6. Cf. Eob. *Laud.* 387 (n.); *Her. Chr.* A 2, 6.

Notes to
DE PUGNA STUDENTUM

Meter: Elegiac distich.

1-2   **Fervidus – Canis** The opening is reminiscent of *Ecl. Theoduli* 1-2: "Ethiopum terras iam fervida torruit aestas, / In Cancro solis dum volvitur aureus axis"; cf. Eob. *Rec.* 1-2; *Laud.* 1-2. For the phrasing cf. Cic. *Arat.* 623-624 (377-378): "Procyon, qui sese fervidus infert / ante Canem"; Hor. *Carm.* 3, 29, 18-19; Celtis, *Am.* 2, 5, 5-6: "rabidos iaculatur Procyon aestus / Et Canis aestivo corpora sole gravat"; Eob. *Laud.* 566-567; *Buc.* 7, 72; *Her. Chr.* 18, 42.

1   **ardentes ... aestus** = Nemes. *Ecl.* 2, 14.

    Prōcyŏn Instead of "Prŏcyōn." Eobanus follows Celtis, *Am.* 2, 5, 5.

2   **ignivomo ... axe** Cf. *Laud.* 211-212 (n.).

3   **solito ... tumultu** = Claud. *in Rufin.* 2, 10.

    tumuerunt bella Ov. *Ep.* 7, 121.

4   **Sophocleo ... pede** Cf. Verg. *Ecl.* 8, 10; Ov. *Am.* 1, 15, 15.

5   **Ut meminisse iuvat** = Ov. *Met.* 9, 485; cf. Stat. *Theb.* 1, 473; Eob. *Her. Chr.* 16, 68. See also *Her. Chr.* 3, 60 (n.).

    victoria maior = Claud. *VI. Cons. Hon.* 248.

6   **commeminisse iuvat** = *Her. Chr.* 22, 48; *Val.* 1, 490; cf. *Her.* 1, 4, 64: "... commeminisse iuvet."

7   **rude ... vulgus** Sen. *Tro.* 67; line 21 below.

    celebrabat honores ≈ Verg. *A.* 12, 840; cf. *A.* 5, 58.

8   **Sacra – Deo** Cf. Mant. *Ecl.* 2, 63: "lux ea sacra fuit Petro"; Eob. *Her. Chr.* 24, 68.

    Panompheo ... Deo Cf. Ov. *Met.* 11, 198, of Jupiter.

9   **consueto more** = *Her. Chr.* B 1, 9.

10   **Quos – sinu** Cf. *Rec.* 52-53 (with notes). Eobanus's pentameter lacks a caesura.

    fovet ... sinu Tib. 1, 8, 30; Verg. *A.* 4, 686; Ov. *Ep.* 19, 62.

11   **carmina voces** For the tag see Ov. *Met.* 9, 300; 12, 157; 14, 341.

13   **argutos ... cantus** Sil. 4, 86.

    fudit ... tybia cantus Cf. Lucr. 4, 585; 5, 1385; Sil. 14, 473.

    cava tybia = Lucr. 2, 620; cf. Ov. *Fast.* 6, 667.

    tybia cantus = Paul. Nol. *Carm.* 27, 80; cf. Catul. 64, 264; Tib. 1, 7, 47; Verg. *A.* 9, 618; Ov. *Am.* 3, 13, 11.

14   **Tritŏn** Instead of "Tritōn."

15   **Quom subito** = *Rec.* 98 (n.).

16   **Tristitia – carent** For this thought see Vulg. *Prov.* 14, 13; Otto 1083; Häussler, pp. 60, 110, 185-186, 240, and 279; Walther 10225; 10599; 10994; Erasmus, *Adag.* 1, 8, 66.

18   **laeticia ... nova** Mart. 8, 11, 4; Eob. *Buc.* 8, 105; *Her. Chr.* 12, 194; 13, 102; 13, 124; *Vict.* 240; 363; app. 1, 23; *Luth.* 1, 6.

    laeticia ... celebrata Vulg. *Esth.* 16, 22: "celebrate eam cum omni laetitia."

19   **subito – furore** Cf. Verg. *A.* 4, 697: "... subitoque accensa furore." For "cumulata" in this sense cf. Caecil. in Cic. *Cael.* 37: "nunc meum cor cumulatur ira."

20	**irata ... manu** = Prop. 3, 25, 10; Ov. *Am.* 3, 6, 36; Eob. *Her. Chr.* 12, 52.
	Martia taela Verg. *Ecl.* 9, 12; Stat. *Theb.* 7, 460; cf. Eob. *Her. Chr.* 1, 190 and *Max.* 114: "Martia ... arma.".
21	**rude vulgus** Line 7 above (n.).
	iners ... turba = Claud. *Cons. Stil.* 2, 79.
	moechanica Note the long second syllable.
22	**nova ... proelia** Verg. *A.* 3, 240.
23	**hastasque verutas** For the verse ending cf. Verg. *G.* 2, 168: "... Volscosque verutos." For the meaning "sharp pikes" cf. Grat. 110-111: "stricta verutis / dentibus ... hastilia."
25	**formata acie** Instead of the more idiomatic "instructa acie."
25-26	**Dorica ... Castra** Verg. *A.* 2, 27; 6, 88; Prop. 2, 8, 32; 4, 6, 34; Ov. *Ep.* 16, 372.
26	**ferus ... Hector** Prop. 2, 22, 31; 2, 22, 34.
	celeres ... equos ≈ Tib. 1, 2, 70; Ov. *Rem.* 788; *Trist.* 3, 10, 54; *Pont.* 1, 2, 80.
27-28	**Tergora – Verberat** Cf. *Nup.* 119-120.
27	**Tergora – crepitant** Cf. Mant. *Somn.*, fol. 214ʳ: "Tergora tensa crepant ..."; Catul. 63, 10; Ov. *Fast.* 4, 342. Hutten twice adopted Eobanus's phrase. See *In exceptionem Moguntinam Alberti panegyricus* 500 (*Opera*, vol. 3, p. 369): "Tergora tensa boum ..."; and *Triumphus Doctoris Reuchlini* 877-878 (*Opera*, vol. 3, p. 442): "dant ... ingentem percussa boatum / Tergora tensa boum."
27-28	**tuba ... clangit** V. Fl. 3, 349; Stat. *Theb.* 4, 342-343.
	tuba ... auras Verberat Cf. Luc. 7, 25; Sil. 5, 189.
27	**tuba ductilis** Eobanus seems to be thinking of a coiled trumpet. Cf. Vulg. *Num.* 10, 2: "tubas argenteas ductiles"; *Psa.* 97, 6: "tubis ductilibus"; Eob. *Psalt.* 81, 6: "Clangite ductilibus carmina laeta tubis"; *Her. Chr.* 1, 186 (n.), of a war trumpet: "curvae ... tubae." The ancient Roman "tuba" or war trumpet, however, had a straight tube. It was the "cornu" or bugle that was coiled.
27-28	**auras Verberat** = Verg. *A.* 10, 892-893 (of hooves); cf. *A.* 5, 377 (a boxer); Juvenc. 4, 375 (a voice): "... verberat auras."
29	**sacras ... Palladis aedes** For this paraphrase of "university" cf. *Rec.* 33-34 (n.). For "sacras aedes" see n. *Buc.* 10, 78.
	venti The past participle is here used in an active sense.
30	**singula verba** = Tib. 2, 1, 32: "... singula verba sonent"; Prop. 4, 11, 84; Ov. *Ep.* 16, 244; et al.; Eob. *Max.* 26; *Her.* 1, 5, 88.
31	**Fit clamor** = *Nup.* 119; *Hod.* 156; cf. Ov. *Met.* 12, 387.
	Stentoreos Proverbial, after Hom. *Il.* 5, 785-786. See Otto 1690; Häussler, pp. 64, 118, and 215; Erasmus, *Adag.* 2, 3, 37.
32	**Quale** An adverbial accusative for "qualiter."
	rapido ... Iovi Cf. Stat. *Theb.* 1, 197: "rapidi ... caeli."
33	**clamore lacessunt** = Verg. *A.* 10, 716; Sil. 17, 386.
34	**rabidis – genis** Cf. Prop. 3, 8, 11: "rabida iactat convicia lingua"; Verg. *A.* 6, 80: "os rabidum"; 6, 102: "rabida ora."
	blactrant ... genis ≈ Brant, *Var. carm.*, sig. A3ʳ (*Texte* 231, 40): "Pollutis blactras verba nefanda genis."
35	**verba vomunt** Bebel, "In laudem Terentianae lectionis," *Carm.*, sig. o2ʳ: "barbara verba vomens"; "Elegia ad Ioannem Nauclerum," sig. r1ᵛ: "talia verba vomunt"; Eob. *Pug.* B 1, 2; cf. Mart. 11, 90, 6.
39	**Scyrona ... saevum** Stat. *Theb.* 12, 577.
41	**Hiis accensa** = Verg. *A.* 1, 29.
	pubes studiosa = *Sylv.* 7, 11, 15; cf. Hor. *Ep.* 1, 3, 6; Eob. *Rec.* 203 (n.); *Laud.* 104-105; *Eleg.* 1, 87-88: "studiosa ... pubes."
41-42	**furores Concipit** = Verg. *A.* 4, 501-502.
42	**rapida – manu** Cf. *Psalt.* 127, 14: "... valida surgit fortis in arma manu"; *Nup.*

	128 (n.): "... consurgit in arma iuventus." For "rapida manu" see Stat. *Theb.* 10, 272; Eob. *Her. Chr.* 18, 56. For the tag "arma manu" see Prop. 2, 16, 42; Ov. *Tr.* 4, 1, 72; 4, 1, 76; et al.; Eob. *Her. Chr.* 12, 112.
	surgit in arma Sil. 7, 591.
43	**enses ... acuti** Ov. *Ep.* 14, 45; *Fast.* 2, 13.
44	**Palladios iuvenes** The phrase occurs also in line 107 below; cf. *Laud.* 533 (n.).
	urget amor = Claud. *Cons. Mall. Theod.*, praef. 10; cf. Sil. 5, 427.
45-46	**furor audaces ... Foecit** Cf. Ov. *Met.* 4, 96; *Fast.* 3, 644; Eob. *Laud.* 247; *Her. Chr.* 8, 112.
45	**iniuria famae** = *Sarmat.* 7: "... Germanae iniuria famae."
46	**immites ... manus** = Prop. 3, 15, 14.
	iussit habere = Prop. 3, 23, 4; Ov. *Fast.* 2, 118; *Tr.* 5, 1, 58; Eob. *Pug.* 58; *Sylv. duae* 1, 56; *Her. Chr.* 10, 140; et al.
47	**miscentque manus** Prop. 2, 27, 8; Sen. *Phoen.* 436; Luc. 4, 773.
48	**Victrices** Instead of "Victores" with the masculine noun "enses."
	ab hoste cruor Stat. *Theb.* 9, 70.
49	**saxa volant** Verg. *A.* 1, 150.
49-50	**densis – humum** For the image cf. Verg. *A.* 9, 666-671.
49	**densis ... imbribus** Luc. 9, 320.
	imbribus aether = Verg. *G.* 2, 325.
50	**multo verbere** Aus. *Protrepticus ad nepotem* 24 (in school); Walter, *Alex.* 1, 385 (of rowers): "... multo castigant verbere pontum."
	verbere ... humum = Maxim. 1, 224: "... verbere pulsat humum."
51	**patulis ... fenestris** = Ven. Fort. *Carm.* 3, 7, 47; 10, 6, 89; Celtis, *Am.* 2, 9, 25; cf. Ov. *Met.* 14, 752; Eob. *Her. Chr.* 20, 103.
53	**suis ... cultoribus** Cf. *Rec.* 16-17.
54	**timidos ... viros** Ov. *Ars* 2, 234.
55	**Delphicus ... Apollo** Enn. *scen.* 361; Cic. *Div.* 1, 81; Plin. *Nat.* 34, 14; et al.
56	**Python tu quoque** Cf. Ov. *Met.* 1, 438.
57	**in ... fugam ... convertimus** Vulg. *Psa.* 88, 24.
58	**timor ... iussit** Sen. *Phaed.* 1089; Eob. *Her. Chr.* 16, 208.
	iussit habere = Line 46 above (n.).
59	**Pallados arma** ≈ Verg. *A.* 8, 435.
60	**molles – manus** Cf. Ov. *Ep.* 14, 56; *Ars* 1, 592. For "fera bella" at this metrical position see also Ov. *Tr.* 2, 360; Mart. 10, 64, 4.
61	**Torva – capilli** See note to line 54 above.
64	**Tutior – est** For the thought cf. Otto 726; Häussler, p. 272. For the phrase "tutior ab hoste" cf. Ov. *Ep.* 11, 44; *Fast.* 3, 424.
66	**clausae ... fores** = Tib. 2, 6, 12; cf. Eob. *Her. Chr.* 2, 64 (n.).
67	**celebres ... triumphos** *Epp. 4,* sig. F4ʳ (25 May 1508): "... celebres felici Marte triumphos"; cf. *Buc.* 4, 52 (n.).
68	**sperato Marte** Cf. line 100 below.
	trophea refers = Ven. Fort. *Carm.* 3, 9, 86.
69	**iam ... decessit Olympo** Cf. Verg. *G.* 1, 450.
	summo ... Olympo = Verg. *A.* 11, 726; Ov. *Met.* 1, 212.
70	**casta Diana** *Laud.* 300; cf. Tib. 2, 5, 122; Eob. *Ama.* A 2, 3 (n.).
73	**vulnus ... ictus** For the idiom cf. Prop. 1, 1, 13: "vulnere rami"; V. Fl. 6, 653: "vulnus ... hastae." The second syllable of "vulnus" is lengthened before the caesura.
74	**viduo ... thoro** = Prop. 2, 9, 16; Ov. *Am.* 3, 5, 42; *Ep.* 5, 106; et al.
76	**promptam ... opem** *Epic.* 9, 62.
77	**festa ... luce** Tib. 2, 1, 29.
78	**Chratifero ... patri** Cf. *Nor.* 1079 (of the St. Lorenz Church in Nuremberg):

"Cratifero sacrum iuveni."

79   **accensis mentibus** = Petr. 124, 283.

80   **varios ... dolos** Prud. *c. Symm.* 1, 75.

      turba prophana = Brant, *Var. carm.*, sig. e3ᵛ (*Texte* 147, 626); Celtis, *Am.* 2, 6, 26: "in medio turba profana foro"; Eob. *Her. Chr.* 6, 156; cf. *Laud.* 384 (n.).

81-82   **iurata ... Bella** Sil. 1, 649.

82   **Bella parant** = Ov. *Fast.* 5, 701.

83   **fatui ... vulgi** = Prud. *c. Symm.* 1, 146.

84   **nomen habes** = Ov. *Rem.* 366; *Pont.* 3, 1, 58; 4, 16, 12; Eob. *Sylv. duae* 2, 200; *Her. Chr.* 18, 118; *Nob.* 336; et al.

85   **Nec mora** = Verg. *A.* 5, 368; Ov. *Am.* 1, 6, 13; 1, 11, 19; and often; Eob. *Her. Chr.* 1, 161; 3, 23; 20, 20; *Vict.* 219; 428; et al.

      correptis ... armis = Petr. 119, 32.

      protinus armis = Claud. *Cons. Stil.* 2, 271.

87   **levis ... Fortuna** Sen. *Med.* 219; Pub. *Sent.* L 4. Fortune was proverbially fickle; see Otto 698; Häussler, pp. 103, 164, and 237.

      incoeptum ... laborem = Verg. *G.* 2, 39; *Culex* 394.

      Fortuna laborem = *Wirt.* 518; cf. Verg. *A.* 1, 628; 2, 385.

88   **certas ... vices** Sen. *Med.* 402; Man. 3, 71.

91   **civilibus armis** = Luc. 1, 44; 1, 325; 3, 313; et al.

92   **Marte – viros** = Ov. *Ep.* 3, 88.

93   **meritas ... poenas** Ov. *Ep.* 12, 119-120; *Met.* 8, 689; *Fast.* 4, 239; Eob. *Buc.* 7, 19.

      Omnibus una = Verg. *A.* 2, 743; 5, 616; Ov. *Met.* 2, 13.

94   **Digna ... tanto crimine** Mart. *Sp.* 12, 3; cf. Eob. *Her. Chr.* 6, 105.

      tanto crimine = Ov. *Ep.* 20, 68.

95   **invidit Fortuna** Verg. *A.* 11, 43.

96   **dea glauca** Pallas's eyes were said to gleam like those of the little owl, the bird sacred to her. Cf., for example, Hom. *Il.* 2, 166, later translated as "dea glauca" in Eob. *Ilias* 2, p. 34; also cf. Hermann von dem Busche, liminary poem to Jacobus Magdalius Gaudensis, *Erarium aureum poetarum* ([Cologne], 1501), sig. A1ʳ: "glauce Pallados"; Eob. *Nup.* 91: "Pallas glauca"; *Her. Chr.* B 1, 40: "glauca ... noctua."

97   **fortibus armis** = Verg. *A.* 10, 735; Ov. *Met.* 1, 456; *Fast.* 5, 587.

99   **collectis viribus** = *Ilias Lat.* 825; Claud. *Cons. Mall. Theod.* 92; *IV. Cons. Hon.* 79.

      viribus arma = *Ilias Lat.* 898.

100   **spaerati ... Martis** Cf. line 68 above.

      copia Martis Ov. *Met.* 13, 208; Sil. 8, 4.

101   **nostrae ... Fortuna saluti** *Val.* 2, 373: "Quem si forte neget nostrae fortuna saluti"; for the tag cf. Verg. *A.* 2, 387; Ov. *Ep.* 12, 73.

102   **nostra futura fuit** = *Her. Chr.* 7, 70.

103-104 **Hos – cecini** Cf. *Buc.* 11, 106, with notes.

103   **palmae victricis** Prop. 4, 1, 139-140; *Laus Pis.* 31; Eob. *Vict.* 441.

105-106 **ego ... struximus** The singular pronoun governs a plural verb.

      Palladia ... arte Germ. *Arat.* 518.

106   **Ōbĕdiens** Instead of "Ŏbēdiens."

107   **Palladii ... iuvenes** Cf. line 44 above (n.).

108   **aeterno nomine** Luc. 8, 139; Sil. 11, 140.

B 1

For the idea that envy is the inescapable companion of virtue and excellence cf. *Laud.* 575-585; *Buc.* B 1, 5-6; *Her. Chr.* 21, 115-116; B 1, 11-74; *Luth.* 2, 57-62; 3, 75-80; 5, 55-66; *Dial.* 2, sig. C3ʳ: "... quae invidia caret virtus, suo nomine indigna est. Semper autem est virtuti comes invidia"; *Sylv.* 4, 9, 8: "Virtuti invidia est comes." The thought was proverbial; see Otto 871; Häussler, pp. 106, 174, and 274; Erasmus, *Adag.* 3, 1, 1, *ASD* 2, 5, pp. 24-27, lines 14-116.

   Meter: Elegiac distich.

1-2	**Zoile – tuis** Cf. Mant. *2. Parthen.* 3, 834-837 (concluding epigram by Franciscus Ceretus Parmensis): "Invide, quid tantum iuvat excandescere, lector, / ...? / ... / Cur iacis in Vatem verba canina pium?"
1	**mordaci ... dente** = Sid. *Carm.* 4, 15: "Non ego mordaci fodiam modo dente Maronem." For the image of detractors as gnawing dogs cf. Hier. *Ep.* 50, 1: "libros ... canino dente rodere"; *Apologia contra Rufinum* 2, 27 (*CCSL* 79, p. 65; *Praef. in Paral.*): "obtrectatoribus meis ..., qui canino dente me rodunt."
1-2	**latras ... verba canina** Ov. *Ib.* 230.
1	**latras dente** Eobanus mixes two familiar images: Envy as a barking dog and the tooth of Envy. He also links them in line 17 below and in *Laud.* 575-578, where "latrator Anubis" is combined with "morsu iniquo" and "rodere versus." For the first image see Otto 316; Häussler, pp. 53, 98, 234, and 264; Eob. *Her. Chr.* B 1, 59; for the second image see Otto 507; Häussler, pp. 55, 100, 152-153, and 268; Eob. *Buc.* B 1, 5-6; *Her. Chr.* B 1, 11-12; *Hymn.* B 14, 1: "Invide, si mordes ...."
2	**vomis ... verba** *Pug.* 35 (n.).
3	**dentes acuis** Hor. *Carm.* 3, 20, 10; [Tib.] 3, 9, 3; Sen. *Phaed.* 346; cf. Verg. *G.* 3, 255. Eobanus mixes his images here too, for it is boars that were thought to whet their tusks before they start fighting.
	latrator Anubis = Verg. *A.* 8, 698; Ov. *Met.* 9, 690; Eob. *Laud.* 215; 575.
4	**doctos ... viros** *Rec.* 93 (n.).
5	**immundae ... cloacae** ≈ Prud. *Psych.* 722.
	versato For the short final syllable cf. line 15 below ("cohibeto"); *Rec.* 145 ("dicito").
6	**siste ... pedem** Ov. *Rem.* 80.
8	**vitreo ... amne** Ov. *Ep.* 15, 157. The epithet "vitreus" is conventionally applied to rivers and streams. See also, for example, Verg. *A.* 7, 759; Aus. *Mosella* 28; Eob. *Laud.* 249; *Ama.* 32, 33; *Buc.* 2, 6; 9, 40; *Her. Chr.* A 3, 10; 15, 74; 24, 56.
	tingier Eobanus uses the archaic passive form in an active sense. He does so also in *Rec.* 67 ("renovarier").
9	**Cecropiae ... Minervae** = Luc. 3, 306; Mart. 1, 39, 3; 7, 32, 3.
10	**ignavum ... pecus** = Brant, *Var. carm.*, sig. C2ᵛ (*Texte* 118, 6), referring to the Jews; Eob. *Her. Chr.* 1, 108; cf. Verg. *G.* 4, 168; *A.* 1, 435.
12	**Noctua** Cf. *Buc.* 10, 30-31 (n.).
15	**Improba lingua** Mart. 2, 61, 2 (in an obscene sense); Brant, *Var. carm.*, sig. A2ᵛ (*Texte* 231, 18); Eob. *Buc.* 10, 58.
	lingua, sile Ov. *Pont.* 2, 2, 59.
	Tantos ... furores Verg. *A.* 4, 501.
	cohibeto furores ≈ Sil. 11, 98.
16	**laceret ... labra proterva** = Brant, *Var. carm.*, sig. A4ᵛ (*Texte* 231, 124): "Haec [volucris] laceret rostro labra proterva suo."
	rabidus ... canis ≈ Ov. *Ars* 2, 374.
17	**dente ... minaci** Ven. Fort. *Mart.* 3, 332: "...latratu et dente minaci."
	dente oblatrare Cf. line 1 above (n.).

19	**Cornua torva** Luc. 1, 612.
	impinget Eobanus plays on two possible senses of the word: "fix onto" (*in* + *pango*) and "paint onto" (*in* + *pingo*).
20	**tempora trunca** Ov. *Ep.* 9, 140.
22	**rhaecia frangit aper** Cf. Hor. *Carm.* 1, 1, 28; Eob. *Laud.* 366-367. For the spelling "rhaecia" instead of "retia" cf. *Laud.* 367 (*Ama.* 35, 45; *Buc.* 3, 146): "Rhetia."
23-25	**Exaedat – Licambes** The model is Brant, *Var. carm.*, sig. A4ᵛ (*Texte* 231, lines 123-124 and 139-140): "Quaeque Promethaeo volucris Tytiove coheret, / Haec laceret rostro labra proterva suo. / [...] / Postmodo (ni cesses) in te mihi saevus iambus / Ibit et Archilocho me experiere parem."
23	**Exaedat** Note the long second syllable of "exaedat" ("exedat"). For the metrical error cf. *Rec.* B 1, 11 ("peraedet").
	volucris ... Promethei ≈ Verg. *Ecl.* 6, 42.
25	**vitam diffunde** Cf. Verg. *A.* 10, 908.
26	**garrula lingua** = Ov. *Am.* 2, 2, 44; [Tib.] 4, 13, 20.

DE LAUDIBUS ET PRAECONIIS INCLITI GYMNASII
APUD ERPHORDIAM

Liminary poem

This epigram was first edited by Eduard Böcking in: Hutten, *Opera*, vol. 1, pp. 4-5.
Meter: Elegiac distich.

1	**multis ... oris** = Verg. *A.* 7, 564.
3	**Caecropiis ... Athenis** ≈ *Aetna* 582; *Anthol. Lat.* 407, 1; Eob. *Her. Chr.* 17, 65; cf. *Rec.* 210 (n.).
4	**Phoebe comose** *Priap.* 36, 2; cf. Eob. *Laud.* 72 (n.).
5	**Urbis Alexandri** = *Her. Chr.* 4, 35; cf. Ov. *Tr.* 1, 2, 79. Alexander the Great founded Alexandria in 332 BC.
	veneranda palacia = Ven. Fort. 7, 7, 65; 7, 16, 25; cf. Mart. 1, 70, 5.
9	**Thurignae – est** Brant, *Var. carm.*, sig. i4ʳ (*Texte* 194, 28), referring to Erfurt: "Thurignae gentis ... caput et domina est." For the spelling "Thurignae" (rather than "Thuringae") see also Brant, *Var. carm.*, sig. e5ʳ (*Texte* 60, 61): "... Phrisiique, Turigni"; Eob. *Orat.*, lim. 7: "... nova Thurignae surgit domus accola Gherae."
12	**puer ... senex** On the topos "Boy and old man" see Curtius, *ELLMA*, pp. 98-101; Eob. *Laud.* 151; B 3, 10; B 5, 1.
	carminis arte Hor. *Ep.* 1, 19, 27.
	arte senex = Ov. *Ib.* 262; Claud. *Carm. minora* 51, 6.

Dedicatory letter

1-2	**Plutarchus – elargiretur** See Plutarch, *Moralia* 174 a. A variation on the story, in which the king graciously accepts a drink of water from a poor man, occurs in Plutarch's dedicatory letter to Emperor Trajan (*Moralia* 172 b). There Plutarch introduces the anecdote to excuse himself for dedicating so small a work to so great a man. Eobanus uses it for the same purpose in the dedication of his *Hymnus paschalis* (1515). Another humanist who tells the anecdote to ingratiate himself with an important patron is Desiderius Erasmus. See *Ep.* 104, lines 48-55 (= *Carm.* 4, ded., *ASD* 1, 7, p. 102, lines 41-47).
1	**humanitatis indicium** V. Max. 5, 1, 1b.
	alacri dantis voluntate Cf. the proverbial "Bis dat, qui cito dat"; Otto 248; Häussler, pp. 70, 97, 140, and 233; Erasmus, *Adag.* 1, 8, 91.
3	**animuli** The word is otherwise found only in the vocative, as a term of endearment.
5	**nihil prorsus – accesserit** Cf. Konrad Celtis, *De origine, situ, moribus, et institutis Norimbergae* 1: "ad vestrae felicitatis cumulum nihil ego ... accedere posse existimavi."
7	**si quid – cognoscam** The model is Cic. *Arch.* 1; cf. Eob. *Nup.*, ded. 12; *Her. Chr.*, ded. 8, 8 (n.).
8	**ex aliqua, licet exigua parte** *Ama.* 20, 6; *Sylv. duae*, ded. 7.
	ineptias An expression of affected modesty; cf. Mart. 11, 1, 14; Plin. *Ep.* 9, 25, 1.

studiorum antistitem Pomponius Porphyrio, *Ars*, praef. 4: "poeta, et studiorum liberalium antistes"; cf. Cic. *de Orat.* 1, 202: "eius artis antistes"; Sen. *Dial.* 10, 14, 5: "antistites bonarum artium"; Eob. *Ama.* 20, 3: "prisci illi literarum antistites." The idea of using "antistes" for a patron of the arts who happens to be a priest occurs also in Erasmus, *Ep.* 49, lines 57-58 (published in 1497), referring to Robert Gaguin, general of the Trinitarian order: "litterarum parente, antistite, principe"; and *Carm.* 35, 1-2 (published in January 1507), thanking a priest for a gift: "Antistes sacer elegantiorum ac / Princeps ... literarum."

9   **Quas – precor** Cf. Mant. *Ecl.*, ded.: "Hoc [carmen tibi] ... dono, ut, quando tetricis illis philosophiae ac theologiae lucubrationibus quibus assidue vacas fatigatus fueris, habeas iucundulam hanc lectiunculam qua tamquam ludo quodam blandulo sed liberali lassum legendo reparetur ingenium"; Eob. *Her.* 3, 4, 5-6: "Aspice, si qua potes praegrandibus ocia curis / Furari"; *Wirt.*, ded. 33-34: "Tu quoque, curarum si quando a mole vacabis / Atque aliud quod agas non erit, ista leges"; *Epp. fam.*, p. 61: "... tibi quos nuper dedimus, Ficine, libellos, / Cum sinet hoc vacui temporis hora, leges"; *Idyl.*, 2. ded. 85-88: "Tu, Ficine, tuae gentis decus, ista videbis, / Si quando a curis ocia liber ages. / Liber ab illustris curarum mole Philippi, / Quod tibi tam raro vix datur, ista leges"; *Sylv.* 6, 9, 23-24: "Ocia sed multo furari pauca labori / Si potes, haec Hesso da, Megabucche, tuo."

11   **Ego – accingar** Cf. Erasmus, *Ep.* 177, lines 101-103 (at the end of the dedicatory letter to *Aliquot declamatiunculae*, written in 1503, but not published until 1519): "Quod si cognoverimus haec nostra praeludia et quasi primicias tibi non displicuisse, tum tuo iudicio tuaque authoritate freti magno animo ad maiora accingemur"; Eob. *Buc.*, ded. 37-38; *Idyl.* 16, 176-177: "Carmina deinde tibi meliora canemus et urbi, / Postquam haec quae dedimus non displicuisse sciemus."

12   **unicum – refugium** Cf. *Ama.* 14, 6: "unicum meae iuventutis refugium."
     tenuitatis refugium Cf. Vulg. *Psa.* 9 A, 10: "refugium pauperi."

13   **Ex caenobio nostro litterario** Cf. Celtis, *Am.*, ded., concluding paragraph: "ex Nurmberga diversorio nostro litterario."

De laudibus

Meter: Hexameter.

tit.   **Deo Optimo Maximo** Cf. the standard cult title of Jupiter, "Optimus Maximus," which the Christian humanists liked to apply to Christ or God.

1-3   **Tercia – Erphordia** Cf. *Buc.* 7, 1-2.

1   **Tercia – aestus** Cf. *Rec.* 216 (n.) and *Pug.* 1-2 (n.). For "tercia messis" see Ov. *Ep.* 6, 57. For the time expression cf. also Mart. 1, 101, 4; 4, 78, 1; et al.; Eob. *Buc.* 4, 82; 9, 3; 9, 52; *Her. Chr.* 7, 27; 7, 53; *Hod.* 31; *Sylv.* 1, 4, 19.

2   **fugit hyems** = *Anthol. Lat.* 227, 1; cf. Ov. *Ars* 3, 186; Mart. 10, 51, 2; Eob. *Ruf.* 1 (*Vict.*, ded. 1): "Fugit hyems. Abiere nives."

4   **dignas ... grates** Verg. *A.* 1, 600; 2, 537.

4-5   **resonantia ... Carmina** = *Culex* 147; *Ilias Lat.* 884.

5   **diversa per** = Verg. *A.* 4, 163.

7   **florentibus ... sylvis** Cf. *Epp. fam.*, p. 184, a letter of 28 January 1537 in which Eobanus refers to an expanded edition of his *Sylvarum libri VI*: "Sylvae nostrae futura aestate reflorescent et regerminabunt in hoc Martiburgensi solo."

8   **promissio** A prosaic word, used here with a short final syllable.

10   **Parturient – ridebimus** Cf. Hor. *Ars* 139.

12   **flamma propiore** = Ov. *Ep.* 18, 177; *Met.* 3, 372.

12-13   **canenti ... fave** Cf. Ov. *Fast.* 4, 723; V. Fl. 1, 11.

13   **Phoebe, fave** = Tib. 2, 5, 1; 3, 10, 19. The Phoebus addressed here is Christ, the "Christian Apollo." Cf. Eob. *Laud.* 375; 395; B 4, 2: "Catholicus ... Apollo"; *Ama.* 35, 113; *Buc.* 3, 13-14; 8, 119-121 (n.); 10, 41; 11, 16-22 (n.); *Vict.* 1-7; 275-281; *Luth.* 5, 17-18; *Idyl.* 2, 84: "maxime Apollo"; *Sylv.* 1, 10, 2-3; 1, 10, 19-20. Also cf. Erasmus, *Carm.* 36, 5: "Unicus ille [*sc.* Christus] mihi venae largitor Apollo." In some later poems Eobanus calls on "Christus Apollo"; see, for example, *Sylv.* 1, 11, 6; 3, 8, 94; 5, 47, 18. Cf. *Nup.* 1-4, where he rejects Phoebus's inspiration and prefers to be inspired by Christ. This posture is common in Christian poetry since Juvenc., praef. 25-27.

     montibus arcis For the hexameter close cf. Verg. *A.* 6, 774.

13-14   **arcis Ethereae** *Rec.* 158 (n.). The image of the "citadel of heaven" is so conventional that Eobanus does not notice the incongruity with "montibus."

15   **Elegi molles** Ov. *Pont.* 3, 4, 85; Eob. *Nup.* 363. Elegiac verse is traditionally "tender," as opposed to the "hard" epic hexameter. Here, however, the epithet "mollis" means "erotic"; cf. Prop. 1, 7, 19; 2, 1, 2; Ov. *Tr.* 2, 307; 2, 349; Mart. 12, 43, 4; Eob. *Nup.* 12; *Her. Chr.* 17, 129; *Idyl.* 10, 29: "mollia carmina."

17   **missam ... salutem** = Ov. *Pont.* 1, 8, 1; 3, 2, 1; cf. *Ep.* 6, 8; 19, 1-2; Eob. *Her. Chr.* 5, 1.

18-19   **turpem ... Venerem** [Sen.] *Oct.* 191; 433.

19-20   **Res – Pectine** A lofty theme demands a style and meter of equal loftiness. Cf. Hor. *Carm.* 4, 2, 33-34; Ov. *Met.* 10, 150; Eob. *Laud.* 454-455; *Vict.*, ded. 24: "Fas erat assueto tangere maius ebur"; *Idyl.* 16, 165: "sublimia plectra." For the phrasing and thought cf. also Verg. *Ecl.* 4, 1.

21   **veteres ... Athenas** Luc. 5, 52; Aus. *Mosella* 388; cf. line 84 below (n.).

22   **Academiaci** Instead of "Academici."

23   **Ausoniae ... gentis** = Sil. 3, 709; cf. Ov. *Met.* 15, 646-647; *Tr.* 5, 2, 48.

24   **Germanus ... orbis** *Epic. Drusi* 391.

     possidet orbis = Ov. *Met.* 7, 59.

25   **Quicquid – Latium** = Trebelius, *Epigr.*, sig. C4ᵛ, poem to Eobanus Hessus (ca. summer 1508): "Quicquid habet Latium, quicquid sacrata Poesis / Continet, ut digytos, Hesse poeta, sapis"; cf. line 97 below.

     studii melioris Cf. *Rec.* 210 (n.).

28   **Arma inter** = Verg. *A.* 7, 453; Sil. 17, 279.

     numen utrumque Ov. *Fast.* 3, 292; 5, 574.

29   **Armigerae ... Minervae** Minerva (Athena) sprang fully armed from the head of Jupiter (Zeus). For the phrase cf. Ov. *Am.* 2, 6, 35 (*Met.* 14, 475; et al.): "armiferae ... Minervae."

31-32   **artes ... Ingenuae** *Rec.* 87 (n.).

31   **crescunt – annis** Cf. Poliziano, *Eleg.* 1, 5: "At tenerae crescent vires crescentibus annis"; Eob. *Laud.* 64; *Buc.* 1, 36-37; *Hod.* 219: "regna tuis crescant crescentibus annis"; *Nor.* 938-939: "crescentibus annis / Crescit"; 1074-1075: "crescentibus annis / Crescere." For the tag "crescentibus annis" see Ov. *Ars* 1, 61; Mart. 1, 88, 1.

32-37   **Nostras – venerabile** For this pride in the achievements of Renaissance Germany cf. Brant, *Var. carm.*, sig. l 8ᵛ (*Texte* 228, 31-36): "Iampridem incoepit doctos nutrire Platones / Theutonia. Invenies mox quoque Maeonidas. / [*2 lines*] / Iam Cicero in nostra reperitur gente Maroque, / Novimus Ascraei et caecucientis opes"; Eob. *Idyl.* 14, 70-75: "sic rediere Latinae / Et Graiae splendore novo sua tempora Musae / Lustrantes, ut iam doctas spes esset Athenas / Huc migraturas et magnae nomina Romae / Virgiliosque viderentur magnosque daturae / Meonidas, Demosthenas, et claros Ciceronas."

35 **Ausonias ... ad urbes** Hor. *Carm.* 4, 4, 56; cf. Verg. *A.* 7, 104-105.
 secum transferret Ov. *Fast.* 6, 428.

40 **oriens e montibus** = *Sylv. duae* 1, 61.

45-46 **Quid – ambages** Cf. Lucr. 6, 919 and 1081; Hor. *Ep.* 1, 7, 82-83; Ov. *Met.* 3, 692; 4, 476; Eob. *Laud.* 467-468; *Her. Chr.* 13, 55 (n.); 21, 15 (n.).

46 **Volvor in ambages** Cf. line 474 below.

49 **Teutonicas ... urbes** Line 69 below.
 inter tot ... urbes Line 415 below.

50 **tantae molis** Verg. *A.* 1, 33; Luc. 6, 483.

50-51 **habenas Flectitis** Verg. *A.* 12, 471; Ov. *Met.* 2, 169; et al.

51 **insignes ... viri** *Buc.* B 2, 36 (n.).

52 **Este ... faciles** Ov. *Am.* 2, 16, 52; *Ars* 1, 617.

56 **Quid loquar** = Verg. *Ecl.* 6, 74; Ov. *Ep.* 19, 39; *Tr.* 2, 399; Eob. *Nup.* 190; *Sylv. duae* 1, 109; et al.; cf. Verg. *A.* 4, 595; Eob. *Buc.* 7, 158.
 sancti ... senatus = *Nor.* 69 and 750; cf. Verg. *A.* 1, 426; Ov. *Pont.* 4, 9, 17.

58 **magnates populi** Vulg. *Eccli.* 33, 19.

59 **carminibus nostris** = Verg. *A.* 7, 733; Eob. *Nor.* 461.

61 **Res – agitur** Cf. Hor. *Ep.* 1, 18, 84.

61-64 **Notissima – Minerva** For the commonplace that poetry confers immortality on those it celebrates see, for example, Tib. 1, 4, 63-66; Prop. 3, 2, 17-26; Hor. *Carm.* 4, 8, 22-28; Ov. *Am.* 1, 10, 61-62; 3, 9, 29-32; Curtius, *ELLMA*, pp. 476-477; Eob. *Laud.* B 1, 1-16; *Buc.* 9, 67-68; *Idyl.* 13, 90-97; *Her. Chr.*, ded. 4, 3; *Her. Chr.* 21, 33-34; *Her.*, ded. 25; 109-110. For the related commonplace that poetry itself is immortal see *Rec.* B 1, 9-13 and note.

62 **tot iam – annis** Cf. line 505 below (n.); *Her. Chr.* 14, 95 (16, 275; *Hod.* 471): "tot euntibus annis." For the proverbial thought that time flies see *Her. Chr.* 17, 55 (n.).

63 **Gloria – diebus** Cf. *Culex* 38: "gloria perpetuum lucens, mansura per aevum"; Alcuin, *Carm.* 76, 1, 21: "Praemia perpetuis semper mansura diebus"; Eob. *Laud.* B 1, 15-16; *Buc.* 8, 56; *Nor.* 970: "Gloria perpetuis non interitura diebus." For "perpetuis diebus" cf. also *Her. Chr.* 17, 64 (n.).

64 **crescet crescente** Cf. line 31 above (n.).

65-66 **Quae – vates** Cf. Cic. *de Orat.* 1, 115.

65 **faciles ... Camenae** = *Buc.* 7, 97; *Epic.* 2, 51; *Sylv.* 5, 36, 9; cf. Filetico, *Theoc.* 1, 64: "Ite, meae Musae, faciles huc ite Camoenae"; Eob. *Buc.* 5, 66 (refrain); line 163 below (n.).

68 **Ausonis ora, vale** The phrase comes from Mutian. *Ep.* 79 (ca. 23 August 1506), where it is used to compliment Eobanus on his poetry. For "Ausonis ora" see also Ov. *Fast.* 2, 94; line 408 below.

69 **Urbes Teutonicae** Line 49 above.

70 **me iudice** = Hor. *Ars* 244; Ov. *Met.* 2, 428; 10, 613.

71 **Sic stat sentencia** = Ov. *Met.* 1, 243.

72 **soror ... pulcherrima Phoebi** Ov. *Ep.* 11, 45, where the phrase refers to the moon-goddess Phoebe; cf. Eob. *Vict.* 88: "soror aurea Phoebi" (Phoebe).
 intonsi Apollo's locks, traditionally unshorn, are a sign of his ageless youth. See, for example, Hor. *Carm.* 1, 21, 2; *Epod.* 15, 9; Tib. 1, 4, 38; Ov. *Met.* 1, 564; cf. Eob. *Rec.* 50 (n.); *Laud.*, lim. 4 (n.).

73 **mutato ... nomine** = Catul. 62, 35; Sil. 2, 647; cf. Hor. *S.* 1, 1, 69; Ov. *Met.* 9, 487; *Fast.* 3, 476; lines 250-251 below.

74 **Iove nata** = Ov. *Met.* 5, 297; 6, 51.

76 **Urbe ... media** = Stat. *Theb.* 12, 481.

78-81 **Tum – Colossi** The model is Mart. *Sp.* 1, 1-6: "Barbara pyramidum sileat miracula Memphis, / Assyrius iactet nec Babylona labor; / [*2 lines*] / aere nec vacuo pendentia Mausolea / laudibus inmodicis Cares in astra ferant." See also Mart. 8, 36, 1-2.

78   **barbara Memphis** = Luc. 8, 542.

81   **Rhodii – Colossi** Cf. Mart. 1, 70, 7-8.

       moles operosa = Ov. *Met.* 1, 258 (in some mss. and early edd.).

82   **At domus interior** = Verg. *A.* 1, 637; 2, 486.

       varios ... colores = Verg. *G.* 1, 452; Ov. *Met.* 1, 270.

83   **vivas ... formas** Cf. Verg. *A.* 6, 848.

       nullo discrimine = Lucr. 5, 1314; Verg. *A.* 1, 574; 10, 108; et al.; Eob. *Ama.* 35, 117; *Her. Chr.* 17, 97.

84   **antiquis ... Athaenis** ≈ Man. 1, 885; cf. line 21 above (n.).

85   **patrios ... vultus** = Verg. *A.* 2, 539; Ov. *Met.* 2, 21; Eob. *Buc.* 9, 85.

86   **Tyriam ... in urbem** Ov. *Ep.* 7, 151; cf. Verg. *A.* 1, 340; 1, 388.

87   **patriae ... terrae** = Stat. *Theb.* 11, 698.

89   **externas ... urbes** *Rec.* 67 (n.).

91   **O domus, o** = V. Fl. 1, 721.

       domus – Minervae Cf. *Rec.* 33-34 (n.) and 45 (n.).

       penetrale Minervae = Ov. *Met.* 13, 337.

94   **Copia librorum** = Locher, *Stult.*, fol. 118ʳ (twice); cf. Hor. *Ep.* 1, 18, 109-110; Ov. *Tr.* 3, 14, 37-38; Eob. *Idyl.* 14, 7.

96   **totum – orbem** = Verg. *A.* 1, 457; cf. Ov. *Met.* 5, 481; Eob. *Laud.* 480. For "totum orbem" at this metrical position see also Ov. *Met.* 12, 63; Eob. *Laud.* 208; *Sylv. duae* 2, 139; *Her. Chr.* B 1, 25; cf. *Laud.* 351 (n.); *Ama.* 35, 7 (n.).

97   **Quicquid – Graii** Cf. line 25 above.

98   **Hebraeis ... vatibus** *Her. Chr.* 4, 25; 9, 78; 10, 91; 21, 1.

99   **grammaticus, rhetor** Juv. 3, 76.

101   **climata terrae** = *Psalt.* 66, 9; 96, 3.

102-103 **totam Encyclopaedian** Mutian. *Ep.* 80, sent to Eobanus Hessus on 27 August 1506: "Est operae pretium tractare totam encyclopaediam."

104   **multo ... labore** = Verg. *G.* 1, 197.

104-105 **studiosa ... Turba** Cf. *Pug.* 41 (n.).

105   **studiis ... honestis** = Hor. *Ep.* 1, 2, 36; cf. Eob. *Nob.* 299: "studiis virtus inolevit honestis."

       studiis insudat *Hod.*, ded. 1: "bonis quidem et rectis studiis aegre insudans."

106-114 **Non secus – laboris** For the bee-image cf. Verg. *A.* 6, 707-709.

106   **Non secus ac** = Verg. *G.* 3, 346; *A.* 8, 243; et al.; Eob. *Nup.* 183; *Her. Chr.* 11, 123.

       vineta Timoli = Ov. *Met.* 6, 15; 11, 86.

107   **Inter odoriferas ... herbas** = Ven. Fort. *Carm.* 8, 6, 7.

       Hyblaei nectaris Stat. *Silv.* 3, 2, 118; Sil. 14, 26. Mount Hybla was proverbial for its honey; cf. Otto 835; Häussler, pp. 105, 172, and 274; Eob. *Buc.* 6, 26; *Her. Chr.* A 3, 50; 17, 124-125; 23, 68; *Luth.* 3, 18: "Arctius haud stipant loculos ... melissae, / Dum vernant humeri, Sicelis Hybla, tui."

108   **Poplite** Cf. Verg. *G.* 4, 181; Plin. *Nat.* 11, 21; Eob. *Sylv. duae* 1, 86 (n.): "Flava laborifero poplite mella locant"; *Wirt.* 140-142: "mellificae volucres ... / ... retinaci poplite florum / Delibant succos."

       volucres Applied to bees also in Ov. *Fast.* 5, 271; Eob. *Buc.* 7, 28; *Wirt.* 140.

109   **fervent** Vergil uses this verb in *G.* 4, 169 and *A.* 1, 436 to describe the work in a beehive.

       strepitantibus alis Tib. 2, 2, 17.

109-110 **strepitantibus ... Murmure** Verg. *A.* 6, 709; Eob. *Nor.* 832 (of a marketplace): "insano strepitat prope murmure turbae."

111   **thymum, casiae** Cf. Verg. *G.* 4, 304.
            cythisi Cf. Verg. *Ecl.* 10, 30; Eob. *Buc.* 2, 50.
112   **Coriciumque crocum** = *Buc.* 9, 60; cf. Hor. *S.* 2, 4, 68; Luc. 9, 809. In
            antiquity, the best saffron came from Corycus in Cilicia. See Plin. *Nat.* 21, 31.
            thymbrae According to Verg. *G.* 4, 31, this aromatic herb (Cretan thyme?) was
            a favorite of bees.
114   **series immensa laboris** ≈ Ov. *Ep.* 9, 5 (of Hercules' labors); cf. *Pont.* 1, 4, 19;
            Eob. *Her. Chr.* 9, 19.
115   **Latiae – linguae** = Ov. *Pont.* 2, 3, 75; cf. *Tr.* 4, 4, 5; Eob. *Laud.* 345 (n.). For
            "Latiae linguae" see also *Her. Chr.* A 3, 61; 10, 1.
116   **Graeca – Latina** Cf. *Orat.*, sig. B4ʳ, referring to Cicero's eloquence: "Attica quo
            veteres Pallas duce liquit Athenas, / Graeca prius, Latio schemate iussa loqui";
            Ilias, praef., sig. α3ᵛ, referring to his translation: "Graeca prius, pueris facta
            Latina legi."
118-119   **Graeca – refert** Cf. Claud. *IV. Cons. Hon.* 398: "Graia ..., ... Romana vetustas";
            Eob. *Epp. 4*, sig. F3ʳ (1508): "Vivunt quos Romana refert et Graeca vetustas";
            lines 349-350 and 416 below.
120   **iacientem fulgura** For the metaphor cf. Cic. *Fam.* 9, 21, 1: "verborum meorum ...
            fulmina"; *Orat.* 29; 234; Quint. *Inst.* 2, 16, 19: "ut non loqui et orare,
            sed, quod Pericli contigit, fulgere ac tonare videaris"; 12, 10, 24; 12, 10, 65;
            Poliziano, *Sylv.* 1, 21-23: "potenti / ... ore tonans, ardentis fulmine linguae /
            Cuncta quatis, Cicero"; Eob. *Her. Chr.*, ded. 18, 3: "non orantem modo, sed
            fulminantem"; *Her. Chr.* 15, 72; *Hod.* 392: "divinae fulmine linguae"; *Dial.* 2,
            sig. B4ᵛ: "detonabunt in nos plus quam Periclaeis fulminibus"; *Her.* 1, 5, 88.
124-125   **Parva – urbes** For the thought cf. Ov. *Am.* 3, 15, 11-14; Vulg. *Mich.* 5, 2; *Matt.*
            2, 6; Eob. *Sylv. duae* 1, 155-156; *Her. Chr.* 21, 227-228; 24, 57-58.
124   **Parva licet** = Ov. *Fast.* 3, 837.
125   **Hessiacas ... urbes** *Buc.*, ded. 7.
128   **velut – Phoebus** For the image cf. Lucr. 3, 1043-1044; Mant. *2. Parthen.* 1,
            503-504: "Non aliter quam sol maiori sidera luce / Umbrat et exoriens alios
            exterminat ignes"; Eob. *Idyl.* 16, 62: "Ut sol ante alios astrorum prominet
            ignes."
129   **virtutis amator** *Rec.* 85 (n.).
132   **legis precepta** = Juvenc. 1, 7.
133   **summo ... vertice** = Verg. *A.* 4, 168; Eob. *Buc.* 4, 101; cf. Lucr. 3, 1001; Catul.
            64, 390; Verg. *A.* 2, 682; et al.; Eob. *Ama.* 16, 9; *Buc.* 1, 83 (n.); 8, 48.
134   **tonsa corona** *Ama.* B 2, 34 (n.).
139   **cura laboris** = Luc. 7, 209.
140   **specimen, laus** = Mutian. *Ep.* 417, line 3, in a verse letter by Eobanus of ca. 25
            August 1506, praising Mutianus: "Inter Teutonicos specimen, laus, gloria
            vates."
142   **Ingenio – acervi** Cf. Pers. 6, 80: "inventus, Chrysippe, tui finitor acervi."
143   **honor studii** *Ruf.* 87: "Surgit honor studii, nostri decus ordinis exit."
144   **grata iuventus** = Ov. *Ars* 2, 733.
146   **Te ... sileant** Verg. *A.* 10, 793; Hor. *Carm.* 1, 12, 21; 4, 9, 30-31; Eob. *Sylv.* 6, 5,
            9: "Cur mea te sileant tam fidum carmina pectus?"
147   **Tam – Pallade** For the panegyric commonplace that the person being praised is
            noble by birth *and* accomplishments see *Rhet. Her.* 3, 13; Quint. *Inst.* 3, 7, 10;
            Eob. *Buc.* B 2, 1-6; *Nup.* 97-102; *Her. Chr.* 6, 63-67; 21, 51-70; *Epic.* 5, 65-68;
            Her., ded. 5-8; *Tum.*, ded. 15-29; *Sylv.* 7, 35, 1-8. For the topos of true nobility
            see *Nup.* 97-99 (n.).
            floribus aevi Cf. *Buc.* 1, 9 (n.).
149   **Bis denos ... annos** = Mart. 7, 14, 9. Eobanus uses the same phrase to indicate

Herbord's age in a verse letter of 25 May 1508: "Bis denos, Hereborde, licet vix egeris annos". See *Epp. 4*, sig. F2ʳ. However in the immediately following section (sig. F6ᵛ) he says that Herbord earned the M.A. at age 23 (in 1504) and is now over 25.

adolescis in annos ≈ Ov. *Am.* 2, 19, 23.

151   **Pene – vir** On the topos "Boy and old man" see *Laud.*, lim. 12 (n.).

151-152   **Margaritanae – honos** Cf. Mutian. *Ep.* 80, sent to Eobanus on 27 August 1506: "Ama meum Herebordum, Margaritanae domus ornamentum singulare."

152   **Stirpis honos** = V. Fl. 2, 562; Eob. *Laud.* 465; *Epp. 4*, sig. F1ᵛ, poem to Herbord, Gerlach, and Wolfgang von der Marthen (1508): "Stirpis honos, Hereborde, tuae ...."

       prole – insignis Cf. V. Fl. 5, 383: "felix prole parens."

       parens ... uterque Her. *Chr.* 12, 197 (n.).

153   **Quo – Immensum** = Ov. *Fast.* 4, 573; cf. Eob. *Hypocr.* 37: "Quo feror huc autem? quia quod non posse canebam / Comprehendi numero, cur numerare velim?"

       Immensum pelagus = Her. *Chr.* 16, 17; cf. Ennod. *Carm.* 1, 7, 53: "Sulcat inmensum pelagus carina."

157   **Quot – puellas** Eobanus alludes to Ov. *Ars* 1, 59.

158   **solvuntur honores** = *Rec.* 195.

159-167   **Hic – canoram** Cf. *Rec.* 211-214 (in Frankenberg).

159   **tripodas Clarii** = Verg. *A.* 3, 360.

       Clarii ... Apollinis Plin. *Nat.* 2, 232; 5, 116.

160   **Aonius vertex** *Rec.* 213 (n.).

       Peneia Daphne Ov. *Met.* 1, 452.

161   **Pierides castae** = Mant. *c. Poet.* 39 (quoted in Eob. *Ama.* 25, 10); Eob. *Sylv. duae* 2, 165.

163   **faciles ... Musae** Aus. *Ep.* 8, 17: "sic tibi sint Musae faciles"; Eob. *Hod.* 466; *Idyl.* 11, 121; et al.; cf. line 65 above (n.): "faciles ... Camenae."

       gelidis ... in umbris Cf. *Buc.* 3, 24 (n.).

       spaciantur in umbris ≈ Mart. 11, 47, 3; cf. Prop. 4, 8, 75; Ov. *Ars.* 1, 67.

164-165   **Cumque – Brachia** Cf. line 306 below; *Buc.* 2, 78.

       nectunt ... Brachia Ov. *Fast.* 6, 329.

165   **albentes – capillos** Cf. *Buc.* 6, 59; 8, 78 (n.). For "albentes capillos" in the sense "blonde hair" see *Buc.* 7, 112; cf. Ov. *Ars* 2, 666 (*Pont.* 4, 12, 30), of gray hair: "albentes ... comas."

165-166   **praecingunt – Innumero** Cf. *Buc.* 2, 91 (n.).

       flore ... Innumero Stat. *Theb.* 8, 300.

166-167   **sub fronde ... Arborea** Ov. *Am.* 3, 5, 8; cf. Eob. *Rec.* 6-7 (n.).

166   **fronde choreas** = Man. 5, 239.

167   **cytharam – canoram** ≈ *Theoc.* 31, sig. L5ᵛ: "... citharam pulsare canoram."

       cytharam pulsante ≈ V. Fl. 5, 693; Mant. *1. Parthen.* 3, 833: "argutam plectro citharam pulsabat eburno."

170-176   **Ac veluti ... Sic** = Verg. *A.* 1, 148-154; 12, 684-690.

170   **sacratas ... aedes** Her. *Chr.* 14, 75.

       virginis aedes = *Rec.* 55; *Laud.* 528.

172   **sacra ... reverentia** Stat. *Silv.* 3, 3, 189.

       virgineae ... vittae Verg. *A.* 2, 168.

176   **divinae ... artis** Verg. *A.* 2, 15; Stat. *Theb.* 7, 61; Eob. *Epic.* 3, 18; *Val.* 2, 6; 2, 292.

177   **palacia regni** = V. Fl. 2, 246.

178   **Ecce sed** = Line 256 below; *Buc.* 3, 82; 4, 105; 8, 101; *Her. Chr.* 3, 75; 4, 137; 5,

86; 6, 111; 22, 73.

	sacras ... aedes *Buc.* 10, 78 (n.).
179	**manibus ... amicis** = Ov. *Met.* 11, 565; *Fast.* 5, 409.
180	**secreta cubilia** = *Lydia* 29; Ov. *Fast.* 1, 427.
182	**Quem metuis** = Luc. 10, 382; V. Fl. 8, 77.
	Tuus – illis Cf. Ov. *Ep.* 18, 85 (Leander's letter to Hero): "... meus ignis in illo est"; Eob. *Her. Chr.* 1, 147.
	hic amor est = Hor. *S.* 1, 3, 24; cf. Verg. *A.* 4, 347; Ov. *Ars* 3, 575; *Met.* 10, 315.
183	**Neu – metus** Cf. Verg. *A.* 7, 438.
	Sic, sic = Verg. *A.* 4, 660; Sil. 4, 506.
184	**Abidenus** = Ov. *Ep.* 18, 1.
	Phrygiam ... urbem ≈ Verg. *A.* 6, 785.
185	**ad Oemonias ... urbes** = Ov. *Ep.* 12, 127.
187	**Adventumque tuum** = Lucr. 1, 7.
188	**Aude animo** = *Eccles.* 35; *Accl.* 2, 153.
189-190	**maiora ... Praemia** Luc. 5, 246-247; Stat. *Theb.* 8, 592.
189	**maiora videbis** = Ov. *Met.* 7, 648: "speque fideque ... maiora videbis."
191	**Dum stupeo** = Ov. *Ep.* 16, 253; Eob. *Her. Chr.* 13, 63.
	titubat lingua Ov. *Ars* 1, 598; *Tr.* 3, 1, 21; Eob. *Sylv.* 2, 2, 53.
	lingua palato = Verg. *G.* 3, 388; Ov. *Met.* 6, 306; *Tr.* 3, 3, 21.
192	**conata loqui** = Ov. *Ep.* 4, 7; *Met.* 13, 569.
	Mirabile dictu = Verg. *G.* 2, 30; 3, 275; *A.* 1, 439; et al.; Eob. *Buc.* 4, 17.
193	**Nescio quem sensi** = Ov. *Ep.* 11, 26.
193-194	**circum ... Tempora** Verg. *A.* 2, 133; 2, 684: "lambere flamma comas et circum tempora pasci" (of Aeneas's son Iulus). Cf. note to lines 199-205 below.
193	**furorem** The poet's divine frenzy ("furor poeticus") is an ancient and medieval commonplace. See Curtius, *ELLMA*, pp. 474-475; and, for example, Plato, *Phdr.* 245 a; Cic. *Div.* 1, 80; *de Orat.* 2, 194; Hor. *Carm.* 3, 4, 5-6; Stat. *Silv.* 2, 7, 76; Marul. *Hymn. nat.* 3, 1, 1-11; Eob. *Buc.* 3, 13 (n.); B 6, 10; *Luth.* 5, 52.
194	**Ganimedis ab urna** = *Sylv.* 3, 6, 25.
195	**Nectareos latices** Cf. Ov. *Met.* 7, 707.
197	**aethereo ... Olympo** = Verg. *A.* 8, 319; Mart. 9, 3, 3.
199	**Numen erat** = Ov. *Met.* 4, 417.
201	**Pectore – aestus** Cf. Ov. *Met.* 2, 640-641.
	Pectore ... calido Pers. 5, 144; Eob. *Ama.* 36, 6.
202	**per – flamma** Cf. Ov. *Met.* 14, 351.
	vaenas ... calentes Sen. *Thy.* 758; Luc. 1, 587.
203	**rapido ... igne** Verg. *G.* 4, 263; Ov. *Met.* 7, 326; et al.
	igne medullae = *Her. Chr.* 4, 95; cf. Ov. *Ep.* 4, 15.
204	**Ossa – penetrat** Cf. Ov. *Met.* 10, 424.
204-205	**lambere ... Flamma comas** Verg. *A.* 2, 684.
206	**caper improbus** Goats were proverbially randy; see Otto 339; Hor. *Epod.* 10, 23.
	"Ite," ait Verg. *A.* 11, 24.
208-210	**Ibimus – honores** Cf. *Buc.* 2, 21-28.
208	**Ibimis, o** = Ov. *Ep.* 15, 175.
	Totum ... orbem = Line 96 above (n.).
209	**Ethiopas ultra Tanaimque** For the conventional hyperbole that a person is eager to go to the ends of the earth for some cause or friend see, for instance, Catul. 11, 1-14; Hor. *Carm.* 2, 6, 1-4; Eob. *Her. Chr.* 18, 37-50; 21, 137-138; *Idyl.* 1, 146-148: "Te quaecunque vocas, Melisaee, in regna sequemur, / Seu tu Sauromatas ultra Tanaimque nivalem / Ire iubes, sive est quicquam quod pascitur ultra"; *Epic.* 9, 85-88: "Ibimus extremos ultra Garamantas et ultra /

Aestivae Solis torrida regna plagae. / Ibimus et Scythiam supra Tanaimque nivalem, / Quaque stat aeterno Tethyos unda gelu"; *Hod.* B 1, 43-48. Cf. further *Ama.* 32, 65-72.

Ethiopas Cf. *Sylv.* 9, 1, 45: "... Aethiopas ultra transibis et Indos."

ultra – nivalem = *Idyl.* 1, 147; cf. Verg. *G.* 4, 517: "... Tanaimque nivalem"; Eob. *Nup.* 83: "Thanaim ... nivalem"; *Epic.* 9, 87: "... supra Tanaimque nivalem"; *Sylv.* 1, 1, 119: "Tanaim ... nivalem"; *Epp. fam.*, p. 86 (in 1519, after hearing a rumor that Erasmus had died): "Curre ad extremos Garamantas et Indos, ultra Scythiam Tanaimque nivalem: non invenies."

210   **priscos ... honores** = [Tib.] 3, 7, 31; Stat. *Ach.* 2, 158; cf. Eob. *Ama.* 32, 44; *Her. Chr.* 12, 62 (n.).

211-212   **sydere ... Ignivomo** Cf. Ven. Fort. *Carm.* 3, 9, 3: "ignivomum solem"; Eob. *Vict.* 262: "ignivomum ... solem"; also cf. *Pug.* 2. The expression paraphrases the familiar "sub sole," used in line 382 below (n.).

213   **divum – poetae** = *Venus* 1, 149; cf. Ov. *Am.* 3, 9, 17: "... sacri vates et divum cura vocamur."

215   **locus in terris** = *Her. Chr.* 6, 100; 21, 198; cf. Verg. *A.* 1, 459-460.

        latrator Anubis = *Pug.* B 1, 3, with notes.

217   **divine poeta** = Verg. *Ecl.* 5, 45; 10, 17.

219   **tristes ... umbras** = Stat. *Theb.* 11, 664; cf. Verg. *A.* 5, 734.

        tentabimus umbras Cf. Ov. *Met.* 10, 12 (of Orpheus).

220   **Elysiis ... campis** Verg. *G.* 1, 38; Tib. 1, 3, 58; Ov. *Ib.* 171.

221   **Threicio ... vati** Ov. *Met.* 11, 2.

223-224   **vincere – Victi** Note the alliteration and play on the root of a word (*annominatio*); cf. *Her. Chr.* 3, 7 (n.).

225   **Spicula – veneno** Cf. line 390 below (n.).

        Nessaeo ... veneno = Ov. *Ep.* 9, 163; cf. *Ib.* 489; Eob. *Her. Chr.* 17, 140; *Rec.* 18-19, with notes: "Nesseo ... Sanguine."

        infecta veneno ≈ Verg. *A.* 7, 341.

228   **Quibus – ureris** Cf. *Buc.* 7, 176 (n.).

229   **Terque – foelix** Sil. 9, 159.

        Terque quater = Verg. *G.* 2, 399; *A.* 4, 589; et al.; Eob. *Nor.* 826.

        mollior aetas = Claud. *Bell. Get.* 160; Sedul. 3, 328; cf. Eob. *Rec.* 132 (n.): "mollis ... aetas."

230   **castos ... amores** Mart. 10, 35, 8; cf. line 240 below (n.).

232   **Foeliciter arde** ≈ Ov. *Rem.* 13.

233   **Hiis – dictis** Cf. Verg. *A.* 4, 54 (in Renaissance edd.): "His dictis incensum animum flammavit amore"; 4, 197; 5, 816; Eob. *Her.* 3, 1, 79-80: "Qualibus ... dictis incenderit ... / ... animum"; *Ilias* 13, p. 322: "Talibus incendit ... pectora dictis."

234   **coniecit in ignes** = Ov. *Met.* 8, 512.

235-239   **Quid – perfodiam** Cf. *Her. Chr.* 17, 35-44.

235   **Quid memorem** = Verg. *A.* 6, 123; 6, 601; 8, 483; Eob. *Nup.* 188; 192; *Max.* 141; *Vict.* 250; *Eccles.* 195; et al.

        antiquos ... amantes = *Ama.* 35, 105; cf. *Her. Chr.* 17, 39; 17, 157.

236   **non ... amor, sed ... error** Cf. Mant. *Ecl.* 1, 52: "nec deus (ut perhibent) Amor est, sed amaror et error." Passionate love is often characterized as "error." See, for example, Prop. 1, 13, 35; Mant. *Ecl.* 7, 66: "error enim communis amor iuvenilibus annis"; Eob. *Ama.* 35, 21; 35, 67; B 2, 33; B 2, 48; *Buc.* 9, 11; *Idyl.* 7, 89: "... quis te malus abiicit error?"; *Her. Chr.* 17, 44.

        torsit amor Ov. *Ars* 1, 176; cf. Eob. *Buc.* 3, 66 (n.).

        inanis ... error *Anthol. Lat.* 464, 7.

237   **versat amor** Ov. *Am.* 1, 2, 8; *Ars* 3, 718.

pallida Pallor is a conventional symptom of lovesickness. See, for example, Tib. 1, 8, 52; Hor. *Carm.* 3, 10, 14; Ov. *Ep.* 11, 27; *Ars* 1, 729; Eob. *Ama.* 1, 1: "vultu pallido"; 10, 1; 23, 1; 35, 27; 35, 53; 36, 5; *Sylv. duae* 2, 48-50; *Her. Chr.* 4, 186; 12, 77-78; *Idyl.* 3, 91-100.

238-239 **Guttura – perfodiam** Cf. Sen. *Phaed.* 259.
              ferro Pectora = Verg. *A.* 12, 540-541; Stat. *Theb.* 5, 160-161; Sil. 6, 480-481.

239   **Venus improba** = *Anthol. Lat.* 633, 9 (traditionally ascribed to Vergil): "Perdidit horrendo Troiam Venus improba bello"; Celtis, *Am.* 1, 14, 35; 3, 8, 9; Eob. *Idyl.* 10, 100: "nescit Venus improba flecti"; cf. Stat. *Silv.* 5, 1, 233; Eob. *Buc.* 7, 175; *Her. Chr.* 6, 102; *Val.* 1, 215: "nec Aonidum Venus improba ludit in hortis."

239-240 **Castum – decet** Cf. *Ama.* B 2, 44 (n.).

240   **Castus amor** Ov. *Ep.* 1, 23; *Fast.* 4, 224; Eob. *Ama.* 35, 112; *Buc.* 5, 67; *Her. Chr.* 4, 148; 5, 125; 7, 144; *Idyl.*, 1. ded. 68 (2. ded. 66); *Sylv.* 2, 13, 16; cf. line 230 above (n.).

240-241 **sacra ... Musica** Line 330 below (n.).

240   **sacra prophanas** = Ov. *Ep.* 7, 129; Eob. *Ama.* B 2, 35; cf. *Eccles.* 195: "... sacra prophanant"; also cf. line 378 below (n.).

241   **Aonio ... fonte** Ov. *Pont.* 4, 2, 47; cf. Camerarius, *Nar.* 14, 1 (with notes).

243   **virginei ... pudoris** = V. Fl. 5, 356; Stat. *Theb.* 12, 205; *Ach.* 1, 765.

246   **Ductrix Thespiadum** Cf. *Buc.* 8, 50 (n.). As the Muse of heroic poetry, Calliope was traditionally the "queen" of the Muses. See Hes. *Theog.* 79; Hor. *Carm.* 3, 4, 2; Ov. *Met.* 5, 662: "e nobis maxima"; Eob. *Ama.* B 2, 1; *Sylv. duae* 2, 162; *Val.* 4, 17: "Musarum maxima."
              sacras ... ad aras = Ov. *Ib.* 463; Eob. *Her. Chr.* 13, 139; cf. Ov. *Tr.* 5, 2, 43; Eob. *Her. Chr.* 1, 137; 13, 81; *Vict.* 243. For "sacras aras" see also *Ama.* B 2, 37; *Nup.* 268; *Her. Chr.* 13, 7; 20, 124; 20, 129; *Nob.* 93; 113; *Nor.* 1111.

247   **Furor – faciebat** Cf. *Pug.* 45-46 (n.).

248   **insania** For the sense "poetic frenzy" cf. Hor. *Carm.* 3, 4, 6.

249   **sacras – undas** Cf. Busch. *Lips.* 14: "... vitreas Permessidis undas"; Jacobus Magdalius Gaudensis, dedicatory poem in *Erarium aureum poetarum* ([Cologne], 1501), sig. A2ʳ: "... liquidas Permessidos undas"; Eob. *Buc.* 8, 47 (n.). For the masculine gender of "Permessis" (normally feminine) see Andrel. *Eleg.* 2, sig. d5ᵛ: "... sacri Permessidos unda"; *Livia* 4, 1, 15: "... exhausti sterilis Permessidos unda." Godelieve Tournoy-Thoen, commenting on the *Livia*-passage, surmises that the tag "Permessidos unda" may ultimately derive from a corrupt reading of Mart. 1, 76, 11: "... Permessidis unda" (instead of "Permesside nuda").
              vitrei For the epithet see *Pug.* B 1, 8 (n.).

250   **Hic – urbem** Cf. *Her. Chr.* 5, 79.

250-251 **mutato ... Nomine** See line 73 above (n.).

250   **mediam ... urbem** = Ov. *Ep.* 9, 123; *Met.* 14, 746; *Tr.* 4, 2, 61; cf. Eob. *Nor.* 333.
              perlabitur urbem ≈ Stat. *Theb.* 6, 1.

251-252 **hedera ... lauro** Cf. Verg. *Ecl.* 8, 12-13; Calp. *Ecl.* 4, 56-57; Mant. *Ecl.* 3, 171: "dignus eras hederis, dignus Parnaside lauro"; *1. Parthen.* 1, 601: "ornataeque comas hederis et virgine lauro"; *2. Parthen.* 1, 13: "Da mihi non hederae, non lauri vimine textam"; Eob. *Buc.* 8, 57-58.

252-253 **viridique ... lauro Tempora** Verg. *A.* 5, 246; cf. Stat. *Silv.* 1, 2, 227-228.
              victricia – Tempora *Epic. Drusi* 459.

253-254 **pandite – liquorem** Cf. Verg. *A.* 10, 163. The "nymphs" are the Muses, as in Eob. *Rec.* 51 (n.).

254   **Clarium ... liquorem** Cf. *Sylv. duae* 2, 158: "Castalio ... liquore"; *Nob.* 9:

"sacros ... liquores."

255 **Finieram** = Mart. 8, 3, 9; Eob. *Her. Chr.* 12, 169; 23, 23; cf. *Her. Chr.* 11, 121.
mediaque ... in voce reliqui Cf. Verg. *A.* 4, 76; 4, 277; 9, 657.

256 **Ecce sed** = Line 178 above (n.).

257 **sacri ... vates** Tib. 2, 5, 114; Hor. *Carm.* 4, 9, 28; Ov. *Am.* 3, 9, 17; 3, 9, 41; *Ars* 3, 539; Eob. *Laud.* 324; *Buc.* 2, 35; *Venus* 1, 149.
ex ordine vates = Juvenc. 1, 47; 1, 122.

261-263 **Rufus – Incolit** Cf. *Buc.* B 2, 7-8.

263-264 **annos Exigit** ≈ Verg. *A.* 1, 74-75; Ov. *Tr.* 3, 4, 43.

264 **insani – vulgi** Cf. *Her. Chr.* 8, 107 (n.).

265-266 **Consilio – probatus** For this pattern of praise – one man combines the virtues of several ancients – see Mant. *Epigr.*, fol. 103ʳ: "Insignis virtute Cato, Pompeius honore, / Tullius eloquio, relligione Numa"; Bebel, "Satyricum carmen," *Carm.*, sig. m4ʳ: "sis / Fabritio gravior defensorique Camillo, / Relligione Numam, vincas pietate Metellum / Et priscos bonitate viros superes"; Eob. *Nup.* 42-45; 56-58.

266 **Numa** Numa Pompilius, the second king of Rome, was proverbially religious. Cf. Erasmus, *Adag.*, prolegomena xiii, *ASD* 2, 1, p. 80, lines 652-653, and *De copia verborum, ASD* 1, 6, p. 106, line 951: "Numa religiosior"; Eob. *Nup.* 57.

267 **Sed – refero** = Ov. *Ep.* 9, 143.

267-268 **Popularis ... Laudis** Cic. *de Orat.* 3, 117; *Agr.* 2, 1; Quint. *Inst.* 8, 3, 2; 10, 2, 27.

268 **odit fastus** Tib. 1, 8, 75.
secum contentus Instead of the expected "suo contentus" or "se contentus."

270 **campos ... apricos** Hor. *Carm.* 1, 8, 3-4; *Ars* 162; Calp. *Ecl.* 5, 8.

271 **Quid – versus** Since this verse presupposes considerable familiarity with Mutianus Rufus, it must have been among those added or rewritten in 1507.

272 **Quid hoc est** = Prud. *Amart.* 628; *Psych.* 694.

273 **venantur honores** = *Psalt.* 73, 19: "Divitiis tumidi primos venantur honores."

274-275 **popularis ... Aura** Cic. *Har.* 44; Hor. *Carm.* 3, 2, 20; Eob. *Buc.* B 2, 13.

275 **blandis ... susurris** Prop. 1, 11, 13.

275-276 **tranquilla ... Ocia** = Luc. 2, 266-267; Eob. *Epic.* 4, 191 (addressing Mutianus Rufus): "Ocia ducebas vitae tranquilla beatae."

276 **monumenta favoris** *Epic.* 7, 73: "monumenta ... nostri ... favoris."

278 **Montibus Hessiacis** = Mutian. *Ep.* 149, line 33 (15 October 1508); Eob. *Sylv.* 7, 4, 1; cf. *Buc.* 4, 40: "Hessiacos ... montes"; *Wirt.* B 1, 5: "Hessiacis ... montibus"; *Epic.* 4, 10: "Hessiacis ... iugis"; 4, 59: "Hessiacos ... colles." Eobanus often mentions the mountains and hills of his homeland. See also, for instance, *Buc.*, ded. 3-4; *Buc.* 1, 10; 4, 40; 7, 127; *Val.* 1, 609; *Epic.* 4, 181; *Sylv.* 2, 4, 23.

279-280 **tam longa ... Nocte** Ov. *Ep.* 16, 317.

280 **Nostris – sylvis** Cf. Verg. *Ecl.* 1, 5; Eob. *Buc.* 1, 24-25; 3, 78; 5, 11; 6, 8-9, where "sylvae" indicate a pastoral world. Here Eobanus is still thinking primarily of his poetic miscellanies (*Sylvae*). See fn. 9 at *Laud.*, ded. 11; and fn. 12 at *Laud.* 5-8. However, the parallel to Verg. *Ecl.* 1, 5 now leads him to contemplate a pastoral tribute to Mutianus Rufus, along the lines of Vergil's fifth eclogue.

281-282 **Quando – Carmina** Cf. *Buc.* 2, 1-2; 11, 4; *Sylv.* 7, 18, 9-10: "Carmina cum faciles mihi pastoralia Musae / Et facili canerent pascua laeta pede."

282 **funere Daphnim** = Verg. *Ecl.* 5, 20.

284 **longum ... aevum** = Ov. *Med.* 49; Luc. 1, 448; Sil. 13, 478.

285 **Dum queror** = Verg. *Ecl.* 8, 19; *Ciris* 405; Eob. *Buc.* 3, 162; *Her. Chr.* 3, 149; 13, 10; 14, 77; *Epic.* 2, 95.
ecce aderat = *Nup.* 174; cf. Stat. *Theb.* 11, 263; Sil. 4, 493; 5, 518.

plectris ... eburnis Cf. Prop. 3, 3, 25; [Tib.] 3, 4, 39; Eob. *Sylv.* 2, 12, 5: "plectro ... eburno"; 4, 19, 14: "plectro ... eburneo"; *Ama.* 33, 2 (n.): "eburno pectine."

286   **magnanimi ... leonis** Ov. *Tr.* 3, 5, 33; Eob. *Buc.* 1, 42; 1, 51; *Her. Chr.* 12, 157. The lion was proverbially great-hearted; see Plin. *Nat.* 8, 48; Stat. *Theb.* 7, 529-532; 8, 124-126; Eob. *Wirt.* 338-341.

288   **moesto pectore** Catul. 64, 202; Sen. *Phaed.* 1255.

288-289   **pectore curas Volvis** Luc. 1, 272; Sil. 15, 19. For the tag "pectore curas" see Catul. 64, 72; Verg. *A.* 1, 227; 4, 448; et al.

289   **lachrimis ... obortis** = Verg. *A.* 3, 492; 4, 30; 6, 867; et al.; Eob. *Laud.* 308 (n.); *Her. Chr.* 12, 207.

290   **Sic ait et** = Verg. *A.* 1, 142; 2, 296; 3, 189; et al.; Eob. *Buc.* 9, 74.

291   **spargentibus umbram** Sen. *Ag.* 94.

292-293   **nuda ... Brachia** Claud. *Rapt. Pros.* 2, 30.

293   **Brachia iactabant** Lucr. 4, 769 (in dreams); Verg. *A.* 5, 376-377 (a boxer); Ov. *Ep.* 14, 69 (during sleep); et al.

    flavus ... Apollo = *Epic.* 4, 61; cf. Ov. *Am.* 1, 15, 35.

294-296   **magis – urit** Cf. Verg. *G.* 1, 85: "levem stipulam crepitantibus urere flammis"; Eob. *Buc.* 7, 132-133 (n.).

294   **in pectora flammas** = Ov. *Met.* 12, 295; cf. *Met.* 6, 466; Eob. *Ama.* 24, 6; B 2, 77; *Buc.* 2, 42; 3, 107; *Sylv.* 1, 8, 23.

297   **In – ocellis** Cf. Quint. *Inst.* 11, 3, 158; Eob. *Theoc.* 8, sig. D2ᵛ: "Defixis in terram oculis ...." For the tag "defixus ocellis" cf. Ov. *Am.* 2, 8, 15.

298   **Fronde ... umbrosa** *Nor.* 317.

299   **stupidas ... aures** = *Her. Chr.* 14, 85; cf. *Buc.* 6, 43.

300   **castae ... Dianae** *Pug.* 70 (n.).

303   **aeternae ... nomina laudis** Mutian. *Ep.* 556, where Eobanus tells Mutianus Rufus in 1516: "Utinam nunc dicas: 'Hesse vir, aeterna nomina laudis habes.'" For the phrase "aeternae laudis" see Juvenc., praef. 17. For the tag "nomina laudis" see also Eob. *Val.* 2, 5; *Epic.* 7, 39; cf. *Sylv. duae* 1, 74.

305   **Aonii nemoris** Prop. 3, 3, 42; Stat. *Ach.* 1, 10.

306   **Et – inter** Cf. lines 164-165 above; *Buc.* 2, 78.

307   **facilis ... Elegeia** Cf. Ov. *Rem.* 379. For the personification see also Ov. *Am.* 3, 1, 7; 3, 9, 3; Stat. *Silv.* 1, 2, 7.

    primos ... honores = V. Fl. 1, 177; cf. Verg. *A.* 11, 219; Ov. *Tr.* 4, 10, 33.

308   **lachrimis – obortis** ≈ Verg. *A.* 3, 492; 11, 41; Ov. *Met.* 7, 689; cf. line 289 above (n.).

309   **faciebat amor** = Ov. *Met.* 4, 96; 6, 469.

312   **optime vates** = Verg. *A.* 6, 669; Eob., verse letter (1508) in Trebelius, *Epigr.*, sig. F2ʳ.

313   **Dic quibus** = Verg. *Ecl.* 3, 104; 3, 106.

314   **patriis ... oris** = Verg. *A.* 10, 198; 11, 281; Eob. *Nup.* 160; 225; cf. *Her. Chr.* 20, 63.

    fatis foelicibus = *Rec.* 192 (n.).

315   **Ne queras ... ultra** Cf. Sen. *Her. O.* 1479.

316   **vitaeque labores** = Hor. *Carm.* 1, 7, 18; *S.* 2, 6, 21; Eob., *Epp. 4*, sig. F3ʳ (1508).

317   **insano ... Oresti** ≈ Ov. *Pont.* 2, 3, 45; cf. Otto 1308.

318   **Pyrithoo Theseus** ≈ Ov. *Pont.* 2, 3, 43.

319   **tibi ego, mihi tu** Cf. Ov. *Ep.* 6, 134: "me tibi teque mihi ..."; 16, 319: "te mihi meque tibi ..."; *Pont.* 3, 6, 12: "tibi me ... teque mihi."

    ille requirit = *Her. Chr.* 7, 121.

320   **taedia vitae** = Ov. *Met.* 10, 482; 10, 625; *Pont.* 1, 9, 31; Eob. *Ama.* 35, 109; *Her. Chr.* 10, 189; 13, 165; 16, 235; 16, 305; 19, 39; cf. *Her. Chr.* 12, 273-274.

321   **Quisquis amat** = Nemes. *Ecl.* 4, 56; Mant. *Ecl.* 1, 81; 1, 114; 3, 79; et al.; Eob.

Ama. 35, 14; B 2, 19; *Buc.* 3, 149; *Her. Chr.* 24, 35. Cf. Prop. 4, 5, 77; Ov. *Rem.* 579; Eob. *Ama.* 36, 5.

causas ... inanes ≈ Ov. *Am.* 2, 2, 31; cf. Verg. *A.* 9, 219.

322   **Dixit et oppositas** ≈ Prop. 2, 29, 39.

322-323   **pueros ... florentibus annis** *Buc.* 8, 72; cf. Stat. *Silv.* 3, 5, 23; Sil. 9, 533.

323   **propter aquas** = *Buc.* 4, 30; cf. Verg. *G.* 3, 14; Eob. *Buc.* 8, 42.

324   **Sacrorum ... vatum** Line 257 above (n.).

      consortia vatum = Hutten, *Querel.* 2, 10, 215: "Plurima praeterea iuvenum consortia vatum."

326   **Aucta bonis** Ven. Fort. *Mart.* 4, 566; Eob. *Her. Chr.* 17, 108.

      Alias ... urbes = Verg. *Ecl.* 1, 24; Eob. *Nor.* 681.

      laudibus urbes = *Nor.* 137.

327   **presenti numine** = Calp. *Ecl.* 4, 84; Eob. *Hod.* 334.

      numine Phoebus ≈ Verg. *A.* 9, 661.

329   **Thersites ... loquaces** [Aus.] *Periocha Iliados* 2: "Thersites ... loquax."

330   **Musica sacra** = *Sylv.* 5, 23, 15; cf. *Laud.* 240-241; *Sylv.* 6, 5, 6; *Theoc.* 27, sig. K6ᵛ: "quicunque poetae / Musica sacra colunt"; Hutten, *Querel.* 2, 5, 14; 2, 10, 182.

      sacra professos ≈ *Eccles.* 171 and *Hypocr.* 79: "... Christi pia sacra professum."

331   **magnos ... poetas** *Ciris* 54; Prop. 1, 7, 24; Ov. *Tr.* 4, 10, 125; *Pont.* 3, 4, 9.

332   **Castalii ... flumina fontis** Cf. Sen. *Oed.* 229; Ov. *Met.* 14, 788.

335-336   **Pergite – Theologiae** = Lines 341-342 below.

335   **Pergite, Pierides** = Verg. *Ecl.* 6, 13.

337   **signanda cedro** Cf. Hor. *Ars* 332: "carmina ... / ... linenda cedro" (that is, with cedar oil, which preserves books from decay); Eob. *Idyl.* 13, 111: "... aeternoque locet tua nomina cedro." Cedarwood was considered especially durable; see Plin. *Nat.* 16, 212-213; Erasmus, *Adag.* 4, 1, 54.

338   **fluctibus undae** ≈ Verg. *A.* 4, 628.

339-340   **Si – regna** Eobanus refers to Noah's Flood (*Gen.* 7, 11-24), but in language more appropriate to Deucalion's flood (Ov. *Met.* 1, 274-310).

340   **Tethym ... vagam** Luc. 1, 414; 6, 67. The form "Tethym" (for "Tethyn") occurs also in Eob. *Hod.* 194 and *Ilias* 14, p. 357.

341-342   **Pergite – Theologiae** = Lines 335-336 above.

343   **sedem – urbe** Cf. Luc. 1, 53: "... in Arctoo sedem tibi legeris orbe."

344   **humanae ... mentis** ≈ Ov. *Met.* 1, 55; Eob. *Her. Chr.* 24, 95; cf. *Her. Chr.* 9, 81.

345   **facundia ... linguae** = Ov. *Pont.* 1, 2, 67; cf. line 115 above (n.).

346   **Relligionis opus** = Ven. Fort. *Carm.* 2, 10, 22; Eob. *Sylv. duae* 2, 212; *Her. Chr.* A 3, 40.

348   **Tot – triumphos** Cf. Mant. *Calam.* 1, p. 34: "... tot egregia partos virtute triumphos."

      magnifica ... virtute Sen. *Ep.* 83, 24.

349-350   **Caldaea – Graecave** Cf. lines 118-119 above (n.).

351   **totum ... orbem** = Verg. *A.* 4, 231; 7, 258; Hor. *Ep.* 2, 1, 254; Eob. *Ruf.* 39; *Laud.* 480; *Ama.* 35, 3 (n.).

352   **asylum** For the image see also lines 497 and 562 below; *Idyl.* 16, 64-65 (of Nuremberg): "velut exilio pulsis hoc tempore Musis / Hospitium dedit et profugis patefecit asylum"; *Sylv.* 9, 18, 25: "... neglectis [*sc.* Camoenis] urbs Norica praestet asylum."

354   **Quis credere posset** = Ov. *Tr.* 1, 2, 81 (where other mss. read "possit"); Mart. 10, 85, 7; Eob. *Sylv.* 2, 10, 23; cf. Ov. *Ep.* 18, 123 and *Met.* 15, 613: "... quis credere possit?"

358   **Quis numerare queat** = Juv. 16, 1.

364   **Zeusinos** This epithet appears to be a neologism.

Chous Apelles Ov. *Ars* 3, 401; Eob. *Epic.* 3, 15; cf. *Her. Chr.* 24, 19.

366-367 **Celeres – Rhetia** Cf. *Pug.* B 1, 22 (n.).

366 **Celeres ... cervi** = Stat. *Theb.* 6, 598.

367 **praeconia laudis** = [Tib.] 3, 7, 177.

368 **Laudis ... umbram** Cf. Otto 1819; Häussler, pp. 27, 65, 219-220, and 290.

374 **Iamque fere** = *Rec.* 159 (n.).

377 **Discaede, prophane** Cf. Verg. *A.* 6, 258; line 384 below (n.).

378 **Manu – prophana** Cf. Ov. *Met.* 2, 755-756.

mysteria sacra = Ven. Fort. *Carm.* 2, 9, 45; Eob. *Sylv.* 9, 12, 3; cf. *Idyl.* 14, 138: "Sancta ... mysteria prodita vulgo."

sacra prophana For this juxtaposition at the hexameter close cf. Hor. *Ep.* 1, 16, 54: "miscebis sacra profanis"; *Ars* 397; Ov. *Ep.* 7, 129; *Met.* 3, 710: "oculis ... cernentem sacra profanis"; Eob. *Laud.* 240; *Ama.* B 2, 35; *Her. Chr.* A 1, 19; *Sylv.* 7, 27, 29; 7, 28, 29. Cf. further *Ama.* B 2, 37 and *Her. Chr.* 11, 36.

379 **semel ... satis est** *Rec.* 165 (n.).

380 **Triviam ... Dianam** Var. *L.* 7, 16; Macr. 1, 9, 6; Mant. *Ecl.* 1, 47; cf. Prop. 2, 32, 10 (= Mutian. *Ep.* 417, line 28, in a verse letter from Eobanus to Mutianus Rufus written in August 1506): "Triviae ... deae"; Ov. *Ep.* 12, 79; Eob. *Her. Chr.* 13, 9.

fonte Dianam ≈ Sil. 12, 366.

381 **In – formam** Cf. Ov. *Met.* 1, 1-2; Paul. Nol. *Carm.* 15, 18; Eob. *Buc.* 3, 54. For the tag "corpora formam" cf. Ov. *Met.* 9, 452.

382 **nil sub sole** Cf. Vulg. *Eccl.* 1, 10; 2, 11. For the familiar phrase "sub sole" see Eob. *Buc.* 7, 140 (n.); cf. lines 211-212 above.

383 **alios ... in annos** = *Nor.* 797; cf. Verg. *A.* 8, 399; Stat. *Silv.* 1, 4, 8; Eob. *Epic.* 4, 207.

durabit in annos = Stat. *Silv.* 3, 3, 38; Eob. *Epp. 4,* sig. F8ᵛ (1508): "aeternos ... durabit in annos"; *Sylv.* 3, 1, 107: "... seros durabit in annos."

384 **Vulgus – prophanum** Cf. Hor. *Carm.* 3, 1, 1; Eob. *Sylv.* 4, 15, 7-8: "procul hinc, profanum / Vulgus, abesto." Cf. also line 377 above (n.); lines 400-401 below; *Her. Chr.*, ded. 1, 2: "prophanum vulgus"; *Pug.* 80 (n.).

arcanis ... arcere Note the wordplay.

386 **Aonias ... Musas** *Rec.* 190 (n.).

386-387 **latrant ... rabulae** Cf. Quint. *Inst.* 12, 9, 12: "a viro bono in rabulam latratoremque convertitur."

387 **adunco stertere naso** Cf. Juv. 1, 57. For "adunco naso" see Ter. *Hau.* 1062; Hor. *S.* 1, 6, 5. Cf. further Eob. *Rec.* B 2, 6 (n.); *Ama.* B 1, 2; Otto 1198; Häussler, pp. 60-61, 76, 112, and 191; Erasmus, *Adag.* 1, 8, 22.

388 **O longum ... miseranda** Cf. Stat. *Silv.* 1, 3, 13.

divae ... Poesis *Ilias Lat.* 890; cf. line 458 below.

390 **Spicula ... tingis ... veneno** Cf. Ov. *Pont.* 4, 10, 31; Sen. *Her. F.* 1195. For "spicula veneno" at this metrical position see Sil. 1, 325; 3, 273; 15, 682; line 225 above.

Lernaeo ... veneno = *Rec.* 105 (n.).

391 **praecordia ferro** = Tib. 1, 1, 63; Ov. *Met.* 6, 251; 13, 476.

394 **revocatus ab umbris** Mart. 11, 5, 13.

395 **triplex ... Apollo** *Buc.* 10, 41, also referring to the Christian Trinity.

396 **teretem ... mundum** = Man. 3, 364.

summo ... ab orbe Man. 3, 378.

397 **tua cura sumus** Mart. 8, 82, 6.

venerabile numen = Ov. *Pont.* 2, 3, 19 (where some mss., however, read "venerabile nomen"); Germ. *Arat.* 102; cf. Stat. *Silv.* 4, 6, 60; Juvenc. 1, 232.

398 **Satis, imo superque** Line 545 below; cf. Pl. *Am.* 168; Verg. *A.* 2, 642; et al.;

Eob. *Ama.* 33, 5.

399 **Salva triumphanti** ≈ Line 419 below.
stat victoria = Ov. *Ep.* 10, 105; cf. Eob. *Buc.* 10, 119 (n.).

400-401 **prophanum – iubes** These words refer back to line 384, where see note.

403 **longa ... taedia** Ov. *Met.* 14, 158; Eob. *Ama.* 35, 109.

405 **triumphales ... palmas** ≈ *Her. Chr.* 4, 233.

406 **cunctas ... gentes** = *Aetna* 573; cf. Luc. 7, 659 and 718.

407 **Tritonia Pallas** = Verg. *A.* 5, 704; Eob. *Laud.* 442.

408 **Ausonis ora** = Line 68 above (n.).

409 **fraternum ... cruorem** Sen. *Med.* 452.

411 **Artibus ingenuis** = Ov. *Pont.* 1, 6, 7; 2, 7, 47; Eob. *Nob.* 272; cf. *Rec.* 87 (n.).

411-412 **ut floribus – aequor** For this type of hyperbolic comparison see, for example, Ov. *Ars* 1, 57-59; *Tr.* 1, 5, 47; 4, 1, 55-56; 4, 10, 107-108; 5, 1, 31-32; 5, 2, 23-26; 5, 6, 37-40; *Pont.* 2, 7, 25-28; 4, 15, 7-10. The trope recurs in Eobanus's works. See, for example, *Her. Chr.* 16, 93-94; 16, 185-186; *Nob.* 245-246; 342; *Eccles.* 167-168; 402.

412 **ut piscibus aequor** = Ov. *Fast.* 1, 493.

415 **Inter tot ... urbes** Line 49 above.
Germani nominis urbes ≈ Brant, *Var. carm.*, sig. i4ʳ (*Texte* 194, 27), of Erfurt: "... in egregia Germani nominis urbe"; Eob. *Nor.* 844: "... Germani nominis oram."

416 **Rhomana vetustas** = Claud. *IV. Cons. Hon.* 398; cf. lines 118-119 above (n.).

419 **Salva triumphantes** ≈ Line 399 above.

424-439 **Urbs – fasces** For a similar encomium (of Nuremberg) see *Idyl.* 16, 118-124.

424 **nimium foelix** = Luc. 8, 139; Stat. *Silv.* 5, 5, 59; cf. Verg. *A.* 4, 657.

426 **Pace ... placida** Lucr. 1, 40; 6, 73; Verg. *A.* 1, 249; 8, 325.
commissas ... moderantur habenas Cf. Ov. *Met.* 2, 169; 6, 223; Eob. *Nob.* 235: "... placidas moderatur habenas"; *Max.* 307: "... moderentur habenas."

427 **Publica cura** Ov. *Fast.* 5, 290; 6, 377.
cura ... quibus est commissa *Sylv.* 2, 1, 23; cf. *Her. Chr.* 11, 165.

428 **respublica floret** Liv. 34, 1, 5, Cic. *Clu.* 107, and Plin. *Ep.* 1, 12, 11: "florente re publica"; Eob. *Sylv.* 2, 1, 97: "studiis respublica floret"; *Epp.* 4, sig. F6ᵛ (1508): "Quorum consiliis respublica floreat ...."

429 **Crescunt divitiae** Hor. *Carm.* 3, 24, 63.
concordia cives = Mant. *Mort.*, fol. 123ᵛ: "Talis enim sanctos pax et concordia cives / Iungit"; Tifernate, *Carm.*, sig. D2ʳ (in heaven): "Dulcis ... sanctos iungit concordia cives"; Eob. *Idyl.* 16, 118, of Nuremberg: "Hinc fovet unanimes stabilis concordia cives."

431-435 **Caedit – fastus** Cf. Alan. *Nat.* 9, 59: "Furta, doli, metus, ira, furor, fraus, impetus, error"; Mant. *2. Parthen.* 3, 46-47: "Furta, arma, rapinae, / Stupra, doli, fraudes"; Hutten, *Vir bonus* 43 (*Opera*, vol. 3, p. 14): "Furta, doli, metus, ira, neces, contagia, caedes." There are similar catalogues in Eob. *Epp.* 4, sig. F6ᵛ (1508): "Insidiae, fraudes, convitia, iurgia, fastus, / Furta, doli, caedes"; *Her. Chr.* 10, 51; *Nob.* 81-86; *Dial.* 3, sig. D1ʳ: "irae, iurgia, convicia, fraudes, rapinae, caedes, adulteria, stupra"; *Sarmat.* 66: "furta, rapina, doli"; *Idyl.* 14, 120: "doli, fraudes, artesque malorum"; *Pod.* 245: "Bella, doli, cedes, periuria, furta, rapinae"; *Sylv.* 2, 2, 67-71 (among the effects of drunkenness): "Iurgia, furta, doli, fraudes, iniuria, caedes, / Incestus, stuprum, raptus, adulterium, / Fastus, avaricies, luxus, gula, livor, et ira, / Pigrities: ista sunt sata iacta manu. / Probra, nefas, rixas, discordia, bella, rapinas, / Semina, si nescis, illius esse scias."

431 **lex Iulia** = Juv. 2, 37.

432 **turpes ... rapinae** Apul. *Met.* 9, 14; 10, 14.

433 **Incestus et stupra** Cf. *Nob.* 99: "stupra incestusque."

433-434 **Meliora ... studia** *Rec.* 210 (n.).

434 **studia et mores** Verg. *G.* 4, 5; Eob. *Dial.* 3, sig. D3ʳ: "praeceptores ... qui iuventutis et studia et mores forment fingantque."

mores ... pudicos Pl. *Capt.* 1029; Ov. *Met.* 7, 734-735; *Tr.* 3, 7, 13.

436-437 **Virtus ... Inclyta** Sen. *Her. O.* 1984; Stat. *Theb.* 11, 412; Eob. *Nob.* 3.

438 **contra – piumque** Cf. Ov. *Ep.* 8, 4.

440 **Dii ... faciles** Ov. *Am.* 2, 14, 43; *Ep.* 12, 84; 16, 282; 18, 3; et al.; Eob. *Nup.* 325; *Her. Chr.* 12, 162.

441 **Hiis ... donis cumulavit** Cf. Verg. *A.* 6, 885; 11, 50; Eob. *Buc.* 11, 79.

Iuppiter urbem = Verg. *A.* 1, 522; Ov. *Fast.* 4, 827.

442 **Tritonia Pallas** = Line 407 above (n.).

446 **turpia ... mendacia** Ov. *Am.* 3, 11, 21.

448 **bifida ... iura** *Buc.* B 2, 17.

monarcham This honorific title for a legal scholar was quite common in the Renaissance. See, for example, *Inventarium Speculi iudicialis* (Padua, 1478), fol. 2ʳ: "Hoc est repertorium iuris utriusque monarche Domini Guil. Durantis"; Brant, *Texte* 67, tit., letter of 1 May 1490 to Andreas Helmut: "Iuris et eloquentie monarcham"; *Perspicacissimi iuris utriusque monarche D. Jasonis de Mayno De operis novi nunciatione* ... (Cremona, 1491); *Excellentissimi utriusque iuris monarche ... Andreae Barbatiae Commentaria in titulo de probationibus* (Bologna, 1497); *Novus tractatus excellentissimi iuris utriusque monarche D. Lauri de Pallatijs ... super statuto quod extantibus masculis femine non succedant* ([Venice], 1500); Jakob Wimpfeling, *Briefwechsel*, ed. Otto Herding and Dieter Mertens (Munich, 1990), vol. 2, no. 203 (a letter published in 1506), p. 533: "Ulricus Krafftus Ulmensis legum monarcha."

449-451 **Qui – rivos** For the image cf. Erasmus, *Carm.* 12, 1-2 (of Arnoldus Beka, professor of law at Louvain from 1481 to 1487): "is / Iuris fons gemini, non modo rivus erat."

450 **fonte perhenni** = Ov. *Am.* 3, 9, 25.

453 **et externas ... urbes** = *Rec.* 67 (n.).

454-455 **non – Pectine** Cf. lines 19-20 above (n.).

455-456 **iusticiae – Cultor** Cf. Luc. 2, 389; Mart. 10, 37, 1.

456-459 **cui se – Homero** Cf. Ov. *Rem.* 395-396; Mart. 14, 195, 1-2; Eob. *Buc.* 6, 10-11 (n.).

456 **cui se – fatentur** Cf. *Her. Chr.* 21, 61 (n.).

457 **Iura – bilance** Cf. *Epp. 4*, sig. F5ʳ (1508): "movet ... recta civilia iura bilance."

iusta – bilance Cf. Adam Werner von Themar, *Contra furibundam Sebastiani Brannt ... Musam ... boatus ... lusus anno Domini 1502 decimo kal. Julii*, line 5: "Quam vellem iusta te rem trutinasse bilance!" See Walther Ludwig, "Matern Hatten, Adam Werner, Sebastian Brant und das Problem der religiösen Toleranz," *Zeitschrift für die Geschichte des Oberrheins* 144 (1996): 287. The phrase occurs also in Eob. *Her. Chr.* 15, 79; cf. *Her. Chr.* 17, 123 (n.) and *Nob.* 103.

458 **Andino ... vati** Cf. *Buc.* B 1, 7; *Theoc.*, ded., sig. A2ᵛ: "Andino ... Maroni." For the epithet see Sil. 8, 594: "cantu / ... Andino" (a variant reading in some mss. and early edd. for "Aonio"); Mant. *Epigr.*, fol. 101ʳ: "Andino ... poetae"; Andrel. *Livia* 1, 1, 53: "tellus Andina"; 2, 6, 30: "Andinam ... tubam"; 3, 1, 15: "Andino ... cothurno"; Eob. *Buc.* 6, 2-3; *Hod.* 342: "Andinum ... nectar."

divina Poesis Cf. line 388 above (n.).

460 **florentis ... gratia linguae** = *Her. Chr.* 19, 27; cf. Mant. *1. Parthen.* 1, 264: "... florentis gloria linguae"; Ov. *Ep.* 12, 12; Marul. *Hymn. nat.* 3, 1, 272: "... divinae gratia linguae"; Eob. *Her. Chr.* 4, 243; B 1, 17.

461   **vulgi Latialis** Cf. Ov. *Met.* 15, 481.
462-463 **ferendus Laude** Cf. Verg. *A.* 1, 625; Eob. *Nor.* 61: "... nulla laude ferendas";
        877: "... laude feratur."
465   **Stirpis honos** = Line 152 above (n.).
466   **strepitus ... forenses** Cic. *Arch.* 12; *Orat.* 32; Eob. *Epic.* 4, 194; *Nor.* 836.
467   **Mite patrocinium** Ov. *Pont.* 1, 2, 68.
467-468 **Quid – sequeris** Cf. lines 45-46 above (n.).
468   **monuit ... Apollo** Cf. Verg. *Ecl.* 6, 3-4.
        Patareus Apollo Hor. *Carm.* 3, 4, 64.
469   **Ebria ... Musa** Ven. Fort. *Carm.* 11, 23, 8; Eob. *Sylv.* 1, 8, 24; 3, 6, 38.
470-472 **perpetuo – ortus** Cf. Vulg. *Eccl.* 1, 7.
470   **perpetuo – cursu** Cf. Ov. *Met.* 15, 179-180.
        flumina cursu = Ov. *Fast.* 4, 467; Stat. *Silv.* 1, 1, 20.
471   **requiem finemque** = [Juvenc.] *Triumph.* 41 (Eob. *Vict.* 238): "Da requiem
        finemque malis ..."; cf. Claud. *in Rufin.* 2, 331: "requiem ... finemque"; Vegius,
        Aen. 12: "... requiem finemque malorum"; Mant. *1. Parthen.* 3, 842: "requiem
        orabat finemque laborum"; Eob. *Vict.* 61: "... requiem finemque laborum."
473   **propositi metam ... laboris** = Hod. 271; cf. *Nor.* 47: "propositi ... vota laboris."
474   **Labor in ambages** Cf. line 46 above.
476   **Maior ... laus ... referenda** Cf. B 1, 8 below.
477-478 **portus – Contigimus** Cf. Ov. *Ars* 3, 748 (after calling for a return to his
        subject): "ut tangat portus fessa carina suas"; *Rem.* 812; Eob. *Laud.* 563-564;
        Val. 1, 653-654: "Plura quidem potui, sed me ceu littore abactum / Longius,
        immensi terruit unda freti"; 2, 381-382: "Et portum video, et longum mare
        restat eundum, / Sed quia praestiterat, littora prima petam"; *Tum.* 231-233:
        "sed me / Proposita brevitate decet traxisse rudentes / Iamdudum, et fessa
        portum petiisse carina." For the nautical metaphor see Curtius, *ELLMA*, pp.
        128-130; Eob. *Sylv. duae* 1, 188.
480   **totumque – orbem** Cf. lines 96 and 351 above, with notes.
481   **gloria famae** = Mart. *Sp.* 17, 1; Eob. *Epp.* 4, sig. F2ʳ (1508); Her. *Chr.* A 4, 17;
        22, 135; *Idyl.* 16, 28; *Nor.* 386.
483   **Et merito** = Lucr. 1, 107; 6, 458; Prop. 1, 17, 1; Ov. *Am.* 3, 12, 9; et al.; Eob.
        Buc. B 2, 17; Her. *Chr.* 3, 56; 21, 67; 21, 199.
        referenda est gratia = Ov. *Pont.* 1, 7, 61.
486   **Barbara – Syna** Cf. Her. 2, 2, 14: "Barbara Christipara distet ab urbe Tyrus."
487   **Costis** The patronymic recurs in Mant. *2. Parthen.* and Eob. Her. *Chr.* 4.
        Eobanus uses it also in line 526 below.
489   **cultu ... paupere** Tib. 1, 10, 19; 3, 3, 31; cf. line 513 below (n.).
489-490 **portus – dedit** Cf. Ov. *Ep.* 2, 108.
491   **meritis cumulavit** ≈ *Sylv.* 6, 5, 17: "meritis cumulatum."
492   **titulos et stemmata** Cf. *Epp.* 4, sig. F5ᵛ (1508): "Stemmata et ... titulos"; Her.
        Chr. 24, 71; Her., ded. 5: "tituli ... et stemmata avorum"; *Sylv.* 2, 8, 12: "titulos,
        stemmata"; Bebel, "In eum qui sine scientia solo titulo et gradu dignitatis
        superbiebat," *Carm.*, sig. o2ᵛ: "doctoris ... stemmata magni."
493   **maiora daturam** ≈ Prop. 1, 8, 37; Stat. *Silv.* 3, 2, 127; Mart. 8, 56, 1.
494   **melioris ... insignia palmae** Cf. lines 520-521 below; Her. *Chr.* 7, 66: "melior ...
        palma."
495-497 **Alma – portus** Imitated in Cordus, *Buc.* 9, 92 (*Ecl.* 10, 146): "Alma inopum
        nutrix tutusque est Hessia [Erffordia *1518*] portus."
495-496 **Alma – fessis** ≈ Lines 552-553 below.
497   **asylum** For the image see line 352 above (n.).
498   **Erudit – inertes** = Line 556 below.
498-499 **ornat ... Moribus** Paul. Nol. *Carm.* 25, 40.

501   chari ... parentes = Line 511 below; cf. Lucr. 3, 85; Verg. *A.* 1, 646; 5, 747.
501-502   cecidere ... Ante diem Cf. Verg. *A.* 4, 620; Eob. *Her. Chr.* 11, 53; *Her.* 1, 6, 190.
502   **Ante diem** = Verg. *A.* 1, 374; Ov. *Ars* 3, 739; et al.; Eob. *Buc.* 6, 74; *Epic.* 6, 10;
             cf. *Rec.* 139 (n.).
             acceptos ... honores Cf. line 520 below. Eobanus uses "honores" to mean
             academic degrees also in lines 507 (n.), 532, and 554 below.
             invidit honores = Claud. *Cons. Stil.* 2, 232.
503   **torvo .... vultu** = Stat. *Silv.* 2, 6, 73; Eob. *Her. Chr.* B 1, 35; cf. Hor. *Ep.* 1, 19,
             12; Ov. *Met.* 2, 270; et al.
504   **divitiis ... beavit** = *Epp. 4,* sig. F6ʳ (1508): "parenti, / Qui te divitiis, qui te
             virtute beavit."
             melior fortuna = Hor. *Carm.* 1, 7, 25; Ov. *Met.* 7, 518.
505   **tot iam − annis** = Verg. *A.* 2, 14; cf. line 62 above (n.).
506   **castra Minervae** Cf. *Rec.* 33-34 (n.).
507   **neque teste opus** *Idyl.* 5, 19; cf. *Her. Chr.* 8, 69.
             profectus honores = *Epp. 4,* sig. F6ᵛ (1508), referring to the baccalaureate
             degree: "Ad gravis aeternos baculi profectus honores"; cf. line 502 above (n.).
509   **Te − annis** Cf. *Buc.* 2, 2-3.
             Pater omnipotens = Lucr. 5, 399; Verg. *G.* 2, 325; *A.* 1, 60; and often.
             melioribus − annis Cf. *Her. Chr.* 16, 129; *Her.* 1, 6, 71: "... melioribus exuit
             annis." For "melioribus annis" see also Verg. *A.* 6, 649; Ov. *Tr.* 4, 10, 93.
510   **Pauper eras** = Mart. 4, 40, 4.
             primo ... aevo = Ov. *Pont.* 1, 2, 137; Eob. *Hod.*, lim. 3; cf. *Her. Chr.* 13, 79 (n.).
511   **chari ... parentes** = Line 501 above (n.).
512   **inertia vitae** = *Culex* 385; Eob. *Her. Chr.* 12, 273.
512-513   **vitae Tempora** = Ov. *Tr.* 4, 9, 5-6.
513   **divite cultu** = *Culex* 95; Ov. *Met.* 5, 49; cf. line 489 above (n.).
514   **Croeso** Croesus was proverbially wealthy. See Otto 468; Häussler, pp. 99, 150,
             and 266; Erasmus, *Adag.* 1, 6, 74.
             portus et aura The image comes from Ov. *Ep.* 1, 110: "tu citius venias, portus et
             aura tuis." Citing among other examples Ov. *Pont.* 2, 8, 68 and Apul. *Met.* 11,
             15, modern editors emend this phrase to "... portus et ara tuis." See further Eob.
             Her. Chr. 5, 40 (n.).
518   **Prima − aetas** ≈ *Epic.* 5, 75: "Prima rudimentis clausa est iuvenilibus aetas."
519   **Ad ... tempus deducta** Cf. Ov. *Met.* 1, 4.
520   **acceptos ... honores** Cf. line 502 above (n.).
521   **Doctoralis ... palmae** Cf. line 494 above, referring to the M.A. degree.
522   **Pontificis − Dei** Cf. *Her. Chr.* 6, 122; 6, 124.
523   **Ecclesian** Eobanus uses the Greek ending to avoid elision.
525   **cantibus odas** = Sedul. 1, 23: "Daviticis adsuetus cantibus odas / ... resonare."
526   **Costis** See note to line 487 above.
528   **ensiferae ... virginis aedes** Cf. *Pug.* 29 (n.). For "ensiferae" cf. line 29 above (n.):
             "Armigerae ... Minervae."
             virginis aedes = *Rec.* 55; *Laud.* 170.
529   **Templa frequentantur** ≈ Ov. *Fast.* 4, 871.
             magnae ... Minervae = *Rec.* 45 (n.); cf. *Rec.* 33-34 (n.).
530   **Atria ... alta** Verg. *A.* 4, 665-666; 12, 474.
531   **venerande pater** Aus. *Ad patrem de suscepto filio* 2 (*Ep.* 17, 2).
532   **pendat honores** Cf. line 554 below. For "honores" in this sense see line 502
             above (n.).
533   **Palladiae ... coronae** = *Laud.* B 2, 1; cf. Ov. *Ars* 1, 727 (olive wreath); Eob. *Pug.*
             44; 107.
             tota cohors = *Rec.* 187 (n.).

cohors collecta *Nup.* 108.

534-537 **Scitis – gentibus** Cf. *Nob.* 287-294.

534 **et externae ... urbes** ≈ *Rec.* 67 (n.).

537 **cunctis ... gentibus** = Luc. 8, 19.

538 **Austriacae ... Viennae** *Accl.* 2, 35.

539 **Agrippinae ... urbis** Cologne (Colonia Agrippinensis) was named for Nero's mother Julia Agrippina (AD 15-59). For another explanation see *Her. Chr.* 17, 201 (n.): "Agrippae ... urbem."

540 **Rhenana Moguntia** = *Hod.* 117.

542 **Musis ... amplificata Latinis** Cf. *Her. Chr.* 24, 131-132, alluding (as here) to Hermann von dem Busche's *Lipsica* [Leipzig, 1504?].

543 **Albioris – recenti** Eobanus alludes to Georgius Sibutus's praise of Wittenberg in his *Silvula in Albiorim illustratam* (Leipzig, [winter 1506/07]). The humanistic name "Albioris" for Wittenberg first occurs on the title page of Nikolaus Marschalk's *Oratio habita ... Thurio Albiori acadaemia* (Wittenberg, 18 January 1503). The colophon of this booklet uses the same word: "Impressum Albiori in Sassonia." See Maria Großmann, *Wittenberger Drucke 1502 bis 1517: Ein bibliographischer Beitrag zur Geschichte des Humanismus in Deutschland* (Vienna, 1971), no. 3, p. 11. Some later occurrences are noted in: Carl G. Brandis, *Beiträge aus der Universitätsbibliothek zu Jena: Zur Geschichte des Reformationsjahrhunderts = Zeitschrift des Vereins für Thüringische Geschichte und Altertumskunde*, N.F., Beiheft 8 (Jena, 1917), pp. 24-26. Eobanus uses the name also in *Sylv.* 2, 25, 3.

544 **Sarmaticae ... gentis** *Nup.* 21 (n.).

Cracovia The reading "Crocavia" in *A* is most likely a misprint. However, cf. the form "Croca" found, for example, in Celtis, *Am.* 1, 3, 18; Eob. *Sarmat.*, lim. 3; and *Epic.*, app. 5, 12: "Pulchra ubi Sarmaticas Croca gubernat opes."

545-546 **studiis ... Ingenuis** *Ama.* A 1, 3; cf. *Rec.* 87 (n.).

545 **satis – superque** Line 398 above (n.).

547 **venditis auro** ≈ Stat. *Theb.* 8, 104; Luc. 3, 160; cf. Verg. *A.* 6, 621.

551 **longa spe** Hor. *Carm.* 1, 4, 15; 1, 11, 7; Eob. *Her. Chr.* 13, 145 (n.).

552-553 **Ast – fessis** ≈ Lines 495-496 above.

554 **impendit honores** = Hutten, *Querel.* 2, 1, 25: "mihi ... impendit honores / Rostochium"; cf. Paul. Nol. *Carm.* 18, 109: "... inpendit honorem"; line 532 above. For "honores" in this sense see line 502 above (n.).

555 **noverca** The stepmother's malignity was proverbial. See Otto 1239; Häussler, pp. 61, 76, 113, 193-194, 241, and 282; Erasmus, *Adag.* 2, 2, 95.

556 **Erudit – inertes** = Line 498 above.

557 **primis ... ab annis** = Verg. *A.* 2, 87; Ov. *Pont.* 2, 2, 1; Eob. *Her. Chr.* 13, 65; cf. *Buc.* 3, 65 (n.); *Her. Chr.* 2, 89; also *Rec.* 86 (n.); *Laud.* B 3, 33.

558 **Patrios ... penates** = Verg. *A.* 4, 598; Prop. 4, 1, 91; cf. Eob. *Rec.* 66 (n.).

558-559 **laude ... Eximia** Verg. *A.* 7, 496.

559 **paupere dives** = Locher, *Stult.*, fol. 10ʳ: "... cum paupere dives." Cf. Eob. *Ama.* 5, 7 (n.): "ex divite pauperem."

561 **properate citi** Verg. *A.* 12, 425.

cura parentum = Juvenc. 3, 492.

562 **asylum** For the image see line 352 above (n.).

563-564 **Et iam – portus** For the nautical metaphor cf. lines 477-478 (n.).

563 **lassatae – carinae** Cf. Ov. *Met.* 11, 559; *Tr.* 1, 2, 2; *Ib.* 17; 275-276.

564 **Hic teneat ... anchora** Ov. *Ars* 1, 772.

565 **requiem sperare** Juv. 6, 106.

566 **Tempus adest** = Prop. 4, 6, 53; Ov. *Am.* 3, 2, 44; *Met.* 14, 808; *Pont.* 2, 2, 67.

566-567 **Fervens – morbos** Cf. *Pug.* 1-2 (with notes).

566	**caelo – ardet** ≈ *Buc.* 7, 72; cf. Verg. *G.* 4, 425-426.
	Procyon See n. *Pug.* 1.
567	**tristes ... morbos** ≈ Ov. *Met.* 7, 601.
568	**succingite tempora** Cf. Verg. *A.* 5, 71; lines 570-571 below.
	tempora lauro = Verg. *A.* 3, 81; 5, 246; 5, 539; *Ciris* 121; *Tib.* 2, 5, 5; et al.; Eob., verse letter (1508) in Trebelius, *Epigr.*, sig. F2ᵛ; *Buc.* 2, 77; 8, 101.
570-571	**fagineo – Tempora** Cf. Ov. *Fast.* 4, 656; line 568 above (n.).
571	**impexos ... capillos** = Ov. *Met.* 1, 529 (in some early edd.); cf. Eob. *Nup.* 187.
572	**serta poetae** = Prop. 3, 1, 19.
574	**ructabo carmina** Cf. Hor. *Ars* 457 (of the crazy poet): "versus ructatur."
	carmina laudis ≈ *Rec.* 77 (n.).
575	**Ite bonis avibus** = Ov. *Met.* 15, 640; cf. *Fast.* 1, 513; Eob. *Buc.* 1, 44 (n.); B 11, 21 (n.). For "bonis avibus" see Erasmus, *Adag.* 1, 1, 75.
575-578	**latrator ... morsu ... rodere** For the combination of images see *Pug.* B 1, 1 (n.).
575	**latrator Anubis** = *Pug.* B 1, 3, with notes.
577	**Tu – solebas** Cf. *Nup.* 368; also cf. *Buc.* B 1, 1.
579	**Livor edax** = Ov. *Am.* 1, 15, 1; *Rem.* 389: "rumpere, Livor edax" (cf. line 581 below); Mart. 11, 33, 3; Eob. *Buc.* B 1, 5; cf. Luc. 1, 288; Eob. *Buc.* 4, 95.
580	**Aequa mente** *Buc.* 10, 70 (n.).
581	**Non – ruperis** = Hor. *S.* 2, 3, 319 (referring to the frog that tried to puff itself up to the size of a calf); cf. Eob. *Buc.* 10, 125 (alluding to the same fable).
583	**volucres ... nubes** V. Fl. 2, 516.
584	**Ex – favos** Cf. Ov. *Ars* 1, 748.
585	**Liget – fratres** Cf. *Psalt.* 133, 1: "... ligat unanimes foelix concordia fratres." The model is Verg. *G.* 2, 496: "... infidos agitans discordia fratres."
	stabilis concordia = *Idyl.* 16, 118 (lauding Nuremberg).
587	**nomen honorque** Ov. *Pont.* 3, 2, 32.
588-590	**faciles – versu** For the modesty formula cf. *Nup.* 356-357: "nobis, si quid versu peccamus inepto, / In veniam faciles ignoscite."
589	**Viciis ignoscite** Hor. *S.* 1, 4, 131.
590	**Non bene tornato ... versu** Cf. Hor. *Ars* 441.

B 1

Meter: Elegiac distich.

1	**toto ... mundo** = Verg. *Ecl.* 4, 9; Ov. *Met.* 15, 254.
2	**Venturae ... posteritatis eris** = *Her. Chr.* 24, 48; cf. Ov. *Tr.* 4, 9, 26; *Pont.* 2, 6, 34.
3	**pendebit – tellus** Cf. Ov. *Met.* 1, 12; 7, 379; Eob. *Vict.* 8-9: "orbis / ... penderet in aere."
4	**Cynthia – equis** Cf. Ov. *Rem.* 258; Eob. *Her. Chr.* 12, 282.
7	**Non tua – umbras** Cf. Verg. *A.* 4, 654.
8	**Clarior ... laus referenda** Cf. *Laud.* 476.
	ad superas ... domos = *Her. Chr.* 19, 140; *Sylv.* 1, 11, 40; cf. Ov. *Fast.* 1, 298; 2, 188; *Met.* 4, 735-736; Eob. *Her. Chr.* 1, 178; *Hod.* 55.
9	**in cineres ... favillas** = Luc. 6, 537.
	in cineres verti Cf. Ov. *Ep.* 1, 24; *Met.* 2, 216; *Tr.* 5, 12, 68; also cf. Hor. *Ep.* 1, 15, 39.
	tenues ... favillas Ov. *Ars* 3, 203 (referring to mascara).
10	**In – habet** Cf. Ov. *Am.* 1, 1, 5; *Tr.* 3, 7, 48; Eob. *Buc.* 9, 7-8; B 9, 6; *Idyl.*, 1. ded. 22 (2. ded. 20): "monumenta ... / In quae Parca nihil iuris habere queat"; *Epic.* 5, 4.

11-16   **Clara – honor** For the commonplace that poetry confers immortality on those it celebrates see *Laud.* 61-64 (n.).
11   **Danais ... Pergama flammis** ≈ Ov. *Met.* 14, 467.
12   **avos** Cf. Verg. *A.* 6, 840: "avos Troiae."
15-16   **perpetuis – Gloria** Cf. *Laud.* 63 (n.).
16   **fama, perhennis** = Ov. *Am.* 1, 10, 62 (different).
        perhennis honor Paul. Nol. *Carm.* 19, 298.
17   **tibi pro meritis** = Ov. *Am.* 3, 6, 105; Mart. 4, 51, 5; et al.; Eob. *Her.*, ded. 90: "Si tibi pro meritis praemia nulla ferant."
        grates – rependo Cf. Juvenc. 1, 96: "laudes ... gratesque rependit."

B 2

Meter: Elegiac distich.

tit.   **Susque deque ferendum** Proverbial; see Otto 1723; Häussler, p. 245; Erasmus, *Adag.* 1, 3, 83.
1   **Palladiae ... coronae** = *Laud.* 533 (n.).
        titulum ... decusque Stat. *Silv.* 2, 7, 62.
2   **Numen habet** = Mart. *Sp.* 33, 7; Eob. *Sylv. duae* 1, 13; cf. *Sylv. duae* 1, 12 (n.).
        numen inane = Hutten, *De virtute* 42 (*Opera*, vol. 3, p. 9).
3   **persolves dignas ... grates** Verg. *A.* 1, 600; 2, 537.

B 3

This epigram and Eobanus's response (B 4) were first edited by Eduard Böcking in: Hutten, *Opera*, vol. 1, pp. 3-4.
        Meter: Elegiac distich.

tit.   **vivacissimi ingenii** *Ama.* 30, 4; cf. Hutten, *Querel.* 2, 8, tit. (early 1510): "Ad Eobanum Hessum, vivacissimum poetam."
2   **fugiunt – rogos** Cf. Ov. *Am.* 3, 9, 28; *Tr.* 4, 1, 102. For the commonplace see Eob. *Rec.* B 1, 9-13 (n.).
3   **putres ... artus** = Stat. *Theb.* 12, 138.
5   **post ... fata superstes** Ov. *Am.* 3, 15, 20; Camerarius, *Nar.* 33, 9 (n.).
        ultima fata Luc. 7, 380; Sil. 7, 224.
6   **spesque decusque** ≈ Ermolao Barbaro, epitaph for Rudolphus Agricola, quoted in Erasmus, *Ep.* 174, line 24, and *Adag.* 1, 4, 39, *ASD* 2, 1, p. 440, line 799: "... Frisii spemque decusque soli."
10   **vafros – senes** On the topos "Boy and old man" see *Laud.*, lim. 12 (n.).
        tenero ... in ore = Mart. 11, 91, 6; cf. Ov. *Am.* 3, 6, 60.
11   **Ergo – mater** Cf. *Buc.* 9, 113. For "pondera" in the sense "unborn child" see, for instance, Lucr. 4, 1250; Prop. 4, 1, 100; Ov. *Am.* 2, 14, 14; *Ep.* 11, 37; Eob. *Buc.* 9, 113; 11, 63 (n.); *Her. Chr.* 1, 205; 2, 48; 2, 74; 13, 4; 13, 76; 13, 129.
12   **enixa – suo** Cf. Ov. *Ep.* 4, 58.
        pignora tanta = Prop. 4, 11, 12.
14   **Ingenii dotes** = Ov. *Ars* 2, 112.
16   **vela secunda** = Prop. 3, 17, 2; Ov. *Ars* 2, 64; *Fast.* 3, 790.
19   **cothurnatus** Cf. Hutten, *Querel.* 2, 8, 1 (early 1510): "Hesse, cothurnati divine poematis auctor."
        curvis ... theatris = Ov. *Ars* 1, 89.
20   **veterum ... ducum** = Mart. 9, 83, 2.
        tristia fata = Ov. *Am.* 3, 9, 2; *Fast.* 6, 748; *Tr.* 3, 3, 38; Eob. *Her. Chr.* 18, 156;

cf. *Rec.* 49; *Buc.* 9, 17 (n.).

21   **modulere poemata** ≈ Aus. *Protrepticus ad nepotem* 56.
22   **Excultum – opus** Cf. Prop. 3, 1, 8.
25   **venturos ... nepotes** Verg. *A.* 3, 158.
27   **natura dedit** = Prop. 2, 18, 25; 4, 11, 47; Juv. 12, 79.
28   **versus ... verba tuos** ≈ Ov. *Fast.* 1, 162.
      barbara verba = Ov. *Pont.* 4, 13, 20; Celtis, *Am.* 1, 4, 32; Eob. *Her. Chr.* 8, 6.
29   **Phrygios ... penates** = Claud. *Rapt. Pros.* 1, 180; Eob. *Nup.* 131; cf. Verg. *A.* 3, 148.
33   **adhuc iuvenis** = Ov. *Ep.* 15, 93.
      primisque sub annis = Ov. *Met.* 13, 596; cf. Eob. *Laud.* 557 (n.).
35   **Vive – nostri** = Ov. *Ep.* 11, 125.

B 4

Meter: Elegiac distich.

1   **Ergo vale** = Aus. *Parent.* 3, 23; cf. Juv. 3, 318: "ergo vale nostri memor ...."
      superis ... secundis = Sil. 11, 504.
2   **Catholicus ... Apollo** See n. *Laud.* 13.
4   **Dimidium nostri** Cf. Hor. *Carm.* 1, 3, 8: "Reddas incolumem precor / Et serves animae dimidium meae." For the image "half of my soul" cf. Eob. *Sylv.* 4, 14, 1: "dimidium mei"; *Her. Chr.* 9, 10 (n.): "Maxima pars ... mei."
5   **viridi ... corona** = Sil. 16, 525.
6   **titulo ... nobiliore** *Her. Chr.* 21, 52.

B 5

Meter: Elegiac distich.

1   **Hesse puer** = Mutian. *Ep.* 79 (epigram on Eobanus Hessus, line 26); Camerarius, *Nar.* 14, 1 (n.).
      puer – poetas On the topos "Boy and old man" see *Laud.*, lim. 12 (n.).
2   **pollice – ebur** Cf. Claud. *Rapt. Pros.* 2, praef. 16: "pollice festivo nobile duxit ebur." In antiquity lyres were often inlaid with ivory. For the metonymy ivory = lyre see also Stat. *Silv.* 1, 2, 3; Mutian. *Ep.* 417, line 1 (a verse letter from Eobanus Hessus to Mutianus Rufus of August 1506): "ebur, plectrum"; Eob. *Vict.*, ded. 24.
3   **immensum ... mundum** Ov. *Met.* 2, 35.
4   **ut perhibent** = Verg. *G.* 1, 247; *A.* 4, 179; et al.; Eob. *Her. Chr.* 10, 83.
      carmina – carent = Ov. *Am.* 1, 15, 32; Eob. *Buc.* 2, 96. For the commonplace see *Rec.* B 1, 9-13 (n.).
5   **Vive diu** = Tib. 1, 6, 63; *Eleg. Maec.* 2, 27; Stat. *Silv.* 2, 3, 43.
      longaevum Nestora Mart. 8, 6, 9. Nestor was proverbial for his longevity. See Otto 1223; Häussler, pp. 61, 112, 192, 241, and 281; Erasmus, *Adag.* 1, 6, 66.
      Nestora vincas ≈ Ov. *Met.* 13, 63.
6   **caedet harena** = Ov. *Ars* 1, 254; cf. Otto 786; Häussler, pp. 57, 73, 104, 169, 237, and 273.

B 6
Meter: Elegiac distich.

1   **nobis ... duobus** = Ov. *Met.* 1, 365.
2   **Unus amor** = *Buc.* 3, 11, where see notes.
           Duo – eadem For the commonplace see Otto 111; Häussler, pp. 52, 69, 95,
           133-134, 232, and 261; Erasmus, *Adag.* 1, 1, 2 ("Amicus alter ipse"); Eob. *Nup.*
           313.

Notes to
DE AMANTIUM INFOELICITATE

Liminary poem

The model for this *propempticon* – the poet's final instructions to his book before sending it out into the world – is Ov. *Tr.* 1, 1. Cf. also Hor. *Ep.* 1, 20; Mart. 3, 4; 3, 5; 7, 84; 10, 104; 12, 3; Eob. *Ama.* B 4; *Buc.*, ded. 7-10; *Buc.* B 11; *Nup.*, lim.; *Accl.*, lim.; *Sylv.* 3, 4.
　　　Meter: Elegiac distich.

1-2	**Vade ... saluta, ... liber** Ov. *Tr.* 1, 1, 15; cf. Eob. *Buc.* B 11, 1 (n.).
1	**Vade ... voce saluta** = *Sylv.* 3, 4, 3.
	tenui ... voce *Epic. Drusi* 108.
	voce saluta = Alcuin. *Carm.* 4, 18: "humili ... voce saluta"; cf. Juvenc. 4, 517: "... blanda cum voce salutat"; Eob. *Hymn.* 64: "Voce salutat."
3	**facilem te prebe** Cic. *Att.* 14, 13 A, 2; Sen. *Ben.* 2, 17, 6.
5-6	**Ut placeas – legi** Cf. *Buc.* B 11, 25-26.
5	**celebres titulos** = *Nup.* 228; cf. Ov. *Fast.* 1, 601-602.
6	**Sic – legi** Cf. Ov. *Tr.* 2, 80; Eob. *Buc.* B 2, 38; *Nup.*, lim. 2.

Dedicatory letter

tit.	**morum – commendabili** If Petrejus Eberbach is to some extent the model for Fronto Fundinus, as I propose in the introduction, the phrase "morum sanctitate commendabili" must be an insider's joke.
1	**Pulchrum ... et preclarum** Pl. *Mil.* 1042; Eob. *Ama.* A 1, 2; B 3, 1; cf. Cic. *Sen.* 43: "pulchrum atque praeclarum."
2	**iusta** This is a variant spelling of "iuxta"; see also *Ama.* 26, 4.
	ne semper – absolvant Cf. [Sen.] *Formula vitae honestae* 2 (= *Martini episcopi Bracarensis opera omnia*, ed. Claude W. Barlow, [New Haven, 1950], p. 240): "Non semper in actu sis, sed interdum animo tuo requiem dato, sed requies ipsa plena sit sapientiae studiis et cogitationibus bonis. Nam prudens numquam otio marcet. Animum aliquando remissum habet, numquam solutum."
	oportunitatem This spelling is common in the late Middle Ages and the Renaissance. See, for example, *Ama.* A 1, 9; cf. *Ama.* 3, 2: "oportune"; *Sylv. duae* 2, 43: "Oportuna."
5	**nulla alia causa – devitarem** For the thought cf. *Her. Chr.*, ded. 8, 2.
	sub dio *Buc.* 11, 15 (n.).
6	**ocium – ignavum** Cf. Sen. *Ep.* 82, 3: "Otium sine litteris mors est."
7	**tanquam – fugiendum** Cf. *Buc.* 6, 69; *Venus* 2, 259: "tanquam aconita fuge."
8	**Libellum – dedicavimus** Cf. *Her. Chr.*, ded. 1, 1 (n.): "Heroidas Christianas ... tibi statim et a principio nuncupare statui, Iobe, pontifex optime."
	Xenocrati – recubanti The anecdote is told in V. Max. 4, 3, ext. 3a, who in turn took it from Diogenes Laertius 4, 7.
	Nasonem – expetentem Cf. Ov. *Am.* 2, 10, 29-38, where the poet, however, is not thinking of his mistress Corinna in particular, but rather of dying while making love.
9	**Sophoclem – abstinentem** In *Sen.* 47 Cicero quotes the aged Sophocles as saying that he has fled from the delights of love as from a brutish and frenzied master: "bene Sophocles, cum ex eo quidam iam adfecto aetate quaereret

uteretur ne rebus veneriis: 'di meliora!' inquit; 'libenter vero istinc sicut ab domino agresti ac furioso profugi.' The anecdote is also told in Plato, *R.* 1, 329 c; V. Max. 4, 3, ext. 2.

Musarum sacerdotes Hor. *Carm.* 3, 1, 3.

hortis Epicuri Cic. *Fin.* 5, 3; *N. D.* 1, 93; cf. Prop. 3, 21, 26 (all referring to the garden where Epicurus taught).

10   **Quamvis – conabuntur** Eobanus similarly anticipates his critics in *Her. Chr.*, ded. 3, 1: "Quanquam futuros non dubito qui dicant ... praecipitanter aeditum."

11   **Tractant – fabri** Quoted from Hor. *Ep.* 2, 1, 116; cf. Erasmus, *Adag.* 1, 6, 15.

12   **De hoc – relinquimus** Cf. *Her. Chr.*, ded. 14, 1: "de his ... erudito lectori iudicandum censeo."

13   **totis viribus** Verg. *A.* 12, 528; Ov. *Met.* 10, 658; Eob. *Ama.* 35, 82.

          hunc libellum ..., quem – consecravimus Cf. *Nup.*, ded. 4 (n.): "... futurae posteritati transmissa aeternitati consecraretur"; *Her. Chr.*, ded. 1, 2: "sub tui sacri nominis tutela secundis ventis in prophanum vulgus abeuntes"; 17, 1: "librum hunc ... tuo sacro nomini nuncupatum dedicatumque publicae lectioni tradere, posteritati transmittere, immortalitatique consecrare non dubitavi." Cf. further Curt. 9, 6, 26: "immortalitati consecretur"; 10, 5, 30: "immortalitati consecrare"; Eob. *Ama.* 34, 4, where "immortalitati me consecrasse" refers to Eobanus's own aspirations.

A 1

tit.   **Doctor** Here the title is equivalent to "Magister" (the title used in the dedicatory letter above). Eberbach had just received his M.A. (in February 1508).

1   **Est ut ais** *Buc.* 7, 25 (n.).

2   **P. Scipionem – ociosi** Cf. Cic. *Off.* 3, 1: "P. Scipionem ... eum, qui primus Africanus appellatus est, dicere solitum scripsit Cato ... numquam se minus otiosum esse, quam cum otiosus ... esset. Magnifica vero vox et magno viro ac sapiente digna"; also cf. *Rep.* 1, 27; Karl Gross, "*Numquam minus otiosus, quam cum otiosus*: Das Weiterleben eines antiken Sprichwortes im Abendland," *Antike und Abendland* 26 (1980): 122-137. For the thought cf. also Eob. *Buc.* 2, 82-83 (n.): "doctam ... segnitiem."

3   **myropolii** The term (applied to the Lateran pharmacy) occurs also in Eobanus's letter of 4 March 1509 to Mutianus Rufus. See Mutian. *Ep.* 643 (vol. 2, p. 337).

          ingenuis studiis *Laud.* 545-546; cf. *Rec.* 87 (n.).

4   **ociosum tempus** Cic. *Amic.* 104; Mart. 5, 20, 3.

7   **in libidinem – adulescentiae** Cf. Cic. *Part.* 34: "adulescentiam procliviorem esse ad libidinem."

9   **oportunitas** For the spelling see *Ama.*, ded. 2 (n.).

A 2

Meter: Elegiac distich.

2   **Davidis** For the genitive form see Juvenc. 1, 151; 1, 166; 2, 105; et al.

3   **virgine ... Diana** Verg. *A.* 4, 511; cf. Eob. *Pug.* 70 (n.).

4   **tetricus ... Cato** Cf. Mant. *c. Poet.* 151: "tetrici ... Catones"; *Ecl.* 2, 134: "tetricos ... Catones"; Eob. *Hod.* 450: "tetrica morosos fronte Catonas"; *Venus* 2, 258: "tetricos ... severa fronte Catones." The censor M. Porcius Cato was proverbial for his rigid sense of morality. See Otto 358; Häussler, pp. 98, 146, and 234.

A 3

The initials "V. I." and "P. D." that precede and follow the epigram probably stand for: "Vir Illustris Petrus Dedit."

Meter: Elegiac distich.

1	**Aurea ... mens** Aus. *Prof.* 20, 11.
	cupidis – puellis Cf. *Priap.* 80, 3: "cupidas ... puellas"; Prop. 1, 11, 29: "... castis inimica puellis."
2	**sine ... crimine vita** Verg. *A.* 4, 550; cf. Eob. *Her. Chr.* 11, 10; 20, 70.
3	**frigora noctis** = Tib. 1, 2, 29; Ov. *Am.* 1, 9, 15.
4	**dominae ... fores** = Prop. 1, 10, 16; cf. Ov. *Am.* 1, 9, 8.
	surdas ... fores = Ov. *Am.* 1, 6, 54.
5	**durae ... sortis** Sen. *Tro.* 524; Claud. *in Rufin.* 2, 89-90.

De amantium infoelicitate

The work stands in the tradition of remedies for passionate (or illicit) love, the ultimate model for which is Ovid's *Remedia amoris*. For some late medieval and Renaissance examples see: "Pseudo-Remedia amoris," ed. Erich J. Thiel in "Mittellateinische Nachdichtungen von Ovids 'Ars amatoria' und 'Remedia amoris,'" *Mittellateinisches Jahrbuch* 5 (1968): 177-180; Aeneas Silvius, "Amoris illiciti medela," letter 106 in his *Opera quae extant omnia* (Basel, 1571), pp. 607-610; and Johann Tröster, *De remedio amoris*, ed. Hans Rupprich, *Die Frühzeit des Humanismus und der Renaissance in Deutschland*, Deutsche Literatur, Reihe Humanismus und Renaissance, vol. 1 (1938; Darmstadt, 1964), pp. 182-197. Eobanus's *Sylvae duae*, poem 2, also stands in this tradition. See further: Mary Frances Wack, *Lovesickness in the Middle Ages: The Viaticum and Its Commentaries* (Philadelphia, 1990); *A Treatise on Lovesickness. Jacques Ferrand*, ed. and trans. Donald A. Beecher and Massimo Ciavolella (Syracuse, NY, 1990).

In both *De amantium infoelicitate* and *Sylvae duae* Eobanus uses an actual love affair as his starting point. He then adds a dollop of scandal in order to turn the everyday, trivial romance into the object of a moralistic attack on illicit love. In *De amantium infoelicitate* he follows Aeneas Silvius by turning Petrejus's girl into a prostitute (see note at 11, 12–12, 4 below); in *Sylvae duae* 2 he changes the humanist-poet Temonius into the priest Collucius, who sordidly celebrates mass while thinking of nothing but his mistress.

1, 1	**saliceta** This form for "salicta" occurs also in Cordus, *Buc.* 1, 135; Eob. *Dial.* 1, sig. A2ᵛ; *Nor.* 1249; *Theoc.* 32, sig. M5ʳ.
	lucus – densus Cf. Ov. *Fast.* 6, 9.
	densus, umbrositate Cf. Verg. *Ecl.* 2, 3 (describing the place where Corydon sings of his hopeless love): "inter densas, umbrosa cacumina, fagos"; Eob. *Buc.* 7, 3-4 (introducing an eclogue on passionate love).
	fontem – habebam Cf. *Buc.* 1, 67-68; Calp. *Ecl.* 1, 11-12: "bullantes ubi fagus aquas radice sub ipsa / protegit et ramis errantibus implicat umbras"; Cic. *Div.* 2, 63: "sub platano umbrifera, fons unde emanat aquaï." The purling spring or babbling brook, where one can take one's ease in the shade of towering trees, is part of the ideal landscape ("locus amoenus") as described in ancient and later European literature. See Curtius, *ELLMA*, pp. 185-200; and, for example, Ov. *Met.* 2, 455-456; *Rem.* 177; Sen. *Phaed.* 514; Nemes. *Ecl.* 4, 47; Eob. *Buc.* 1, 65-71 (n.); 2, 82-86; 3, 1-2; 3, 83-84; 4, 37-40; 5, 1-3; 7, 74-75; 7, 123-125; *Her. Chr.* 4, 62; 20, 21-26.
	patulae fagi Echoing the opening line of Vergil's eclogues ("... patulae recubans sub tegmine fagi"), this phrase evokes an Arcadian scene. Cf. Eob. *Val.* 1, 443:

"patulae sub tegmine fagi"; also cf. *Buc.* 3, 83 (n.); 7, 123-124.

sacrum habebam Eobanus affects the ancient belief that all springs are sacred.

1, 1-2 **apparuit iuvenis – edidit** Cf. the quite similar scene in *Buc.* 3, 82-87.

1, 1 **vultu pallido** Pallor is a conventional symptom of lovesickness. See n. *Laud.* 237.

1, 2 **ex imo – ducens** Cf. Verg. *A.* 2, 288; Ov. *Met.* 10, 402-403; Eob. *Sylv. duae* 2, 149 (n.).

1, 3 **lucano** The adjective (formed from "lucus") appears to be a neologism. A contemporary manuscript note in the Strasbourg copy glosses it with "silvestri."

2, 1-6 **Et quis – remedium** Unhappy lovers shun the company of their fellows and prefer to grieve in communion with nature. See, for example, Verg. *Ecl.* 2, 4-5; Prop. 1, 18; Ov. *Ep.* 15, 137-138; Nemes. *Ecl.* 4, 12-13; Mant. *Ecl.* 3, 143-144; Eob. *Buc.* 3, 109-110; 3, 151-152.

2, 3 **convictus ... miseris solatium prebet** Cf. Sen. *Ben.* 4, 18, 3: "[societas] solacia contra dolores dedit"; Walther 29943: "Solamen miseris socios habuisse malorum."

2, 4 **Solitudo – mater est** Cf. Walther 29962a2: "Solitudo est mater sollicitudinis."

2, 5 **Loca – potes** Ov. *Rem.* 579-580.

3, 1 **Sic effatus conticui** Cf. Verg. *A.* 6, 53-54; 6, 197; 7, 135; 9, 22.

arrectis auribus Verg. *A.* 1, 152; 2, 303; 12, 618; Otto 215; Häussler, pp. 96 and 138; Erasmus, *Adag.* 3, 2, 56.

3, 2 **oportune** For the spelling see *Ama.*, ded. 2 (n.).

4, 1 **finem loquendi faciebat** Sal. *Jug.* 14, 25; Caes. *Gal.* 1, 46, 2; Vulg. *Deut.* 20, 9.

4, 3 **contubernalem** Cf. *Ama.* 28, 1.

5, 1 **dii nemorum** Ov. *Met.* 7, 198; *Fast.* 3, 309.

5, 2-6 **O Fortuna – exerces** For this image of Fortuna see Howard R. Patch, *The Goddess Fortuna in Mediaeval Literature* (1927; New York, 1967); Eob. *Sylv.* 1, 4, especially lines 31-42:

> Insidet instabili Fortuna volubilis orbi
>   Et nigra tectum sindone lumen habet.
> Passibus incertis et in haec et in illa vagatur,
>   Nec minimum constans temporis esse potest.
> Tam fovet indignos quam dignos deprimit; errat,
>   Non videt, errorem quo tueatur habet.
> Deiicit elatos, deiectos tollit in altum,
>   Pessima saepe bonis, optima saepe malis.
> Nulli fida diu, nulli constanter amica,
>   Nunc prius osa cupit, nunc adamata fugit.
> Ludit et ostentat vires lasciva potentes,
>   Utque oculo orbata est, sic ratione caret.

See also *Sylv. duae* 1, 166 (n.); *Sylv.* 1, 1, 86; 2, 1, 11-12; 4, 2, 15-20; 4, 14, 37-40.

5, 4 **Bonis – erigis** Cf. *Sylv.* 4, 2, 18, referring to Fortuna: "Bonis iniqua est, aequa semper improbis."

5, 5 **Rotae – insistis** See Otto 695; Häussler, pp. 2, 103, 164, and 236-237.

5, 6 **Caeca** Fortune was proverbially blind; see Otto 694; Häussler, pp. 103, 164, and 236. Also see Eob. *Her. Chr.* 5, 154; 8, 7-8; *Sylv.* 1, 1, 98; 3, 7, 10.

5, 7 **ex divite pauperem** Paul. Nol. *Carm.* 21, 530; Eob. *Ama.* 19, 15; cf. *Laud.* 559 (n.); *Buc.* 7, 83.

5, 8 **quis te – pessimus** Cf. Mant. *Ecl.* 2, 111-113: "miserande puer, quis te deus istas / misit in ambages? sed non deus, immo Satanum / pessimus ...."

quis te – compulit Cf. *Ama.* 7, 9 (n.): "Quis me hinc deorum eripiet?"

6, 1   **medium sermonem interrupit** *Ama.* 19, 1; cf. Verg. *A.* 4, 388.

6, 2   **Surdo – canis** Eobanus combines Verg. *Ecl.* 10, 8 ("non canimus surdis") with Ter. *Hau.* 222 ("surdo narret fabulam"). Cf. Otto 1715; Häussler, pp. 80 and 245.

6, 3   **non audit** Boeth. *Consol.* 2, m. 1, 5 (of Fortuna): "Non illa miseros audit."

6, 5   **mille pericula** *Buc.* 10, 169 (n.).

7, 1   **Extorsit mihi ... lachrimas** Cf. Sen. *Con.* 9, 6, 8: "illi extorquebo lacrimas."

7, 6   **animi turbine** Cf. Ov. *Am.* 2, 9, 28.

7, 9   **syrtes** For the image of the "shoals" of love cf. Mant. *Ecl.* 1, 40: "quis in syrtes Auster te impegerat istas?"
Quis me – eripiet Cf. Aen. Silv. *Hist.*, p. 129, line 13: "Quis me hinc vivum eripiet?"; Verg. *A.* 6, 341-342: "quis te, Palinure, deorum / eripuit nobis ...?"; Eob. *Ama.* 5, 8: "quis te huc deorum compulit?"; 16, 8: "Utinam deorum aliquis mihi vitam eriperet!"

8, 1   **Clavo – sum** Cf. Pl. *As.* 156: "fixus ... clavo Cupidinis."

8, 3-6 **Dii – cogis** All-powerful Love is a commonplace in erotic literature. Besides the examples cited by Eobanus, see, for instance, Verg. *A.* 4, 412; Ov. *Met.* 13, 758-759; Mant. *Ecl.* 2, 33: "... Veneris nihil esse potentius igne"; Eob. *Ama.* 35, 1-4; B 2, 14; B 2, 25; *Buc.* 3, 58-59; 7, 139-140; *Venus* 1.

8, 5   **Regnat – deos** Ov. *Ep.* 4, 12, of Amor. Ovid's text has "dominos" instead of "superos." Cf. Eob. *Sylv. duae* 2, 140.

8, 6   **Improbe – cogis** Verg. *A.* 4, 412.

8, 7–9, 8 **Multos – venit** Cf. *Buc.* 7, 119-121 (n.).

8, 7   **invia lustra** Verg. *A.* 4, 151.
densissimos vepres Cf. *Buc.* 10, 49 (n.).

9, 1-8 **Occurrunt – venit** The first two verses are adapted from Mant. *Mort.*, fol. 122ᵛ (where we find "animos" instead of "animum"). The remaining verses are Ovidian. For lines 3-4 cf. Ov. *Ep.* 9, 37-38: "inter serpentes aprosque avidosque leones / iactor et esuros cerno per ora canes"; for lines 5-8 cf. Ov. *Ep.* 13, 103-108: "Sive latet Phoebus seu terris altior exstat, / tu mihi luce dolor, tu mihi nocte venis. / [*2 lines*] / aucupor in lecto mendaces caelibe somnos; / dum careo veris gaudia falsa iuvant."

9, 1   **variae – figurae** Cf. Claud. *Rapt. Pros.* 3, 124: "somnia ... variis infausta figuris"; Eob. *Buc.* 8, 29; *Her. Chr.* 5, 71. For "variae figurae" cf. Ov. *Met.* 15, 172; *Ib.* 423. For "somnia vana" see Ov. *Met.* 11, 614.

9, 5   **viridi ... cespite** Verg. *A.* 3, 304; *Culex* 393; Ov. *Ars* 3, 688; et al.; Eob. *Her. Chr.* 14, 94.

10, 1   **nunc huc – curro** Quoted from Ov. *Ep.* 10, 19.
sylvestribus – contentus Cf. Mant. *Ecl.* 3, 149-150 (of the mad lover Amyntas as he wanders about in the woods): "raro silvestria poma / carpentem et potu contentum simplicis undae."
sylvestribus ... cibis *Her.* 1, 6, 12.

10, 4   **morborum** The image of passionate love as a disease recurs in ancient literature. See, for instance, Pl. *Cist.* 71; *Mil.* 1272; Catul. 76, 25; Tib. 2, 5, 110; Prop. 2, 1, 58.

10, 9-10 **Pyramus – dedit** For these standard exempla of unfortunate lovers cf. *Ama.* 35, 17-40; *Her. Chr.* 17, 133-144.

11, 5   **de infoelici amoris exitu** Cf. the subtitle of Mant. *Ecl.* 3: "De insani amoris exitu infelici."

11, 10 **conscisseres** A variant spelling of "conscisceres."

11, 11 **Ad te ... redi** Ter. *Ad.* 794.

11, 12–12, 4 **Valde – deperierit** Cf. Aen. Silv. *Ep.* 106 ("Amoris illiciti medela"), in *Opera* *quae extant omnia* (Basel, 1571), p. 607: "Dixisti te nec virginem nec nuptam nec viduam amare, sed mulierem quamvis pulchram, meretricem tamen."

12, 4   **efflictim ... deperierit** Pl. *Am.* 517; Apul. *Met.* 3, 16.

12, 6   **scissitarer** A variant spelling of "sciscitarer."

      doctam – animas Cf. *Her. Chr.* 11, 84 (of the courtesan Thais): "Mirantes vultu fallere docta procos." Thais's confessor, by contrast, is addressed in *Her. Chr.* 11, 93 as "Errantes revocare animas doctissime."

12, 8   **effusis – habenis** Eobanus uses the same phrase in a public lecture on his *Sylvae duae* (1514): "[amor] virtus ... est, quamdiu nos in vitium non convertimus. Fit enim plaerunque, dum effusis continentiae habenis virtutem hanc amplectimur, ut in vitium decidamus." See *Epp. fam.*, p. 247 (reprinted in the introduction to *Sylv. duae* in vol. 2 of the present edition). Cf. Verg. *A.* 12, 499; also cf. *A.* 5, 818.

      supra – modum Cf. Vulg. *2. Macc.* 9, 8: "supra humanum modum."

      mihi ... applauderem Cf. *Ama.* 20, 8.

12, 9-10   **quottidie ornatior – collo margaritae** Cf. Aen. Silv. *Hist.*, p. 85, lines 17-20: "indies ornatior ... reddebatur .... Nunc auro illitis, nunc muricis Tiri sanguine tinctis, nunc filis que ultimi legunt Seres textis vestibus utebatur."

12, 10   **calamistro crispati** Hier. *Ep.* 52, 5.

      involuti auro crines Cf. Verg. *A.* 4, 138; Eob. *Accl.* 1, 213: "Textile compositis e crinibus emicat aurum."

12, 11   **Nunc fasciis – occultari velle videretur** Cf. *Epp. 1*, sig. H7^r (ca. 1530): "... quaedam mulierculae sic corporis quasdam partes tegunt, ut videri illas cupiant."

      cerussa purpurissoque Cf. Hier. *Ep.* 107, 5: "Cave ... ne cerussa et purpurisso ... ora depingas"; 108, 15: "facies, quam ... purpurisso et cerussa ... saepe depinxi"; Eob. *Ama.* 35, 97 (n.).

      incautum A lover who fails to see the dangers of passion is "incautus." See Verg. *G.* 4, 488; *A.* 4, 70; Ov. *Rem.* 148; Eob. *Ama.* 19, 19; 35, 10; 35, 44; B 2, 7; *Buc.* 3, 34; 3, 39; *Sylv. duae* 2, 113-116; cf. *Her. Chr.* 9, 107. The prudent man, of course, is "cautus." See *Buc.* 7, where the lusty Caldus is confronted by the non-sentimental, clear-eyed Cautus.

      amoris labyrinthum Cf. Erasmus, *Adag.* 2, 10, 51, *ASD* 2, 4, p. 310, lines 626-628.

      labyrinthum inextricabilem Plin. *Nat.* 36, 91; Boeth. *Consol.* 3, 12, 30; Erasmus, *Enchiridion*, *LB* 5, col. 21 A: "e labyrintho quodam inextricabili emergere"; Eob., public lecture on his *Sylvae duae* (1514), in *Epp. fam.*, p. 247 (of passionate love): "nemo unquam ... hunc ... inextricabilem labyrinthum effugerit"; *Her. Chr.*, ded. 19, 2; cf. Verg. *A.* 6, 27; Otto 897; Häussler, pp. 107, 175, and 239.

14, 1   **non haberem – pascerem** Cf. Ov. *Rem.* 746.

14, 2   **percitus oestro** Mant. *Calam.* 1, p. 35; Erasmus, *Adag.* 2, 8, 54.

      oculis obiiciens Verg. *A.* 5, 522.

14, 3   **torvis oculis** Ov. *Met.* 5, 92; Eob. *Buc.* 7, 7; 7, 10.

14, 5   **talibus – compellans** Cf. Verg. *A.* 2, 372; Ov. *Met.* 8, 787.

14, 6   **unicum meae – mea hera** Cf. Aen. Silv. *Hist.*, p. 115, line 10: "mea Lucrecia, mea hera, mea salus, meum refugium."

      unicum meae – refugium Cf. *Laud.*, ded. 12.

      cordis habitaculum This old image became very popular in medieval Latin and vernacular poetry. See Friedrich Ohly, *"Cor amantis non angustum.* Vom Wohnen im Herzen,"* in his: *Schriften zur mittelalterlichen Bedeutungsforschung* (Darmstadt, 1977), pp. 128-155. Cf. Eob. *Buc.* 7, 156.

      mea lux *Buc.* 3, 90 (n.).

hera Catul. 68, 136; Ov. *Ep.* 9, 78.
14, 8   **meum suavium** Pl. *Poen.* 366; Ter. *Eu.* 456.
14, 11   **plus quam – amantem** Cf. Ter. *Ad.* 903: "qui te amat plus quam hosce oculos"; Catul. 3, 5. The expression was proverbial; see Otto 1264; Häussler, pp. 19, 61, 77, 194-195, and 242.
15, 2   **Operam omnem perdidi** Pl. *Epid.* 132; *Poen.* 880.
15, 3   **Illa – superbivit** Cf. Mant. *Ecl.* 4, 65: "virgo superbivit mox, ut se audivit amari."
15, 4   **Abi – rem** Cf. Pl. *Capt.* 877; *Epid.* 78; *Per.* 288; Ter. *An.* 317.
16, 4   **Veneris sacerdoti** Pl. *Rud.* 430.
16, 8   **Utinam – eriperet** Cf. *Ama.* 7, 9 (n.).
16, 9   **summo vertice** *Laud.* 133 (n.).
17, 2   **summis labris** Sen. *Ep.* 10, 3.
17, 4   **Ego – efficatius** Cf. *Buc.* 7, 173-175 and notes.
18, 5   **aura vitali vesci** Cf. Lucr. 5, 857; Verg. *A.* 1, 546-547.
18, 9   **Vivit – amat** For the paradox cf. Alan. *Nat.* 9 (metrum 5), 10: "[Est amor] mors vivens, moriens vita"; Eob. *Buc.* 7, 171 (n.); *Sylv. duae* 2, 82, with note: "[amor est] exitium ... placens." The oxymoron of the living dead was popular in Renaissance and Baroque literature; see Leonard Forster, *The Icy Fire: Five Studies in European Petrarchism* (Cambridge, 1969), pp. 17-20.
19, 1   **medium – interrumpens** *Ama.* 6, 1 (n.).
19, 5   **Sperare ... iubemur** Cf. Otto 1681; Häussler, pp. 40, 64, 80, and 117.
19, 6   **sperandum – sepultis** Cf. Filetico, *Theoc.* 4, 42: "Rebus sperare secundis / Est opus humanis. Spes est carpentibus auras / Vitalis; spes nulla datur modo lumine cassis."
19, 12-15 **Animam – fecit** The consequences of licentiousness were often enumerated. See, for example, Alan of Lille, *Summa de arte praedicatoria* 5, *PL* 210, col. 122 A: "bursam evacuat, corpus enervat, animum inebriat, statum mentis effeminat, animum commaculat, famam perdit, proximum offendit, Deum amittit"; Wimpfeling, *Adol.*, pp. 198-199; Jacob Hartlieb, *De fide meretricum* (ca. 1500), in: *Die Deutschen Universitäten im Mittelalter*, ed. Friedrich Zarncke (Leipzig, 1857), p. 80: "Amor mulierum Deum offendit, angelos contristat, daemones laetificat, hominem excaecat, rationem enervat, visum obnubilat, memoriam debilitat, fantasiam lacerat, marsupium evacuat, infamat, vilem abiectum et inconstantem facit, anxium et sollicitum omni tempore reddit, podagram cyragram arteticam vertiginem generat"; Erasmus, *Enchiridion*, *LB* 5, col. 57 B (of carnal lust): "patrimonium exhaurit, corporis simul et vires et speciem interimit. Valetudinem vehementer laedit, morbos innumerabiles parit, eosque foedos .... Ingenii vigorem tollit, mentis aciem hebetat et quasi pecuinam mentem inserit ... et, quod hominis erat proprium, eripit rationis usum." See also Eob. *Ama.* 25, 1-5 (with notes).
19, 12   **puteum Acherontis** Cf. *Ama.* 35, 45 (n.).
19, 15   **Ex divite pauperem** *Ama.* 5, 7 (n.).
              ex homine bestiam fecit Since passionate love is a form of madness, it reduces sufferers to the level of unreasoning beasts. For the thought see, for example, Cic. *Off.* 1, 105; Serv. *A.* 7, 19: "Circe ... libidine sua et blandimentis homines in ferinam vitam ab humana deducebat, ut libidini et voluptatibus operam darent"; Alan of Lille, *Summa de arte praedicatoria* 5, *PL* 210, col. 123 A: "luxuria ... hominem in pecudem mutat"; Aen. Silv. *Hist.*, p. 125, lines 27-28: "ex amoris flamma sic mens hominis alienatur ut parum a bestiis differat"; Mant. *c. Am.*, fol. 176ʳ: "Fit pecus omnis amans, dum pro ratione libido / Iudicium nutu temperat omne suo. / Quisquis enim vivit sine lumine mentis et usu, / Fert hominis vultus ingeniumque ferae"; *Ecl.* 3, 158: "aequiperans

hominem pecudi"; 7, 111-114; Erasmus, *Enchiridion, LB* 5, col. 56 F-57 A; Eob. *Ama.* 21, 2-4; *Sylv. duae* 2, 229-242.

19, 19 **incaute** *Ama.* 12, 11 (n.).

19, 20 **Nemo – cognoscit** For the inverse cf. *Her. Chr.* 9, 72.

19, 24 **Tu – requiem** Cf. *Her. Chr.* 9, 99-114, with notes.

vadis ad interitum *Her. Chr.* 9, 101; cf. *Ama.* 35, 47.

20, 2 **Chymeram** The Chimera of ancient myth was a fire-breathing monster with the head of a lion, the body of a she-goat, and the tail of a serpent; see Hom. *Il.* 6, 181; Hes. *Theog.* 319-324; Serv. *A.* 6, 288. Late-medieval descriptions, in part influenced by Hor. *Ars* 1-5, sometimes give the creature a woman's head. Cf. Alan of Lille, *Summa de arte praedicatoria* 5, *PL* 210, col. 122 A, describing Lust: "in capite suo gerit faciem virginis et imaginem voluptatis, in medio capram foetosae libidinis, in fine lupam, depraedatione virtutis"; 17, *PL* 210, col. 146 C (also in *PL* 40, col. 1250 and *PL* 217, col. 760 A-B): "chimera ... initium habet a ratione, finem in sensualitate. Cum sic agitur: *Humano capiti cervicem pictor equinam* [Hor. *Ars* 1] .... Sunt quidam quorum vita monstrum mirabile facit, cuius initium bonum, quasi caput hominis praetendit, medium vero in luxuriam descendens, ventrem caprae ostentat, ad ultimum in rapacitatem devians, lupae pedes habet." Eobanus's moral interpretation of the Chimera ultimately derives from Fulg. *Myth.* 3, 1: "Cymera ... quasi cymeron, id est fluctuatio amoris .... Ideo etiam triceps Cymera pingitur, quia amoris tres modi sunt, hoc est incipere, perficere et finire. Dum enim amor noviter venit, ut leo feraliter invadit .... At vero capra quae in medio pingitur perfectio libidinis est, illa videlicet causa, quod huius generis animal sit in libidine valde proclivum .... At vero quod dicitur: 'postremus draco,' illa ratione ponitur, quia post perfectionem vulnus det penitentiae venenumque peccati."

20, 3 **literarum antistites** Cf. *Laud.*, ded. 8 (n.).

20, 6 **ex aliqua, licet exigua parte** *Laud.*, ded. 8 (n.).

20, 7 **iugum ... suave** Vulg. *Matt.* 11, 30.

20, 8 **Nobis applaudimus** Cf. *Ama.* 12, 8.

20, 10 **insanire** For the folly of lovers – "amentes amantes" – see Otto 79; Häussler, pp. 129-130, 232, and 260; Walther 912; 914; 918; 936; 937; 8777; 20186-20188; 29131; Locher, *Stult.*, fol. 24ᵛ: "Quisquis amat, ratione caret"; Eob. *Buc.* 3, 88; 7, 171; cf. also *Her. Chr.* 17, 39-50.

22, 1 **Hii – coinquinati** Vulg. *Apoc.* 14, 4.

22, 1-2 **quales olim – turpia** Cf. Celtis, *Am.* 2, 9, 43-48: "Corpore maturo tunc nupsit mascula virgo, / Quattuor ut lustris vita peracta fuit. / Colloquium castum iuvenis servabat in agris / Robustoque fuit corpore sera Venus. / Sed nunc bis quinos ubi vix transegerit annos, / In Venerem et Bacchum docta puella ruit." Celtis's and Eobanus's source is Caes. *Gal.* 6, 21, 5: "Intra annum vero vicesimum feminae notiriam habuisse in turpissimis habent rebus."

22, 3-5 **Ita – refertissimus** The sexual continence practised by the ancient Germans is lauded by Tacitus in *Germania* 18-19 and by Celtis in *Amores* 2, 9. Praise of the Germanic past is a recurrent theme in Eobanus's works. See especially *Nob.* 151-190 and *Nor.* 304-316.

22, 3 **virtus ..., quae nos – praetulit** Cf. Caes. *Gal.* 5, 54, 5: "ei qui virtute belli omnibus gentibus praeferebantur."

22, 4 **Quandoquidem – Italicus** Celtis, *Am.* 2, 9, 62.

22, 6 **vetustatis inquisitor** Locher, *Stult.*, ded., fol. 2ᵛ: "Philippus Beroaldus Bononiensis, ... omnis ... vetustatis candidissimus inquisitor."

cuius manes – deploravimus Eobanus's contribution, as reported in Mutian. *Ep.* 78, was as follows:

Lector, ave, magni reliquum visure poetae,
　Quo fuit in toto doctius orbe nihil.
Hac humili doctus requiescit Celtis in urna,
　Quem merita lugeat Musica turba chely.

22, 7, 1-8 **Mos – dabant** Celtis, *Am.* 2, 9, lines 67-70 and 73-76.

22, 7, 1 **castum – cubile** ≈ Verg. *A.* 8, 412.

22, 7, 5 **Arborei foetus** = Verg. *G.* 1, 55; Ov. *Met.* 4, 125.

22, 7, 7 **Pars hominum** = Hor. *S.* 2, 7, 6; *Ep.* 1, 1, 77.

23, 1 **Lemnii** See Erasmus, *Adag.* 1, 9, 27, *ASD* 2, 2, p. 352, lines 589-590: "Lemniae mulieres, graveolentia maritorum offensae, eos universos sustulerunt auxilio Thoantis."

24, 1 **tanquam ex speculo** Cf. Ter. *Ad.* 415 and 428: "tamquam in speculum"; Erasmus, *Adag.* 2, 3, 50.

24, 2 **Exemplis – vetustas** Cf. Boeth. *Consol.* 3, 5, 2: "plena est exemplorum vetustas"; Eob. *Her. Chr.* 15, 143: "Magna habet haec aetas, maiora exempla vetustas."

24, 5 **montem Lyciae** Chimera was also the name of a volcano near Phaselis in Lycia. Cf. Plin. *Nat.* 2, 236; 5, 100; Serv. *A.* 6, 288.

24, 6 **Excute – infoelix** Taken from Ov. *Met.* 7, 17-18, as quoted in Aen. Silv. *Hist.*, p. 87, lines 19-20 (where "flammas" and "pectore" are reversed, contrary to the meter). For the phrasing and thought cf. Eob. *Ama.* 35, 61; also *Ama.* B 2, 55.

25, 2-7 **Marsilius – volat** In *De vita* 1, 7, Marsilio Ficino list five "monsters" that prey especially on scholars: phlegm, black bile, sexual intercourse, gluttony, and sleeping late. In the present passage Eobanus quotes liberally from Ficino's remarks about sexual intercourse: "Primum quidem monstrum est Venereus coitus, praesertim si vel paulum vires excesserit; subito namque exhaurit spiritus praesertim subtiliores, cerebrumque debilitat, labefactat stomachum atque praecordia. Quo malo nihil ingenio adversius esse potest. Cur nam Hippocrates coitum comitiali morbo similem iudicavit, nisi quia mentem, quae sacra est, percutit; ... ut non iniuria prisci Musas atque Minervam virgines esse voluerint. Huc Platonicum illud spectat: cum Venus Musis minitaretur, nisi sacra Venerea colerent, se contra illas suum filium armaturam, responderunt Musae: 'Marti, O Venus, Marti talia minitare; tuus enim inter nos Cupido non volat.'" Eobanus also adapts this passage in *Sylv. duae* 2, 131-170; and *Val.* 1, 209-210 and 213-218.

25, 4 **Subito – potest** For these effects cf. *Ama.* 19, 14-15, with note to lines 12-15.

25, 5 **Hippocrates** See Gel. 19, 2, 8 (= Macr. 2, 8, 16).

25, 6 **prisci – poaetae** According to an ancient and patristic commonplace, poets like Homer and Orpheus were regarded as theologians. See Curtius, *ELLMA*, chapter 12, pp. 214-227. The topos remained popular in the Renaissance. See, for example, Bocc. *Gen.* 15, 8: "Gentiles poetas mithicos esse theologos"; Poliziano, preface to a translation of Plato's *Charmides*, in: *Opera omnia* (Basel, 1553), p. 448: "prisci illi theologi Homerus, Orpheus, Hesiodus"; Mutian. *Ep.* 77 (vol. 1, p. 114); Eob. *Ama.* 33, 6 (n.).

25, 7 **Platonicum illud** Carol V. Kaske and John R. Clark point out in a note to Ficino, *De vita* 1, 7 (p. 415), that the source for this story is Diogenes Laertius 3, 33, quoting *Anthol. Pal.* 9, 39. See further James Hutton, *The Greek Anthology in Italy* (Ithaca, NY, 1935), pp. 110-111.

25, 8 **Pierides – satas** Taken from Mant. *c. Poet.* 39-42: "Pierides castae, castae Libetrides undae. / Tota pudiciciam vera poesis amat: / est Helicon virgo, virgo Peneia Daphne, / Castalides aiunt virgine matre satas."

26, 1 **diobolari scorto** Pl. *Poen.* 270.

          quae corpus suum publicavit Pl. *Bac.* 863.

26, 3   **Forma – suo** Ov. *Ars* 2, 113-114. On the brevity of youthful beauty see *Buc.* 7, 168-170 (n.).

26, 4   **iusta** A variant spelling for "iuxta," as in *Ama.*, ded. 2.

          lyrici Davidis Cf. *Her. Chr.* 6, 56 (of King David).

          oculos – avertisti See Vulg. *Psa.* 118, 37.

26, 6   **quod – sanguinem** Cf. *Ama.* 35, 97-98 (n.).

26, 7, 1   **viridi ... in herba** = *Culex* 115; Ov. *Met.* 3, 502.

          latet anguis in herba = Verg. *Ecl.* 3, 93.

26, 7, 2   **blanda ... in meretrice** *Ama.* 35, 95; cf. Ov. *Am.* 1, 15, 18.

27, 1   **soporatos** This detail derives from the medieval bestiaries. See, for example, *Physiologus Latinus, éditions préliminaires, versio B*, ed. Francis J. Carmody (Paris, 1939), chapter 12, 4-7 (p. 25); Brant, *NS* 108, 40-44.

27, 2   **mortis ... amariciem** Cf. Vulg. *1. Reg.* 15, 32: "amara mors."

27, 3   **Has – devitemus** Cf. Hier. *Praef. in libro Jos.*: "mortiferos Sirenarum cantus surda debeamus aure transire."

27, 4   **Omnes – sunt** In the euhemeristic tradition the Sirens were interpreted as prostitutes. See Serv. *A.* 5, 864: "secundum veritatem [Sirenes] meretrices fuerunt, quae transeuntes quoniam deducebant ad egestatem, his fictae sunt inferre naufragia"; Pierre Courcelle, "L'interprétation evhémériste des Sirènes-courtisanes jusqu'au XIIᵉ siècle," in: *Gesellschaft. Kultur. Literatur: Rezeption und Originalität im Wachsen einer europäischen Literatur und Geistigkeit. Beiträge Luitpold Wallach gewidmet*, ed. Karl Bosl (Stuttgart, 1975), pp. 33-48.

27, 5   **Si vero – commertium** Cf. Vulg. *1. Cor.* 7, 9.

27, 6   **Pelle – iugo** Mant. *c. Poet.* 31-32.

27, 6, 2   **subtrahe colla iugo** = Prop. 2, 5, 14; Ov. *Rem.* 90; cf. Eob. *Ama.* 35, 62. For the tag "colla iugo" see *Ama.* 35, 48 (n.).

28, 1   **optimos – efficere** Cf. Mutianus Rufus's advice to Eobanus in August 1506 (*Ep.* 80): "debes ... dare ... operam, ut utriusque linguae praestantissimos auctores varia tibi multiplicique lectione vel digitis tuis notiores efficias." Also cf. Juv. 7, 231-232.

29, 1-8   **Non amor – opes** The verses come from Tifernate, "Triumphus Cupidinis"; see *Carm.*, sig. A8ʳ.

29, 1-2   **Non amor – malum** This distich is also quoted, albeit with some variants, in Bebel, *Prov.* 555, to illustrate the familiar proverb, "Ubi amor, ibi dolor." The paradoxes of love expressed in these lines recur in late-medieval literature. See Harry Vredeveld, "Some Remarks on Heinrich Bebel's *Proverbia Germanica*, 555: 'Ubi amor, ibi dolor,'" *Daphnis* 17 (1988): 347-351. See also Eob. *Ama.* 35, 9 (n.) and *Sylv. duae* 2, 81-82 (n.).

29, 5-6   **Sunt – timor** Cf. Ter. *Eu.* 59-61.

29, 7   **studiis melioribus** = *Rec.* 210 (n.).

29, 8   **Exiguo – opes** = *Sylv.* 1, 3, 92.

30, 4   **vis ingenii** Cic. *de Orat.* 1, 172; *Phil.* 5, 49.

          ingenii ... vivacis *Laud.* B 3, tit. (n.).

          cytharae cantus Hor. *Carm.* 3, 1, 20.

31, 1   **dicto citius** For this proverbial phrase see Otto 528; Häussler, pp. 55, 72, 101, 154, and 268.

32, 1-84 **Heu – lugeant** Meter: Fourth Asclepiadean strophe.

32, 1   **taela Cupidinis** = *Ama.* 32, 36; cf. *Ama.* 35, 63 (n.).

32, 3-4   **Saevo – impio** Cf. Verg. *Ecl.* 8, 47-50; also cf. Eob. *Ama.* 32, 37.

32, 3   **Saevo saevior angue** Mant. *c. Am.*, fol. 177ʳ (referring to Amor); Eob. *Her. Chr.* 16, 44; cf. *Her. Chr.* 1, 121.

32, 6-7   **integer Vita** Cf. Hor. *Carm.* 1, 22, 1.
32, 13   **lachrimis ... dabis modum** Cf. Petrarch, *Africa* 5, 683 (Walther 21907a; Eob. *Ebn.* 131): "Pone modum lacrimis"; Eob. *Ama.* 32, 42.
32, 14   **fata mori ... iubent** *Ama.* 32, 28; for "fata iubent" see *Rec.* 94 (n.).
32, 16   **dulce – mori** Prud. *Amart.* 153-154; cf. Eob. *Her. Chr.* 7, 56 (n.).
32, 18   **Plorantes ... genas** *Her. Chr.* 3, 44.
32, 19   **Saevum ... Amorem** Verg. *Ecl.* 8, 47; Ov. *Am.* 1, 6, 34; et al.; Eob. *Ama.* 33, 11, 2.
32, 21-22 **harundinis – Amor** Cf. *Buc.* 3, 91 (n.).
32, 28   **fata iubent mori** *Ama.* 32, 14 (n.).
32, 31   **Moestum ... carmen** Ov. *Ep.* 2, 118.
          dicite carmen *Buc.* 9, 109 (n.).
32, 32   **Cantent ... tybiae** Ov. *Fast.* 6, 659-660.
          Cantent flebile Ov. *Rem.* 36; cf. Eob. *Ama.* 32, 57.
32, 33   **Fontes ... vitreos** Ennod. *Carm.* 2, 19, 5; Ven. Fort. *Carm.* 7, 8, 18; Eob. *Her. Chr.* 15, 74. For the epithet see n. *Pug.* B 1, 8.
32, 34   **siccis – currite** Cf. Ov. *Met.* 14, 50.
32, 36   **taela Cupidinis** = *Ama.* 32, 1; cf. *Ama.* 35, 63 (n.).
32, 37   **At tu – puer** Cf. *Ama.* 32, 3-4 (n.). Cupid is often called "puer"; see, for instance, Catul. 64, 95; Prop. 1, 6, 23; 1, 9, 21; Ov. *Am.* 2, 9, 2; 3, 15, 15; *Ars* 1, 165; 2, 15; Eob. *Ama.* 35, 60; *Buc.* 3, 36 (n.); *Sylv. duae* 2, 99; *Her. Chr.* 17, 101; 24, 36.
          saeva Venus = *Ama.* 32, 77.
32, 38   **Quid adhuc non** *Buc.* 4, 6 (n.).
32, 40   **Dempto fine** Ov. *Ep.* 1, 50; *Tr.* 3, 11, 2; Sen. *Phaed.* 553; Eob. *Her. Chr.* 1, 91.
32, 41   **Miserum – exitus** Cf. Ov. *Met.* 9, 726 (the lover speaks): "quis me manet exitus?"
32, 42   **finem lachrimis ponet** Cf. *Ama.* 32, 13 (n.).
          lachrimis ... inanibus Verg. *A.* 4, 449; 10, 465.
32, 44   **Priscis ... honoribus** *Laud.* 210 (n.).
32, 45-48 **Quin – venerabiles** Cf. *Buc.* 3, 163-170, with notes.
32, 46   **densa ... lustra** Sil. 4, 302-303.
32, 49   **cura ... pectoris** Ov. *Pont.* 4, 5, 36.
          cura ... maxima Verg. *G.* 4, 354; *A.* 1, 678; Prop. 2, 16, 2; Ov. *Ep.* 17, 198; et al.
32, 51   **spernis amantem** Tib. 1, 8, 61.
32, 53   **patulae ... arbores** Ov. *Met.* 1, 106; Stat. *Silv.* 3, 1, 70; cf. Eob. *Ama.* 1, 1 (n.): "patulae fagi."
32, 54   **Verni ... temporis** Hor. *Ars* 302.
          tota ... gratia Maxim. 2, 32; Eob. *Her. Chr.* 4, 163; 23, 78; *Sylv.* 1, 7, 42.
32, 57   **flebile cantilant** Cf. *Ama.* 32, 32 (n.).
32, 58-59 **Arrident – rident** Cf. *Buc.* 1, 3-5.
32, 58   **nitidis ... fontibus** V. Fl. 3, 553.
32, 59   **nunc omnia rident** Verg. *Ecl.* 7, 55; Eob. *Ruf.* 25; *Buc.* 9, 14.
32, 61-62 **Seu – doloribus** Cf. Ov. *Ep.* 13, 103-104 (adapted in Eob. *Ama.* 9, 7-8).
32, 65-72 **Insani – beatior** Cf. *Her. Chr.* 12, 233-234; 13, 39-40. For the hyperbolic motif of journeying to the ends of the earth see n. *Laud.* 209.
32, 65   **Insani ... turbinis** Sen. *Phoen.* 420; Stat. *Theb.* 1, 366.
32, 66   **divitis Indiae** Hor. *Carm.* 3, 24, 2. The riches of India were proverbial. See Otto 862; Häussler, p. 106; Eob. *Buc.* 2, 36-37; *Her. Chr.* 16, 239 (n.).
32, 69   **vicina ... sydera** Ov. *Met.* 2, 507; *Tr.* 5, 3, 41.
32, 70-71 **miser ... Prometheus** Mart. 11, 84, 9.
32, 75   **Saevi ... dracones** Enn. *scen.* 274; V. Fl. 8, 438; Claud. *Epith.* 193.
32, 77   **saeva Venus** = *Ama.* 32, 37.

flebilibus modis = Hor. *Carm.* 2, 9, 9; cf. Sen. *Her. O.* 1091; Eob. *Her. Chr.* 20, 90.

32, 81 **lyrici ... modi** Ov. *Ep.* 15, 6; *Fast.* 5, 386.
dulce decus Hor. *Carm.* 1, 1, 2; Stat. *Silv.* 3, 1, 161; Mart. 9, 28, 1; Eob. *Buc.* 2, 58.

32, 82 **Post ... cineres** *Buc.* 6, 75 (n.).

32, 83-84 **saera ... saecula** Luc. 10, 263-264.

33, 2 **eburno pectine** Verg. *A.* 6, 647; Eob. *Vict.* 292-293; cf. *Laud.* 285 (n.).

33, 4 **flebilibus elegis** Cf. Ov. *Am.* 3, 9, 3.

33, 5 **Satis superque** *Laud.* 398 (n.).

33, 6 **Insanus amor** Verg. *Ecl.* 10, 44; *A.* 2, 343; Hor. *Carm.* 3, 21, 3; Prop. 2, 14, 18; Ov. *Ars* 1, 372; et al.; Eob. *Ama.* 35, 1; *Buc.* 3, 95; 4, 64.
qui primas – obtinet Cf. the argument prefacing Marsilio Ficino's translation of *Mercurii Trismegisti liber de potestate et sapientia Dei* (Venice, 1491), sig. a1ᵛ, speaking of Hermes Trismegistus: "Primus de maiestate Dei, daemonum ordine, animarum mutationibus sapientissime disputavit. Primus igitur theologiae appellatus est auctor. Eum sequutus Orpheus secundas antiquae theologiae partes obtinuit." For Orpheus as a theologian see n. *Ama.* 25, 6.

33, 7 **montes – flexisse dicatur** Cf. Prop. 3, 2, 3-4; Hor. *Carm.* 1, 12, 7-12; Ov. *Ars* 3, 321-322; *Met.* 11, 1-2; 14, 338-340; *Tr.* 4, 1, 17-18; Eob. *Her. Chr.* 19, 29-30; 21, 39-40; *Idyl.* 1, 50-53; *Accl.* 2, 4: "Cum [Orpheus] traheret sylvas, flumina, saxa, feras"; *Epic.* 2, 103-104.

33, 9 **Satis – periisse** Cf. *Her. Chr.* 15, 86 (n.).

33, 11, 1 **flagrantes – flammae** Cf. *Ama.* B 2, 53; *Nup.* 201.
viscera flammae = Ov. *Rem.* 105.

33, 11, 2 **Saevus ... amor** *Ama.* 32, 19 (n.).
in ardenti pectore = Mutian. *Ep.* 417 (vol. 2, p. 77, line 32), a verse letter by Eobanus written in August 1506: "Talis in ardenti pectore fervor erat"; cf. Stat. *Silv.* 2, 3, 19-20.

34, 1 **tui ordinis** Cf. *Ruf.* 87: "nostri decus ordinis."
qui dum in Foro – obstrepebat Cf. Ov. *Tr.* 4, 10, 19-34.
tabernariorum operarios The phrase also occurs in Mutian. *Ep.* 45 (1 October 1506), in which Mutianus Rufus compliments Eobanus on his *De pugna studentum*: "Legi nuper motum repentinum inter scholasticos et operarios tabernariorum."
ut ... scribere non dubitarit Cf. *Her. Chr.* 24, 103 (n.).

34, 2 **Sponte – erat** Ov. *Tr.* 4, 10, 25-26.

34, 4 **immortalitati ... consecrasse** *Ama.*, ded. 13 (n.).

34, 5 **poaeticas fores** Sen. *Dial.* 9, 17, 10: "frustra poeticas fores compos sui pepulit."

34, 7 **lilileta** A variant of "lilieta." Cf. the comparable form "tililetum" in *Nor.* 317 and 354.

34, 10 **lyra ... increpui** Hor. *Carm.* 4, 15, 2.

35, 1–36, 6 **Heu – Amor** Meter: Elegiac distich.

35, 1-4 **Heu – Amor** For the omnipotence of Amor cf. *Ama.* 8, 3-6 (n.).

35, 1 **Heu dolor** = Stat. *Theb.* 11, 616; 12, 210; Sil. 5, 190; et al.; Eob. *Her. Chr.* 10, 141; 12, 250.
insano ... Amori = *Buc.* 3, 95; cf. *Ama.* 33, 6 (n.).

35, 2 **superum ... quis** Luc. 5, 86; Stat. *Theb.* 5, 710; Eob. *Nup.* 204 (n.).
volucri ... deo = Tifernate, *Carm.*, sig. A7ʳ: "Vincitur a volucri sexus uterque deo"; cf. Eob. *Ama.* 35, 68.

35, 3 **Regnat – orbem** Cf. *Ama.* 8, 5 (n.).
totum ... occupat orbem Ven. Fort. *Carm.* 2, 3, 1: "Virtus celsa crucis totum recte occupat orbem"; cf. Ov. *Met.* 6, 147; Eob. *Laud.* 351 (n.); *Sylv. duae* 1, 23:

"Prussiacum ... occupat orbem."

35, 5   **dira lues** = Stat. *Theb.* 1, 601; cf. Ov. *Met.* 7, 523; 15, 626.

           inextinguibilis To make the word fit the meter, Eobanus lengthens the fourth syllable.

35, 6   **quantis viribus** = Ov. *Tr.* 1, 4, 24.

35, 7   **Nulla ... toto ... truculentior orbe** = Ov. *Pont.* 2, 7, 31. For "toto orbe" at this metrical position see also Eob. *Her. Chr.* 15, 95; *Nob.* 231; *Vict.* 479; cf. *Laud.* 96 (n.); *Her. Chr.* 1, 57.

           pestis The image is often applied to passionate love. See, for example, Catul. 76, 20; Verg. *A.* 1, 712; 4, 90; V. Fl. 7, 252; Eob. *Sylv. duae* 2, 51.

35, 8   **levis ... Amor** = Ov. *Ep.* 3, 42.

           ex omni – Amor Cf. Ov. *Rem.* 42; 358; Tifernate, *Carm.*, sig. A7ᵛ: "... ex omni parte triumphat Amor." For "ex omni parte" at this metrical position see also Ov. *Fast.* 5, 4; 5, 158; Eob. *Buc.* B 11, 20; *Her. Chr.* 9, 52; 17, 24; 24, 30; cf. *Her. Chr.* 14, 110.

35, 9   **Dulce – virus** For these oxymora cf. *Ama.* 29, 1-2 (n.).

           Dulce malum = *Anthol. Lat.* 494a, 1: "Dulce malum pelago Sirenae ..."; Alan. *Nat.* 9 (metrum 5), 7, referring to love; cf. Sen. *Ag.* 589; Tifernate, *Carm.*, sig. A8ʳ (quoted in Eob. *Ama.* 29, 2).

35, 10   **Incautos** *Ama.* 12, 11 (n.)

           precipitanter agit = *Her. Chr.* 9, 108 (referring to the garden path of pleasure).

35, 11   **Intrat – lapsu** = *Idyl.* 3, 116; cf. Mant. *2. Parthen.* 1, 30-31: "tacitoque in pectora lapsu / Intrantes"; *Calam.* 1, p. 48: "[Venus] placido per pectora lapsu / Se insinuans."

           serpit per viscera ≈ *Ama.* B 2, 53 (n.).

           viscera lapsu = Sil. 4, 384.

35, 12   **clausis ... sensibus** Cf. Catul. 51, 5-6; Mant. *Ecl.* 1, 48: "Ludit Amor sensus"; Eob. *Buc.* 3, 100.

           haeret amor ≈ Ov. *Rem.* 430; cf. *Met.* 3, 395.

35, 13-14   **Sed – prius** Cf. *Buc.* 3, 39-40.

35, 14   **Quisquis amat** = *Laud.* 321 (n.).

35, 15   **Quis – vexat** Cf. Sedul. 1, 245: "Quis furor est? quae tanta animos dementia ludit"; Verg. *A.* 5, 465; Luc. 1, 8; Eob. *Venus* 1, 217: "Quis furor hic? Saevae quae tanta potentia pestis?"; Cordus, *Buc.* 10, 107 (*Ecl.* 5, 72): "Quae mala te rabies, quae te vesania [dementia *1518*] vexat?"

           Quis furor est? Quae = Ov. *Am.* 3, 14, 7; [Tib.] 3, 9, 7.

           Quae – daementia ≈ Verg. *A.* 5, 465; cf. Eob. *Her. Chr.* 17, 99 (n.).

35, 16   **tam – pati** Cf. *Venus* 1, 200-201: "quas durus Amor tam saeva coegit / Vincla pati."

           saeva ... vulnera Ov. *Ars* 3, 744; *Met.* 7, 849; *Pont.* 2, 2, 23.

35, 17-40   **Ad Seston – faces** For this catalogue of ancient lovers cf. *Ama.* 10, 9-10 (n.).

35, 17   **iuvenem ... natantem** Ov. *Ep.* 19, 145.

35, 18   **sunt in amore** = Prop. 2, 15, 12; cf. Eob. *Sylv. duae* 2, 125 (n.).

35, 20   **misit in arma** = *Nux* 110: "... Aonium misit in arma virum."

35, 21   **quis – error** Cf. Verg. *Ecl.* 8, 41 (*Ciris* 430; Ov. *Tr.* 2, 109): "me malus abstulit error"; Eob. *Idyl.* 7, 89: "... Quis te malus abiicit error?" For "error" in the language of love see *Laud.* 236 (n.).

35, 22   **prius – rubent** Cf. *Val.* 1, 415: "Alba prius, nunc rubra tuo de sanguine, Thysbe."

           sanguine mora rubent = Mant. *Sylv.* 3, fol. 287ᵛ: "... Tysbeo sanguine mora rubent"; cf. Ov. *Tr.* 4, 6, 34.

35, 23   **miserum funus** Ov. *Am.* 2, 6, 9.

35, 24   **impatiens ... latus** Ov. *Am.* 3, 7, 36 (in an obscene context).

35, 25   **patrium ... honorem** Verg. *A.* 5, 601.

35, 26   **preter – nihil** = Ov. *Ep.* 19, 16.

35, 28   **Cur – aper** Cf. Verg. *Ecl.* 2, 59.

35, 29   **Fraena pati** = *Venus* 1, 216; cf. Ov. *Ep.* 4, 22; *Ars* 1, 472; Sil. 3, 387.

35, 31   **Tyrinthius heros** = Ov. *Ars* 2, 221; *Met.* 7, 410; *Fast.* 2, 349.

35, 32   **Oechali – tuos** Cf. Ov. *Ep.* 16, 128, referring to Helen of Troy: "... in terras, Oebali nympha, tuas"; cf. *Ep.* 9, 50.

35, 33-34 **Arma – opus** Cf. *Eleg. Maec.* 1, 79-80: "clava torosa tua pariter cum pelle iacebat, / quam pede suspenso percutiebat Amor."

35, 34   **Debile – opus** Cf. Ov. *Ep.* 9, 77. For "debile opus" see Mart. 8, 6, 8.

          pollice – opus ≈ Ov. *Med.* 14; *Ibis* 74.

35, 35   **Omnia – Iole** Cf. Prop. 3, 11, 16; Ov. *Ep.* 9, 2; 9, 25-26.

35, 37   **Chyronis ... antro** = V. Fl. 1, 407; Stat. *Silv.* 1, 4, 98; cf. Ov. *Met.* 2, 630.

35, 38   **longa – toga** Cf. Ov. *Ars* 1, 689-690.

35, 41   **Tot mala perpessi** ≈ [Tib.] 3, 2, 8.

35, 43   **Gaudet amans** = Ov. *Met.* 2, 862.

35, 44   **Incautos** *Ama.* 12, 11 (n.).

35, 45   **Rhetia** For the image see, for example, Lucr. 4, 1146-1148 and Prop. 2, 32, 20.

          puteum ... abyssi = *Her. Chr.* 11, 69; cf. *Ama.* 19, 12: "puteum Acherontis." The phrase comes from Vulg. *Apoc.* 9, 1-2.

35, 47   **Vadit ad interitum** ≈ *Her. Chr.* 9, 101; cf. *Ama.* 19, 24.

          crudeli ... tyranno Paul. Nol. *Carm.* 26, 263; Mant. *2. Parthen.* 3, 633; Eob. *Her. Chr.* 4, 221; 12, 23; cf. *Her. Chr.* 1, 121; 11, 51.

35, 48   **libera colla iugo** = Claud. *Carm. minora* 18, 6; Eob. *Eccles.* 270; cf. *Ama.* 27, 6, 2 (n.).

35, 49   **Cupidinea ... sagitta** ≈ Ov. *Rem.* 157.

          nimium nimiumque = [Tib.] 3, 6, 21; Mart. 8, 3, 17; Eob. *Buc.* 6, 6.

35, 50   **Paphias ... fores** = *Sylv. duae* 2, 224.

35, 51-52 **Heu – tui** Lovesickness destroys youthful beauty and vigor. See, for example, Ov. *Ep.* 11, 27; Petrarch, *Secret.* 3, p. 403: "Hinc pallor et macies et languescens ante tempus flos aetatis"; Eob. *Buc.* 7, 141-143; *Her. Chr.* 12, 75-80; *Idyl.* 3, 107-109.

          Heu, ubi ... pectoris ille tui ≈ Ov. *Am.* 3, 8, 18.

35, 51   **Heu, ubi nunc** = Ov. *Ep.* 4, 150; Stat. *Theb.* 5, 350; Eob. *Hod.* 343.

          nunc iuvenile decus = *Laus Pis.* 260.

          gloria formae = *Culex* 408.

35, 53   **Quid ... miserande puer** = Verg. *A.* 10, 825; cf. *A.* 11, 42; Eob. *Rec.* 125 (n.); *Ama.* B 2, 75.

          Quid palles Pallor was considered typical of lovers; see n. *Laud.* 237.

35, 53-54 **inania ... Gaudia** Aus. *Parent.* 9, 21; *Cupido cruciatus* 35.

35, 55   **Liber – ibas** Cf. *Sylv. duae* 2, 53-54.

          Liber eras, memini Cf. Ov. *Am.* 3, 6, 5.

35, 56   **tacita fraude** = *Hypocr.* 54; cf. Stat. *Theb.* 10, 721; Mart. 5, 65, 5.

35, 57-58 **inhospita ... Avia** = *Idyl.* 11, 178-179.

          lustras Avia Ov. *Met.* 1, 479.

35, 58   **vulnera tanta** Ov. *Ib.* 252.

35, 59-60 **Acrior – puer** Cf. *Ruf.* 57-58: "Numen habent sylvae; saepe illic nudus Apollo / Et levis errat Amor." "Puer" is a conventional term for Cupid; see *Ama.* 32, 37 (n.).

35, 60   **callidus ... puer** = Tib. 1, 4, 76.

35, 61   **Excute – aestus** Cf. *Ama.* 24, 6 (n.); B 2, 55.

          pectoris aestus = Luc. 8, 166; Eob. *Ama.* B 2, 55.

35, 62   **Subtrahe ... colla ... iugo** *Ama.* 27, 6, 2 (n.).

colla – iugo = Mant. *c. Am.*, fol. 176ʳ.

35, 63   taela Cupidinis = Ov. *Ars* 1, 261; cf. Eob. *Ama.* 32, 1; 32, 36.

35, 64-66 Sanari – erit Cf. Ov. *Rem.* 503-504; Sen. *Phaed.* 249, addressed to the enamored Phaedra: "pars sanitatis velle sanari fuit"; Eob. *Val.* 1, 105-108: "Sit tibi praecipue simplex et recta voluntas, / Velle animi sana conditione frui. / Quo si non valeas, frustra servare laboras / Corpora, quae medicae munere mentis egent."

35, 64   sanus eris = Ov. *Rem.* 794; Eob. *Val.* 1, 214: "Si possis Venerem spernere, sanus eris"; *Sylv.* 5, 43, 8.

35, 66   Semper – erit Cf. *Ama.* B 2, 49-50.

35, 67   error Cf. *Laud.* 236 (n.).

35, 68   volucrem ... deum ≈ *Ama.* 35, 2 (n.).

virus habere = Jakob Dornberg, epigram in Wimpfeling, *Adol.*, p. 352: "lascivum carmen virus habere puta"; Eob. *Her. Chr.* 5, 140; 17, 132.

35, 71   vaela carinae = Ov. *Met.* 3, 639; *Ib.* 493; Luc. 8, 48; et al.

35, 72   Grandis – mari Cf. Ov. *Ep.* 21, 66; Eob. *Her. Chr.* 24, 22; *Epic.* 4, 120: "... in Ionia cognita Lesbos aqua"; *Sylv.* 1, 9, 24: "Mater in Idaeis cognita diva iugis."

Ionio ... mari = Ov. *Tr.* 2, 298.

35, 74   Graecia tota = Prop. 2, 6, 2; Ov. *Rem.* 164; 468.

35, 75   mollis amor = Ov. *Ep.* 15, 179; cf. *Ars* 2, 152.

secura voluptas = Claud. *Epith.* 82: "... non secura Voluptas."

35, 76   in plumis ... Venus ≈ Mart. 10, 13, 6. For "plumis" meaning "a feather bed" see Eob. *Buc.* 8, 20; *Val.* 1, 196; *Sylv.* 6, 13, 18; 7, 8, 4: "de plumis vix relevatus eram."

35, 79   Ocia ... dulcia Man. 5, 173; Aus. *Ep.* 4, 31; Eob. *Her. Chr.* 19, 166.

magnanimus ... Achilles ≈ Ov. *Met.* 13, 298.

35, 80   Dii superi = *Buc.* 8, 26; *Nup.* 198; cf. *Buc.* 6, 83 (n.).

35, 81   reluctantes ... flammas Cf. *Ama.* 35, 90: "repugnantes ... faces."

vincla tenacia = Paul. Nol. *Ep.* 8, 3; cf. Verg. *G.* 4, 412.

35, 82   totis viribus *Ama.*, ded. 13 (n.).

35, 83   Pluma levis Cf. Otto 1438; Häussler, pp. 202 and 284; Eob. *Buc.* 8, 62; *Her. Chr.* 17, 59.

facili ... reflectitur aura Cf. *Buc.* 4, 78. For "facili aura" see Eob. *Her. Chr.* 15, 113 (n.).

35, 84   missa sagitta = Prop. 4, 6, 68.

35, 86   vires – tuas = Ov. *Ars* 2, 180.

35, 87-88 Protinus – amor Cf. *Ama.* B 2, 77-78.

35, 89   animum – potentem Cf. *Her. Chr.* 23, 91.

35, 90   repugnantes ... faces Cf. *Ama.* 35, 81: "reluctantes ... flammas."

mens animosa = Eobanus, verse letter (1506) in Trebelius, *Epigr.*, sig. F2ʳ: "Quam lateat vili mens animosa domo."

35, 91   niveum ... pudorem *AH* 4, 93, 5; 50, 96, 9; Eob. *Buc.* 2, 73.

35, 92   putri ... luto = *Her. Chr.* 11, 116; 15, 38.

35, 93   fata gemis = *Idyl.* 6, 17: "Qui fletus! Quae fata gemis tam tristia ...?"; cf. Catul. 65, 14; Verg. *A.* 1, 221-222; Ov. *Fast.* 3, 862; *Tr.* 3, 4, 37.

35, 95-96 Stulte – ope Cf. *Buc.* 7, 168.

35, 95   Stulte, quid = Ov. *Am.* 2, 9, 41; *Tr.* 3, 8, 11; Mart. 3, 85, 3; Walther 30388b-30390; Mant. *Ecl.* 2, 76; Eob. *Buc.* 7, 168.

in blanda ... meretrice *Ama.* 26, 7, 2 (n.).

35, 96   formae luxuriantis *Her.*, ded. 40: "forma ... luxuriante."

35, 97-98 Quae – olet Cf. Vulg. *Matt.* 23, 27-28; Claud. *Cons. Stil.* 2, 135-136 (allegorical image of *luxuries*): "blanda quidem vultus, sed qua non taetrior ulla / Interius: fucata genas et amicta dolosis"; Eob. *Ama.* 26, 6; *Her. Chr.* 15,

35-36, of the courtesan Pelagia.

35, 97   **vultum – cerussa** Cf. Hier. *Ep.* 127, 3: "Illae enim solent purpurisso et cerussa ora depingere"; Eob. *Ama.* 12, 11 (n.).

35, 98   **mephytin olet** = *Her. Chr.* 9, 106 (referring to the garden path of pleasure).

35, 99-100 **Sic – bibit** Cf. Juv. 10, 25-27; Eob. *Buc.* 6, 69; *Her. Chr.* 5, 141-142; 20, 121-122.

35, 99   **Sic aliquis** = Ov. *Ib.* 271; Juv. 15, 24; Eob. *Her. Chr.* 15, 193; 15, 199.

35, 100   **poenas exiciumque** = *Her. Chr.* 19, 10; *Pod.* 60.

35, 101   **brevis ... voluptas** Ov. *Ep.* 19, 65; *Met.* 9, 485; *Pont.* 1, 2, 51; Eob. *Her. Chr.* 15, 107; 17, 53; *Idyl.* 17, 207: "Quam brevis illa fuit, quam non sincera voluptas."

35, 103   **largum ... amorem** Paul. Nol. *Carm.* 18, 445: "voce pia largum testatur pauper amorem / debitor."
          vendit amorem = Tib. 1, 4, 67.

35, 105   **antiquos ... amantes** = *Laud.* 235 (n.).

35, 106   **Iudice – amans** See *Ama.* 18, 8.

35, 107   **flammas extingue** Ov. *Ars* 3, 463; *Met.* 15, 778.

35, 109   **Longa ... taedia** *Laud.* 403 (n.).
          taedia vitae = *Laud.* 320 (n.).

35, 110   **Sit – nefas** = *Sylv.* 2, 2, 90 (referring to drunkenness).
          Sit pudor ... degenerasse Cf. Ov. *Ars* 1, 496; Eob. *Buc.* 8, 83 (n.).
          tantum ... nefas = Ov. *Am.* 3, 9, 44; Eob. *Her. Chr.* 18, 26.

35, 111   **divae ... Camoenae** Gel. 1, 24, 2; Eob. *Buc.* 6, 58.

35, 112   **casti ... amoris** *Laud.* 240 (n.).
          lumen amoris habent ≈ Alan. *Parab.* 2, *PL* 210, col. 585 A: "Qui clarum gemini lumen amoris habet."

35, 114   **praedominatur amor** = Mant., *De natura Amoris*, vol. 1, fol. 178ᵛ; Eob. *Her. Chr.* 21, 108; *Psalt.* 4, 10. The verb "praedominatur" is a medievalism.

35, 115   **Vade – flammis** Cf. Vulg. *Joan.* 8, 11, where Jesus tells the adulterous woman: "vade et iam amplius noli peccare."
          turpibus ... flammis Ennod. *Carm.* 2, 112, 9; Eob. *Buc.* 9, 7; *Val.* 1, 216.
          urere flammis = Verg. *G.* 1, 85; *A.* 2, 37; Luc. 1, 591.

35, 116   **Ad vitam – redi** Cf. *Her. Chr.* 9, 99.

35, 117   **Nullo – laesus** ≈ *Her. Chr.* 17, 97.
          Nullo discrimine = *Laud.* 83 (n.).

35, 118   **Consilio – meo** ≈ *Her. Chr.* 5, 160; cf. Ov. *Ep.* 6, 12.

36, 2   **Sit satis** = Verg. *A.* 9, 653; Tib. 1, 10, 61; Ov. *Tr.* 1, 1, 56; Eob. *Buc.* 5, 111; 8, 127.

36, 3   **Rumpite ... languentia fila** *Her.* 1, 6, 179-180: "languentia fila senectae / Rumpere."
          fila sorores = Ov. *Ep.* 12, 3 (in some mss.); Luc. 6, 703; 9, 838; Stat. *Silv.* 1, 4, 123; Eob. *Vict.* 161 (of the Parcae): "Territa lanificae ponebant fila sorores."

36, 5   **quisquis amas** Cf. *Laud.* 321 (n.).

36, 6   **Priscus – amor** Cf. *Sylv. duae* 2, 247. For "priscus amor" see Maxim. 2, 15.
          calido pectore *Laud.* 201 (n.).

B 1

1   **Libuit – videremur** Eobanus expresses the same thought in *Hymn.* B 13.
2   **absque figurato naso** Cf. *Laud.* 387 (n.).
      Sylvarum – libros See *Laud.*, ded. 11, with fn. 9.
      ex officina nostra Erasmus, *Adag.* 2, 6, 66.

B 2

Meter: Elegiac distich.

1   **Maxima Pieridum** As the Muse of heroic poetry, Calliope was queen of the
        Muses. See n. *Laud.* 246.
2   **subito ... ore** Prop. 2, 32, 16.
        tales – sonos = *Her.* 1, 6, 76; cf. Ov. *Ep.* 11, 94; *Fast.* 1, 434; *Ib.* 222.
3   **solito ... tristior** Vulg. *Gen.* 40, 7; Eob. *Her. Chr.* 12, 211; *Dial.* 2, sig. B4ᵛ:
        "Salve, Misologe, quid solito videris tristior?"
5   **nostri ... causa doloris** *Her. Chr.* 9, 44.
        causa doloris = Prop. 1, 16, 35; Verg. *A.* 9, 216; Ov. *Met.* 1, 509; et al.
6   **vati – tuo** ≈ Ov. *Ep.* 15, 58.
7   **incautus** *Ama.* 12, 11 (n.).
8   **Dulce ... garrit** *Copa* 9.
        dextra A transferred epithet. Venus spoke so "dexterously" to Eobanus that he
        fell in love.
        garrit in aure Cf. Pers. 5, 96 and Mart. 5, 61, 3: "garrit in aurem." Eobanus uses
        the ablative (instead of the accusative) to make the phrase fit the meter.
9-10   **libera – Libera** Note the alliteration. For "libera lingua" see Ov. *Pont.* 3, 3, 22.
10   **vincula ... Amor** = Tib. 2, 2, 18; Prop. 1, 15, 16.
14   **Omnipotens ... Amor** For the omnipotence of Amor cf. *Ama.* 8, 3-6 (n.).
15-18   **Polluit – genus** For the thoughts cf. lines 57-60 below. For lines 17-18 cf.
        Eobanus's public lecture on his *Sylvae duae* (1514), in *Epp. fam.*, p. 247:
        "Artifex ... amor est, ... artificium pulcherrimum exercet .... Mores docet,
        formam componit, gestus indicat, humanitatem ostendit, frontem variat,
        animum levat, denique ex stultis sapientes reddit. Quorum omnium
        exemplum in uno Cymone Boccatii videre licet."
16   **Egregias mentes** Prud. *Psych.* 386.
18   **omne genus** = Ov. *Fast.* 4, 94; *Tr.* 2, 264; *Pont.* 4, 16, 24; Eob. *Her. Chr.* 6, 158;
        11, 52.
19   **Quisquis amat** = *Laud.* 321 (n.).
        tacito ... aestu Sen. *Phaedr.* 362; cf. Eob. *Buc.* 3, 132 (n.).
20   **ineptus amans** Cf. *Ama.* B 2, 78 (n.): "... ineptus amor."
22   **Quid sit amor** = Ov. *Met.* 13, 762; Eob. *Sylv. duae* 2, 25; cf. *Buc.* 3, 58 (n.).
23-24   **poma – Tantale** ≈ Ov. *Am.* 2, 2, 43-44; cf. Eob. *Vict.* 174, referring to Tantalus:
        "Pomaque ... fugientia prehendit."
24   **languet amor** = Ov. *Ars* 2, 436.
25   **Quem – Amor** ≈ Mart. 5, 48, 1. For the omnipotence of Amor cf. *Ama.* 8,
        3-6 (n.).
        non Venus aurea = Verg. *A.* 10, 16. For "Venus aurea" at this metrical position
        see also Ov. *Ep.* 16, 35; 16, 291; *Met.* 10, 277; Eob. *Ruf.* 59; *Nup.* 255; *Sylv.*
        duae 2, 117.
27   **Mentitur – amores** Cf. *Her. Chr.* 1, 151-152.
28   **Falsa ... numina** *Her. Chr.* 4, 218 (n.).
        Falsa deum = *Her. Chr.* 17, 9.
        vincit amor = Verg. *Ecl.* 10, 69; Ov. *Am.* 3, 11, 34; *Ep.* 9, 26.

29   **Iuppiter Europam** = Ov. *Ep.* 4, 55.
31   **Quid mirum** = Lucr. 5, 1238; Ov. *Ars* 3, 110; *Fast.* 6, 289; et al.
        demens ... vetustas = *Her. Chr.* 17, 51; cf. *Her. Chr.* 1, 151.
32   **Plena malis** = Juv. 10, 191.
34   **Paphias ... faces** *Sylv.* 1, 7, 10.
        tonsa corona = *Sylv. duae* 2, 206; *Her. Chr.* 17, 224; *Eccles.* 102; cf. *Laud.* 134;
        Nup. 267.
35   **Christi ... sacra** *Her. Chr.* 17, 9 (n.).
        sacra prophanas = *Laud.* 240 (n.).
37   **Sacra prophanat** Cf. *Laud.* 378 (n.).
        sacras ... aras = *Laud.* 246 (n.).
38   **tetricus ... cucullus** *Her. Chr.* 11, 91; cf. Celtis, *Am.* 3, 10, 41, of the monk's
        cowl: "taetrum ... cucullum." Here the cowl stands for the monks who wear it.
39-40   **O, nostri – videt** Cf. *Her. Chr.* 6, 101 (n.); 13, 111-112.
40   **Crimina ... tanta** Ov. *Tr.* 2, 508.
        lumine ... videt = *Her. Chr.* 8, 8; 12, 108; 13, 112; 15, 198.
41   **Languet ... virtus** *Her. Chr.* 19, 59.
        libidine virtus = *Ilias Lat.* 92: "... superata libidine virtus"; Eob. *Tum.* 2, 151:
        "... insana quam victa libidine virtus."
42   **totas ... opes** = Mart. 11, 5, 12.
43   **talibus aures** = Ov. *Met.* 6, 1.
44   **Verba – loqui** The theme is central to Mant. *c. Poet.* Cf. further Catul. 16, 5:
        "castum esse decet pium poetam"; Marul. *Epigr.* 1, 62, 5-6: "Casta placent
        Phoebo, castissima turba sororum est, / Casta pios vates Pieriosque decent";
        Mutian. *Ep.* 77 (vol. 1, p. 114), paraphrasing Catul. 16, 5; Eob. *Laud.* 239-240;
        244; *Ama.* B 2, 59; *Buc.* 1, 91; 3, 35-36; *Sylv.* 1, 7, 44.
        non nisi casta = Mart. 6, 45, 2; cf. Ov. *Am.* 3, 4, 41.
45   **Quid ulterius** = *Epp.* 4, sig. F2ᵛ (1508): "Parce. Quid ulterius te iuvat esse
        trucem?"
46   **tantos ... viros** ≈ Ov. *Pont.* 2, 6, 30; cf. Eob. *Her. Chr.* 18, 13 (n.).
49-50   **Vulnere – diu** Cf. *Ama.* 35, 66 (with notes to *Ama.* 35, 64-66).
51   **armat ... mentem** Sil. 4, 249.
        sententia mentem = Ov. *Met.* 9, 517; Sil. 12, 507; cf. Eob. *Buc.* 10, 151 (n.).
52   **causas invenit** = Ov. *Pont.* 3, 2, 76.
        omnis amans = Ov. *Am.* 1, 9, 1 and 2; *Ars* 1, 729; Eob. *Ama.* B 2, 76; *Buc.* 7,
        171; *Sylv. duae* 2, 50; *Her. Chr.* 4, 146.
53   **indomitae ... flammae** Sen. *Phaed.* 187.
        serpunt – flammae ≈ Ov. *Rem.* 105; cf. Eob. *Ama.* 35, 11.
        viscera flammae = *Ama.* 33, 11, 1 (n.).
54   **Causa prior** = Ov. *Met.* 15, 37.
55   **Supprime – aestus** Cf. *Ama.* 24, 6 (n.); 35, 61, where see notes.
57-60   **Prosunt – amas** For the thoughts cf. lines 15-18 above (n.).
59   **Sacra – poaetae** Cf. *Ama.* B 2, 44 (n.).
        Sacra canunt = Verg. *A.* 2, 239.
        canunt ... Veneris ... furta *Vict.* 278; cf. Ov. *Tr.* 2, 440.
61   **te Cynthia – Properti** Cf. Mart. 8, 73, 5.
62   **Ussit – suum** Cf. Mart. 14, 193, 1.
66   **Et tua – erat** Cf. Verg. *Ecl.* 10, 22; Mart. 8, 73, 6.
71   **sacer ... vates** Ov. *Am.* 3, 9, 41 (of the poet Tibullus).
74   **Nos ... vates ... sumus** *Her. Chr.*, lim. 6; cf. Ov. *Am.* 1, 1, 6.
        Nos ... conditione sumus *Eleg. Maec.* 1, 118.
75   **miserande puer** = *Ama.* 35, 53 (n.).
        Tibi dexter Apollo = *Idyl.* 1, 54: "tibi dexter Apollo / Spirat"; *Icones*, sig. B2ᵛ:

"memorans, quam dulcia Musae / Carmina contulerint, quam sit tibi dexter Apollo"; cf. Prop. 3, 2, 9: "... Apolline dextro"; Ov. *Tr.* 5, 3, 57; Stat. *Theb.* 3, 454 and *Silv.* 5, 1, 13: "... dexter Apollo."

76	**miser ... amans** *Buc.* 7, 129 (n.).
	omnis amans = *Ama.* B 2, 52 (n.).
77-78	**Toto – amor** Cf. *Ama.* 35, 87-88.
77	**Toto ... pectore flammae** Cf. Verg. *A.* 7, 356; Eob. *Laud.* 294 (n.).
78	**ineptus amor** = Tib. 1, 4, 24; cf. Eob. *Ama.* B 2, 20; *Her. Chr.* 19, 60.

B 3

1	**succisivis horis** Similarly Eobanus explains on the title page of *Laud.* that he composed the poem "succisivis horis." Cf. *Her. Chr.*, ded. 8, 4, where he says that the book was finished "horis subcisivis." See further Otto 1294; Häussler, p. 282; Erasmus, *Adag.* 2, 1, 22.
	pulchrum ... et praeclarum Cf. *Ama.*, ded. 1 (n.).
4	**Ex – nuncii** Cf. *Ama.* B 1, 4 (n.).

B 4

For the *propempticon* to the book cf. *Ama.*, lim., with introductory note (p. 433 above). Meter: Elegiac distich.

1	**Vade, liber** = Ov. *Tr.* 1, 1, 15.
	vana ... convicia Ov. *Met.* 9, 302-303.
2	**in urbe manet** = Tib. 2, 3, 2.
4	**placida ... manu** ≈ Ov. *Tr.* 3, 1, 2 (the book speaks): "da placidam fesso, lector amice, manum."
5	**Erphordia clara** Cf. *Rec.* 230.

Liminary epigram

Meter: Elegiac distich.

1 **Rustica ... Musa** Verg. *Ecl.* 3, 84; Claud. *Cons. Stil.* 1, 181; Eob. *Buc.* 6, 10-11. **Siculi ... poetae** Hor. *Ars* 463.
  Musa poetae = Pers. 1, 68; Eob. *Her. Chr.* 24, 133; cf. *Buc.* 3, 29.

2 **uterque Maro** Cf. epigram by Eobanus Hessus in *Thomae Wolphii Iunioris In Psalmum tercium et trigesimum expositio* (Erfurt, [Wolfgang Stürmer], 1507), sig. a2ᵛ: "Mantua non tantum gemino Tyberina Marone / Laudis habet."

4 **Me – locum** Cf. *Her. Chr.* 5, 146. For the tag "habere locum" see Ov. *Fast.* 1, 518; 4, 28; Eob. *Sylv. duae* 1, 178.

5 **Primus Teutonico** ≈ *Epp. 4*, sig. F3ᵛ (1508): "Otto per orbem / Primus Teutonicis hoc nomine notus in oris." Eobanus was proud of being the first German to write pastoral poetry. See *Buc.* 3, 28-32; 6, 6-9; *Sylv. duae* 1, 181-182; *Her. Chr.* 24, 112; *Eleg.* 1, 67-68; *Wirt.* B 1, 5-6; *Sylv.* 1, 4, 79-80; 3, 5, 1-2. His claim is echoed by Crotus Rubianus in *Buc.* B 7, 7-8, Johann Pistoris of Kirchberg in *Buc.* B 10, 3-4, and Lotich. *Eleg.* 6, 30, 37-38. In truth, however, he was not the very first German to try his hand at the genre. Bartholomew of Cologne had published an "Ecloga bucolici carminis" as early as 1485; and Heinrich Bebel had followed with eclogues printed in 1495 and 1504. Eobanus admits as much in a public lecture on his *Sylvae duae* (early 1514), where he notes that there were "practically" no pastoral poets in Germany before him ("ante me fere nullus in Germania"). See *Epp. fam.*, p. 246. The claim to being the first German pastoralist, then, is a matter of degree. Eobanus certainly was the first in Germany to compose a whole cycle of eclogues, in the manner of Vergil, Baptista Mantuanus, and Fausto Andrelini.
  For the claim of having originated a genre or being the first in one's country to write in a given style see, for example, Lucr. 1, 922-930; Verg. *G.* 2, 174-176; 3, 10-12; Hor. *Carm.* 3, 30, 12-14; Prop. 3, 1, 3-4; also cf. Calp. *Ecl.* 4, 62-63. **Teutonico – Latinum** Cf. *Buc.* B 11, 22; *Wirt* B 1, 5-6: "agnas / Quas ego Teutonico primus in orbe dedi"; *Epp. 3*, sig. C7ᵛ (in a letter of 9 July 1536, referring to his translation of Theocritus's *Idylls*): "Nos Latio Siculum pavimus orbe pecus"; Lotich. *Eleg.* 6, 30, 38: "Teutonico Latios pavit in orbe greges."

6 **Sive – nihil** Cf. *Eleg.* 1, 66: "... sive aliqua est, sive ea fama nihil." For the verse structure cf. *Her. Chr.* 17, 274 (n.).

Dedicatory letter

Meter: Elegiac distich.

1 **sol ... finderet arvum** Cf. Ov. *Am.* 2, 16, 3; *Met.* 3, 151-152; Eob. *Buc.* B 6, 2 (n.).
  sol ... lampade Cf. Lucr. 5, 610. For the sun regarded as the torch of Phoebus see, for example, also Lucr. 5, 402; 6, 1198; Verg. *A.* 3, 637; Eob. *Buc.* 9, 95.

2 **multo lumine** Verg. *A.* 3, 151; Stat. *Theb.* 5, 666; *Silv.* 4, 5, 14.

3-4	**Has – habet** Cf. Filetico, *Theoc.*, ded., sig. A1ᵛ: "Has ego Trinacriis errantes montibus agnas / Eduxi Latio ... solo"; Eob. *Buc.* 7, 127; *Wirt.* B 1, 5 (referring to some of his pastorals dealing with Hessian themes): "Perlege in Hessiacis errantes montibus agnas"; *Sylv.* 6, 11, 3-4 (about his Theocritus-translation): "Nunc tandem Siculis ductas e montibus agnas / Pascere Romani iussimus arva soli"; 7, 4, 1: "Montibus Hessiacis errantes ... capellas."
3	**in montibus agnas** = *Buc.* 11, 1; *Sylv.* 7, 9, 17; *Theoc.* 11, sig. D7ʳ; 36, sig. N5ᵛ; cf. Verg. *Ecl.* 2, 21.
4	**belliger Hessus** Cf. *Buc.* B 3, 1 (n.).
5	**gelida – umbra** The model is Mant. *Ecl.* 1, 1: "gelida ... pecus omne sub umbra / ruminat"; cf. Eob. *Buc.* 9, 19. For "gelida umbra" see also *Laud.* 163; *Buc.* 3, 24 (n.); and, for example, Lucr. 5, 641; Verg. *A.* 11, 210; Mant. *Ecl.* 5, 2; 9, 19; 9, 68. For "pecus omne" see also, for instance, Verg. *G.* 2, 371; 3, 445; *A.* 12, 718; Mant. *Ecl.* 9, 160; 9, 225; Eob. *Buc.* 8, 4; 8, 33; 11, 96.
6	**messe ... ager** = Ov. *Ars* 3, 82; Eob. *Her. Chr.* 10, 134; 12, 226.
7	**Ibitis ... urbem** For the idiom cf., for example, Verg. *A.* 3, 254: "ibitis Italiam"; Ov. *Ep.* 10, 125. For the *propempticon* cf. Ov. *Tr.* 1, 1, 1: "sine me, liber, ibis in urbem"; see further Eob. *Ama.*, lim. (n.).
	Hessiacam ... urbem Cf. *Laud.* 125.
	servet – Iuppiter Cf. Pl. *Ps.* 934; Ter. *Ph.* 807.
9	**obliquo** For the epithet see *Rec.* 178 (n.).
10	**in partes ... duas** = Ov. *Fast.* 6, 84; *Tr.* 5, 5, 36.
12	**Munera ... vatis** *Nor.* 1371: "te ... munera vatis / Accipere ista tui ... decebit."
13	**spes patriae** *Laud.* B 3, 6.
14	**lacte – damus** = Mart. 13, 38, 2.
20	**quae – erat** = Ov. *Ep.* 3, 48.
21	**honor patriae** = *Buc.* B 2, 23 (referring to Englender); *Epic.* 4, 130: "Cordus, honor patriae deliciumque suae."
22	**munere – eras** ≈ Mart. 1, 101, 8.
23	**quo se potius iactet** Cf. *Buc.* 6, 10-11 (n.).
26	**Virtutis ... praemia** Sil. 16, 157-158.
	praemia ferre tuae = Mart. 1, 25, 6; cf. Eob. *Wirt.*, ded. 32: "Debes ... meriti praemia ferre tui"; *Sylv.* 9, 19, 12: "Quae possum meritis praemia ferre tuis?"
27	**Teste Deo** Prop. 4, 9, 13; Ov. *Ep.* 6, 30.
	virtus manifesta = Juvenc. 2, 326.
	manifesta negari ≈ Ov. *Ep.* 4, 111; Mart. 2, 8, 7.
28	**Quae – deus** For the proverbial expression "as plain as day" see Otto 999; Häussler, pp. 59, 75, and 180-181.
29	**Macte – annos** Cf. *Sylv.* 3, 1, 73 (to Duke John Frederick of Saxony): "Macte animo, veteres duce te revocabimus annos"; *Buc.* 3, 31.
32	**nostra Thalia** = Mart. 4, 8, 12; 9, 26, 8; Eob. *Tum.*, ded. 10; *Hypocr.* 10; *Sylv.* 2, 1, 6; 7, 9, 24; 7, 35, 16; and 9, 17, 2.
33	**celebri ... in aula** = *Calum.* 13; cf. Paul. Nol. *Carm.* 19, 256: "...celebri Felicis in aula."
	capras numerabis Cf. *Buc.* 1, 29 (n.).
34	**Donēc** Instead of "Donĕc."
	copia grandis Bocc. *Ecl.* 1, 23; 4, 10.
35	**alacrem ... iuventam** *Idyl.* 16, 77.
	formosa Halerina Eobanus takes this phrase from Mutian. *Ep.* 149, line 34, an "Ecloga pastoralis" urging him to seek Englender's patronage: "Magniloquo formosa viro coniuncta Halerina."
36	**prole – parens** Cf. V. Fl. 5, 383; Eob. *Her. Chr.* 4, 36; 13, 134; 20, 17 (n.); *Vict.* 244: "prole beatus"; *Her.* 1, 6, 108: "... prole beate senex." The idea of wishing

Englender and his wife good luck in obtaining offspring comes from Mutian. *Ep.* 149, lines 37-41.

37-38   **Addere – nostra** For the thought cf. *Laud.*, ded. 11 (n.).

38   **Munera – nostra** Cf. Verg. *Ecl.* 2, 44; Eob. *Her. Chr.* 22, 1; *Idyl.* 13, 20-21: "ni mea forsan / Sordeat ... Musa."

Bucolicon

1

The spelling "aegloga" in the title of this poem was common in the Middle Ages and the Renaissance, owing to an imagined connection with αἴξ, αἰγός ("goat"). See Helen Cooper, "The Goat and the Eclogue," *Philological Quarterly* 53 (1974): 363-379. See also Eob. *Her. Chr.* 24, 111.

Meter: Hexameter.

1-6   **Alma – veniunt** Besides its evident function of delighting the reader, the evocation of spring serves as the lead-in to Paniscus's argument that Camillus should take advantage of the springtime of his life. Hence the verses should not be taken too literally, as if Christiani were persuading Eobanus to leave Frankenberg already in the spring of 1504 rather than the summer. In line 66 Eobanus suggests that it is, in fact, summer already ("calor aestivus"). In line 117, however, we are again reminded that it is springtime.

    For other evocations of spring in Eobanus's works see *Ruf.* 1-28 and *Sylv.* 4, 4, 1-20, in both cases introducing an exhortation to make good use of the springtime of life; *Buc.* 6, 17-30; and *Her. Chr.* 3, 137-145, *Hymn.* 85-128, and *Vict.*, ded. 1-10 (the renewal of nature at Easter).

1-2   **Alma – paritura** For the description of mother Nature in the spring cf. Lucr. 1, 250-251; Verg. *G.* 2, 324-331; Ov. *Met.* 15, 91-92; [Sen.] *Oct.* 404-405: "tellus laeta fecundos sinus / pandebat ultro"; *Anthol. Lat.* 567, 1 (traditionally attributed to Vergil): "Vere sinum tellus aperit"; Ven. Fort. *Carm.* 3, 9, 9: "terra favens vario fundit munuscula fetu"; Mutian. *Ep.* 66 (vol. 1, p. 90), written in the spring of 1508: "Omniparens mater nostra diva tellus laxavit sinum"; Eob., *Epp. 1*, sig. R8ᵛ (1534?): "Plena sinu vario germine turget humus."

1   **Alma ... Mater** Lucr. 2, 992-993 (mother Earth); Ov. *Fast.* 4, 1 (Venus).

2   **Ore renidenti** = Ov. *Met.* 8, 197; V. Fl. 4, 234.

3-4   **Vernat – Pascua** Cf. *Ecl. Theoduli* 285: "Prata virent, silvae frondent, nunc omnia rident"; Eob. *Ama.* 32, 59 (n.).

3   **Vernat – sylvae** = *Vict.*, ded. 7.

    Vernat humus = Ov. *Met.* 7, 284; Eob. *Ruf.* 99; cf. *Her. Chr.* 23, 2 (n.).

    frondent sylvae Verg. *Ecl.* 3, 57 (in springtime).

3-5   **viridantia – luxuriant** Cf. *Ama.* 32, 58-59.

4   **salientibus ... rivis** Verg. *Ecl.* 5, 47.

    undique rivis = Verg. *A.* 5, 200.

4-5   **rivis Gramina** Verg. *Ecl.* 10, 29.

5-6   **omnibus – veniunt** Cf. Verg. *Ecl.* 4, 39 (in the coming golden age).

5   **omnibus omnia** = Lucr. 1, 172; 2, 337; et al.; cf. Eob. *Buc.* 6, 24 (n.).

6   **Sponte sua veniunt** = Verg. *G.* 2, 11. For "sponte sua" at this metrical position see Verg. *Ecl.* 4, 45; 8, 106; *G.* 2, 47; et al.; Eob. *Her. Chr.* 1, 194; 15, 205; 24, 101; *Vict.*, ded. 6; *Vict.* 15; 84.

    Patria – umbra Cf. Verg. *Ecl.* 1, 4.

8   **pingui ... arvo** *Buc.* 4, 111 (n.).

9   **flore – aevi** Cf. *Ilias* 8, p. 204: "Ut pueros qui flore virent impuberis aevi." For

"flore aevi" see Sil. 15, 34; Eob. *Laud.* 147.

puberis aevi = Nemes. *Ecl.* 2, 81; cf. Eob. *Hod.* 147: "... impuberis aevi."

10   **Montibus et sylvis** = Verg. *Ecl.* 2, 5. The mountains and hills of Hesse are often mentioned in Eobanus's works; see n. *Laud.* 278.

sylvis – abundat Cf. *Wirt.* 441: "... sylvae et fluvii quibus Hessia dives abundat." For "Hessia dives" see also *Buc.* B 8, 10; *Idyl.* 1, 129.

dives abundat Ov. *Ep.* 16, 356.

11   **Digna – Musae** Cf. Verg. *Ecl.* 8, 10.

cothurnatae ... Musae Cf. Ov. *Am.* 2, 18, 18; Eob. *Buc.* 3, 28, with notes.

modularis carmina ≈ Ov. *Met.* 14, 341. The phrase is often used for pastoral singing and piping. See, for instance, Verg. *Ecl.* 10, 51; *A.* 1, 1a; *Culex* 100; Tib. 2, 1, 53-54; Ov. *Met.* 11, 154; Eob. *Buc.* 8, 44-45; cf. *Buc.* 4, 74 (n.); 7, 137.

carmina Musae = Nemes. *Ecl.* 1, 70.

12   **Et ... summa ... culmina** = Verg. *Ecl.* 1, 82; cf. *A.* 2, 695; Eob. *Buc.* 1, 116.

14   **sterilem ... Camaenam** Cf. Andrel. *Ecl.* 7, 33: "steriles Musae."

16   **inter pecudes** Verg. *A.* 3, 656; Eob. *Buc.* 4, 99 (n.).

17   **dulces annos, ... tempora** ≈ Erasmus, *Carm.* 2, 75: "O dulces anni, o felicia tempora vitae." For "dulces annos" see, for example, Ov. *Met.* 7, 752; Stat. *Theb.* 4, 354.

florida tempora Her. *Chr.* 18, 111; *Epic.* 3 A, 6: "Florida ... tempora veris"; cf. Catul. 68, 16; Erasmus, *Carm.* 2, 34: "floridam iuventam."

tempora perdis = Mant. *3. Parthen.*, fol. 108ᵛ; Eob. *Her. Chr.* 4, 65 (n.); cf. Ov. *Fast.* 1, 143; Mant. *Ecl.* 1, 37; 6, 136.

18   **Nos – tenemus** Cf. Verg. *Ecl.* 1, 3.

alios fines = Verg. *A.* 11, 324.

melioraque rura Cf. Mant. *Ecl.* 9, 232: "... coge pecus melioraque pascua quaere."

rura tenemus ≈ Ov. *Met.* 3, 2; Eob. *Rec.* 75.

20   **Fortunate puer** Verg. *Ecl.* 5, 49.

21   **tali – terra** Cf. Verg. *A.* 1, 572; 4, 349; Eob. *Buc.* 3, 7; Cordus, *Buc.* 9, 38 (*Ecl.* 10, 70), referring to Italy: "[vellem] ... novus in tali considere rure colonus [terra considere pastor *1518*]."

22   **Et – casas et** Cf. Verg. *Ecl.* 2, 29; Eob. *Buc.* 6, 13.

22-23   **dites – soles** Cf. Mant. *Ecl.* 5, 6-7: "Vos quibus est res ampla domi, quibus ubera vaccae / plena ferunt, quibus alba greges mulctraria complent"; Eob. *Buc.* 7, 89-91.

plena ... Ubera Ov. *Rem.* 180; *Fast.* 4, 769; *Tr.* 1, 8, 44.

23   **totos ... soles** = Mart. 10, 12, 7.

replent mulctralia Cf. Verg. *G.* 3, 177.

24   **nostrae ... sylvae** = Calp. *Ecl.* 7, 2; cf. Eob. *Buc.* 6, 8.

resonabunt ... sylvae Cf. Verg. *Ecl.* 1, 5.

dulcia See n. *Buc.* 2, 106.

25   **iucundius aevo** ≈ *Buc.* 4, 33.

27   **Apollineas laurus** Ov. *Fast.* 6, 91.

27-28   **nondum – quando** Cf. Ov. *Ep.* 5, 9.

28   **Talis eras** = Ov. *Am.* 1, 10, 7.

29   **numerare capellas** = *Sylv.* 2, 4, 33. Herders count their animals every so often to make sure that none of them has wandered off. Cf. Verg. *Ecl.* 3, 34; 6, 85; *G.* 4, 436; Tib. 1, 5, 25; Ov. *Met.* 13, 824; Calp. *Ecl.* 3, 64; Eob. *Buc.* 1, 125; B 6, 5.

30   **ego – memini** = Ov. *Met.* 15, 160; Eob. *Nor.* 620.

34   **Nemo – evadit** = *Ilias* 6, p. 160: "Mortem nemo effugit unquam, / Nemo vir evadit."

34-37   **omnes – senectus** Cf. *Idyl.* 10, 16-18: "satis insanitum est mollibus annis. /

Nunc sapere et meliora sequi provectior aetas / Admonet."

34-35   **omnes – annis** Based on Mant. *Ecl.* 1, 118 (referring to the passion of love): "semel insanivimus omnes." The saying quickly became proverbial; see Wilfred P. Mustard, *The Eclogues of Baptista Mantuanus* (Baltimore, 1911), pp. 40-48. Eobanus quotes it in *Ama.* B 2, 69 and paraphrases it in *Idyl.* 10, 16 (see preceding note). Interestingly, Eobanus's verse became proverbial in its own right, being cited as: "A primis et nos pueriliter egimus annis." See Walther 65.

35   **primis ... annis** = *Buc.* 3, 65 (n.).

    aegimus annis ≈ Ov. *Met.* 8, 708.

36-37   **Atque – Crescat** For the underlying thought that advancing age brings wisdom cf. Vulg. *Luc.* 2, 52; Ter. *Ad.* 832: "aetate sapimus rectius"; Erasmus, *Adag.* 3, 9, 57. For the phrasing cf. Eob. *Laud.* 31 (n.): "crescunt crescentibus annis."

36   **Atque utinam** = Verg. *Ecl.* 10, 35; *A.* 1, 575; Prop. 1, 9, 8; et al.; Eob. *Her. Chr.* 9, 53; 11, 37; 11, 161; 17, 251; and often.

37   **et ingrediens – senectus** Cf. Mant. *Somn.*, fol. 209ʳ: "... et ad fragilem veniat cum laude senectam."

39   **Qui canat in triviis** That is, Paniscus is no run-of-the-mill poet. Cf. Verg. *Ecl.* 3, 26-27; Calp. *Ecl.* 1, 28-29; Nemes. *Ecl.* 4, 3; Eob. *Buc.* 4, 73 (with note to lines 73-75); 7, 104; 8, 99-100.

    in triviis = Aus. *Epigr.* 76, 1; Eob. *Buc.* 11, 72 (n.), in a different sense; *Nor.* 52 (crossroads).

40-41   **Orphea ... Thamiras, Amphion** For these legendary singers cf. line 50 below (n.). For the scansion "Orphĕă" see Verg. *Ecl.* 6, 30; Ov. *Pont.* 3, 3, 41; Mant. *Ecl.* 9, 215-216; Eob. *Epic.* 2, 100.

40   **fatum deflesse** Ov. *Met.* 7, 388; 7, 698.

42   **magnanimum ... leonem** The lion was proverbially great-hearted; see *Laud.* 286 (n.).

43-44   **talem – Saecula** Cf. Verg. *A.* 1, 605-606; Ov. *Tr.* 4, 10, 125; Stat. *Silv.* 1, 1, 81-82; Eob. *Her. Chr.* 24, 141; *Nob.* 243-244: "quos nostra tulerunt / ... saecula"; *Nor.* 689: "Felices, quos illa tulit ... aetas / Aurea."

44   **Nate bonis avibus** *Idyl.* 16, 76; cf. *Accl.* 1, 149: "Orte bonis avibus"; also cf. *Laud.* 575 (n.).

    tibi ... rident = Calp. *Ecl.* 4, 51; cf. Lucr. 1, 8.

45-46   **dumosis – lacer** Cf. *Ama.* 8, 7: "per hos densissimos vepres infoelix erro, lacer et informis."

45   **convallibus erres** Cf. Ov. *Met.* 13, 821; Stat. *Theb.* 5, 523; Eob. *Her. Chr.* 14, 119.

46   **sola ... sub rupe** Verg. *Ecl.* 10, 14; Catul. 64, 154; cf. Eob. *Buc.* 7, 162. Shepherds enjoy singing in the cool shade beneath a cliff. For the motif see Verg. *Ecl.* 1, 56; *G.* 4, 508; Calp. *Ecl.* 4, 16; Eob. *Buc.* 4, 69.

    totis ... diebus = Mart. 1, 19, 3; 2, 5, 1; et al.

47-48   **Carmina – Concinis** Cf. *Idyl.* 15, 26-27: "sub ipsas / Talia cantabat resonantia carmina valles."

47   **Carmina per ... resonantia cautes** ≈ *Culex* 147.

    duras ... cautes = Ov. *Met.* 4, 672; Stat. *Theb.* 8, 233; cf. Eob. *Buc.* 10, 153 (n.).

    longe resonantia Verg. *G.* 1, 358.

48-49   **aeterna – Pierides** Cf. *Her.*, ded. 17-18: "Dignus eras cui perpetua de fronde coronam / Inciperent nostrae nectere Pierides."

48   **aeterna ... fronde** Cf. Lucr. 1, 118: "perenni fronde coronam"; Ov. *Tr.* 3, 1, 45; Eob. *Buc.* 8, 49 (n.).

    fronde coronent ≈ Verg. *A.* 4, 506; Hor. *Ep.* 1, 18, 64; cf. Eob. *Buc.* 11, 85.

50   **Orphea – cantu** Cf. Mant. *Fed. Spagn.*, fol. 140ᵛ: "Non Thamyras, non Amphion, non Thracius Orpheus, / Non Linus, et magno veniens Museus ab

Orpheo"; Eob. *Buc.* 1, 40-41; *Venus* 1, 152-153: "Orpheus et Thamyras, Linus et Musaeus et ille, / Qui mediis placidos flexit delphinas in undis."

51   **magnanimum ... leonem** *Laud.* 286 (n.).
      quisquis fuit ille = Ov. *Met.* 1, 32; 15, 104; Juv. 8, 274.

54-56 **Haec – papyro** Since shepherds are supposed to be untutored folk, their occasionally more than pastoral knowledge has to be accounted for. Cf. *Adnot.*, sig. I 8ʳ, commenting on Verg. *Ecl.* 3, 40: "Meminisse autem convenit raro fieri ut rusticis et pastoribus sermo tribuatur de philosophis aut alioqui magnis rebus, quas illi non intelligant. Itaque ut decorum personarum servetur, fieri haec fere semper cum quadam excusatione." For the motif cf. Mant. *Ecl.* 7, 154-155: "sic docuit rediens aliquando ex urbe sacerdos / Iannus, et in magno dixit sibi codice lectum"; 5, 101: "haec me iam pridem memini didicisse sub Umbro." For other examples see Mant. *Ecl.* 6, 58-59; 6, 155-162; 7, 10; 8, 87-97; 9, 200; Eob. *Buc.* 2, 39; 7, 47-48; 7, 99-103; 10, 104-108; Cordus, *Ecl.* 3, 96-97: "sic doctus ... / rettulit Arnophilax"; 4, 47-48: "Non anus hoc Phillis docuit, sed maximus Auson / in grandique mihi legisse volumine dixit." Camillus, however, stands out from the average shepherd in that he has learned to read.

57   **Verum age, quando** ≈ Verg. *A.* 11, 587.

57-60 **quando ... Dic** Cf. Verg. *Ecl.* 3, 55; Mant. *Ecl.* 10, 13: "Dicite, quandoquidem tepidos admovit ad ignes / nos hiberna dies ..."; cf. also *Ecl.* 1, 1-2.

57-58 **breves – facit** For this paraphrase of noontime cf. Ov. *Met.* 3, 50 and 14, 53-54; also *Ars* 3, 723; *Met.* 3, 144; Calp. *Ecl.* 4, 169; Eob. *Her. Chr.* 6, 35-36; *Sylv.* 1, 9, 9-10: "medium cum sol ascenderit orbem / Et brevis ex omni facta erit umbra loco."

58   **lustra capellae** ≈ Calp. *Ecl.* 5, 14.

59   **tenent loca** Verg. *A.* 6, 434; Ov. *Met.* 4, 436; Eob. *Buc.* 10, 48; *Idyl.* 5, 9.

60   **Dic age** = Verg. *A.* 6, 343; *Ciris* 234; Ov. *Am.* 3, 5, 31; et al.; Eob. *Buc.* 1, 63; 8, 110 (n.).

61   **doctos ... pastores** *Idyl.* 12, 100.

62   **patrios ... remearis ad agros** Mant. *Dionys.* 1, fol. 171ʳ: "... patrios remeavit ad agros"; cf. Verg. *A.* 11, 793. For "patrios agros" see also line 122 below (n.).

63   **Dic – herbas** The model is Mant. *Ecl.* 1, 1-2: "gelida quando pecus omne sub umbra / ruminat, antiquos paulum recitemus amores." Cf. further Verg. *Ecl.* 6, 54; Ov. *Am.* 3, 5, 17.
      lectas ... herbas = Ov. *Fast.* 5, 401; cf. Ov. *Met.* 14, 347.

65-71 **Quin – vates** For the "motif of bucolic repose" (Curtius, *ELLMA*, p. 191), with its invitation to take one's ease in the shade of a tree next to a babbling brook or spring, cf. Theoc. 1, 21-23; 5, 31-34; Verg. *Ecl.* 1, 1-5; 3, 55-59; 5, 1-7; 7, 9-13; Calp. *Ecl.* 1, 6-12; 2, 4-6; 5, 2; 6, 65-68; Nemes. *Ecl.* 1, 30-34; Eob. *Buc.* 4, 66-71; 5, 1-10; 7, 27-29; 7, 74-75; 8, 30-33. For the idealized landscape see n. *Ama.* 1, 1.

65   **Quin – umbrae** Cf. Calp. *Ecl.* 1, 6; Eob. *Buc.* 4, 67.
      gelidae ... umbrae *Buc.*, ded. 5 (n.); 3, 24 (n.).
      succedimus umbrae Verg. *G.* 3, 418; 3, 464; Calp. *Ecl.* 1, 6; 1, 19; Eob. *Buc.* 4, 13; 4, 67.

67-68 **hiis – scaturit** Cf. *Ama.* 1, 1 (where see notes): "ad fontem, quem inibi ex patulae fagi radicibus limpide scaturientem ... sacrum habebam."

67   **dulces saliunt ... undae** Cf. Verg. *Ecl.* 5, 47; *G.* 2, 243; Ov. *Rem.* 632; Eob. *Buc.* 2, 13 (n.).

68   **sacri latices** Sil. 7, 163-164 (of wine).

70   **Hic – quies** Cf. Mart. 11, 26, 1; Hor. *Ep.* 1, 17, 6; Eob. *Buc.* 3, 6 (n.). For "grata quies" see also Ov. *Ars* 3, 695; *Met.* 14, 52.

Alia ... parte = Verg. *A.* 4, 153; Stat. *Theb.* 6, 177.

72-82   **Proxima – bidentes** This praise of Thuringia echoes Vergil's praise of Italy in *G.* 2, 136-154.

72   **montanis ... Hessis** Cf. line 10 above; n. *Laud.* 278.

72-73   **terminat ... Imperium** Alcuin. *Carm.* 1, 103: "imperium latum tibi terminat undis"; cf. Eob. *Her. Chr.* 2, 25.

73-74   **dives – nemorum** Cf. line 107 below (n.).

73   **florentibus arvis** = Sedul. 1, 90; cf. Ov. *Met.* 2, 791.

74   **Laeta ..., sed ... laetior** Cf. Ov. *Met.* 14, 337: "rara ..., sed rarior."
         iugis nemorum Verg. *A.* 11, 544-545.

75   **flava Ceres** = Mant. *1. Parthen.* 2, 867; cf. Verg. *G.* 1, 96; Tib. 1, 1, 15; Ov. *Am.* 3, 10, 3.

76   **pingui ... arista** = Verg. *G.* 1, 8; cf. *Ecl.* 4, 28; Ov. *Met.* 1, 110.

77   **gravidae ... uvae** Claud. *Cons. Stil.* 2, 466; Boeth. *Consol.* 1, m. 2, 21.
         in collibus uvae Verg. *Ecl.* 9, 49; Tib. 1, 4, 19; cf. Stat. *Silv.* 2, 2, 103.

78   **dum viret annus** *Eras.* 8: "Dum viret et varias parturit annus opes." For "annus" in this sense see Verg. *Ecl.* 3, 57; Hor. *Carm.* 3, 23, 8; *Epod.* 2, 29.

79   **abruptos montes** Sen. *Her. O.* 1167.

79-80   **summa – iuga** Cf. Ov. *Rem.* 179; *Ep.* 16, 55: "amantis saxa capellae." For "summa iuga" see, for example, *Culex* 46; Ov. *Ep.* 4, 42.

80-81   **herbas ... foetas serpente** Cf. *Buc.* 4, 107 (n.): "loca foeta venenis."
         herbas ... carpunt Verg. *G.* 3, 465; Tib. 2, 5, 55; Eob. *Buc.* 3, 64.

82   **innumeras ... bidentes** = Vegius, *Aen.* 398 (in the printed version).
         pratum – bidentes Cf. Lucr. 2, 317-318 and 661-662; *Culex* 50; Ov. *Rem.* 178. "Bidentes" are sheep having two (permanent) front teeth, characteristic of two-year-olds.

83-84   **Iamque – stupet** The shepherd's favorite post is a hilltop or cliff from where he can easily survey his flock. Cf. Verg. *A.* 2, 307-308; Sil. 6, 324; 7, 366; 16, 10; Eob. *Buc.* 5, 44 (n.); 8, 32-33; 9, 114-115; 11, 87-88.

83   **summo ... a vertice** Ov. *Met.* 12, 433; Eob. *Buc.* 8, 48; cf. Verg. *A.* 2, 682; Eob. *Laud.* 133 (n.).

84   **plena omnia** = Juv. 2, 4; Eob. *Nup.* 338; *Sylv.* 6, 2, 13.

85   **miseros ... amores** = Tib. 1, 2, 89; 1, 9, 1.
         deflet amores = *Idyl.* 10, 10; cf. *Buc.* 3, 84-85; cf. also *Buc.* 3, 170.

86   **resonant ... cantu** Verg. *A.* 7, 12.

87-88   **Mammosae – salaces** Cf. *Sylv.* 2, 4, 43: "Cum satyris illic mammosae Naiades errant; / Hessiacum Phyllis non colit una nemus."

87   **Phillides** The ending "-es" is short (as in the Greek nominative plural). "Phyllis" is a stock name in bucolic poetry since Verg. *Ecl.* 3, 76; see also Eob. *Buc.* 6, 62.

88-89   **Sylvani – Napeae** Cf. Ov. *Met.* 1, 192-193; Eob. *Ruf.* 17-20: "Dryades mollesque Napee / Monticolaeque deae, / Sylvanus, satyri, monstrosaque numina fauni, / Semihominesque ferae." Cf. also Lucr. 4, 580-589 and, for example, Ov. *Fast.* 1, 397; Nemes. *Ecl.* 3, 25.

88   **Sylvani – salaces** ≈ Celtis, *Ludus* 27: "Silvanus Satyrique leves Faunique salaces"; cf. Eob. *Venus* 1, 62-63: "Venit et agrestum promiscua turba deorum: / Capripedes faunique leves satyrique salaces."
         satyrique leves Ov. *Ars* 1, 542; cf. Eob. *Idyl.* 16, 7: "satyris levibusque ... faunis."

89   **nymphae – Napeae** Cf. *Buc.* 6, 61; *Idyl.* 7, 141: "Nymphae, Naiades, Dryades, mollesque Napaeae."

90   **mammosa ... Phillide** Cf. *Epp. fam.*, p. 87 (1523), referring to the nuns of Erfurt: "Nulla Phyllis nonnis est nostris mammosior."

91   **Absint – omnes** For the thought cf. *Sylv.* 1, 7, 44: "Nequitia a versu debet

abesse meo"; *Ama.* B 2, 44 (n.).

nostris – omnes ≈ Mant. *Ecl.* 4, 175: "leves prohibete puellas / pellanturque procul vestris ab ovilibus omnes"; cf. Verg. *Ecl.* 1, 8; Eob. *Buc.* 9, 98.

92   **Macte, puer** Verg. *A.* 9, 641.

93   **Nunc coepta sequemur** = *Nor.* 91; 813; cf. Petrarch, *Africa* 4, 45: "... sed grata magis nunc cepta sequamur"; Eob. *Buc.* 10, 92; *Idyl.* 14, 93: "... dum coepta sequuntur"; *Eleg.* 3, 47: "ut coepta sequar"; *Sylv.* 3, 11, 14: "... mea coepta sequar."

94   **in media ... regione** Lucr. 5, 534; Ov. *Fast.* 6, 273.

95   **credere durum est** = Tib. 1, 6, 7.

97   **duri ... labores** = Stat. *Ach.* 2, 153.

      peperere labores = Enn. *var.* 7.

99   **donat – merces** Cf. Paul. Nol. *Carm.* 21, 788: "pro munere munus ... / ... referam"; Bocc. *Ecl.* 1, 49: "... reddant pro munere munus"; 4, 104: "... statuet pro munere munus."

100   **Illa etiam, si** = Verg. *A.* 11, 653.

      pro ... nummos = Hor. *S.* 1, 2, 43.

101   **Vorat – reddit** Cordus, *Buc.* 7, 62 (*Ecl.* 9, 104): "... vorat omnia, reddit egenos."

102   **pro tribulis spinas** Cf. Vulg. *Gen.* 3, 18: "spinas et tribulos."

103   **Ergo – aetas** Cf. *Buc.* 2, 60; 2, 67; *Ruf.* 43: "Dum vigor est ..., dum pullulat aetas"; *Her. Chr.* 10, 163.

      Ergo age = Verg. *A.* 2, 707; Ov. *Ars* 1, 343; et al.; Eob. *Buc.* 8, 88; *Her. Chr.* 11, 109; 22, 157.

      viridi succo The epithet "viridis" is frequently used to describe the vigor of youth. See, for example, Verg. *Aen.* 5, 295; Ov. *Ars* 3, 557; Boeth. *Consol.* 1, m. 1, 7. For succo" in this figurative sense cf. Ter. *Eu.* 318: "corpus solidum et suci plenum"; Ov. *Pont.* 1, 10, 27.

      pullulat aetas = [Cyprian.] *Carm.* 2, 10 and 6, 161 (*CSEL* 3, 1, pp. 289 and 314); Cordus, *Buc.* 4, 77 (*Ecl.* 1, 113): "... tua pullulat aetas."

104   **parvi – peculi** Cf. Andrel. *Ecl.* 9, 37: "tam grandis congesti summa peculi." As the adjective "parvi" shows, "peculi" is here used in the medieval sense "flock," "small farm animals." Cf. Petrarch, *Ecl.* 6, 165: "Cura gregis, rurisque labor, studium peculi"; Bocc. *Ecl.* 2, 13 (a shepherd leaves his flock to follow his beloved): "nec cura potest retinere peculi"; 4, 114: "nunc cura peculi / nulla tibi"; 8, 19: "quantum septis augere peculi"; 12, 179: "grandis cura peculi"; Eob. *Buc.* 7, 51; *Idyl.* 4, 108: "nostri ... septa peculi"; 7, 10: "cura peculi"; 16, 167: "parvi septa peculi"; *Theoc.* 32, sig. M4ᵛ: "cuique ipse greges armentaque tota / Auxit et eximii dedit incrementa peculi."

105-106 **Foelices – Quaere** Cf. Hor. *Epod.* 16, 41-42.

105   **Foelices ... campos** Ov. *Fast.* 5, 197; V. Fl. 1, 445.

      pinguia rura Juvenc. 3, 460.

106   **Nocent pecori** Hor. *Epod.* 16, 61; Ov. *Rem.* 614.

      vepres – achantus Cf. *Idyl.* 5, 8-9 (referring to Erfurt): "et tristis acanthus / Invisaeque tenent vepres loca."

      tristis achantus = *Idyl.* 3, 140; 5, 8. The form "achantus" is a medievalism for "acanthus" (the spelling that Eobanus uses in the *Idyllia* and the Theocritus-translation). See, for example, Bocc. *Ecl.* 3, 16; 5, 94; 10, 88; Eob. *Buc.* 10, 8.

107-110 **Hessia – Nemphim** For the pattern of comparison cf. *Buc.* 3, 21-24 (n.).

107   **Hessia – sylvis** Eobanus imitates the structure of Verg. *A.* 1, 14: "ostia, dives opum studiisque asperrima belli." For the thought cf. Eob. *Epic.* 4, 56: "nemorum sylvis Hessia dives"; *Wirt.* 441: "... sylvae et fluvii, quibus Hessia dives abundat."

      dives agris ... -que = Stat. *Theb.* 5, 305: "insula dives agris opibusque ..."; cf.

Hor. *S.* 1, 2, 13; *Ars* 421.

densisque – sylvis For the idiom cf. Ov. *Met.* 4, 89; *Tr.* 4, 10, 3; Mant. *Ecl.* 10, 30: "... vitreis uberrimus undis."

densis ... sylvis = Ov. *Met.* 15, 488.

108-109 **agnum Imbellem** *Buc.* 10, 122; *Her. Chr.* 22, 105; cf. Sil. 2, 685; Eob. *Rec.* 42.

109   **furibunda – thaurus** Cf. Ov. *Met.* 13, 871.

    in praelia thaurus = Verg. *A.* 10, 455; 12, 103.

110   **Ut – Nemphim** Cf. Mant. *Ecl.* 9, 218: "[hic alios] exsuperat quantum Tiberim Padus, Abdua Macram."

    vagus Aedera = *Epic.* 4, 171; cf. *Buc.* 3, 1; 11, 5; *Her. Chr.* 24, 128. "Vagus" is a conventional epithet of rivers. See, for instance, Hor. *Carm.* 1, 2, 18; 1, 34, 9; Prop. 2, 19, 30; 3, 11, 51; Eob. *Nup.* 152; *Sylv. duae* 1, 59 and 1, 144.

111   **Aedera ... aurifer** *Idyl.* 5, 51; *Epic.* 4, 81; *Wirt.* 36; 439; cf. *Wirt.* 475: "Aedera ... aureus"; Franciscus Irenicus, *Exegesis historiae Germaniae* (1518; Hannover, 1728) 7, 9: "Aiunt et in aurifero fluvio aliquibus Edera dicto, in partibus Hassiae, maxime tempore hyemali aurorum crustas reperiri."

    Hermo Cf. Verg. *G.* 2, 137: "auro turbidus Hermus"; Luc. 3, 209-210; Mart. 6, 86, 5.

114   **Pingue solum** = Verg. *G.* 1, 64; *A.* 4, 202.

    Viret omnis ager *Ruf.* 6: "Nunc viret omnis ager"; cf. *Rec.* 5 (n.); *Buc.* 9, 15.

115   **Stagna – fontes** = Petrarch, *Ecl.* 2, 93; cf. Ov. *Met.* 1, 38; Stat. *Theb.* 5, 522; Eob. *Buc.* 2, 24.

116   **summa procul ... culmina** = Verg. *Ecl.* 1, 82.

118   **Hos – linquam** Cf. Verg. *Ecl.* 1, 3.

119   **Dulces curae** Stat. *Silv.* 2, 1, 71; Eob. *Buc.* 3, 9.

    loca nota = *Rec.* 89 (n.).

120-123 **Tu – frondes** Cf. Verg. *Ecl.* 1, 74-78; Mant. *Ecl.* 9, 54-55: "heu, pecus infelix, quod lacte et prole solebas / affluere, in nostris licuit dum pascere campis."

120-121 **infoelix ... pecus** Verg. *Ecl.* 3, 3; Mant. *Ecl.* 8, 111; 9, 54; 9, 184; Eob. *Buc.* 7, 9; cf. *Buc.* 3, 64.

122   **patrios ... agros** = Mant. *Dionys.* 1, fol. 171ʳ; cf. Hor. *Carm.* 1, 1, 11-12; Ov. *Met.* 14, 476; Eob. *Buc.* 1, 62; 6, 7; *Her. Chr.* 10, 134.

    errare per agros *Buc.* 3, 118-119 (n.).

123   **consuetas ... frondes** Cf. *Idyl.* 11, 6: "non pastas aliena fronde capellas."

    carpere frondes = Calp. *Ecl.* 2, 45; cf. Eob. *Buc.* 8, 34; 10, 164.

124   **Sol ruit interea** = Verg. *A.* 3, 508. Many bucolic poems close with the end of day. See Curtius, *ELLMA*, pp. 90-91; Eob. *Buc.* 4; 5; 9; and 11.

125   **Sume pedum** Verg. *Ecl.* 5, 88 (as a gift); cf. Mant. *Ecl.* 9, 20 and 10, 45: "pone pedum ...."

    compelle gregem ≈ Calp. *Ecl.* 5, 57; cf. Eob. *Buc.* 7, 113-114.

    numeraque capellas Cf. *Buc.* 1, 29 (n.).

126   **Ne – hircus** For the motif cf. Vulg. *Gen.* 22, 13: "arietem inter vepres haerentem cornibus"; Mant. *Calam.* 3, p. 93 (referring to *Gen.* 22, 13): "caprum ..., qui cornibus altis / Vepribus haerebat."

2

The argument to this poem in the 1539-edition informs us that Pudicus ("Chaste") is Eobanus's friend Georg Spalatin (1484-1545). This identification is challenged by a contemporary gloss in the Strasbourg copy, which identifies Pudicus as Crotus Rubianus (see fn. 71 at Camerarius, *Nar.* 17, 17; cf. introductory note to Eob. *Buc.* 3). Internal and external evidence, however, confirms that it is indeed Spalatin who is meant here. From lines 5-14 we know that Pudicus herds sheep in a valley sacred to St. George – a clear allusion to the monastery of Georgenthal, south of Gotha, where Spalatin worked from 1505 to 1508. In lines 72-74 Pudicus says that he is taking a vow of chastity. This fits Spalatin, who took holy orders in July 1508, but not Crotus Rubianus, who was ordained priest in about 1510. And in *Sylv.* 9, 29, lines 1-2 and 9-10 (written in ca. 1530) Eobanus reminds Spalatin that he had once praised him in bucolic song: "Qualis eras in flore tuae, Spalatine, iuventae, / Talem nunc etiam gratulor esse virum. / .... / ... puero nihil es mutatus ab illo, / Quem mea bucolico carmine Musa canit." This can only refer to the present eclogue.

Meter: Hexameter.

1-2	**Carmina – canerent** Cf. *Laud.* 281-282; *Buc.* 11, 4; *Her. Chr.* 24, 105; *Sylv.* 7, 18, 9-10: "Carmina cum faciles mihi pastoralia Musae / Et facili canerent pascua laeta pede."
1	**Carmina ... pastoralia** = Nemes. *Ecl.* 4, 15-16.
	Carmina cum primum = Ov. *Tr.* 4, 10, 57.
1-2	**divae Pierides** = *Ciris* 93-94; Eob. *Buc.* 8, 114.
2-3	**me – indueret** Cf. Calp. *Ecl.* 2, 89-90; Eob. *Laud.* 509.
2	**florente iuventa** = Hor. *Ars* 115; *Eleg. Maec.* 1, 7; Sil. 16, 455.
4	**charo ... amico** Mart. 4, 10, 3; 10, 44, 7.
	iam pastor By the time he wrote this eclogue, Eobanus had probably already finished *Buc.* 1, 3, 5, 6, and 7.
5	**Vallis erat ... secreta recessu** = *Sylv.* 5, 22, 7; cf. Verg. *A.* 11, 522; Eob. *Buc.* 4, 27; *Her. Chr.* 4, 57; 16, 259; *Nor.* 115.
	Vallis erat = Ov. *Met.* 3, 155.
6	**vitreo** For the epithet see *Pug.* B 1, 8 (n.).
7	**Stat domus ... veneranda** Mart. 9, 20, 5; cf. Verg. *A.* 8, 192.
8	**requies gratissima** = Maxim. 1, 249.
9-10	**domini ... servaret oves** Cf. Bocc. *Ecl.* 8, 7: "domini servare greges."
11	**mollibus annis** = Ov. *Ep.* 1, 111; cf. *Ars* 1, 10; *Tr.* 3, 4, 43; Eob. *Buc.* 10, 52.
12	**dulces ... Musas** *Buc.* 2, 15 (n.).
13	**Ad – veniret** ≈ *Nor.* 621: "Ad fontem salientis aquae cum saepe venirem."
	rivum salientis aquae Cf. Lucr. 2, 30; Verg. *Ecl.* 5, 47; 8, 87; Vulg. *Joan.* 4, 14: "fons aquae salientis"; Paul. Nol. *Carm.* 21, 691: "venam / aeternum salientis aquae ..."; Eob. *Buc.* 1, 67 (n.).
	cum sepe veniret Cf. Verg. *Ecl.* 5, 88; Eob. *Buc.* 2, 33; 4, 82; 4, 98.
14	**sic est auditus** = *Idyl.* 11, 12: "... saxo sic est auditus ab alto"; *Theoc.* 11, sig. D6ᵛ: "... scopulo sic est auditus ab alto"; cf. Cordus, *Buc.* 5, 4 (*Ecl.* 7, 4): "... sic Casselio Linus [Singlesio Pius *1518*] est auditus in agro."
15	**Musae – Musae** The line becomes a refrain – a common feature in pastoral poetry. See, for example, Theoc. 1 and 2; Verg. *Ecl.* 8; Nemes. *Ecl.* 4; Bocc. *Ecl.* 6; Eob. *Buc.* 2, 20 (n.) and *Buc.* 5 (in the contestants' strophes).
	Musae, noster amor Cf. Verg. *Ecl.* 7, 21: "Nymphae, noster amor ..." (where "Nymphae" = "Musae"); Eob. *Her. Chr.* 1, 29 (n.).
	dulces – Musae = *Epith.* 18; cf. Verg. *G.* 2, 475; line 12 above.
16	**Pro Iove ... Christum** *Her. Chr.*, ded. 9, 3; *Her. Chr.* 9, 64.
16-19	**rura – pomum** The Christian Muses dwell in the earthly Paradise where Adam,

at the serpent's and Eve's bidding, ate from the forbidden fruit; see Vulg. *Gen.* 3. Paradise was traditionally believed to lie far away in the East, on a high mountain that rises up to the lunar sphere. Cf. *Ezech.* 28, 13-16; and, for example, Dante, *Purgatorio* 28, 91-102; Bocc. *Ecl.* 14, 170-175; Mant. *Ecl.* 8, 45-49; *2. Parthen.* 3, 264-303; Eob. *Her. Chr.* 23, 45-46, with notes; *Vict.* 392-396; *Epic.* 6, 35-36: "Est locus Aurorae primo surgentis in ortu, / Aeriae supra lucida regna plagae." For the idea that the Christian Muses dwell in Paradise cf. *Buc.* 2, 93-95; 8, 119-121 (n.); 11, 18-19 (with note to lines 16-22); *Epic.* 1, 17-18: "omnis ... / Qui chorus Aonidum regna beata colit."

17	**Aeoum ... orbem** = Luc. 8, 289; cf. Ov. *Fast.* 3, 466; 5, 557; *Pont.* 4, 9, 112.
	longe – orbem Cf. Ov. *Tr.* 5, 1, 13; Eob. *Sylv.* 1, 1, 157: "... gelidam longe proiecta sub Arcton."
18-19	**ab arbore – pomum** Cf. [Tiro Prosper], *De providentia divina* 285, *PL* 51, col. 623 D: "... a vetitis pomum decerpere ramis"; Ov. *Met.* 5, 536: "decerpserat arbore pomum"; *Pont.* 3, 5, 19. For "vetitum pomum" see Sedul. 1, 70: "vetiti dulcedine pomi"; Avit. *Carm.* 1, 316: "... vetitum praesumpserit arbore pomum."
20	**Ite – Camaenae** For the refrain see note to line 15 above. The verse echoes the refrain in Filetico, *Theoc.* 1: "Ite, meae Musae, faciles huc ite Camoenae." Cf. also Eob. *Buc.* 5, 61 (refrain); 9, 20.
	Ite ... ite = Verg. *Ecl.* 1, 74; 7, 44; 10, 77; cf. Eob. *Buc.* 10, 162.
	novos ... flores Lucr. 1, 928; 4, 3; Stat. *Silv.* 3, 1, 66-67.
	flores legite Verg. *Ecl.* 3, 92; Ov. *Met.* 4, 315; 5, 554. The flowers are to be woven into garlands for immortal poets; see lines 87-92 below.
21-28	**Vos – profundas** Cf. Hor. *Carm.* 3, 4, 29-36; Eob. *Laud.* 208-210 (with note to line 209). For the catalogue of natural elements and phenomena, typical of medieval and Renaissance poetry (including Baptista Mantuanus's), see Curtius, *ELLMA*, pp. 92-93.
23	**Rura – nemora** Cf. *Eccles.* 154 (*Tum.* 7, 142): "villas, oppida, rura, casas"; *Tum.* 4, 76-77: "villas, / Rura, casas, nemora."
24	**Stagna, lacus** = *Buc.* 1, 115 (n.).
26	**Frigora dura** Lucr. 5, 818.
27	**Hirsutas ... hyemes** Cf. Ov. *Met.* 2, 30; Eob. *Sylv. duae* 1, 44: "Hirsutus Boreas."
	arva pruinas ≈ *Buc.* 7, 143 (n.).
28	**tenebras – profundas** Cf. *Vict.* 319: "... tenebris et nocte profunda."
	noctesque profundas ≈ Verg. *A.* 4, 26; 6, 462.
30-33	**O utinam – venirem** Cf. *Her. Chr.* 10, 131-136 (n.); *Idyl.* 15, 85: "O utinam subitas addat mihi Iuppiter alas! / Protinus ad te abeam sublimis."
30	**utinam – alas** The model is Ov. *Ep.* 18, 49.
	volucres ... alas Ov. *Ib.* 290.
31	**Cyrrham** According to Isid. *Orig.* 14, 8, 11, Cyrrha is one of the two peaks of Mount Parnassus. Here it stands for Mount Parnassus itself. Cf. Brant, *Var. carm.*, sig. l 8ᵛ (*Texte* 228, 39): "Cyrrha Heliconque sacer"; Eob. *Sylv. duae* 2, 173 (n.): "Phocaicae ... culmina Cyrrhae"; *Hod.* 238: "Collibus Aoniis et ab altae culmine Cyrrhae."
	Helicona, Cytheron Cf. *Sylv.* 1, 9, 15: "Heliconve ... sanctusve Cytheron."
33	**Prepetibus pennis** = Verg. *A.* 6, 15 (of Daedalus's wings); cf. Eob. *Hod.* 14.
	sepe venirem = *Buc.* 4, 82; *Nor.* 621; cf. line 13 above (n.).
35-36	**Carmina – honor** Cf. Gigas, *Sylv.* 2, sig. C8ʳ: "... pereunt aes, purpura, et aurum. / Culta Thalia manet nescia sola mori." For the commonplace that poetry is immortal see Eob. *Rec.* B 1, 9-13 (n.).
35	**sacrorum ... vatum** *Laud.* 257 (n.).

36	**Immortalis honor** ≈ Mant. *Calam.* 3, p. 70: "Immortalis honos ...."
36-37	**gemmae – Indis** Cf. Tifernate, *Carm.*, sig. C1ᵛ: "Haec [carmina] ego non auro, non cunctis comparo gemmis / Quas mercatores ex oriente vehunt." The wealth of India was proverbial; see Eob. *Ama.* 32, 66 (n.).
37	**Quas – Indis** Cf. Hor. *Ep.* 1, 1, 45; Ov. *Ars* 1, 53; Eob. *Her. Chr.* 15, 95.
38	**dactilothecis** A medievalism for "dactyliothecis," which does not fit the meter. The form also occurs in Cordus, *Ecl.* 7, 48: "... quos Inda alios huc dactylotheca lapillos / mittit."
39	**docuit mater** See n. *Buc.* 1, 54-56.
	viridemque smaragdon ≈ Tib. 2, 4, 27.
40	**collo – corallia** Cf. Ov. *Ep.* 9, 57: "suspensa monilia collo."
41	**Omnia pretereunt** = Paul. Nol. *Carm.* 16, 3.
42	**Vos – flamma** Cf. *Buc.* 8, 46-47 (n.).
	dulci ... pectora flamma = *Anthol. Lat.* 446, 3; cf. Eob. *Her. Chr.* 17, 47; *Her.* 3, 6, 93. For the tag "pectora flamma" see n. *Laud.* 294.
43-44	**Despitio – sordent** Cf. *Her. Chr.* 24, 95-96, where Eobanus describes his excitement at learning that there were still living poets.
43	**mortalibus usquam** = Verg. *A.* 2, 142; Sil. 11, 3.
44	**Nec mirum** = Lucr. 2, 338; 6, 130; Catul. 62, 14; Prop. 1, 13, 29; Eob. *Her. Chr.* 17, 191.
	omnia sordent = Stat. *Silv.* 5, 5, 51.
46-52	**Luxuriant – Musae** For the series of pastoral analogies cf. Verg. *Ecl.* 2, 63-65; 5, 32-34; and 7, 65-68.
46	**nova gramina rivis** *Rec.* 8 (n.).
46-50	**gramina rivis ... fronde capellae ... apis cythiso** Cf. Verg. *Ecl.* 10, 29-30.
47	**vitali pluvia** *Nor.* 1301.
48	**Littoribus – alnus** Cf. Verg. *G.* 2, 110.
	procera ... alnus Verg. *Ecl.* 6, 63.
	paludibus alnus ≈ *Theoc.* 7, sig. C5ʳ: "... assuetaeque paludibus alni."
49	**lascivae ... capellae** Verg. *Ecl.* 2, 64; Filetico, *Theoc.* 3, 3: "Tityre, lascivas virgultis pasce capellas"; Eob. *Buc.* 3, 62.
49-50	**fronde – cythiso** Cf. Verg. *Ecl.* 10, 30.
50	**apiastro** This variety of balm (*melissophyllon*) is so named because bees are fond of it. Cf. *Nup.* 53.
51	**mea sola voluptas** = Ov. *Ep.* 19, 17; cf. Verg. *A.* 3, 660; 8, 581.
51-52	**voluptas, ... requies, ... Musae** Cf. Lucr. 6, 93-94.
52	**Vita – requies** *Her. Chr.* 6, 7; cf. Lucr. 4, 506 (Luc. 5, 685; 7, 639): "vita salusque"; Eob. *Hod.* B 8, 12: "... spes, via, vita, salus."
	omnia, Musae = Verg. *G.* 2, 475: "... dulces ante omnia Musae."
54-57	**Non ita – moretum** Imitated by Cordus, *Ecl.* 7, 117-118: "Non ita pingue sapit mihi lac, non suave moretum, / non molles ita castaneae, non mitia poma."
54	**mellitae ... placentae** Hor. *Ep.* 1, 10, 11.
55	**segmina porri** = *Val.* 1, 521.
56	**oleata Ceres** Cf. Vulg. *Num.* 11, 8: "panis oleati."
	cocta polenta Cf. Ov. *Met.* 5, 450 (in some mss. and early edd.): "coxerat polenta"; Mant. *Ecl.* 6, 5: "polenta coquit."
57	**hesterno – lacte** Cf. Stat. *Theb.* 1, 508: "lacte novo perfusus."
	lacte moretum = Cordus, *Ecl.* 6, 147: "... mixtum lacte moretum." The ancient "moretum" was a rustic dish of pounded herbs mixed with oil and cheese.
58	**dulce decus** *Ama.* 32, 81 (n.).
60	**Sum puer, et** = Locher, *Stult.*, fol. 15ʳ; cf. Eobanus, in Mutian. *Ep.* 417, line 34 (August 1506): "Sum puer, at ...."
	viridi – aetas ≈ *Buc.* 1, 103 (n.).

61   **Ut – vitis** Cf. Verg. *Ecl.* 7, 48; Ov. *Fast.* 1, 152; Stat. *Silv.* 5, 1, 48.
62-65   **Et mihi – Adonim** For the motif cf. Theoc. 6, 34-38; Verg. *Ecl.* 2, 25-27; Ov.
           Met. 13, 840-841; Calp. *Ecl.* 2, 88-89; Nemes. *Ecl.* 2, 74-81.
62   **forma decens** Ov. *Am.* 3, 1, 9.
62-63   **pectine – Comeret** Calp. *Ecl.* 4, 69; Eob. *Val.* 1, 155; cf. Ov. *Met.* 4, 311.
63   **dixit – mater** Cf. Filetico, *Theoc.* 4, 9: "Et me dicebat mater mea credula
           quondam / Pollucem superare deum, quod fortior essem."
           sedula mater = Walter. *Alex.* 4, 409; Pontano, *Ecl.* 1, 50; *De amore coniugali* 1,
           1, 25; cf. Phaed. 4, 5, 13.
65   **Vicinum** Verg. *Ecl.* 3, 53; Calp. *Ecl.* 6, 83; 6, 91; Nemes. *Ecl.* 1, 9.
           forma superas ... Adonim For the motif cf. Verg. *Ecl.* 2, 26-27; Calp. *Ecl.* 3,
           61-62; Nemes. *Ecl.* 2, 78-79; Eob. *Buc.* 3, 111-112. For "forma superas" see
           Ov. *Fast.* 5, 85.
66   **quicquid id est** *Nup.* 15 (n.).
67   **mea – aetas** ≈ *Buc.* 1, 103 (n.).
70   **Sicut – rubentes** Cf. Otto 1552; Häussler, pp. 63-64, 79, 116, and 286.
72   **referetis honorem** ≈ Stat. *Theb.* 12, 819.
73   **stabit – pudoris** Cf. *Her. Chr.* 8, 67.
           nivei flos ... pudoris Cf. *Nup.* 244; *Her. Chr.* 13, 97. For "nivei pudoris" see
           Ama. 35, 91 (n.); for "flos pudoris" see *Buc.* 11, 22 (n.).
76   **Dicite, quae ... maior** Cordus, *Buc.* 2, 40 (*Ecl.* 3, 44): "dicite quae maior
           Veneris dicione potestas?"
           quae maior in orbe Cordus, *Buc.* 6, 94: "quae maior in orbe / nequicia esse
           potest?"
77   **sacra ... tempora lauro** = Verg. *A.* 3, 81; Eob. *Idyl.* 2, 28: "[Musae] ... sacra
           redimitae tempora lauro"; cf. *Laud.* 568 (n.).
           velatis – lauro Cf. Verg. *A.* 5, 72; 5, 246; Ov. *Met.* 5, 110; *Fast.* 3, 861.
78   **Musarum amplexibus** *Dial.* 1, sig. A2ᵛ: "Hesiodo ... in Musarum ...
           amplexibus cum obdormisset"; cf. *Laud.* 164-165 and 306.
79   **Vivere apud Musas** *Sylv.* 6, 2, 40: "Nos ..., / Queis nisi apud Musas vivere poena
           fuit."
           doctis ... Musis Ov. *Ars* 3, 411-412.
80   **inanis ... formae** *Buc.* 3, 127; *Her. Chr.* 17, 71.
           gaudia formae = Ov. *Met.* 14, 653; Stat. *Ach.* 1, 167; Eob. *Val.* 2, 145:
           "... fugientis gaudia formae."
81   **genus, tituli** = Gigas, *Sylv.* 1, sig. B4ᵛ: "Fama, genus, tituli, pereunt brevis ocia
           vitae. / Musae perire nesciunt" (cf. lines 35-36 above and note).
82-86   **in viridi – umbram** For the *locus amoenus* see n. *Ama.* 1, 1.
82   **in viridi ... gramine** Ov. *Am.* 1, 14, 22.
82-83   **doctam ... segnitiem** Cf. Stat. *Silv.* 1, 3, 108-109: "docta ... / otia." See further
           Eob. *Ama.* A 1, 2 (n.).
83-84   **tactis – aurae** Cf. Ov. *Met.* 11, 603-604; Eob. *Buc.* 7, 124-125.
84   **Unda sonat** = Ov. *Met.* 8, 139.
           lābans Wrongly for "lābens." Eobanus confounds the forms elsewhere too. In
           Her. Chr. 20, 15 he writes "genu lābente" (instead of the expected, but here
           metrically impossible "genu lābante"); in *Her. Chr.* 16, 31 (*A B*) he has "genu
           lābante" (changed to "genu lābante" in *O*).
           admurmurat aurae ≈ Stat. *Silv.* 5, 1, 153.
86   **levem ... umbram** Tib. 2, 5, 96; Ov. *Met.* 5, 336; Eob. *Rec.* 4 (n.); *Buc.* 8, 62.
           populus umbram ≈ Verg. *A.* 8, 276; Ov. *Met.* 10, 555; Nemes. *Ecl.* 4, 23.
88-90   **Samsucos – nepenthe** For the flower catalogue cf. Verg. *Ecl.* 2, 45-50; Ov. *Fast.*
           4, 437-442; Eob. *Buc.* 9, 59-60 (n.); *Idyl.* 15, 89-91: "[sinum] Floribus
           implerem violisque rosisque thimoque / Et quae mille meis superant in

montibus herbis. / Lilia praecipue ferrem rubrumque papaver"; Cordus, *Buc.* 2, 46-48 (*Ecl.* 3, 50-52).

89 **Lilia verna** Mant. *c. Poet.* 106; Eob. *Sylv.* 6, 9, 2; cf. *Buc.* 6, 19-20 (n.); 11, 42.

91 **Cingite – poaetas** For the motif cf. Lucr. 1, 928-930 (4, 3-5); Prop. 3, 1, 19-20; Eob. *Laud.* 165-166; *Buc.* 6, 54-59; 8, 78; cf. further *Buc.* 8, 55-59.
Cingite ... flore Ov. *Fast.* 3, 254.

92 **Inter – haberem** Imitated in Cordus, *Buc.* 1, 107, referring to pastoral poets: "inter quos utinam quota pars ego dicerer olim"; cf. Prop. 2, 34, 94: "hos [poetas] inter si me ponere Fama volet."
Inter quos utinam Cf. Hor. *S.* 2, 2, 92.
quota pars = Mart. 5, 65, 7; cf. Ov. *Am.* 2, 12, 10; *Ep.* 12, 89; *Met.* 7, 522; et al.; Eob. *Her. Chr.* 1, 96 (n.); 4, 234; 11, 4; also cf. *Her. Chr.* 11, 24 (n.): "quota ... portio."
nomen haberem ≈ Prop. 2, 26, 7; Ov. *Met.* 11, 760.

93 **Valle ... viridi** *Sylv. duae* 2, 136; 2, 146; *Epith.* 19.

94-95 **Qui – Sydereo** Cf. lines 16-19 above, with notes.

94 **monte quiescis** ≈ Luc. 8, 695.

96 **Carmina – carent** = *Laud.* B 5, 4 (n.).

96-98 **Gaudete – lavabo** Eobanus imitates Filetico, *Theoc.* 5, 142-146: "gaudete, capellae, / ... / ... / Foelicem sperate diem vitamque, capellae. / Cras ego vos omnes Sybaritis fonte lavabo."

98 **si vivam** Pl. *Mos.* 4; *Per.* 786; Eob. *Her. Chr.* 5, 8; 7, 28.
liquido ... fonte lavabo Cf. *Theoc.* 16, sig. F5^r: "liquido ... fonte lavare"; 36, sig. N4^r: "liquido ... in fonte lavaro." For "liquido fonte" see Verg. *Ecl.* 2, 59; *G.* 2, 200; 3, 529; 4, 18; 4, 376; Ov. *Met.* 10, 122. For the tag "fonte lavabo" see Verg. *Ecl.* 3, 97; cf. *A.* 7, 489; Ov. *Ep.* 21, 177; Calp. *Ecl.* 4, 134; Eob. *Her. Chr.* 6, 121 (n.).

100 **parvo – colle** *Sylv.* 1, 2, 114.

102 **Ite – capellae** Cf. Verg. *Ecl.* 1, 74; Eob. *Buc.* 10, 162.

103 **Sic – cecinit** Cf. *Idyl.* 15, 120: "Sic bonus ille canens compescuit Eurytus ignem."

104 **subter – latebat** ≈ Ov. *Fast.* 2, 587.

105 **Omnia concepit** The motif appears also in Mant. *Ecl.* 8, especially *Ecl.* 8, 152-154.

105-106 **illo – erat** Tranquillus is praised for his wisdom also in *Buc.* 5, 11. For the idiom cf. Hor. *S.* 1, 5, 42; Verg. *A.* 1, 544-545; 6, 164; 7, 649-650; 9, 179-180; 9, 772; Eob. *Buc.* 3, 111; 9, 48; 9, 63; *Her. Chr.* 2, 15; 16, 52; 16, 135-136; 21, 198.

106 **suaves ... versus** Bucolic verses are conventionally "sweet." Cf., for example, Verg. *Ecl.* 5, 45-47; Calp. *Ecl.* 2, 6; 4, lines 9, 55, 61, 150, and 160; 7, 19-22; Eob. *Buc.* 1, 24-25.
incidit in arbore Carving names, verses, even entire poems into the bark of trees is a favorite pastime in the bucolic world. See, for instance, Verg. *Ecl.* 5, 13-14; 10, 53-54; Calp. *Ecl.* 1, 20-25; 3, 43-44; 3, 89; Nemes. *Ecl.* 1, 28-29; Eob. *Buc.* 9, 61-63.
in arbore versus = Calp. *Ecl.* 3, 89; line 108 below.

107 **Extat – littera** Cf. Calp. *Ecl.* 1, 22-23; Nemes. *Ecl.* 1, 29. For the phrase "extat littera" see Ov. *Ib.* 3-4.

107-110 **Foelix – poetae** Cf. Verg. *Ecl.* 10, 53-54; Ov. *Ep.* 5, 25-27; Bocc. *Ecl.* 6, 136-137: "Crescent ea nomina quantum / ipsa quidem fagus crescet." Eobanus's lines were twice imitated. Cf. Cordus, *Buc.* 3, 130-131 (*Ecl.* 4, 183-184): "Crescite crescenti dulces cum [in *1518*] cortice versus / perpetuosque dies nostro supereste Menalcae"; Lotich. *Eleg.* 1, 8, 101-104: "Tu tamen haec serva nostri monumenta doloris, / Arbor, et incisis cresce videnda notis. / Quas aliquis viridi spectans in cortice, tempus / Militiae possit flebile scire meae."

108   **in arbore, versus** = Line 106 above (n.).

109   **Atque – dicet** Cf. Ov. *Am.* 2, 10, 37; 3, 15, 11-13: "atque aliquis spectans ... / moenia ... / ... dicet"; *Ars* 3, 341; Eob. *Her. Chr.* 13, 35; *Her.*, ded. 105-106: "Atque aliquis nostri spectans monumenta laboris, / 'Hoc Paulus,' dicet, 'nomine dignus erat'"; *Epic.* 3, 149-150: "Quos olim spectans aliquis, 'tua gloria,' dicet, / 'Vivit'"; *Sylv.* 9, 2, 27-28: "Atque aliquis spectans Ebnerum in carmine nostro / Dicet ...."

3

Introducing the first portion of this poem in the 1539-edition (*Idyl.* 3), Eobanus remarks that it is pointless to identify the speakers because the focus is on literary and amatory themes, not specific individuals. This certainly holds true for Narcissus. A first cousin to the mythical Narcissus (Ov. *Met.* 3, 339-510), he serves to warn the reader about the unhappy consequences of unbridled passion. Cygnus, however, is clearly Eobanus himself, for the swan was his lifelong emblem; see Camerarius, *Nar.* 31, 7-8, with fn. 137. Can we also identify Philaegon ("One who loves goats")?

According to a manuscript note in the margin of the Strasbourg copy of the *Bucolicon*, Philaegon is Dr. Johann Englender, the patron to whom Eobanus dedicated his book. This identification is quite unlikely. Eobanus, who knew Englender only via Mutianus Rufus's letter of 15 October 1508 (*Ep.* 149), could hardly have adopted the familiar tone with him that he does here or have invited him, a happily married man, to take his ease at Erfurt among the rustic matrons and girls and enjoy the sweet cares of love (lines 8-9). It seems far more plausible to identify Philaegon with Eobanus's friend Crotus Rubianus, whom we met already as the writer of the liminary poem to *De laudibus* and who appears in *Buc.* 8 as Iarbas, perhaps also in *Buc.* 9 as Iucundus. For his life see fn. 71 at Camerarius, *Nar.* 17, 17. An older and more mature shepherd than Cygnus, Philaegon evidently has a Christian humanist's eye for poets and poetry, he praises Cygnus as Germany's first pastoralist (lines 30-32), and he is chaste (cf. line 42). This description fits Crotus perfectly. He was some eight years Eobanus's senior, having been born around 1480. In *Laud.* 297-307 Eobanus singles him out for his humanist learning, his poetry, and ... his chastity. Besides writing the liminary epigram for *De laudibus* in 1507, he composed two commendatory poems for the *Bucolicon* in 1509. In *Buc.* B 7, 7-8 Crotus praises Eobanus for introducing pastoral to Germany, just as Philaegon does in lines 30-32 of the present eclogue. The revision of 1528/39 adds a further clue. Philaegon, we read in *Idyl.* 3, 11-19, has come back to Erfurt after an unpleasant stay in Fulda. As it happens, Crotus lived in Fulda from 1510 to 1515 and again from 1522 to 1524.

The eclogue was first edited and annotated in: Harry Vredeveld, "A Neo-Latin Satire on Love-Madness: The Third Eclogue of Eobanus Hessus' *Bucolicon* of 1509," *Daphnis* 14 (1985): 673-719.

Meter: Hexameter.

1-6   **Hic ... Hic ... Hic** For the anaphora cf. Verg. *Ecl.* 10, 42-43.

1   **Hic – herbas** Cf. *Buc.* 9, 56-57 (n.).

    vagus For the epithet see *Buc.* 1, 110 (n.).

2   **virides ... alni** Verg. *Ecl.* 10, 74.

2-3   **quae – echo** Cf. *Sylv.* 4, 17, 26-28: "tauros videas ... / Lata mugitu resonare circum / Pascua rauco."

2   **littora circum** = Lucr. 4, 220; Verg. *A.* 3, 75; 6, 329.

3   **Crebra – echo** The line was imitated by Hutten, *In exceptionem Moguntinam Alberti panegyricus* 165 (*Opera*, vol. 3, p. 358): "Multa repercussis modulatibus

insonat echo"; and Lotich. *Ecl.* 1, 107: "Moesta repercussis gemuit quoque rupibus Echo." Cf. *Anthol. Lat.* 227, 13: "... sonat pecudum mugitibus Echo"; Eob. *Her. Chr.* 4, 166; 4, 213.

4-9   **Hic – vitam** The description is reminiscent of the one given by Paniscus in *Buc.* 1, 72-89.

4   **foelices – pagos** Cf. *Epp. 4,* sig. F7ᵛ (1508): "... multiplici ditantur messe coloni"; *Hod.* 165: "... ditant vineta colonos"; *Nor.* 85: "... multa ditavit messe colonos"; *Wirt.* 459-460: "plena messe colonos / Ditat."

5   **casas – tecta** = Calp. *Ecl.* 2, 60 (also quoted in Mant. *Ecl.* 3, 6); cf. Eob. *Buc.* 4, 35 (n.).

6   **Hic – quies** = *Her. Chr.* 14, 91; cf. *Buc.* 1, 70.
    mihi parta quies = Verg. *A.* 7, 598; cf. *A.* 3, 495.

7   **Num – terra** Cygnus – consciously or unconsciously – echoes Paniscus's words of *Buc.* 1, 21 (where see note).

9   **dulces curas** *Buc.* 1, 119.
    inertem ... vitam Tib. 1, 1, 5, where the phrase stands in opposition to the "vita activa" of the rich man and the soldier. For Tibullus, the "vita iners" is an ideal: a life of simplicity, tranquillity, contentment, and love. To the moralist, of course, idleness is not an ideal at all, but rather the mother of wantonness. Cf., for instance, [Sen.] *Oct.* 562-563: "amor ... iuventa gignitur, luxu, otio / nutritur"; Mant. *c. Am.*, fol. 177ᵛ: "[amans] inertia laudat / Ocia"; *2. Parthen.* 2, 247: "lasciva ... inertia"; Eob. *Nor.* 630: "inertia pectora amantum." See further Ov. *Rem.* 135-150. Cygnus's dream is noticeably at odds with Pudicus's ideal of "docta segnities" in *Buc.* 2, 82-83 (n.).
    ducere vitam = Verg. *A.* 2, 641; 4, 340.

10   **nihil – requiescere** Cf. Verg. *Ecl.* 1, 79; 7, 10; Nemes. *Ecl.* 4, 46; Eob. *Buc.* 10, 42 (n.).

10-12   **quando – orbis** Cf. Mant. *Dionys.* 3, fol. 190ʳ: "quando / Una sit ambobus Christi cultura fidesque, / ... / ... atque viri comites se voce fatentur / Ingenua, quos relligio coniunxerat una"; Eob. *Sylv.* 1, 11, 9-12 (to his friend Sturnus): "[Gratulor] Quod mihi par studium te coniunxisse fateris. / Caussa pari nobis convenit ista modo, / Scilicet unus amor vatum, Deus unus, et unum / Quod studium coelo nos docet esse satos."

11   **Unus amor** = *Laud.* B 6, 2; cf. Verg. *A.* 9, 182; 12, 282; Stat. *Silv.* 5, 3, 241.
    amor, studium commune Cf. Mant. *Ecl.* 3, 42 (of erotic love): "res vulgaris amor, studium commune iuventae." Philaegon, by contrast, is talking of love for the Christian Muses. Cf. Eob. *Sylv.* 1, 4, 23-24: "Ad studia accedunt animi communia nostri, / Palladia est nobis unus in arce locus"; Pontano, *Parthen.* 2, 1, 43-44: "communes igitur Musae, communia nobis / sunt studia." For "amor, studium" see also Verg. *A.* 11, 739; Ov. *Met.* 14, 634.

12   **Salutifer orbis** ≈ Ov. *Met.* 2, 642 (Mant. *1. Parthen.* 2, 602): "... salutifer orbi."

13-14   **Numine – Poaetes** Philaegon's description of the Christian poet is echoed in *Vict.* 275-281 (referring to the Hebrew prophets): "Vobis ille quidem divinam in carmina mentem / Influxit magni lustrator Spiritus orbis, / Enthea sanctorum quem spirant pectora vatum – / Non qui furta canunt Veneris turpesque deorum / Concubitus tenerique insana Cupidinis arma, / Sed qui de superis non impia, qualia vobis / Carmina caelestes inspiravere Camoenae." Cf. also *Sylv.* 1, 12, 13-16: "Ille [Deus] regit vates, divinum inspirat amorem / .... / Et nisi divini fallunt oracla Platonis, / Esse nequit vates quem fugit ille Deus."

13   **vatum ... pectora** Ov. *Pont.* 4, 2, 25.
    flammantia pectora Their hearts are "flaming," because inspired by the fire of the Holy Spirit. For the phrase cf. Nemes. *Ecl.* 2, 14: "flammati pectoris"; Stat. *Silv.* 5, 1, 197: "flammatus pectora"; Sil. 14, 120: "flammato pectore";

Petrarch. *Ecl.* 1, 39 (of the poet): "flammata mente"; Eob. *Her. Chr.* 6, 175. This is the Christian answer to the poetic frenzy of the ancients (see *Laud.* 193, with note). Cf. Ov. *Fast.* 6, 5: "est deus in nobis; agitante calescimus illo," turned around in Eob. *Sylv.* 1, 10, 19-20: "Est Deus in nobis, non qualem Naso canebat: / Christo, non Phoebo, pectora nostra calent." Cf. Eob. *Buc.* 8, 119-121 (n.).

14   **sublime rapit** = Sil. 6, 235.
    coeli terraeque = Lucr. 5, 98; Ov. *Met.* 2, 96; Paul. Nol. *Carm. app.* 1 ([Prosper], *Poema coniugis ad uxorem*), 79: "... caeli terraeque creator" ; Juvenc. 1, 35: "... dominus caeli terraeque repertor"; cf. Vulg. *Gen.* 24, 3 and often: "Deum caeli et terrae." The form "poaetes" is a transliteration of the Greek word for "maker."

15   **Numine ... raptus** *Her. Chr.* 24, 76.
    raptus sublimis Cf. Verg. *A.* 5, 255; Ov. *Met.* 4, 363; 7, 222.

15-16   **Tityrus ... pulsabat sydera canna** Cf. Mant. *Ecl.* 5, 86-88: "Tityrus ... / rura, boves et agros et Martia bella canebat / altius et magno pulsabat sidera cantu." For "pulsabat sydera" see also Verg. *A.* 3, 619-620; Sil. 5, 394.

16   **Ardua ... sydera** Ov. *Met.* 1, 730-731; Stat. *Silv.* 1, 4, 116-117; Eob. *Her. Chr.* 1, 73; *Nor.* 113-114.

17-18   **foelix – Mantua** Cf. Mart. 1, 61, 2: "Marone felix Mantua est"; Tifernate, *Carm.*, sig. D3ʳ ("In Virgilium vatem"): "Hunc etenim foelix produxit Mantua cignum."

18   **Ocneis** Ocnus was the mythical founder of Mantua (Verg. *A.* 10, 198-200), the city where Vergil was born. Cf. Andrel. *Livia* 2, 2, 1: "Ocnaeis ... campis"; 4, 3, 24, of Vergil: "Ocnaeo vate"; *Ecl.* 9, 25: "Ocnaeique lacus"; Eob. *Buc.* 6, 1; B 11, 23.
    ubi – agris Cf. Verg. *G.* 3, 14-15; Mant. *Ecl.* 2, 37-38: "ubi Mincius ... / alluit ... agros."
    errat in agris Verg. *G.* 3, 249; Ov. *Am.* 1, 10, 5 (in most mss.): "... erravit in agris"; *Ars* 2, 473; *Met.* 2, 490; cf. Luc. 9, 939: "... errat in arvis"; lines 118-119 below (n.).

19-27   **Ille – Faustum** In his day, Baptista Mantuanus was often called "the Christian Vergil." See Erasmus, *Ep.* 49, lines 96-103; Wilfred P. Mustard, introduction to his edition of *The Eclogues of Baptista Mantuanus* (Baltimore, 1911), pp. 30-34. Clearly influenced by Eobanus is the discussion in Cordus, *Ecl.* 2, 56-64 (cf. Cordus, *Buc.* 1, 51-55). There Candidus represents Baptista Mantuanus, who in his first eclogue sang of Faustus's courtship of Galla:

> *Aegon.* Candidus est, gelida qui Faustum lusit in umbra,
> ut retulit veteres Gallam quibus arserat ignes.
> *Mopsus.* Nunc age, dic, isto tibi quid de vate videtur.
> *Aegon.* Omnia consequitur magnas per ovilia laudes.
> At fuerat foelix in eisdem Tityrus arvis,
> non levibus tantum silvestria ludere cannis,
> sed fera magnorum doctus quoque proelia regum
> ingenti cantare tuba lituoque sonoro,
> debita cui cessit victoria iudice Pane.

19   **deos veteres** Verg. *A.* 8, 187; 9, 786; Prud. *Psych.* 29; Eob. *Her. Chr.*, ded. 11, 2; *Her. Chr.* 10, 75; 10, 172; 11, 58; 23, 113; *Vict.* 6.

20   **Spiritibus** That is, both Mantuans are divinely inspired. Cf. Hor. *Carm.* 2, 16, 38; 4, 6, 29; Verg. *Ecl.* 4, 54; Prop. 3, 17, 40.
    dubiam ... carmina palmam = Juv. 11, 181. Philaegon finds it impossible to prefer the one Mantuan over the other.

21-24 **Ut lentas – umbra** For this traditional pattern of comparison cf. Verg. *Ecl.* 1, 24-25; 5, 16-18; Bocc. *Ecl.* 1, 32-34; 5, 70-72; Mant. *Ecl.* 9, 217-219; Eob. *Buc.* 1, 107-110; 10, 8-9.

21 **securibus ilex** = Verg. *A.* 6, 180.

22 **humiles ... genistas** Verg. *G.* 2, 434; Mant. *Ecl.* 9, 94.

23 **meus ... Tityrus** Cf. Mant. *Ecl.* 2, 8-9 and 3, 173-174: "noster / Tityrus."

24 **gelida ... in umbra** = Calp. *Ecl.* 3, 16. Eobanus, however, is thinking here in particular of the famous opening line of Mantuanus's eclogues, *Ecl.* 1, 1: "Fauste, ... gelida quando pecus omne sub umbra / ruminat." For "gelida umbra" see also Eob. *Buc.*, ded. 5 (n.).

  resupinus in umbra = Filetico, *Theoc.* 1, 2: "Et tu dulce sonas grata resupinus in umbra"; also Filetico, *Theoc.* 3, 38 and 7, 89; cf. Verg. *A.* 3, 624.

26 **Magnus uterque** = Hor. *S.* 1, 4, 67.

  maiestate verendus = Gianfrancesco Pico della Mirandola, "Deprecatoria ad Deum," in his *Opera omnia* (Basel, 1557; repr. Hildesheim, 1969, vol. 1), p. 339: "Deus ... maiestate verendus"; Eob. *Nup.* 208: "... maiestate verendus"; cf. *Nor.* lines 798 and 1095; *Val.* 2, 37.

28 **breviore ... gradiare cothurno** Cf. Prop. 3, 17, 39; Claud. *Cons. Mall. Theod.* 315: "... graditur maiore cothurno"; Eob. *Buc.* 1, 11 (n.). For the sense cf. also the revised version in *Idyl.* 3, 34: "Tu quoque non gravibus quamvis utare Camoenis."

29 **Mantoos** Instead of the classical "Mantuanos." The adjective is derived from "Manto," the mother of Ocnus who founded Mantua. Cf. *Max.* 87: "... propior Mantoae Myncius urbi."

  Musa poaetas ≈ *Buc.*, lim. 1 (n.).

30 **Hic – audes** The awkwardness of "efferris" with its negative implications and the neologism "beatiter" caused Eobanus to revise the line in *Idyl.* 3, 36: "Per tua rura tamen non infoeliciter audes."

31 **carmina pastor** = *Idyl.* 2, 94; cf. Verg. *Ecl.* 6, 67.

32 **Rhomula Teutonicas** Cf. *Tum.* 7, 114: "Romula Teutonico milite tecta petit"; *Sylv. duae* 1, 182: "Teutona Rhomanum duxit in arva gregem"; *Buc.*, lim. 5; *Nob.* 279: "Teutona Romulidas quis duxit in arva Camaenas?"; *Idyl.* 8, 2: "primi Latias in Teutona pascua Musas / Ducimus."

33 **inurbanas – puellas** = Line 8 above.

34 **incaute** *Ama.* 12, 11 (n.).

  puer Eobanus was sixteen or seventeen years old at the time described here. The word is repeatedly used in the *Bucolicon* to characterize the adolescent who is still enchanted with erotic, passionate love. Cf. also *Ama.* 35, lines 13, 53, 57, and 63; B 2, lines 11, 21, 23, 63, and 75; *Sylv. duae* 2, 125-130; 208; *Sylv.* 1, 6, 35-36.

34-35 **talibus ... Illecebris** = *Idyl.* 10, 24-25.

35-36 **Non debent – Cupido** For the thought see *Ama.* B 2, 44 (n.).

36 **Sit – Cupido** Cf. *Ama.* 25, 8-9.

  Sit procul a = Marul. *Epigr.* 1, 62, 15: "Sit procul a nobis obscoena licentia scripti"; cf. also Ov. *Ep.* 4, 75; 15, 176; *Ars* 2, 107.

36-40 **puer – amores** For this description of Cupid cf. especially Prop. 2, 12, 1-12, with an allegorization of his various traits. "The childlike appearance symbolizes the 'senseless' behaviour of lovers, the wings indicate the volatile instability of amorous emotions, and the arrows the incurable wounds inflicted upon the human soul by love" (Erwin Panofsky, *Studies in Iconology* [New York, 1967], p. 104).

36 **puer – Cupido** = *Her. Chr.* 17, 101. For "puer ille" at this metrical position see Ov. *Am.* 1, 1, 25 (Cupid): "... certas habuit puer ille sagittas." Cupid is often

called "puer"; see Eob. *Ama.* 32, 37 (n.).

37   **Quem ... aiunt portare** = Verg. *A.* 4, 598.

        volucres ... sagittas = Aus. *Precationes variae* 1, 11; Prud. *c. Symm.* 1, 363.

        portare sagittas = *Priap.* 9, 7: "num pudet auratas Phoebum portare sagittas?"

38   **Est alacer** = Bocc. *Ecl.* 14, 204.

        volat Hor. *Carm.* 1, 2, 34: "volat ... Cupido"; Ov. *Ars* 3, 4.

39-40   **ferit – amores** Cf. *Ama.* 35, 9-14.

39   **ferit incautos** *Rec.* 37 (referring to the plague).

        dulcia vulnera Cf. Apul. *Met.* 4, 31: "tuae sagittae dulcia vulnera"; Eob. *Her. Chr.* 17, 85; 18, 125. For the image see, for example, Lucr. 1, 34; Hor. *Carm.* 1, 27, 11-12; Prop. 2, 22, 7; Ov. *Ep.* 4, 20; Verg. *A.* 4, 2; 4, 67.

        vulnera nutrit = Sedul. 4, 77: "sua vulnera nutrit / Qui tegit"; cf. Verg. *A.* 4, 2; and, for instance, Ov. *Ars* 3, 579; Ov. *Met.* 1, 496.

40   **Et tantum – amores** Cf. Aeneas Silvius, "In effigiem Amoris" 13: "qui sapit evitat malesana Cupidinis arma, / et tantum pueros intrat ineptus amor." See Adrianus van Heck, ed., *Enee Silvii Piccolominei ... carmina* (Vatican City, 1994), no. 117, p. 188.

        qui sapit odit amores For the obverse see *Ama.* 20, 10 (n.); *Buc.* 7, 171 (n.).

41-51   **Foelix – antro** The simple life of contentment and tranquillity, untroubled by passion or involvement in public affairs, is an ancient ideal often taken up in the Renaissance. It was championed especially by Eobanus's mentor, Mutianus Rufus; see *Buc.* 6. The theme is typically associated with the praise of country life and embellished with reminiscences of the golden age. Cf. Verg. *G.* 2, 458-474 and 493-540; Hor. *Epod.* 2; also Tib. 1, 1, 1-5; Poliziano, *Sylv.* 2, 17-24; Andrel. *Ecl.* 5, 6-52; Eob. *Val.* 1, 229-242; *Sylv.* 5, 29, 39-50; 9, 4, 23-40.

41   **Foelix rure suo** For the ideal cf. Verg. *Ecl.* 1, 46-58; also cf. Hor. *Carm.* 2, 16, 37; *S.* 2, 6, 1-5. For the phrase "rure suo" see Ov. *Fast.* 6, 671.

        parvo – agello Cf. Andrel. *Ecl.* 7, 31: "O ego vixissem patrio contentus agello"; Poliziano, *Sylv.* 2, 23: "... ac modico contentus acervo"; Bebel, "De miseria humanae conditionis," *Carm.*, sig. l 5ᵛ: "... modicis contentus agellis"; Eob. *Pod.* 203: "modico ... contentus agello"; *Her. Chr.* 22, 31. See also Otto 1926; Walther 8957: "Felix, qui didicit contentus vivere parco"; Tib. 1, 1, 25; Mart. 10, 96, 5-6; Mant. *Ecl.* 5, 117-119. Eobanus subscribed to the ideal himself; cf. his letter to Georg Spalatin of 12 April 1512, in Mutian. *Ep.*, vol. 2, p. 368: "Parvo contentus ero, modo detur ad litteratiores literas reditus."

43-45   **Dummodo – edet** Milk, fruit, and acorns were the staple foods of the Arcadians; cf. Verg. *Ecl.* 1, 80-81; also Ov. *Met.* 1, 103-106 (in the golden age); 15, 96-98. For "arbuta" see Lucr. 5, 941 and 965; cf. Verg. *G.* 1, 148; 2, 520; Ov. *Met.* 1, 104. For "nuces" (especially acorns) see, for example, Tib. 2, 1, 38; 2, 3, 69; Verg. *G.* 1, 8 and 159; Ov. *Am.* 3, 10, 9; *Fast.* 1, 676; 4, 399; Eob. *Buc.* 6, 4.

44   **famem solabitur** Verg. *G.* 1, 159; Calp. *Ecl.* 4, 32.

45-46   **oci ... amor** Cf. Verg. *Ecl.* 5, 61. For the ideal (here only implied) of leisure for literary pursuits cf. Eob. *Buc.* 2, 82-83 (n.). This ideal contrasts with Cygnus's hedonistic attitude in line 9 above.

46   **Dulcis amor** = *Vict.* 118: "Dulcis amor patriae"; cf. Catul. 66, 6; 68, 24; 68, 96; Verg. *G.* 3, 291-292; Eob. *Buc.* 4, 49; *Her. Chr.* 15, 93; 20, 150.

        amor ... voluptas = Prud. *Apoth.* 396: "castus amor, pulchra species, sincera voluptas."

        secura – voluptas = Mant. *Somn.*, fol. 218ᵛ, of heaven. Cf. *Culex* 89 (of shepherd life): "dulcis ... requies et pura voluptas"; Poliziano, *Sylv.* 4, 145: "Musa quies hominum divumque aeterna voluptas"; Mant. *Mort.*, fol. 121ᵛ, of heaven: "Hic aeterna quies, hic est aeterna voluptas."

secura quies Verg. *G.* 2, 467.

47-51 **O igitur – antro** Cf. Hor. *Epod.* 2, 39-46; Tib. 1, 1, 5-6.

47 **chara soror** Ov. *Met.* 9, 368.

frigida mater = *Her. Chr.* 12, 277. She is "frigida" because she has reached the winter of old age, when the body's "innate heat" is nearing extinction. Cf. Verg. *A.* 5, 395-396; Sedul. 1, 109: "Frigidus annoso moriens in corpore sanguis"; Eob. *Buc.* 6, 73 (n.); *Her. Chr.* 14, 162.

According to ancient and medieval physiology, the body's innate heat is fueled by the "radical moisture." As we age, more and more of this fuel is consumed, so that the body becomes progressively drier and cooler and the spirits and powers of the soul weaken. The process was frequently compared to the way a burning lamp consumes oil. See Peter H. Niebyl, "Old Age, Fever, and the Lamp Metaphor," *Journal of the History of Medicine* 26 (1971): 351-368; Eob. *Val.* 1, 267-274, with notes.

48 **Instruat – popinam** Cf. *Sylv.* 9, 4, 32: "[uxor] coquat ad tenuem prandia parca focum." For "instruat focum" see Juv. 5, 97; for "ardentem focum" see Tib. 2, 1, 22.

tenuemque popinam Cordus, *Buc.* 4, 12: "tenuem ... popinam"; cf. *Ecl.* 6, 94 (Eob. *Idyl.* 3, 54): "... tenuemque culinam."

50 **Ipse – secter** Cf. Tib. 1, 10, 41.

lactantes agnas Cf. Ov. *Pont.* 4, 8, 41.

51 **pace bona** = *Max.* 111: "Utere pace bona nobiscum ...."

tranquillo ... antro Petrarch, *Ecl.* 1, 1.

tutus in antro = *Idyl.* 12, 40 (in the 1528-version).

52 **Aut – Amorem** Cf. Aen. Silv. *Hist.*, praef., p. 75, lines 4-5: "Qui nunquam sensit amoris ignem aut lapis est aut bestia"; Cic. *Amic.* 48.

lapis est = Tib. 1, 10, 59; cf. Otto 911; Häussler, pp. 58, 74, 107-108, 176, and 239.

truncus iners = Mant. 1. *Parthen.* 2, 155: "iacuit ceu truncus iners"; cf. Ov. *Am.* 3, 7, 15 (in an obscene sense): "truncus iners iacui"; Otto 1695; Häussler, pp. 80, 118, and 215.

qui nescit Amorem Cf. [Tib.] 3, 4, 73: "nescis quid sit amor"; Ov. *Met.* 4, 330; line 58 below (n.).

53 **terdecimum** Eobanus, following Servius, understands "alter ab undecimo ... annus" in Verg. *Ecl.* 8, 39 to mean "thirteenth." Modern commentators generally take it to mean "twelfth."

54 **Dic ubi** = Ov. *Met.* 8, 861; Luc. 9, 123; Mart. 4, 66, 17; et al.; Eob. *Buc.* 3, 56; *Her. Chr.* 6, 81; 17, 63.

mutatis corpora formis Cf. *Laud.* 381 (n.).

56-57 **Dic – Aeditur** An allusion to Verg. *Ecl.* 8, 43-45: Amor is hard-hearted because he was born amidst rocks and crags.

57 **gratos ... amores** [Sen.] *Oct.* 763; cf. Eob. *Idyl.* 5, 60 (a bull's lust for a heifer): "grato ... amore."

tecum – amores The implication is that Philaegon too, in his younger days, was bewitched by love's spell. But that is human nature, as Fortunatus in Mant. *Ecl.* 1, 118 ruefully admits: "Id commune malum, semel insanivimus omnes." (Cf. Eob. *Buc.* 1, 34-35, with note.)

58 **Dicere – Amor** *Sylv. duae* 2, 28.

quid sit Amor = Verg. *Ecl.* 8, 43; [Tib.] 3, 4, 73; cf. Eob. *Ama.* B 2, 22 (n.).

fortis et impiger = Walter, *Alex.* 8, 3: "fortis et impiger ille / Terrarum domitor"; Eob. *Psalt.* 19, 31: "... quam fortis et impiger heros." On the omnipotence of Amor see n. *Ama.* 8, 3-6.

impiger ales ≈ Stat. *Theb.* 1, 292 (Mercury) and Sil. 4, 510: "... impiger alis."

For "impiger" applied to Cupid see Ov. *Met.* 1, 467; cf. line 38 above, where he is termed "alacer." For "ales" referring to Cupid see Prop. 2, 30, 31; Sen. *Phaed.* 301; line 76 below.

59   **in papilionibus** Vulg. *2. Reg.* 11, 11 (of tents).

60-61   **Hinc – Ito** The dialogue is interrupted by Philaegon, the "good" shepherd who watches over his flocks and – unlike the love-struck Cygnus – notices that the goats are going astray. The motif of interrupting a pastoral conversation with a reference to or description of the herdsman's real business of tending the flock goes back to Theoc. 4, 44-49. It also occurs in Mantuanus's moral-satiric eclogues; see *Ecl.* 1, 175-176; 4, 87-88; 6, 41-42: "ante tamen paulum pecus et praesepia vise. / vade, redi; calor est post frigora dulcior; ito"; cf. Eob. *Buc.* 10, 112-113. The motif has several functions here. On the literal level it reminds the reader of the pastoral setting and serves as a bridge to the Narcissus-tale and Cygnus's own love plaint. On the tropological level it signals the reader that being in love and being a good shepherd are ultimately incompatible: both lover and beasts go astray as they follow their appetites.

60   **errantes ... capellas** = *Sylv.* 2, 4, 33.

     hinc age ... capellas Cf. Verg. *Ecl.* 3, 96: "reice capellas" (used in the 1528/39 version of the present line: "capellas / Reiice").

62   **Lascivum pecus** = Mart. 13, 39, 1 (a kid); cf. Calp. *Ecl.* 5, 23 (she-goats). Goats were proverbially randy. Here, however, the dominant (literal) sense points to their frolicsome nature; cf. next note.

     lasciva capella = Verg. *Ecl.* 2, 64: "florentem cytisum sequitur lasciva capella"; cf. Eob. *Buc.* 2, 49 (n.).

63-76   **Vos sata – Philaegon** Cygnus's lament is uttered *after* he has spoken with his friend Narcissus; cf. lines 90-95 below. We should imagine a considerable lapse of time between line 62 and line 63 and a shorter break between line 76 and line 77.

63-66   **Vos sata – amore** Cf. Verg. *Ecl.* 2, 64-65. For lines 63-64 cf. also Verg. *Ecl.* 1, 77-78; Filetico, *Theoc.* 5, 128: "... hic viridem carpunt cythisumque capellae"; Eob. *Buc.* 7, 21-22.

63   **Vos sata – capellae** The line was imitated by Lotich. *Eleg.* 6, 30, 67 (addressing goats): "Vos thyma, vos cytisus, vos arbuta frondea pascant."

     gramina – capellae = Boiardo, *Ecl.* 9, p. 685; cf. *Ciris* 300: "... gramina nota capellas."

     gramina laeta = Filetico, *Theoc.* 4, 17; cf. Verg. *G.* 2, 525.

63-64   **capellae – pecus** Cf. Verg. *Ecl.* 1, 74; line 104 below.

64   **florentes ... herbas** Verg. *Ecl.* 9, 19; *G.* 3, 126; Ov. *Fast.* 3, 253.

     carpitis herbas *Buc.* 1, 80-81 (n.).

65   **primis ... ab annis** = Verg. *A.* 8, 517; Ov. *Tr.* 4, 4, 27; Mant. *Ecl.* 3, 167; Eob. *Her. Chr.* 11, 9; 18, 55; 18, 99; 24, 75; cf. Mant. *Ecl.* 1, 11 (as Faustus begins his tale of love): "Hic ego, dum sequerer primis armenta sub annis, / ..."; Eob. *Laud.* 557 (n.); *Buc.* 1, 35.

     custos Verg. *Ecl.* 3, 5; 5, 44; 10, 36; *G.* 1, 17.

66   **infinito ... amore** V. Max. 5, 7, ext. 1: "infinito amore correptus."

     Foenilia The unusual name ("hayloft") reappears in Cordus, *Ecl.* 9, 66: "Foenilia coniux."

     torquet amore = Tib. 1, 4, 81; cf. Ov. *Ars* 2, 124; Eob. *Laud.* 236 (n.).

67   **Quamvis – ignes** The verse is borrowed in part from Mant. *Ecl.* 1, 54: "quamvis illa meo miserata faveret amori." Cf. Eob. *Theoc.* 3, sig. B5ʳ: "Respiciat si forte meos miserata dolores"; *Idyl.* 15, 46: "nec tu miserata dolentem / Respicis." For "miserata" cf. line 158 below (n.).

67-69   **illa – Viderit** Eobanus conflates two models: Bocc. *Ecl.* 1, 35-36 (the girl, smitten with another man, has forgotten her old flame; the hapless lover now recalls their affair under the same beech trees that once witnessed the trysts): "Hec [nympha] facilem placidis quondam me cepit in annis / has inter fagos"; and Mant. *Ecl.* 1, 6-8 (where the love recalled is deemed "honestus," because it led to marriage): "Hic locus, haec eadem sub qua requiescimus arbor / scit quibus ingemui curis, quibus ignibus arsi / ante duos vel ... quattuor annos."

68	**Saepius has mecum** ≈ Line 156 below.
69-70	**O dulces – illa** Cf. *Lydia* 9-10: "O fortunati [agri] ..., / in quibus illa pedis nivei vestigia ponet."
	herbae – sedens Cf. *Buc.* 4, 39.
70-71	**delapsa – papillas** Cf. Catul. 64, 65-66; 66, 81; Celtis, *Am.* 4, 13, 15-22: "Ergo age, solve animos roseisque recinge corollis, / Barbara, flaventes, Cimbrica, laeta comas! / ... / ... / Nunc disiunge pedes herboso caespite torpens / Concerpens flores, Barbara, odoriferos. / Abice, quaeso, tuam niveo de corpore pallam / Subque umbris densis corpore nuda sede!"
70	**delapsa – palla** Cf. *Idyl.* 15, 45 (a motif not derived from Theoc. 11, on which the idyll is based): "... delapsam a corpore pallam."
71	**Explicuit ... papillas** The motif, familiar to the erotic elegy, also occurs in Pontano, *Ecl.* 1, 8: "Hic mihi tu teneras nudasti prima papillas"; 1, 34-38; 4, 68.
	Explicuit ... comas Claud. *in Rufin.* 1, praef. 8, referring to trees: "explicuere comas." For the erotic implications of a girl's unbinding her locks see, for instance, Ov. *Ars* 3, 141-154 and 783-784. Cf. also Eob. *Buc.* 7, 112 (n.). Virgins and matrons, by contrast, are admonished not to let their hair flow freely over their shoulders, but to keep it bound up; cf. *Sylv.* 3, 5, 21-22.
	flavasque – papillas Cf. Bebel, "Carmen in pestem," *Carm.*, sig. m5ᵛ: "Flavaque caesaries nec non teretesque papillae." Also cf. Bebel, "Elegia de praemeditatione senectutis et mortis" 5, in: Gustav Bebermeyer, *Tübinger Dichterhumanisten: Bebel, Frischlin, Flayder* (1927; repr. Hildesheim, 1967), p. 24: "... teretesque papillas"; Eob. *Her. Chr.* 4, 225 (n.).
	flavas ... comas Tib. 1, 5, 44; 2, 1, 48; Hor. *Carm.* 1, 5, 4.
	comas ... papillas = Poliziano, *Sylv.* 2, 219: "... resoluta comas nudata papillas."
72	**mea cura, capellae** = Bocc. *Carm.* 1, 25: "et si forte pecus non sit mea cura, capelle / iamdudum stabant"; Filetico, *Theoc.* 5, 1: "Effugite audentes nimium, mea cura, capellae."
73	**An – aevi** Cf. Verg. *A.* 7, 53; Eob. *Her. Chr.* 4, 41 (n.).
	duro ... viro Ov. *Am.* 3, 4, 1; *Ep.* 7, 84; *Rem.* 554; et al.
	coniuncta viro = Lucr. 5, 1012; Verg. *Ecl.* 8, 32.
74	**interclusa** Her husband would keep her guarded and prevent her from leaving the house to continue her amours. For this motif cf., for example, Prop. 2, 6, 37-40; Ov. *Am.* 2, 19; 3, 4; Juv. 6, 346-348; Aen. Silv. *Hist.*, p. 117, lines 13-15; Brant, *NS* 32.
	meos ... amores = Tib. 1, 3, 81; Prop. 1, 16, 19.
	lugebit amores *Ilias Lat.* 71.
75-76	**Hei – Alite** Cf. Verg. *A.* 2, 274; Ov. *Met.* 14, 15; Eob. *Buc.* 7, 139-140 (n.). For "alite" see line 58 above (n.).
75	**Hei – perii** Cf. Verg. *Ecl.* 8, 41; *Ciris* 430; Ov. *Ep.* 12, 33.
	Hei mihi, quam = *Epic. Drusi* 9; 88; 176.
76	**pharetram ... gestare** Verg. *A.* 1, 336; Stat. *Silv.* 5, 1, 130. Philaegon did not mention the quiver explicitly (line 37), but it is a conventional attribute of Cupid.
77-78	**Cygne – quereris** Cf. Petrarch, *Ecl.* 1, 6: "Silvi, quid quereris?"
77	**pecus – arces** ≈ Verg. *G.* 4, 168; *A.* 1, 435.

78 **Totis – sylvis** Cf. Mant. *Ecl.* 3, 184: "... et audita est totis querimonia campis"; cf. also Verg. *Ecl.* 1, 5; Prop. 1, 18, 31.

79 **Perfidus ille** = Ov. *Ars* 1, 536; 3, 489; cf. Verg. *Ecl.* 8, 91. In the moral-satiric eclogue – unlike purely idyllic pastoral – the animals too are addressed and judged in moral terms. Cf. Eob. *Buc.* 4, 62-63; 7, 17-24.
potum – amnem Cf. *Buc.* 7, 114 (n.).
descendit ad amnem Cf. Stat. *Theb.* 11, 195; Juv. 6, 522; line 101 below.

80 **Quem – molli** Cf. Verg. *G.* 3, 464.
molli ... clivo = Verg. *Ecl.* 9, 8; *G.* 3, 293.
via pendula clivo Cf. Prud. *Cath.* 9, 50 (of Christ's walking on the water): "mobilis liquor profundi pendulam praestat viam"; Gunther, *Lig.* 8, 413: "difficili ... loca pendula clivo."

81 **cognita flumina** Cf. Verg. *Ecl.* 1, 51; Eob. *Buc.* 3, 101.

82-87 **Ecce – ignes** Cf. the scene described in *Ama.* 1, 1-2.

82 **Ecce sed** = *Laud.* 178 (n.).
horrendum – dictu Cf. Verg. *A.* 3, 621; Mant. *Calam.* 1, p. 25: "dictu horrendum visuque tremendum"; *Georgius*, fol. 219ᵛ: "dictu mirabile, visu / Terrificum."
horrendum visu = Stat. *Theb.* 6, 892; cf. Verg. *A.* 9, 521; Stat. *Theb.* 6, 939.
miserabile dictu = Hrotsv. *Gesta Ottonis* 502; *Passio Pelagii* 38; Walter, *Alex.* 7, 274.

83 **Sub rupe aerea** Verg. *G.* 4, 508.
fagi ... in umbra Cf. *Buc.* 7, 123-124. The beech is the pastoral tree par excellence since Verg. *Ecl.* 1, 1. See also Eob. *Buc.* 2, 97; 6, 51; 9, 61; *Ama.* 1, 1; *Idyl.* 4, 2.

84 **Ad fontem** Like his Ovidian counterpart, Narcissus is seated beside a spring. Here the motif remains allusion only.
longos ... amores Line 120 below (n.).

84-85 **amores Deflebat** *Buc.* 1, 85 (n.).

87 **despectos – ignes** Cf. Claud. *III. Cons. Hon.* 104: "... ultrices in se converterat iras."

88-89 **Dum – Rubinam** The motif comes from Filetico, *Theoc.* 1, 78-93. For line 88 cf. especially Filetico, *Theoc.* 1, 92: "ille nihil, nimio sed amore perustus / Infoelix iam lugentes properabat ad agros."

88 **moeroris causam** Mart. 2, 11, 10.
nihil ille, sed = Stat. *Theb.* 9, 343; cf. Verg. *A.* 2, 287; Ov. *Met.* 7, 743; 12, 232-233; *Fast.* 2, 797; Stat. *Theb.* 12, 367.
amens Cf. the proverbial "amens, amans"; see Otto 79; Häussler, pp. 129-130, 232, and 260.

89 **Centenam – Rubinam** Cf. Bocc. *Ecl.* 2, 23-24: "Pampineam, o! quotiens nequicquam vocibus usque / in celum totis clamavi vallibus imis"; lines 119-120 below. The tautological "Centenam ... repetita voce" is avoided in the revised version of this line: "Centenam loquitur solamque Philantida clamat."
repetita voce = Avit. *Carm.* 3, 296.

90-91 **Hinc – iaculo** Narcissus's lament has rekindled Cygnus's love. For the contagiousness of passion see Ov. *Rem.* 609-616.

90 **mea spes, mea lux** Cf. Verg. *A.* 2, 281. For "mea spes" see Pl. *Bac.*, fragment 13; *Rud.* 247; *St.* 583; Eob. *Eccles.* 383: "mea spes, mea vita, Luthere." For "mea lux" at this metrical position see, for example, Prop. 2, 14, 29; 2, 28, 59; 2, 29, 1; Ov. *Am.* 1, 8, 23; line 159 below; cf. Eob. *Ama.* 14, 6.
Me quoque = Verg. *Ecl.* 9, 33; *G.* 3, 8.

91 **Fixit – iaculo** Cf. Prop. 2, 13, 2; Ov. *Met.* 1, 472; Eob. *Ama.* 32, 21-22; *Buc.* 3, 151 (n.); *Her. Chr.* 17, 86.

91-92 **Nec – plectro** As they pine away for unrequited love, swains can no longer sing their ditties tempered to the oaten flute. See Mant. *Ecl.* 1, 18-19; Eob. *Buc.* 7, 159-163; cf. line 122 below (n.).
Nec tu me ... videbis Amplius Cf. Verg. *A.* 12, 679-680; 12, 810.
laeta ... carmina Verg. *G.* 2, 388; Calp. *Ecl.* 1, 35.

92 **arguto ... plectro** *Vict.* 273.
meditari – plectro = Sabell. *In natal.* 5, sig. b1ᵛ; cf. *In natal.* 2, sig. a3ᵛ: "...meditatus carmina plectro"; Eob. *Buc.* 11, 107. For "meditari carmina" see *Lydia* 6. For the tag "carmina plectro" see Prop. 2, 3, 19; Eob. *Her. Chr.* 24, 161.

93 **mihi finiat** = Ov. *Met.* 15, 874; *Tr.* 3, 7, 49; cf. Eob. *Her. Chr.* 18, 181.

94 **Ni – amo** Cf. Mant. *Ecl.* 3, 91: "da quod amo; nostro haec una est medicina dolori." For the proverbial saying that only possession of the beloved offers a cure for lovesickness see Otto 101; Häussler, pp. 52, 69, 132, and 232; Aen. Silv. *Hist.*, p. 109, lines 30-31: "unicum remedium est, si copia sit amati"; p. 149, line 23: "nulla re magis curatur ista pestis quam dilecti copia"; Eob. *Buc.* 7, 146 (n.).
sperare senectam = Sil. 15, 54.

95 **Insano ... Amori** = *Ama.* 35, 1; cf. *Ama.* 33, 6 (n.).
servimus Amori Cf. *Buc.* 3, 148; 4, 64; 7, 159.

96 **Ambo – canendi** Cf. Verg. *Ecl.* 7, 4-5; Calp. *Ecl.* 2, 3-4; Nemes. *Ecl.* 2, 16; Filetico, *Theoc.* 6, opening lines: "Ambo florentes aetate ..."; Eob. *Buc.* 5, 4-5; 5, 114; *Idyl.* 10, 7-8: "quando mihi proximus annis / Et forma prior et me maior es arte canendi." In *Theoc.* 8, sig. D1ʳ Eobanus recalls the present line: "Ambo aetate pares tenera, flaventibus ambo / Crinibus, et pulchro docti contendere cantu."

97 **fata vocant** = Verg. *A.* 6, 147; Ov. *Ep.* 7, 1; cf. Verg. *G.* 4, 496; *A.* 10, 472; 11, 97; Ov. *Ep.* 6, 28.

98 **levis** Cf. line 141 below (n.).
blando ... vultu Tib. 1, 6, 1; Stat. *Silv.* 1, 1, 31.

99 **Mortis – trahit** Cf. *Rec.* 43-44 (n.); Erasmus, *Enchiridion, LB* 5, col. 55 F–56 F: "[libido], quo malo nullum aliud ... plures in exitium trahit." For love as a living death see *Ama.* 18, 9 (n.).

100 **Una ... foemina sensus** = Prop. 2, 1, 55.
cunctos ... sensus Cf. Ov. *Rem.* 307: "totos ... sensus" (= Eob. *Idyl.* 7, 71, the revised version of the present line).
concludit ... sensus Cf. *Ama.* 35, 12 (n.).

101 **Quin potius** = Lucr. 1, 798; 4, 127; Verg. *A.* 4, 99.
notum ... amnem Cf. line 81 above (n.).
descendis ad amnem ≈ Line 79 above (n.).

102 **sol – transcendit** Cf. Verg. *A.* 8, 97; Ov. *Met.* 11, 353-354; Avit. *Carm.* 3, 1: "Tempus erat, quo sol medium transcenderet axem"; Eob. *Her. Chr.* 3, 133 (n.).
axem Ov. *Ep.* 4, 160; *Met.* 2, 59; and often.

103 **medio temone** Stat. *Theb.* 12, 751. The sun's chariot is now at the zenith of its course. Hence its yoke-beam is level, pointing neither up nor down. Cf. Ov. *Met.* 11, 257-258, nearing sunset: "inclinato ... temone"; Eob. *Nup.* 282 (n.), near sunset: "prono temone." Cf. further Ov. *Met.* 10, 447.
Gregem – aquatum Cf. *Ecl. Theoduli* 25 (following Vulg. *Gen.* 29, 8 and 29, 11): "adaquare gregem [venit]." In this sense "aquatum" seems to be unparalleled.

104 **Ite – pecudes** Cf. lines 63-64 above (n.).
liquidum ... amnem = *Nor.* 1246; cf. Ov. *Met.* 6, 400.

105-106 **Me – potem** For the image of love as unquenchable thirst cf. especially Ov. *Met.* 3, 415 (Narcissus): "dumque sitim sedare cupit, sitis altera crevit"; also Mant.

Ecl. 2, 84-85: "sors tua Narcisso similis: Narcissus in undis / dum sedare sitim properat, sitit amplius"; Ov. *Rem.* 533-534; Eob. *Buc.* 7, 173-175.

105   **Me coquet** Ov. *Ep.* 15, 12: "me calor Aetnaeo non minor igne coquit."

106   **extingui** Ov. *Met.* 7, 569: "nec sitis est exstincta prius quam vita bibendo."
        Nerea For the metonymy ("Nereus" = "sea") see, for instance, Ov. *Met.* 1, 187; Luc. 2, 713.

107   **urunt – flammae** Cf. Ov. *Met.* 7, 803; Eob. *Laud.* 294 (n.).

108   **Cygne, viden** Cf. Mant. *Ecl.* 1, 175: "Fauste, viden? ..."

109   **O salve** = Ov. *Met.* 12, 530.

109-110   **Quid – nostri** Like his Ovidian counterpart, Narcissus shuns the company of his fellows and frequents lonely places where he can vent his sorrow in laments to nature. The motif is conventional; see *Ama.* 2, 1-6 (n.).

111-173   **Donec – reliquit** Narcissus's lament falls into three sections. The first (lines 111-144) tells how his love started as mere coquetry à la Galatea (Theoc. 6, 17), but ended as a passion unto death. At the end of this part Narcissus presents himself as the wronged party and seeks to arouse our indignation against the fickleness of women and the baseness of Rubina's new paramour. The middle section (lines 151-164) aims to arouse pity – in the reader as well as in the beloved. In the conclusion (lines 165-173) Narcissus addresses the flock, his fellow shepherds, and (in the epitaph) lovers like himself. Here he imagines himself dying for love like Vergil's Gallus (*Ecl.* 10, 9-20) or the Daphnis of Theoc. 1.

111-113   **Donec – Cantando** Cf. Mant. *Ecl.* 2, 151-152: "tunc animo, tunc vi, tunc ore valebam, / nec mihi sese alius poterat componere pastor."

111   **Donec – alter** Cf. Ov. *Tr.* 3, 6, 3; Petrarch, *Ecl.* 10, 378: "Dives eram in silvis, nec me felicior alter."
        Donec eram foelix ≈ Ov. *Tr.* 1, 9, 5.

112-113   **nec qui – Cantando** Cf. *Buc.* 10, 12; 10, 160-161; Filetico, *Theoc.* 5, 24: "Et mecum si tunc audes contendere tenta"; Cordus, *Ecl.* 6, 6: "iam potes alterno mecum contendere versu"; Eob. *Theoc.* 8, sig. D1ʳ: "Num libet alterno mecum contendere cantu." Narcissus alludes to the shepherds' pastime of testing their skill in piping and singing against each other. See, for instance, Theoc. 5; Verg. *Ecl.* 3 and 7; Calp. *Ecl.* 2; Eob. *Buc.* 5 (with note at *Buc.* 5, 13).

113   **Cantando** = Verg. *Ecl.* 3, 25; 6, 71; 9, 52.

113-114   **Mea – Optabant** Cf. Catul. 62, 42; Ov. *Met.* 3, 353 (Narcissus): "multi illum iuvenes, multae cupiere puellae."

113   **hylares ... nymphae** = Sil. 8, 182.
        connubia nymphae = Stat. *Ach.* 1, 241.

114   **malesanus** = Ov. *Met.* 3, 474 (Narcissus).

114-115   **amantes Sprevi** Tib. 1, 8, 61; cf. Calp. *Ecl.* 3, 25.

115   **nigram** Cf. Verg. *Ecl.* 2, 16; Ov. *Ars* 2, 657-658; *Rem.* 327.

116-123   **Quas – sequeretur** She pursues him, just as Echo pursued the mythical Narcissus.

117-118   **veluti – Vacca** For the image cf. Verg. *Ecl.* 8, 85-89. For the comparison girl-heifer see Hor. *Carm.* 2, 5, 6; Ov. *Am.* 3, 5, 37; *Ep.* 5, 117-124; Calp. *Ecl.* 3.

117   **verna** Literally, "in springtime" – that is, in the mating season. In the 1539-version "verna" is changed to "lasciva."

118-123   **totos – sequeretur** Cf. Bocc. *Ecl.* 2, 9-24: "Me miserum male sanus amor per devia solum / distrahit, et longos cogit sine mente labores / ut subeam, victusque sequar vestigia nondum / cognita Pampinee. Dixi 'sequar' inscius, imo / perscruter; nec cura potest retinere peculi / quin montes celsos densosque per invia lucos / discurram ... / [...] / [*line 23*] Pampineam, o! quotiens nequicquam vocibus usque / in celum totis clamavi vallibus imis."

118-119 **totos – Errabat** Cf. Ov. *Met.* 14, 422: "... latos [*or* Latios] errat vesana per agros." For the motif cf. line 152 below (n.); for the wording cf. Ov. *Met.* 7, 534-535: "per agros / errasse"; Tib. 1, 3, 61; Sen. *Phoen.* 561-562; Eob. *Buc.* 1, 122; 3, 18; 5, 87-88.

119 **clamans Narcissum** Cf. Verg. *Ecl.* 6, 43-44; *Mor.* 31.
nomine tantum = Hor. *S.* 1, 9, 3; Juv. 8, 31.

120 **longum ... amorem** = Catul. 76, 13; Verg. *A.* 3, 487; cf. *A.* 1, 749; *Ciris* 383; Prop. 1, 19, 26; Ov. *Am.* 1, 6, 5; et al.; Eob. *Buc.* 3, 84.

121-122 **Non illam – custodia** Cf. Ov. *Met.* 3, 437-438 (Narcissus).
Non illam ... Non ≈ Verg. *G.* 3, 140-141.

121 **duri ... parentes** = *Sylv.* 9, 1, 31; cf. Nemes. *Ecl.* 2, 10.

122 **Non – custodia** Lovesick swains and shepherdesses neglect their pastoral duties; cf. Ov. *Met.* 2, 683-685; 13, 763; Bocc. *Ecl.* 2, 13: "nec cura potest retinere peculi"; Mant. *Ecl.* 2, 107; 4, 25-26; cf. lines 91-92 above (n.).
commissa – custodia Cf. *Buc.* 4, 24: "pecudum commissa ... custodia."

122-126 **sola – flammae** Cf. Nemes. *Ecl.* 4, 5-10.

122-123 **per omnes ... sylvas** Ov. *Met.* 14, 418-419.

124 **nemora et saxa** *Her. Chr.* 13, 13; *Sylv.* 5, 22, 21.
nemora ... aspera Verg. *A.* 11, 902.
saxa aspera = Stat. *Silv.* 2, 2, 31; cf. Lucr. 4, 147; Ov. *Met.* 6, 76; et al.

125 **ut peius amaret** The trick is recommended in Ov. *Am.* 2, 19, 33-36; cf. also *Met.* 9, 724-725. For "peius amaret" see Ov. *Ep.* 4, 26; 7, 30.

127 **Heu – inani** Cf. *Her. Chr.* 17, lines 71 and 83; Prop. 3, 24, 1; Ov. *Ars* 1, 707.

128 **credit amari** = Ov. *Met.* 7, 823; cf. *Ars* 3, 673.

129 **indigno ... furore** Cf. line 172 below (n.): "indigno ... amore."
consumpta furore Cf. Filetico, *Theoc.* 1, 138: "Dixerat et scaevo consumptus amore quievit"; 3, 12: "Aspice quam tenero sim iam consumptus amore"; 3, 53: "... consumptus amore iacebo"; 6, 26: "placido dominae consumptus amore / Alterius."

131 **aversa recessit** = Lucr. 5, 413; cf. Verg. *A.* 4, 362 (Dido).

132-139 **Occului – flammae** Cf. Ov. *Met.* 4, 64.

132 **tacitum ... amorem** At this point Narcissus is still unaware of the depth of his passion. For this use of "tacitus" cf. Ov. *Rem.* 105; Verg. *A.* 4, 67; Eob. *Ama.* B 2, 19 (n.); *Sylv. duae* 2, 35.
confessus amorem = Ov. *Met.* 14, 703.

133-135 **Ut essem – Comere** Cf. Ov. *Met.* 13, 764-767 (Polyphemus).

134 **didici – componere** Cf. Mant. *Ecl.* 4, 228: "discit ... vultum componere vitro"; [Tib.] 3, 13, 9; Ov. *Met.* 13, 767.
componere, crinem Cf. Prop. 1, 15, 5.

134-135 **crinem Comere** = Stat. *Theb.* 9, 901-902.

135-136 **non – Mens mea** Cf. Ov. *Met.* 9, 520. For "intellexerat ignem" see *Met.* 9, 457. For "mens mea" at this metrical position see Tib. 1, 2, 98; Ov. *Ep.* 16, 73; Eob. *Her. Chr.* 10, 36; 18, 156; cf. Ov. *Ep.* 12, 212; *Met.* 9, 520; 13, 957; *Pont.* 4, 9, 90; Eob. *Her. Chr.* 2, 8.

137-138 **si quis – Diceret** Cf. Verg. *Ecl.* 9, 33-34.

138-139 **Interea – flammae** Cf. Ov. *Rem.* 105.
totum Exurunt – flammae Cf. Catul. 64, 92-93; Sen. *Ag.* 132.

138 **Venus ignea** = Maxim. 3, 7.

139 **Tum denique** = Verg. *G.* 2, 369; Ov. *Ep.* 10, 43; *Met.* 3, 629; et al.

141 **O mulierum – ventis** Cf. Calp. *Ecl.* 3, 10. The fickleness of women was proverbial. See Otto 1153; Häussler, pp. 17, 111, and 280.
muliērum This medieval scansion lingers in early Renaissance verse. See, for example, Bocc. *Ecl.* 7, 124; Mant. *Ecl.* 4, 70; 4, 206; 4, 245; 6, 57; Celtis, *Am.*

2, 2, 5; 2, 7, 45; Eob. *Buc.* 9, 11. Eobanus did not recognize the medievalism until many years later, when Joachim Camerarius pointed it out to him in Nuremberg. See *Epp. 1*, sig. H5ᵛ.

ventis Winds are proverbially changeable; see Otto 1863; Häussler, pp. 81, 223, and 246.

142   **Adonim** A shepherd already mentioned in *Buc.* 2, 65 (n.).

transtulit ignes Cf. Ter. *Hec.* 169-170: "huc transtulit / amorem"; Hor. *Epod.* 15, 23; Ov. *Met.* 10, 83-84.

143   **furatus** The motif "theft" occurs also in ancient pastoral. See Theoc. 5, 2 (fleece); 5, 4 (flute); Verg. *Ecl.* 3, 16-18; Calp. *Ecl.* 3, 74.

144   **teretes calamos** *Idyl.* 7, 64; 10, 28.

145   **Infoelix puer** = Verg. *A.* 1, 475; Mant. *Ecl.* 1, 129; cf. Eob. *Rec.* 119 (n.); *Buc.* 9, 50.

146   **Rhetia – incidis** Proverbial; see Otto 917; Häussler, pp. 176 and 275; Mant. *Ecl.* 2, 137-138: "incautus sibi multa tetendit / retia et in foveam cecidit quam fecerat."

Rhetia ... tendis Prop. 2, 32, 20; Ov. *Am.* 1, 8, 69; *Ars* 1, 45; *Rem.* 202; *Met.* 8, 331.

Atque ita = Lucr. 2, 227; 4, 890; 6, 201; Verg. *G.* 4, 409; *A.* 5, 382; et al.

147   **alma Venus** = Ov. *Met.* 10, 230; 14, 478; 15, 844; Stat. *Silv.* 1, 2, 159; cf. Lucr. 1, 2; Verg. *A.* 1, 618; et al.; Eob. *Ruf.* 38 and 39; *Buc.* 7, 108; *Sylv. duae* 2, 168.

fastum – omnem Cf. Hor. *Carm.* 3, 10, 9-10. For "fastum omnem" see Tib. 1, 8, 75.

148-149   **Quam – famulatur** That the lover is a slave to his mistress is an old commonplace. See, for example, Cic. *Parad.* 36; Tib. 2, 4, 1-4; Mant. *Ecl.* 1, 114-116: "Quisquis amat servit: sequitur captivus amantem, / fert domita cervice iugum, fert verbera tergo / dulcia"; Brant, *NS* 92, 81-82.

148   **dominae ... servire puellae** Lotich. *Eleg.* 2, 1, 25: "Nonne fuit melius dominae servire puellae?"; cf. Ov. *Am.* 2, 17, 1.

liceat, servire Verg. *A.* 4, 103. For "liceat" used parenthetically see Ov. *Met.* 8, 38; Luc. 1, 202.

149   **Quisquis amat** = *Laud.* 321 (n.).

151   **Palepaphia** *Ciris* 88; Eob. *Her.* 2, 1, 99 (a temple of Venus): "Templa Palae-paphio ... scorto"; *Sylv.* 2, 6, 35: "Linque Palaepaphios ignes, Citheraea." Venus was said to have come ashore at Palaepaphos (Old Paphos) on Cyprus; see Mela 2, 102.

percussus harundine = Ov. *Ep.* 9, 161; Eob. *Nup.* 10: "Paphia percussus arundine."

solus See n. *Ama* 2, 1-6.

152   **Per – rura** The wounds of passion force the sufferer to wander about ceaselessly. Cf. Verg. *A.* 4, 68-69; 4, 300-303; *Ciris* 167; Ov. *Met.* 13, 872; Nemes. *Ecl.* 4, 6; Mant. *Ecl.* 3, 143-144; note to lines 118-123 above. This restlessness is in sharp contrast to the tranquillity of soul envisaged by Philaegon (lines 45-51 above).

sylvas et rura = *Buc.* 10, 1; cf. Ov. *Met.* 11, 146.

sepe videntes = Verg. *G.* 1, 354.

153   **Fleverunt Dryades et ... nymphae** Cf. Ov. *Met.* 3, 505-507 (at Narcissus's death); 13, 689; Verg. *Ecl.* 5, 20-21 (at Daphnis's death).

vulnera nymphae = Claud. *Carm. minora* 30, 175.

154-155   **Ut – potant** Cf. Theoc. 1, 74-75; Verg. *Ecl.* 5, 25-26 (at Daphnis's death); Nemes. *Ecl.* 2, 29-30.

154   **magnos ... dolores** Ov. *Met.* 8, 517; Luc. 9, 889.

155   **Gramina – potant** Cf. Mant. *Ecl.* 1, 35: "[iuvenca] gramina non carpit nec

fluminis attrahit undam"; Eob. *Buc.* 10, 164.
Gramina ... carpunt Ov. *Tr.* 4, 8, 20.
dulcia flumina Cf. Verg. *G.* 3, 445.
flumina potant ≈ Ov. *Met.* 1, 634; Eob. *Nor.* 419.

156 **Saepius haec mecum** ≈ Line 68 above.

157 **Quo fugis?" exclamo ... revertere** = Ov. *Ep.* 10, 35; cf. *Met.* 3, 383-384 and 3, 477 (Narcissus); Eob. *Her. Chr.* 20, 65.

158 **Quem fugias** = Ov. *Met.* 1, 515; cf. Verg. *Ecl.* 2, 60.
miserere ... amantis Sen. *Phaed.* 671; cf. line 67 above (n.).
impatienter amantis Cf. Mant. *Ecl.* 7, 65: "nimis impatienter amabat"; Ov. *Ep.* 19, 4; Eob. *Her. Chr.* 24, 25.

159 **Huc ades, o** = Verg. *Ecl.* 2, 45; 7, 9; 9, 39; Ov. *Am.* 2, 12, 16; Eob. *Buc.* 5, 9; 7, 129; cf. *Buc.* 5, 10 (n.).
mea lux = Line 90 above (n.).

161 **spe fallis inani** = *Theoc.* 3, sig. B5ʳ. For "spe inani" see Verg. *A.* 10, 627; 10, 648; 11, 49; Ov. *Met.* 7, 336; Eob. *Her. Chr.* 14, 143; *Idyl.* 15, 47: "... aut saltem spe consolaris inani." For the tag "fallis inani" see Prop. 3, 6, 3.

162 **Dum queror** = *Laud.* 285 (n.).
impediunt lachrimae Ov. *Met.* 9, 328-329; 13, 745; cf. Eob. *Her. Chr.* 5, 38.
lumen et auras = Verg. *A.* 6, 363; Eob. *Theoc.* 17, sig. F8ᵛ: "vidisti lumen et auras / Vitales."

163-170 **Quid – ignes** Wearied by misfortune and unrequited passion, Narcissus now finds solace in contemplating his own death and funeral and thinking how the herd and his fellow shepherds will mourn him. In this he follows the example of Gallus in Verg. *Ecl.* 10, 31-34. Cf. also Bocc. *Ecl.* 2, 135-155; Mant. *Ecl.* 3, 103-124; Eob. *Ama.* 32, 25-84.

163 **Quid – superis** Cf. Maxim. 1, 231: "nil mihi cum superis: explevi munera vitae." For "superis" in this sense see also Eob. *Her. Chr.* 3, 6.
Quid mihi cum = Ov. *Am.* 2, 19, 57; *Ep.* 6, 47; 14, 65; et al.
Iuvat ire et = Verg. *A.* 2, 27; Stat. *Theb.* 1, 616; Eob. *Hod.* 73; cf. Verg. *A.* 4, 660; Mant. *Ecl.* 3, 143-144, in similar context: "me rapit impatiens furor et iuvat ire per altos / solivagum montes, per lustra ignota ferarum."
perdere vitam = Ov. *Tr.* 5, 10, 51. Narcissus is not about to commit suicide (cf. Theoc. 3, 25-27; Verg. *Ecl.* 8, 59-60); but he longs for death and is pining away, much like his mythical namesake. See Ov. *Met.* 3, 469-473; cf. also Theoc. 1, 66-141 (Daphnis); Verg. *Ecl.* 10, 9-69 (Gallus); Bocc. *Ecl.* 1, 17; 1, 132-135; 2, 123-155; Eob. *Ama.* 10, 7-12.

164 **Tormentum – venenum** Cf. *Sylv. duae* 2, 81-82.
durus amor Verg. *G.* 3, 259; *A.* 6, 442.
Venus acre venenum = Mant. *3. Parthen.*, fol. 107ʳ (different): "Venus acre venenum / Influit in mentem."
acre venenum = Lucr. 4, 637; 4, 640; 5, 900; 6, 974; Mant. *Ecl.* 9, 140. For the traditional image of love as poison see, for example, Prop. 2, 12, 19; Verg. *A.* 1, 688; Walther 7979; Mant. *Ecl.* 1, 119; Eob. *Ama.* 23, 5; 36, 4; *Sylv. duae* 2, 81; *Idyl.* 15, 24: "hoc ... plusquam letale venenum."

165 **placida ... morte quiescam** Cf. Verg. *A.* 9, 445; Eob. *Her. Chr.* 7, 156.

166 **Lanigerae pecudes** = Lucr. 2, 661; Ov. *Met.* 13, 781. Cf. Eob. *Buc.* 8, 21 (n.).
mea funera = Ov. *Pont.* 1, 9, 17; Stat. *Theb.* 12, 383; *Ach.* 1, 631.

167 **Nec salices – myricas** Cf. *Buc.* 8, 34.
Nec salices, caprae, ... captate Cf. Verg. *Ecl.* 1, 77-78; Nemes. *Ecl.* 1, 6-7.

168-173 **Vos – reliquit** For these motifs – burial, the strewing of flowers on the grave, epitaph – cf. Verg. *Ecl.* 5, 40-44; Bocc. *Ecl.* 1, 132-135; Mant. *Ecl.* 3, 117-124; 3, 182-189; Eob. *Buc.* 9, 56-63.

168 **Vos ... pastores** = *Buc.* 9, 107.
date membra quieti ≈ Ven. Fort. *Carm.* 6, 10, 29 (= Bocc. *Ecl.* 2, 72; Mant. *1. Parthen.* 2, 469): "... dare membra quieti"; Eob. *Idyl.* 15, 33: "... cum placidae demisi membra quieti." For "quieti" in the sense "eternal rest" see, for example, Lucr. 3, 211; Verg. *A.* 10, 745; Prop. 2, 28, 25.

169 **Flore ... cognomine** The narcissus; cf. Ov. *Met.* 3, 509-510.
signatam ... terram ≈ Stat. *Theb.* 6, 904. For "signatam" see also Verg. *A.* 3, 287; Ov. *Met.* 2, 326; 8, 540.
spargite terram For the time-honored custom of decking the grave with flowers and herbs see, for instance, Verg. *Ecl.* 5, 40; *A.* 5, 79; 6, 883-886. Cf. also Eob. *Rec.* 135; *Buc.* 9, 58-61; *Epic.* 1, 109: "Spargimus hic frustra tumulum redolentibus herbis"; 8, 79-80.

170 **Et deflete meos ignes** Cf. Verg. *Ecl.* 10, 33-34.
aevoque futuro ≈ [Tib.] 3, 4, 47.

171 **Si quis amator erit** Cf. Prop. 3, 16, 13; Ov. *Rem.* 13.
quod – carmen Cf. Ov. *Tr.* 3, 3, 71.
addite carmen = Verg. *Ecl.* 5, 42: "... tumulo superaddite carmen." For "carmen" in the sense "epitaph" see Eob. *Rec.* 136 (n.).

172 **Cum – periret** Cf. Verg. *Ecl.* 10, 10 (in many mss. and Renaissance edd.): "... indigno cum Gallus amore periret"; Eob. *Idyl.* 15, 12: "... insano cum nuper amore periret"; *Theoc.* 1, sig. A5ᵛ: "... indigno cum Daphnis amore periret." For "indigno amore" see also Verg. *Ecl.* 8, 18.
Cum miser ... periret = *Epic.* 2, 137 (in a concluding epitaph): "Cum miser ingrato Nesenus in amne periret."

173 **Exemplo – reliquit** Narcissus now offers his interpretation of this tale of woe: Love is an irresistible force that we withstand only at our peril. Cf. Ov. *Ep.* 4, 11: "quidquid Amor iussit, non est contemnere tutum"; Aen. Silv. *Hist.*, p. 123, lines 23-24: "Nil peius est quam obstare cupidini nostre"; line 147 above: "Venus fastum ... vindicat omnem." Narcissus's view of passion as a natural force that must not be withstood is, of course, perfectly at home in the pastoral idyll: "omnia vincit Amor: et nos cedamus Amori," as Gallus concludes in Verg. *Ecl.* 10, 69. But in Eobanus's moral-Mantuanesque pastoral, which inverts the hedonistic pastoral dream, such a way of thinking represents the mind of the natural man – not that of a Christian like Philaegon who rejects passionate love precisely because it is so seductive and overpowering. Hence the good shepherd follows Philaegon's example and vigilantly watches over his flock, lest he become a bad shepherd and suffer Narcissus's fate.
Exemplo ... reliquit *Idyl.* 14, 111: "... ut exemplo ipse reliquit."
contendat amare Literally: "refuse to love." In this sense "contendat" is a medievalism. For the thought cf. Verg. *A.* 4, 38: "... placitone etiam pugnabis amori?"; Filetico, *Theoc.* 1, 97-98, where Venus says: "solebas / Dicere me contra et dulcem contendere natum." In the 1528/39 version the verb is changed to "contemnat." The Strasbourg copy, however, glosses the phrase with: "velit [*sc.* amare] insipienter."

4

Meter: Hexameter.

1-3 **Montibus – curas** Cf. Mant. *Ecl.* 5, 1-2: "Candide, nobiscum pecudes aliquando solebas / Pascere et his gelidis calamos inflare sub umbris."

1 **Montibus hiis** = Verg. *Ecl.* 7, 56; Ov. *Fast.* 1, 517; 5, 652.

 mecum quondam ... solebas = Her. *Chr.* 16, 237; cf. Ov. *Fast.* 3, 613; *Trist.* 3, 14, 3.

2 **Pascere oves** = *Buc.* 8, 86; 9, 39; cf. Verg. *Ecl.* 6, 5; Ov. *Fast.* 1, 204; *Pont.* 1, 8, 52.

2-3 **alterna ... Carmina** Ov. *Ep.* 15, 5-6 (referring to elegiacs); cf. Eob. *Buc.* 5, 13 (n.): "Alternis ... modis."

3 **urgentes ... curas** V. Fl. 8, 24.

 depellere curas = Bocc. *Ecl.* 2, 97: "graves ... depellere curas"; cf. Tib. 1, 5, 37; Prud. *c. Symm.* 2, 124: "... terrenas animo depellite curas."

4 **tenent ... te** Cf. Tib. 1, 3, 3: "me tenet ... Phaeacia"; Hor. *Carm.* 1, 7, 19-21; Ov. *Ep.* 16, 295; *Tr.* 3, 4, 47-48; *Pont.* 1, 3, 65; 1, 6, 1-2; Eob. *Buc.* 4, 27; 4, 41 (n.); *Her. Chr.* 19, 3.

5 **Usque adeo solus** = Luc. 3, 118.

6 **quid ... deseris agros** = Luc. 7, 821.

 quid adhuc non = *Sylv. duae* 2, 227; cf. *Ama.* 32, 38.

8-9 **Hic – surgunt** Cf. Verg. *Ecl.* 5, 36-39 (the landscape degenerates after Daphnis's death).

8 **tribuli, lolium** Ov. *Met.* 5, 485.

11 **vota morantur** = Ov. *Ep.* 18, 5; cf. *Ep.* 7, 21; 19, 95; *Met.* 8, 71.

12-26 **Pascua – ipso** The model is Mant. *Ecl.* 9, 130-152, describing the weed-choked fields of Rome, where snakes, foxes, and wolves roam in search of prey.

12-14 **Pascua – anguis** Cf. Verg. *Ecl.* 3, 93.

13 **Heu, fuge** = Verg. *A.* 2, 289; 3, 44; line 107 below.

 vicinae ... successeris umbrae Cf. Calp. *Ecl.* 1, 6; 1, 19; Eob. *Buc.* 1, 65 (n.).

14 **pedem tenerum** Ov. *Am.* 1, 4, 44; *Ars* 1, 162; 2, 212; cf. Eob. *Her. Chr.* 18, 40 (n.).

 calcata ... anguis Cf. Ov. *Met.* 10, 23-24; 13, 804.

15 **Vera refers** = Ov. *Met.* 5, 271; Mant. *Ecl.* 7, 51.

16 **Hesterna ... luce** = Ov. *Am.* 2, 2, 3; cf. Eob. *Her. Chr.* 9, 37; *Sylv.* 1, 8, 1.

 saturas ... capellas ≈ Verg. *Ecl.* 10, 77; Ov. *Met.* 15, 472.

 mulgerem – capellas Cf. *Buc.* 7, 94; 10, 98.

17-18 **longum ... colubrum** Verg. *G.* 2, 320.

17 **mirabile dictu** = *Laud.* 192 (n.).

18-19 **colubrum – petentem** For the wording cf. Verg. *A.* 3, 424-425. For the motif cf. Mant. *Ecl.* 10, 138-140: "ecce caput tollit coluber linguaque trisulca / sibilat, inflantur fauces, nepa livida [*cf. line 23 below*] tendit / brachia, ventrosus profert vestigia bufo [*cf. line 44 below*]."

18 **colubrum ... latentem** Ov. *Met.* 11, 775.

19 **Ora exertantem, et** = Verg. *A.* 3, 425.

21 **Credo – nec** = Verg. *A.* 4, 12; Eob. *Her. Chr.* 14, 127. For "credo equidem" at the hexameter opening see also Verg. *A.* 6, 848; Stat. *Theb.* 12, 77; Eob. *Her. Chr.* 4, 199.

 mira videntur ≈ Verg. *A.* 10, 267.

23 **Incustoditas ... caulas** Cf. Ov. *Tr.* 1, 6, 10.

 nepa livida = Mant. *Ecl.* 10, 139 (see note to lines 18-19 above).

24 **Est – custodia** Cf. Ter. *Eu.* 832: "scelesta, ovem lupo commisisti." The expression was proverbial; see Otto 983; Häussler, pp. 178-179; Erasmus,

Adag. 1, 4, 10.

pecudum commissa ... custodia Cf. *Buc.* 3, 122; for "pecudum custodia" see
Verg. *G.* 4, 327 (in some mss. and many edd., including Eob. *Adnot.*, sig. H2ᵛ);
Juvenc. 1, 158.

25   **cede tepent** Verg. *A.* 8, 196; Ov. *Met.* 4, 163.

25-26   **sanguine ... Innocuo** *Her. Chr.* 16, 113 (n.).

25   **sanguine postes** = Sil. 13, 208.

26   **voratius ipso** ≈ Ov. *Met.* 8, 839.

27   **Me – recessu** Cf. *Sylv.* 6, 13, 13: "Me iuvat umbrifero viridantia prata recessu /
Visere."

        Me tenet = Tib. 1, 3, 3; Ov. *Met.* 14, 379; *Tr.* 3, 4, 48; cf. line 4 above (n.).

        vallis – recessu Cf. *Buc.* 2, 5 (n.); *Epp. 4*, sig. F5ᵛ (1508), referring to the Von
der Marthen estate outside Erfurt: "Arcem in secessu ..., quam quartus ab urbe /
Thuringa Latio signatus more lapillus / Dividit."

28   **Ad – urbe** Cf. Ov. *Fast.* 2, 682; Mart. 1, 12, 4; 10, 79, 1; Camerarius, *Nar.* 24,
16.

30-32   **Hic – armenta** For this image of pastoral tranquillity cf. Tib. 1, 10, 9-10 (in the
golden age); Eob. *Buc.* 1, 80-81, with note to line 81.

30   **ego ... viridi ... in antro** = Verg. *Ecl.* 1, 75; cf. *A.* 8, 630; Calp. *Ecl.* 4, 95; line 70
below.

        propter aquas = *Laud.* 323 (n.).

        requietus in antro Cf. *Culex* 113.

31   **Saepe – somnos** Cf. Verg. *Ecl.* 1, 55; Eob. *Val.* 1, 464: "Saepe leves somnos
conciliare solet." For "leves somnos" see Hor. *Carm.* 2, 16, 15; *Epod.* 2, 28;
Verg. *A.* 5, 838; Ov. *Fast.* 4, 332. For "capio somnos" see Ov. *Fast.* 4, 530; cf.
Eob. *Buc.* 6, 48 (n.).

31-32   **Secura vagantur ... armenta** Cf. Stat. *Theb.* 10, 824.

33   **nostro ... aevo** Ov. *Ars* 1, 241; *Met.* 15, 868; *Pont.* 1, 8, 21.

        iucundior aevo ≈ *Buc.* 1, 25.

35-36   **Ipse – forensi** Cf. *Nor.* 1307-1308.

35   **silvestresque – tecta** Cf. *Buc.* 3, 5 (n.); Ov. *Fast.* 4, 803-804: "tectis agresti-
bus ... / et ... casae."

37-40   **Et me – montes** Cf. *Epic.* 4, 171: "Me ... nascentem primum vagus Aedera
vidit"; *Her. Chr.* 24, 49-62.

37   **me chara parens** = *Her. Chr.* 10, 133; cf. *Rec.* 152 (n.).

        viridi ... umbra Verg. *Ecl.* 9, 20; *Ciris* 4; Eob. *Her. Chr.* B 1, 7; *Vict.* 415.

38-39   **Floralia ... Dona** Cf. *Her. Chr.* 4, 64.

39   **Dona tulit** = Verg. *A.* 9, 407.

        teneraque ... in herba = Ov. *Met.* 3, 23.

        sedens ... in herba Cf. *Buc.* 3, 69-70.

40   **Gemmeus** Calp. *Ecl.* 2, 57; Plin. *Ep.* 1, 3, 1.

        Hessiacos ... montes *Laud.* 278 (n.).

41   **Nunc tenet ... Erphurdia** Cf. Brant, *Var. carm.*, sig. bc4ᵛ (*Texte* 35, 9): "Nunc
tenet australis domus ..."; Eob. *Her.* 1, 5, 3: "Nam tenet ... Tyatira"; line 4 above
(n.).

        infoelix Erphurdia = Line 45 below; cf. *Rec.* 13.

42   **mala ... pascua** *Idyl.* 3, 14 (referring to Fulda).

        bona pascua = [Tib.] 3, 9, 1.

43   **amantes saxa** = Ov. *Ep.* 16, 55 (of goats).

44   **Plena ... per ovilia** Verg. *A.* 9, 339; cf. Eob. *Rec.* 41.

        ventrosus ... bufo = Mant. *Ecl.* 10, 140 (see note to lines 18-19 above).

45   **infoelix Erphurdia** = Line 41 above (n.).

46   **male servatos ... honores** = *Idyl.* 17, lines 106 and 107 (referring to the troubles

at Erfurt in the early 1520's).

47   **Dum loquimur** Hor. *Carm.* 1, 11, 7.

47-63 **tuus – iuvenca** For the motif – two bulls fighting over a heifer – cf. Verg. *G.* 3, 219-241; Ov. *Am.* 2, 12, 25-26; Nemes. *Ecl.* 4, 34. Cf. further Verg. *A.* 12, 101-106 and 715-722; Ov. *Met.* 9, 46-49; Eob. *Buc.* 10, 68.

48   **cornuta fronte** Alan. *Parab.* 2, *PL* 210, col. 585 B: "taurus, / ... qui cornuta fronte ferire potest."

49   **dulci ... amore** *Buc.* 3, 46 (n.).

    possit amore ≈ Verg. *A.* 4, 85.

50   **Cernis ut ecce** = Calp. *Ecl.* 1, 4. For "cernis ut" at the hexameter opening see also, for example, Verg. *A.* 10, 20; Ov. *Tr.* 5, 14, 37; Eob. *Buc.* 5, 50; 9, 36; *Ruf.* 97; *Her. Chr.* 14, 163.

    ecce iterum *Rec.* 149 (n.).

52   **O montana Pales** = Nemes. *Ecl.* 2, 55. The tutelary deity of flocks and herds, Pales is called "montana" because so much pasturing occurs in the hills and mountains.

    celebrem ... triumphum *Pug.* 67 (n.); *Her. Chr.* 12, 103.

53   **Mulctram** Milk was the standard offering to Pales; see Tib. 1, 1, 36; Ov. *Fast.* 4, 746; Nemes. *Ecl.* 1, 68.

    capies ... coronam Ov. *Fast.* 2, 105. In antiquity, people used to adorn images of the gods with garlands.

56   **niveae ... iuvencae** = Ov. *Am.* 3, 13, 13; cf. [Tib.] 3, 4, 67; Ov. *Am.* 2, 12, 25. Ancient literary descriptions often describe the most beautiful cattle as snowy white.

57   **tibi ... videtur** = Lucr. 4, 406; Prop. 1, 8, 3; Hor. *S.* 1, 4, 90.

60-61 **pedum – Sentiet** For the motif cf. Theoc. 4, 49; Cordus, *Buc.* 3, 32 (*Ecl.* 4, 33): "non sapies, nisi torva pedum tibi cornua vellat [frangat *1518*]."

60   **inter cornua** = Verg. *A.* 4, 61; 5, 479; 6, 245; Ov. *Met.* 7, 594; 15, 133.

61   **ut – concurrere** Cf. Ov. *Met.* 9, 46; Stat. *Theb.* 4, 397.

62   **coronam** A "crown" of welts raised by the beating.

63   **I nunc et** = Prop. 2, 29, 22; Hor. *Ep.* 2, 2, 76; Ov. *Ep.* 3, 26; et al.; Eob. *Her. Chr.* 1, 163 (n.); 13, 116; 17, 157-158; 23, 90.

    pugna pro pulchra The alliteration is expressive of the anger in Phileremus's voice.

64   **Ah – pecus** Cf. *Buc.* 7, 9 (n.); 1, 120-121 (n.).

    Insano ... amori *Ama.* 33, 6 (n.).

    servis amori = *Buc.* 7, 159; cf. *Buc.* 3, 95.

65   **Fers – tantum** Cf. Mant. *Ecl.* 1, 115: "... fert verbera tergo"; also cf. Ov. *Am.* 1, 2, 13.

66-71 **Sol – Philereme** For the "motif of bucolic repose" see n. *Buc.* 1, 65-71.

66   **Sol – campos** Cf. Verg. *G.* 1, 65-66.

    corpora fuscat Cf. Ov. *Ars* 1, 513; Mant. *Ecl.* 1, 75-76: "quia sole perusta / fusca fit."

67   **Umbra iuvat** Ov. *Rem.* 406.

    Gelidae – umbrae Cf. *Buc.* 1, 65, with notes.

68   **Gratior ... locus** *Nor.* 1242.

    hic locus est = Verg. *A.* 6, 390; Eob. *Sylv.* 6, 2, 19.

68-69 **tilias – agit** Cf. Ov. *Am.* 2, 16, 36; *Ep.* 14, 40; Eob. *Nor.* 406-407: "tilias hic frigida leves / Aura movet." For "tilias laeves" see Verg. *G.* 2, 449.

    frigida ... Aura Lucr. 3, 290; Prop. 1, 16, 24; Ov. *Am.* 2, 16, 36: "frigidaque arboreas mulceat aura comas"; *Ep.* 14, 40.

69   **summa ... rupe** = Mart. 13, 98, 1; cf. Verg. *Ecl.* 1, 56; *G.* 4, 508, where Orpheus sings "rupe sub aeria"; Eob. *Buc.* 1, 46 (n.).

70   **viridi ... antro** Line 30 above (n.).

consedimus antro = Bocc. *Ecl.* 3, 66; cf. Verg. *Ecl.* 5, 19: "... successimus antro"; Calp. *Ecl.* 1, 8-9; 6, 65.

71-72   **Lude – Camaenis** Cf. *Idyl.* 17, 23-27.

Levant – Carmina Cf. Nemes. *Ecl.* 4, 19: "... levant et carmina curas."

73-75   **Magna – Apollo** Cf. Calp. *Ecl.* 4, 5-10. For lines 73-74 cf. also Ov. *Met.* 15, 146-147; Mant. *Ecl.* 8, 87: "Candide, mira canis nullis pastoribus umquam / cognita"; Eob. *Buc.* 1, 39 (n.); 8, 99-100.

73   **Magna canam** = Ov. *Ars* 2, 536; Mant. *Ecl.* 7, 10.

73-74   **canam ... moduletur harundine** Singing and flute-playing are frequently mentioned together in pastoral poetry. See, for instance, Verg. *Ecl.* 5, 2; 5, 48; Calp. *Ecl.* 1, 93; 6, 10-11; Eob. *Buc.* 7, 137.

74   **moduletur harundine** ≈ *Culex* 100; Ov. *Rem.* 181; *Met.* 11, 154; Eob. *Buc.* 7, 137; cf. Verg. *Ecl.* 10, 51; Eob. *Buc.* 1, 11 (n.).

75-76   **Incipe – Camaenae** Cf. *Buc.* 5, 60; *Idyl.* 1, 54-55: "tibi dexter Apollo / Spirat, et Aoniae veniunt ad plectra sorores." For line 75 cf. also Cordus, *Buc.* 4, 55 (*Ecl.* 1, 83): "Tu prior incipias, praesens tibi spirat Apollo."

75   **tibi – Apollo** Cf. *Buc.* 10, 40-41; *Nup.* 353 (n.).

76   **vicinia tota** = Ov. *Met.* 2, 688; cf. Eob. *Her. Chr.* 3, 135.

77   **aereo ... vertice montem** ≈ *Sylv. duae* 2, 135.

aereo ... vertice = Tib. 1, 7, 15 (in some mss.); Sil. 1, 128.

vertice montem ≈ Catul. 68, 57: "aerii ... vertice montis"; Verg. *A.* 5, 35; 11, 526.

78   **levis – aura** Cf. *Ama.* 35, 83. The reference "occidui" indicates that the mountain is to the west of the shepherds. For "levis aura" at this metrical position see Ov. *Met.* 1, 529; cf. *Ep.* 5, 53; *Ars* 3, 100; et al.; Eob. *Her. Chr.* 6, 112.

aura Favoni = Lucr. 1, 11.

79   **Horrisonum** Cf. Franciscus Irenicus, *Exegesis historiae Germaniae* (1518; Hannover, 1728) 7, 24: "Memoratur mons in Turingiae partibus, haud procul ab Isenacho, quem ideo Horrisonum Eobanus dixit, Teutonice Hirselberg, ubi sylvanos satyrosque inhabitare fama divulgavit."

Latio – dicit Cf. *Her. Chr.* 6, 38. For the tag "nomine dicit" see Verg. *G.* 4, 356; Eob. *Sylv. duae* 1, 189.

Latio ... nomine Sil. 16, 306.

80   **bibit** With the name of a river as direct object, "bibit" (or a synonym) is a conventional paraphrase for living in a certain place. See, for instance, Verg. *Ecl.* 1, 62; 10, 65; *A.* 7, 715; Hor. *Carm.* 3, 10, 1; 4, 15, 21; Ov. *Ep.* 12, 10; *Tr.* 5, 3, 24; Eob. *Nup.* 166-167.

82   **ante duas messes** *Buc.* 9, 3; *Idyl.* 10, 11. For the time expression see *Laud.* 1 (n.).

cum saepe venirem ≈ *Buc.* 2, 13 (n.).

84   **Per nemora et montes** ≈ Lucr. 5, 41.

84-85   **nocturna ... Terriculamenta** Cf. Ov. *Fast.* 5, 421: "nocturna Lemuria" (the malevolent souls of the dead that flit about by night).

85-96   **pueros terrere – putares** The "lamiae" of ancient folklore were witches or vampires who, when at home, store their eyes in a jar, but put them back in their sockets when they go outside. See Plutarch, *De curiositate* 515 f–516 a. As in lines 89-94 below, Plutarch likens them to malicious meddlers who can see everybody else's faults, but are blind to their own. Eobanus's immediate source, however, is the introductory paragraph of Angelo Poliziano, *Praelectio in Priora Aristotelis Analytica, titulus Lamia* (1492): "Lamiam igitur hanc Plutarchus ille Cheroneus ... habere ait oculos exemptiles, hoc est quos sibi eximat detrahatque cum libuit rursusque cum libuit resumat atque affigat, quemadmodum senes ocularia specilla solent, quibus hebescenti per aetatem visui opitulantur; nam et cum quid inspectare avent, insertant quasi forfici nasum, et cum satis inspectarunt, recondunt in theca. ... Sed enim Lamia haec quoties domo egreditur, oculos sibi suos affigit vagaturque per fora, per plateas, per quadrivia, per angiportus, per delubra, per thermas, per ganeas, per conciliabula omnia circumspectatque singula, scrutatur, indagat, nihil tam bene obtexeris ut eam lateat. Milvinos esse credas oculos ei aut etiam emissicios sicuti Plautinae aniculae. Nulla eos praeterit quamlibet individua minuties, nulla eos evadit quamlibet remotissima latebra. Domum vero ut revenit, in ipso statim limine demit illos sibi oculos abicitque in loculos. Ita semper domi caeca, semper foris oculata. ... Vidistisne, obsecro, unquam Lamias istas, viri Florentini, quae se et sua nesciunt, alios et aliena speculantur? Negatis? Atqui tamen sunt in urbibus frequentes etiamque in vestra, verum personatae incedunt: homines credas, Lamiae sunt." See Angelo Poliziano, *Lamia: Praelectio in Priora Aristotelis Analytica*, ed. Ari Wesseling (Leiden, 1986), pp. 3-4, with the commentary on pp. 22-26. Eobanus alludes to this passage also in *Praef.*, sig. C1ᵛ: "Vidistis, opinor, Angelum Policianum ... interspergere ... larvas et lamias cum exemptilibus oculis et id genus monstra."

85	**terrere paventes** For the hexameter close cf. Ov. *Met.* 2, 398 and 13, 230.
86-88	**Quas – talpas** Adapted in *Dial.* 2, sig. B4ʳ, where the lines take aim at the evangelical preachers in Erfurt.
87	**vigiles ... lynces** Lynxes were reputedly the most sharpsighted of all animals. See Plin. *Nat.* 28, 122.
91-92	**Lyncea ... Lumina** Petrarch, *Ecl.* 2, 107-108, referring to Argus: "lumina centum / Lincea"; Mant. *2. Parthen.* 3, 95, of Aristotle: "Lyncea in aethereos attollens lumina tractus"; Brant, *Var. carm.*, sig. g7ᵛ (*Texte* 175, 3). The adjective, derived from "lynx," is a medievalism. Cf. the classical "Lyncēus" (Ov. *Fast.* 5, 709), referring to the proverbially keen-sighted Argonaut Lynceus.
91	**qui** The masculine form (rather than the expected "quae") indicates that Argus associates the "vampires" with the oligarchs of Erfurt.
	per rura, per urbes = Claud. *Rapt. Pros.* 3, 326; Eob. *Idyl.* 17, 121.
92-93	**per plateas – diaetas** Cf. *Her. Chr.* 22, 56 (n.).
94	**ad unguem** = Hor. *S.* 1, 5, 32; *Ars* 294; Eob., *Epp. 4*, sig. F6ᵛ (1508), referring to Gerlach von der Marthen: "Novit et hoc ... ad unguem"; *Nup.* 67; 88; *Her. Chr.* 24, 163. The proverbial expression originally referred to the sculptor's test for perfect smoothness. See Otto 1827; Häussler, pp. 65, 80-81, 119, 220-221, and 290; Erasmus, *Adag.* 1, 5, 91.
95	**Livor, edax animal** Cf. *Laud.* 579 (n.): "Livor edax ..."; *Her. Chr.* B 1, 65.
99	**pecudes inter** = Calp. *Ecl.* 4, 44; cf. Eob. *Buc.* 1, 16 (n.).
	sub rupe iacerem Verg. *Ecl.* 10, 14; Eob. *Buc.* 7, 162; cf. *Buc.* 1, 46 (n.).
100-101	**Obscuram – sulphur** Cf. Verg. *G.* 2, 308-309; *A.* 3, 571-574; Sil. 14, 57.
100	**Obscuram ... flammam** Cf. Verg. *A.* 4, 384: "atris ignibus"; 8, 198-199; 11, 186; Hor. *Carm.* 4, 12, 26; *Epod.* 5, 82.
100-101	**flammam Surgere** Ov. *Ep.* 13, 114.
101	**summo ... vertice** = *Laud.* 133 (n.).
102-109	**Tum – recludunt** Cf. Stat. *Theb.* 2, 50-54 (of the supposed entrance to the underworld).
102-103	**Tum – aether** Cf. Verg. *A.* 11, 745 (12, 462); 11, 832-833; Eob. *Vict.* 141 (in hell): "Tum vero audisses tristes mugire cavernas / Mortifero gemitu."
102	**Tum vero** = Verg. *Ecl.* 6, 27; *G.* 3, 505; *A.* 1, 485; and often; Eob. *Her. Chr.* 12, 155.
	aereas ... ad auras = Ov. *Met.* 14, 127.

103   **clamoribus – aether** Cf. Ov. *Ars* 3, 375 (Eob. *Her. Chr.* 1, 93): "... resonat
           clamoribus aether"; Verg. *A.* 8, 239: "... intonat aether."
104   **Obstupui retroque** ≈ Verg. *A.* 2, 378. For "obstupui" at the hexameter opening
           see Verg. *A.* 2, 560; 2, 774; 3, 48; 3, 298; Ov. *Ep.* 16, 67; Eob. *Her. Chr.* 2, 63;
           4, 187; 12, 131; cf. *Her. Chr.* 9, 39; 14, 87.
105-106   **Ecce – inquit** Cf. Verg. *Ecl.* 7, 6-8. For the motif of looking for a lost animal see
           also Calp. *Ecl.* 3, 1-2; Mant. *Ecl.* 2, 53-56; Eob. *Buc.* 7, 1-4; 8, 111 (of Heliades,
           looking for a runaway bull).
105   **Ecce sed** = *Laud.* 178 (n.).
           in valle iuvencam ≈ Sil. 4, 310.
107   **Heu, fuge** = Line 13 above (n.).
           loca foeta = *Vict.* 133: "... putri loca foeta mephiti"; cf. Verg. *A.* 1, 51; Ov. *Met.*
           14, 103. For "loca foeta venenis" cf. Eob. *Buc.* 1, 80-81.
107-108   **venenis Tartareis** V. Fl. 7, 632; 8, 83.
108-109   **Nigri – Panditur** Cf. Prop. 4, 11, 2; Verg. *A.* 6, 127; Ov. *Fast.* 4, 449.
108   **Nigri ... Ditis** Ov. *Met.* 4, 438. In ancient Roman belief, Dis was the lord of the
           underworld. To maintain the play on words in line 113, I have rendered the
           name as "Pluto" (the Greek equivalent of Dis).
109   **Acheronta recludunt** Cf. Stat. *Theb.* 5, 156; cf. also Verg. *A.* 8, 244-245.
110   **Coge pecus** Verg. *Ecl.* 3, 20.
110-111   **graminis – Attigerit** Verg. *Ecl.* 5, 26. For the tag "graminis herbam" cf. Ov.
           Met. 10, 87; Eob. *Sylv. duae* 1, 85.
111   **pingui – arvo** Verg. *Ecl.* 3, 100, which Eobanus read as follows: "Eheu, quam
           pingui macer est mihi taurus in arvo"; see *Adnot.*, sig. B1ʳ; cf. Eob. *Buc.* 1, 8.
112   **Haec ubi** = Verg. *A.* 1, 81 (et al.): "Haec ubi dicta ..."; Claud. *Rapt. Pros.* 3, 137
           (likewise with ellipsis of the verb): "Haec ubi, digreditur templis ...."
           sylvam ... in altam Ov. *Am.* 3, 9, 23; 3, 10, 35; *Ep.* 11, 89; et al.
113   **dites** A play on words: "dites" are the filthy rich (plutocrats); but "Dis" (Pluto)
           is the god of the underworld (and hence of the treasures buried in the earth).
114   **Vidimus – carnes** Cf. Verg. *A.* 3, 626-627; Mant. *Ecl.* 2, 122: "[sunt qui]
           humanos absumant dentibus artus."
           fracta stipe Cf. Ov. *Fast.* 4, 350; *Pont.* 1, 1, 40; Eob. *Sylv.* 3, 21, 14: "exigua pro
           stipe."
115   **sine lege modoque** = Locher, *Stult.*, fol. 24ᵛ: "Quisquis amat, ratione caret; sine
           lege modoque / Discurrit"; fol. 27ᵛ; Eob. *Theoc.* 15, sig. E8ʳ: "Agmen ... sine
           lege modoque / Immensum."
117-118   **Frigida – agnas** Cf. Nemes. *Ecl.* 2, 88-90: "Sic ... canebant / frigidus e silvis
           donec descendere suasit / Hesperus et stabulis pastos inducere tauros"; Mant.
           Ecl. 3, 192-194; Eob. *Buc.* 11, 109-111 (with notes). For the concluding motif
           see n. *Buc.* 1, 124.
117   **Frigida nox** Hor. *Carm.* 3, 7, 6-7; Man. 2, 421; Eob. *Nup.* 334-335.
           thauros ... pastos Verg. *Ecl.* 7, 39.
118   **errantes ... agnas** = *Buc.* 11, 1; cf. Calp. *Ecl.* 5, 15.
           ovilibus agnas ≈ *Buc.* 8, 12.

5

Two shepherds compete for a prize by singing in responsive stanzas. This form of bucolic verse, known as "amoebean contest," goes back to Theoc. 5. Eobanus's immediate models, however, were Vergil's third and seventh eclogues; see also Calp. *Ecl.* 2, *Ecl. Theoduli*, Bocc. *Ecl.* 13, Boiardo, *Ecl.* 3, and Gerald. *Ecl.* 5 (a poem concerning Christ's miracles).

Meter: Hexameter.

1-17	**Pastores – honores** The model is Verg. *Ecl.* 7, 1-19. For lines 1-6 cf. also Calp. *Ecl.* 2, 1-7. For the "motif of bucolic repose" see n. *Buc.* 1, 65-71.
1	**Pastores – ulmo** Cf. Verg. *Ecl.* 5, 1-3; Eob. *Idyl.* 10, 3: "Pastores duo conveniunt de montibus ...."
	viridi ... ulmo *Buc.* 6, 52.
2	**pictas ... ripas** Cf. Prop. 1, 2, 13.
	ubi plurima = Verg. *A.* 12, 690; Stat. *Theb.* 10, 59; Eob. *Buc.* 7, 3; 8, 112.
2-3	**plurima ... unda** = Verg. *G.* 4, 419-420.
3	**dulces ... unda susurros** Cf. Mant. *1. Parthen.* 2, 736-737: "nitidis e fontibus undae / volvebant dulces cursu crepitante susurros"; Eob. *Ruf.* 55: "Qua dulci veniens admurmuret unda susurro."
4-5	**Una – parati** Cf. *Buc.* 3, 96 (n.).
4	**Una – erat** ≈ Mant. 1. Parthen. 2, 806: "Una aetas ambobus erit ...."
	formosus uterque = Ov. *Met.* 9, 713; *Fast.* 2, 395.
5	**certare parati** = Verg. *A.* 5, 108; Mant. *Ecl.* 10, 3.
6	**studio intenti** *Her. Chr.* 11, 83 (n.).
	calamosque ligabant After cutting the reeds of their panpipes to the right length, shepherds fasten them together with wax. See Verg. *Ecl.* 2, 32; 3, 25-26; Tib. 2, 5, 32; Ov. *Met.* 1, 711-712; Calp. *Ecl.* 3, 26; 4, 19-20; Nemes. *Ecl.* 1, 58; lines 36-37 below.
7	**Tranquillus – supervenit** For the motif of the umpire who happens to come by see Verg. *Ecl.* 3, 50; 7, 8-10; Calp. *Ecl.* 6, 28.
8	**Ut ... videre** = Verg. *A.* 8, 107.
	prior ... inquit Verg. *A.* 1, 321.
9-11	**Huc – sylvas** Cf. *Ecl. Theoduli* 28-29, to the umpire Fronesis ("Prudence"): "huc ades, o Fronesis! nam sufficit hora diei, / ut tua iam nostro postponas seria ludo."
9	**Huc ades, o** = Verg. *Ecl.* 7, 9 (addressed to the umpire); Eob. *Buc.* 3, 159 (n.).
	Pecus – umbra At noontime, the herd seeks relief from the heat in the shade or by a stream. For the motif cf. Verg. *Ecl.* 2, 8; *G.* 3, 327-334; Calp. *Ecl.* 5, 56-59; Eob. *Buc.* 1, 57-59; 7, 72-73; 10, 48-49.
	dormit in umbra = *Buc.* 11, 86.
10	**Huc ades et** = Tib. 1, 7, 49; 3, 10, 1; Ov. *Am.* 1, 6, 54; 3, 2, 46; et al.; Eob. *Buc.* 5, 108; 7, 122; cf. *Buc.* 3, 159 (n.).
	iudex certaminis = Bocc. *Ecl.* 13, 70: "Sed quis erit ... iudex certaminis huius?"; cf. Calp. *Ecl.* 2, 9.
11	**tua – sylvas** The motif of praising the umpire is foreign to idyllic pastoral, but recurs in the allegorical variety. See in particular Mant. *Ecl.* 10, 6-12 (praise of the umpire Bembus).
12-14	**Audaces ... audatia ... temeraria** Cf. Ov. *Met.* 10, 544-545: "in audaces non est audacia tuta. / parce meo, iuvenis, temerarius esse periclo." For the thought cf. Eob. *Buc.* 10, 120; *Her. Chr.* 5, 164; *Hod.* 72-73: "prudens audacia laudem / Inveniet."
12	**Audaces pueri** ≈ Stat. *Theb.* 12, 127.
	pueriliter ausi ≈ *Psalt.*, ded. 43.
13	**Alternis – modis** Cf. Verg. *Ecl.* 3, 59; 7, 18; *Cat.* 9, 19; Stat. *Silv.* 1, 2, 248;

Calp. *Ecl.* 2, 25; 4, 79; 6, 2; Eob. *Buc.* 3, 112-113 (n.); 4, 2-3; 10, 12; 10, 160-161.

Alternis ... modis = Arator, *Epistola ad Vigilium* 21.

audatia laus est Prop. 2, 10, 5-6.

15   **Quae – ergo** Cf. Verg. *Ecl.* 3, 31; Eob. *Buc.* 5, 18; 5, 57; 10, 7. For the practice of putting up stakes and praising one's own contribution see Theoc. 5, 21-30; 8, 11-24; Verg. *Ecl.* 3, 29-48; Calp. *Ecl.* 2, 7-8; 6, 32-57.

16   **Ipse ego ... flumina** ≈ Verg. *A.* 8, 57.

quandoquidem = Verg. *Ecl.* 3, 55 (the umpire speaks): "Dicite, quandoquidem in molli consedimus herba ..."; Mant. *Ecl.* 10, 13 (the umpire speaks): "Dicite, quandoquidem tepidos admovit ad ignes / nos hiberna dies ...."

stant – thauri = *Theoc.* 1, sig. A6ʳ.

17   **meritos ... honores** = Verg. *A.* 3, 264; 8, 189; Ov. *Met.* 13, 594; cf. Eob. *Nup.* 275 (n.).

largibor honores ≈ Hor. *Ep.* 2, 1, 15.

18   **Hunc tibi** = Lucr. 6, 225; Verg. *A.* 8, 514; Ov. *Met.* 13, 855.

lunatum ... arcum Mant. *Georgius,* fol. 202ᵛ, at this metrical position: "lunato ... arcu"; cf. Ov. *Am.* 1, 1, 23: "lunavit ... arcum."

19   **stipite pomi** = *Ecl. Theoduli* 51.

20   **Foecimus hiis manibus** Cf. *Theoc.* 8, sig. D1ᵛ: "fecimus illam [fistulam] / Iam pridem his manibus"; also cf. Calp. *Ecl.* 3, 76.

torno Verg. *Ecl.* 3, 38 (in similar context); *G.* 2, 449.

21   **Distinctum – bubulis** Cf. Ov. *Pont.* 1, 2, 19.

visco ... tenaci Var. *Men.* 27.

23   **Herculeis ... sagittis** ≈ V. Fl. 1, 393; 5, 136; Stat. *Theb.* 10, 261. Hercules' arrows always hit their mark; see Sen. *Her. O.* 1650-1659; Brant, *NS* 75, 53-56.

ferit ille = Verg. *Ecl.* 9, 25.

24   **quot – numerare** Cf. *Her. Chr.* 16, 79.

non est numerare = Ov. *Tr.* 3, 12, 25.

26   **Saepe – lepores** ≈ Calp. *Ecl.* 3, 77.

capreasque fugaces Cf. Verg. *A.* 10, 724-725; Ov. *Met.* 1, 442.

27-28   **Phillirides – Achilli** Cf. Ov. *Ars* 1, 11.

27   **caelatus** For the motif cf. lines 49-54 below; Theoc. 1, 28-56; Verg. *Ecl.* 3, 37 and 3, 45-46.

28   **Spicula ... pharetra** = Ov. *Ars* 3, 516.

32   **invidit – Adonis** Cf. Verg. *Ecl.* 2, 39.

33   **mecum – certes** Cf. Verg. *Ecl.* 4, 58; cf. also *Ecl.* 2, 57 (different).

34-54   **En ista – nymphae** Imitated by Cordus, *Buc.* 2, 5-20 (*Ecl.* 3, 5-28), describing the flute bought from Battus (Eobanus Hessus) for four fleeces and a lamb. In the 1518-edition Cordus raises the price to seven fleeces, a lamb, and a large cheese. Made of boxwood, the instrument is delicately carved with an image of Phoebus amidst the Muses.

34   **pendet – pinu** Cf. Verg. *Ecl.* 7, 24; Tib. 2, 5, 29-30; Nemes. *Ecl.* 1, 14; 3, 5. A flute is also put up as the stake in the singing contests of [Theoc.] 8 (not known to Eobanus until much later) and *Ecl. Theoduli* 18.

36   **calamis – cicutis** Cf. Verg. *Ecl.* 2, 36-37; Ov. *Met.* 13, 784. For "cicutis" (reeds made from the stem of hemlock) see also Lucr. 5, 1383; Verg. *Ecl.* 5, 85; Calp. *Ecl.* 7, 12; Eob. *Buc.* 10, 4; 10, 19.

37   **cera connexa** See note to line 6 above.

38   **Pan – poetas** Pan was the inventor and first teacher of the syrinx (panpipe); see Ov. *Met.* 1, 689-712; Verg. *Ecl.* 2, 32-33. He is "impius" because he attempted to rape the nymph Syrinx. However, she was changed into reeds before he could

carry out his plan.

Pan deus = Verg. *Ecl.* 10, 26; *G.* 3, 392.

agrestes – poetas Cf. Lucr. 5, 1383.

docuit resonare Verg. *Ecl.* 1, 5.

39   **buxo tornata** Cf. Verg. *G.* 2, 449. For "buxus" in the sense "boxwood flute" see Verg. *A.* 9, 619; Ov. *Met.* 4, 30; 12, 158; et al.; Eob. *Buc.* 10, 6 (n.).

41   **Longa – foecit** Cf. Calp. *Ecl.* 1, 26; also cf. Ov. *Met.* 11, 793.

42-43   **Hanc – capellam** Cf. Theoc. 1, 57-58 (the beautifully carved bowl was bought with a goat and a large cheese).

42   **Hanc ego** = Verg. *A.* 9, 287.

43   **raptamque – capellam** Cf. Verg. *A.* 7, 484.

44-48   **Hac – flatu** As soon as Floridus plays his flute, all nature blooms and listens intently. Cf. Calp. *Ecl.* 2, 10-20; 4, 60-67, of the flute that once belonged to Tityrus (Vergil).

44   **Hac – alto** ≈ *Idyl.* 11, 26: "Haec ubi personuit scopulo vocalis ab alto"; cf. Petr. 122, 177: "Haec ubi personuit ..."; Eob. *Buc.* 1, 83-84 (n.).

    scopulo ... alto = Ov. *Tr.* 3, 9, 29.

45   **Floruit omne nemus** Cf. Verg. *Ecl.* 7, 59; Eob. *Rec.* 5 (n.).

    omne nemus = Verg. *A.* 5, 149; 8, 305; Ov. *Met.* 3, 44; Eob. *Buc.* 9, 40; cf. *Buc.* 7, 109 (n.); *Sylv. duae* 1, 102 (n.).

45-46   **flores – humus** Cf. Verg. *Ecl.* 9, 41; Eob. *Ilias* 14, p. 362: "florum genus omne ... / Fundebat genialis humus."

46-47   **gravis – ibat** For the motif cf. Theoc. 2, 38; Verg. *Ecl.* 9, 57-58; Hor. *Carm.* 1, 12, 9-10; Calp. *Ecl.* 2, 16.

47   **Spirabant Zephiri** Verg. *A.* 4, 562.

    Zephiri ... Favonius Cf. *Buc.* 7, 152.

48   **circum – tempora** = Ov. *Am.* 2, 12, 1.

50   **Cernis ut** = *Buc.* 4, 50 (n.).

51   **Daemens – certamina** Cf. Verg. *A.* 6, 172, of Misenus.

53   **Misenum in littore** = Verg. *A.* 6, 162 and 212.

54   **Arrident ... nymphae** Cf. Verg. *Ecl.* 3, 9; Hor. *Carm.* 2, 8, 13-14.

    cava littora = Pontano, *Ecl.* 1, 2, 76; 1, 3, 13; cf. Eob. *Buc.* 9, 54.

55   **tecum deponimus** Verg. *Ecl.* 3, 32.

56   **Quis prior incipiat** Cf. Cordus, *Buc.* 4, 55 (*Ecl.* 1, 83): "Tu prior incipias ..."; Eob. *Buc.* 5, 60 (n.).

57   **Ludite – dictum** Cf. Verg. *Ecl.* 3, 111; 6, 24; also cf. line 112 below.

58-60   **Ludite – Incipe** Imitated by Cordus, *Ecl.* 3, 40-42: "Aspicis ut summae motare cacumina silvae / cessant ...? / Incipe." For lines 58-59 cf. Verg. *Ecl.* 6, 27-28.

58   **ut incipiant – sylvae** Quoted in *Dial.* 3, sig. C3ᵛ.

    incipiant ... sylvae Verg. *Ecl.* 6, 39; Eob. *Buc.* 6, 8-9.

    cacumina sylvae = Ov. *Met.* 1, 346; *Fast.* 2, 439; 3, 329.

59   **Blandaque – nymphae** Cf. *Sylv.* 2, 12, 15, referring to Vergil: "Cuius blanda novem saltant ad plectra sorores."

    Blanda ... carmina Stat. *Theb.* 8, 58.

    ad carmina nymphae = Pontano, *Ecl.* 1, 72: "at circum attonitae stupuere ad carmina nymphae"; 1, 5, 67: "... sociae plaudunt ad carmina nymphae."

60   **Incipe – aetas** Cf. Alcuin. *Carm.* 57, 4: "Incipe tu, senior ... Menalca, prior."

    Incipe ... prior = Verg. *Ecl.* 5, 10: "Incipe, Mopse, prior ..."; cf. *Ecl.* 3, 58; Calp. *Ecl.* 2, 27; 4, 81; Eob. *Buc.* 4, 75, with note to lines 75-76; 5, 56 (n.).

    tua ... dignior aetas = Verg. *A.* 9, 212; Eob. *Idyl.* 13, 14: "tua dignior aetas / Pace fuit."

61   **Dicite – Musae** Cf. *Theoc.* 19, sig. G5ᵛ: "Dicite, Sicelides, lugentes dicite

Musae." Each singer repeats the opening and concluding verses from stanza to
stanza. For the refrain see n. *Buc.* 2, 15.

Dicite, Pierides, ... dicite = Filetico, *Theoc.* 1, 64 (the opening line of Thyrsis's
song): "Dicite, Pierides, pastorum dicite cantus"; cf. Verg. *Ecl.* 8, 63; [Tib.] 3,
1, 5; Ov. *Ars* 2, 1; *Fast.* 2, 269; 6, 799.

certantes ... Musae Cf. *Idyl.* 17, 138: "... certantes secum deducere Musas";
Theoc. 1, sig. A4ʳ: "si pro pignore Musae / Certantes mereantur ovem."

62-64   **Quis fuit – regnum** Cf. Mant. *2. Parthen.* 3, 38-40: "Quis fuit ante Iovem [*cf.
line 62*], qui lucida volveret astra [*cf. line 63*]? / Qui regeret coeli cursum, qui
clauderet undas / Littore, qui laeto vestiret gramine campos [*cf. lines 92-93*]?"
Vernus's praise of God in these and the following lines influenced Cordus,
Ecl. 7, 148-153: "Quis iubet eruptis segetes assurgere glebis? / Quis volucres
tenui suspendit in aere nubes? / Quis pluviam decribrat aquam? Quis fulmina
mittit? / Denique quis tantae sustentat pondera terrae, / ne cadat et medias ne
praecipitemur in undas? / Unus ab antiquo qui talia providet aevo."

62   **ante cahos** Prud. *Amart.* 44 (of Christ): "Ante chaos genitus."

         prima exordia = Verg. *A.* 4, 284.

63   **Quis mare – foecit** ≈ Prud. *Apoth.* 153: "qui mare, qui terras, qui lucida sidera
fecit." Cf. Eob. *Hod.* 43.

         Quis ..., quis lucida sydera = Mant. *Mort.*, fol. 119ᵛ: "Quis regit hos orbes? quis
lucida sydera torquet?" For "lucida sydera" see also Eob. *Buc.* 7, 101 (n.).

64   **contrahit omnia** = Luc. 9, 776.

66   **faciles ... Camaenae** *Laud.* 65 (n.).

67-68   **Virginis ... Christophorae** Cf. *Her. Chr.* 6, 187 (n.): "Christiferae ... puellae."
The epithet "Christophorae" is a Graecism for "Christifer," formed after the
name of St. Christopher ("Christ-bearer").

67   **Virginis intactae** = Aldh. *De laudibus virginum, PL* 89, col. 271 D; Hrotsv.
Maria 536; *Theoph.* 196; cf. Catul. 62, 45.

         castum ... amorem *Laud.* 240 (n.).

         referemus amorem ≈ Ov. *Met.* 4, 170.

68   **genialis – lecti** For the paraphrase cf. *Her. Chr.* 7, 152 (n.). For "genialis lecti"
see, for example, Hor. *Ep.* 1, 1, 87; Eob. *Nup.* 79.

69   **arcano ... semine** Paul. Nol. *Carm.* 18, 187; cf. Eob. *Her. Chr.* 2, 104; 22, 18.

         conceptum semine ≈ Col. 10, 144: "... concepto semine partum"; Mant. *1.
Parthen.* 1, 308 (the Virgin): "... concepto semine Mater"; cf. Ov. *Met.* 10, 328.

         semine natum ≈ Lucr. 2, 733; Cic. *Div.* 1, 20.

72   **Quis – molem** Cf. *Her. Chr.* 18, 116. For "molem" in the sense "moles mundi"
see Lucr. 5, 96; 6, 567.

         terminat orbem = *Sylv.* 2, 7, 39: "... Teutonicum qua Prussia terminat orbem."

73   **rutilum ... ignem** Verg. *G.* 1, 454; *A.* 8, 430; Ov. *Ep.* 3, 64; *Met.* 4, 403; 11, 436
(lightning bolts).

         fissis ... nubibus For the image cf. Lucr. 6, 203; Verg. *A.* 3, 199; Stat. *Theb.* 12,
709-710; Eob. *Her. Chr.* 13, 100.

         iaculatur nubibus ignem ≈ Verg. *A.* 1, 42; Stat. *Theb.* 7, 158.

74   **aeterna – ratione** ≈ Man. 1, 64; cf. Boeth. *Consol.* 3, m. 9, 1.

77   **Vidit et incaluit** = Ov. *Met.* 2, 574; 3, 371; *Fast.* 2, 307; cf. *Met.* 2, 641; Eob.
Her. Chr. 6, 125.

78   **Nobilis ... Virgo** Hor. *Carm.* 3, 11, 35-36; Prud. *Cath.* 11, 53.

         flagravit For the image cf. Brant, *Var. carm.*, sig. A8ʳ (*Texte* 103, 87-88),
comparing Mary to the burning bush (Vulg. *Exod.* 3, 2): "Flagrat et intactum
permansit ab igne rubetum? / Urit amor matrem nec tamen igne perit."

         nomine Virgo = Ov. *Pont.* 3, 2, 81.

79   **Ut – horto** Cf. *Her. Chr.* 1, 154. The Virgin Mary is traditionally compared to
            a flower in an enclosed garden. The image goes back to the Mariological
            interpretation of Vulg. *Cant.* 2, 1-2; 4, 14 (flower) and *Cant.* 4, 12 (enclosed
            garden). See further Salzer, pp. 14-15 and 145-150 (Mary as flower); pp. 15-16
            and 281-284 (Mary as garden). See also Eob. *Buc.* 11, 31-33.
            pingui ... horto Verg. *G.* 4, 118.

82-83   **Quis prohibet – arctum** Cf. Vulg. *Job* 26, 8-9.

82   **Quis prohibet – torquet** Cf. Mant. *Ecl.* 3, 12: "Nescio quis ventos tempesta-
            tesque gubernat."
            ventos ... rauca tonitrua = *Nor.* 286.
            Quis rauca – torquet ≈ *Ilias* 1, p. 27: "Iuppiter omnipotens, qui rauca tonitrua
            torquet." For "rauca tonitrua" at this metrical position see Stat. *Theb.* 2, 40. For
            "tonitrua torquet" cf. the standard phrase "fulmina torquet" (Verg. *A.* 4, 208;
            Ov. *Pont.* 3, 6, 27; and often).

83   **Quis nebulam spargit?** August. *Enarrationes in Psa.*, 147, 2 (*CCSL* 40): "quis
            nebulam spargit, nisi Deus?"; cf. Vulg. *Psa.* 147, 16: "Qui dat nivem sicut
            lanam, Nebulam sicut cinerem spargit"; Hor. *Carm.* 3, 15, 6.
            Quis nubes – arctum ≈ *Ilias* 14, p. 362, of Jupiter: "... qui nubes densat in
            arctum." For the phrase "nubes denset" cf. Verg. *G.* 1, 419.

84   **Unus qui** = Verg. *A.* 6, 846; Ov. *Ars* 2, 646.
            rerum discrimina = Luc. 4, 104.

87-88   **Dum – Errat** Cf. *Her. Chr.* 4, 105-106, of St. Catherine of Alexandria. Both
            Catherine and Mary become the bride of Christ and weave their own bridal
            garlands.
            sola – Errat Cf. Verg. *G.* 3, 249; Ov. *Ars* 2, 473; *Met.* 7, 534-535; Eob. *Buc.* 1,
            122; 3, 118-119 (n.).

88-89   **ab Eoa – tumorem** The image recalls the familiar verses edited in *AH* 54, 221,
            3: "Auster lenis te perflavit / Et perflando fecundavit." See also *AH* 54, 219, 7;
            54, 273, 7.

88   **perflavit – aura** Cf. *Her. Chr.* 4, 157 (in a paradisiacal landscape). The image is
            based on Vulg. *Luc.* 1, 35: "Spiritus sanctus superveniet in te."
            Spiritus aura = Man. 1, 818; cf. Ov. *Met.* 8, 524; 12, 517.

89   **afflata** Cf. Mant. *1. Parthen.* 2, 666-667: "Virginis aures / aliger afflavit caelesti
            nuntii ore"; Eob. *Buc.* 8, 116 (n.).
            tumorem = Mant. *1. Parthen.* 2, 878, referring to Christ in the womb: "nec
            celare tumorem / cura fuit: numquam fecundi pondera ventris / dissimulavit."

92   **has segetes** = Verg. *Ecl.* 1, 71.
            campum ... arista Verg. *Ecl.* 4, 28.
            campum pingit Cf. Ven. Fort. *Carm.* 3, 9, 11: "mollia purpureum pingunt
            violaria campum"; Eob. *Epic.* 6, 41: "Aurea foelicem pingunt violaria
            campum"; cf. further Lucr. 5, 1396; Ov. *Fast.* 4, 430; Eob. *Her.* 3, 8, 80:
            "florigeram gratia pingat humum."

93   **frondibus ornat** ≈ Ov. *Met.* 6, 163: "... sua tempora frondibus ornant."

94   **propria ... virtute** = *Wirt.* 38; cf. *Ecl. Theoduli* 349 (in many mss.): "Quique
            regis cuncta propria virtute sub una"; Eob. *Idyl.* 4, 110: "Omnia nanque potes
            propria virtute ...."
            virtute secundum = Verg. *A.* 5, 258; cf. Eob. *Rec.* 156 (n.).

97   **Interea dulci** ≈ Verg. *G.* 2, 523.
            dulci – venter Cf. Mart. 14, 151; Eob. *Her. Chr.* 13, 129.
            tumuit ... venter Ov. *Met.* 10, 505.

99   **Virgineum – pudorem** Cf. Paul. Nol. *Carm.* 6, 112: "virgo [Maria] inlibatum
            servabat casta pudorem"; 32, 82: "... castum servare pudorem"; Ov. *Met.* 13,

480: "... castique decus servare pudoris." For "virgineum pudorem" see Tib. 1, 4, 14; Stat. *Theb.* 12, 205; *Ach.* 1, 765; Eob. *Her. Chr.* 4, 131; 13, 97.

102   **Quis veteres faunos** Cf. Verg. *A.* 7, 254.

          trusit ad umbras Cf. Verg. *A.* 7, 773.

103   **numina ... deorum** = Ov. *Ep.* 2, 43.

104   **Unus – gubernat** Cf. Nikolaus Marschalk, *Enchiridion poetarum clarissimorum* (Erfurt, 1502), vol. 1, sig. A5ʳ ("Ex Orpheo"): "Unus perfectus deus est qui cuncta creavit"; Brant, *Var. carm.*, sig. d2ʳ (*Texte* 147, 35): "Unus enim solus Deus et rex cuncta gubernans."

          qui cuncta gubernat = Man. 4, 892; Celtis, *Am.* 4, 14, 55; cf. Mant. *Ecl.* 6, 192: "... qui cuncta gubernant."

107   **pia ... Virgo** Ov. *Pont.* 3, 2, 81; Paul. Nol. *Carm.* 6, 151 (Mary). The phrase is often applied to Mary; see Salzer, p. 361; Eob. *Buc.* 11, 50; *Hod.* B 7, 11.

          coronae See Vulg. *Apoc.* 12, 1, traditionally interpreted to refer to Mary's crown. See further Eob. *Buc.* 11, 91-92 (n.).

108   **Huc ades et** = Line 10 above (n.).

          floribus arvum ≈ Ven. Fort. *Carm.* 9, 3, 7.

109   **Fistula – silebit** Cf. Nemes. *Ecl.* 1, 80: sooner will the impossible happen "quam taceat ... tuas mea fistula laudes."

111-116 **Sit satis – thauros** The umpire stops the singing-match and declares both contestants winners. For the motif and the wording cf. Verg. *Ecl.* 3, 108-111 and Calp. *Ecl.* 2, 98-100; cf. also Bocc. *Ecl.* 13, 147-150: "Iurgia pastorum non est compescere parvum: / et tu dignus eras vitula, tu dignus et hyrco. / Sat dictum, pueri: duras componite lites; / ibo ego nunc agnis tonsuris forfice lanam"; Eob. *Buc.* 8, 127-130.

111   **Sit – suadet** Cf. Mant. *Ecl.* 10, 187-188 (the umpire Bembus ends the debate): "Parcite; iam satis est lis intellecta diesque / inclinata cadit, iam post iuga summa ruit sol." For the motif (the poem ends with the close of day) see Eob. *Buc.* 1, 124 (n.).

          Sit satis = *Ama.* 36, 2 (n.).

          suadet Cf. Verg. *A.* 2, 9: "suadentque cadentia sidera somnos"; Nemes. *Ecl.* 2, 89-90.

112   **Claudite – cannas** ≈ *Epith.* 245: "Claudite vocales, Nymphae, iam claudite cantus"; cf. Verg. *Ecl.* 3, 111; 6, 55-56; also cf. line 57 above.

113   **Vicit uterque** Hier. *Ep.* 77, 10: "Vicit uterque, et uterque superatus est. Ambo se victos et victores fatentur." Cf. Gerald. *Ecl.* 5, 148 (at the end of an amoebean contest): "Victores ambo ...."

114   **Vos – aetas** Cf. *Buc.* 3, 96 (n.); 5, 4-5.

116   **concordes** = Calp. *Ecl.* 2, 99 (cf. note to lines 111-116 above).

          pascite thauros ≈ Verg. *Ecl.* 3, 86; cf. Eob. *Buc.* 8, 130.

6

The poem was first edited by Karl Gillert in Mutian. *Ep.* 148.
      Meter: Hexameter.

1   **Ocnaeo** *Buc.* 3, 18 (n.).

2   **longo ... intervallo** Verg. *A.* 5, 320; Eob. *Her. Chr.* 22, 69.

          Andinas *Laud.* 458 (n.).

3-5   **Modo – vetet** Cf. Sedul. 1, 97-98: "silvamque patentem / Ingrediens aliquos nitor contingere ramos."

3   **sylvas ... patenteis** *Rec.* 5 (n.).

4	**colurnas** Verg. *G.* 2, 396.
5	**arbusta – myricas** Cf. Verg. *Ecl.* 4, 2; Eob. *Idyl.* 13, 3-4: "Si vestrum decuit teneras sprevisse myricas / Tityron et cecinisse suas in consule sylvas ...."
6	**nimium nimiumque** = *Ama.* 35, 49 (n.).
7	**patrios agros** *Buc.* 1, 122 (n.).
8-9	**Nunc – resonare** Eobanus is now fulfilling his earlier promise to celebrate Mutianus in pastoral song. See *Laud.* 280-284.
8	**nostrae ... sylvae** *Buc.* 1, 24 (n.).
8-9	**sylvae Incipient** Verg. *Ecl.* 6, 39; Eob. *Buc.* 5, 58.
9	**ignoscite, Musae** = Ov. *Trist.* 5, 7, 55.
10-11	**quo se ... tantum Iactat** = Mant. *Ecl.* 4, 246-247: "senex, quo se vetus Umbria tantum / iactat"; cf. Verg. *Ecl.* 6, 73; Eob. *Laud.* 456-459 (n.); *Buc.*, ded. 23.
	rustica ... Musa *Buc.*, lim. 1 (n.).
11	**te, Tityre** = Verg. *Ecl.* 1, 38. Here Tityrus is Vergil himself. For this identification see *Buc.* 3, 15-16, with fn. 28.
12-14	**Non tu – notissime** Mutianus is invited to enter the world of shepherds and singers; that is, he is exhorted to publish pastoral poetry of his own. Cf. Verg. *Ecl.* 10, 17, addressed to the urbane poet Gallus: "nec te paeniteat pecoris, divine poeta." As Servius comments, "allegoricos hoc dicit: nec tu erubescas bucolica scribere."
12	**Non – montes** Cf. Calp. *Ecl.* 4, 88.
13	**Et – sacras** Cf. *Buc.* 1, 22 (n.).
	habitare – silentes Cf. *Epp.* 4, sig. F7ᵛ (25 May 1508): "... lucos habitare silentes"; Verg. *Ecl.* 10, 58; *G.* 1, 476; 4, 364.
14	**Rufe – notissime** Cf. *Epic.* 4, 59: "Rufe, per Hessiacos quondam notissime colles."
	Aonios colles = Sid. *Carm.* 22, 96; cf. Eob. *Hod.* 238.
15	**Cictiaco** Literally, "of Citium (Cittium)," the seaport in Cyprus where the Stoic philosopher Zeno was born. The epithet is a neologism for "Cittiensis." In the 1528/39 version Eobanus changed it to "Socratico."
	dulcem ... vitam Lucr. 2, 997; 3, 66; Catul. 64, 157; Verg. *A.* 6, 428; Eob. *Buc.* 6, 85.
	trutinas – vitam Cf. *Anthol. Lat.* 644, 9 ("De viro bono"): "... iusto trutinae se examine pendit"; Eob. *Buc.* 8, 89; *Tum.* 2, 5: "Indicis excusso trutinare examine librae."
16	**Ingredere et ... assuesce** = Verg. *G.* 1, 42.
	sylvis ... iugosis = Ov. *Ep.* 4, 85; cf. *Am.* 1, 1, 9.
17-30	**En tibi – serenet** Cf. *Ruf.* 99-104: "Vernat humus meliore nemus clangore resultat, / Dum venis, ergo veni. / Adventus rus omne tuos presentit et omni / Se parat arte tibi. / Ut venias te prata rogant et vernus Apollo / Pieridumque chorus." As soon as Mutianus enters this pastoral landscape, all nature rejoices. Cf. Calp. *Ecl.* 4, 132-136; 4, 97-111; Eob. *Buc.* 11, 24-27 (n.).
17-19	**En tibi – Omnis** For this description of springtime cf. Verg. *Ecl.* 3, 56-57; Eob. *Buc.* 1, 1-6 (with notes).
17	**omnia pleno** ≈ Lucr. 1, 376; 4, 162; et al.; Verg. *Ecl.* 3, 60; *G.* 1, 371; 2, 4.
18	**Fundit ... tellus** Verg. *Ecl.* 4, 19-20; *G.* 1, 13; 2, 460; cf. *Ecl.* 9, 41.
	aperta For the meaning cf. Ov. *Fast.* 4, 87: "ver aperit tunc omnia, densaque cedit / frigoris asperitas, fetaque terra patet."
18-19	**tibi – Omnis** Cf. Ov. *Met.* 13, 820; Verg. *Ecl.* 3, 56.
18	**germinat arbos** = Calp. *Ecl.* 4, 111; Eob. *Nor.* 1239; cf. *Her. Chr.* 23, 77.
19-20	**lilia ... vernantia** Col. 10, 270; Eob. *Buc.* 11, 42; cf. *Buc.* 2, 89 (n.).
21	**gelidi fontes** = Verg. *Ecl.* 10, 42; *Lydia* 17.

fontes manant Ov. *Met.* 9, 664-665.

rupibus altis = Verg. *G.* 3, 273; Ov. *Ep.* 7, 37; Eob. *Vict.* 73; *Sylv.* 2, 29, 29.

22   **Frigida ... flumina** Verg. *Ecl.* 5, 25; Hor. *Epod.* 13, 13-14.

flumina lapsu = Claud. *in Rufin.* 1, 159.

23   **Per ... amaena silentia** Stat. *Silv.* 2, 6, 100; Eob. *Ruf.* 9.

virides ripas ≈ Aus. *Mosella* 141; cf. Verg. *Ecl.* 7, 12; *G.* 4, 121; Ov. *Met.* 2, 371.

24-25   **fugit – serpens** For the motif, with its implicit promise of a new golden age, see
          n. *Buc.* 1, 81.

24   **omnibus omnis** = Lucr. 1, 876; cf. Eob. *Nup.* 302; cf. Lucr. 4, 708 (Eob. *Nob.*
          133): "... omnibus omnes"; Eob. *Buc.* 1, 5 (n.).

26   **Siculam ... Hyblen** ≈ Ov. *Ib.* 197; cf. Eob. *Her. Chr.* 17, 125. Mount Hybla in
          Sicily was proverbial for its bees; see n. *Laud.* 107.

27   **lascivit humus** Geoffrey of Vinsauf, *Poetria nova* 906, in: *The* Poetria nova *and
          its Sources in Early Rhetorical Doctrine*, ed. Ernest Gallo (The Hague, 1971),
          p. 60.

29   **Aspice quam** = Prop. 1, 17, 6; Ov. *Fast.* 1, 104; Eob. *Buc.* 9, 85; *Her. Chr.* B 1,
          35; *Hod.* B 1, 5.

toto – anno Cf. Verg. *Ecl.* 7, 43.

30   **splendore serenet** = Vegius, *Aen.* 458: "Titan / ... aurato caelum splendore
          serenet"; cf. Eob. *Theoc.* 4, sig. B7ʳ: "[Iupiter] ... claro coelum splendore
          serenat."

31-32   **Hoc erat – Optabam** Cf. Verg. *A.* 12, 259; Ov. *Met.* 11, 694; Eob. *Idyl.* 3, 137:
          "Hoc erat, o superi, quod vos ego saepe rogabam."

31   **Hoc erat, hoc** = *Her. Chr.* 12, 213.

saepe per agros = Ov. *Met.* 14, 397.

33   **Saxa – rupes** Cf. *Nor.* 477: "Antra salebrosas subter squalentia rupes." Notice
          the alliteration.

Saxa ... squalentia Petr. 120, 74.

salebrosas ... rupes Cf. *Her. Chr.* 10, 173 (n.).

34   **pratis ... virentibus** Aus. *Ep.* 24, 85.

35   **assiduo – carmine** Cf. Verg. *Aen.* 7, 12: "adsiduo resonat cantu."

resonantem ... Rufum Cf. Verg. *Ecl.* 1, 5.

37-38   **Dum nemora – manebunt** For this assurance of perpetuity cf., for example,
          Tib. 1, 4, 65-66; Verg. *Ecl.* 5, 76-78; *A.* 1, 607-609. For the closely related type
          "sooner will something unchangeable come to an end than ..." see Eob. *Her.
          Chr.* 8, 53-54.

37   **Dum ... sylvae stabunt** = Bocc. *Ecl.* 7, 107.

nemora et sylvae = Ov. *Am.* 3, 6, 84.

dum flumina current ≈ Ov. *Met.* 8, 558.

38   **mare ... tellus** = Lucr. 1, 1014; Ov. *Met.* 1, 257; *Pont.* 1, 10, 9.

ventus et aura Ov. *Am.* 1, 8, 106; *Ib.* 106.

40-43   **Ipsa – stupidis** The model is Verg. *Ecl.* 8, 1-5.

40   **armenta feraeque** = Lucr. 2, 343; 2, 921; 4, 1197; 5, 228.

41   **avidi ... lupi** Ov. *Tr.* 1, 1, 78; Stat. *Theb.* 11, 30.

sevique leones = *Her. Chr.* 19, 125; cf. Lucr. 3, 306.

43   **Auribus ... stupidis** *Laud.* 299 (n.).

Auribus accipient Ov. *Met.* 10, 62-63; *Tr.* 4, 1, 90; Calp. *Ecl.* 6, 76.

omnis ad auras ≈ V. Fl. 3, 350.

43-44   **ad auras ... canet** Verg. *Ecl.* 1, 56.

44   **Carmina ... canet** ≈ Verg. *Ecl.* 1, 77.

Carmina nostra = Ov. *Met.* 10, 149; *Tr.* 5, 11, 24.

montibus altis = Lucr. 4, 1020; et al.; Verg. *Ecl.* 7, 66; and often; Eob. *Buc.* 8,

15; *Hod.* 186.

45   **Aereae rupes** = Sil. 1, 371.

    concava – sonabunt Verg. *G.* 4, 49-50; cf. *A.* 5, 677-678; 5, 866; Ov. *Ep.* 10, 22.

46-47   **O tantum ... sordida ... Rura** Verg. *Ecl.* 2, 28.

47   **redolentia regna** = *Anthol. Lat.* 2, 25: "... mellis redolentia regna."

48   **dulcem ... somnum** = Aus. *Ecl.* 20,14 ("De viro bono"); cf. Verg. *A.* 4, 185; *Ciris* 206.

    captare ... somnum Calp. *Ecl.* 5, 64; cf. Eob. *Buc.* 4, 31 (n.).

    sub arbore somnum ≈ Verg. *G.* 2, 470.

49   **vivoque – fonte** Cf. Verg. *Ecl.* 5, 47; Mant. *Ecl.* 5, 84: "... plenoque sitim restinguere vitro." For "vivo fonte" see Ov. *Met.* 3, 27; *Fast.* 2, 250.

50   **cantu – auras** Cf. Verg. *A.* 7, 34; Ov. *Fast.* 1, 155; Eob. *Nor.* 426-427: "volucres ... vocibus auras / Dulcisonis mulcent."

50-51   **opacas Quercus** Cf. Verg. *A.* 6, 208-209; 11, 851.

51   **fagineumque – decoras** Cf. Verg. *Ecl.* 8, 22.

52   **virides ulmos** *Buc.* 5, 1.

    sine nomine = Verg. *A.* 2, 558; 6, 776; 9, 343; et al.; Eob. *Buc.* 7, 144.

53   **urbanum – tribunal** Cf. *Epic.* 4, 194 (on Mutianus's death): "Nulla tibi strepitus cura forensis erat."

54   **virgineae laurus** *Sylv.* 5, 9, 3; cf. Sabell. *In natal.* 3, sig. a4ʳ: "virgineas ... lauros" (to be placed around the Virgin's altar); Mant. *1. Parthen.* 1, 601: "virgine lauro"; Eob. *Laud.* 568, with fn. 84: "puellari ... lauro."

54-55   **frigida ... lactuca** According to ancient and contemporary medical thinking, lettuce belongs to the class of "cold and moist" plants that induce slumber (cf. line 48 above). See Paul. Aeg. 1, 74 (trans. Guillaume Cop): "Lactuca manifeste refrigerat et humectat, atque iccirco somnum quoque allicit"; Eob. *Val.* 1, 463-464: "Hortorum lactuca decus, quia friget et humet, / Saepe leves somnos conciliare solet." The same properties were also believed to cool sexual desire; cf. lines 63-69 below; *Her. Chr.* 16, 265 (the Virgin eats "cold" herbs from her garden).

55   **Saeminibus ... piis** Plin. *Nat.* 20, 68 says that lettuce seeds are an antidote to scorpion bites. Powdered lettuce seeds, taken with wine, he adds, ward off lustful dreams.

    tonsile buxum Cf. Mart. 3, 58, 3.

57-59   **Lecta – capillos** For the motif see *Buc.* 2, 91 (n.).

57   **Lecta corona** Prop. 4, 10, 4.

    castos ... crines Ov. *Met.* 15, 675-676.

    quae plurima = Verg. *G.* 1, 184; 4, 274; *A.* 4, 333; 8, 427; et al.

58   **divae ... Camaenae** *Ama.* 35, 111 (n.).

    dicunt bona verba Cf. Tib. 2, 2, 1; Ov. *Fast.* 1, 72; Eob. *Her. Chr.* 6, 135. In antiquity "words of good omen" were used to introduce a sacred action or ceremony.

59   **Vernantes – capillos** Cf. *Buc.* 8, 78 (n.).

60   **Quem tibi** = Verg. *A.* 3, 340; 6, 764.

    meditantur honorem ≈ Bocc. *Ecl.* 12, 109: "... nemorum meditatur honores"; Mant. *1. Parthen.* 2, 533: "... caeli aeternos meditatur honores"; Eob. *Her.*, ded. 25: "Pierides / ... aeternos meditantur honores."

61   **Nulla – Oraeas** Cf. *Buc.* 1, 89 (n.).

    mollis Oraeas Trebelius, *Epigr.*, sig. D2ᵛ, letter to Eobanus (ca. July 1508): "... cum Sylvano mollis Oreas adest."

62   **Phillis ... Lycoris** The names are mentioned together in Verg. *Ecl.* 10, 41-42; Mant. *Ecl.* 4, 176; Cordus, *Buc.* 6, 50-51 (*Ecl.* 8, 83-84): "Lycoris / et fucata

genas Phillis." Phyllis is a stock name in pastoral poetry since Verg. *Ecl.* 3, 76; cf. Eob. *Buc.* 1, 87. Lycoris, the mistress of the ancient poet Gallus, is mentioned three times in Verg. *Ecl.* 10.

64-69 **Non ita – gemmis** Cf. Mant. *Ecl.* 4, 193-195: "Si fugiunt aquilam fulicae, si retia cervi, / si agna lupum, si damma canem, muliebria cur non / blandimenta fugis tantum tibi noxia, pastor?"

64 **Non ita – umbrae** According to Plin. *Nat.* 16, 64, snakes avoid the shade of ash trees.

65 **Non sic agna lupos ... fugit** Cf. Hor. *Epod.* 12, 25-26; Ov. *Ars* 1, 118; *Met.* 1, 505-506; Eob. *Buc.* 10, 122 (n.); *Idyl.* 15, 35-36 (translating Theoc. 11, 24).

66 **incommoda vitae** = V. Fl. 4, 86; Juv. 13, 21.

67 **Acidalio** The epithet comes from Verg. *A.* 1, 720, where it is applied to Venus; see also Mart. 6, 13, 5; 9, 13, 3; Eob. *Her. Chr.* 6, 104. The Acidalian spring in Boeotia is associated with Venus because the Graces – daughters of Venus – used to bathe there. See Serv. *A.* 1, 720.
 generosam ... mentem Ov. *Tr.* 3, 5, 32; Sen. *Tro.* 1064.
 caumate Vulg. *Job* 30, 30.

68 **animos – volentes** ≈ *Sylv.* 8, 21, 17: "... animum maiora volentem"; cf. *Buc.* 6, 95; Prud. *Psych.* 307.

69 **Tu – gemmis** Cf. *Ama.*, ded. 7 (n.): "tanquam ... venenum fugiendum." The image of the poison proffered in gem-studded cups comes from Juv. 10, 25-27; cf. Eob. *Ama.* 35, 99-100 (n.).

70 **O vitae – beatae** Cf. *Pod.* 267: "O vitae secura quies, o summa beatae"; *Venus* 2, 224-225: "Fastibus vulgi caruisse vitae est / Summa beatae."
 vitae ... beatae Hor. *S.* 2, 4, 95; Eob. *Buc.* 11, 101; *Epic.* 4, 191 (referring to Mutianus Rufus): "Ocia ducebas vitae tranquilla beatae, / Nec Venus in partes venerat ulla tuas."
 vitae – quies Sen. *Her. F.* 159-160; for "tranquilla quies" see also Luc. 1, 250; Eob. *Nup.* 352.

71 **Sic ... preteritos ... annos** = *Her. Chr.* 14, 45.
 Sic ... exuat ≈ Ov. *Met.* 9, 268.
 mihi – annos Cf. Verg. *A.* 8, 560; Ov. *Pont.* 1, 2, 143; Celtis, *Am.* 1, 12, 23: "Et mihi praeteritos animus si computet annos"; Eob. *Her. Chr.* 14, 45.
 exuat annos ≈ Tib. 1, 4, 35 (Eob. *Nup.* 71): "... exuit annos"; cf. Eob. *Her. Chr.* 16, 129; *Her.* 1, 6, 71: "Iam me vita senex melioribus exuit annis."

72 **Talem – me** Cf. *Her. Chr.* 9, 149.
 sera dies = Calp. *Ecl.* 5, 120; Mant. *3. Parthen.*, fol. 103ʳ: "Postquam sera dies saeclis labentibus aetas / Intulit extremos."

72-74 **seu mihi – sanguis** Cf. Hor. *S.* 2, 1, 57-59.

72-73 **longos ... dies** Vulg. *3. Reg.* 3, 14; *Prov.* 28, 16; cf. Eob. *Her. Chr.* 3, 128 (n.). 7

73 **Invideant ... fata** For the complaint against malicious fate that begrudges us a long life see, for example, Ov. *Pont.* 2, 8, 59: "nobis invidit inutile fatum"; Verg. *A.* 11, 43; Eob. *Buc.* 9, 50-51.

73-74 **frigidus – sanguis** Cf. Verg. *A.* 5, 395-396; Juv. 10, 217; Sedul. 1, 109: "Frigidus annoso moriens in corpore sanguis"; Eob. *Her. Chr.* 7, 122.

73 **frigidus annis** = *Aetna* 432; Filetico, *Theoc.* 4, 58: "frigidus annis / Ille senex"; Mant. *1. Parthen.* 2, 209 (of Joseph). Cf. Eob. *Buc.* 3, 47 (n.): "frigida mater."

74 **Ante diem ... moriatur** *Rec.* 139 (n.); cf. *Laud.* 502 (n.).
 corpore sanguis = Lucr. 2, 194; Ov. *Met.* 14, 754; *Fast.* 3, 331.

75 **Non – sepulchri** The theme is worked out at some length in Brant, *NS* 85, 97-155.
 post cineres = Prop. 3, 1, 36; Ov. *Pont.* 4, 16, 3; Eob. *Ama.* 32, 82.
 cura sepulchri = Ov. *Fast.* 5, 657; Stat. *Theb.* 9, 159.

76 **corporea ... mole** August. *C. D.* 11, 5; *Ep.* 120, 4; 162, 9; and, for example, Marul. *Hymn. nat.* 1, 1, 28: "Corpoream iussi molem compage tueri"; Mant. *7. Parthen.*, fol. 158ᵛ: "Corporeae molis memores." For the commonplace that the body is a burden for the soul see, for example, Plato, *Phd.* 81 c; Sen. *Ep.* 24, 17; 65, 16; 102, 22; Eob. *Her. Chr.* 21, 70. For the related concept of the body as the soul's prison see *Her. Chr.* 14, 133 (n.); 16, 258.

77-78 **Caedat – Vermibus** Cf. *Rec.* 142-143 (n.).

78 **volucres ... sublime volantes** *Theoc.* 15, sig. F2ʳ: "... volucrum sublime volantum"; cf. Lucr. 6, 97.

volucres pascat Ov. *Ars* 3, 35-36; Luc. 4, 810: "nobile corpus, / Pascit aves ... Curio."

79 **Cura eadem** = *Her. Chr.* 5, 69.

79-80 **Stultus – Collocat** Cf. Locher, *Stult.*, fol. 95ᵛ, alluding to [Sen.] *De remediis utriusque fortuitorum* 5: "Sarcophagum facias quid prodest marmore et auro? / Qui bonus est, coelo tegitur si non habet urnam"; Luc. 8, 859-860: "templis auroque sepultus / Vilior umbra fores."

79 **foeda cadavera** = Prud. *Dittochaeon* 3, 3; Mant. *1. Parthen.* 2, 271; cf. Ov. *Met.* 7, 548.

80 **vanis** For the sense "lifeless" cf. Hor. *Carm.* 1, 24, 15 (of the ghost of a dead man): "vanae ... imagini."

81 **Daemens et** = Verg. *A.* 6, 172.

miseros ... artus = Verg. *G.* 3, 483; Eob. *Her. Chr.* 12, 75; cf. Verg. *A.* 2, 215; *Ciris* 482.

amplectitur artus = Ov. *Ep.* 12, 173; Stat. *Silv.* 5, 1, 194. For the gesture of embracing the dead see Verg. *A.* 11, 150; Prop. 2, 9, 9; Ov. *Met.* 2, 627; and often.

82 **simulachra virum** = Sil. 13, 650 and Petr. 121, 118 (both referring to spirits); Eob. *Nor.* 858: "... simulachra virum de marmore sculpta."

82-83 **defunctaque ... Corpora** = Ov. *Ep.* 14, 125-126; cf. Verg. *G.* 4, 475; *A.* 6, 306.

83 **dii superi** = Hor. *Ep.* 2, 1, 138; cf. Eob. *Ama.* 35, 80 (n.).

85 **Gloria debetur** Phaed. 3, praef. 61; Prud. *c. Sym.* 2, 756; Eob. *Her.* 1, 5, 141; *Sylv.* 9, 3, 14.

dulcis ... vitae Line 15 above (n.).

85-86 **post ... vitae Tempora** Calp. *Ecl.* 4, 138-139.

86 **tellure quiescam** ≈ Sil. 7, 297.

87 **Tu modo** = Verg. *Ecl.* 4, 8; *G.* 3, 73; *A.* 2, 160; et al.; Eob. *Buc.* 6, 93; *Her. Chr.* 6, 205; 12, 279; et al.

magno ... iubila Christo = *Sylv.* 1, 7, 21. For "magno Christo" at this metrical position see also *Her. Chr.* 18, 65; cf. *Her. Chr.* 19, 9; 21, 183; *Sylv. duae* 1, 37; *Hymn.* 113; *Vict.* 295; *Hod.* 260; also cf. *Her. Chr.* 6, 103: "magnum ... Iesum." For "iubila Christo" at this metrical position see also *Vict.*, app. 1, 25: "... reduci paschalia iubila Christo"; app. 2, 23: "... resurgenti paschalia iubila Christo"; *Epic.* 4, 193 (to Mutianus Rufus): "Sancta salutifero psallebas iubila Christo."

88 **Nocturnis ... sacris** Ov. *Ars* 1, 567; Prud. *Perist.* 2, 71.

89 **Percurris** Cf. Ov. *Am.* 2, 4, 27: "habili percurrit pollice chordas."

90 **Vatis Iessei** Bebel, "De laude et utilitate poaetices," *Carm.*, sig. q3ʳ: "Iessei ... vatis"; Eob., epigram in *Thomae Wolphii Iunioris In Psalmum tercium et trigesimum expositio* (Erfurt, [Wolfgang Stürmer], 1507), sig. a2ᵛ: "Castum est / Quicquid Iessaei carmina vatis habent." The Psalmist David was the son of Jesse. For the adjective see also [Juvenc.] *Triumph.* 50: "notissima proles / Stirpis Iessaeae"; Mant. *1. Parthen.* 2, 446: "stirpis Iessaeae princeps"; 2, 684: "nomina clara / gentis Iessaeae"; *c. Poet.* 16: "Iessei regia Musa senis"; Eob. *Her. Chr.* 10, 148; *Vict.* 294.

91   **libros mille inter** Cf. Sen. *Dial.* 9, 6: "inter tot milia librorum oscitanti"; Mant. *Fed.Spagn.*, fol. 141ʳ: "Inter mille libros."

       solis ad ortum = Cic. *Div.* 1, 20; cf. Verg. *G.* 3, 277; Ov. *Ib.* 427; Luc. 9, 76.

92   **Leniter afflantem** *Culex* 155.

       afflantem ... pectora Ov. *Rem.* 434.

93   **Tu modo** = Line 87 above (n.).

93-94 **olim – Carmina** Cf. *Sylv. duae* 2, 243.

95-96 **Maiora – Pangere** Cf. Verg. *Ecl.* 4, 1.

96   **pastorem – harundo** Cf. *Idyl.*, 2. ded. 102: "Fistula pastores, non tuba rauca decet." On the need to maintain pastoral decorum see also *Idyl.* 13, 99-104; 16, 51-53; 16, 160-163.

97   **averso ... Apolline** Prop. 4, 1, 73; Eob. *Idyl.* 11, 179.

7

With its bipartite structure, the eclogue resembles Mant. *Ecl.* 8. In lines 1-71 of that eclogue the herdsmen debate the advantages of lowland and upland pastures. Realizing that their debate is leading nowhere, they start conversing about Pollux's love for the Virgin Mary. Cf. also Calp. *Ecl.* 2, which starts off as an amoebean contest between a shepherd and a gardener concerning their respective livelihoods before moving on to the subject of love.

    The first part of the eclogue was imitated by Cordus in *Ecl.* 8, a non-allegorical pastoral that begins by describing how a dog was killed by a boar and continues with other rustic topics. Cautus's wooing song in the second half of the poem (lines 107-153) is reminiscent of Verg. *Ecl.* 2, 6-68 and Ov. *Met.* 13, 789-869.

    Meter: Hexameter.

1-4   **Tercius – nemus** For the motif of searching for a lost animal cf. *Buc.* 4, 105-106 (n.). In keeping with Mantuanesque pastoral, however, this Arcadian motif is given an unhappy ending in order to introduce the eclogue's main theme: Like the goat, the foolish lover goes astray because of his carnal appetites and runs the risk of eternal death. Cf. Mant. *Ecl.* 4, 1-75.

1-2   **Tercius – postquam** Closely paralleled in *Laud.* 1, 1-2. Cf. also *Buc.* 8, 1-2.

1   **Tercius ... Lucifer** = Stat. *Theb.* 12, 50; cf. Ov. *Fast.* 2, 149-150; Mant. *Ecl.* 2, 1: "... iam septima lux est"; Eob. *Vict.* 433-434: "Iam tertius ibat / Lucifer." In verse, "Lucifer" often has the broader meaning "morning" or "day," as it does here.

       immenso ... orbi ≈ Ov. *Pont.* 2, 8, 23; Eob. *Buc.* B 11, 5 (n.).

2   **Altera nox** = Stat. *Theb.* 8, 16.

       nox abiit = Ov. *Am.* 1, 5, 6; cf. *Fast.* 4, 721.

3   **Quaeritur in sylvis** = Petr. 119, 14.

       ubi plurima = *Buc.* 5, 2 (n.).

3-4   **plurima – nemus** Cf. *Theoc.* 1, sig. A7ʳ: "quem circum plurima densent / Umbrosum querceta nemus."

4   **Umbrosum ... nemus** Ov. *Met.* 7, 75; Eob. *Idyl.* 7, 51-52.

4-5   **Dic – vidisti** Cf. Calp. *Ecl.* 3, 1-2.

6-7   **Niger – torvos** Cf. Mant. *Ecl.* 4, 89-90: "O aries, aries, qui tortis cornibus atrum / daemona praesentas."

7   **Cornua – redeuntia** Cf. Ov. *Am.* 3, 13, 17; *Fast.* 5, 119.

       oculos ... torvos *Ama.* 14, 3 (n.).

8   **Quorum – solebat** Cf. Mant. *Ecl.* 9, 46: "hic aries qui fronte lupos cornuque petebat."

       Quorum ope = Ov. *Met.* 7, 199; Juv. 14, 183.

occursare Verg. *Ecl.* 9, 25.

9   **Ah, pecus infoelix** Cf. Mant. *Ecl.* 8, 111: "si pecus infelix erit ..."; 9, 54 and 9, 184: "heu, pecus infelix ..."; cf. also Verg. *Ecl.* 3, 3; Eob. *Buc.* 4, 64.
    Non te tua ≈ Verg. *A.* 2, 429; 9, 486; 12, 894.

10   **torvi ... oculi** *Ama.* 14, 3 (n.).
    Tibi vera fatebor = Ov. *Ep.* 8, 97; Mant. *Ecl.* 8, 5; cf. Verg. *A.* 2, 77-78; Ov. *Ep.* 14, 47; Eob. *Idyl.* 7, 43: "nec me tibi vera fateri / ... pudet."

11   **decus nemorum** = Bocc. *Ecl.* 8, 34 (Pontano, *Parthen.* 2, 9, 15): "Nympha, decus nemorum ..."; Eob. *Idyl.* 10, 7: "Thyrsi, decus nemorum ..."; cf. Ov. *Met.* 8, 317; Stat. *Theb.* 9, 383; Eob. *Buc.* 9, 62.

12   **volucrum ... nidos** Verg. *A.* 8, 235; Ov. *Met.* 12, 15.
    scrutabar ... nidos Mant. *Ecl.* 1, 23. For the motif see also Mant. *Ecl.* 3, 84; 4, 13; 4, 34; 10, 117-118.
    arbore nidos = Juv. 14, 80; cf. Mant. *Ecl.* 3, 84.

14   **Nisi forte fuissem** ≈ *Sylv. duae* 1, 131.

15   **ora petisset** ≈ Lucr. 5, 1319.

16   **Ne doleas – necesse est** For this bit of proverbial wisdom cf. Otto 654; Häussler, pp. 43, 56, 161, and 271; *AH* 33, 226, 8, 1: "Laeto fer animo, quaecumque ferre necesse"; Walther 9325: "Fer patienter onus, ferre quodcumque necesse est"; Erasmus, *Adag.* 1, 3, 14; Eob. *Her. Chr.* 7, 135; 16, 303.
    quod fata iubent = Luc. 8, 520; cf. Ov. *Met.* 15, 584; Eob. *Rec.* 94 (n.).
    ferre necesse est = Petrarch, *Ecl.* 2, 53.

19   **Nunc – poenas** Cf. Verg. *A.* 10, 617; also cf. *A.* 9, 422-423; Ov. *Fast.* 4, 239; Eob. *Tum.* 7, 31: "Ille tamen meritas persolvit sanguine poenas." For "meritas poenas" see also n. *Pug.* 93.

20   **viridem ... terram** Juvenc. 1, 162.

21   **cythisum – cyperon** Cf. Bocc. *Ecl.* 10, 48: "... cythisum salicesque novas frondesque recentes"; Verg. *Ecl.* 1, 78; 2, 64.
    tiliasque leves Verg. *G.* 1, 173; Sen. *Oed.* 538.

22   **solus abibas** = Ov. *Ars* 2, 361; cf. Eob. *Her. Chr.* 5, 135.

24   **Qui – audet** Quoted as a proverb in Walther 24356; cf. Ov. *Met.* 10, 544: "non est audacia tuta"; Bebel, *Prov.* 269: "Audentiores saepius vulnerantur"; Eob. *Her. Chr.* 5, 164.

25   **Est ut ais** = Mant. *Ecl.* 4, 84; cf. Eob. *Ama.* A 1, 1.

26   **hanc – repende** For the thought cf. Verg. *A.* 1, 239.

27-29   **mecum – flores** For the "motif of bucolic repose" see n. *Buc.* 1, 65-71. For the *locus amoenus* see n. *Ama.* 1, 1; cf. especially Verg. *Ecl.* 1, 53-55 and 7, 12-13; Eob. *Buc.* 7, 74-75.

27   **mecum ... succede salicto** Cf. Verg. *Ecl.* 5, 6; 5, 19; Cordus, *Ecl.* 3, 38: "... Vicinum mecum succede sub antrum."

28   **thaurigenae ... volucres** Cf. Poliziano, *Sylv.* 1, 188: "Taurigenae ... aves."
    stipant ... mella Verg. *G.* 4, 163-164; *A.* 1, 432-433.
    volucres *Laud.* 108 (n.).

29   **stridunt** Verg. *G.* 4, 310; 4, 556; cf. *A.* 7, 65.

30   **per superos** = Verg. *A.* 2, 141; Ov. *Pont.* 4, 12, 39; Stat. *Theb.* 12, 103; Eob. *Buc.* B 1, 8; *Her. Chr.* 8, 79; 12, 47.
    res digna cachinno Catul. 56, 1-2; cf. Mant. *Ecl.* 4, 77: "... o res risu celebranda bimestri"; Prud. *c. Symm.* 2, 403: "... digna cachinno."

32   **Quam rudis es** Cf. Mant. *Ecl.* 6, 113: "sed tu tam rudis es ...."
    diuturno ... usu Cic. *Amic.* 85; cf. line 52 below (n.).

33   **cautissime** Caldus repeats the wordplay in line 95 below. Cautus gets his revenge in line 159.

36	**vere rosas** Cf. Lucr. 1, 174; Verg. *G.* 4, 134.
	rubra papavera = Filetico, *Theoc.* 7, 157.
37-38	**Deus ... natura** Ov. *Met.* 1, 21; Camerarius, *Nar.* 6, 9.
41	**Adonis** See *Buc.* 2, 65 (n.).
42	**Hoc leve** = Mant. *Ecl.* 5, 142.
	naturae specimen Cic. *Tusc.* 1, 32; Plin. 36, 97; Prud. *Apoth.* 635.
43-47	**Populeis – ovem** Cf. Vulg. *Gen.* 30, 37-41.
43	**canalia** The neuter form is common in medieval Latin.
45-46	**colorem ... niveum** Hor. *Carm.* 2, 4, 3; Ov. *Fast.* 2, 763.
47-48	**Sic – scriptum** The model is Mant. *Ecl.* 7, 154-155: "sic docuit ... sacerdos / Iannus et in magno dixit sibi codice lectum." For Caldus's explanation of his more than pastoral knowledge see n. *Buc.* 1, 54-56.
49-50	**Sic etiam – coloris** Calp. *Ecl.* 2, 36-39.
51	**incrementa peculi** = *Theoc.* 32, sig. M4ᵛ: "eximii dedit incrementa peculi." For the meaning of "peculi" see n. *Buc.* 1, 104.
52	**longo ... usu** = Ov. *Pont.* 3, 6, 53; cf. *Am.* 1, 8, 105; *Ars* 3, 791; *Tr.* 3, 5, 9; 3, 6, 19; Mant. *Ecl.* 4, 190; Eob. *Buc.* 7, 32; *Her. Chr.* 16, 15; *Vict.* 119; *Salom.* 4, sig. B3ʳ: "Longo me docuit facta experientia ab usu."
53-65	**Eheu – artus** The passage imitates Theoc. 4, 50-55.
53	**spina – momordit** = *Theoc.* 4, sig. B7ʳ: "dum sequor ipse iuvencam / Incauto miserum pede spina offensa momordit."
54	**Aspicis ut** = Ov. *Tr.* 1, 9, 7; 5, 14, 35; Calp. *Ecl.* 4, 97; Eob. *Ruf.* 35; *Her. Chr.* 9, 63.
55	**Affer opem** = Ov. *Met.* 8, 601.
	dente tenaci = Verg. *A.* 6, 3 (of an anchor).
60	**sanguine vulnus** = Sil. 5, 368.
63	**Pignora chara** = Verg. *Ecl.* 8, 92, of pledges; Claud. *Cons. Olyb. et Prob.* 143, of children; Filetico, *Theoc.* 7, 4, of children; cf. Ov. *Met.* 3, 134; *Fast.* 3, 218; Eob. *Her. Chr.* 4, 50; 21, 26.
	messis in agro = Andrel. *Ecl.* 1, 41.
65	**humanos ... artus** *Ciris* 198.
	dolor occupat artus = Jacobus Magdalius Gaudensis, "Epistola Dive Marie Magdalene ad Christum in infirmitate Lazari fratris," in *Erarium aureum poetarum* ([Cologne], 1501), sig. H2ʳ: "Tantus ... teneros dolor occupat artus"; cf. Verg. *G.* 4, 190; *A.* 7, 446; et al.; Eob. *Her. Chr.* 13, 63 (n.).
66-103	**Nunc – recordor** The debate between a shepherd and a goatherd goes back to Theoc. 5 and Verg. *Ecl.* 7 (an eclogue that, like Eobanus's seventh, opens with the motif of searching for a lost animal).
67	**perge fateri** = *Sylv.* 1, 10, 37; 8, 25, 19.
69	**inter amicos** = Hor. *S.* 1, 3, 1; *Ep.* 1, 5, 24; Ov. *Pont.* 1, 5, 1.
71	**seria** *Buc.* 10, 91 (n.).
72-76	**Incipe – Camoenae** Cf. Verg. *Ecl.* 3, 55-59 (after some skirmishing between two herdsmen and just before an amoebean contest). For the "motif of bucolic repose" see n. *Buc.* 1, 65-71. For the repetition of "Incipe" see Verg. *Ecl.* 5, 10-12.
72-73	**Incipe ... dum ... Dum ... dum** Cf. Verg. *Ecl.* 10, 6-7; Nemes. *Ecl.* 1, 6-8. For the anaphora cf. also Eob. *Her. Chr.* 10, 163-164.
	coelo – capellis Cf. Hor. *Carm.* 3, 29, 18-22.
72	**coelo – ardet** ≈ *Laud.* 566 (n.); cf. *Pug.* 1 (with notes).
73	**Dum – pecus** Cf. *Ruf.* 106: "Dum iuvat umbra deos."
	grata capellis = Bocc. *Ecl.* 16, 13: "...vepreta hic grata capellis."
74-75	**Hic – herba** For the *locus amoenus* see n. *Ama.* 1, 1.
75	**platano** The plane tree is specifically mentioned in a pastoral context also in

Calp. *Ecl.* 4, 2; Nemes. *Ecl.* 2, 18; Eob. *Idyl.* 7, 82.

molli ... herba = Verg. *Ecl.* 3, 55; Eob. *Sylv. duae* 1, 85.

78-79   **Sed tamen – usus** Cf. Filetico, *Theoc.* 5, 26, on the superiority of wool over goat's hair: "Quis molli duras pro vellere setas / Tondeat?"

78   **bidentum** *Buc.* 1, 82 (n.).

83   **divite pauper** = Paul. Nol. *Carm.* 21, 530: "... ex divite pauper"; cf. Eob. *Ama.* 5, 7 (n.): "ex divite pauper."

84   **murice ... et ostro** In antiquity, garments dyed with costly purple were symbols of status and wealth. Cf. *Buc.* B 8, 6.

murice tingit Tib. 2, 4, 28; Hor. *Carm.* 2, 16, 36; Ov. *Ars* 1, 251; et al.

88   **Caseolos – dona** Cf. *Idyl.* 7, 15-16: "Caseolos butyrumque, boni duo maxima lactis / Commoda."

duo maxima dona Cf. Mant. *Ecl.* 8, 62-63 (of bread and wine): "duo sustentacula vitae / maxima"; *1. Parthen.* 3, 264: "... tua maxima dona."

89-91   **ubera plena ... complent mulctralia** Mant. *Ecl.* 5, 6-7 (also imitated in Eob. *Buc.* 1, 22-23, where see notes).

89-90   **ubera ... Lactis oves** Tib. 1, 3, 46.

90   **seroque ... vespere** = Ov. *Met.* 4, 415.

ad mulctram ... ductae Cf. Calp. *Ecl.* 4, 25.

91   **distentis ... mammis** Cf. Lucr. 1, 259; Verg. *Ecl.* 4, 21-22; 7, 3; Hor. *Epod.* 2, 46.

93   **Lactis – reportat** Cf. Verg. *Ecl.* 4, 21-22.

94   **Bisque – capellae** Cf. Verg. *Ecl.* 3, 34: "bisque die ..."; 3, 5 (of an incompetent shepherd): "bis mulget in hora."

mulgentur – capellae Cf. *Buc.* 4, 16.

95   **Ha ... nescis** = Bocc. *Ecl.* 4, 13: "Ha! miserum rides; nescis quibus ipsa reservet / te fortuna dolis."

mentiri nescis Juv. 3, 41.

cautissime Caute For the wordplay see line 33 above.

97   **Perge, precor** = Bocc. *Ecl.* 1, 24; Erasmus, *Carm.* 64, 92.

Faciles ... Camoenae = *Laud.* 65 (n.).

Faciles ... risere = Verg. *Ecl.* 3, 9. The sense is twofold: "The Muses laugh at your joke"; "the Muses smile on you with favor." For the latter meaning cf. *Sylv.* 7, 18, 9-14: "Carmina cum faciles mihi pastoralia Musae / Et facili canerent pascua laeta pede / [*2 lines*], / Tum mihi ridebant per carmina laeta Camoenae, / Tunc fuit ingenii gratia plena mei."

98-102   **Capra – auro** For a similar display of astronomical-mythological lore see Mant. *Ecl.* 8, 81-86. Though quite beyond the average shepherd, the knowledge is carefully accounted for, both in Mantuan's and in Eobanus's eclogues. Cf. n. *Buc.* 1, 54-56 above.

99   **Docto ... Iarbae** Cf. Calp. *Ecl.* 4, 59: "doctus Iollas."

100   **Oleniae ... caprae** Sen. *Med.* 313; cf. Eob. *Her. Chr.* 10, 69 (n.).

suxit ... ubera *Buc.* 9, 117-118.

101   **Lucida ... sydera** = Sen. *Oed.* 504; cf. Eob. *Buc.* 5, 63 (n.).

Phryxaeum pecus Cf. Ov. *Ep.* 6, 104; 12, 8; *Fast.* 3, 852; Mart. 10, 51, 1; Eob. *Epic.* 3 A, 5: "Vellera Phryxaeae pecudis iam Phoebus obibat."

sydera fulget = Ov. *Met.* 2, 722.

102   **fulvum ... vellus** Ov. *Am.* 2, 11, 4; *Ep.* 6, 14.

rutilo ... auro = Claud. *Cons. Stil.* 3, 230.

103   **Sic – recordor** Cf. Mant. *Ecl.* 5, 101: "haec me iam pridem memini didicisse sub Umbro."

104   **nec sunt trivialia** Cf. *Buc.* 1, 39 (n.).

106   **Lycaeum** This term properly refers to the gymnasium near Athens where

Aristotle taught. Here, as so often in Renaissance literature, it means "university."

108 **canna texit ... palustri** Cf. Ov. *Met.* 8, 630 (of a dwelling). For "canna palustri" see also Ov. *Rem.* 142; *Met.* 4, 298; *Pont.* 4, 3, 47. In *Met.* 1, 706 Syrinx is said to be transformed into "calamos ... palustres."
Venus alma *Buc.* 3, 147 (n.).

109 **Ut – ignes** An allusion to Verg. *Ecl.* 1, 5: "formosam resonare doces Amaryllida silvas" and Prop. 1, 18, 31: "resonent mihi 'Cynthia' silvae"; cf. Eob. *Buc.* 7, 138. What Tityrus did for Amaryllis, and Propertius for Cynthia, Caldus now wants to do for Canace.
nemus omne Verg. *Ecl.* 6, 11; 7, 59; et al.; cf. Eob. *Buc.* 5, 45 (n.).
intelligat ignes ≈ Ov. *Met.* 9, 457.

110 **En venit** Calp. *Ecl.* 4, 78; cf. Verg. *Ecl.* 3, 50; Calp. *Ecl.* 6, 28; 6, 91.

111-112 **niveae – capilli** For the motif in an erotic context cf. Ov. *Met.* 1, 528-529 (of Daphne as she flees from Apollo); *Fast.* 5, 609 (of Europa, borne away by Jupiter in the shape of a bull); cf. also Eob. *Her. Chr.* 3, 151 (Mary Magdalene, hoping to catch a glimpse of her beloved Jesus).
niveae ... Albentes ... lactea With her white clothes, blonde hair, and fair skin, Canace makes a luminous impression on her love-struck admirer. The emphasis on brightness is typical of ancient descriptions of feminine beauty. See, for example, Catul. 13, 4: "candida puella"; Prop. 2, 29, 30: "candida forma"; 3, 11, 16; Ov. *Fast.* 3, 493; and the examples given in the note to line 112 below.

111 **niveae ... vestes** Ov. *Met.* 10, 432.
molli – vestes Modeled on Ov. *Met.* 2, 875 (of Europa, being carried off to Crete).
molli ... flamine Claud. *Carm. minora* 30, 201.

112 **Albentesque – capilli** Blonde hair flowing down over white shoulders is a regular feature in poetic descriptions of beauty. Cf., for instance, Verg. *G.* 4, 337; Filetico, *Theoc.* 5, 91: "Cumque movet flavos per candida colla capillos"; also cf. Eob. *Her. Chr.* 2, 59. For the erotic implications of unbound hair see *Buc.* 3, 71 (n.); see further Prop. 2, 3, 13; Ov. *Met.* 1, 477 (Daphne); 10, 592: "tergaque iactantur crines per eburnea ..."; *Fast.* 2, 772; Poliziano, *Eleg.* 7, 81: "Aura quatit fusos in candida terga capillos." For "albentes capilli" see Eob. *Laud.* 165 (n.).
post ... terga Verg. *A.* 2, 57; 11, 81; Ov. *Am.* 1, 2, 31; *Met.* 3, 575; Eob. *Her. Chr.* 3, 152.
terga capilli ≈ Ov. *Ars* 1, 541.

113 **virga** Cf. Bocc. *Ecl.* 11, 13: "virga cogebat ... capellas."

114 **poto – amne** Cf. Mant. *Ecl.* 1, 97: "... potum compellat ad amnem"; Eob. *Buc.* 3, 79; *Idyl.* 10, 37: "... potum compellit ad undas."

116 **Nympharum decus** = *Idyl.* 17, 11.
ante omnes formosa Cf. Verg. *A.* 5, 570.

119-121 **Nulla – noctes** For these symptoms of lovesickness see *Ama.* 8, 7–9, 8. It is a commonplace that lovers are preoccupied night and day with the beloved. See, for example, Tib. 2, 4, 11; Ov. *Ep.* 7, 26; 13, 103-104; Eob. *Her. Chr.* 5, 69-70.

120 **Dies ... totos consumimus** Mant. *Calam.* 1, p. 40: "... totos hac arte dies consumit et annos."

121 **Longa insomnia** V. Fl. 7, 6.
turbant – noctes = *Sylv. duae* 2, 95; cf. Damasus, *Epigr.*, ed. Maximilian Ihm (Leipzig, 1895), 27, 9: "nocte soporifera turbant insomnia mentem"; Landino, *Xandra* 2, 11, 1: "Tristia ... turbant insomnia pectus"; Eob. *Buc.* 8, 25; *Her. Chr.* 14, 105. For the motif cf. also Verg. *A.* 4, 9.

insomnia noctes = *Consol.* 93: "Et quae multa ferunt monstrosae insomnia noctes"; cf. Mant. *Dionys.* 3, fol. 189ᵛ: "... insomnia noctis"; Eob. *Buc.* 8, lines 25, 35 (n.), and 98.

122-129   Huc ades – Huc ades Modeled on Verg. *Ecl.* 9, 39-43.

122   Huc ades ... formosa Cf. Verg. *Ecl.* 2, 45.

           Huc ades et = *Buc.* 5, 10 (n.).

123-125   Tum – susurrant For the *locus amoenus* see n. *Ama.* 1, 1.

123   una sub umbra Ov. *Fast.* 2, 87.

124   Faginea See n. *Buc.* 3, 83.

124-125   latices – faciunt Cf. *Buc.* 2, 83-84 (n.).

125   tremulumque For the adverbial "tremulum" see Mart. 14, 203, 1; Aus. *Ep.* 21, 14: "cumque suis loquitur tremulum coma pinea ventis."

126-131   Hic tibi – altis Cf. Cordus, *Ecl.* 3, 117-125, where the lover promises pears, nuts, a young hare, a turtle dove, and other rustic gifts.

126   tibi castaneae = Ov. *Met.* 13, 819 (among the gifts that Polyphemus offers to Galatea). Chestnuts are typically rustic gifts to a beloved; see Verg. *Ecl.* 2, 52; *Copa* 19; Ov. *Ars* 2, 268; Calp. *Ecl.* 2, 82; Bocc. *Ecl.* 1, 111.

           allia As a "hot and dry" food, garlic was considered an aphrodisiac; see *Val.* 1, 513-514.

127   pyra For pears as a lover's present see Lucr. 5, 965; Poliziano, *Sylv.* 2, 375: "cumque piris miserorum munus amantum."

           vicinis – Hessi Cf. *Buc.*, ded. 3-4 (n.).

           vicinis montibus = Paul. Nol. *Carm.* 26, 417.

           montibus Hessi = *Val.* 1, 609: "Quique suis alacres habitant in montibus Hessi"; *Sylv.* 2, 4, 23. Cf. *Laud.* 278 (n.).

128   servamus Verg. *Ecl.* 2, 42; Ov. *Met.* 13, 837.

129   Huc – amantis Cf. Verg. *A.* 4, 429; Ov. *Met.* 13, 839.

           Huc ades, o = *Buc.* 3, 159 (n.).

           Miseri ... amantis Pl. *Bac.* 208; *Cur.* 152; Verg. *A.* 4, 429; Tib. 1, 8, 61 and 71; Prop. 1, 16, 45; Eob. *Ama.* B 2, 76; *Her. Chr.* B 1, 29.

130   leporem ... palumbem The rabbit and the dove were sacred to Venus and hence are traditional lover's gifts. See Ov. *Met.* 13, 832-833; Calp. *Ecl.* 3, 76-77; Nemes. *Ecl.* 2, 67-68; Mant. *Ecl.* 1, 68-69. See further Theoc. 5, 96; 5, 133; Verg. *Ecl.* 3, 68-69.

           turdosque duos For thrushes as lover's gifts see Ov. *Ars* 2, 269.

           castamque palumbem Cf. *Her.* 1, 6, 150: "castam ... avem." The dove – especially the turtledove, to which the ringdove is closely related – was reputed to be chaste and loyal to its mate until death. See *Her. Chr.* 5, 54, with note. Eobanus uses "palumbem" (literally, "wild wood-pigeon") in the sense "columbam" ("domestic pigeon," "dove"); for this he had the authority of Verg. *Ecl.* 1, 57 (with Servius's note).

131   quae – altis *Theoc.* 11, sig. D7ᵛ: "... lustris ea sum venatus in altis." References to hunting recur in Arcadian pastoral; see Verg. *Ecl.* 2, 29; 2, 40-41; 5, 60-61; 7, 29-30; 10, 55-60.

132-133   Uror – autumni The image is based on the ancient practice of burning the straw left on the fields after harvesting. See, for example, Verg. *G.* 1, 84-85. Ovid uses it as an image of love in *Met.* 1, 492-496. Cf. Verg. *G.* 3, 99; Celtis, *Am.* 1, 8, 34-39; Eob. *Laud.* 294-296; *Sylv. duae* 2, 127-129; *Sylv.* 3, 7, 23-25: "Sicut enim stipulae multo iam sole perustae / In flammas totae, si quis adurat, eunt, / Sic tua iam calidam succendit epistola mentem."

133   Sole sub autumni Cf. *Rec.* 2 (n.).

           ille fatigat = Verg. *A.* 6, 79.

134   corda sagitta = *Sylv. duae* 2, 83.

135-138   **O si – sonarent** Cf. Calp. *Ecl.* 3, 53-54; Nemes. *Ecl.* 2, 47-49.
135   **respiciat** Nemes. *Ecl.* 4, 20: "Respice me tandem ...."
136   **Ut quondam** = Verg. *G.* 3, 99; *A.* 5, 588; Hor. *S.* 1, 2, 55; Eob. *Nup.* 9.
137-138   **Dulcisona – sonarent** In his misery, he has stopped singing; cf. lines 159-163
          below. For the motif see *Buc.* 3, 91-92 (n.).
137   **laetos – versus** Cf. Mant. *Calam.* 1, p. 47: "... cum laetos modulatur tibia
          cantus"; Eob. *Buc.* 1, 11 (n.); 4, 74 (n.). Singing and flute-playing are often
          mentioned together; see n. *Buc.* 4, 73-74.
138   **cantu – sonarent** Cf. *Buc.* 7, 109; 8, 107.
          omne sonarent ≈ Verg. *Ecl.* 6, 44.
139-140   **Heu – Pectora** Cf. Verg. *A.* 3, 56; 4, 412; Ov. *Met.* 6, 472; Eob. *Buc.* 3, 75-76
          (n.).
139   **crudelis Amor** = Verg. *A.* 6, 24; cf. *Ecl.* 10, 29.
140   **Nulla – potestas** On the omnipotence of Amor see n. *Ama.* 8, 3-6.
          sub sole = Lucr. 5, 714; Verg. *G.* 2, 512; Luc. 2, 584. For the phrase in this sense
          see Vulg. *Eccl.* 1, 3; 1, 10; 1, 13-14; and often; cf. Eob. *Laud.* 382 (n.); *Buc.* 11,
          96 (n.); also *Her. Chr.* 23, 75.
141-143   **Sic me – pruinis** The cares of love have robbed of him of his youth and aged
          him prematurely. Cf. *Ama.* 35, 51-52 (n.); *Sylv.* 4, 14, 15-19: "Sic, sic perit
          vernans iuventa, / Ante diem subit heu senectus. / Curae frequentes et labor et
          dolor / Corpus perurunt, ut nova Sirius / Exhaurit implacatus arva." For the
          thought that grief makes us grow old before our time see *Her. Chr.* 18, 111-112
          (n.).
141   **Sic ... sic posito** ≈ Verg. *A.* 2, 644.
          posito – honore Cf. Ov. *Tr.* 4, 10, 93: "pulsis melioribus annis"; Eob. *Her. Chr.*
          16, 129.
          vitae – honore For the wording cf. Verg. *G.* 4, 326: "... vitae mortalis
          honorem"; Mant. *1. Parthen.* 1, 5: "... mundi melioris honores"; Eob. *Her. Chr.*
          8, 135. For "honore" in the sense "best part of [youth]" cf. *Ruf.* 37-38 (in a
          carpe-diem exhortation): "Hoc in flore sumus. Quem ne perdamus honorem /
          Nos monet alma Venus."
          vitae melioris = Sil. 12, 316; cf. Eob. *Her. Chr.* B 1, 3.
142   **Cogis** Said of Amor also in Verg. *A.* 4, 412.
          ante diem = *Rec.* 139 (n.).
143   **arva pruinis** = Avit. *Carm.* 1, 221: "... canescunt arva pruinis"; Mant. *Ecl.* 1,
          135; 8, 191; cf. Verg. *G.* 4, 518; Eob. *Buc.* 2, 27; *Hod.* 69: "... urebant arva
          pruinae."
144   **sine nomine** = *Buc.* 6, 52 (n.).
145-146   **maiora – propter** Cf. *Her. Chr.* 18, 53.
145   **maiora ... tormenta** *Aetna* 555.
146   **mei medicina furoris** ≈ Verg. *Ecl.* 10, 60; cf. Mant. *Ecl.* 3, 91: "da quod amo;
          nostro haec una est medicina dolori." For the proverbial idea that only the
          beloved can heal the wounds of love see Eob. *Buc.* 3, 93-95, with note to line
          94.
147   **Huc olim properans** = Line 151 below.
147-148   **oscula – Endimioni** Cf. Ov. *Am.* 2, 5, 23-28: "oscula ... / [*3 lines*] / qualia
          credibile est ... / ...Venerem Marti saepe tulisse suo"; Eob. *Sylv.* 1, 9, 21-22:
          "Oscula libabunt [Musae], non qualia Cypris Adoni, / Sed quale Endimion,
          frigida Luna, tibi."
149-150   **Qualibus – Idae** With his lover Oenone, Paris lived as a shepherd on Mount Ida
          until he was recognized as the son of King Priam.
149   **Pariden** This form (instead of the correct "Paridem") occurs in early editions of
          Verg. *A.* 5, 370. Eobanus maintains the spelling in the *Idyllia* of 1528/39.

complexa lacertis = *Buc.* 9, 69 (n.).

150   **Servantem – Idae** Cf. Ov. *Ars* 1, 28.

Phrygiae – Idae = *Nup.* 115; Cordus, *Buc.* 2, 72 (*Ecl.* 3, 75): "Phrygiae sub vallibus Idae / paverat armentum Paris"; cf. Claud. *Rapt. Pros.* 2, 267: "... Phrygiis in vallibus Idae." For "Phrygiae Idae" see also Verg. *G.* 4, 41; *A.* 3, 6; Ov. *Fast.* 4, 79; Eob. *Buc.* B 2, 41 (n.); *Nup.* 89; *Sylv.* 1, 7, 7.

vallibus Idae = Ov. *Am.* 1, 14, 11; *Ep.* 16, 53; 17, 115; et al.

151   **Huc olim properans** = Line 147 above.

152   **leves Zephyri** *Ciris* 25; Sen. *Oed.* 38; 884; *Oct.* 973.

Zephyri ... Favoni Cf. *Buc.* 5, 47. In Apul. *Met.* 4, 35 and elsewhere, it is Zephyrus that bears Psyche to Cupid's house. The warm breezes known as Zephyr or Favonius are the traditional harbingers of spring, the season of love.

153   **Ferte ... ferte** = Prop. 1, 1, 28.

154   **Lingua – anhelus** Cf. Catul. 51, 6-9.

Lingua stupet *Her.* 1, 6, 4.

155   **saliunt praecordia** Erasmus, *Carm.* 64, 81: "Qualibus o mihi nunc saliunt praecordia votis!"

propinquat This turn of events – the prayer unexpectedly answered – is reminiscent of Verg. *Ecl.* 8, 108-109, where a series of spells cast on the beloved concludes with his return.

156   **Quae – antro** For the image see *Ama* 14, 6 (n.).

sub pectoris antro Prud. *Psych.* 774; cf. *Psych.* 6.

157-158   **Quo fugiam – loquar** Cf. Pl. *Aul.* 729: "Nunc mi incertumst, / abeam an maneam an adeam an fugiam"; Bocc. *Ecl.* 9, 152: "quo fugiam? quo tristis eam? ..."; Mant. *Ecl.* 9, 179: "quid faciam? quo me vertam? ..."

158   **Quid ... loquar** *Laud.* 56 (n.).

Pudor obstat Ov. *Ars* 2, 720; *Rem.* 352; *Met.* 7, 145.

obstat amori = *Ciris* 180: "... ubi enim rubor, obstat amori"; Stat. *Theb.* 2, 270.

159   **Caldus ... calido** For the wordplay cf. lines 33 and 95 above.

servis Amori = *Buc.* 4, 64; cf. *Buc.* 3, 95.

161-162   **Mirabar – iaceres** See lines 135-138 above. Cf. Calp. *Ecl.* 7, 7-9; Nemes. *Ecl.* 4, 15-16.

161   **Mirabar quid** = Verg. *Ecl.* 1, 36.

161-162   **modos et ... Carmina** Stat. *Ach.* 1, 573.

162   **deserta – iaceres** Cf. Verg. *Ecl.* 10, 14; Eob. *Buc.* 1, 46 (n.).

deserta ... rupe *Culex* 51.

163   **barbam squalentior** Cf. Verg. *A.* 2, 277.

164   **ergo – canemus** Ironically quoting line 107 above.

168   **Stulte – formae** Cf. *Ama.* 35, 95-96; *Her. Chr.* 17, 73.

168-170   **quid – iuventae** The brevity of youthful beauty was proverbial. See Otto 688; Häussler, pp. 40 and 163; Eob. *Ama.* 26, 3; *Her. Chr.* 7, 109-110; 17, 71-72. The standard symbol of fleeting beauty and youth was the rose, which (in its pre-modern form) blooms in the morning and wilts in the evening. See, for example, Prop. 4, 5, 61-62; [Aus.] *De rosis nascentibus* 43-46; Walther 32539c; 32540; Erasmus, *Carm.* 2, 87-88.

168   **imagine formae** = Verg. *A.* 6, 293; Ov. *Met.* 3, 416; 4, 676.

169-170   **Ut rosa – iuventae** Cf. Aen. Silv. *Ep.* 106 ("Amoris illiciti medela"), in *Opera quae extant omnia* (Basel, 1571), p. 609: "Forma ... uti flos agri decidit. Rosa mane rubet, sero languescit"; Eob. *Sylv.* 3, 3, 21-22 (on the death of Heinrich Eberbach's baby son Cosmas in ca. 1515): "Tam cito vere novo vix dum rosa nata pruinis / Aut matutino frigore tacta cadit"; *Theoc.* 36, sig. N4ᵛ: "Quam cito ... / ... rosa sicca perit, tam flos cadit ille iuventae."

169   **vespere tacta** Cf. Ov. *Met.* 3, 729: "... frondes autumni frigore tactas."

170   **Quam cito** = Tib. 1, 4, lines 28, 29, 30; Prop. 1, 5, 26; et al.; Eob. *Max.* 143.
       bulla The comparison varies the proverbial "homo bulla" – "man is a bubble."
       See Otto 275; Häussler, p. 141; Erasmus, *Adag.* 2, 3, 48; Eob. *Her. Chr.* 15,
       115; *Sylv.* 1, 4, 65-66: "[Mens] res humanas pereunti comparat umbrae / Et
       bullae scopulos percutientis aquae."
       flos – iuventae Cf. *Her. Chr.* 16, 270; *Theoc.* 7, sig. C8ʳ: "hic tibi ... aevi / Flos
       cadit." For "flos iuventae" see V. Fl. 1, 101; Stat. *Theb.* 7, 301; et al.; Eob. *Her.
       Chr.* 7, 111.
       flos ... ille = Ov. *Tr.* 5, 8, 19, referring to youth: "... sed flos erat ille caducus."

171   **Desipit – vivo** Cf. *Buc.* 3, 96-100 (Philaegon speaking). For passionate love as
       a form of insanity see *Ama.* 20, 10 (n.).
       Desipit omnis amans = *Her. Chr.* 17, 83; cf. *Ama.* B 2, 52 (n.).
       moriturque – vivo Cf. Aen. Silv. *Hist.*, p. 97, line 25 (a sententia also quoted in
       the margin of the Strasbourg copy): "Semper moritur et nunquam mortuus est
       qui amat"; Locher, *Stult.*, fol. 56ʳ: "pars ... ingens / Stultorum moritur terreno
       in corpore semper"; Eob. *Ama.* 18, 9 (n.).
       corpore vivo = Lucr. 2, 703.

172   **Caprarum ... pastor** As his name suggests, Philaegon (like Cautus) is a
       goatherd.
       sic ille monebat *Her. Chr.* 2, 31; cf. Verg. *A.* 7, 110; Bocc. *Ecl.* 4, 109: "... sic
       ante monebas"; Eob. *Her.* 1, 3, 79: "... sic ante monebat."

173-175 **Ut nequit – monitus** Cf. Ov. *Ep.* 15, 12; *Met.* 13, 867-869; Otto 34; Häussler,
       pp. 21, 52, and 258; Mant. *Ecl.* 2, 105-106: "ignes qui nec aquis perimi potuere
       nec umbris / diminui"; Eob. *Ama.* 17, 3-4 (in a humorous inversion); *Buc.* 3,
       105-106 (n.); *Venus* 1, 67-68: "ignes, / Quos non ipse queat Nereus
       extinguere"; 2, 333-335: "incendia, / Quae non refusa grandis unda Nerei /
       Restinguat."

173   **fluctibus Aethna** = Mantuan, *Calam.* 1, p. 20. Mount Etna was often
       associated with the fires of love; see Otto 34; Häussler, pp. 21, 52, and 258;
       Cordus, *Buc.* 2, 129 (*Ecl.* 3, 179).

174   **gravis ... ardor** Catul. 2, 8; Eob. *Her.* 3, 1, 86.
       qui – sustulit = *Idyl.* 15, 88; cf. Poliziano, *Eleg.* 5, 18: "Dextera quae miserum
       me mihi subripuit."

175   **Venus impia** Cf. *Laud.* 239 (n.): "Venus improba."

176   **quibus immergor – uror** Cf. Mant. *Ecl.* 1, 7: "... quibus ingemui curis, quibus
       ignibus arsi"; Eob. *Laud.* 228. For "ignibus uror" cf. also Ov. *Ars* 3, 567; *Met.*
       4, 194.

177-179 **Interea – tempus** The ending, with its tropological overtones, is based on
       Mant. *Ecl.* 2, 172-174 (a thunderstorm portends a disastrous end to passionate
       love): "Cernis ut a summo liventia nubila Baldo / se agglomerent? oritur
       grando; ne forte vagantes / tempestas deprendat oves, discedere tempus"; cf.
       also *Ecl.* 3, 192-194.

177   **pluvias ... undas** Cf. Ov. *Ars* 3, 174; *Met.* 1, 82; *Fast.* 2, 219.
       attrahit undas ≈ Mant. *Ecl.* 1, 35: "... attrahit undam."

178   **Et Libs – Auster** Cf. Stat. *Theb.* 5, 705; *Silv.* 3, 3, 96; Sil. 16, 97.
       luctantur Cf. Verg. *A.* 1, 53; Eob. *Her. Chr.* 9, 13; *Idyl.* 17, 195: "luctantes ...
       venti." For the image cf. also *Buc.* 9, 35 (n.).
       humidus Auster = Verg. *G.* 1, 462; cf. *G.* 3, 429; Ov. *Met.* 1, 66; Eob. *Her. Chr.*
       17, 185; 18, 43.

179   **Tempestas oritur** = Sil. 6, 177.
       Pastu – tempus Cf. Verg. *G.* 4, 186.
       discedere tempus = Prop. 2, 5, 9; Mant. *Ecl.* 2, 174 (see note to lines 177-179
       above).

8

The story of Eobanus's short-lived aspirations to the laurel wreath during the summer of 1508 is recorded in Mutianus Rufus's correspondence. After their mutual friend Hermann Trebelius had been crowned poet laureate by Elector Frederick the Wise, Eobanus too began to thirst for the privilege and badgered Mutianus to make appeals to this end at the Saxon court. See Mutian. *Ep.* 70 (2 July 1508) and *Ep.* 72 (4 July 1508). Nothing, however, came of these initiatives. By late July 1508 Mutianus had to console his protégé by giving him a garland of wheat spikes. "With this," he wrote Herbord von der Marthen, "he will be content until the emperor gives him the poet's [wreath]." See Mutian. *Ep.* 77 (vol. 1, p. 115). For the practice of crowning poets with the laurel wreath in Germany see Karl Schottenloher, "Kaiserliche Dichterkrönungen im Heiligen Römischen Reiche Deutscher Nation," in: *Papsttum und Kaisertum: Forschungen zur politischen Geschichte und Geisteskultur des Mittelalters, Paul Kehr zum 65. Geburtstag dargebracht* (Munich, 1926), pp. 648-673.

The precise date when Hermann Trebelius was crowned poet laureate at Wittenberg has been a matter of dispute. The traditional date is early summer 1508; see Krause, *HEH*, vol. 1, pp. 72-73; Gillert, in Mutian. *Ep.*, vol. 1, p. 98, n. 1. Subsequent research, however, uncovered a poem by Trebelius in which he mentions that the laureation took place during Petrus Lupinus's term as rector at Wittenberg, that is to say, sometime between May 1506 and May 1507. See Trebelius, *Epigr.*, sig. E6^v; Krause, "Beiträge," pp. 45-46; Gustav Bauch, "Trebelius," in *Allgemeine Deutsche Biographie*, vol. 38 (Leipzig, 1894), pp. 549-550, and *Die Universität Erfurt im Zeitalter des Frühhumanismus* (Breslau, 1904), p. 156, n. 4.

Placing the date of Trebelius's coronation in 1506/07, however, conflicts with too many other circumstances to be tenable.

(a) A plague forced the University of Wittenberg to close on 4 July 1506 and move to Herzberg an der Elster until December 9. Gustav Bauch concludes from this circumstance that the laureation took place either shortly before 4 July 1506 or in the winter of 1506/07. The earlier date, however, can be ruled out immediately, for Mutianus Rufus (apparently unaware of the plague in Wittenberg) was still urging Trebelius in late August 1506 to travel to Wittenberg to accept the honor. See Mutian. *Ep.* 79.[1]

(b) The poem in which Trebelius mentions that he was laureated during the rectorship of Petrus Lupinus was not written in Wittenberg, as one might expect, but rather in his hometown Eisenach, for on sig. E5^r he says: "Sunt haec Isiaco carmina facta solo." He had been living in Wittenberg until early July 1506, but was then forced to return to Eisenach, partly because of a conflict with his humanist rival Georgius Sibutus and partly because of the plague. He would remain in Eisenach until the summer of 1508. Since the laureation, as we saw, had not yet taken place by the end of August 1506, Trebelius must have composed his paean of thanks to the Elector *in anticipation* of his formally receiving the laurel crown at Wittenberg during Lupinus's rectorship. In other words, the poem was intended to be presented at a formal ceremony to be held later, but then was not published until 1509.

(c) The winter 1506/07 may likewise be ruled out as the date of Trebelius's laureation ceremony. Two letters by Mutianus Rufus, demonstrably written in early July 1508, refer to the ceremony as a very recent event. See *Epp.* 71 and 72.

(d) Mutian. *Ep.* 70, written on 2 July 1508, and *Ep.* 72, dated 4 July 1508, both indicate that the honor granted to Trebelius inspired Eobanus to lust after the same privilege. This sudden ardor is understandable only if Trebelius was crowned in late June 1508.

(e) Placing Mutian. *Epp.* 70-72 in early July 1506, as Bauch proposes in *Die Universität Erfurt*, p. 156, n. 4, is out of the question, not only because *Ep.* 70 alludes to

[1]For the date of *Ep.* 79 see the introduction to *De recessu studentum*, p. 96, with fn. 3.

Maximilian's Italian campaign of winter-spring 1508, but also because by July 1506 the still teen-aged Eobanus had not yet published any verse and hence could not very well have been crowned poet laureate. As a matter of fact, he had not even introduced himself to Mutianus Rufus by then. See the introduction to *De recessu studentum* (pp. 95-97).

(f) Two further clues confirm that Trebelius was indeed formally laureated in June 1508. According to the present eclogue, the laureation has just taken place (lines 101-116). Furthermore, Eobanus's dream about his own dashed aspirations occurs around July 23, when the sun enters the sign of Leo (line 45). This sequence fits 1508, but not 1506. Other indications hint that Eobanus took at least another six months to get over his disappointment and write the present eclogue with the necessary distance. In lines 91-92 the poet indicates that he is now twenty-two years old. Since Eobanus at the time believed he was born on 6 January 1487 (see fn. 13 at Camerarius, *Nar.* 5, 15), the age reference points to 1509 as the eclogue's composition date. This date is confirmed in lines 90-94 and 122-123, where Eobanus alludes to his obtaining the degree of Master of Arts, an event that took place in early February 1509.

How are we to resolve the conflict between Trebelius's unequivocal statement that he received the laurel during the rectorate of Petrus Lupinus (1506/07) and the many pieces of evidence pointing to the early summer of 1508? I propose the following solution. Trebelius was indeed granted the title of poet laureate early in the summer semester of 1506. However, the laureation ceremony had to be postponed because of the plague then raging in Wittenberg and could not be arranged until late June 1508. The intrigues of his rival Georgius Sibutus in 1506 may also have played a part in the long delay.

As for Eobanus's eclogue, which reflects on his own, ultimately doomed hopes for the laurel wreath, it was composed shortly after his graduation as M.A. in early February 1509 – some seven or eight months after Trebelius's crowning.

Meter: Hexameter.

1-12	**Surgit – agnae** Cf. Pers. 3, 1-7; Aus. *Ephem.* 1, 1-5.
1	**Surgit ... Titan** [Sen.] *Oct.* 3.
2	**pulsa ... nocte** Stat. *Silv.* 1, 2, 52; cf. Ov. *Fast.* 6, 729-730; Eob. *Her. Chr.* 12, 46 (n.).
	reserantur pascua Cf. V. Fl. 1, 655: "emicuit reserata dies"; Stat. *Theb.* 5, 479; Boeth. *Consol.* 1, m. 3, 8; cf. line 19 below (n.).
3	**Colludunt teretes ... guttae** [Aus.] *De rosis nascentibus* 9.
	gramina guttae = *Buc.* 11, 109 (n.).
4	**Omne pecus** *Buc.*, ded. 5 (n.).
	patulis ... arvis = Sil. 4, 545; cf. Luc. 4, 743.
5	**Et matutinae** = Calp. *Ecl.* 5, 55; cf. Verg. *A.* 8, 456; Calp. *Ecl.* 3, 17.
6	**Solus ... antro** = Bocc. *Ecl.* 11, 167; cf. Petrarch, *Ecl.* 1, 1: "Monice, tranquillo solus tibi conditus antro."
	Polipheme, sub antro ≈ Verg. *A.* 3, 641.
7	**somnolenti glires** Cf. Mart. 3, 58, 36; Walther 30035b: "Somnolentior glire." For the scansion "somnŏlenti" see Mant. *Ecl.* 3, 59.
	glires – marini = Antonius Codrus Urceus, *Epigrammata*, in: *In hoc Codri volumine haec continentur: Orationes seu sermones ...* (Bologna, 1502), sig. h6ᵛ: "Dormitis nimium glires vitulique marini." For "vitulique marini" see also Juv. 3, 238.
8	**mille – voces** = *Vict.* 405.
	avium voces = Lucr. 5, 1379; Claud. *in Eutr.* 1, 317.
8-9	**soporem ... excutere** Ov. *Met.* 11, 677-678.
10-11	**Iam – Oceano** Cf. Cordus, *Ecl.* 8, 104-105: "Iamque exorta dies fuit et sex altior ulnis / sol tepidos nonam radios dispersit in horam." In Cordus's calculation, the sun has risen six ells in three hours (two ells per hour, from

sunrise to 9 a.m.). If this calculation holds true for the present passage, it is now about 8 a.m. and Polyphemus has overslept by two hours. Cf. line 31 below: the shepherds want to talk until 10 a.m.

	sol extat ... Altus ab Oceano Cf. Ov. *Ep.* 13, 103.
11	**terras ... omnes** = Verg. *A.* 10, 3; Ov. *Met.* 5, 474; *Pont.* 3, 3, 61.
	supereminet omnes = Verg. *A.* 1, 501; 6, 856; Ov. *Met.* 3, 182; *Tr.* 1, 2, 49.
12	**balant – agnae** Cf. Calp. *Ecl.* 2, 68; Ov. *Met.* 13, 827.
	ovilibus agnae ≈ *Buc.* 4, 118.
13	**dulci somno** Verg. *A.* 4, 185; *Ciris* 206.
15	**montibus altis** = *Buc.* 6, 44 (n.).
17	**lucis pars** = Ov. *Met.* 7, 662.
18	**clauso ... lecto** Cf. line 41 below (n.).
	requiescere lecto = Tib. 1, 1, 43; Prop. 1, 8, 33.
19	**Ut – orbem** Cf. Ov. *Met.* 9, 795; *Ilias Lat.* 650: "Ut nitidum Titan radiis patefecerat orbem."
20	**plumis** See *Ama.* 35, 76 (n.).
21	**Lanigeris ... ovibus** Verg. *A.* 3, 660; Ov. *Fast.* 1, 334; cf. Eob. *Buc.* 3, 166 (n.).
21-22	**campos – damus** ≈ Calp. *Ecl.* 5, 29-30. For "dumeta capellis" see also Calp. *Ecl.* 5, 5; Eob. *Buc.* 9, 114.
22	**Gaudent – iuvenci** Cf. Verg. *Ecl.* 8, 15; *G.* 3, 326; Calp. *Ecl.* 5, 52-55.
23	**alio ... tempore** = Lucr. 5, 1081; V. Fl. 2, 361; Sil. 17, 387.
24	**animum ... movent** Verg. *G.* 3, 521; Ov. *Ep.* 12, 89; *Pont.* 1, 2, 113; Eob. *Her. Chr.* 7, 38.
	res digna relatu = Mant. *Ecl.* 7, 57 (also referring to a dream-vision); cf. Ov. *Met.* 4, 793 and *Fast.* 3, 541: "... digna relatu."
25	**praeteritam – noctem** Cf. *Buc.* 7, 121 (n.); *Her. Chr.* 5, 77 (n.).
26	**Dii superi** = *Ama.* 35, 80 (n.).
	certa fides Prop. 3, 8, 19; Ov. *Fast.* 6, 609; et al.; Eob. *Her. Chr.* 6, 118; 13, 68; *Vict.* 308.
	Oracula Cf. *Epic.* 3 A, 45, where Eobanus calls his dream about Albrecht Dürer an "oraclum."
28	**Dic igitur** = Juv. 7, 106.
29	**quae mira – figuris** Cf. *Ama.* 9, 1; *Her. Chr.* 5, 71.
	novis ... figuris = Stat. *Silv.* 1, 3, 56; cf. Ov. *Met.* 15, 169.
	simulachra figuris = Aus. *Cupido cruciatus* 99: "nocturnis ... simulacra figuris"; Celtis, *Am.* 1, 14, 54: "... noctivagis simulacra figuris"; 3, 4, 37: "Dum nos sub variis ludunt simulacra figuris."
30-31	**Interea – Pascetur** Cf. Verg. *Ecl.* 10, 6-7; Nemes. *Ecl.* 1, 6-8; Eob. *Buc.* 8, 34-35. For the phrasing cf. also *Buc.* 10, 115.
31	**decimam – horam** Cf. Mant. *Ecl.* 1, 121 (referring to the "noon" hour, according to late-medieval usage): "... in nonam dum lux attollitur horam." In the present passage the time reckoning is the modern one, where the hours begin at midnight (rather than at sunrise, as in the ancient Roman system). For this usage cf., for example, Cordus, *Ecl.* 8, 105 (see note to lines 10-11 above); Eob. *Sylv.* 7, 11, 9-10: "Cras, ubi purpureos Aurora reduxerit ortus / Nonaque iam clarum fecerit hora diem." The shepherds intend to converse until 10 a.m. (the fourth hour after sunrise), when it is time to drive the flock to water. See Verg. *G.* 3, 327-330; Calp. *Ecl.* 5, 56-57.
32-33	**Et nos – videre** For the "motif of bucolic repose" see n. *Buc.* 1, 65-71. Cf. in particular *Idyl.* 3, 20-21: "... postquam consedimus antro, / Unde pecus patet atque oculis vicinia nostris."
32	**Et nos – recubabimus** Cf. Verg. *Ecl.* 1, 14; 5, 3.
33	**velut e tumulo** In the 1528/39 version this phrase is changed to the more

familiar "velut e specula," perhaps in response to Erasmus, *Adag.* 4, 3, 95.
pecus omne = *Buc.*, ded. 5 (n.).

34 **Pascite – capellae** Cf. Nemes. *Ecl.* 1, 6-7.

35 **monstriferae ... somnia noctis** = *Psalt.* 73, 55; cf. *Theoc.* 25, sig. I 4ᵛ: "... monstrosae somnia noctis." For the tag "somnia noctis" see Petrarch, *Africa* 2, 7; Erasmus, *Carm.* 2, 83; Eob. *Buc.* 7, 121 (n.).

36-40 **Tempus – silet** Cf. Ov. *Met.* 7, 185-187.

36-37 **Tempus erat ... Quo ... prima quies** Verg. *A.* 2, 268.

36 **Tempus erat** = *Rec.* 1 (n.).

sacros ... ignes = *Ilias Lat.* 34. For "ignes" meaning "stars" see, for example, Hor. *Carm.* 1, 12, 47; Verg. *A.* 2, 154; Eob. *Nor.* 17. The stars are "sacred" because the heavens are home to the gods.

nox caeca Lucr. 1, 1115-1116; Catul. 68, 44; Verg. *G.* 3, 260; *A.* 2, 397; et al.; Eob. *Her. Chr.* 14, 103.

reduxerat ignes = *Her. Chr.* 3, 67.

37 **gravidos – artus** Cf. Verg. *A.* 5, 857; Stat. *Silv.* 1, 4, 56-57.

38 **Cum – canorae** Cf. Verg. *A.* 4, 525; Stat. *Theb.* 1, 339; *Silv.* 5, 4, 3.

volucresque canorae = Ov. *Fast.* 3, 17.

39 **Totaque ... tellus** = Luc. 1, 654.

Tartareo ... numine Cf. Prud. *Perist.* 13, 52: "tartareae caliginis."

circumdata – tellus = *Idyl.* 17, 235: "Cuncta tridentifero circumdata numine tellus"; cf. Ov. *Met.* 2, 272.

39-40 **tellus ... conversa** Ov. *Met.* 1, 87-88.

40 **Me somnus habebat** Ov. *Pont.* 3, 3, 7.

41 **clauso ... antro** = Juv. 4, 21; cf. line 18 above.

42-59 **Propter – corona est** The dream of being crowned poet on Mount Helicon is ancient. See, for example, Hes. *Th.* 22-34; Verg. *Ecl.* 6, 64-73 (of Gallus); Prop. 3, 3; Petrarch, *Ecl.* 3 (the poet dreams that he is being crowned by the Muses).

42 **Propter aquas** ≈ Verg. *G.* 3, 14; cf. Eob. *Laud.* 323 (n.). That Eobanus is strolling along a brook at the start of his dream is part of the tradition of poet-crownings on Mount Helicon. Thus Gallus in Verg. *Ecl.* 6, 64 walks beside the Permessis; and Propertius (3, 3, 1-2) dreams he is lying beside the Hippocrene. Similarly in Petrarch, *Ecl.* 3, 87-88, Stupeus happens to be wandering along a brook when the Muses appear to him and grant him the laurel. Heliades, in lines 112-113 below, reports that he too was walking beside a "sacred spring" when he was enraptured and made poet laureate.

42-43 **herbosis ... Aggeribus** Ov. *Met.* 14, 445.

42 **errare videbar** = Enn. *Ann.* 41; cf. Hor. *Carm.* 3, 4, 6-7.

43 **frondesque – capellis** Leafy twigs were cut and stored to serve as fodder during the winter months; see, for example, Calp. *Ecl.* 2, 44-45; 5, 98-115; Serv. *Ecl.* 1, 56. However, this was not normally done in mid-summer, but only toward the end of the pasturing season.

44-45 **arguta – Carmina** Cf. *Idyl.* 7, 63: "... arguta meditari carmina buxo."

44 **arguta ... canna** Sil. 7, 439; cf. Verg. *Ecl.* 7, 24; Calp. *Ecl.* 7, 12.

44-45 **modulari ... Carmina** *Buc.* 1, 11 (n.).

44 **modulari ... canna** Calp. *Ecl.* 4, 45.

44-45 **dultia ... Carmina** = *Culex* 146-147.

45 **ira Leonis** = Maxim. *Eleg.* 1, 271; cf. Ov. *Tr.* 4, 6, 5; Luc. 6, 487. For the sense cf. Hor. *Carm.* 3, 29, 18-19: "iam Procyon furit / et stella vesani Leonis"; Ov. *Met.* 2, 81.

46 **mihi, nescio quo** = Ov. *Ep.* 3, 78.

46-47 **succenso – undae** Cf. Verg. *G.* 3, 291-292; Eob. *Buc.* 2, 42.

46 **succenso – amore** Cf. Verg. *A.* 3, 298; Eob. *Her. Chr.* 17, 81; *Hod.* 32-33:

"Mirifico ... studiorum pectus amore / Accensus." For "succenso amore" see Verg. *A.* 7, 496; Ov. *Ep.* 15, 167.

47   **sacrae – undae** ≈ Andrel. *Eleg.* 2, sig. d5ᵛ: "... sacri Permessidos unda"; Eob. *Nor.* 7: "... sacrae Permessidos undas"; *Ebn.* 173: "... sacrae Permessidos unda"; cf. Locher, "Ad S. Brant," in *Stult.*, fol. 3ᵛ: "Permessidos unda / Sacra"; Eob. *Laud.* 249 (n.).

48   **Culmine ab aereo** = *Sylv.* 2, 26, 3; cf. *Sylv. duae* 2, 151 (of Mount Parnassus): "aereo de culmine"; *Coluth.*, sig. A4ᵛ: "... ab aerio Parnassi culmine montis"; also cf. *Sylv. duae* 2, 135.

      summoque ... vertice = Verg. *A.* 11, 526; Ov. *Met.* 6, 204; cf. Eob. *Buc.* 1, 83 (n.).

      vertice Musae ≈ Verg. *G.* 3, 11.

49   **Desuper ostentant** ≈ Verg. *A.* 6, 678.

      lauri – coronam Cf. Lucr. 1, 118: "Ennius, ... qui primus amoeno / detulit ex Helicone perenni fronde coronam"; Mant. *2. Parthen.* 1, 14: "... de fronde coronam"; Eob. *Buc.* 1, 48 (n.); *Sylv.* 6, 5, 29: "... lauri de fronde coronas."

50   **ductrixque – verendi** Cf. Stat. *Theb.* 4, 34-35: "tuque o nemoris regina sonori, / Calliope"; Petrarch, *Ecl.* 3, 121-122 (Calliope crowns him poet): "Regina sonori / Hunc michi prima chori ramum dedit arbore vulsum"; Bocc. *Ecl.* 14, 119-120: "nemoris custos regina canori / Caliopes"; Eob. *Laud.* 246 (n.).

51   **summa ... ab arce** Verg. *A.* 2, 41; Ov. *Rem.* 57.

52   **Qui – coerces** Cf. Hes. *Th.* 22-23, where we learn that Hesiod was tending his flock in the valley when the Muses made him a poet.

53   **ovium custos** = Verg. *G.* 1, 17.

55-58 **Huc – bacca** Cf. Verg. *Ecl.* 6, 64-71; Petrarch, *Ecl.* 3, 102-105: "'accipe ramum / Hunc prius,' et tenero frondosum pollice ramum / Decerpsit cupidoque michi porrexit et, 'Ibis, / Ibis,' ait, 'dicesque novem vidisse sorores'"; Eob. *Buc.* 6, 57-59.

55   **praemia fronti** Cf. Hor. *Carm.* 1, 1, 29 (of the poet's wreath).

56   **perpetuis ... victura diebus** Cf. *Laud.* 63 (n.).

58   **Cinge – bacca** In antiquity the poet's wreath was made of ivy, sacred to Bacchus, or of laurel, sacred to Apollo; see n. *Laud.* 251-252. Here "bacca" stands for "lauri baca" (Verg. *G.* 1, 306) and hence, by metonymy, for the laurel wreath.

      Cinge – hedera Cf. Ov. *Am.* 1, 7, 36: "cinge comam lauro"; *Tr.* 1, 7, 2; line 109 below.

      viridi bacca Hor. *Carm.* 2, 6, 15-16.

      tege tempora = Verg. *A.* 4, 637; cf. Ov. *Fast.* 2, 26.

      tempora bacca ≈ Ov. *Met.* 10, 116.

59   **En ultro** Verg. *A.* 3, 155.

      ultro porrecta Ov. *Met.* 3, 458.

60   **"Accipe," cum dixisset** Cf. Verg. *Ecl.* 6, 69; Calp. *Ecl.* 2, 34; Eob. *Her. Chr.* 4, 125.

      in sublime ferebar Cic. *N. D.* 2, 44; 2, 140; Aus. *Ephem.* 3, 38; cf. Eob. *Her. Chr.* 15, 37 (n.).

61   **solito ... velotior** Cf. Ov. *Met.* 14, 388.

      magis velotior The double comparative is quite common in later Latin.

62   **Umbra levis** *Buc.* 2, 86 (n.).

      pluma Proverbially light. See Otto 1438; Häussler, pp. 202 and 284.

      pernitior Euro Cf. *Rec.* 37 (n.).

63   **Iamque – eram** Cf. Ov. *Ep.* 11, 71; Eob. *Her. Chr.* 11, 68.

      Iamque adeo = Lucr. 2, 1150; Verg. *A.* 2, 567; et al.

      antri For the Muses's grotto on Mount Helicon cf. Hor. *Carm.* 3, 4, 40; Mart. 12, 11, 3; Juv. 7, 59-60; Claud. *Rapt. Pros.* 2, praef. 51; Eob. *Nob.* 10; *Sylv.* 4,

19, 8: "ex Heliconis antro"; line 115 below.

64   **Unde prius** = Lucr. 1, 930; 4, 5; Verg. *G.* 1, 74.

    nostras ... ad aures = Ov. *Ep.* 12, 137.

65   **cursu ... anhelo** = Ov. *Met.* 11, 347; Stat. *Theb.* 9, 222; 10, 686; et al.

67   **Passis ... lacertis** *Her. Chr.* 6, 13.

    mea colla lacertis ≈ Ov. *Am.* 1, 4, 35; 2, 18, 9; *Ep.* 8, 93.

67-68   **colla – Complexus** Ov. *Met.* 1, 734; cf. Eob. *Rec.* 130 (n.); *Buc.* 9, 69 (n.).

68   **Quo – abis** = Mant. *Ecl.* 1, 90.

68-69   **Iuvenilibus – ponis** Cf. *Buc.* 10, 140, with notes.

71-72   **maiora – Praemia** Luc. 5, 246-247.

72   **pueri – annis** Cf. *Laud.* 322-323 (n.).

74-75   **Despiciunt – lauri** Cf. Pontano, *Parthen.* 1, 17, 15: "Stultus ego, fieri credam qui fronde poetam: / Non laurus vatem, sed sua Musa facit"; lines 125-126 below.

75   **bona carmina** = *Buc.* 10, 82; cf. Ov. *Am.* 3, 9, 39.

77   **mirantur** This rare passive is replaced with "celebrantur" in the 1528/39 version.

78   **vernant – capilli** = Poliziano, *Sylv.*, praef. 9 (of garlands): "Crescit fronde torus, vernant in flore capilli." For this phrase – a figurative way of expressing the poets' youthfulness – cf. Eob. *Buc.* 6, 59; *Sylv.* 7, 7, 3: "Quae puer annorum vernans in flore reliqui"; cf. further *Theoc.* 11, sig. D6ᵛ: "Vernarentque leves iuvenili in fronte capilli"; *Idyl.* 16, 77: "vernantem in flore iuventae"; *Sylv.* 1, 4, 15: "... vernans in flore iuventa"; *Sylv.* 7, 9, 1 and *Consol.* 77: "... vernans in flore iuventae."

    flore capilli = Ov. *Ep.* 4, 71; cf. Eob. *Laud.* 165.

79   **coelum – pulsant** Cf. Hor. *Carm.* 1, 1, 36; Ov. *Met.* 7, 61; Mart. 8, 36, 11; Otto 289; Häussler, pp. 97, 143, and 234; Eob. *Her. Chr.* 6, 191; 16, 290.

    vertice pulsant ≈ Ov. *Met.* 5, 84; *Ilias Lat.* 376.

81   **primatibus herent** Cf. *Tum.* 3, 77-78: "haerens / Principibus."

82-83   **seque – praetulerint** Cf. *Idyl.* 11, 102-103: "te / ... praeferres omnibus unum."

83   **pudor est** (with following infinitive) = Ov. *Met.* 14, 18; Eob. *Epic.* 3 B, 11; cf. *Ama.* 35, 110 (n.).

86   **Pascere oves** = *Buc.* 4, 2 (n.).

    dominis ... superbis = Lucr. 2, 1091; Verg. *A.* 12, 236.

87   **Ferre iugum** = Stat. *Theb.* 10, 233; *Silv.* 1, 2, 78; 5, 3, 160; Juv. 6, 208.

    quaerere victum = Claud. *in Eutr.* 2, 371; Eob. *Idyl.* 14, 117; cf. Ter. *Hau.* 447; *Eu.* 261; Eob. *Her. Chr.* 16, 120.

88   **Ergo age** = *Buc.* 1, 103 (n.).

    siste gradum = *Ilias Lat.* 1063; cf. Verg. *A.* 6, 465; Ov. *Ep.* 13, 102.

    obstare furori = Verg. *A.* 4, 91.

89   **vitam trutinare** *Buc.* 6, 15.

90   **Nos te** = Verg. *A.* 3, 156; Stat. *Theb.* 7, 98.

92   **aetas ... compleverit annos** Macr. 1, 6, 83: "cum aetas tua quinquagesimum et sextum annum compleverit."

94   **libertatis honorem** ≈ Sil. 10, 645.

96   **Tantum effatus** Verg. *G.* 4, 450; *A.* 6, 547; 10, 256 and 877.

97   **Horrendum clamans** = *Ilias* 5, p. 139; 8, p. 189; cf. Verg. *A.* 6, 288.

    orto iam sole Vulg. *4. Reg.* 3, 22; *Marc.* 16, 2. According to an ancient belief, dreams that come after midnight are truthful. See, for example, Hor. *S.* 1, 10, 33; Eob. *Theoc.* 20, sig. H1ʳ: "Tempus erat, iam sydereae pars tertia noctis / Transierat, prope erat roseis Aurora quadrigis, / Tempore quo mollis gratissima munera somni / Irrepunt vinclisque ligant praedulcibus artus / Veraque per cunctas pascuntur somnia terras"; cf. also Verg. *A.* 6, 893-896.

98   **quae – noctem** Cf. *Theoc.* 26. sig. I 8ʳ: "Talia per tacitae quae vidi insomnia noctis." For "vidi somnia" see Ov. *Met.* 9, 475; for the tag "somnia noctem" cf. Eob. *Buc.* 7, 121 (n.).

99-100   **Mira – pastor** Cf. *Buc.* 1, 39 (n.); 4, 73-74 (with note to lines 73-75).

99   **Mira refers** = Calp. *Ecl.* 1, 31.

100   **tractet – pastor** *Sylv.* 3, 2, 57: "Sacra bonus tractet Verbi mysteria pastor."

101   **Ecce sed** = *Laud.* 178 (n.).
          Aonia ... tempora lauro = Lotich. *Eleg.* 2, 6, 11: "Cincta quod Aonia non sunt mea tempora lauro."
          redimitus – lauro = Verg. *A.* 3, 81; [Tib.] 3, 4, 23; cf. Eob. *Buc.* 2, 77 (n.).

104   **Salvete aeternum** Verg. *A.* 11, 97; Eob. *Theoc.* 1, sig. A8ʳ: "Musae, / Aeternum salvete."

105   **laetitiam ... novam** *Pug.* 18 (n.).
          celebrate faventes = Verg. *A.* 1, 735; 8, 173.

106   **Nunc – leves** Cf. Verg. *Ecl.* 5, 2; Eob. *Buc.* 10, 18.

107   **Sonent – cantu** Cf. *Buc.* 7, 138.
          omnia cantu = Sil. 13, 347.

108   **Quis te, ... puer** Mant. *Ecl.* 2, 111: "miserande puer, quis te deus istas / misit in ambages?"
          tanto ... honore Verg. *A.* 8, 617.
          dignatus honore = Ov. *Met.* 3, 521; 8, 569; Sil. 11, 272.

109   **cinxit ... fronde capillos** Cf. Verg. *A.* 8, 274: "... cingite fronde comas"; Mart. 4, 54, 2; line 58 above.

110   **Dic age dic** = Calp. *Ecl.* 7, 19; 7, 78; cf. Eob. *Buc.* 1, 60 (n.).
          Aliquis superum = *Her. Chr.* 1, 43; cf. *Her. Chr.* 17, 202; *Luth.* 2, 44.
          pastor agrestis Ennod. *Carm.* 1, 8, praef.

111   **Dum – thaurum** Cf. *Buc.* 4, 105-106 (n.), where Heliades is looking for a runaway heifer.
          lustra ... per inhospita Sil. 16, 103.
          amissum ... thaurum ≈ Stat. *Theb.* 3, 52.

112-113   **Monte – aquas** Cf. Calp. *Ecl.* 4, 16; Eob. *Idyl.* 1, 77-78: "puri latices, quos plurima quercus inumbrat." For the trees overshadowing the Muses's spring cf. Prop. 3, 3, 13.

112   **Monte sub obscuro** = *Sylv.* 3, 3, 48 and *Epic.* 1, 86 (both referring to Mount Helicon).
          ubi plurima = *Buc.* 5, 2 (n.).

113-116   **raptum – Musas** Imitated by Cordus, *Ecl.* 2, 167-172: "O si quis medias raptum me turbo per auras / sisteret umbrosum Parnassi in rupe sub antrum, / ut prope congressus Phoebumque deasque viderem / imbiberetque meum praesentia numina pectus! / Contigit hoc patriae cuidam sub vallibus Ascrae / et sacer hinc subito cecinit nova carmina vates."

113   **super ardua** = Verg. *A.* 6, 515; 7, 562; Eob. *Her. Chr.* 1, 73; 9, 113.
          ardua montis = Verg. *A.* 8, 221; 11, 513; Ov. *Met.* 8, 692.

114   **Divae Pierides** *Buc.* 2, 1-2 (n.).
          Pierides – foecere Cf. Verg. *Ecl.* 9, 32-33; Mart. 8, 73, 5.

115   **Ascraeo – antro** Changed to "Ascraeis pascenti in vallibus agnas" in the 1528/ 39 version, because Hesiod's herd consisted of lambs, not cattle ("armenta"); see Hes. *Th.* 22-23. For the Muses' grotto on Mount Helicon see line 63 above (n.).

116   **afflatus numine** Verg. *A.* 6, 50; Mant. *2. Parthen.* 3, 153-154: "afflata ... / Numine"; cf. Eob. *Buc.* 5, 89.

117   **vidisse puto** Verg. *A.* 6, 454; Ov. *Ep.* 18, 32.
          daemona This unpastoral word occurs also in Mant. *Ecl.* 1, 50 and 4, 90.

118   **Pierides ... Musae** *Rec.* 74 (n.).
           delyramina Cf. Paul. Nol. *Carm.* 15, 30: "Castalidas, vatum phantasmata,
           Musas."
119-121   **Vana – numen** Since Christian poets are inspired by the Holy Spirit, they
           cannot invoke the pagan Muses except on a symbolic level. See Paul Klopsch,
           Einführung in die Dichtungslehren des lateinischen Mittelalters (Darmstadt,
           1980), pp. 20-30; Eob. *Sylv.* 1, 10, 23-30 (where Eobanus defends himself for
           invoking Christ instead of Apollo and the Muses in *Nup.* 1-7): "Sed tamen est
           ratio cur Phoebum agnoscere possis / Et Musas dicas carminis esse duces – /
           Non ut honore Deo, non ut virtutibus aeques, / Non ut adorandum numen
           habere putes. / Musae, Mercurius, Phoebus, Pan, Liber, Apollo, / Nomina sunt
           uni contribuenda Deo. / Ludere nominibus licuit semperque licebit; / Credere
           nequaquam numen habere licet." See further n. *Laud.* 13; *Buc.* 2, 16-19 (n.); 3,
           13-14 (with notes); 11, 16-19 (with note to lines 16-22).
119   **Vana ... fabula** *Her. Chr.* 20, 140 (n.).
121   **unum – numen** Cf. Gianfrancesco Pico della Mirandola, "Deprecatoria ad
           Deum," in his *Opera omnia* (Basel, 1557; repr. Hildesheim, 1969, vol. 1), p.
           339: "Alme Deus ... qui ... / Vere unum in triplici numine numen habes." For
           "triplici numine" see also Prud. *Cath.* 5, 163.
124   **de rebus agemus** ≈ Verg. *A.* 11, 445.
125   **Non – cucullus** Eobanus's line, as printed in the 1528/39 version, became
           proverbial. See Walther 10138: "Fuscina non facit unca cocum, monachumve
           cucullus."
           Non – coquum Proverbial; see Walther 17383: "Non cocus ex cultro longo ...
           probatur"; 17404-17406.
           monachumve cucullus Proverbial; see Walther 1010-1011; 17778-17779;
           17845-17846.
126   **Nec laurus vatem** ≈ Pontano, *Parthen.* 1, 17, 16 (quoted in note to lines 74-75
           above). Cf. also the Neo-Latin epigram quoted in Walther 18621: "Non tituli
           faciunt nec laurea serta poetam, / Non in fronde, sed in fronte poeta sedet."
           Sua – monstrat Cf. Cic. *Tusc.* 1, 41: "bene enim illo Graecorum proverbio
           praecipitur: 'quam quisque norit artem, in hac se exerceat'"; Erasmus, *Adag.* 1,
           6, 15; Otto 167; Eob. *Buc.* 10, 111.
127-130   **Sit – capellas** Closely paralleled in *Buc.* 5, 111-116, where see notes.
127   **Sit satis hoc** = *Ciris* 455; Aus. *Parent.* 23, 19.
128   **res est divina** Erasmus, *Carm.* 38, 30 (of music).
           divina poetam ≈ Verg. *Ecl.* 5, 45; 10, 17.
129   **nostris – pagis** Cf. Calp. *Ecl.* 4, 13.
           non enarrabile = Verg. *A.* 8, 625; Pers. 5, 29.
130   **pascite ... capellas** Cf. Verg. *Ecl.* 9, 23; Eob. *Buc.* 5, 116.

9

The lament for the dead Iolas (Landgrave William II of Hesse) stands in the tradition of
pastoral eulogies that begins with Theoc. 1 and continues with Verg. *Ecl.* 5, Nemes. *Ecl.* 1,
and Petrarch, *Ecl.* 2. On the genre see Ellen Zetzel Lambert, *Placing Sorrow: A Study of the
Pastoral Elegy Convention from Theocritus to Milton* (Chapel Hill, 1976). Bion's "Lament
for Adonis" and Pseudo-Moschus's "Lament for Bion" were unknown to Eobanus at the
time he wrote the present eclogue.
      Eobanus's poem strongly influenced Cordus's pastoral lament for Landgrave
William II and encomium of his son Philip. See Cordus, *Buc.* 4 (*Ecl.* 1). In *Buc.* 4, 39
Cordus refers to William as "Iollas."
      Meter: Hexameter.

1	**flavae ... puellae** Ov. *Am.* 2, 4, 39; Juv. 6, 354.
	cura puellae = Prop. 3, 21, 3; [Tib.] 3, 17, 1; Ov. *Am.* 1, 9, 43; et al.
2	**dulces – ignes** Cf. *Idyl.* 1, 39: "... placidos liquisti invitus amores."
3	**ante duas ... messes** = *Idyl.* 10, 11; cf. *Buc.* 4, 82. For the time expression see *Laud.* 1 (n.).
	potuisti linquere = Verg. *A.* 9, 482; Prop. 3, 12, 1.
4	**Germania Rhenum** = *Her. Chr.* 24, 51; cf. Mart. 2, 2, 3.
5	**compressus – laborum** ≈ *Psalt.* 18, 17: "... oppressus mole laborum"; 72, 33: "... depressos mole laborum"; cf. line 64 below; *Vict.* 266: "... obruta mole laborum."
6	**Quidve doles** ≈ Verg. *A.* 1, 9.
7-8	**nihil ... iuris habent** *Laud.* B 1, 10 (n.).
7	**turpes ... flammae** *Ama.* 35, 115 (n.).
7-8	**fortia ... Pectora** = Verg. *A.* 8, 150-151.
10	**Aetas – annum** Cf. Verg. *Ecl.* 8, 39; Eob. *Her. Chr.* 24, 119.
11	**amor ... error** For the wordplay see *Laud.* 236 (n.).
	muliērum For this medieval scansion see n. *Buc.* 3, 141.
	inutilis error = *Ilias* 20, p. 505: "... animi te ludit inutilis error"; cf. Verg. *Ecl.* 8, 41 and *Ciris* 430 (of passionate love): "malus ... error."
12	**alius ... dolor** Sen. *Phaed.* 99.
12-13	**alta ... Pectora** = V. Fl. 5, 594-595; cf. Stat. *Silv.* 1, 4, 48-49.
	curis ... mordacibus Luc. 2, 681.
14-16	**Nunc omnia – resultant** Nature mourns the death of Iolas, as it once mourned the death of Daphnis; cf. Theoc. 1, 71-75; 7, 74-75; Verg. *Ecl.* 5, 27-28. For the pathetic fallacy cf. also Verg. *Ecl.* 10, 13-15; Stat. *Theb.* 5, 333-334; Nemes. *Ecl.* 1, 72-74; Eob. *Buc.* 9, 53-55; *Her. Chr.* 3, 45-56; *Epic.* 3, 47; 3, 123-130; 4, 35-56; 4, 77-100; 6, 105-108; *Ebn.* 79-84.
14	**Nunc omnia moerent** Cf. *Ama.* 32, 59 (n.): "nunc omnia rident."
14-15	**omnia – prius** Cf. *Idyl.* 3, 139-140: "omnia fient / Candida, nigra prius"; 15, 81-82: "omnia ponam / Cara prius."
15-16	**Nunc omnis – Tristantur** A reversal of the idyllic state of nature as depicted in Verg. *Ecl.* 3, 56-57; Eob. *Ruf.* 5-8.
15	**omnis – patentes** *Rec.* 5, where see notes.
16	**montes – resultant** Cf. Verg. *A.* 5, 150; Eob. *Nor.* 594: "... valles plangore resultant."
17	**fata ... tam tristia** Sen. *Phoen.* 244; cf. Ov. *Am.* 3, 9, 2; *Met.* 10, 163; et al.; Eob. *Rec.* 49; *Laud.* B 3, 20 (n.); *Her. Chr.* 12, 144 (n.); 16, 117; 20, 36.
18	**Dic, precor** = Ov. *Pont.* 3, 3, 53; V. Fl. 7, 275; Mart. 6, 10, 9.
	interea calidus ≈ Verg. *A.* 9, 422.
19	**pecus – umbra** Cf. Mant. *Ecl.* 1, 1-2: "quando pecus omne sub umbra / ruminat"; 9, 19: "dum grex in gelida procumbens ruminat umbra"; Eob. *Buc.*, ded. 5 (n.); 1, 63 (n.).
	illustri A gloss in the Strasbourg copy says that the epithet here means "opaca." If so, the epithet is used in the unusual sense "in-lustri." In the 1528/39 version Eobanus changed it to "ilicea" (literally: "of an oak tree").
20	**Flete – Camaenae** Cf. Filetico, *Theoc.* 1, 64: "Ite, meae Musae, faciles huc ite Camoenae"; Eob. *Buc.* 2, 20 (n.); Hutten, *Querel.* 2, 7, 1: "Flete meae maestae et lachrimas confundite Musae."
21	**ante diem** = *Rec.* 139 (n.).
	fato concessit = *Epp. fam.*, p. 86, letter of ca. March 1519: "... fato concessit Erasmus"; cf. Plin. *Pan.* 11, 3: "fato concessit."
22	**Dicite – Parcae** = *Eras.* 135; cf. *Her. Chr.* 16, 225; *Ebn.* 27: "Dicite crudeles, infamia numina, Parcae".

crudelia – Parcae = *Epic.* 1, 81; cf. Poliziano, *Sylv.* 3, 84-85: "crudelia divum / Numina, crudeles Parcas." For the hexameter close cf. Verg. *Ecl.* 4, 47 and *Ciris* 125: "... numine Parcae"; Stat. *Theb.* 8, 191; Eob. *Epic.* 2, 71: "... mala numina Parcae."

23 **Ausurae – deos** Cf. *Buc.* B 3, 6 (n.), on the death of William II of Hesse. For "violare deos" cf. Verg. *A.* 12, 797; Ov. *Met.* 4, 613.

24-28 **Iuvenis – reddi** The Fates repent of their deed. The motif reappears in *Epic.* 4, 63-72 (at the death of Mutianus Rufus).

25 **Lanificae ... sorores** = *Epic.* 4, 63: "Lanificae corpus videre exangue sorores"; cf. Mart. 4, 54, 5; 6, 58, 7; Juv. 12, 64-66; Eob. *Vict.* 161: "... lanificae ponebant fila sorores."
   procul ... rupe = Verg. *Ecl.* 1, 76.

26 **vires ... suas odere** Petr. 120, 84; cf. Eob. *Tum.* 5, 96.

27 **humili ... manu** Ov. *Ars* 2, 254.
   ni fata negarent Sil. 6, 115-116; cf. Ov. *Met.* 10, 634; Sil. 1, 107.

28 **relabentes – reddi** Cf. Verg. *A.* 6, 719-721.

29 **Somnus ... Laethaeus** Verg. *G.* 1, 78; Hor. *Epod.* 14, 3. Sleep is a conventional euphemism for death; see, for example, Verg. *A.* 10, 746; 12, 310; Hor. *Carm.* 3, 11, 38.
   ut extinctum ... Iolam = *Idyl.* 13, 34 (recalling the present eclogue); cf. line 67 below; Verg. *Ecl.* 5, 20.

30 **Ferrea – agros** For the motif cf. Verg. *G.* 1, 466-468 (at the death of Julius Caesar); Petrarch, *Ecl.* 2, 7-9 (in a pastoral elegy): "tum fusca nitentem / Obduxit Phebum nubes, precepsque repente / Ante expectatum nox affuit."
   Ferrea nox *Epic.* 1, 35; cf. Verg. *A.* 10, 745-746 (12, 309-310).

31-32 **Et lupus – praedam** Cf. Mant. *Ecl.* 3, 23-24: "latro insidias intentat ovili / atque lupus milesque lupo furacior omni"; Andrel. *Ecl.* 2, 4-6: "Ne forsan miles nostri populator agelli / Tristia damna ferat; nihil est a milite tutum / Prodiga cui desit consumpti copia nummi"; Eob. *Buc.* 11, 97-98; *Idyl.* 4, 108-109: "nostri custodi septa peculi, / Ne lupus et rapidi turbent armenta latrones."

31 **Et lupus et miles** Cf. Mant. *Ecl.* 3, 24: "atque lupus milesque ...."
   praedator ovilia ≈ Calp. *Ecl.* 1, 40.
   ovilia lustrans ≈ Calp. *Ecl.* 5, 28 (in a different sense).

32 **agens ... praedam** Ov. *Tr.* 5, 10, 20.
   effuso sanguine Verg. *A.* 7, 788; Eob. *Her. Chr.* 4, 216 (n.); cf. *Her. Chr.* 12, 122 (n.).
   sanguine praedam = Ov. *Tr.* 1, 11, 29; Sil. 4, 124.

33-34 **Non – Pascua** Cf. *Buc.* 1, 80-81 (n.); 4, 31-32 (n.); *Idyl.* 1, 95: "Incustoditae per pascua tuta vagantur / Lanigerae pecudes."

33 **passim vagantur** Verg. *A.* 6, 886; Ov. *Met.* 12, 54.

33-34 **tuta ... Pascua** = Lines 89-90 below.

34 **custode tuentur** *Psalt.* 127, 3: "Ni Deus invigilet, frustra custode tuentur"; cf. Verg. *A.* 1, 564. Eobanus uses "tuentur" in an unusual passive sense; cf. Luc. 1, 26: "... nulloque domus custode tenentur."

35 **Certantes – venti** For the motif – storms at the death of a shepherd – cf. Petrarch, *Ecl.* 2, 9-11: "horruit ether / Grandine terribili; certatim ventus et imber / Sevire et fractis descendere fulmina nimbis." The image of the brawling winds is ancient; cf. Lucr. 6, 98: "pugnantibus ventis"; Verg. *G.* 1, 318; *A.* 1, 53; 4, 442-443; Ov. *Tr.* 1, 2, 27-30; V. Fl. 4, 270: "ventis certantibus"; Eob. *Buc.* 7, 178; *Her. Chr.* 9, 13; 15, 169; *Idyl.* 17, 195: "luctantes ... venti."

36-37 **Cernis – motu** The motif is developed at length in *Epic.* 4, 77-90: at the death of Mutianus Rufus all the rivers and streams of Hesse pour forth their sorrow.

36 **Cernis ut** = *Buc.* 4, 50 (n.).

obscuro For the epithet see Ov. *Fast.* 4, 758.
turbatus flumine = Stat. *Theb.* 9, 286.

37 **saxa indignantia** *Her.* 1, 5, 75.

39 **Pascere oves** = *Buc.* 4, 2 (n.).

40 **omne nemus** = *Buc.* 5, 45 (n.).
vitreus Aedera For the epithet see *Pug.* B 1, 8 (n.). Cf. *Rec.* 177 and *Her. Chr.* 24, 56.

41 **Fulda – Rhenusque** Mutian. *Ep.* 79, line 19 (in an epigram to Eobanus Hessus): "Vulda, Lanus, Rhenus ...," quoted in Eobanus's response (Mutian. *Ep.* 417, line 13).
Moenusque biformis Cf. Verg. *A.* 8, 727 (perhaps because the Rhine has two mouths): "... Rhenusque bicornis."

42 **sepe superbos** = Verg. *G.* 3, 217.

43 **Vicerat – certamine** Cf. Ov. *Ep.* 16, 361.
agresti ... certamine Verg. *A.* 7, 523; cf. *G.* 2, 531.

44 **castrata** The image is criticized as unseemly in Cic. *de Orat.* 3, 164 and Quint. *Inst.* 8, 6, 15.
Nisi Nisus is also the name of the mythical king of Megara whose daughter cut off the red lock on which the country's safety depended. Cf. *Ama.* 35, 25.

46 **Poeni ... leones** Verg. *Ecl.* 5, 27: "tuum Poenos etiam gemuisse leones / interitum"; *Ciris* 135; Ov. *Tr.* 4, 6, 5.

47 **fugere lupi** = Luc. 6, 627.

47-48 **Non ... Alter erat ... maior** For the idiom see *Buc.* 2, 105-106 (n.).

47 **Non tempore nostro** = Ov. *Tr.* 5, 6, 5.

49 **Nunc iacet** = Lucr. 5, 1275; Prop. 1, 16, 33; Ov. *Ep.* 5, 106; Eob. *Sylv. duae* 2, 169.
tantum decus *Nup.* 174; *Val.* 2, 358; *Tum.* 5, 32; *Epic.* 3 A, 2.

49-52 **Et iam – messes** For the lament that fate has taken the deceased in his prime cf. *Epic.* 2, 25-30; 5, 207-214; *Ebn.* 23-26; *Eras.* 27-34.

49 **iam fortior aetas** = *Tum.* 3, 124; cf. Ov. *Ep.* 1, 107; Luc. 10, 134; Stat. *Theb.* 4, 253; et al.

50 **infoelix puer** *Buc.* 3, 145 (n.).

50-51 **pessima – tibi** For the commonplace see *Buc.* 6, 73 (n.).

51 **fortibus utilis annis** ≈ Ov. *Am.* 2, 3, 7; cf. *Met.* 11, 222.
utilis annis = Ov. *Tr.* 4, 8, 21; Mart. 11, 81, 3.

52 **messes** For this time-expression see *Laud.* 1 (n.).

53-55 **Fleverunt – ubique est** For the pathetic fallacy cf. lines 14-16 above (n.); for the motif that streams and nymphs weep for the deceased cf. Verg. *Ecl.* 5, 20-21; Ov. *Met.* 3, 505-507 (at Narcissus's death); 11, 47-49 (at the death of Orpheus); 13, 689-690; Mant. *Ecl.* 3, 180-182 (followed by an exhortation to the shepherds to bestrew the grave with fragrant herbs); Eob. *Epic.* 3, 127-130; 4, 77-80.

53 **Fleverunt – fragosi** The verse has seven feet – a blemish not removed until the 1539-edition, where Eobanus changes "sylvarumque deae" to "Naiades."
sylvarumque deae V. Fl. 1, 106.

54 **cava ... littora** *Buc.* 5, 54 (n.).
sonuerunt – planctu Sen. *Tro.* 107; cf. Eob. *Ilias* 16, p. 410: "... resonabant littora planctu."

55 **quicquid ubique est** = Verg. *A.* 1, 601; cf. Hor. *S.* 1, 2, 60; Ov. *Fast.* 1, 117; Eob. *Her. Chr.* 1, 78 (n.).

56 **Nunc – damus** Cf. Sil. 13, 714-715.
tumulo damus Ov. *Met.* 2, 326; Tib. 2, 4, 48; line 58 below.

56-63 **hic – arvis** Cf. *Rec.* 134-146; *Buc.* 3, 168-173, with notes; *Epic.* 1, 107-112:

"Hic ubi flaventes exaestuat Albis arenas / Palladiaeque recens alluit urbis opus, / Spargimus hic frustra tumulum redolentibus herbis, / Carmine signantes marmora celsa brevi: / 'Hac situs exigua Dux est Friderichus in urna, / Quem sua non totum Teutona coepit humus'"; 7, 95-102. The model for lines 58-63 is Verg. *Ecl.* 5, 40-44 (followed by a two-line epitaph for Daphnis); cf. also *A.* 6, 883-885.

56-57   **hic – agros** Cf. Verg. *G.* 3, 14-15; Mant. *Ecl.* 2, 37-38: "nitidis ubi Mincius undis / alluit herbosos fugiens perniciter agros"; Eob. *Buc.* 3, 1; *Her. Chr.* 5, 79; Cordus, *Threnod.*, sig. A4ʳ: "Hic ubi prelabens sacram Lanus alluit aedem."

58   **tumulo date** Cf. line 56 above (n.).

     spargite flores ≈ Hor. *Ep.* 1, 5, 14.

59-60   **Narcissos – puellam** For the flower catalogue cf. *Buc.* 2, 88-90 (n.); Mant. *Calam.* 1, p. 35: "Lilia, narcissos, violas, flentes hyacinthos, / Purpureisque crocum foliis."

59   **violas – hyacinthos** = Man. 5, 257; Eob. *Nup.* 51; cf. Verg. *A.* 11, 69.

60   **Coriciumque crocum** = *Laud.* 112 (n.).

     Cyniraeque puellam = Mantuan. *1. Parthen.* 1, 650.

61   **in viridi – fago** Cf. Verg. *Ecl.* 5, 13. For the motif cf. Eob. *Buc.* 2, 106 (n.). For the beech tree in pastoral poetry see n. *Buc.* 3, 83.

62-63   **Gloria – arvis** Like Mopsus's lament in Verg. *Ecl.* 5, 20-44, Sylvius's ends with an epitaph.

62   **Gloria sylvarum** Cf. *Buc.* 7, 11 (n.): "decus nemorum."

     situs est hic A standard formula in epitaphs. See for example [Tib.] 3, 2, 29; Luc. 8, 793; Mart. 12, 52, 3.

     pastor Iolas = Gerald. *Ecl.* 4, 2 (where the phrase refers to Jesus).

63   **Quo – foelicior** Cf. Verg. *A.* 9, 772; Eob. *Buc.* 2, 105-106 (n.).

     omnibus arvis = Luc. 9, 341.

64   **amore – laborum** Cf. lines 1-6 above, especially lines 5-6, with notes.

65-66   **recta – tui** Cf. Juv. 9, 90-91.

67-68   **Non sic – videtur** For the commonplace that poetry immortalizes those whom it celebrates see *Laud.* 61-64 (n.).

67   **extinctus Iolas** Cf. line 29 above (n.).

69   **niveis ... complexa lacertis** Mant. *2. Parthen.* 2, 153: "... niveis complexa lacertis"; cf. Ov. *Fast.* 6, 497; Eob. *Buc.* 7, 149. For "niveis lacertis" at this metrical position see Verg. *A.* 8, 387; Sil. 14, 496; cf. Ov. *Am.* 2, 16, 29.

69-70   **complexa ... Corpus inane viri** Cf. Verg. *Ecl.* 5, 22-23; Ov. *Met.* 13, 488.

70   **Corpus – viri** = *Ilias* 18, p. 466; 23, p. 562; cf. Prop. 3, 18, 32; Ov. *Am.* 3, 9, 6; *Ep.* 15, 116; et al.

     coniunx pulcherrima = Mant. *Dionys.* 2, fol. 179ʳ; cf. Verg. *A.* 10, 611; Ov. *Ep.* 3, 71-72.

71-72   **Urite – Elysium** She hopes to follow the example of Evadne, who threw herself on the funeral pyre of her husband Capaneus, and of Laodamia, who wanted to accompany her husband Protesilaus into the underworld. Cf. Ov. *Ars* 3, 17-22.

71   **Urite – flammis** Cf. Verg. *A.* 2, 37.

74   **Sic ait et** = *Laud.* 290 (n.).

     nivea ... fronte = Ov. *Met.* 10, 138; Sil. 7, 446.

     fronte coronam = Ov. *Met.* 8, 178.

75   **Illa – ruricolarum** Cf. Antonius Codrus Urceus, *Aegloga*, in: *In hoc Codri volumine haec continentur: Orationes seu sermones ...* (Bologna, 1502), sig. F6ᵛ: "Galatea ..., / Ruricolas inter satis est formosa puellas."

76-77   **Quam – peperit** Cf. Nikolaus Marschalk, *Enchiridion poetarum clarissimorum* (Erfurt, 1502), vol. 1, sig. C5ᵛ ("ex Porphyrio de oraculis Apollinis"), referring to Aesculapius: "Quem mater peperit compressa ab Apolline magnum"; Ov. *Ib.*

212: "quem peperit magno lucida Maia Iovi."

76   **Galathea** This name is not in apposition to "parens" (line 76) but to "Illa" (line
      75). Cf. the marginal note in the 1534-version of the present eclogue,
      published as an appendix to *De victoria Wirtembergensi*: "Matrem Phil.
      intelligit"; *Idyl.*, 2. ded. 92 (explaining the name): "Mater [Philippi] ... est
      Galatea mihi."
      septem ... trioni = Verg. *G.* 3, 381; cf. Ov. *Met.* 2, 528.
      compressa = Prop. 2, 30, 35; Celtis, *Am.* 3, 3, 11: "Ursa per Arcadium
      quondam compressa Tonantem."

77   **Formosior – est** = Ov. *Ep.* 18, 73; Eob. *Nup.* 92.

79   **Nunc – urna** The contrast "small grave, great fame" is ancient. See, for
      example, Ov. *Met.* 12, 615-616.
      brevi – urna = Guarino, *Carm.*, sig. l 7ᵛ; cf. Ov. *Am.* 3, 9, 40; 3, 9, 67; *Met.* 4,
      166; Eob. *Rec.* 133 (n.); epitaph for Konrad Celtis, quoted in n. *Ama.* 22, 6;
      Epic. 1, 111: "Hac situs exigua Dux est Friderichus in urna"; 5, 9: "iaces,
      clauditque tuum brevis urna cadaver"; 5, 35: "brevi clausum est breve corpus in
      urna"; 8, 77: "Nunc tamen ille brevem tantus tenuatur in urnam"; *Ebn.* 181:
      "Molliter exigua corpus requiescat in urna"; *Eras.* 155: "Quod reliquum magni
      bustum breve clausit Erasmi."

80-81 **Illa – Plorat** Cf. *Her. Chr.* 13, 29, revised in *Her.* 2, 3, 29 as: "Ipsa domo vidua
      perturbatos hymenaeos / ... feram"; Mant. *Ecl.* 1, 31: "... plorans infelices
      hymenaeos."

80   **Illa domo vidua** ≈ Ov. *Ep.* 9, 35; Eob. *Her. Chr.* 16, 259; cf. Ov. *Fast.* 1, 36;
      Eob. *Her. Chr.* 20, 94; 21, 26; 21, 89.

81   **niveos lacerat ... capillos** Cf. Ov. *Met.* 13, 534; 14, 420; Juv. 6, 490; Eob. *Her.
      Chr.* 5, 95 (n.). For "niveos capillos" meaning "blonde hair" see Boiardo, *Ecl.* 8,
      p. 683 (of a beautiful girl); cf. Eob. *Laud.* 165 (n.); *Buc.* 7, 112 (n.).

82   **Digna ... thalamis** [Sen.] *Oct.* 544.
      digna marito = Mant. *2. Parthen.* 3, 737: "... tu Caesare digna marito"; Eob.
      Epp. 4, sig. F5ʳ (1508): "tanto mulier ... digna marito."

83-84 **Nobis – puellam** Imitated by Cordus, *Ecl.* 1, 56-58 (a pastoral elegy for
      William II): "Bina tamen moriens nobis hic pignora liquit, / audentem specie
      Nymphis certare puellam / et iuvenem patriae haeredem virtutis Adonin."

84   **Spem generis** = Stat. *Theb.* 2, 165 (different); Eob. *Idyl.* 13, 36, quoting from
      the present eclogue.
      puerum ... marem *Ilias* 19, p. 488.
      teneram ... puellam Prop. 2, 25, 41; Ov. *Ep.* 14, 87; et al.; Eob. *Her. Chr.* 12,
      259.

85-86 **Aspice – matrem** Imitated in Cordus, *Threnod.*, sig. B1ʳ: "Sunt duo nanque tibi
      patrios imitantia vultus / Pignora, de diva nobile stirpe genus. / Parvus in
      augusta tibi ludit filius aula / Et summi thalamo digna puella Iovis."

85   **Aspice quam** = *Buc.* 6, 29 (n.).
      quam – vultus Cf. Lucr. 4, 1219; 4, 1224; Verg. *A.* 4, 329; Ov. *Ep.* 13, 152;
      Sen. *Tro.* 647-648; Cordus, *Buc.* 4, 74 (*Ecl.* 1, 98): "Quam similem ad generosa
      refers patris ora decorem!"
      patrios ... vultus = *Laud.* 85 (n.).

86   **filia matrem** = *Rec.* 32 (n.).

88   **Clarissime sanguis** = *Luth.* 4, 21; *Accl.* 2, 165; *Wirt.* 435; *Sylv.* 3, 2, 7.

89   **magni ... parentis** V. Fl. 4, 186; Stat. *Theb.* 2, 715; Sil. 2, 477.

89-90 **tuta ... Pascua** = Lines 33-34 above.

90   **misse – astris** Cf. line 111 below (n.). Eobanus associates Philip with the
      heaven-sent Child in Verg. *Ecl.* 4 who is to inaugurate a new golden age. See in
      particular Verg. *Ecl.* 4, 6-7. Praising a new or future ruler for restoring the

golden age is a commonplace in panegyrics. See, for example, Calp. *Ecl.* 1, 42-45; Andrel. *Ecl.* 4, 124-129; Erasmus, *Carm.* 4, 51-54.

patentibus astris A gloss in the Strasbourg copy indicates that "patentibus" means "claris." Cf. Stat. *Theb.* 10, 374-375 (in all the mss.): "fulgure claro / astra patent"; Eob. *Buc.* B 11, 6: "astra patent." The unusual phrase is changed to "faventibus astris" in *Idyl.* 6, 93.

92	**Indolis egregiae** = Celtis, *Am.* 4, 15, 23: "Indolis egregiae iuvenis ..."; Eob. *Sylv.* 3, 3, 19.
92-93	**virtutis – Signa** Cf. Tifernate, *Carm.*, sig. D2ʳ: "tanta ... virtutis signa futurae"; Eob. *Her. Chr.* 13, 141.
93	**vultu ... sereno** Lucr. 3, 293; Catul. 55, 8; Hor. *Carm.* 1, 37, 26; Verg. *A.* 2, 285-286; Ov. *Tr.* 1, 5, 27; Eob. *Buc.* 11, 52 (n.).
	iubes sperare Verg. *G.* 4, 325.
94	**Optima quaeque** = Verg. *G.* 3, 66; cf. Eob. *Epic.* 2, 80; *Sylv.* 3, 3, 30.
	nec – numine = Stat. *Silv.* 1, 4, 23.
95	**nitet facies** = Avit. *Carm.* 1, 228: "terrae ... / blanda nitet facies."
	Phoebeae – instar = Verg. *A.* 3, 637. For the comparison of the ruler with the sun see, for example, Hor. *Carm.* 4, 5, 5-8; Erasmus, *Carm.* 4, 51-56; *Panegyricus ad Philippum, ASD* 4, 1, p. 29, lines 106-109; p. 50, lines 758-760; cf. *Adag.* 1, 3, 1, *ASD* 2, 1, p. 308, lines 132-133.
96-97	**Claude – mundo** Imitated in Cordus, *Ecl.* 1, 100-104:

> *Lycidas.* Claude tuos oculos radiosaque lumina conde;
> quis tantum poterit vel nivens ferre nitorem? [...]
> *Faustulus.* Immo aperi et tristi profer nova gaudia mundo.

For line 96 cf. also Cordus, *In natalem Christi hymnus,* in: *Opera poetica omnia* [Frankfurt am Main? 1550?], fol. 37ᵛ: "Tectos condite vultus, / Quis tantos radios ferat?"

96	**Claude oculos** = Mant. *Ecl.* 2, 83.
97	**da gaudia** = Ov. *Ars* 2, 459; Stat. *Silv.* 4, 1, 20.
	gaudia mundo = Claud. *IV. Cons. Hon.* 642; Eob. *Her. Chr.* 6, 21; *Her.* 1, 6, 83: "Adferet ille puer toti nova gaudia mundo."
98	**ab ovilibus omnes** = *Buc.* 1, 91 (n.).
99	**Raptoresque lupique** Cf. Ov. *Met.* 10, 540.
	frigidus anguis Verg. *Ecl.* 3, 93; 8, 71.
100	**Atque – dracones** Cf. Verg. *G.* 4, 13.
101	**tetri ... veneni** Lucr. 4, 685; Prop. 2, 24, 27.
102-103	**Si quis – aspis** Cf. Vulg. *Psa.* 90, 13.
102	**nostra ... harena** Cf. *Idyl.* 17, 70: "per nostras ... arenas."
	basiliscus harena = Luc. 9, 726.
103	**Occidet, et** = Verg. *Ecl.* 4, 24: "occidet et serpens ..."; Stat. *Theb.* 12, 819.
104	**securos praestabunt** Juv. 8, 170-171.
	pabula foetus ≈ Verg. *Ecl.* 1, 49.
105	**Spargite humum ... floribus** Cf. Verg. *Ecl.* 5, 40; 9, 19-20.
105-106	**in qua – plantae** Cf. *Lydia* 10: "[O fortunati agri,] in quibus illa pedis nivei vestigia ponet."
106	**niveae ... plantae** Stat. *Ach.* 1, 100; Claud. *Epith.* 152.
	vestigia plantae = Ov. *Fast.* 4, 463; Man. 1, 657; 4, 631; Sil. 9, 390; 15, 505.
107	**Vos ... pastores** = *Buc.* 3, 168.
108	**Thure vaporato** ≈ Stat. *Theb.* 1, 556; cf. Verg. *A.* 11, 481.
	circumlustrate quotannis Cf. Tib. 1, 1, 35. For "circumlustrate" see Lucr. 5, 1437.
	quotannis = Verg. *Ecl.* 5, 67; 5, 79; Mant. *Ecl.* 3, 186: "atque sacerdotum

cantus ac tura quotannis / ducite, et aeternam requiem cantate poetae."

109 **Et carmen – carmen** Cf. Verg. *Ecl.* 5, 42.

dicite carmen ≈ Verg. *Ecl.* 6, 5; Prop. 1, 9, 9; cf. Eob. *Ama.* 32, 31.

110-112 **Salve – paternum** Cf. Verg. *A.* 8, 301-302.

110 **Salve – Iolae** Cf. *Wirt.* 528 (to Landgrave Philip): "Salve, semideum sanguis generose Philippe"; *Luth.* 4, 23: "Carole, semideum sate stirpe ab utroque parente"; *Accl.* 1, 28; "Carole, semideum regibus orte genus"; 1, 99: "... semideum sanguis clarissime regum."

111 **a magno – missus** Cf. Verg. *Ecl.* 4, 7; *A.* 4, 574; Calp. *Ecl.* 4, 137-138; Otto 287; Häussler, pp. 53, 70, 97, 142, 233, and 264; Mant. *1. Parthen.* 1, 493: "... summo genus aethere missum"; 2, 797; Eob. *Her. Chr.* 16, 81; line 90 above.

magno ... aethere = Stat. *Theb.* 7, 77; cf. Verg. *A.* 10, 356.

112 **pecudes ... defende** Cf. *Buc.* 11, 97.

rus ... paternum Ov. *Am.* 2, 16, 38; *Tr.* 4, 8, 10; Eob. *Vict.* 288.

113 **Ergo – mater** Cf. *Laud.* B 3, 11 (n.).

114-115 **Quae – montis** Cf. Calp. *Ecl.* 5, 5. For the pastoral scene cf. also Verg. *Ecl.* 1, 74-76; Eob. *Val.* 1, 235-236: "Nunc errare greges pecudum spectabis ab alto / Vertice."

114 **dumeta capellas** ≈ *Buc.* 8, 21, where see note.

115 **summi – montis** V. Fl. 4, 260; cf. Verg. *A.* 4, 186; Sil. 12, 622.

117-118 **suxit Ubera** Cf. Vulg. *Luc.* 11, 27: "Beatus venter qui te portavit et ubera quae suxisti"; Eob. *Buc.* 7, 100.

118 **magnis ... divis** Verg. *A.* 12, 296; Ov. *Met.* 6, 526; *Tr.* 3, 3, 31.

119 **Et – sol** Cf. *Buc.* 1, 124 (n.); *Ilias* 7, p. 182: "ibat / Iam Sol Oceano propior."

Oceano propior = Verg. *G.* 2, 122.

Plura canemus For this conclusion cf. *Idyl.* 9, 95: "plura et meliora canemus, / Crastina Phoebaeos ubi lux reparaverit ignes"; *Her. Chr.* 24, 166 (n.).

10

Meter: Hexameter.

1 **sylvas – colunt** Ov. *Met.* 11, 146; cf. Eob. *Buc.* 3, 152.

2 **flumine Rheni** = *Her. Chr.* 17, 211; *Hod.* 155; *Sylv.* 8, 3, 31.

3 **Scythicum Tanaim** ≈ Luc. 9, 414.

4 **cicutis** *Buc.* 5, 36 (n.).

5 **levi ... carmen avena** = *Theoc.* 19, sig. G6ᵛ; cf. Calp. *Ecl.* 4, 63; Nemes. *Ecl.* 1, 63.

6 **Multiforem buxum** Ov. *Met.* 12, 158; Mant. *Ecl.* 1, 163; cf. Eob. *Buc.* 5, 39 (n.).

dulcem – monaulon = *Sylv.* 7, 21, 5; cf. *Nup.* 295 (*Luth.* 1, 3): "... sufflare monaulon."

7 **Pignoribus positis** See *Buc.* 5, 15 (n.).

pro – vitae = Mant. *Consol.*, fol. 129ᵛ; cf. Juvenc. 4, 455: "... munere vitae"; Eob. *Her. Chr.* 14, 97 (n.): "... munera vitae."

8-9 **ego – ligustrum** For the pattern of comparison see *Buc.* 3, 21-24 (n.).

8 **ego tam supero** Cf. Ov. *Met.* 13, 368.

achantum For the spelling see n. *Buc.* 1, 106.

9 **rosa ... Pestana** Ov. *Pont.* 2, 4, 28; Mart. 4, 42, 10. Paestum in Lucania was famed for its roses; cf. Eob. *Her. Chr.* 23, 66.

septivagum For this unusual epithet cf. Mant. *2. Parthen.* 3, 773 (of snakes): "sepivagis."

10 **barbara rura** Lines 159-160 and 166 below; *Sylv.* 2, 23, 6 (contrasting Italy and Germany): "Illic Pierides Musaea per oppida regnant; / Numinibus tantis

barbara rura vacant"; *Sarmat.* 2.

rura poaetas = Line 154 below.

12   **Nemo – pastor** Cf. *Buc.* 3, 112-113 (n.).

mecum – contendere *Theoc.* 8, sig. D1ʳ: "Num libet alterno mecum contendere cantu?"; cf. Calp. *Ecl.* 2, 6: "... contendere cantu."

13   **longinquas ... oras** = *Ilias* 22, p. 540.

14   **monstrante viam** = Verg. *A.* 1, 382.

pannosus et = Mant. *Ecl.* 2, 150.

15   **quis nescit** = Ov. *Am.* 1, 5, 25.

15-16   **laeta ... Pascua** = *Vict.* 288-289; cf. Ov. *Fast.* 4, 476; Juv. 12, 13; Mant. *Ecl.* 10, 148.

16-39   **Grex – cantus** The model is Mant. *Ecl.* 5, 171-181, a satire on court poets. Cf. especially *Ecl.* 5, 176-178: "postquam trivialibus ora cicutis / applicuere, sibi applaudunt, sua carmina iactant / insulsi, illepidi, indociles, improvidi, inepti."

17   **nivei ... lactis** Verg. *Ecl.* 2, 20; Ov. *Met.* 13, 829; *Fast.* 4, 151; 4, 780; Eob. *Vict.* 252.

copia lactis = Verg. *Ecl.* 1, 81; *G.* 3, 308.

18-19   **vix – cicuta** Cf. Cordus, *Buc.* 1, 61-63 (cf. *Ecl.* 2, 23-25): "nonne pudet vos doctos credere vates, / qui modo vix orsi fragili garrire cicuta / nescitis laxum distendere flatibus utrem?" For the insult cf. also Verg. *Ecl.* 3, 26-27; Cordus, *Buc.* 9, 19-20 (*Ecl.* 5, 34-35): "tenui [Fragili *1518*] solitus garrire cicuta, / ridiculus toto fuit hoc in rure poeta." For "cicuta" see Eob. *Buc.* 5, 36 (n.).

18   **libros – colurnos** Cf. *Buc.* 8, 106 (n.).

19   **Confusum ... murmur** Sil. 15, 138.

20   **fastu turges** Cf. note to line 125 below.

23   **nostris ... Camoenis** = *Her. Chr.* 24, 57; *Nor.* 1384; *Sylv.* 6, 5, 89; cf. Stat. *Silv.* 4, 7, 21; and, for example, Eob. *Her. Chr.* 10, 113; *Hod.* 411; 463.

25   **nemorum saltus** Verg. *Ecl.* 6, 56.

29   **Inter – canentes** Cf. Cordus, *Buc.* 10, 108 (*Ecl.* 5, 73): "Inter tot celebres ut fex et amurca poetas / ... / usque adeo falsis te extollas [tollas *1518*] laudibus, ut te / non pudeat tanto mendatia dicere fastu."

30-34   **Ut quae – palustri** For these derogatory comparisons cf. Filetico, *Theoc.* 1, 136: "lenta stridens nyctimen in umbra, / Iam cantus philomena tuos imitetur amoenos"; 5, 136-137: "Luscinia dulci raucos contendere turdos / Nec fas est epopas cygnis obstare canoris"; Verg. *Ecl.* 8, 55; Calp. *Ecl.* 6, 7-8; Otto 496; Häussler, pp. 100, 151, 235, and 267; Andrel. *Ecl.* 10, 29-32: "Scilicet incedens puerili inflatus honore / Corvus et argutum crocitans si tentet olorem, / Aufigit explosus totisque irrisus ab agris, / Lucifuga obscuro latitat ceu noctua luco"; line 39 below (n.). Cf. also Eob. *Hod.* 15 (in a comparison with Homer): "Non talem infoelix aequabit noctua palmam."

30-31   **volucrum ... despectissima ... noctua** In ancient times regarded as a harbinger of death and disaster, the owl in the Middle Ages and Renaissance was despised as the lowest, most despicable of birds – an emblem of vainglory. Cf. *Pug.* B 1, 11-14; Paul Vandenbroeck, "Bubo significans: Die Eule als Sinnbild von Schlechtigkeit und Torheit, vor allem in der niederländischen und deutschen Bilddarstellung und bei Jheronimus Bosch I," *Jaarboek van het Koninklijk Museum voor Schone Kunsten Antwerpen* (1985): 19-135.

certet – cantando Cf. Verg. *Ecl.* 5, 9: "certet Phoebum superare canendo"; 3, 21: "cantando victus"; Eob. *Buc.* 11, 16-17.

31   **morientes ... cygnos** Cf. Sen. *Phaed.* 302: "moriente cycno." For the old belief that swans sing a melancholy, but marvelously beautiful song just before they die, see Otto 497; Häussler, pp. 19, 55, 72, 151, 235, and 267; Erasmus, *Adag.* 1, 2, 55; Eob. *Her. Chr.* A 3, 60; 23, 39-40; *Epic.* 4, 51-53; 4, 137-138.

32-34   **Ut mille – palustri** Cf. Filetico, *Theoc.* 7, 41: "ut crepitans resonanti rana cicadae / Vocibus est impar, sic nunc ego vatibus istis."

33   **calamita** Instead of the standard form "calamites."

    rana Seriphi *Sylv.* 4, 17, 40, applied to a friend who has remained silent too long; cf. *Sylv.* 5, 5, 20: "nec nos / Decet silere Seriphias uti ranas / Et esse mutos." The frogs on the island of Seriphos in the Cyclades were proverbially dumb. Erasmus, however, compares them to unskilled singers and speakers in *Adag.* 1, 5, 31. It is this sense that Eobanus has in mind here.

36   **lucifugum** Verg. *G.* 4, 243 (at this metrical position); Andrel. *Ecl.* 10, 32 (quoted in note to lines 30-34 above).

    carmine vatem ≈ *Buc.* 11, 34 (n.).

37   **Vernantes – pubere** *Sylv.* 7, 26, 2-3: "primo / Vernas pubere"; cf. Mart. 2, 61, 1: "vernarent dubia lanugine malae."

    pueri – possunt Note the alliteration.

38   **Vade – rupes** The verse prepares for the concluding lines 167-174.

39   **Inter – cantus** Cf. *Idyl.* 1, 19: "Inter Phoebaeos ut ineptit noctua cantus"; lines 30-31 above.

    noctua, cantus = Verg. *G.* 1, 403.

40-41   **Si tibi – Apollo** Cf. Prop. 2, 24, 5; Eob. *Buc.* 4, 75 (n.); 10, 93.

41   **triplex ... Apollo** *Laud.* 395.

42   **sub hac – umbra** Cf. Andrel. *Ecl.* 1, 18: "Hac mecum aesculea paulum requiesce sub umbra"; Verg. *Ecl.* 1, 79; 7, 10; *Culex* 157; Eob. *Buc.* 3, 10 (n.); line 45 below. An invitation to a shepherd-poet to sit down in the shade is tantamount to inviting him to sing together. See, for instance, Theoc. 1, 12-14; 1, 21-25; Verg. *Ecl.* 5, 1-3.

44   **Aoniae ... coronae** = Poliziano, *Sylv.* 1, 26 (referring to a wreath).

46   **Experiar – improbe** Cf. Verg. *Ecl.* 3, 28-29. For the taunting "improbe" see Calp. *Ecl.* 6, 19; 6, 25.

    Experiar quid = Stat. *Theb.* 10, 847.

46-47   **iactes Carmina** Ov. *Met.* 11, 153; Mant. *Ecl.* 5, 177 (in a satire on court poets): "sua carmina iactant."

47   **potuisti – vatem** = *In Ed. Leeum*, sig. A4ᵛ: "Tam tu veridicum potuisti spernere vatem."

48-49   **Huc – agnae** Cf. *Buc.* 5, 9, with notes.

48   **Huc ... concede** = Verg. *A.* 2, 523.

    Tenent loca *Buc.* 1, 59 (n.).

    loca tuta = *Her. Chr.* 22, 63; cf. *Her. Chr.* 5, 157.

49   **densis ... vepribus** Mutian. *Ep.* 79, line 10 (in an epigram to Eobanus Hessus): "... densis vepribus uva tumet"; Eob. *Ama.* 8, 7: "densissimos vepres."

51   **Non – puero** = Mant. *Ecl.* 10, 124: "non tibi cum puero res est ..."; cf. Eob. *Idyl.*, 1. ded. 86 (2. ded. 84): "Rem non cum pueris sentiet esse sibi."

    puero ... impubere Ov. *Fast.* 2, 239.

52   **molles ... annos** *Buc.* 2, 11 (n.).

    aetas ... annos = *Her. Chr.* 14, 45; 18, 91.

53   **genas ... vestiat umbra** Cf. Verg. *A.* 8, 160. For "umbra" in this sense see Stat. *Theb.* 4, 336; Alan. *Parab.* 5, *PL* 210, col. 590 B: "Surgentem Drusus festinat radere barbam, / Ne noceat lippae noctibus umbra genae"; also cf. Stat *Silv.* 3, 4, 79.

54   **barbam tractaveris** Tugging at someone's beard is a proverbially insulting gesture. See Otto 239; Häussler, p. 233; Erasmus, *Adag.* 2, 4, 69.

55   **Sis licet** = *Her. Chr.* 4, 10; cf. *Her. Chr.* 23, 116.

    nulli – caedas Cf. *Her. Chr.* 24, 155-156; Camerarius, *Nar.* 8, 1-3, of Eobanus Hessus.

56-57 **Est – poetae** The model is Mant. *Ecl.* 10, 126-127: "Da veniam, Myrmix; 'amitam' proferre volenti / nescio quis mihi misit in os malus error 'amatam.'"

56 **Est aliquid** = Ov. *Ep.* 3, 131; 4, 29; *Rem.* 480; *Met.* 12, 93; et al.; Eob. *Her. Chr.* 2, 87; 4, 39; 4, 154; 5, 98; 5, 144; 10, 146.

58 **sponte sua** = Lucr. 4, 736; 5, 79; 5, 804; Hor. *Ep.* 1, 12, 17.
    improba lingua *Pug.* B 1, 15 (n.).

59 **Non – ignarus** = Cordus, *Buc.* 1, 74 (*Ecl.* 2, 75).
    scommate ... isto Mant. *Ecl.* 6, 114: "... isto te scommate carpi."

60 **Quis ridere queat** Cf. Mart. 7, 18, 11.

61 **scabros ... dentes** Suet. *Aug.* 79, 2.
    nudantia dentes = Lucr. 5, 1064.

62 **canis** For the insult see Otto 315; Häussler, pp. 145 and 264; cf. line 66 below.

63 **Verba probant animum** Cf. Ven. Fort. *Carm.* 3, 27, 4: "dulces animos dulcia dona probant"; Erasmus, *Adag.* 1, 6, 50: "Qualis vir, talis oratio."

64 **difficilis naturae** Ov. *Ep.* 15, 31; Eob. *Idyl.*, 1. ded. 13 (2. ded. 11); cf. *Nup.* 88 (n.): "facilis ... Natura."

65 **Non – venustat** Cf. Sen. *Ep.* 66, 4: "scire possemus non deformitate corporis foedari animum, sed pulchritudine animi corpus ornari"; Erasmus, *Adag.* 3, 3, 1.
    mens formosa *Her. Chr.* 4, 193; cf. Sen. *Ep.* 66, 3, arguing that a beautiful soul can spring from an ugly body: "formosus animus."

66 **Invidia est** = Verg. *A.* 4, 350; [Tib.] 3, 3, 20; Stat. *Ach.* 1, 146.

67 **obliquos ... ocellos** *Priap.* 73, 1; cf. Hor. *Ep.* 1, 14, 37; Eob. *Her. Chr.* 12, 108 (n.).

68 **cum – abhorret** For the motif – two bulls fighting over a heifer – see *Buc.* 4, 47-63 (n.).

69 **Indicat iram oculis** Cf. Vulg. *Esth.* 15, 10: "ardentibus oculis furorem pectoris indicasset"; Lucr. 3, 288-289; Verg. *A.* 12, 102; Ov. *Met.* 8, 355-356.

70 **Quis tam** = Verg. *A.* 6, 501.
    aequa mente = *Idyl.* 11, 11; 11, 27: "Famae damna ferens non aequa mente ..."; cf. Hor. *Carm.* 2, 3, 1-2; Ov. *Ars* 2, 438; *Pont.* 4, 14, 39; Eob. *Laud.* 580.

71-72 **Omnia – cavillo** Cf. *Dial.* 1, sig. A5ᵛ: "Ubi igitur modestia tua et patientia quam plenis buccis semper predicas, si ne tantillum quidem (etiam si falsum sit) ferre potes?"

71 **Omnia fert sapiens** For the Stoic wisdom that we should face adversity and success with equal tranquillity see, for example, Cic. *Tusc.* 4, 65-66; 5, 30; *Off.* 1, 90; Hor. *Carm.* 3, 3, 1-8; *S.* 2, 7, 83-88; Sen. *Ep.* 66, 6; 78, 29; 113, 27-31.
    Omnia fert = Verg. *Ecl.* 9, 51 (different).

73 **Allatrata – rellatrat** Cf. Hartmann von Aue, *Iwein* 875-878: "ichn wil mich mit dem munde / niht glichen dem hunde / der dâ wider grînen kan, / sô in der ander grînet an." The expression may still have been proverbial in Eobanus's day.
    morsa remordet Cf. Hor. *Epod.* 6, 4; Sen. *Dial.* 4, 34, 1: "Pusilli hominis et miseri est repetere mordentem"; Walther 15058: "Mordeo mordentem."

75 **Concava ... vallis** Ov. *Met.* 8, 334.
    carminibus – remugit Cf. Verg. *Ecl.* 6, 84; Stat. *Theb.* 1, 346-347; Eob. *Buc.* 11, 88; cf. further *Buc.* 1, 47-48.

76 **Verum – negat** = *Idyl.* 13, 199: "Verum nemo negat nisi vanus et ater et excors."

77 **Omnia – sylvae** Cf. Verg. *Ecl.* 10, 8; Nemes. *Ecl.* 1, 73-74.
    procerae ... sylvae ≈ Ov. *Ep.* 16, 109.

78 **Liniger ... sacerdos** = Claud. *IV. Cons. Hon.* 573.
    sacra ... in aede sacerdos *Her. Chr.* 15, 103. For "sacra in aede" see Ov. *Met.* 14, 316; cf. *Met.* 14, 315; Eob. *Pug.* 29; *Laud.* 178; *Her. Chr.* 9, 138; 16, 153; *Nob.*

107. For the tag "aede sacerdos" see Ov. *Fast.* 1, 587.

80   **Garrula – coaxat** Cf. *Anthol. Lat.* 762, 64: "Garrula limosis rana coaxat aquis"; Andrel. *Ecl.* 4, 56: "Garrula limoso quid gurgite rana coaxas?"; Eob. *Idyl.* 11, 52: "... in limo placeat sibi rana palustri"; 17, 144: "... in viridi limo mihi rana coaxat."

    Garrula ... rana *Dirae* 74.

    limosa ... palude Sen. *Ag.* 768; Sil. 4, 750.

81   **magnis ... clangoribus** = Verg. *A.* 3, 226.

82-83   **Si bona – echo** Proverbial; cf. Walther 23231b; 29606: "Sicut silva personat, sic echo resultet"; 29626; 29634: "Silvis immissum solet echo remittere bombum"; 32645: "Ut vox insultat tua, sic tibi silva resultat"; and the familiar German proverb: "Wie man in den Wald hineinruft, so schallt es wieder heraus."

82   **bona carmina** = *Buc.* 8, 75 (n.).

84   **qui – bene** Cf. Quint. *Inst.* 1, proem. 9: "Oratorem autem instituimus illum perfectum, qui esse nisi vir bonus non potest."

85   **mala carmina** = Hor. *S.* 2, 5, 74; Mart. 12, 40, 1.

86-87   **Si – possit** Cf. Euripides, *Medea* 518-519 (not known to Eobanus directly).

86   **Si bonus es** = Lines 93 and 149 below.

    fronti ... tabellam Cf. Cic. *Planc.* 16.

87   **Ut – videat** = Ov. *Ars* 1, 738.

    qui – possit Cf. Verg. *Ecl.* 4, 27: "... quae sit poteris cognoscere virtus." For the tag "cognoscere possit" cf. Lucr. 2, 462; 3, 117; et al.

88   **Mille – testes** Proverbial; see Otto 421; Erasmus, *Adag.* 1, 10, 91: "Conscientia mille testes"; Eob. *Nup.*, postscript; *Epic.* 5, 43: "Quanquam teste egeat nullo mens conscia recti"; *Epp.* 2, sig. B8ʳ, letter of 25 July 1524 to Philip Melanchthon: "conscientia mille testes."

    recti mens conscia Cf. Verg. *A.* 1, 604; Ov. *Fast.* 4, 311; Eob. *Her. Chr.* 8, 99 (n.); 13, 44; 15, 25-26 (n.); *Hypocr.* 89: "Mens ... recti sibi conscia." For "mens conscia" at this metrical position see Luc. 7, 784 and V. Fl. 3, 301.

90   **Hora fugit** Ov. *Am.* 1, 11, 15; Pers. 5, 153; Sil. 15, 64.

    Cupidae ... menti Catul. 64, 147; 64, 398; Ov. *Ep.* 6, 71.

    nectis ludibria Cf. *Idyl.* 7, 29: "Ergo quid ambages nectis?"; *Tum.* 1, 43-44: "frivola vincula nectit / Mentibus humanis."

    ludibria menti = *Salom.* 3, sig. B1ʳ: "Haec Deus humanae immisit ludibria menti."

91   **seria ludo** = Verg. *Ecl.* 7, 17; Hor. *S.* 1, 1, 27; *Ars* 226; cf. Eob. *Buc.* 7, 71.

92   **Coepta sequi** *Buc.* 1, 93 (n.).

93   **Si bonus es** = Line 86 above and line 149 below.

    si te – Apollo Cf. lines 40-41 above (n.).

94   **inaudaces ... Musas** Cf. *Sylv.* 3, 8, 11 (9, 17, 7): "inaudaces ... Camoenas."

    pulchra ... certamina Cf. Sen. *Ben.* 3, 36, 3: "pulchro certamini"; Eob. *Theoc.* 1, sig. A4ʳ: "Ipse feres foetam pulchro e certamine capram."

95-96   **Ut – palestram** Cf. Ov. *Tr.* 2, 17; *Pont.* 1, 5, 37-38.

95   **maiora ... vulnera** Ov. *Pont.* 3, 7, 25-26; Stat. *Silv.* 2, 6, 7.

    bonam ... famam Camerarius, *Nar.* 33, 21 (n.).

    redimat – famam Cf. Mart. 1, 8, 5.

96   **athleta palestram** ≈ *Her. Chr.* 18, 165.

98-101   **Antea -- palmam** For this figure of speech (*adynaton*), which emphasizes the impossibility of an event by referring to events even more unlikely to happen, see, for example, Verg. *Ecl.* 1, 59-63; Eob. *Buc.* 10, 156-158; *Her. Chr.* 8, 53-55; 15, 81-85; 19, 49-50; 19, 153-154.

98   **mulgere capellas** *Buc.* 4, 16.

99   **venum – urbem** = *Idyl.* 7, 4. For the motif cf. Verg. *Ecl.* 1, 19-21; 1, 33-35; 9, 1-6; 9, 62-65; Mant. *Ecl.* 6, 156-157.
100   **apes ... capellae** Verg. *Ecl.* 10, 30.
            lita Cf. Verg. *G.* 4, 39.
            salsa capellae Cf. Boiardo, *Ecl.* 5, p. 677: "nec tantum [placent] salsa capellis / Gramina."
101   **certamine palmam** = *Idyl.* 17, 125; *Sylv.* 1, 7, 19; cf. *Her. Chr.* 4, 233.
104-105   **Urbica – urbem** The model is Mant. *Ecl.* 6, 155-156, where the one shepherd asks, "Unde urbanarum tibi tanta peritia rerum?" and the other answers, "Haec didici quondam ductis in moenia capris." For the explanation of more than pastoral knowledge see n. *Buc.* 1, 54-56 above.
107   **Tempore ab illo** = Paul. Nol. *Carm.* 18, 85; Eob. *Her. Chr.* 13, 119; cf. Lucr. 3, 114; Ov. *Ep.* 21, 65; *Met.* 1, 314.
109-111   **Pastorem – oportet** Cf. Prop. 2, 1, 43-46; Hor. *Ep.* 2, 1, 114-116; Erasmus, *Adag.* 1, 6, 15, *ASD* 2, 2, p. 40, lines 377-387.
            Pastorem curare greges ... oportet Cf. Verg. *Ecl.* 6, 4-5.
109   **armenta tueri** Verg. *G.* 2, 195.
110   **tractare rudentes** = Juv. 6, 102.
111   **Sutorem crepidas** Proverbial; see Plin. *Nat.* 35, 85; Otto 462; Häussler, p. 150; Erasmus, *Adag.* 1, 6, 16.
            sua – oportet See n. *Buc.* 8, 126.
112-114   **Florales – hircum** Cf. Mant. *Ecl.* 1, 175-176: "Fauste, viden? vicina pecus vineta subintrat; / iam (ne forte gravi multa taxemur) eundum est." For the motif see further Eob. *Buc.* 3, 60-61 (n.).
113   **Dominus ... horti** Calp. *Ecl.* 2, 2.
115   **boves – pascunt** Cf. *Buc.* 8, 30-31.
116   **duris ... rebus** = Ov. *Pont.* 2, 7, 53; Sil. 2, 596.
118   **quo iudice** *Theoc.* 8, sig. D1ᵛ: "Ecquis erit sub quo victoria iudice constet?"
119   **Debita – recto** Cf. Cordus, *Ecl.* 2, 64: "debita cui cessit victoria iudice Pane."
            stabit victoria Ov. *Ars* 2, 539-540; cf. Eob. *Laud.* 399 (n.).
120   **Sepe – hostem** Cf. *Buc.* 5, 12-14 (n.).
            Sepe solet = Lucr. 4, 606. Many medieval proverbs open with this phrase; see Walther 27283-27307.
            qui provocat hostem = Luc. 4, 275.
121   **victoria caessit** Verg. *A.* 12, 183; Stat. *Theb.* 6, 530.
122-123   **Ut lupus – anguem** Cf. Mant. *Ecl.* 4, 193-194: "Si fugiunt aquilam fulicae, si retia cervi, / si agnum lupum, si damma canem ...." For this type of ironic comparison cf. also Mant. *Ecl.* 5, 146-147: "nostri curant ita carmina reges / ut frondes Aquilo, mare Libs, vineta pruinae"; Eob. *Idyl.* 3, 97-100; *Her.* 3, 5, 35-36.
122   **Ut lupus – agnum** Cf. Verg. *Ecl.* 8, 52; Otto 981; Häussler, pp. 178, 239, and 277; Eob. *Buc.* 6, 65 (n.).
            lupus ... insatiabilis Ov. *Ib.* 170.
            imbellem ... agnum ≈ *Her. Chr.* 22, 105; cf. *Buc.* 1, 108-109 (n.).
123   **Ut leporem canis** Ov. *Met.* 1, 533.
            captum – anguem For the image cf. Verg. *A.* 11, 751-756; Hor. *Carm.* 4, 4, 11-12; Ov. *Met.* 4, 362-364 and 714-717.
            Iovis aliger = Stat. *Silv.* 3, 3, 80 (in a different grammatical relationship). Cf. Verg. *A.* 1, 394; 12, 247; Hor. *Carm.* 4, 4, 1; Eob. *Buc.* B 4, 2 (n.).
124   **Teque tuasque** ≈ Verg. *A.* 2, 661; Sil. 6, 510.
125-126   **immane – laborat** For the well-known fable of the frog and the ox see Hor. *S.* 2, 3, 314-320; Phaed. 1, 24; Otto 1504 and 1558; Häussler, pp. 204, 208, and 244; Andrel. *Ecl.* 10, 3-5: "garrulus Idas / Omnia disperdens raucum per

compita carmen / Ingenti simulata bovi ceu rana tumebat."

125   **immane tumes** Cf. line 20 above: "fastu turges immanius"; *Idyl.* 14, 92-93: "fastu / Intumuisse." For the image see, for instance, Cic. *Tusc.* 3, 19: "inflatus et tumens animus"; Phaed. 1, 3, 4: "Tumens inani ... superbia."
       si te ruperis = Hor. *S.* 2, 3, 319 (fable of the frog and ox); cf. Eob. *Laud.* 581.

126   **rana – esse** = Alan. *Parab.* 5, *PL* 210, col. 590 A: "Inflando se rana bovi par esse volebat."
       esse laborat ≈ Calp. *Ecl.* 4, 64: "... si Tityrus esse laboras"; Mart. 12, 94, 7; Eob. *Nob.* 273: "... nobilis esse laboret."

127   **Et nunc** = Prop. 2, 21, 7 and Verg. *A.* 4, 215 (contemptuously). See further Verg. *Ecl.* 3, 56; 9, 57; *A.* 2, 180; 3, 491; et al.
       Adriacae ... ranae Hutten, *Epigr.* 15, 1; 37, 1. Comparing the Venetians to frogs was quite popular in Germany at the time. See Mutian. *Epp.* 69, 70, and 160; Hutten, *Epigr.* 21, 1-4; 23, lines 1 and 12; 27, 1; 35, lines 2 and 4; and so forth; *Marcus,* passim; Eob. *Buc.* B 4; B 5.

128   **vago ... ponto** Tib. 2, 3, 39.
       brachia ponto = Sil. 3, 414.

129   **Non contenta** Hutten, *Marcus* 14 (*Opera,* vol. 3, p. 296): "[Rana] iam non contenta paludes / Et luteas habitare casas."

130   **terras habitant** Ov. *Met.* 1, 195; *Tr.* 5, 2, 51.
       candida lilia = Ov. *Met.* 4, 355; 5, 392; Calp. *Ecl.* 3, 53. For the lilies (fleurs-de-lis) of France see also Eob. *Buc.* 10, 133; B 4, 2; *Nup.* 37: "fortis lilia Galli."

131   **Iovis arbore** = Ov. *Met.* 1, 106 (an oak).

132   **patrias ... undas** Ov. *Fast.* 6, 733; Stat. *Theb.* 7, 319.

133   **Grandia ... quassantes lilia** Verg. *Ecl.* 10, 25.
       aquilae ... lilia Cf. *Nup.* 37.

134-135 **Quas – paludem** Cf. Mutian. *Ep.* 160 (late spring? 1509). After describing how the Venetian lion will be an easy prey for the imperial eagles, now that it has been crushed by France and the papacy, Mutianus Rufus writes: "Quem mare, quem tellus, quem non capiebat Olympus, / Cum ranis miserum nunc capit una palus." He then alludes to the fable of the frog and the ox.

135   **Antiquam ... paludem** This derisive reference to Venice occurs also in *Max.* 75; cf. *Max.* 227: "Ante coegerimus Venetum in sua stagna rebellem."

136   **proprio ... sanguine** V. Fl. 5, 476.

138   **Ut – dicam** Sen. *Phoen.* 297.

138-139 **quando – cicadae** Cf. *Idyl.* 14, 148-150, referring to the enemies of humanistic learning: "Taliter inflati, monstra ignavissima, paulo / Ante breves ranae, coeperunt esse Gigantes, / Ipsum excisuri vel ab irato Iove coelum."

140   **Discite – superbae** Cf. *Nob.* 17: "Discite, mortales, menti dare fraena superbae"; *Buc.* 8, 68-69.
       Discite, pastores = *Buc.* B 7, 15.
       fraena For this common image see, for instance, Hor. *Carm.* 4, 15, 10; Juv. 8, 88; Eob. *Her. Chr.* 18, 74.

141   **Altius – cadit** Proverbial; see Otto 73 (with the addendum on p. XLII); Häussler, pp. 42, 52, 69, 94, 128-129, and 259; Hor. *Carm.* 2, 10, 10-11.

141-142 **Omne – superis** Cf. *Idyl.* 14, 107-108: "omnis sapientia mundi / Exosa est superis."

141   **Omne superbum** = Prud. *Psych.* 285: "... frangit Deus omne superbum"; Eob. *Psalt.* 113, argument 3: "[Christus] humiles animo relevat, domat omne superbum."

142   **Invisum superis** ≈ Ov. *Ep.* 20, 138.
       pietas gratissima coelo Cf. Stat. *Silv.* 3, 3, 1: "Pietas, cuius gratissima caelo /

rara profanatas inspectant numina terras"; Verg. *A.* 8, 64.

143-146 **Aspicis – turbant** Cf. Hor. *Carm.* 2, 10, 9-12.

143-144 **Aspicis – harundo** For the contrast (usually between the rigid oak and the pliant reed) cf., for example, Aesop. 71 (Hausrath); Macr. *Sat.* 7, 8, 6; Eob. *Sylv.* 4, 14, 29-32 (in reverse): "palustrem flectat arundinem / Quantumlibet vis parva Favonii, / Pinus resistit fortiores / Despiciens Cerealis Euros."

143   **annosas ... pinus** Ov. *Met.* 12, 357.
          convelli turbine Cf. Verg. *G.* 2, 293-294.

145-146 **Fulmina – turbant** Proverbial; see Otto 727; Häussler, pp. 57, 104, 165, and 272; Walther 9338 (with further references).
          Fulmina ... summa petunt Ov. *Rem.* 370; cf. *Met.* 2, 206.

146   **coelo proxima** *Sylv. duae* 2, 111 (n.); *Her. Chr.* 12, 222 (n.).

148   **tristem – ruinam** Cf. *Idyl.* 13, 163: "... tristi doleat cecidisse ruina." For "tristem ruinam" see Verg. *A.* 1, 238; Sil. 15, 692.

149   **Si bonus es** = Lines 86 and 93 above.
          patiare parem Cf. line 21 above and line 166 below.

150   **Non – soli** Proverbial. See Otto 1288; Häussler, pp. 113, 195, and 282; Walther 18657a: "Non uni dat cuncta Deus"; cf. Mant. *Ecl.* 5, 59-60: "hoc vult Deus; omnia non dat / omnibus"; Eob. *In Ed. Leeum,* sig. C2ʳ: "Non uni dat cuncta loco natura, sed aequa / Munera quae confert dividit ista manu"; *Ilias* 13, p. 344: "uni non dat deus omnia, verum / Dotibus hos illis, alios his dotibus auget, / Nec ratione pari dispensat cuncta."

151   **potior – menti** Cf. Verg. *A.* 2, 35: "... melior sententia menti." For the tag "sententia menti" see also Verg. *A.* 11, 314; V. Fl. 1, 548; cf. Eob. *Ama.* B 2, 51 (n.).
          potior sententia = Hor. *Ep.* 1, 17, 17; cf. *Epod.* 16, 17.

152-153 **Sepe – aurum** Proverbial; cf. Walther 27317: "Sepe sub incultis reperitur gemma lapillis: / Sepe cadus vilis nobile nectar habet."

152   **immundo ... pulvere** = Verg. *A.* 12, 611; cf. Ov. *Fast.* 4, 238.

152-153 **pulvere gemmae ... aurum** ≈ Mant. *2. Parthen.* 1, 238-239, where St. Catherine is said to draw treasures from pagan literature: "quasi collectum de sordibus aurum / Et quasi fulgentes Gangis de pulvere gemmas."

153   **Sepe ... duris ... cotibus** Verg. *G.* 4, 203; cf. Prop. 1, 3, 4; Eob. *Buc.* 1, 47 (n.).
          fulvum ... sub ... aurum = Verg. *A.* 7, 279.

154   **Nunc – experior** Mutian. *Ep.* 643, letter from Eobanus to Mutianus Rufus of 4 March 1509 (vol. 2, p. 339): "Quid hominis sit, nunc primum experior."
          rura poaetas = Line 10 above.

155   **barbara tellus** = Ov. *Met.* 7, 53; Luc. 8, 392; Stat. *Silv.* 5, 2, 46.

156-157 **Sydera – flammas** For the adynata see note to lines 98-101 above.

156   **Sydera cuncta** = Verg. *A.* 3, 515; cf. Eob. *Her. Chr.* 1, 17 (n.).

157   **Nerea – flammas** Cf. Ov. *Tr.* 1, 8, 4; Eob. *Her. Chr.* 19, 49-50.

158   **Carmina ... dii, qualia** *Sylv.* 6, 1, 35: "Funebres vidi – dii, qualia carmina! – Musas"; cf. *Hod.* 375 (*Idyl.* 16, 132; *Epic.* 3, 33; *Nor.* 163; *Sylv.* 3, 13, 7): "dii, qualia."

159   **Invideo ... Musas ... Latinas** Cf. lines 173-174 below.
          Invideo vobis ..., o rura Cf. *Lydia* 1 (also lines 8 and 20): "Invideo vobis, agri ...."

159-160 **rura ... Barbara** Line 10 above (n.).

160-161 **Iam – Carmine** Cf. *Idyl.* 11, 25 (expanding the introduction to the present poem): "quando / Audeat hic nemo mecum contendere pastor"; *Buc.* 3, 112-113 (n.).

161-162 **patrias – Aspiciam** Cf. Verg. *A.* 11, 793; Claud. *in Rufin.* 1, 141.

161   **patrias ... urbes** = V. Fl. 4, 171; 5, 562; cf. Eob. *Rec.* 102 (n.).

162   **Ite, meae – capellae** Cf. *Buc.* 2, 102 (n.).

163   **umbrosos ... colles** Ov. *Ars* 2, 420; Luc. 2, 396.

        iniquo sydere = Walter. *Alex.* 2, 532.

164   **Non libate – carpite** Cf. Verg. *Ecl.* 5, 25-26 (at Daphnis's death); Eob. *Buc.* 3, 155 (with notes at lines 154-155 and 155).

165   **dulces ... patriae ... agros** Cf. Verg. *Ecl.* 1, 3.

166   **Barbara rura** Line 10 above (n.).

        pares – ferre Cf. Luc. 1, 125-126: "Nec quemquam iam ferre potest Caesarve priorem / Pompeiusve parem"; Locher, *Stult.*, fol. 78ᵛ: "Non vult ferre parem, maiorem ferre recusat"; Walther 9347a: "Ferre parem nequeo, maiorem ferre recuso."

        non possum ferre = Juv. 3, 60; Tifernate, *Carm.*, sig. A6ᵛ: "Odi mendacem, non possum ferre protervum"; Celtis, *Am.* 3, 6, 57 (imitating Prop. 2, 34, 18): "Ursula, rivalem non possum ferre Tonantem."

167-174   **Iam – cucullo** For this conclusion cf. Mant. *Ecl.* 5, 188-190: "Vade malis avibus numquam rediturus, avare, / et facias subito quidquid tractaveris aurum / more Midae, quando virtus tibi vilior auro." Cf. line 38 above.

167   **tumidas – ranas** Cf. lines 125-126 above (n.).

168   **Aedite – saemine** Cf. *Sylv.* 3, 2, 77: "Aedite magnorum regum de sanguine ...";
Boeth. *Consol.* 4, m. 3, 5: "Solis edita semine."

        per aestum = Verg. *Ecl.* 5, 46.

169   **Per iuga, per valles** = Ov. *Met.* 14, 425; Sil. 7, 360; cf. Eob. *Her. Chr.* 18, 45.

        per mille pericula = V. Fl. 7, 271; Mant. *Ecl.* 6, 169: "... per mille pericula vadens"; cf. Luc. 1, 299; Juv. 3, 8; Eob. *Ama.* 6, 5.

170   **nuda – pascua** Cf. Verg. *Ecl.* 1, 47-48; Eob. *Idyl.* 5, 11 (of weeds): "pecori ... obducunt pascua."

        nuda silex Verg. *Ecl.* 1, 15.

172   **omne ... numen** Ov. *Fast.* 5, 29-30; Mart. 10, 92, 13.

        numen Olimpi = Alcuin. *Carm.* 1, 535.

173-174   **invideas ... Latinas Pierides** Cf. line 159 above.

174   **Bardiaco – cucullo** Cf. Eobanus's letter of 6 January 1515 to Johann Reuchlin, in: *Illustrium virorum epistolae ... ad Ioannem Reuchlin Phorcensem ... liber secundus* (Haguenau, 1519), sig. y3ᵛ, referring to the inquisitor Jacob of Hoogstraten: "Quid tibi cum doctis, bardo signate cucullo, / Hostrate, nate pessimis auguriis?" The form "Bardiacus" for "Bardaicus" ("Vardaicus") was quite common in the Renaissance. See, for example, Jacobus Magdalius Gaudensis, *Erarium aureum poetarum* ([Cologne], 1501), sig. D2ʳ, where "Bardiacus" is defined as "sagum ex pilis caprarum." See further Egidio Forcellini, *Lexicon totius latinitatis*, s.v. "Bardaicus." The term was considered a synonym for "bardocucullus." Cf. Capitol. *Pertinax* 8, 3: "cuculli Bardiaci [Bardaici]."

11

In part modeled on Mant. *Ecl.* 7 and 8, this eclogue in its turn influenced Euricius Cordus, *Buc.* 5 (*Ecl.* 7).

Eobanus often lauds the Virgin, especially in his earlier writings. See *Buc.* 5; *Hod.* B 7 (= *Sylv.* 3, 8) and B 8; and *Sylv.* 2, 27. She is also prominently featured in *Her. Chr.*, letters 1, 2, 13, and 16.

On the Mariology of the Renaissance humanists see Hanna-Barbara Gerl, "Geschenk der Natur und des Himmels," in: *Maria – für alle Frauen oder über allen Frauen?*, ed. Elisabeth Gössmann and Dieter R. Bauer (Freiburg i. Br., 1989), pp. 116-145. See further Walter Delius, *Geschichte der Marienverehrung* (Munich, 1963), pp. 191-195.

Meter: Hexameter.

1-12   **Hactenus – agros** Like a shepherd counting his sheep at the end of the day (*Buc.* 1, 29 n.), Eobanus now lists the opening lines of the preceding ten eclogues and, as it were, commends them into the hands of the Virgin. For the pastoral incipits cf. Verg. *Ecl.* 5, 86-87.

1-2   **Hactenus – Diximus** Cf. *Idyl.* 13-17, praef. 1-2, referring to the preceding twelve idylls: "Hactenus agresti iuvenilia carmina plectro / Pinximus."

1   **errantes – agnas** Cf. Verg. *Ecl.* 2, 21; 5, 8; *A.* 9, 92; Calp. *Ecl.* 5, 15; Eob. *Buc.*, ded. 3-4, with notes; 4, 118; 10, 16-17; *Wirt.* B 1, 5: "Perlege in Hessiacis errantes montibus agnas."

2   **audaci calamo** Cf. Stat. *Silv.* 4, 7, 27: "audaci fide"; Eob. *Vict.*, ded. 14: "audaci pectine."

4   **mihi – Musae** = *Laud.* 281; *Sylv.* 7, 18, 9; cf. *Buc.* 2, 1.

13   **ordine carmen** = Ov. *Met.* 5, 335.

14-15   **deducite ... Carmina** Hor. *Carm.* 3, 30, 13-14; cf. line 20 below (n.), in a different sense.

14   **nymphae** The Muses; see *Rec.* 51 (n.).

15   **urbanum** Eobanus's poem is at once "urbane" and "urban." In the latter sense, the word contrasts with "rus" of the preceding verse and alludes to the allegorical character of these eclogues (which in effect deal with urban, not rustic matters).

          sub dio = Mant. *Dionys.* 2, fol. 185^v: "... sub dio ad sydera somnum / Carpere"; cf. Hor. *Carm.* 3, 2, 5 (where some Renaissance edd. print "sub dio"); Eob. *Ama.*, ded. 5.

16-22   **Ludite – pudoris** Eobanus rejects the pagan Muses and instead invokes the Christian Muses. Cf. Juvenc. 1, praef. 25-27; Paul. Nol. *Carm.* 15, 30-33: "non ego Castalidas, vatum phantasmata, Musas / nec surdum Aonia Phoebum de rupe ciebo; / carminis incentor Christus mihi, munere Christi / audeo peccator sanctum et caelestia fari"; Mant. *Calam.* 1, p. 19 (opening lines); *1. Parthen.* 1, 1-28; Eob. *Buc.* 2, 16-19 (n.); 8, 119-121 (n.); *Vict.* 275-281, where it is the "caelestes Camoenae" who inspire the Old Testament prophets.

16-17   **vicisse – Cantando** *Buc.* 10, 31 (with note to lines 30-31).

17   **gentilia numina** = Prud. *c. Symm.* 1, 449.

18   **divinam ... mentem** Cic. *Div.* 1, 17; et al.; Lucr. 3, 15; Verg. *G.* 4, 220; Eob. *Her. Chr.* 19, 25; 21, 75; *Vict.* 275.

19   **Caelestes animae** = Mant. *Mort.*, fol. 121^r; Eob. *Psalt.* 148, 1; cf. *Vict.* 401: "Caelestes ... animae."

          sanctorum ... vatum = Ven. Fort. *Carm.* 8, 1, 65: "sanctorum carmina vatum"; cf. Eob. *Vict.* 277; *Eleg.* 1, 113.

          numina vatum = Ov. *Ars* 3, 347; *Met.* 15, 622; Eob. *Sylv. duae* 2, 165.

20   **virgineae mentes** Ov. *Met.* 5, 274.

deducite carmen Ov. *Met.* 1, 4; cf. lines 14-15 above (n.).

21   **vestrae ... prima coronae** Just as Calliope is queen of the pagan Muses (*Buc.* 8, 50, with notes), so Mary is queen of the Christian Muses.
     prima coronae = Sil. 16, 505; Eob. *Hod.* 262.

22   **mater – pudoris** Cf. *Buc.* 5, 97-99.
     flore pudoris = Paul. Petr. 4, 591; 4, 643; cf. Eob. *Buc.* 2, 73; *Nup.* 244; *Her. Chr.* 13, 97.

23   **ubi ... cecinissem** For "ubi" with the subjunctive see Hor. *Carm.* 3, 6, 41-42; Eob. *Her.* 2, 1, 111.
     populea ... in umbra = Pontano, *Ecl.* 1, 7, 64: "... populea vacuus cantabit in umbra"; cf. Verg. *G.* 4, 511; Nemes. *Ecl.* 4, 1.
     cecinissem – umbra Cf. Filetico, *Theoc.* 1, 13-14: "... laetus moduleris in umbra." For "laetus in umbra" cf. also Verg. *Ecl.* 1, 4 (= line 106 below): "... lentus in umbra."

24-27   **Purior – numina** For the epiphany and its effect on nature cf. Mant. *1. Parthen.* 3, 476-478 (when Jesus enters Egypt): "praesentia numina tellus / sensit et illius radiis felicibus aether / intima maiori complevit viscera partu"; Eob. *Buc.* 6, 17-30; *Her. Chr.* 4, 151-162 (n.), after St. Catherine of Alexandria sees a vision of Jesus and his mother.

24   **Purior – aether** Cf. Ov. *Ars* 3, 55-56.
     radiis ... aether = Mant. *1. Parthen.* 3, 477 (see above).
     resplenduit aether = Avit. *Carm.* 4, 527.

25   **Sol stetit** = Sedul. 1, 163; cf. Eob. *Vict.* 450-451 (on Easter morning): "Stabat ... / Sol."
     superi ... limina mundi Cf. Ov. *Tr.* 5, 11, 25: "caeli ... limina"; Eob. *Sylv.* 4, 2, 36: "mundi ... limina."

26   **calor ... subitus** Stat. *Silv.* 1, praef.; Eob. *Nup.*, ded. 3 (n.).
     mentem incendia Cf. Catul. 64, 226; V. Fl. 7, 243.

27   **O Virgo** = Verg. *A.* 6, 104; 11, 536; Mant. *Ecl.* 7, 70.
     sentimus ... numina Verg. *A.* 3, 359-360; 5, 466; Hor. *Ep.* 2, 1, 134; Ov. *Ars* 3, 55; et al.; Mant. *1. Parthen.* 3, 476-477 (see note to lines 24-27 above).
     nova numina = Claud. *Rapt. Pros.* 2, 371; Prud. *c. Symm.* 2, 359.

28   **Spes miserum** *Psalt.* 38, 60: "Mi Deus, o miserum spes rata, certa salus"; cf. line 54 below (n.): "terrae spes."
     quae – rerum ≈ *Psalt.* 51, 1: "Summe pater, qui sceptra tenes altissima rerum."
     sceptra tenes Cf. Salzer, pp. 443 and 447-467; cf. Eob. *Her. Chr.* 4, 111.

31-33   **Quam – Signifero** Three traditional symbols of the Virgin, drawn from the Song of Songs. For the enclosed garden and sealed fountain see Vulg. *Cant.* 4, 12; and, for example, Brant, *Var. carm.*, sig. B7ʳ (*Texte* 115, 73-74): "Tu fons signa gerens, ortus conclusus ab omni / Parte." For the flowers see Vulg. *Cant.* 2, 1-2; 4, 14. See also Eob. *Buc.* 5, 79 (n.).

31-32   **pictus ... Monstravit paries** Cf. Mant. *Ecl.* 8, 93-94 (in similar context): "'ista sacer paries,' ait, 'omnia monstrat.' / pictus erat paries signis et imagine multa"; cf. also *Ecl.* 7, 42-47; Prop. 2, 6, 34; Eob. *Her. Chr.* 12, 205.

32   **in fonte lavantem** For the phrasing cf. *Buc.* 2, 98 (n.). Here the gesture is intended to evoke the Virgin's purity.

33   **Signifero** In the sense "signatus" this epithet seems to be unparalleled.
     Tunc illa Mant. *1. Parthen.* 2, 766 (to Mary): "... Tunc illa propago ...?"
     Dei – Mater Brant, *Var. carm.*, sig. E4ᵛ (*Texte* 110, 1), paraphrasing the antiphon "Salve, regina" (*AH* 50, 245): "O regina, Dei mater castissima, salve"; cf. Alcuin. *Carm.* 109, 4, 1: "Virgo Maria, Dei genitrix, castissima virgo." See further Salzer, pp. 103-104; Eob. *Her. Chr.* 8, 85.

34   **veteres ... vates** Ov. *Am.* 3, 6, 17; Prud. *Apoth.* 234 (of the Hebrew prophets);

Eob. *Sylv. duae* 2, 217 (n.).

typico For this word in the theological sense "typological," "prefigurative" see also *Her. Chr.* 16, lines 123 and 164.

cecinerunt ... vates = Verg. *A.* 5, 524.

carmine vates = *Anthol. Lat.* 2, 24; Sabell. *In natal.* 1, sig. a2ʳ: "Venturam cecinere pii te carmine vates"; Eob. *Vict.* 317; cf. *Buc.* 10, 36; *Her. Chr.* 4, 21.

36   **Quicquid agit** = Tib. 1, 6, 66; Mart. 1, 68, 1.

37   **mari terraque** = *Hod.* B 7, 3: "Virgo, mari terraque potens ..."; cf. Hor. *Saec.* 53; *Epod.* 9, 27; Erasmus, *Adag.* 1, 4, 25; Eob. *Her. Chr.* 18, 33.

pates, Dea Cf. Verg. *A.* 1, 405.

Dea ... dearum For this term of praise see *Mariale*, q. 162, 14, in: *Opera b. Alberti Magni*, vol. 37 (Paris, 1898), pp. 235-236. Cf. Enn. *Ann.* 22, referring to Juno: "dia dearum"; Vulg. *Psa.* 49, 1: "Deus deorum." In Renaissance literature the Virgin is often honored with the title "dea"; see, for instance, Landino, *Xandra* 2, 10, 14: "Christiferae ... deae"; Sabell. *In natal.* 3, sig. a5ʳ; Brant, *Var. carm.*, sig. C1ʳ (*Texte* 95, 6); Mant. *Ecl.* 8, 122 and 146; Eob. *Her. Chr.* 14, 79; line 89 below.

38   **Non – aiunt** Cf. Ov. *Am.* 2, 4, 33; *Ars* 1, 713.

39   **conferre puellas** ≈ Ov. *Rem.* 709.

40   **magni – mundi** Cf. Ov. *Met.* 2, 35. For "magni mundi" see Lucr. 2, 1144; 5, 433; et al.; Eob. *Vict.* 269; 330. For "lux mundi" at this metrical position see Brant, *Var. carm.*, sig. H6ʳ (*Texte* 144, 47), of St. Augustine: " lux ... clarissima mundi." The phrase was frequently applied to the Virgin Mary; see Salzer, pp. 431-434; cf. Salzer, pp. 391-399. In Vulg. *Joann.* 8, 12 and 9, 5 it is applied to Jesus; cf. also *Joann.* 11, 9.

41   **Pulchra nimis** Vulg. *Gen.* 12, 14; 41, 18; *3. Reg.* 1, 4; *Esth.* 2, 7; *Dan.* 13, 2. Mary is often praised for her beauty, symbolic of her soul; see Salzer, pp. 443-444; Eob. *Her. Chr.* 4, 110; cf. *Her. Chr.* 2, 83-86.

dilecta Tonanti = Bebel, "Ad divam Virginem," *Carm.*, sig. p4ᵛ: "Virgo ... dilecta Tonanti"; cf. Hor. *Carm.* 1, 21, 4; Eob. *Her. Chr.* 16, 1 (n.). Eobanus applies Jupiter's title "Tonans" (Ov. *Ep.* 9, 7; *Met.* 1, 170; etc.) to the Christian God. He does so also in *Her. Chr.* 1, 157; 2, 7; 4, 251; and often. This usage is sanctioned by a tradition dating back to the earliest Christian poets. See, for example, Juvenc. 2, 795; 4, 553; 4, 672; 4, 786; Paul. Nol. *Carm.* 22, 149; Prud. *Cath.* 12, 83; *Apoth.* 171.

42-43   **Lilia ... vincis ... Mixta rosis** Cf. [Ven. Fort.] "In laudem sanctae Mariae" 233 (*MGH, Auctores antiquissimi*, vol. 4, 1, p. 377): "inde rubore rosas, candore hinc lilia vincens"; Tifernate, *Carm.*, sig. A4ʳ, praising the Virgin: "Tu niveas formosa rosas, tu candida vincis / Lilia." The lily and rose are favorite symbols of Mary; see Salzer, pp. 162-170 and 183-192.

Lilia ... Mixta rosis Ven. Fort. *Carm.* 2, 9, 24; 6, 1, 108; 9, 2, 122; Eob. *Epic.* 4, 40; cf. Verg. *A.* 12, 68-69; Ov. *Am.* 2, 5, 37.

42   **Lilia ... vernantia** *Buc.* 6, 19-20 (n.).

Lilia ... vincis = Mart. 8, 28, 11.

43   **niveae ... columbae** ≈ Ov. *Met.* 15, 715; cf. *Met.* 13, 674. The epithet "nivea" was commonly applied to the Virgin; see Salzer, pp. 335-336; Eob. *Her. Chr.* 1, 142; 4, 109-112.

similis – columbae Cf. Vulg. *Cant.* 2, 13-14: "speciosa mea ..., columba mea"; Salzer, p. 138, lines 25-26: "speciosa quasi columba"; p. 138, line 30: "velut columba speciosa"; p. 351, line 10, quoting Gregory the Great (*PL* 78, col. 798 A): "speciosam sicut columbam." "Speciosa" is a common term of praise for the Virgin; see Salzer, pp. 349-353 and 444. For "columba" see Salzer, pp. 134-140 and 501-502.

44	**Corpora – mendae** Cf. Ov. *Am.* 1, 5, 18; Tifernate, *Carm.*, sig. A4ʳ (referring to Mary): "... nec in toto corpore menda sedet"; Salzer, pp. 366-367.

44   **Corpora – mendae** Cf. Ov. *Am.* 1, 5, 18; Tifernate, *Carm.*, sig. A4ʳ (referring to Mary): "... nec in toto corpore menda sedet"; Salzer, pp. 366-367.
eburnea For this epithet see, for example, Prop. 2, 1, 9; Ov. *Am.* 3, 7, 7; *Ep.* 20, 57; *Met.* 3, 422; 4, 335; 10, 592; Mant. *1. Parthen.* 3, 704 (of Mary): "eburnea membra"; Eob. *Her. Chr.* 1, 159 (Mary).

45-46 **Tu ... Deum ... deducis Olimpo** Cf. Ov. *Fast.* 3, 317; Eob. *Her. Chr.* 2, 80.

45   **mortalibus aegris** = Lucr. 6, 1; Verg. *G.* 1, 237; *A.* 2, 268; et al.

46   **res mira** = *Sylv. duae* 1, 83; *Her. Chr.* B 1, 33; cf. Ov. *Met.* 13, 893.

47-48 **paris – mundo** Cf. *Her. Chr.* 1, 103-104.

47   **immensum – Christum** For the paradox of Almighty God in a tiny crib cf. *Her. Chr.* 1, 107-108 (n.). Also cf. *Her. Chr.* 1, 138 (n.).
immensum ... Christum ≈ Paul. Nol. *Carm.* 14, 43: "inmensi ... gloria Christi."
ad praesaepia = Verg. *G.* 3, 214 and 495; Tib. 2, 1, 7; Mant. *Ecl.* 7, 34: "... Christo ad praesepia nato"; Erasmus, *Carm.* 42, 49; cf. Vulg. *Luc.* 2, 16.

48   **toti ... mundo** = Luc. 2, 383; 3, 393.

49-50 **Quem – Deum** The ox and ass, traditionally believed to have been present at Jesus' birth. Cf., for example, Hier. *Ep.* 108, 10: "stabulum in quo 'agnovit bos possessorem suum, et asinus praesepe Domini sui' [Vulg. *Isa.* 1, 3]"; Eob. *Her. Chr.* 1, 108.

50   **Cognovere Deum** *Her. Chr.* 23, 91.
pia Virgo = *Hod.* B 7, 11; cf. *Buc.* 5, 107 (n.).

51   **populem ... agrestem** Hor. *Carm.* 3, 30, 11-12; Eob. *Her.* 1, 1, 75.
non spernit ≈ Verg. *Ecl.* 3, 74.

52-53 **Flecte – iacentes** A reminiscence of the antiphon "Salve, regina" (*AH* 50, 245), lines 4-7: "Ad te suspiramus gementes et flentes / In hac lacrimarum valle. / Eia ergo, advocata nostra, / Illos tuos misericordes oculos ad nos converte."

52   **Flecte ... oculos** Ov. *Met.* 8, 696; 10, 57; Juv. 13, 144.
pios oculos Ennod. *Carm.* 2, 9, 11: "Huc oculos converte pios."
vultumque serenum = Walter. *Alex.* 7, 270; cf. Eob. *Buc.* 9, 93 (n.).

53   **lachrymarum valle** Vulg. *Psa.* 83, 7.

54   **Virgo, decus coeli** = Tifernate, *Carm.*, sig. A4ʳ; Bebel, "Ad Virginem tetrastichon," *Carm.*, sig. q1ʳ: "Virgo, decus coeli, ... spes miserorum." For "decus coeli" at this metrical position see Verg. *A.* 9, 18 (of Iris); cf. Hor. *Saec.* 2; Eob. *Her. Chr.* 1, 129 (of Mary); Salzer, p. 420, line 36 and p. 422, line 4: "decus coeli civium." "Decus" is a traditional term of praise for the Virgin; see Salzer, pp. 344 and 420-422. It is used again in line 105 below.
terrae spes Mary is often addressed as the hope of the world; see Salzer, pp. 574-577; Eob. *Her. Chr.* 2, 46; *Hod.* B 7, 1: "spes unica mundi." Cf. line 28 above (n.): "Spes miserum."
terror abyssi For this term of praise cf. Salzer, pp. 589-591; Eob. *Hod.* B 7, 4: "Terror ... infernae ... domus."

55-64 **Stella – orant** Cf. Vulg. *Psa.* 106, 4-29; Mant. *1. Parthen.* 1, 270-284: the Virgin helps sailors in storms, the wounded in battle, prisoners, the hungry, sinners; Tifernate, *Carm.*, sig. A4ᵛ, to Mary: "Tu das optatam languenti sepe salutem, / Eripis e duro carcere saepe reum. / Te vocat in partu mulier, te miles eandem / Subvenias querulo saucius ore rogat. / Saepe procelloso iactatis aequore nautis / Dirigis in portum stella serena ratem. / Erigis afflictos, aegris solacia praebes, / Saepe venis terra, saepe vocata mari"; Erasmus, *Paean Virgini Matri*, LB 5, col. 1232 D-1233 A.

55-57 **Stella – miserae** As "star of the sea" Mary is the patron saint of sailors. They appeal to her when storms rend the sails; tropologically, she guides her people through the storms of life to the safe harbor. See Salzer, pp. 400-418 and

527-531; Eob. *Her. Chr.* 5, 43-44; *Hod.* B 7, 19-28; B 7, 43-44: "Naufragus urgenti te navita clamat in alto / Et salvis placidam mercibus intrat humum."

55 **Stella maris** According to a well-known medieval explanation, "Mary" means "stella maris" – a corruption of "stilla maris." Cf. Hier. *Liber interpretationis hebraicorum nominum, CCSL* 72, p. 76: "Maria inluminatrix mea ... aut stilla maris"; and, for example, Isid. *Orig.* 7, 10, 1: "Maria inluminatrix, sive stella maris. Genuit enim lumen mundi."

   medio ... profundo = Ov. *Met.* 4, 537; V. Fl. 1, 574; Sil. 7, 418; 14, 16.

56-59 **Ut ventos – agrum** Cf. Mant. *Ecl.* 8, 98-109 (referring to the Virgin): "ista potest nigro depellere nubila caelo, / ista potest siccis fluvios dare frugibus imbres. / cum volet, ista novos duris emittere campis, / cum volet, emissos poterit restringere fontes. / qui modo sunt steriles et nudi gramine campi, / si volet, in pingues poterit convertere glaebas. / [*5 lines*] / si favet haec nobis, complebunt horrea messes."

56 **Ut ventos nymbosque** ≈ Stat. *Theb.* 8, 423.

   ventos – serves Cf. V. Fl. 1, 584.

56-57 **naufraga ... Membra ratis** Ov. *Ars* 1, 412; Andrel. *Eleg.* 1, sig. a7ʳ, in a poem to the Virgin: "Sustineat [tua pietas] nostre naufraga membra ratis."

57 **rure colonus** ≈ Luc. 1, 170; 2, 635; 6, 277; Eob. *Ruf.* 7: "... in rure coloni."

58 **ruptis – ymbres** Cf. Ov. *Met.* 11, 516; Verg. *Ecl.* 6, 38; *A.* 3, 199; V. Fl. 4, 661; Sen. *Med.* 533; Stat. *Theb.* 12, 709-710; Mant. *1. Parthen.* 2, 132: "... largus de nubibus imber."

   largos ... ymbres = Luc. 4, 76; cf. Lucr. 1, 282; Hor. *Epod.* 16, 53-54.

59 **plenis ... messibus agrum** *Nor.* 559: "Vicinos plenis flavescere messibus agros"; cf. Ov. *Met.* 8, 781; *Fast.* 4, 707; Eob. *Sylv. duae* 1, 69.

   sterilem ... agrum Verg. *G.* 1, 84; *A.* 3, 141; Ov. *Ars* 1, 450; Luc. 8, 829.

60 **ardentes ... ad aras** = Mant. *1. Parthen.* 1, 304; 2, 11; Eob. *Her. Chr.* 2, 91.

   supplex – aras = *Her. Chr.* 4, 217; cf. Ov. *Am.* 1, 7, 61; *Met.* 10, 415; Mant. *Georgius,* fol. 207ʳ: "semper ad aras / Procubuit ... supplex."

61 **Te vocat – carcere** Cf. *Hod.* B 7, 47-48, addressing the Virgin: "Illum durus habet graveolenti carcer in umbra / Ferrea, ceu pulvis, te duce, vincla cadunt."

   Te vocat = Ov. *Tr.* 5, 4, 26; Tifernate, *Carm.,* sig. A4ᵛ (see note to lines 55-64 above); Mant. *Bapt.,* fol. 230ᵛ: "Languidus auxilium medicae cui defuit artis, / Te vocat"; Sabell. *In natal.* 11, sig. c1ᵛ: "Te vocat ille senex ...."

   damnatus carcere ≈ Prud. *c. Symm.* 1, 470: "lugebas longo damnatos carcere centum."

62 **magis exorabile** ≈ *Her. Chr.* 5, 173.

   exorabile numen = Stat. *Silv.* 5, 1, 164; Juv. 13, 102.

63-64 **Te gravidae – orant** Expectant mothers pray to the Virgin because she not only bore a perfect son but did so without labor pains. For the prayer cf. Ov. *Fast.* 2, 451-452: "parce, precor, gravidis, facilis Lucina, puellis / maturumque utero molliter aufer onus." For the phrasing cf. Mant. *Bapt.,* fol. 230ᵛ, to John the Baptist: "At mulier gravida quae pignora sustinet alvo, / Nonaque iam celeri luna propinquat equo, / 'Da facilem,' dicit, 'iuvenis sanctissime, partum / Ponere cum ventris pondera tempus erit.'"

63 **pondera ventris** = Ov. *Ep.* 11, 37; Mant. *1. Parthen.* 2, 879; cf. *1. Parthen.* 2, 753: "... pondere ventris"; Eob. *Her. Chr.* 13, 129; cf. *Laud.* B 3, 11 (n.).

64 **Tunc cum tempus erit** Cf. Verg. *Ecl.* 3, 97; Mant. *1. Parthen.* 2, 112 (Eob. *Hod.* 416): "Tunc, ubi tempus erit ...."

66 **cerimonia** For the neuter plural form (with a short first syllable) see Ven. Fort. *Carm.* 1, 11, 23; *Mart.* 3, 53; 4, 308.

67-83 **Si qua – mystes** Cf. Cordus, *Buc.* 5, 34-41 (*Ecl.* 7, 30-37), at Pentecost: the people rest from their labors, go to church, bring offerings to the altars, while the priests celebrate the feast.

67 **redeunt solennia** = Aus. *Versus paschales* 1: "Sancta salutiferi redeunt sollemnia Christi / et devota pii celebrant ieiunia mystae."

68-74 **Festo – uvas** Cf. Catul. 64, 38-42 (at the wedding of Peleus and Thetis); Tifernate, *Carm.*, sig. C3ᵛ (on New Year's Day): "Omnis hanc lucem celebrat iuventus, / Fervidum cessant mare navigantes / Navitae, curis hodie solutis / Cessat arator."

68 **Festo – cessant** Cf. *Her. Chr.* 11, 81-82.
Festo ... die Pl. *Aul.* 380; *Poen.* 758; 848; Hor. *Carm.* 3, 28, 1.
sacra ... fiunt *Her. Chr.* 4, 211 (n.).
opera omnia = Verg. *A.* 4, 607; 12, 699.

69 **Navita ... sulcat mare** Cf. *Ruf.* 21-22: "navita ... / Per mare sulcat iter"; *Her. Chr.* 14, 69 (n.): "sulcantes ... vada cerula nautas." For "sulcat mare" see Verg. *A.* 10, 197; cf. also, for example, *A.* 5, 158; Ov. *Pont.* 2, 10, 33; Sil. 17, 155. Eobanus often uses the image; see also, for example, *Her. Chr.* 5, 46; 15, 179; 17, 163.

71-72 **magister ... in triviis** *Her. Chr.* 24, 97.

72 **in triviis** = Bebel, "In laudem Terentianae lectionis," *Carm.*, sig. o2ʳ, referring to performances of Terence's plays in schools: "Personet in triviis ..."; Eob. *Buc.* 1, 39 (n.), in a different sense. For the sense "school" see also *Her. Chr.* 24, 97 and *Eleg.* 1, 45: "triviis popularibus."

72-73 **fumantia ... Terga** = Sil. 9, 602-603; cf. Ov. *Met.* 14, 363, where some early editions read "fumantia terga"; Verg. *A.* 12, 337-338.

73 **stivam ... arator** Ov. *Met.* 8, 218.

74 **vinitor uvas** = Sedul. 1, 91: "Sordidus ... calcabit vinitor uvas"; cf. Verg. *Ecl.* 10, 36.

75 **explorant – racemos** Cf. Calp. *Ecl.* 1, 2.

76 **Confluit ... vulgus** = *Her. Chr.* 17, 221; *Hod.* B 7, 59.
totum ... vulgus Sen. *Tro.* 1077-1078.

77 **Imberbes – senilis** For the phrasing cf. Mart. 9, 8, 9; Eob. *Psalt.* 148, 36: "Imberbes pueri, iuvenes, teneraeque puellae, / Imbelles aevo iam graviore senes"; for the thought cf. Mant. *Ecl.* 8, 179: "Virgine laetetur pubes et cana senectus"; Prud. *Cath.* 9, 109-111. For the expression "young and old" see Eob. *Rec.* 24 (n.).

78 **venerantur Iesu** For the tag cf. *Her. Chr.* 6, 103.

79 **cumulant – altaria** Verg. *A.* 11, 50. For "cumulant donis" cf. Eob. *Laud.* 441.

79-80 **puellae Innuptae** Verg. *G.* 4, 476; *A.* 2, 238; 6, 307; Sabell. *In natal.* 3, sig. a4ᵛ: "Stent pueri circum ... innuptaeque puellae."

81 **ardentes ... lychnos** *Theoc.* 31, sig. L4ʳ.

82 **veneranda dies** = Paul. Nol. *Carm.* 27, 44 (the day Christ was born).
dies ... illuxerit orbi *Hod.* 358-359: "Iam tertia luxerat orbi / Orta dies"; for "dies illuxerit" cf. Pl. *Per.* 712 and 780; Verg. *G.* 2, 337; Ov. *Met.* 7, 431; for "illuxerit orbi" cf. Vulg. *Psa.* 76, 19; 96, 4; Mant. *1. Parthen.* 3, 254: "... Deus illucesceret orbi."

83 **sacra – mystes** Cf. *Sylv. duae* 2, 195; *Accl.* 2, 205: "Sancta coronati tractent libamina mystae." For "sacra libamina" see Tiro Prosper, *Epigr.* 72, 1, *PL* 51, col. 520 B: "Magnum praesidium est sacro libamine pasci."

84 **salutares ... herbas** = Mant. *Ecl.* 9, 8; cf. Ov. *Rem.* 45.
pascunt – herbas = *Theoc.* 36, sig. N5ᵛ; *Psalt.* 8, 33; cf. Verg. *G.* 3, 162; Ov. *Met.* 4, 635.

85 **Fronde coronantur** For the phrase cf. *Buc.* 1, 48 (n.). The Strasbourg copy, glossing "Fronde" with "querna," indicates that the youths' garlands are made

of oak leaves.
liber in arvis = V. Fl. 6, 330.
86 **et dulci ... in umbra** = *Culex* 122.
dormit in umbra = *Buc.* 5, 9.
87 **Iamque – voces** Cf. *Buc.* 1, 83, with note to lines 83-84.
summo ... de culmine Verg. *G.* 1, 402; *A.* 7, 512.
tales ... voces = Verg. *A.* 5, 723; V. Fl. 4, 24.
88 **Incipit, et** = Verg. *A.* 1, 721; 2, 269; 8, 373.
cantu – remugit Cf. *Buc.* 10, 75 (n.).
89-105 **O Dea – mundi** For the shepherd's prayer to the Virgin cf. Mant. *Ecl.* 8, 122-151, which opens with the verse: "O Dea, quae servas urbes et rura, precamur."
89 **O Dea** = Verg. *A.* 1, 372; Ov. *Met.* 14, 841. For the title "dea" see note to line 37 above.
rura ... servas Ov. *Fast.* 2, 662.
90 **Numine sub** = Ov. *Met.* 15, 546.
series – rerum = Verg. *A.* 1, 641.
91-92 **aurato – stellas** Based on Vulg. *Apoc.* 12, 1, traditionally interpreted as referring to the Virgin. See further Salzer, pp. 373-377; Mant. *Ecl.* 8, 85: "et sacram bis seno sidere frontem / cinxit"; *1. Parthen.* 3, 825-826: "textam Phoebi de lumine vestem, / claraque bissenis Matri diademata flammis"; 3, 955-956: "Ipsa tenens sceptrum et nitido diademate fulgens / cincta caput"; *Votum*, fol. 54ʳ: "Lucida bisseno tibi frons innectitur astro"; Eob. *Buc.* 5, 107; *Her. Chr.* 4, 109: "... comas auro rutilante coactas."
91 **diademate crines** = Luc. 5, 60; Stat. *Theb.* 9, 163.
93 **Gnosiacae ... coronae** = Mant. *2. Parthen.* 2, 169, after St. Catherine has received her wedding ring from Jesus: "Hic neque Gnosiacae sequimur figmenta coronae"; cf. Stat. *Silv.* 1, 6, 88: "vincens Gnosiacae facem coronae."
similis fortuna = Verg. *A.* 1, 628; Juv. 12, 29.
94 **serenatae ... frontis** ≈ Aus. *Precationes variae* 1, 3.
pulcherrima lumina = *Coluth.*, sig. C2ʳ: "... illa solo pulcherrima lumina figens"; cf. *Her. Chr.* 3, 78, of the angel's eyes: "pulchro lumine."
95 **Aspice nos** = Verg. *A.* 2, 690; Eob. *Her. Chr.* 17, 145; cf. *Her. Chr.* 14, 81.
Tua turba sumus Ov. *Am.* 1, 1, 6; Stat. *Silv.* 1, 2, 70; cf. Eob. *Her. Chr.* 12, 60; 12, 98.
96 **omne ... pecus** *Buc.*, ded. 5 (n.).
sub lumine mundi Cf. *Salom.* 1, sig. A5ʳ: "... sub aperti lumine solis"; 8, sig. C2ʳ: "sub magni lumine solis." The expression varies the standard phrase "sub sole"; see *Buc.* 7, 140 (n.).
lumine mundi = Man. 1, 68.
97-98 **pecus – ovili** Cf. *Buc.* 9, 31-32 (n.). Here the soldier and wolf stand for the devil and his minions.
97 **pecus defende tuum** Cf. *Buc.* 9, 112.
98-99 **lupus ... Fures** Wolves and thieves are mentioned in the same breath also in Tib. 1, 1, 33; Verg. *G.* 3, 407; Mant. *Ecl.* 9, 230: "iste potest servare gregem, depellere morbos, / ... / conciliare Iovem, fures arcere luposque."
98 **lupus insidias** = Verg. *Ecl.* 5, 60; *G.* 3, 537.
insidias ... componat Tib. 1, 6, 4; Prop. 2, 32, 19.
99-100 **Fures ... stabulis** Verg. *G.* 3, 407.
averte ... A stabulis Verg. *A.* 8, 207-208.
100-104 **Da tuta – cursu** For the conclusion to this prayer cf. Boeth. *Consol.* 3, m. 9, 22-24: "Da, pater, augustam menti conscendere sedem, / da fontem lustrare boni,

da luce reperta / in te conspicuos animi defigere visus."

100   **greges in pascua duci** ≈ *Theoc.* 32, sig. M1ʳ: "... greges in pascua ducis"; cf. Verg. *G.* 3, 323.

101   **laetas segetes** Verg. *G.* 1, 1.
      vitae ... beatae *Buc.* 6, 70 (n.).

102   **Da facilem** = Verg. *G.* 1, 40: "da facilem cursum ...."
      facilem victum Verg. *G.* 2, 460.

103   **Vota iuvant** = *Rec.* 62.
      vitae ... presentis The phrase, which draws attention to the life to come, is very common in Christian prose and poetry. See, for example, Lact. *Inst.* 7, 5, 21; 7, 27, 1; Paul. Nol. *Carm.* 10, 325; 21, 348; Prud. *c. Symm.* 2, 216 and 908; Eob. *Her. Chr.* 13, 165 (n.); 14, 97.

104   **facili ... cursu** Verg. *G.* 1, 40; Stat. *Theb.* 5, 544; Sil. 17, 211; Mart. 10, 104, 3.
      patriam For the commonplace that our true homeland is heaven see, for example, Cic. *Tusc.* 1, 24; Sen. *Ep.* 86, 1; August. *Enarrationes in Psa.*, 55, 6: "caelestem patriam, ubi anima nostra impleatur securitate, impleatur quiete et sempiterna felicitate"; Eob. *Her. Chr.* 21, 67-70; *Epic.* 3, 5; 9, 105-108.

105   **O decus, o ... requies** Claud. *Rapt. Pros.* 3, 416; cf. Verg. *G.* 2, 40; Ov. *Ep.* 16, 273; *Fast.* 6, 810; *Tr.* 5, 2, 49; Mant. *1. Parthen.* 3, 538 (Mary addressing Christ on the cross); Eob. *Her. Chr.* 12, 168; 20, 68; *Nor.* 968. For "decus" as a term of praise for the Virgin see note to line 54 above.
      miseri ... mundi = Prud. *Amart.* 844; cf. Luc. 5, 469; Sabell. *In natal.* 8, sig. b4ᵛ: "... miseri spes unica mundi."

106-111   **Hos – pastos** This coda is modeled on the conclusion of Vergil's last eclogue (*Ecl.* 10, 70-77).

106-107   **Hos – plectro** Cf. Verg. *G.* 4, 559-560 and 565-566; Mart. 9, 84, 3; Eob. *Val.* 2, 409-410 (at the end of the poem): "Haec ... cecini ... / Dum ...."

106   **Hos – cecini** Cf. *Pug.* 103-104.
      lentus in umbra = Verg. *Ecl.* 1, 4.

107   **Carmina – plectro** Cf. *Buc.* 3, 92, with notes.
      Carmina ... iuvenilia = Ov. *Tr.* 4, 10, 57; cf. Eob. *Her. Chr.* 24, 113 (n.).

109   **Nox ruit, et** = Verg. *A.* 8, 369; cf. *A.* 6, 539. For the concluding motif see n. *Buc.* 1, 124.
      gelidae – guttae ≈ Mant. *1. Parthen.* 2, 1009: "... gelidi veniunt in gramina rores."
      in gramina guttae ≈ Calp. *Ecl.* 5, 55; cf. Eob. *Buc.* 8, 3.

110   **tellus ... humida** = Ov. *Met.* 8, 563.

111   **Ite – pastos** Cf. Bocc. *Ecl.* 11, 238 (conclusion): "Ite domum, pueri, pastas revocate capellas"; Nemes. *Ecl.* 2, 90: "frigidus ... suasit / Hesperus ... stabulis pastos inducere tauros"; Eob. *Buc.* 4, 117-118 (n.).
      boves ... pastos Verg. *Ecl.* 5, 24-25.

B 1

For this attack on unspecified carping critics cf. *Pug.* B 1, with notes.
Meter: Elegiac distich.

tit. **Teste conscientia** Cf. *Buc.* 10, 88 (n.).
1 **Nunc age, qui ... solebas** = *Nup.* 368; *Luth.* 7, 1; cf. Verg. *A.* 7, 37.
 qui quondam ... solebas = *Laud.* 577 (to an abusive critic).
 mea – scripta Cf. Ov. *Rem.* 361; *Pont.* 3, 9, 2; Mart. 1, 91, 1.
3 **censurae campum ... apertum** = *Eleg.* 3, 29: "Nunc age, censurae campum
 subeamus apertum." For "campum apertum" (in the literal sense) see, for
 example, Verg. *G.* 2, 280 and *A.* 11, 493.
4 **perfida lingua** = Mart. 7, 24, 2; Eob. *Her. Chr.* 8, 140.
5 **Livor edax** = *Laud.* 579 (n.).
 turba – illa Cf. Ov. *Ep.* 4, 101.
6 **vipereo – soles** Cf. Hor. *Carm.* 4, 3, 16; *Ep.* 1, 18, 82; Ov. *Pont.* 3, 4, 74; Eob.
 Psalmus CXVIII, ex ipsius M. Lutheri scholiis (Nuremberg, 1530), ded., sig. A2ʳ:
 "Quod si forte volet, sicut solet omnia, Livor / Haec quoque vipereo rodere
 dente, veta." The image of the tooth of Envy was proverbial; see n. *Pug.* B 1, 1.
 For "vipereo dente" see, for example, Ov. *Ep.* 6, 33 and *Met.* 3, 103.
 rodere dente = *Sylv. duae* 2, 130.
7 **Andinus vates** *Laud.* 458 (n.).
 magnus Homerus Hor. *S.* 1, 10, 52; Ov. *Am.* 1, 8, 61; *Rem.* 365; et al.
8 **per superos** = *Buc.* 7, 30 (n.).

B 2

In *Ep.* 119, written to Crotus Rubianus on 17 January 1509, Mutianus Rufus says that he
has just received a copy of this poem from Englender himself. Mutianus then praises the
work profusely, calling it a "poema mirae suavitatis" and highlighting lines 1 and 39-44.
 Meter: Elegiac distich.

1-18 **Cum – thoro** Eobanus uses virtually the same pattern to introduce the
 dedicatory letter of his *Idyllia*, lines 1-12. Here is the 1528-version:

> Cum tua non uno virtus, Bilibalde, feratur
> Nomine, Pieria vivere digne cheli,
> Cum tua certatim populi praeconia linguae
> Laudibus aeternis hic et ubique vehant,
> Cum (si vera fides populari adhibenda favori est)
> Multorum laudes unus habere queas –
> Et merito, cum sis tam multa dote beatus,
> Non est de meritis fama maligna tuis – [*2 lines*]
> Dignus honorata mihi visus es esse Camoena,
> Quae victura tuum nomen in astra levet.

Cf. also *Her.*, ded. 15-18: "Cum tibi sint et opes, cum sis et sanguine clarus, /
Nec tamen has partes deseruisse queas, / Dignus eras cui perpetua de fronde
coronam / Inciperent nostrae nectere Pierides"; *Sylv.* 7, 35, 1-14: "Cum tua non
uno virtus praecone feratur, / Nobilis o gentis laus Iacobe tuae, / Cum sit
imaginibus domus inclyta, cuius honori / Natales debes, vir memorande,
tuos /[...:] / Crede mihi, virtus haec est quae laude perhenni / Debeat et coelos
et super astra vehi. / Ergo tot Aonidum cultores inter et Hessum / Praeconem

laudis fer, precor, esse tuae"; 8, 1, 1-8.

1   **vir praestantissime** Cic. *Pis.* 64; *Phil.* 11, 19; *Sest.* 89.

2   **illustres ... avos** = Prop. 2, 13, 10.

3   **tua – feratur** Cf. Cic. *Arch.* 24: "O fortunate ... adulescens, qui tuae virtutis Homerum praeconem inveneris!"

4   **superent laudes** [Tib.] 3, 7, 28.

    laudes – tuae ≈ Celtis, *Ludus* 159: "Cantabo laudes hic et ubique tuas"; and his concluding epigram in Gunther, *Lig.*, p. 16, line 4: "Germania ... / ... referet laudes hic et ubique tuas".

6   **Quem – cheli** Cf. Eobanus's epigram to Euricius Cordus, line 4, in the latter's *Contra maledicum Thiloninum Philymnum defensio* (Erfurt, 1515), edited in: Cordus, *Epigr.*, p. 110: "Quem stupeat posita noster Apollo chely."

    noster Apollo = *Val.* 1, 264; *Sylv.* 6, 8, 2; 7, 28, 32; cf. Ov. *Rem.* 251; Stat. *Theb.* 3, 628.

7   **Laudabat – Rufus** See Mutian. *Ep.* 149, dated 15 October [1508].

7-8   **Rufus – Gothae** Cf. *Laud.* 261-263 (n.).

8   **colit ... moenia celsa** *Ebn.* 38.

    moenia celsa = Ov. *Fast.* 3, 92.

9   **praeconia linguae** = *Idyl.*, 1. ded. 3 (2. ded. 3); *Epic.* 1, 29: "In tua nec deerunt faciles preconia linguae."

10   **Non intermissa** ≈ Ov. *Pont.* 1, 4, 16.

12   **teste caret** = Ov. *Ars* 3, 398; cf. Eob. *Her. Chr.* 4, 108; *Eras.* 71: "Nec mea teste caret vox haec ...."

13   **si vera fides** Luc. 7, 192; Eob. *Her. Chr.* 4, 52.

    populari ... aurae *Laud.* 274-275 (n.).

14   **Saecula – nihil** Cf. *Luth.* 1, 22: "Saecula quo cernunt doctius ista nihil."

    doctius ... nihil Pl. *Mos.* 279; Eob. *Her. Chr.* 21, 73.

15   **in ... principis aula** *Her. Chr.* 5, 51-52. For "principis aula" see [Sen.] *Oct.* 668; 689; 948.

    in augusta ... aula Mart. 7, 40, 1.

17   **Et merito** = *Laud.* 483 (n.).

    bifidi ... iuris *Laud.* 448.

    laus maxima *Hod.* 462: "... tui laus maxima et unica saecli."

    maxima iuris = Ov. *Met.* 3, 622.

18   **in primo ... thoro** = Prop. 3, 20, 14.

19   **aeternum ... nomen** = Verg. *A.* 6, 235; Eob. *Nor.* 878; cf. Verg. *A.* 6, 381; *Ciris* 40; Eob. *Sylv. duae* 1, 156; *Her. Chr.* 12, 120 (n.).

20   **barbara lingua** = Ov. *Ars* 3, 482; cf. *Tr.* 5, 2, 67.

21   **Adde quod** = Lucr. 1, 847; 3, 829; and often; Eob. *Her. Chr.* 8, 105; 11, 47; 17, 77; *Nob.* 303; et al.

23   **honos patriae** = *Buc.*, ded. 21 (n.), also of Englender.

24   **Ingenii candor** Cf. Ov. *Tr.* 3, 6, 7: "animi ... candor"; Eob. *Ebn.* 50: "candor pectoris."

25   **Quam bene** = Lucr. 3, 1071; Tib. 1, 3, 35; Ov. *Ep.* 7, 187; *Met.* 9, 488-489; *Fast.* 6, 187; Eob. *Her. Chr.* 2, 105; 3, 108; 3, 118; 9, 109; 12, 87; 12, 99; 21, 182; *Nob.* 201; et al.

    sub tanto ... principe Claud. *Cons. Mall. Theod.* 159; cf. Eob. *Buc.* B 2, 47; *Her. Chr.* 5, 52 (n.).

26   **Nobile ... opus** = Mart. *Sp.* 8, 2 (in the mss. and early edd.); cf. Eob. *Her. Chr.* 24, 132 (n.).

    maximus orbis = *Sylv. duae* 1, 10 (n.).

27   **Ortus et occasus** = Ven. Fort. *Carm. app.* 2, 82; cf. Ov. *Met.* 1, 354. But the phrase is very common in prose.

	nomen adorant ≈ Juvenc. 3, 96: "... genitoris nomen adorat"; Eob. *Max.* 17: "... Augustum nomen adoras"; *Accl.* 2, 193: "... nomen adorat."
29	**Scit ... Rhenus** Mart. 8, 11, 1. For this manner of speaking cf. Mant. *Sylv.* 3, fol. 283ᵛ: "Scit Rhenus, scit Gallus Arar, scit Lydius Arnus, / Scit Tyberis"; Eob. *Her. Chr.* 6, 164; *Max.* 85-87: "Exiguo quoties numerosas milite turmas / Fudimus et parva maxima castra manu / Scit Padus et ... Myncius"; 147-148: "Quam funesta tibi fuerint Thrasimena tempe / Scit Trebia et Ticino proxima rura tuo."
	innumero ... milite Ov. *Pont.* 1, 8, 18.
	milite Rhenus = Claud. *Carm. minora* 25, 91.
30	**forti ... manu** = Ov. *Ep.* 6, 14; Claud. *Rapt. Pros.* 2, praef. 30.
31-32	**Ergo – innocuam** Cf. *Buc.*, ded. 25-30.
31	**magno ... sub Caesare** Prop. 2, 1, 26 and Ov. *Fast.* 4, 859, both referring to Caesar Augustus. For "magni Caesaris" see also Verg. *G.* 4, 560; Hor. *Carm.* 1, 12, 50-51; Prop. 2, 7, 5; 2, 31, 2; Ov. *Fast.* 4, 124.
33	**Suspicis ingenuas ... arteis** Ov. *Am.* 3, 8, 1. For "ingenuas artes" see Eob. *Rec.* 87 (n.).
	studiis melioribus = *Rec.* 210 (n.).
34	**Diceris – loqui** Cf. Locher, *Stult.*, fol. 3ᵛ: "Audes magnifico cum Cicerone loqui"; Bebel, "Epitaphium Ioachimi Humellii," *Carm.*, sig. n1ʳ: "Noverat et magno cum Cicerone loqui"; Eob. *Eras.* 70: "Dixisses magno cum Cicerone loqui."
	Cicerone loqui = Mart. 5, 69, 8.
35	**studiis ... probatis** = *Sylv.* 6, 2, 9: "Docte vir et studiis et honoribus aucte probatis."
	studiis virtus = *Nob.* 299: "ubi cum studiis virtus inolevit honestis, / Ipsa decus verae nobilitatis habet."
36	**insignes ... viros** = Ov. *Tr.* 4, 10, 16; cf. Eob. *Laud.* 51.
	lingua Latina = *Anthol. Lat.* 605, 4; Ven. Fort. *Carm.* 6, 2, 98; Eob. *Val.* 1, 316.
37	**Docte vir** *Rec.* 93 (n.).
	in tantum ... honorem = Prop. 3, 11, 17.
	provectus honorem ≈ Hrotsv. *Agn.* 133: "... summo provectus honore"; cf. *Theoph.* 15: "Digno confestim provectus honore ...."
38	**poteris – candidiore** = *Ama.*, lim. 6 (n.).
	candidiore frui = Ov. *Tr.* 3, 4, 34.
40-42	**Cui – velit** Cf. Prop. 2, 2, 13-14; Eob. *Nup.* 89-92.
41	**Vincere – Ida** Cf. *Sylv.* 1, 7, 7: "Nulla Venus Phrygia formosior esset in Ida"; 7, 1, 52: "uxorem ..., / Quam forma Venerem vincere posse ferunt."
	Phrygia ... in Ida = Verg. *A.* 9, 80; Sil. 7, 437; cf. Eob. *Buc.* 7, 150 (n.).
42	**regia Iuno** Verg. *A.* 1, 443; 4, 114; et al.
44	**Praemia ... prima ferat** Hor. *Ep.* 1, 3, 25.
	vel Sexto iudice Cf. Hor. *S.* 1, 2, 134: "Fabio vel iudice."
45	**divesque – foelix** Cf. *Idyl.* 16, 78-79: "auctum / Praeter opes etiam fortunatis hymenaeis."
	coniuge foelix = Ov. *Met.* 6, 681; 7, 60; 9, 333; *Tr.* 5, 5, 21.
46	**iure beatus** = Bebel, "De miseria humanae conditionis," *Carm.*, sig. i4ᵛ: "Et potuit dici iure beatus item."
47	**Ergo nec immerito** = *Her. Chr.* 13, 143; cf. Ov. *Pont.* 4, 9, 133-134.
	princeps ... tantus Line 25 above (n.).
49	**nomine laudis** = *Val.* 2, 377; *Ilias* 2, p. 39; 18, p. 476.
50	**faciunt divos** = *Her. Chr.* 10, 52.

B 3

Meter: Elegiac distich.

1 **Exue ... cultus** Stat. *Theb.* 4, 199.
   bellipotens ... Hessia Cf. Mutian. *Ep.* 79, line 13 (epigram for Eobanus Hessus,
   written in 1506): "Armipotens ... Hessia"; Eob. *Buc.*, ded. 4; *Her. Chr.* 24, 54.
   Hessia cultus ≈ *Rec.* 90.
2 **Taedigeno – caput** Cf. *Ebn.* 34: "[luget patria,] Lugubre funereo pulvere sparsa
   caput." For this ancient gesture of mourning see, for example, Catul. 64, 224;
   Verg. *A.* 10, 844; 12, 611; Vulg. *Jos.* 7, 6; *Esth.* 4, 1. The word "taedigenus"
   occurs at this metrical position in an epigram by Jakob Locher to the printer
   Johann Bergmann, as a paraphrase of Sebastian Brant's last name: "nostro ... /
   Thaedigenae." See Locher, *Stult.*, fol. 144ʳ. Brant applies the word to his son in
   the dedicatory letter to his edition of Aesop's *Fabulae* (Basel, 1501): "Onophrio
   Thedigene"; see *Texte* 374, 1. Cf. Eob. *Epith.* 8: "Tedigenas ... flammas"; 169:
   "tedigenis ... flammis."
   moestum ... caput Luc. 6, 625; Sen. *Tro.* 1133.
3 **superos ... adivit** Sen. *Her. F.* 17.
4 **belli ... togae** = *Epic.*, app. 5, 18: "... seu belli tempore sive togae"; *Tum.* 7, 128:
   "...belli nescia, gnara togae."
   fama togae Cf. Mart. 2, 90, 2. As the formal outer garment of free-born
   Romans, the toga came to symbolize peacetime.
5 **ferales ... cupressi** Verg. *A.* 6, 216; Ov. *Tr.* 3, 13, 21; Eob. *Vict.* 184; *Epic.* 1, 5;
   cf. *Her. Chr.* 18, 96. The cypress is an ancient symbol of death and mourning.
   februa The sense "exequies" appears to be unparalleled.
6 **deos – mori** Eobanus reuses this line in a letter to Johann Lang, after hearing a
   (false) report of Erasmus's death in ca. March 1519; see *Epp. fam.*, p. 70. It then
   appears in slightly modified form in *Eras.* 50 (refrain): "Pene deos cogent impia
   fata mori." For the thought cf. Poliziano, *Eleg.* 7, 225-226: "Hoc licuit vobis, o
   ferrea pectora, Parcae: / Credo ego iam divum numina posse mori"; Eob. *Buc.*
   9, 23.
   cogunt ... mori Verg. *Ecl.* 2, 7; Ov. *Ep.* 3, 140.
   impia fata = *Sylv.* 3, 20, 8; cf. *Rec.* 119 (n.).

B 4

Meter: Elegiac distich.

tit. **scrupus** Literally, "a sharp stone."
2 **Armiger** The eagle is Jupiter's armorbearer because it carries his thunderbolts.
   Cf. Verg. *A.* 5, 255; 9, 564; Hor. *Carm.* 4, 4, 1; Ov. *Met.* 15, 386; Eob. *Nob.*
   291: "Iovis armiger"; *Hymn.* B 12, 1; *Hod.* 13: "fulminis armiger ales"; *Idyl.* 11,
   142: "Iovis armiger."
3 **Adria** Cf. *Nob.* 202, also referring to Venice as an Adriatic power: "Trux licet
   iratas Adria tollat aquas"; similarly *Max.* 72; B 15, 3; B 15, 5.
   Rhodanum – Tybrimque Cf. Ov. *Met.* 2, 258-259; *Fast.* 4, 571.
4 **Et minor est** = *Sylv. duae* 1, 136.
   quam fuit ante = Ov. *Fast.* 1, 94; *Tr.* 5, 12, 22; *Pont.* 2, 1, 4; 3, 1, 50 and 98.
5 **Oedipodas** This form occurs also in Ov. *Tr.* 1, 1, 114; Mart. 9, 25, 10. For
   Oedipus as a proverbial solver of enigmas see Otto 1280; cf. Mant. *Ecl.*, ded.:
   "Audi, o Pari, aenigma perplexum quod Oedipodes ipse non solveret"; Eob.
   Sylv. 5, 11, 2: "Solutor eia gloriose aenigmatum / Maiorque quovis Oedipo"; 5,
   13, 25.

6   **Forsitan – erit** Cf. Jacobus Magdalius Gaudensis, dedicatory poem in *Erarium aureum poetarum* ([Cologne], 1501), sig. A2ᵛ: "Forsitan e vulgo qui leget unus erit"; Ov. *Ars* 3, 422.

B 5

A hitherto unknown epigram by Eobanus on the same topic was published by his friend and fellow student Johann Möller (Molitoris, Mylius) of Würzburg in: *Palladii de insitione carmen. Παραινέσεις duae de famuli legibus. Πρόγνωσις in Venetos* ... [Erfurt, Joh. Knappe the Elder, 1509?], sig. B2ᵛ-B3ʳ. The poem consists of 6 elegiac distichs:

ΠΡΟΓΝΩΣΙΣ IN VENETOS ANNI NONI
SUPRA SESQUIMILLESIMUM

Forma viri ignoti visa est. Mihi forte roganti
    Quis foret, "Orator," plebs ait, "est Venetus."
Vitta coercebat Germano more capillos,
    Velabat Venetum Gallica crista caput,
5   Et thorax Hispanus erat Romanaque vestis.
    Quaerenti varius quid sibi vult habitus
Rettulit, "Hoc omnis rapuit praedator, et omne
    Quod tenet imperium quid nisi preda fuit?"
Verus ego vates, faveant modo numina vati,
10   Esopi merito graculus alter erit:
Vittam Germani, rapiet at Gallica cristam,
    Thoraca Hyspanus, Martia Rhoma togam.

Meter of **B 5**: Alcmanian strophe, as in Hor. *Epod.* 12, consisting of a dactylic hexameter followed by a dactylic tetrameter.

2   **Per Styga** = Ov. *Ars* 1, 635; 2, 41. Jupiter swore his most solemn oaths by the Styx.
4-6   **pollice presso .... pollice verso** Cf. Erasmus, *Adag.* 1, 8, 46, *ASD* 2, 2, p. 268, lines 742-745: "Qui faveret, pollicem premebat, qui minus faveret, pollicem convertebat. Qui gestus in proverbium abierunt, ut iam *premere pollicem* dicatur, qui quoquo pacto favet, *convertere* qui male vult." Cf. also Juv. 3, 36; Otto 1445.

B 6

Meter: Hexameter.

1   **pia turba** = [Tib.] 3, 10, 25; Ov. *Fast.* 2, 507; *Tr.* 5, 3, 47; Luc. 8, 79.
2   **Findebatque – campos** Cf. Verg. *G.* 2, 353; Tib. 1, 7, 21. For the image cf. also Eob. *Buc.*, ded. 1 (n.).
          undique campos = Ov. *Fast.* 2, 227.
3   **Falce ... deposita ... messor** Claud. *Bell. Get.* 463-464.
          festa ocia ... agebat *Her. Chr.* 12, 65.
4   **taela** For the old image of poetry as weaving see n. *Her. Chr.* A 2, 10-11.
5   **numeravit oves** Cf. *Buc.* 1, 29 (n.).
          armentarius omneis ≈ Lucr. 6, 1252.
6   **Quam dives pecoris** = Verg. *Ecl.* 2, 20.
9   **Esopa** The word (= "oesopa," "oesypa") occurs also in *Sylv. duae* 2, 230: "inter

olentes / Esuriens hyrcos aesopa spurca voras." Cf. Filippo Beroaldo, [*Orationes et poemata*] (Bologna, 1491), sig. h1ʳ: "Esopa non spirat, Pharii nec stercora piscis."

subter ... coryleta capellas Cordus, *Buc.* 4, 120.

10   **sancto ... furore** Poetic frenzy; see n. *Laud.* 193.

11   **Lene susurrantes** Prud. *Apoth.* 846.

      percurrite visu ≈ Prud. *Amart.* 892.

12   **sublimis ... cathedrae** Ennod. *Carm.* 2, 79, 5.

      sileat compago ≈ Juv. 3, 304.

13   **Grande – pretium** = Juv. 12, 127; 14, 281.

B 7

Meter: Elegiac distich.

2   **simum ... gregem** Cf. Verg. *Ecl.* 10, 7: "simae ... capellae."

5   **ignaros ... agrestes** Verg. *G.* 1, 41.

7-8   **Primus – patriam** Cf. Verg. *G.* 3, 10-11; Ov. *Trist.* 3, 7, 15.

7   **Aonia ... rupe** = Paul. Nol. *Carm.* 15, 31: "nec surdum Aonia Phoebum de rupe ciebo."

      rupe capellas = Ov. *Pont.* 1, 8, 51.

8   **pascua – gregi** Cf. V. Fl. 4, 363.

9   **magno ... ore** Verg. *G.* 3, 294; *A.* 12, 692; Ov. *Ars* 1, 206.

10   **terra superba** = Ov. *Am.* 3, 10, 20; *Pont.* 2, 9, 54.

12   **cornu divite** Sen. *Med.* 65; cf. Ov. *Met.* 9, 91.

15   **Discite, pastores** = *Buc.* 10, 140.

16   **gloria ruris** = Mart. 6, 80, 6; 9, 60, 4.

19   **avertere morbos** = Paul. Nol. *Carm.* 19, 45; cf. Hor. *Ep.* 2, 1, 136.

21   **ovium ... magistri** Verg. *Ecl.* 2, 33.

22   **memori – cuncta** Hor. *S.* 2, 4, 90; cf. Ov. *Ep.* 13, 66 (*Fast.* 3, 178; et al.): "memori pectore"; Eob. *Sylv. duae* 2, 200; *Her. Chr.* 16, 162 (n.).

23   **lux ... diei** = *Anthol. Lat.* 645, 20.

      lux alma = *Rec.* 196 (n.).

24   **querulae ... aves** Sen. *Phaed.* 508-509; Eob. *Her. Chr.* 8, 36.

B 8

Meter: Elegiac distich.

1   **laeto ... vultu** = Sil. 5, 227; cf. Eob. *Her. Chr.* 17, 1 (n.).

      nova gaudia = Verg. *A.* 10, 325; Ov. *Pont.* 4, 4, 21; Eob. *Nup.* 328; *Her. Chr.* 1, 111; *Vict.*, ded. 1; cf. *Her. Chr.* 3, 93.

      gaudia vultu = Catul. 64, 34; *Culex* 120; Luc. 2, 373.

2   **se – habet** Cf. Ov. *Fast.* 1, 32; Mant. *1. Parthen.* 1, 232: "habent quo se tueantur"; Eob. *Her. Chr.* 7, 58.

4   **lingua diserta** Arator 1, 460; Eob. *Her. Chr.* 11, 129; *Sylv.* 5, 29, 15.

5   **fulvo ... metallo** = Lact. *De ave Phoenice* (= *Anthol. Lat.* 485a), lines 131 and 141; cf. Sen. *Ag.* 857-858; Mutian. *Ep.* 149, line 35, referring to Englender's wealth.

      saciata metallo = Stat. *Silv.* 1, 2, 153 (a gilded house).

6   **Aebria – togae** Cf. Mart. 14, 154, 1.

7   **sylvestris Musa** Lucr. 4, 589; Verg. *Ecl.* 1, 2.

9-10   **Ergo – erit** Cf. Grat. 251: "ergo semper eris, dum carmina dumque manebunt /

silvarum dotes atque arma Diania terris."
10   **pecoris ... dives** Verg. *Ecl.* 2, 20; Sil. 1, 393.
            Hessia dives *Buc.* 1, 10 (n.).
11   **Tempora ... tacito labentia cursu** Cf. Ov. *Tr.* 4, 10, 27; *Trist.* 3, 3, 11-12.
            tacito ... cursu = Stat. *Theb.* 10, 139; cf. Ov. *Met.* 14, 601.
12   **magno foenore** = Tib. 2, 6, 22; Prop. 1, 7, 26.
            foenore ... honor = Prop. 3, 1, 22.

B 9

The poem was first edited by Gustav Kawerau, *Der Briefwechsel des Justus Jonas* (Halle, 1884), no. 1, p. 1.
            Meter: Elegiac distich.

3-4   **Nomen – facis** For the commonplace that poetry, which itself is immortal, confers immortality on the poet and others cf. *Rec.* B 1, 9-13 (n.).
6   **Te – habere** Cf. Ov. *Tr.* 3, 7, 48; Eob. *Laud.* B 1, 10 (n.).
9   **Prisca ... aetas** Sid. *Carm.* 2, 183; Eob. *Her. Chr.* 17, 35.
12   **nomen habet** = *Sylv. duae* 1, 24 (n.).
13   **botrosa** A medieval variant for "botruosa." Cf. Isid. *Orig.* 17, 8, 11, where one ms. reads "butrosum semen."
21   **Teutonis ora** Celtis, *Germania* 2, 30; Eob. *Sylv. duae* 1, 128 (n.).
22   **Dissimulare suum** = Ov. *Tr.* 4, 9, 32.

B 10

Meter: Elegiac distich.

1   **Oleniam ... capellam** ≈ *Her. Chr.* 10, 69 (n.).
4   **primus** See *Buc.*, lim. 5 (n.).
            arva soli = *Sylv. duae* 1, 154; *Her. Chr.* 13, 168; 17, 260.

B 11

For the propempticon form see introd. *Ama.*, lim.
            Meter: Elegiac distich.

1   **Vade – liber** Cf. Mart. 1, 70, 1; Ov. *Tr.* 3, 7, 1-2; Eob. *Ama.*, lim. 1-2 (n.); *Sylv.* 2, 9, 17: "Perge salutatum ... amicos."
            Ite, capellae = Verg. *Ecl.* 1, 74; 10, 77.
3   **Ire licet** = Hor. *S.* 1, 6, 105; Stat. *Theb.* 12, 154.
5   **immensum ... orbem** = Ov. *Am.* 2, 9, 17; *Met.* 3, 77; Eob. *Epp. 4*, sig. F1ᵛ (1508); *Sylv.* 2, 19, 5; cf. *Buc.* 7, 1 (n.).
6   **non tellus sufficit** Cf. Luc. 5, 356.
            astra patent Stat. *Theb.* 10, 375.
7   **descendite ad umbras** ≈ Verg. *A.* 6, 404; Stat. *Theb.* 10, 404; *Silv.* 3, 3, 206.
8   **Stygio ... Iovi** Verg. *A.* 4, 638; Ov. *Fast.* 5, 448; Sil. 1, 386; Eob. *Her. Chr.* 1, 180.
10   **tucior esse potest** ≈ Ov. *Rem.* 580 (quoted in Eob. *Ama.* 2, 5).
11   **raptorum ... luporum** Verg. *A.* 2, 355-356; Ov. *Met.* 10, 540.
13   **canis** Cf. *Pug.* B 1, 1 (n.).
15   **corvi – contemnite** Note the alliteration. The "croaking ravens" are the

enemies of humanism at Erfurt. Cf. *Luth.* 5, 57: "Quis sapiens corvos timeat crocitare molestos?"; *Hypocr.* 34: "Praetereo fraudes, improbe corve, tuas."

19   **Fallor, an** = Ov. *Am.* 3, 1, 34; *Met.* 13, 641; *Fast.* 1, 515; 5, 549; et al.; Eob. *Sylv. duae* 2, 71; *Her. Chr.* 6, 207.

20   **nihil – potest** Cf. Hor. *Carm.* 2, 16, 27-28; Ov. *Ep.* 15, 45; Eob. *Her. Chr.*, ded. 8, 6: "quid enim ex omni parte beatum?"; *Her. Chr.* 17, 24; *Eleg.* 3, 93-94: "Adde quod ex omni tam nemo est parte beatus, / Ut nunquam peccet."
    ex omni parte = *Ama.* 35, 8 (n.).

21   **Ite bono auspitio** Cf. *Sylv.* 1, 5, 3: "Vade bono auspicio ..."; also cf. *Laud.* 575 (n.). For "bono auspitio" at this metrical position see also *Nup.* 258; cf. Catul. 45, 19; Ov. *Am.* 1, 12, 28; Eob. *Her. Chr.* 12, 178; *Max.* 218.
    Totus ... orbis = Ov. *Ep.* 16, 375; *Met.* 1, 203; *Fast.* 1, 123; et al.; cf. Eob. *Laud.* 96 (n.).

22   **Hessiacum – pecus** Cf. *Buc.*, lim. 5 (n.).

23-26   **Si tamen – honos** Cf. Stat. *Theb.* 12, 816-819.

23   **Ocnaeas** See n. *Buc.* 3, 18.

24   **Caedite** = Prop. 2, 2, 13; 2, 34, 65; Eob. *Her. Chr.*, lim. 5.
    Sunt illo ... loco ≈ Ov. *Fast.* 6, 46.

25-26   **Este – honos** Cf. *Ama.*, lim. 5-6.

25   **gloria maior** = Luc. 8, 78; Stat. *Silv.* 1, 2, 180; et al.

26   **manebit honos** ≈ Ov. *Tr.* 5, 9, 10.

27   **I, pecus, i** ≈ Verg. *A.* 6, 546.

28   **Te precor** = Verg. *A.* 10, 461 and 525; Ov. *Rem.* 75; *Pont.* 2, 5, 4; Eob. *Her. Chr.* 5, 123.

LIST OF ABBREVIATIONS

INDEX OF MEDIEVAL AND NEO-LATIN WORDS

GLOSSARIAL INDEX

GENERAL INDEX

LIST OF ABBREVIATIONS

Abbreviations of ancient and patristic works as well as books of the Vulgate follow the ones given in P.G.W. Glare, ed., *Oxford Latin Dictionary* (Oxford, 1983); Charlton T. Lewis and Charles Short, *A Latin Dictionary* (1879; Oxford, 1966); and Henry G. Liddell and Robert Scott, *A Greek-English Lexicon*, revised by Henry S. Jones (1968; Oxford, 1985). To distinguish *Baebi Italici Ilias* from Eobanus Hessus's translation of Homer's *Iliad*, the ancient abridgment is referred to as *Ilias Lat.* As for *Anthologia Latina* (Shackleton Bailey, fasc. 1; Riese, fasc. 2) and *Anthologia Palatina*, they are cited as *Anthol. Lat.* and *Anthol. Pal.*, respectively.

Other works cited in abbreviated form are given below.

A. Patristic, Medieval, and Renaissance Authors and Works

Aen. Silv. *Hist.*	Aeneas Silvius, *Historia de duobus amantibus*. In: *Aeneas Silvius Piccolomini (Pius II) and Niklas von Wyle, The Tale of Two Lovers, Eurialus and Lucretia*, ed. Eric J. Morrall (Amsterdam, 1988).
AH	*Analecta hymnica medii aevi*, ed. Guido M. Dreves, Clemens Blume, and Henry M. Bannister (Leipzig, 1886-1922; repr. New York, 1961). 55 vols. Cited by volume, poem, and strophe numbers.
Alan. *Nat.*	Alan of Lille, *De planctu Naturae*, ed. Nikolaus M. Häring. In: *Studi Medievali* 19 (1978): 797-879.
Alan. *Parab.*	Alan of Lille, *Liber parabolarum*. In: *PL* 210, col. 581-594.
Alcuin. *Carm.*	Alcuinus, *Carmina*, ed. Ernst Dümmler. In: *MGH, Poetae Latini aevi Carolini*, vol. 1, pp. 169-351.
Andrel. *Ecl.*	Fausto Andrelini, *Eclogae*. In: *The Eclogues of Faustus Andrelinus and Ioannes Arnolletus*, ed. Wilfred P. Mustard (Baltimore, 1918).
Andrel. *Eleg.*	Fausto Andrelini, *Elegiae* (Paris, [1496]).
Andrel. *Livia*	Fausto Andrelini, *Livia*. In: *Publi Fausti Andrelini "Amores" sive "Livia,"* ed. Godelieve Tournoy-Thoen (Brussels, 1982).
Arator	Arator, *De actibus apostolorum*, ed. Arthur P. McKinlay. In: *CSEL* 72.
Avit. *Carm.*	Alcimus Ecdicius Avitus, *Carmina*, ed. Rudolf Peiper. In: *MGH, Auctores antiquissimi*, vol. 6, 2.
Bebel, *Carm.*	Heinrich Bebel, poems in: *Oratio ad regem Maximilianum de laudibus atque amplitudine Germaniae* (Pforzheim, 1504).
Bebel, *Prov.*	Heinrich Bebel, *Proverbia Germanica*, ed. Willem H.D. Suringar (Leiden, 1879; repr. Hildesheim, 1969).
Bocc. *Carm.*	Giovanni Boccaccio, *Carmina*. In: *Opere latine minori*, ed. Aldo F. Massèra (Bari, 1928), pp. 89-105.
Bocc. *Ecl.*	Giovanni Boccaccio, *Buccolicum carmen*. In: *Opere latine minori*, ed. Aldo F. Massèra (Bari, 1928), pp. 3-85.
Bocc. *Gen.*	Giovanni Boccaccio, *Genealogie deorum gentilium libri*, ed. Vincenzo Romano. In: *Giovanni Boccaccio, Opere*, vols. 10 and 11 (Bari, 1951).
Boiardo, *Ecl.*	Matteo M. Boiardo, *Bucolicon carmen*. In: *Tutte le opere di Matteo M. Boiardo*, ed. Angelandrea Zottoli, vol. 2 (n.p., 1944), pp. 667-689.
Brant, *NS*	Sebastian Brant, *Das Narrenschiff*, ed. Friedrich Zarncke (Leipzig, 1854; repr. Hildesheim, 1961).

Brant, *Texte*   *Sebastian Brant, Kleine Texte*, ed. Thomas Wilhelmi (Stuttgart–Bad
                          Cannstatt, 1998). 2 vols. in 3.
Brant, *Var. carm.*   Sebastian Brant, *Varia carmina* (Basel, 1498).
Busch. *Lips.*   Hermann von dem Busche, *Lipsica* [Leipzig, 1504?]. In: *Helius
                          Eobanus Hessus, Noriberga illustrata und andere Städtegedichte*, ed.
                          Joseph Neff (Berlin, 1896), pp. 73-91.
Camerarius, *Nar.*   *Narratio de H. Eobano Hesso, comprehendens mentionem de
                          compluribus illius aetatis doctis et eruditis viris, composita a Ioachimo
                          Camerario Pabebergensi* (Nuremberg, 1553); Eob. *Poetic Works,*
                          vol. 1, pp. 10-91.
Celtis, *Am.*   Konrad Celtis, *Amores*, ed. Felicitas Pindter (Leipzig, 1934).
Celtis, *Germania*   Konrad Celtis, *De situ et moribus Germaniae additiones*. In: *Conradi
                          Celtis quae Vindobonae prelo subicienda curavit opuscula*, ed. Kurt
                          Adel (Leipzig, 1966), pp. 55-64.
Celtis, *Ludus*   Konrad Celtis, *Ludus Dianae*. In: Conrad Celtis, *Ludi scaenici*, ed.
                          Felicitas Pindter (Budapest, 1945), pp. 1-6.
Cordus, *Buc.*   Euricius Cordus, *Bucolicon per decem aeglogas iucundissime
                          decantatum* (Erfurt, 1514). In: Ioanna Paschou, *Euricius Cordus,
                          Bucolicon: Kritische und kommentierte Ausgabe* (Hamburg, 1997).
Cordus, *Ecl.*   Euricius Cordus, *Bucolicum ludicrum* (Leipzig, 1518). In: Ioanna
                          Paschou, *Euricius Cordus, Bucolicon: Kritische und kommentierte
                          Ausgabe* (Hamburg, 1997).
Cordus, *Epigr.*   Euricius Cordus, *Epigrammata (1520)*, ed. Karl Krause (Berlin,
                          1892).
Cordus, *Threnod.*   Euricius Cordus, *Funebris threnodia in mortem illustrissimi Hessie
                          Principis Guilielmi, Philippi patris* (Erfurt, [1515]).
[Eberbach], *Ebriet.*   [Petrejus Eberbach], *De generibus ebriosorum et ebrietate vitanda*
                          [Erfurt, 1516], ed. Friedrich Zarncke, in: *Die Deutschen
                          Universitäten im Mittelalter* (Leipzig, 1857), pp. 116-154, with
                          notes on pp. 254-257.
Ecl. Theoduli   *Ecloga Theoduli*. In: *Seven Versions of Carolingian Pastoral*, ed. R.P.H.
                          Green (Reading, 1980), pp. 111-149.
Ennod. *Carm.*   Magnus Felix Ennodius, *Carmina*, ed. Wilhelm Hartel. In: *CSEL* 6,
                          pp. 507-609.
Eob.   Eobanus Hessus.
Eob. *Dichtungen*   Helius Eobanus Hessus, *Dichtungen: Lateinisch und Deutsch. Dritter
                          Band: Dichtungen der Jahre 1528-1537*, ed. and trans. Harry
                          Vredeveld (Bern, 1990).
Eob. *Poetic Works*   *The Poetic Works of Helius Eobanus Hessus*, ed., trans., and annotated
                          by Harry Vredeveld.
Erasmus, *Adag.*   Desiderius Erasmus, *Adagia*. In: *Desiderii Erasmi Roterodami opera
                          omnia*, ed. Joannes Clericus, vol. 2 (Leiden, 1703; repr. Hildesheim,
                          1961), and in *ASD*, ordo 2.
Erasmus, *Carm.*   Desiderius Erasmus, *Carmina*, ed. Harry Vredeveld. In: *ASD* 1, 7.
Erasmus, *Ep.*   Desiderius Erasmus, *Opus epistolarum*, ed. P.S. Allen, H.M. Allen,
                          and H.W. Garrod (Oxford, 1906-1958). 11 vols.
Ficino, *De vita*   Marsilio Ficino, *Three Books on Life*, ed. and trans. Carol V. Kaske
                          and John R. Clark (Binghamton, N.Y., 1989).
Filetico, *Theoc.*   Martino Filetico, translation of Theocritus, *Idylls* 1-7. In: *Theocriti
                          Bucolicum e Graego* [sic] *traducta .... Hesiodi Ascraei Georgica per
                          Nicolaum de Valle ... e Graeco in Latinum conversa .... Hesiodi
                          Theogonia per Boninum Mombritium ... e Graeco in Latinum conversa
                          ...* (n.p., n.d.). Cited according to the poem and line numbers of

Theocritus's Greek text.

Gerald. *Ecl.*   Antonio Geraldini, *Eclogues*, ed. Wilfred P. Mustard (Baltimore, 1924).

Gigas, *Sylv.*   Johannes Gigas (Heune), *Sylvarum libri IIII* (Wittenberg, 1540).

Guarino, *Carm.*   Battista Guarino, *Carmina* (Modena, 1496).

Gunther. *Lig.*   Gunther der Dichter, *Ligurinus*, ed. Erwin Assmann. In: *MGH, Scriptores rerum Germanicarum in usum scholarum separatim editi*, vol. 63 (Hannover, 1987).

Hrotsv.   Hrotsvit von Gandersheim, works in: *Hrotsvitae opera*, ed. H. Homeyer (Munich, 1970).

Hrotsv. *Agn.*   Hrotsvit von Gandersheim, *Passio Agnetis*.

Hrotsv. *Maria*   Hrotsvit von Gandersheim, *Historia nativitatis laudabilisque conversationis intactae dei genitricis*.

Hrotsv. *Theoph.*   Hrotsvit von Gandersheim, *Lapsus et conversio Theophili vicedomini*.

Hutten, *Epigr.*   Ulrich von Hutten, *Ad Caesarem Maximilianum epigrammatum liber unus*. In: Hutten, *Opera*, vol. 3, pp. 205-268.

Hutten, *Opera*   *Ulrichi Hutteni opera quae reperiri potuerunt omnia*, ed. Eduard Böcking (Leipzig, 1859-1870; repr. Aalen, 1963). 5 vols. and 2 supplementary vols.

Hutten, *Querel.*   Ulrich von Hutten, *Querelarum libri duo*. In: Hutten, *Opera*, vol. 3, pp. 19-83.

[Juvenc.] *Triumph.* Pseudo-Juvencus, *Triumphus Christi heroicus*. In: *PL* 19, 385-388.

Landino   Cristoforo Landino. Poems in: *Carmina omnia*, ed. Alexander Perosa (Florence, 1939).

Locher, *Stult.*   Jakob Locher Philomusus, *Stultifera navis* (Basel: Bergmann von Olpe, 1497).

Lotich. *Ecl.*   Petrus Lotichius Secundus, *Eclogae*. In: *Petri Lotichii Secundi poemata omnia*, ed. Friedrich T. Friedemann (Leipzig, [1842]), pp. 227-244.

Lotich. *Eleg.*   Petrus Lotichius Secundus, *Elegiae*. In: *Petri Lotichii Secundi poemata omnia*, ed. Friedrich T. Friedemann (Leipzig, [1842]), pp. 1-188.

Mant.   Baptista Mantuanus. Unless otherwise noted, his works are cited according to his *Opera omnia* (Antwerp, 1576). 4 vols.

Mant. *Bapt.*   Baptista Mantuanus, *In laudibus Ioannis Baptistae*. In: *Opera omnia* (Antwerp, 1576), vol. 2, fol. 229^r-231^r.

Mant. *Calam.*   Baptista Mantuanus, *De calamitatibus temporum*, ed. Gabriele Wessels (Rome, 1916).

Mant. *c. Am.*   Baptista Mantuanus, *Elegia contra Amorem*. In: *Opera omnia* (Antwerp, 1576), vol. 1, fol. 175^v-178^r.

Mant. *Consol.*   Baptista Mantuanus, *Consolatio in morte Collae Asculani*. In: *Opera omnia* (Antwerp, 1576), vol. 1, fol. 124^r-134^r.

Mant. *c. Poet.*   Baptista Mantuanus, *Contra poetas impudice loquentes, cum Sebastiani Murrhonis interpraetacione*, ed. Mariano Madrid Castro. In: *HL* 45 (1996): 93-133.

Mant. *Dionys.*   Baptista Mantuanus, *De Dionysii Areopagitae conversione, vita et agone*. In: *Opera omnia* (Antwerp, 1576), vol. 2, fol. 159^r-200^v.

Mant. *Ecl.*   Baptista Mantuanus, *Eclogae*, In: *Adulescentia: The Eclogues of Mantuan*, ed. and trans. Lee Piepho (New York, 1989).

Mant. *Epigr.*   Baptista Mantuanus, *Epigrammata ad Falconem*. In: *Opera omnia* (Antwerp, 1576), vol. 1, fol. 100^r-118^r.

Mant. *Fed. Spagn.* Baptista Mantuanus, *De morte Federici Spagnoli*. In: *Opera omnia* (Antwerp, 1576), vol. 1, fol. 139^r-143^r.

Mant. *Georgius*	Baptista Mantuanus, *De vita et agone D. Georgii Martyris*. In: *Opera omnia* (Antwerp, 1576), vol. 2, fol. 201ʳ-219ᵛ.
Mant. *Lud. Morb.*	Baptista Mantuanus, *De vita D. Ludovici Morbioli Bononiensis*. In: *Opera omnia* (Antwerp, 1576), vol. 2, fol. 220ʳ-229ʳ.
Mant. *Mort.*	Baptista Mantuanus, *De contemnenda morte*. In: *Opera omnia* (Antwerp, 1576), vol. 1, fol. 118ᵛ-123ᵛ.
Mant. *1. Parthen.*	Baptista Mantuanus, *Parthenice prima sive Mariana*, ed. and trans. Ettore Bolisani (Padua, [1957]).
Mant. *2. Parthen.*	Baptista Mantuanus, *Parthenice secunda (Catharinaria)*. In: *Vitae Sanctae Katharinae, Pars secunda*, ed. A. P. Orbán, Corpus Christianorum, Continuatio Mediaevalis 119 A (Turnhout, 1992), pp. 351-435.
Mant. *3. Parthen.*	Baptista Mantuanus, *Parthenice tertia*. In: *Opera omnia* (Antwerp, 1576), vol. 2, fol. 101ʳ-114ʳ.
Mant. *4. Parthen.*	Baptista Mantuanus, *Parthenice quarta*. In: *Opera omnia* (Antwerp, 1576), vol. 2, fol. 114ᵛ-121ʳ.
Mant. *5. Parthen.*	Baptista Mantuanus, *Parthenice quinta*. In: *Opera omnia* (Antwerp, 1576), vol. 2, fol. 121ᵛ-128ʳ.
Mant. *6. Parthen.*	Baptista Mantuanus, *Parthenice sexta*. In: *Opera omnia* (Antwerp, 1576), vol. 2, fol. 129ᵛ-141ᵛ.
Mant. *7. Parthen.*	Baptista Mantuanus, *Parthenice septima*. In: *Opera omnia* (Antwerp, 1576), vol. 2, fol. 142ʳ-158ᵛ.
Mant. *Somn.*	Baptista Mantuanus, *Somnium Romanum*. In: *Opera omnia* (Antwerp, 1576), vol. 3, fol. 208ᵛ-220ᵛ.
Mant. *Sylv.*	Baptista Mantuanus, *Sylvae*. In: *Opera omnia* (Antwerp, 1576), vol. 3, fol. 242ᵛ-317ᵛ.
Mant. *Votum*	Baptista Mantuanus, *Votum ad divam Virginem*. In: *Opera omnia* (Antwerp, 1576), vol. 2, fol. 54ʳ-55ʳ.
Marul. *Epigr.*	Michael Marullus, *Epigrammaton*. In: *Michaelis Marulli carmina*, ed. Alessandro Perosa (Zürich, 1951), pp. 1-102.
Marul. *Hymn. nat.*	Michael Marullus, *Hymni naturales*. In: *Michel Marulle, Hymnes naturels*, Travaux d'Humanisme et Renaissance 296, ed. Jacques Chomarat (Geneva, 1995).
Mutian. *Ep.*	Conradus Mutianus Rufus, *Epistulae*. In: *Der Briefwechsel des Conradus Mutianus*, Geschichtsquellen der Provinz Sachsen 18, ed. Karl Gillert (Halle, 1890). 2 vols.
Nar.	See Camerarius, *Nar.*
Petrarch, *Africa*	Francesco Petrarca, *Africa*, ed. Nicola Festa (Florence, [1926]).
Petrarch, *Ecl.*	Francesco Petrarca, *Eclogae*, ed. Antonio Avena (Padua, 1906; repr. in: *Petrarch's "Bucolicum Carmen"*, trans. Thomas G. Bergin [New Haven, 1974]).
Petrarch, *Secret.*	Francesco Petrarca, *De contemptu mundi, colloquiorum liber, quem Secretum suum inscripsit*. In: *Francisci Petrarchae opera quae extant omnia*, vol. 1 (Basel, 1554; repr. Ridgewood, N.J., 1965), pp. 373-416.
Poliziano, *Eleg.*	*Elegiae*. In: Angelo Poliziano, *Prose volgari inedite e poesie latine e greche edite e inedite*, ed. Isidoro del Lungo (Florence, 1867), pp. 227-256.
Poliziano, *Sylv.*	*Sylvae*. In: Angelo Poliziano, *Prose volgari inedite e poesie latine e greche edite e inedite*, ed. Isidoro del Lungo (Florence, 1867), pp. 285-427.
Pontano, *Ecl.*	Giovanni Pontano, *Eclogae*. In: *Ioannis Ioviani Pontani carmina*, ed. Johannes Oeschger (Bari, 1948), pp. 1-62.
Pontano, *Parthen.*	Giovanni Pontano, *Parthenopeus*. In: *Ioannis Ioviani Pontani*

	carmina, ed. Johannes Oeschger (Bari, 1948), pp. 63-121.
Prud. *Amart.*	Aurel. Prudentius Clemens, *Amartigenia.*
Prud. *Apoth.*	Aurel. Prudentius Clemens, *Apotheosis.*
Prud. *Perist.*	Aurel. Prudentius Clemens, *Peristefanon.*
Sabell. *In natal.*	Marcantonio Sabellico, *In natalem diem divae virginis Mariae.* Cited according to the edition Deventer: R. Pafraet, 1490.
Sedul.	Caelius Sedulius, *Paschale carmen,* ed. J. Huemer. In: *CSEL* 10, pp. 1-146.
Tifernate, *Carm.*	Gregorio Tifernate, *Carmina.* In: *Hoc volumine haec continentur: P. Gregorii Tipherni poetae illustris opuscula. Francisci Octavii poetae Elegiae …* (Venice, 1498; quoted according to the reprint, Strasbourg, 1509).
Trebelius, *Carm.*	Hermann Trebelius, *Carmina* (Frankfurt an der Oder, 1509).
Trebelius, *Epigr.*	Hermann Trebelius, *Epigrammaton et carminum liber primus* [Frankfurt an der Oder, 1509?].
Vegius, *Aen.*	Mapheus Vegius Laudensis, *Aeneidos liber XIII.* In: *Das Aeneissupplement des Maffeo Vegio,* ed. Bernd Schneider (Weinheim, 1985).
Ven. Fort. *Carm.*	Venantius Fortunatus, *Carmina,* ed. Friedrich Leo. In: *MGH, Auctores antiquissimi,* vol. 4, 1.
Ven. Fort. *Mart.*	Venantius Fortunatus, *Vita S. Martini,* ed. Friedrich Leo. In: *MGH, Auctores antiquissimi,* vol. 4, 1, pp. 293-370.
Walter, *Alex.*	Walter of Châtillon, *Alexandreis,* ed. Marvin L. Colker (Padua, 1978).
Wimpfeling, *Adol.*	Jakob Wimpfeling, *Adolescentia,* ed. Otto Herding (Munich, 1965).

B. Eobanus Hessus's Works

Accl.	*Divo ac invicto Imp. Caes. Carolo V. Augusto Germaniam ingredienti urbis Norimbergae gratulatoria acclamatio. Ad eundem de bello contra Turcas suscipiendo adhortatio* (Nuremberg, 1530); Eob. *Dichtungen,* vol. 3, pp. 73-101.
Adnot.	*In P. Virgilii Maronis Bucolica ac Georgica adnotationes* (Haguenau, 1529).
Ama.	*De amantium infoelicitate, contra Venerem, de Cupidinis impotentia* (Erfurt, 1508); Eob. *Poetic Works,* vol. 1, pp. 200-263.
Buc.	*Bucolicon* (Erfurt, 1509); Eob. *Poetic Works,* vol. 1, pp. 272-381.
Calum.	*Descriptio Calumniae, ad doctissimum virum Philippum Melanthonem* (Marburg, 1539).
Coluth.	*Coluthi Lycopolitae Thebani vetusti admodum poetae de raptu Helenes ac iudicio Paridis poema* (Erfurt, 1534).
Consol.	*Ad optimum virum M. Philippum Nidanum, in morte Barbarae uxoris consolatio.* In: *Helii Eobani Hessi descriptio Calumniae, ad doctissimum virum Philippum Melanthonem. Ad optimum virum M. Philippum Nidanum, in morte Barbarae uxoris consolatio, eodem authore* (Marburg, 1539).
Dial.	*Dialogi tres, Melaenus, Misologus, Fugitivi* (Erfurt, 1524).
Ebn.	*In funere clariss. quondam viri, D. Hieronymi Ebneri, Urbis Noribergae aerario praefecti supremi etc.* (Nuremberg, [1532]); Eob. *Dichtungen,* vol. 3, pp. 485-499.
Ebriet.	Verses by Eobanus Hessus contained in: [Eberbach], *Ebriet.*
Eccles.	*Ecclesiae afflictae epistola ad Lutherum* (Haguenau, 1523).

Eleg.	*Elegiae tres* (Nuremberg, 1526).
Epic.	*Illustrium ac clarorum aliquot virorum memoriae scripta epicedia* (Nuremberg, 1531); Eob. *Dichtungen*, vol. 3, pp. 103-181.
Epith.	*Epithalamion seu ludus gratulatorius in nuptiis et receptione insigniorum Doctoratus Iurium humanissimi et eruditissimi viri, D. Iusti Studaei* (Frankfurt am Main, 1539).
Eras.	*In funere clariss. et incomparabilis eruditionis viri, D. Erasmi Roterodami, epicedion* (Marburg, 1537); Eob. *Dichtungen*, vol. 3, pp. 541-551.
Her.	*Heroidum libri tres* (Haguenau, 1532); Eob. *Dichtungen*, vol. 3, pp. 269-483.
Her. Chr.	*Heroidum Christianarum epistolae* (Leipzig, 1514).
Hod.	*A profectione ad Des. Erasmum Roterodamum hodoeporicon carmine heroico* (Erfurt, [1519]).
Hymn.	*Hymnus paschalis nuper ex Erphurdiensi Gymnasio Christianae victoriae acclamatus* (Erfurt, 1515).
Hypocr.	*In hypocrisim vestitus monastici* [Nuremberg, 1527].
Icones	*Homericae aliquot icones insigniores, Latinis versibus redditae* (Nuremberg, 1533).
Idyl.	*Bucolicorum idyllia XVII.* In: *Operum farr.* 1, pp. 2-55.
Ilias	*Poetarum omnium seculorum longe principis Homeri Ilias* (Basel, 1540).
In Ed. Leeum	Epigrams by Eobanus Hessus in: *In Eduardum Leeum quorundam e sodalitate literaria Erphurdiensi Erasmiaci nominis studiosorum epigrammata* (Erfurt, 1520).
Laud.	*De laudibus et praeconiis incliti atque tocius Germaniae celebratiss. Gymnasii litteratorii apud Erphordiam ... carmen succisivis horis deductum* (Erfurt, 1507); Eob. *Poetic Works*, vol. 1, pp. 140-191.
Luth.	*Habes hic, lector: In evangelici Doctoris Martini Lutheri laudem defensionemque elegias IIII. Ad Iodocum Ionam Northusanum cum eodem a Caesare redeuntem elegiam I. Ad Udalricum Huttenum Equitem Germanum ac poetam nobilissimum de causa Lutheriana elegiam I. In Hieronymum Emserum Lutheromastiga conviciatorem invectivam elegiam I.* (Erfurt, 1521).
Max.	*Responsio Maximiliani Aug.* In: *Quae in hoc libello nova habentur: Epistola Italiae ad divum Maximilianum Caes. Aug. Ulricho Hutteno Equite Germano autore. Responsio Maximiliani Aug. Helio Eobano Hesso autore* (Erfurt, 1516).
Nar.	See Camerarius, *Nar.*
Nob.	*Helii Eobani Hessi de vera nobilitate et priscis Germanorum moribus. Ad Georgium Spalatinum libellus carmine elegiaco* [Erfurt, 1515].
Nor.	*Urbs Noriberga illustrata carmine heroico per Helium Eobanum Hessum anno M.D.XXXII* [Nuremberg, 1532]; Eob. *Dichtungen*, vol. 3, pp. 183-267.
Nup.	*Encomium nuptiale divo Sigismundo, regi Poloniae, scriptum anno Christiani calculi M.D.XII* (Cracow, 1512).
Orat.	*Oratio sive praelectio in auspicio Officiorum M. Tullii Ciceronis et M. Accii Plauti comoediarum in Academia Erphurdiensi per Magistrum Eobanum Hessum in eadem Academia bonas litteras publice profitentem habita M.D.XV* [Erfurt, 1515].
Pod.	*Ludus de podagra* (Mainz, 1537).
Praef.	*Praefatio in epistolas Divi Pauli Apostoli ad Corynthios Erphurdiae ad Christianae philosophiae studiosorum ordinem habita ab eximio viro*

	D. Iodoco Iona Northusiano .... *Huic addita est non multum dissimili argumento Eobani Hessi praefaciuncula in Enchiridion Christiani militis* (Erfurt, 1520).
Psalt.	*Psalterium universum* (Schwäbisch Hall, 1538).
Pug.	*De pugna studentum Erphordiensium cum quibusdam coniuratis nebulonibus* (Erfurt, 1506); Eob. *Poetic Works,* vol. 1, pp. 122-133.
Rec.	*De recessu studentum ex Erphordia tempore pestilenciae* [Erfurt, 1506]; Eob. *Poetic Works,* vol. 1, pp. 98-115.
Ruf.	*Ad Mutianum Rufum elegia.* In: Harry Vredeveld, "A Forgotten Poem by Eobanus Hessus to Mutianus Rufus," "*Der Buchstab tödt – der Geist macht lebendig": Festschrift zum 60. Geburtstag von Hans-Gert Roloff von Freunden, Schülern und Kollegen,* ed. James Hardin and Jörg Jungmayr (Bern, 1992), vol. 1, pp. 1067-1083.
Salom.	*Salomonis Ecclesiastes carmine redditus* (Nuremberg, 1532).
Sarmat.	*In poetam Sarmatam Germanos ignaviae insimulantem invectiva* [Erfurt, 1523/24].
Sylv.	*Sylvarum libri IX.* In: *Operum farr.* 1, pp. 179-340.
Sylv. duae	*Sylvae duae nuper aeditae: Prussia et Amor* [Leipzig, 1514].
Theoc.	*Theocriti Syracusani idyllia triginta sex, Latino carmine reddita* (Haguenau, 1531).
Tum.	*De tumultibus horum temporum querela. Priscorum temporum cum nostris collatio. Omnium regnorum Europae mutatio. Bellum servile Germaniae. Haec omnia carmine heroico. Ad Germaniam afflictam consolatio paraenetica, elegia una. Roma capta, elegiae duae* (Nuremberg, 1528); Eob. *Dichtungen,* vol. 3, pp. 7-71.
Val.	*Bonae valetudinis conservandae rationes aliquot. Simplicium ciborum facultates quaedam. Medicinae encomion. Chorus illustrium medicorum. Novem Musae* [Frankfurt am Main, 1531].
Venus	*Venus triumphans, ad Ioachimum Cam. Qu. ... In nuptiis Ioachimi Cam. epithalamion seu ludus Musarum* (Nuremberg, 1527).
Vict.	*Victoria Christi ab inferis carmine heroico* (Erfurt, 1517).
Vitanda ebriet.	*De vitanda ebrietate elegia, additis super eadem re aliquot epigrammatis* (Erfurt, 1516).
Wirt.	*De victoria Wirtembergensi, ad illustrem et inclytum heroa Philippum, Hessorum omnium ac finitimarum aliquot gentium principem, gratulatoria acclamatio* (Erfurt, 1534); Eob. *Dichtungen,* vol. 3, pp. 501-539.

C. Eobanus's Correspondence and Collected Works

Epp. fam.	*Helii Eobani Hessi, poetae excellentiss., et amicorum ipsius epistolarum familiarium libri XII,* ed. Johannes Drach (Marburg, 1543).
Epp. 1	*Narratio de H. Eobano Hesso ..., composita a Ioachimo Camerario Pabebergensi. Epistolae Eobani Hessi ad Camerarium et alios quosdam,* ed. Joachim Camerarius (Nuremberg, 1553).
Epp. 2	*Libellus alter, epistolas complectens Eobani et aliorum quorundam doctissimorum virorum, necnon versus varii generis atque argumenti,* ed. Joachim Camerarius (Leipzig, 1557).
Epp. 3	*Tertius libellus epistolarum H. Eobani Hessi et aliorum quorundam virorum autoritate, virtute, sapientia, doctrinaque excellentium,* ed. Joachim Camerarius (Leipzig, 1561).
Epp. 4	*Libellus novus, epistolas et alia quaedam monumenta doctorum*

superioris et huius aetatis complectens, ed. Joachim Camerarius (Leipzig, 1568).

Operum farr.   *Operum Helii Eobani Hessi farragines duae, nuper ab eodem qua fieri potuit diligentia contractae et in hanc, quam vides, formam coactae, quibus etiam non parum multa accesserunt, nunc primum et nata et aedita* (Schwäbisch Hall, 1539).

D. Other Abbreviations

add.	*addidit, addiderunt,* added (in).
app.	appendix.
ASD	Desiderius Erasmus, *Opera omnia* (Amsterdam, 1969-).
b.	born (in).
BL	British Library.
BNU	*Bibliothèque Nationale et Universitaire,* National and University Library.
ca.	*circa,* approximately.
Carm.	*Carmen, Carmina.*
CCSL	*Corpus Christianorum, series Latina* (Turnhout, 1953-).
cf.	*confer,* compare.
CSEL	*Corpus scriptorum ecclesiasticorum Latinorum* (Vienna, 1866-).
col.	column, columns.
Curtius, *ELLMA*	Ernst Robert Curtius, *European Literature and the Latin Middle Ages,* trans. Willard R. Trask (Princeton, 1990).
d.	died (in).
ded.	*dedicatio,* dedicatory letter.
del.	*delevit, deleverunt,* deleted (in).
Ecl.	*Ecloga, Eclogae.*
ed.	edited by; editor.
edd.	editions
e.g.	*exempli gratia,* for example.
Ep., Epp.	*Epistula, Epistulae.*
Epigr.	*Epigrammata.*
et al.	*et alii, et alia,* and others.
fn.	footnote.
fol.	folio, folios.
Gillert	See Mutian. *Ep.*
Häussler	Reinhard Häussler, ed., *Nachträge zu A. Otto: Sprichwörter und sprichwörtliche Redensarten der Römer* (Hildesheim, 1968).
HL	*Humanistica Lovaniensia.*
introd.	introduction (to).
Kleineidam	Erich Kleineidam, *Universitas studii Erffordensis,* Erfurter Theologische Studien 14, 22, 42, and 47 (Leipzig, 1981-1992). 4 vols.
Krause, "Beiträge"	Karl Krause, "Beiträge zum Texte, zur Chronologie und zur Erklärung der Mutianischen Briefe mit besonderer Berücksichtigung der Gillert'schen Bearbeitung," *Jahrbücher der Königlichen Akademie gemeinnütziger Wissenschaften zu Erfurt,* N.F. 19 (1893): 1-94.
Krause, *HEH*	Carl Krause, *Helius Eobanus Hessus, sein Leben und seine Werke: Ein Beitrag zur Cultur- und Gelehrtengeschichte des 16. Jahrhunderts* (Gotha, 1879; repr. Nieuwkoop, 1963). 2 vols.
Kreyssig	Johann Theophil Kreyssig, ed., *Ioachimi Camerarii narratio de Helio*

	Eobano Hesso. Accesserunt Christ. Theoph. Kuinoelli oratio de Helii Eobani Hessi in bonas literas meritis et Helii Eobani Hessi carmina: De pugna studentum Erphordiensium cum quibusdam coniuratis nebulonibus et in bonarum artium detractorem (Meissen, 1843).
LB	Desiderius Erasmus, *Opera omnia*, ed. J. Clericus (Leiden, 1703-1706; repr. Hildesheim, 1961-1962). 10 vols.
lim.	liminary epigram, epigram on the title page.
m.	metrum (in Boeth. *Consol.*).
MGH	*Monumenta Germaniae Historica.*
ms., mss.	manuscript, manuscripts.
n.	note (to).
n.d.	no date.
n.p.	no place.
n.pr.	no printer.
no., nos.	number, numbers.
om.	*omisit, omiserunt,* omitted (in).
ÖNB	*Österreichische Nationalbibliothek,* Austrian National Library.
Otto	A. Otto, *Die Sprichwörter und sprichwörtlichen Redensarten der Römer* (Leipzig, 1890; repr. Hildesheim, 1971). References are to the proverb number.
PL	J.-P. Migne, ed., *Patrologiae cursus completus, series Latina* (Paris, 1844-1865). 221 vols.
praef.	*praefatio,* preface.
repr.	reprinted.
Salzer	Anselm Salzer, *Die Sinnbilder und Beiworte Mariens in der deutschen Literatur und lateinischen Hymnenpoesie des Mittelalters* (Seitenstetten, 1886-1894; repr. Darmstadt, 1967).
sc.	*scilicet,* namely.
sig.	signature, signatures.
SB	*Staatsbibliothek,* State Library.
StadtB	*Stadtbibliothek,* Municipal Library.
SUB	*Staats- und Universitätsbibliothek,* State and University Library.
s.v.	*sub verbo, sub voce,* under the word.
tit.	title, heading.
t.p.	title page.
trans.	translated (by), translator (of).
UB	*Universitätsbibliothek,* University Library.
vol., vols.	volume, volumes.
Von Hase	Martin von Hase, *Bibliographie der Erfurter Drucke von 1501-1550* (Nieuwkoop, 1968³).
Walther	*Proverbia sententiaeque Latinitatis medii aevi,* ed. Hans Walther (Göttingen, 1963-1969). 6 vols.

INDEX OF MEDIEVAL AND NEO-LATIN WORDS

This index lists words that occur neither in *Thesaurus Linguae Latinae* nor in Forcellini's *Lexicon totius Latinitatis*. Words, in the sense indicated here, that are also found in dictionaries of later Latin are marked with an asterisk. For proper names and their derivatives see the Glossarial Index.

GLOSSARIAL INDEX

All references are to the Latin text. References to proper names that are alluded to, but not explicitly mentioned in the text, are enclosed in square brackets. The names "Eobanus Hessus Francobergius" and "Helius Eobanus Hessus" are omitted when they occur in the titles and headings of his works. For a key to the abbreviations see pp. 553-557 above.

ABIDENUS, a, um, *from Abydos, a town opposite Sestos on the Hellespont:* Laeander *Laud.* 184.

ACADAEMIA *or* ACADEMIA, *the gymnasium near Athens where Plato taught:* quondam celebrata *Rec.* 207; — *a university: Nar.* 19, 6; 20, 3; 25, 1; Erphordiana *Nar.* 18, 1-2; Lipsica *Nar.* 11, 2.

ACADEMIACUS, a, um, *of the Academy in Athens:* Plato *Laud.* 22.

ACADEMICUS, a, um, *of a university:* administratio *Nar.* 17, 17.

ACHERON, *one of the rivers in the underworld; hence, the underworld: Ama.* 19, 12; *Buc.* 4, 109.

ACHILLES *(see also Aeacides), the Greek hero in Homer's* Iliad*: Buc.* 5, 28; ferus *Ama.* 35, 19; fortis *Laud.* 318; magnanimus *Ama.* 35, 79; non victus *Laud.* 265.

ACHILLAEUS, a, um, *of Achilles:* ferrum *Laud.* 391.

ACIDALIUS, a, um, *of Venus:* cauma *Buc.* 6, 67.

[ADAM], *the first man: Buc.* 2, 19.

ADONIS, *a shepherd lad: Buc.* 3, 142; [3, 143-144]; sceleratus *Buc.* 7, 41; stultus *Buc.* 5, 32; vicinus *Buc.* 2, 65.

ADRIA, *the Adriatic Sea: Buc.* B 4, 3.

ADRIACUS, a, um, *of the Adriatic Sea:* ranae *Buc.* 10, 127.

AEACIDES *(see also Achilles), Achilles: Laud.* 459; *Ama.* 35, 38; 35, 73.

AEDERA, *see Edera.*

[AENEAS], *the Trojan hero, ancestor of the Romans: Laud.* 86-90; *Ama.* 35, 69-70.

AEOUS, a, um, *see Eous.*

AESTICAMPIANUS, IOANNES, *Johannes Rhagius (Rack) of Sommerfeld (ca. 1460-1520): Nar.* 11, 3.

AETHIOPES, *see Ethiopes.*

AETHNA, *Mount Etna in Sicily: Buc.* 7, 173; Sicelis *Pug.* 32.

AGAMEMNON *(see also Atrides), the commander of the Greek forces at Troy:* [*Rec.* 167]; nullus *Rec.* 169.

AGRIPPINUS, a, um, *of Agrippina:* urbs *(Cologne) Laud.* 539.

ALBIORIS *(see also Witeberga), Wittenberg:* studio vulgata recenti *Laud.* 543.

ALBIS, *the Elbe River: Nar.* 11, 3.

ALCIBIADES, *Athenian general and statesman (ca. 450-404 BC): Nar.* 9, 18.

ALCON, *a Cretan archer:* Gnosius *Buc.* 5, 29.

ALEXANDER, *Alexander the Great (356-323 BC): Laud.,* lim. 5.

[ALEXANDRIA], *a city in Egypt, founded by Alexander the Great: Laud.,* lim. 5.

ALPES, *the Alps: Buc.* 10, 3.

ALPHENI, *men like the jurisconsult P. Alfenus Varus, consul suffectus in 39 BC: Laud.* 445.

AMALTHAEUS, a, um *(see also Olenius), of the she-goat Amalthea that suckled the young Jupiter on Crete; one of her horns was placed among the stars:* sydus *Buc.* 7, 99.

[AMALTHEA] *(see also Olenius), the she-goat Amalthea that suckled the young Jupiter on Crete: Buc.* B 11, 8.

AMBROSIUS, *St. Ambrose (ca. 339-397): Laud.* 356.
AMOR *(see also Cupido), the god of love: Ama.* 8, 3; 8, 4; [8, 5]; 10, 2; 10, 12; 11, 3; 16, 7;
    32, 2; [35, 2-3]; 35, 4; 35, 56; B 2, 10; B 2, 11; B 2, 25; B 2, 37; *Buc.* 3, 52; [3,
    56-57]; 3, 58; 3, 91; [7, 139-140]; calidus *Buc.* 7, 159; crudelis *Buc.* 7, 139;
    improbus *Ama.* 8, 6; insanus *Ama.* 35, 1; *Buc.* 3, 95; levis, ex omni parte
    timendus *Ama.* 35, 8; omnipotens *Ama.* B 2, 14; saevus *Ama.* 32, 19; saevus et
    improbus *Ama.* 32, 22; venenosus *Ama.* 36, 4.
AMPHION, *a legendary lyrist: Buc.* 1, 41; clarus *Buc.* 1, 50.
ANDINUS, a, um, *of Andes, the birthplace of Vergil:* vates *(Vergil) Laud.* 458; *Buc.* B 1, 7;
    Pierides *Buc.* 6, 2.
ANGLIA, *England:* nobilis *Buc.* B 2, 19.
ANGRIVARII, *a Germanic tribe on both sides of the Weser River:* veteres *Nar.* 5, 2.
[ANNA], *Anna von Mecklenburg (1485-1525), the second wife of William II of Hesse: Buc.*
    9, 69-82; 9, 86; 9, 113-120.
ANTIPATRI, *men like the jurist and historian L. Caelius Antipater (second century BC):*
    Laud. 444.
ANUBIS, *an Egyptian god with the head of a dog; hence, a captious critic: Pug.* B 1, 3; *Laud.*
    215; 575.
AONIA, *the part of Boeotia containing Mount Helicon: Buc.* 2, 31.
AONIUS, a, um *(see also Heliconius), of Mount Helicon, Heliconian:* chorus *Nar.* 33, 4;
    corona *Buc.* 10, 44; fons *Laud.* 241; laurus *Buc.* 8, 101; nemus *Laud.* 305; rupes
    Buc. B 7, 7; vertex *Rec.* 213; *Laud.* 160; colles *Buc.* 6, 14; Musae *Rec.* 190; *Laud.*
    386; viri *Laud.* B 3, 4.
APELLES, *celebrated Greek painter (fourth century BC), who lived for a long time on the
    island of Cos: Pug.* B 1, 19; Chous *Laud.* 364.
APERBACHUS, PETREIUS, *see Eberbachus, Petrus.*
APHRICANUS, a, um, *see Scipio Aphricanus.*
APOLLINEUS, a, um, *of Apollo:* horti *Buc.* 8, 103; laurus *Buc.* 1, 27; opes *Buc.* B 9, 14.
APOLLO *(see also Phoebus, Phoibos), god of the sun, patron of poetry and the Muses: Laud.*
    B 3, 36; *Ama.* 30, 5; B 2, 75; *Buc.* 1, 41; 6, 97; Clarius *Laud.* 159; crinitus *Rec.*
    50; Delphicus *Pug.* 55; flavus *Laud.* 293; foelix *Buc.* 4, 75; ipse *Rec.* 190; noster
    Buc. B 2, 6; Patareus *Laud.* 468; — *Christ:* caelestis *Laud.* 375; Catholicus
    Laud. B 4, 2; summus *Ama.* 35, 113; triplex *Laud.* 395; *Buc.* 10, 41; verus *Buc.*
    10, 93.
[APOLLONIUS MOLON], *a famous Greek rhetor and grammarian (second/first century
    BC), who taught Cicero and other Romans: Laud.* 34.
ARGIVUS, a, um, *Greek:* Argo *Ama.* 35, 39; dux *(Agamemnon) Rec.* 167.
ARGO, *the ship in which Jason and his Argonauts sailed to Colchis in quest of the Golden
    Fleece:* Argiva *Ama.* 35, 39.
ARGUS, *a pastoral name ("sharp-eyed") for Eobanus Hessus: Buc.* 4, tit.; 4, *passim as speaker;*
    4, 6; 4, 73.
ARISTEUS, a, um, *of the mythical hero Aristaeus, who taught the art of beekeeping:* volucres
    Laud. 108.
ARISTOTELES, *the Greek philosopher (384-322 BC):* doctus *Rec.* 206.
ARMENIUS, a, um, *of Armenia:* Georgius *(St. George) Buc.* 4, 29.
ARNOLDUS, HARTOMANUS, *Eobanus Hessus's cousin: Nar.* 6, 3; [6, 5].
ARTAXERXES, *Artaxerxes II (Mnemon), king of Persia from 404 to 358 BC: Laud.,* ded. 1.
ASCRAEUS, a, um, *of Ascra near Mount Helicon, birthplace of Hesiod:* antrum *Buc.* 8, 115.
ATHAENAE *or* ATHENAE, *Athens: Nar.* [21, 2]; 24, 16; [*Rec.* 210]; *Laud.* 67; antiquae
    Laud. 84; Caecropiae *Laud.,* lim. 3; Teutonicae *Laud.* 413; veteres *Laud.* 21.
ATRIDES *(see also Agamemnon), Agamemnon, commander of the Greek forces at Troy: Laud.*
    265.
AUBANUS, GREGORIUS (GEORGIUS), *Gregor (Georg) Käl of Aub in Franconia*

(d. 1515): Nar. 11, 4.
AUGUSTINIANUS, a, um, *Augustinian:* familia *Nar.* 17, 3; 19, 8.
AUGUSTINUS, AURELIUS, *St. Augustine (354-430): Laud.* 355.
AUSONIS, idis, *Italian:* ora *Laud.* 68; 408; Musae *Buc.* 6, 10.
AUSONIUS, a, um, *Italian:* gens *Laud.* 23; urbes *Laud.* 35.
AUSTER, *the south wind, the south: Nar.* 1, 13; humidus *Buc.* 7, 178.
AUSTRIACUS, a, um, *in Austria:* Vienna *Laud.* 538.

BACCHUS *or* BACHUS, *the god of wine; hence, wine: Pug.* 9; *Ama.* B 2, 29; *Buc.* 5, 103; immodicus *Rec.* 227.
BALTHIACUS, a, um, *Baltic:* mare *Buc.* 10, 4.
BAPTISTA MANTUANUS, *see Mantuanus, Baptista.*
BARDIACUS, a, um, *Illyrian:* cucullus *Buc.* 10, 174.
BARTHOLOMEUS, *Bartholomew Arnoldi of Usingen (d. 1532): Laud.* 139.
BAUMGERTNERUS, HIERONYMUS, *Hieronymus Baumgartner (1498-1565): Nar.* 24, 8
BELGICUM, *the Duchy of Brabant: Nar.* 15, 3; 16, 3.
BERLERUS, VITUS, *Veit Werler of Sulzfeld: Nar.* 11, 4.
BERTERUS, *Johann von Werther: Nar.* 15, 3.
BIBLIS, *Byblis, daughter of Miletus; after falling in love with her brother Caunos, she was changed into a spring:* liquida *Ama.* 35, 28.
BILBILITANUS, *the epigrammatist Martial of Bilbilis in Spain (first century AD): Laud.* B 3, 32.
[BOCKENDORF], *village near Frankenberg in Hesse: Nar.* 5, 10.
[BONEMILCH, JOHANN], *see Lasphe, Ioannes.*
BOREAS, *the north wind: Buc.* 7, 178.
BOREUS, a, um, *northern:* axis *Nar.* 9, 17.
BORUSSIA, *Prussia: Nar.* 7, 5; 8, 4; 10, 17; 19, 6.
[BREITENGRASER, WILHELM], *see Vilhelmus.*
BUDEUS, GUILIELMUS, *Guillaume Budé (1468-1540): Nar.* 32, 5.
[BUSCHIUS, HERMANNUS], *Hermann von dem Busche (ca. 1468-1534): Laud.* 542.
BYBLIS, *see Biblis.*
BYRMUSTUS, IOANNES, *Johann Biermost of Erfurt (d. 1512): Laud.* 454-456; [457-462].

CACUS, *a giant killed by Hercules for stealing some of the cattle of Geryon: Pug.* 40.
CAECROPIUS, a, um, *see Cecropius.*
CAESAR AUGUSTUS, *the Roman emperor (27 BC–AD 14): Ama.* 34, 1; antiquus *Buc.*, ded. 30; magnus *Buc.* B 2, 31.
CAESAREUS, a, um, *of the emperor, imperial:* leges *Laud.* 425.
CALCHAS, *chief seer among the Greeks before Troy: Rec.* 28.
CALDAEUS, a, um, *Chaldaean:* vetustas *Laud.* 349.
CALDUS, *a shepherd ("hotblooded"): Buc.* 7, tit.; 7, *passim as speaker;* 7, 66; 7, 72; 7, 159; optimus *Buc.* 7, 4.
CALLIMACHUS, *the famous poet of Cyrene (third century BC): Nar.* 17, 13.
CALLIOPE *(see also Musa), Muse of epic poetry, "queen" of the Muses: Rec.* 51; *Laud.* 228; 233; 244; [245-246]; *Ama.* B 2, *passim as speaker;* [*Buc.* 8, 50-60]; mea *Laud.* 5; tua *Laud.* 270.
CALUMNIA, *Calumny (personified): Nar.* 17, 20.
[CALYPSO], *the nymph who kept Ulysses for seven years on the island Ogygia: Ama.* 35, 71-72.
CAMAENA, CAMENA, *or* CAMOENA *(see also Musa), a Muse; hence, poetry: Laud.* 475; *Buc.* 2, 20; [2, 21-28]; 2, 34; 2, 41; [2, 42-44]; 2, 53; 2, 68; 2, 87; 7, 76;

B 7, 13; inexperta *Buc.* 1, 52; sterilis *Buc.* 1, 14; tua *Buc.* 4, 76; agrestes *Rec.* B 1, 4; audaces *Buc.* 6, 6; dispositae *Buc.* 4, 72; divae *Ama.* 35, 111; *Buc.* 6, 58; faciles *Laud.* 65; *Buc.* 5, 66; 5, 70; 5, 76; 5, 80; 5, 86; 5, 90; 5, 96; 5, 100; 5, 106; 5, 110; 7, 97; insontes *Laud.* 379; lyricae *Ama.* 36, 1; meae, et si rudes *Buc.* 6, 39; nostrae *Laud.* 482; 588; *Buc.*, ded. 31; *Buc.* 10, 23; tristes *Buc.* 9, 20; vestrates *Buc.* 10, 35.

CAMERARIUS PABEBERGENSIS, IOACHIMUS, *Joachim Camerarius of Bamberg (1500-1574): Nar.*, tit.; *Nar.*, [*passim*].

CAMILLUS, *a pastoral name ("adolescent") for Eobanus Hessus: Buc.* 1, tit.; 1, *passim as speaker;* 1, 2.

CANACE, *a shepherdess: Buc.* 7, 110; [7, 111-156]; 7, 129; 7, 135; 7, 145; formosa *Buc.* 7, 122; mea *Buc.* 7, 153.

CANCER, *the Crab, a sign of the zodiac that the sun enters at the summer solstice:* calidus *Buc.*, ded. 2.

CANICULA *(see also Canis), the Dog Star (Sirius), whose rising marks the start of the dog days of summer in July and August:* furibunda *Laud.* 567.

CANIS *(see also Canicula), the Dog Star (Sirius), associated with the hottest time of the year: Buc.* B 6, 2; gravis *Pug.* 2.

CAPELLA, VALENTINUS, *Valentin Sifridi of Cappel in Hesse (d. 1528): Nar.* 17, 9.

CAPITOLIUM, *the temple of Jupiter on the Capitoline hill:* regia *Laud.* 92.

CAPNIO, IOANNES, *Johann Reuchlin of Pfzorzheim (1454/55-1522): Nar.* 17, 13.

CARIUS, a, um, *in Caria, a country in south-west Asia Minor:* sepulchrum *(Mausoleum) Laud.* 79.

CAROLUS V, *Charles V (1500-1558), Holy Roman Emperor since 1519: Nar.* 17, 17.

[CARTHAGE], *city on the north coast of Africa: Laud.* 86.

CASSELA, *Kassel, residence of the landgraves of Hesse since the thirteenth century:* [*Buc.*, ded. 7]; princeps *Buc.*, ded. 9.

CASTALIDES *(see also Musa), the Muses: Ama.* 25, 8.

CASTALIUS, a, um, *Castalian, of the spring Castalia on Mount Parnassus, sacred to Apollo and the Muses:* fons *Laud.* 332; *Ama.* 34, 7; undae *Rec.* 211.

CATHARINA *(see also Costis), St. Catharine of Alexandria, daughter of Costus: Laud.* 487; — *Katharina Später (d. 1540/43), who married Eobanus Hessus in late 1514: Nar.* 14, 7; [30, 2].

CATO, *M. Porcius Cato, censor in 184 BC: Ama.* A 1, 2; tetricus difficilisque *Ama.* A 2, 4.

CATONES, *men like the censor M. Porcius Cato: Laud.* 443.

CATTI *(see also Hessus), the Hessians; hence, Hesse: Nar.* 5, 2; 12, 13; 28, 4.

CATULA, *a shepherdess: Buc.* 3, 115.

CAUCASEUS, a, um, *of the Caucasus mountains:* ferae *Pug.* B 1, 24.

CAUCASUS, *the Caucasus mountains: Ama.* 32, 69.

CAUTUS, *a shepherd ("cautious"): Buc.* 7, tit.; 7, *passim as speaker;* 7, 11; 7, 53; 7, 69; 7, 158; cautissimus *Buc.* 7, 95.

CECILII, *men like the Roman advocate and writer Pliny the Younger (C. Plinius Caecilius Secundus; ca. AD 61-113/14): Laud.* 445.

CECROPIUS *or* CAECROPIUS, a, um, *Athenian, Attic:* Minerva *Pug.* B 1, 9; urbs *(Athens) Rec.* 210; Athenae *Laud.*, lim. 3; — *learned:* iuvenes *Rec.* 164.

CELTIS, CONRADUS, *the German "archhumanist" (1459-1508): Ama.* 22, 6.

CERES, *goddess of grain and fruits; hence, crops, wheat, bread: Ama.* 22, 7, 8; *Buc.* 2, 47; flava *Buc.* 1, 75; laeta *Rec.* 1; oleata *Buc.* 2, 56.

CHALCIS, *Schmalkalden in Hesse: Nar.* 28, 4.

CHALDAEUS, a, um, *see Caldaeus.*

CHARITES Χάριτες, *the Graces: Nar.* 34, 1.

CHEZIMANUS, IOANNES, *Johann Ketzmann (1487-1542): Nar.* 22, 1.

CHIMAERA, *see Chymera.*

CHIRON, *see Chyron.*

CHOREB, *Mount Horeb (Sinai), the "mountain of God": Laud.* 133.

CHOUS, a, um, *Coan, of the island Cos in the Dodecanese:* Apelles *Laud.* 364; vestes *Rec.* B 1, 8.

CHRISEIS, *the daughter of Chryses:* [*Rec.* 167]; abducta *Rec.* 28.

CHRISTIANUS, a, um, *Christian:* ritus *Nar.* 26, 4.

CHRISTIANUS FRANCOBERGIUS, IOANNES, *a student at Erfurt: Laud.* B 6, tit.

CHRISTIANUS, LUDOVICUS *(see also Paniscus), Ludwig Christiani (1480-1553), Eobanus Hessus's teacher at Erfurt: Nar.* 7, 1; *Rec.* 84; [85-87].

CHRISTICOLA, ae, *Christian:* Pallas *Laud.* 486; poetae *Buc.* 2, 32.

CHRISTOPHORUS, a, um, *Christ-bearing:* Virgo *(the Virgin Mary) Buc.* 5, 68.

CHRISTUS *(see also Apollo, Deus, Iesus, Tonans), Jesus Christ: Nar.* 28, 5; *Laud.*, ded., tit.; *Laud.* 131; 218; [488]; *Ama.* B 2, 28; B 2, 33; B 2, 35; B 2, 64; *Buc.* 2, 16; [3, 12]; 3, 19; [5, 69; 11, 49-51]; immensus *Buc.* 11, 47; magnus *Buc.* 6, 87; noster *Ama.* B 2, 39.

CHRYSIPPUS, *Stoic philosopher (third century BC), particularly interested in logic: Laud.* 142.

CHYMERA, *the Chimera, a mythological monster in Lycia; hence, a wild fancy:* Licia *Laud.* 365; *Ama.* 20, 2; [20, 3-4]; 24, 2-5; — *a mountain in Lycia:* [*Ama.* 24, 5].

CHYRON *(see also Phillirides), the centaur Chiron, tutor of Achilles: Ama.* 35, 37.

CICERO, *the Roman orator and statesman (106-43 BC): Nar.* 1, 11; *Laud.* 32; 34; 36; 461; doctus *Laud.* 117; magnus *Buc.* B 2, 34.

CICTIACUS, a, um, *of Zeno (335-263 BC), born in Citium (Cyprus), founder of the Stoic school; hence, Stoic:* examen *Buc.* 6, 15.

CIGNUS, *see Cygnus.*

CINYRAS, *see Cyniras.*

CIRCE, *the enchantress who detained Ulysses on his voyage back to Ithaca: Ama.* 27, 2.

CIRRHA, *see Cyrrha.*

CITHERON, *see Cytheron.*

CLARIUS, a, um, *Clarian, of Claros in Ionia where Apollo had a temple and oracle:* Apollo *Laud.* 159; liquor *Laud.* 254; rus *Laud.* 302.

COLCHIS, idis, *of Colchis:* Phasias *(Medea) Laud.* 185.

[COLONIA AGRIPPINENSIS], *Cologne: Laud.* 539.

COLOSSUS, *the gigantic statue of the sun-god at Rhodes:* Rhodius *Laud.* 81.

CONRADUS CELTIS, *see Celtis, Conradus.*

CORDUS SIMUSIUS, EURICIUS (HENRICUS), *Euricius Cordus of Simtshausen (1486-1535): Nar.* 12, 1; [12, 2-3]; 12, 4; [12, 5-10]; 12, 11-12; 20, 10.

CORDUS, VALERIUS, *natural scientist (1515-1544), son of Euricius Cordus: Nar.* 12, 5; [12, 6].

CORICIUS, a, um, *of Corycus in Cilicia, famous for its saffron:* crocum *Laud.* 112; *Buc.* 9, 60.

CORYNNA, *Corinna, the poetical name of Ovid's mistress: Ama.*, ded. 8; pulchra *Ama.* B 2, 62.

COSTIS *(see also Catharina), St. Catherine of Alexandria, daughter of Costus: Laud.* 487; 526.

COUS, a, um, *see Chous.*

CRACOVIA, *Cracow in Poland: Laud.* 544.

CRASSI, *men like the Roman orator L. Licinius Crassus (140-91 BC): Laud.* 445.

CRATINUS, *Athenian comic poet (fifth century BC): Laud.* 242.

CRATO FULDENSIS, ADAMUS, *Adam Krafft of Fulda (1493-1558): Nar.*, tit.; *Nar.* 1, 1; [2, 2; 3, 1; 3, 4; 4, 4; 4, 8; 4, 10]; 12, 15; 15, 2; 16, 1; 19, 3; 26, 2; 32, 1.

CROCUS BRITANNUS, RICARDUS, *Richard Croke of London (ca. 1489-1558): Nar.* 2, 4; 15, 1.

CROESUS, *a fabulously rich king of Lydia (sixth century BC): Laud.* 514.

CROTUS RUBIANUS, IOANNES, *or* IOANNES DORNHEIM VENATORIUS *(see also Iarbas, Iucundus, Philaegon, Vernus), German humanist (ca. 1480-ca. 1545): Nar.* 17, 17; 19, 5; [19, 6-7]; *Laud.,* t.p.; *Laud.* 299; [300-322]; 302; 310; *Buc.* B 7, tit.; [B 8, tit.].

CUPIDINEUS, a, um, *of Cupid:* sagitta *Ama.* 35, 49.

CUPIDO *(see also Amor), the son of Venus, god of love: Ama.,* t.p.; ded. 5; *Ama.,* tit.; 8, 1; 11, 2; 16, 7; 18, 4; [32, 4; 32, 6]; 32, 36; [32, 37-40; 32, 80]; 34, 5; [35, 2; 35, 47; 35, 60]; 35, 63; [35, 68]; *Buc.* 3, 36; [3, 37-39; 3, 75-76; 7, 167]; ferus *Ama.* 32, 1; pharetratus *Ama.* 27, 6; tuus *Ama.* 25, 7.

CYGNUS *or* CIGNUS, *a pastoral name ("swan") for Eobanus Hessus: Buc.* 3, tit.; 3, *passim as speaker;* 3, 10; 3, 60; 3, 77; 3, 98; 3, 108.

CYNIRAS, *Cinyras, a mythical king of Assyria and Cyprus, father of Myrrha: Buc.* 9, 60.

CYNTHIA *the poetical name of Propertius's mistress: Ama.* B 2, 61.

CYNTHIUS, a, um, *of Mount Cynthus on Delos, where the moon-goddess Diana was born:* Luna *Laud.* B 1, 4.

CYPRIGENA, *Venus, so called because she came ashore in Cyprus: Ama.* A 3, 2.

CYPRIS, *Venus:* lasciva *Ama.* B 2, 15.

CYRIACUM OVILE, *the cloister of St. Cyriacus in Erfurt: Laud.* 130.

CYRRHA, *one of the two peaks of Mount Parnassus: Buc.* 2, 31.

CYRUS IUNIOR, *Cyrus II (423-401 BC), the brother of Artaxerxes II: Laud.,* ded. 1.

CYTHERON, *Cithaeron, a mountain in Boeotia, sacred to the Muses and Bacchus: Buc.* 2, 31.

DACI, *the Transylvanians:* Istricolae *Laud.* 452.

DAEDALUS, *a mythical Athenian architect and inventor, who escaped from the Labyrinth in Crete by making wings for himself and his son Icarus: Buc.* 2, 30.

DANAI, *the Greeks: Rec.* 26.

DANAUS, a, um, *Greek:* flammae *Laud.* B 1, 11.

DANTISCANUS, *Johannes Dantiscus (Jan Dantyszek) of Danzig (1485-1548): Nar.* 10, 1; [10, 2]; 10, 3; [10, 4]; 10, 5; [10, 6-16].

DAPHNE, *the daughter of the river-god Peneus, loved by Apollo and changed into a laurel tree:* [*Ama.* B 2, 26]; Peneia *Laud.* 160.

DAPHNIS *(see also Mutianus), a pastoral name for Mutianus Rufus: Laud.* 282.

DAVID *(see also Iesseus), the second king of the Jews:* [*Buc.* 1, 42-43; 1, 51-52; 6, 89-90]; lyricus *Ama.* 26, 4; vester *Ama.* A 2, 2.

DAVIDICUS, a, um, *of David:* Psalmi *Nar.* 26, 5.

DEIDAMIA, *a princess of Scyros and mother of Pyrrhus by Achilles:* dilecta *Ama.* 35, 73.

DELIA, *the poetical name of Tibullus's mistress: Ama.* B 2, 65.

DELOS, *an island in the Aegean Sea, birthplace of Apollo: Nar.* 24, 16.

DELPHICUS, a, um, *Delphic, of Delphi, where Apollo had a famous oracle:* Apollo *Pug.* 55; laurus *Rec.* 212; rura *Rec.* 75.

DEUS *(see also Apollo, Christus, Iesus, Iuppiter, Spiritus, Tonans), the triune God, God the Father, Christ: Nar.* 6, 9; 6, 18; 26, 6; [29, 5]; 32, 1; *Rec.* 54; *Pug.* B 1, postscript; *Laud.* 133; 339; [395-398; 509]; 522; *Ama.* 26, 1; B 2, 73; *Buc.,* ded. 27; *Buc.* [3, 14-17; 5, *passim*]; 5, 104; 6, 71; 6, 77; [8, 121]; 10, 150; [11, 18]; 11, 33; 11, 45; aeditus virginea alvo *Rec.* 12; aeternus *Nar.* 26, 6; 29, 6; ipse *Buc.* 7, 37; nascens *Buc.* 11, 50; optimus maximus *Laud.,* tit.; Panompheus *Pug.* 8.

[DIABOLUS] *(see also Dis, Pluto), the devil,* Lucifer: *Buc.* 2, 18.

DIANA *(see also Luna), the virgin goddess of the hunt and the moon; the moon: Rec.* 196; *Ama.* A 2, 3; casta *Pug.* 70; *Laud.* 300; Trivia *Laud.* 380.

DIDO, *the mythical foundress and queen of Carthage, lover of Aeneas: Ama.* 10, 10; 35, 69; regia *Ama.* 35, 24.

15; *Ama.* B 3, 4; [B 4, 2]; *Buc.* 1, 94; [1, 95-102; 3, 1-9; 4, *passim*]; clara *Rec.*
230; *Ama.* B 4, 5; docta *Rec.* 52; 218; *Pug.* 10; foelix *Laud.* 325; infoelix *Rec.* 13;
Buc. 4, 41; 4, 45; magna *Laud.* 3; nova *Laud.* 43; sublimata *Laud.* 532; victrix
Laud. 48.

ERPHORDIANUS, a, um, *of Erfurt:* Academia *Nar.* 18, 1-2; Petrus Eberbachus *Ama.*,
ded., tit.; schola *Nar.* 26, 1; eruditi *Nar.* 15, 14.

ERPHORDIENSIS *or* ERPHURDIENSIS, e, *of Erfurt:* gymnasium *(the University of*
Erfurt) Ama. B 3, 1; magister *Buc.*, t.p.; Mercurius *(the "Engelshaus", a*
dormitory in Erfurt where Eobanus lived in 1508) Ama. B 1, 4; opusculum *Ama.*,
t.p.; *Ama.*, tit.; Petreius Aperbachus *Nar.* 17, 10; studium *Laud.*, ded. 10; virgo
(Katharina Später) Nar. 14, 7; amici *Nar.* 25, 1; studentes *Pug.*, t.p.; *Pug.*, tit.;
Sylvae *(a miscellany) Ama.* B 1, 2.

ERYDANUS *(see also Padus), Eridanus, a Greek name for the Po River in Italy: Laud.* 39.

[ESCHENAU], *a village near Nuremberg: Nar.* 25, 4.

ETHIOPES, *the Ethiopians: Laud.* 209.

EUMENIDES *(see also Erinnis, Furiae), the Furies: Rec.* 163.

EUROPA, *the princess whom Jupiter, disguised as a bull, carried across the sea to Crete: Ama.*
B 2, 29.

EURUS, *the east wind: Rec.* 37; *Buc.* 8, 62; leniter afflans *Buc.* 6, 92.

EURYDICE *or* EURIDICE, *the wife of Orpheus: Buc.* 1, 41; quaesita *Laud.* 223.

FALERNUM, *see Phalernum.*

FASTUS, *a pastoral name ("arrogance") for Riccardo Sbruglio of Cividale di Friuli (ca. 1480*
– after 1525): Buc. 10, tit.; 10, *passim as speaker;* 10, 35; 10, 45; 10, 67; 10, 85;
10, 112; 10, 118; 10, 147; noster *Buc.* 10, 104.

FATUM *(see also Parcae), Fate, destiny, death: Rec.* 94; 221; *Pug.* B 1, 25; *Laud.* 313; B 1,
10; *Ama.* 32, 14-15; 32, 28; 32, 45; 32, 84; *Buc.* 2, 41; 3, 97; 7, 16; 9, 21; 9, 27;
B 8, 2; nefandum *Buc.* 1, 40; perniciosum *Ama.* 33, 8; tuum *Pug.* B 1, 26;
cognata *Ama.* 35, 93; foelicia *Rec.* 192; *Laud.* 314; impia *Rec.* 119; *Buc.* B 3, 6;
mea *Rec.* 145; *Buc.* 6, 73; meliora *Rec.* 229; pessima *Buc.* 9, 50; tristia *Rec.* 49;
Laud. B 3, 20; *Buc.* 9, 17; tua *Rec.* 125; ultima *Laud.* B 3, 5.

FAUNUS, *a deity of the fields and woods: Buc.* 1, 90; salaces *Buc.* 1, 88; veteres *Buc.* 5, 102;
— *the satyr Marsyas:* rudis *Buc.* 6, 97.

FAUSTINA, *a shepherdess: Buc.* 3, 115.

FAUSTUS *(see also Mantuanus), a shepherd in the eclogues of Baptista Mantuanus; hence,*
Mantuanus himself: Buc. 3, 27; ille *Buc.* 3, 24.

FAVONIUS *(see also Zephyrus), the west wind of spring:* mollis *Buc.* 5, 47; occiduus *Buc.* 4,
78; venerandus *Buc.* 7, 152.

FICINUS, MARSILIUS, *the Italian humanist and philosopher Marsilio Ficino (1433-*
1499): Ama. 25, 2.

FIDILLA, *a shepherdess:* nigra *Buc.* 3, 115.

FIRMICUS, *Julius Firmicus Maternus (fourth century AD): Nar.* 5, 16.

FLACCUS, *the Roman poet Horace (65-8 BC): Laud.* 9.

[FLAVIA], *a poetical name for Eobanus Hessus's sweetheart in Erfurt: Buc.* 9, 1; 11, 11.

FLORALIS, e, *of Flora, the goddess of flowers:* dona *Buc.* 4, 38; horti *Buc.* 10, 112.

FLORIDUS, *a pastoral name ("blooming") for Petrejus Eberbach: Buc.* 5, tit.; 5, *passim as*
speaker; 5, 2; 5, 8; 5, 19; 5, 115; noster *Buc.* 11, 29.

FOENILIA, *a shepherdess loved by Cygnus:* [*Buc.* 3, 66-74; 3, 90]; levis *Buc.* 3, 98; mea *Buc.*
3, 150; pulchra *Buc.* 3, 66.

[FORCHHEIM], *see Heltus Vorhemius.*

FORTUNA *(see also Rhamnusia), the blind goddess Fortune, Lady Luck: Nar.* 6, 11; 21, 3;
Pug. 95; 101; *Ama.* 5, 2; [5, 3-7]; 6, 1; [6, 3-5]; inimica bonis *Rec.* 96; levis *Pug.*
87; melior *Laud.* 504.

FORUM RHOMANUM, *the main public square in ancient Rome: Ama.* 34, 1.
FRANCFORDIA, *Frankfurt an der Oder:* tua *Laud.* B 4, 3.
FRANCOBERGIA *or* FRANCOPERGA, *Frankenberg in Hesse: Nar.* 6, 5; *Rec.* 86; [174-227]; cincta niveis muris, foveis circumvallata profundis *Rec.* 174.
FRANCOPERGENSIS, e, *of Frankenberg in Hesse:* patria *Nar.* 7, 1.
FRANCUS, *a Franconian: Nar.* 11, 4; 16, 7.
FRANCUS PORTUNUS, IOANNES, *Johann Frank of Burgtonna (ca. 1499–after 1568): Nar.* 18, 1.
FRIBURGUM, *Freiburg im Breisgau: Laud.* 540.
FRONTO FUNDINUS, *a lovesick young man: Ama.*, [*passim*]; 4, 3; 7, 2; 17, 3; 19, 1; charissimus *Ama.* 5, 8; 11, 7; meus *Ama.* 34, 6.
FULDA, *river in Hesse: Buc.*, ded. 9; *Buc.* 9, 41; turbatus *Buc.* 9, 36; — *town in Hesse: Nar.* 19, 6.
FULVIA, *a prostitute in Erfurt: Ama.*, [*passim*]; illa *Ama.* 12, 6.
FUNDINUS, *see Fronto Fundinus.*
FURIAE *(see also Erinnis, Eumenides), the Furies, who harried the guilty:* tristes *Buc.* 4, 109.

GALATHEA, *a pastoral name for Anna von Mecklenburg (1485-1525), the second wife of William II of Hesse: Buc.* [9, 69-75]; 9, 76; [9, 77-82; 9, 86; 9, 113-120].
GALLA, *a shepherdess: Ama.* B 2, 69.
GALLIA, *France: Buc.* 9, 4; [10, 130; 10, 133].
GALLUS, *the Roman poet (first century BC):* sacer *Ama.* B 2, 66; — *Christian priest:* foelices *Ama.* A 2, 1.
GANGES, *the Ganges River in India: Ama.* 32, 67.
GANIMEDES, *Ganymede, Jupiter's cupbearer: Laud.* 194.
GEDANENSIS, e, *of Danzig (Gdansk):* cervisia *Nar.* 9, 10; quidam aequalis *(Johannes Dantiscus) Nar.* 10, 1.
GEDANUM *(see also Dantiscum), Danzig (Gdansk): Nar.* 9, 4.
GEMUNDA, *Gemünden, a town in Hesse: Nar.* 6, 3.
GEMUNDINUS, a, um, *of Gemünden in Hesse:* oppidum *Nar.* 5, 4.
[GEORGENTHAL], *a Cistercian abbey south of Gotha: Buc.* 2, 5-10; 2, 93.
GEORGIANA [FAMILIA], *the "Georgenthaler Hof," a house in Erfurt maintained by the abbey of Georgenthal: Nar.* 17, 1.
GEORGIUS, *St. George:* Armenius *Buc.* 4, 29; divus *Buc.* 2, 7; 2, 93; — *Duke George of Saxony (1471-1539): Nar.* 18, 3; — *Margrave George of Brandenburg-Ansbach (1484-1543): Nar.* 24, 6.
GERA *or* GERHA, *the Gera, a tributary of the Unstrut in Thuringia: Laud.* [39-42]; 73; 251; *Buc.* 8, 54; noster *Laud.* 39; spumans *Laud.* 573; vagus *Buc.* 3, 1; 11, 5.
GERICOLUS, a, um, *dwelling by the Gera River :* Minerva *Laud.* 506; Pallas *Laud.* 20.
[GERLACH VON DER MARTHEN], *father of Herbord von der Marthen (1465-1515): Buc.* 4, 29.
GERMANI, *the ancient Germans: Ama.* 22, 1.
GERMANIA, *ancient Germany: Ama.* 22, 5; — *modern Germany (see also Teutonicus, Teutonis, Teutonus): Nar.* 2, 4; 13, 10; 15, 1; 19, 9; [*Laud.* 24; 32; 415]; *Ama.* B 3, 1; *Buc.* [lim. 5; *Buc.* 3, 32; 6, 7-8]; 9, 4; [10, 1-29; 10, 154-160; B 9, 21; B 10, 4]; laudata *Laud.* 535; tota *Nar.* 13, 10; *Laud.*, t.p.
GERMANICUS, a, um, *Germanic:* virtus *Ama.* 22, 3; 22, 4; vetustas *Ama.* 22, 6.
GERMANUS, a, um *(see also Teutonicus, Teutonis, Teutonus), German:* iuventus *Rec.* 166; nomen *Laud.* 415; orbis *Laud.* 24; solum *Buc.* B 10, 4; vates *Buc.*, lim. 3; *Buc.* B 9, 15; oppida *Laud.* 30.
GIGANTES, *the Giants, sons of Heaven and Earth, who stormed the heavens, but were struck by Jupiter's lightning bolts and buried under Mount Etna: Buc.* 10, 138.
GNOSIACUS, a, um, *Cretan:* corona *(Ariadne's crown, made into a constellation) Buc.* 11,

93.

GNOSIUS, a, um, *of Gnosos in Crete:* Alcon *Buc.* 5, 29.

[GÖDE, HENNINGUS], *see Henningus.*

GOSUS, *the Goßberg, a hill north of Frankenberg:* [*Rec.* 182-183]; frondens *Buc.* 1, 116.

GOTHA, *city in Thuringia: Nar.* 12, 12; 12, 14; 13, 10; 14, 3; affinis *Buc.* B 2, 8; condita parvo collo *Buc.* 2, 101; finitima *Laud.* 262.

GOTHANUS, a, um, *of or in Gotha:* collegium *Nar.* 12, 13.

GRAECI *(see also Graii), the Greeks: Nar.* 1, 5; *Laud.*, ded. 1.

GRAECIA, *Greece:* docta *Laud.* 420; tota *Ama.* 35, 74.

GRAECULUS, a, um, *Greek:* vir *(Apollonius) Laud.* 34.

GRAECUS, a, um, *Greek:* facundia *Laud.* 116; iuventus *Rec.* 166; lingua *Nar.* 2, 3-4; nomen *Nar.* 7, 6; vetustas *Laud.* 118; 350; autores *Nar.* 22, 4; litterae *Nar.* 15, 1; sylvae *Rec.* 208; urbes *Laud.* 36; versus *Nar.* 25, 8.

GRAII *(see also Graeci), the Greeks: Laud.* 97.

GRAIUS, a, um, *Greek:* faces *Ama.* 35, 40.

GREGORIUS, *Pope Gregory the Great (590-604):* sacer *Laud.* 357.

GRONINGUS, *Johann Algesheim of Gröningen (d. 1553): Nar.* 17, 9; 25, 3; noster *Nar.* 4, 6.

GRUDII, *an ancient people in present-day Belgium; hence, Brabant: Nar.* 15, 11.

GUILIELMUS *(see also Iolas), William II of Hesse (1468-1509):* [*Nar.* 12, 13]; *Buc.* B 2, 15; [B 2, 25]; B 2, 27; [B 2, 30]; B 3, tit.; B 3, 3.

HACUS, CHRISTOPHORUS, *Christoph Hack of Jerichow: Nar.* 17, 9.

HAEMONIUS, a, um, *see Oemonius.*

[HAINA], *a Cistercian monastery in Hesse: Nar.* 5, 4; 5, 9; 6, 1.

HALERINA, *the wife of Johann Englender:* [*Buc.* B 2, 39-45]; formosa *Buc.*, ded. 35.

HASSIA, *see Hessia.*

HEBRAEUS, a, um, *Hebrew:* vetustas *Laud.* 349; vates *Laud.* 98.

HECTOR, *the Trojan hero:* ferus *Pug.* 26.

HEIDENA, SEBALDUS, *Sebald Heyden of Bruck (1499-1561): Nar.* 22, 1.

HEINENSIS, e, *of Haina, a Cistercian monastery in Hesse:* conventus *Nar.* 5, 4; 5, 9.

HELENE, *King Menelaus's wife, abducted by Paris:* [*Laud.* 184]; *Ama.* 35, 19.

HELIADES, *a pastoral name ("offspring of Helios") for the poet Hermann Trebelius (Surwynt) of Eisenach, crowned poet laureate in 1508: Buc.* 4, 106; [4, 107-112]; 8, tit.; 8, *passim as speaker;* 8, 102.

HELICON, *a mountain in Boeotia, sacred to Apollo and the Muses: Buc.* 2, 31; [8, 48-51].

HELICONIUS, a, um *(see also Aonius), of Mount Helicon:* sacra *Laud.* 162.

HELIUS EOBANUS HESSUS, *see Hessus, Helius Eobanus.*

HELTUS VORHEMIUS, GEORGIUS, *Georg Helt of Forchheim (ca. 1485-1545): Nar.* 7, 13; 11, 5; 12, 2.

HENNINGUS, *the legal scholar Henning Göde (d. 1521): Laud.* 448; [449-453].

[HERCULES], *the mythical Greek hero: Ama.* 35, 31-36.

HERCULEUS, a, um, *of Hercules, Herculean:* ops *Laud.* 377; sagittae *Buc.* 5, 23.

HEREBORDUS MARGARITUS LEOBURGIUS *(see also Phileremus), Herbord von der Marthen und Löwenburg (ca. 1480-1529): Laud.* [146-152]; B 5, tit.; *Buc.* B 6, tit.; disertus *Laud.* 146.

HERMUS, *a gold-bearing river in Asia Minor:* vetus *Buc.* 1, 111.

HERODOTUS, *the Greek historian (fifth century BC): Nar.* 5, 7.

HESIODUS, *Hesiod of Ascra in Boeotia (ca. 700 BC): Nar.* 3, 8; [*Buc.* 8, 115].

HESSIA *or HASSIA, Hesse:* [*Nar.* 5, 2; 5, 4; 29, 2; 33, 1-2]; *Laud.* 123; [B 3, 6-7; B 6, 1]; *Buc.*, ded., tit.; [ded., *passim; Buc.* 1, *passim;* 9, *passim;* B 2, 23; B 3, 4; B 7, 8]; B 7, 12-13; B 8, tit.; B 8, 10; bellipotens *Buc.* B 3, 1; dives *Buc.* 1, 10; dives agris densisque uberrima sylvis *Buc.* 1, 107; eadem *Buc.* B 7, 11; inclyta *Rec.* 90.

HESSIACUS *(see also Hessus), a Hessian: Nar.* 12, 1; 28, 5.
HESSIACUS, a, um, *of Hesse, Hessian:* ditio *Nar.* 5, 2; pecus *Buc.* B 11, 22; terra *Buc.*, ded.
19; territorium *Nar.* 5, 4; urbs *(Kassel) Buc.*, ded. 7; montes *Laud.* 278; *Buc.* 4,
40; urbes *Laud.* 125.
HESSICUS, a, um, *of Hesse:* sceptra *Buc.* B 2, 16.
HESSUS *(see also Catti, Hessiacus), a Hessian: Nar.* 26, 1; *Buc.* B 3, tit.; belliger *Buc.*, ded.
4; fortes *Buc.* 7, 127; montani *Buc.* 1, 72; tui *Laud.* B 3, 8; *see Hessus, Helius
Eobanus.*
HESSUS, HELIUS EOBANUS *(see also Argus, Camillus, Cygnus, Mannus, Poliphemus,
Sylvius, Vernus): Nar.*, tit.; *Nar., passim; Pug.* 105; *Laud.*, lim. 11; [*Laud.,
passim*]; 181; 231; 315; *Laud.* B 3, tit.; [B 3, *passim*]; B 5, 1; B 6, 1; *Ama.* A 1,
tit.; [A 1, *passim*]; *Ama.*, [*passim*]; 6, 1; 7, 6; 18, 1; 33, 3; B 1, 3; B 2, *passim as
speaker;* B 2, 3; B 2, 48; *Buc.* B 6, 4; [B 7, *passim*]; B 7, 3; B 7, 5; B 7, 17; B 7,
22; B 7, 26; B 9, 3; B 9, 21; B 10, 2; B 10, 6; doctus *Ama.* A 3, 6;
expectatissimus *Ama.* 3, 2; impudicus *Ama.*, ded. 11; meus *Ama.* 6, 7; noster
Buc. B 9, 14; proclivis in umbra *Buc.* 2, 3; suus *Laud.* B 5, tit.; tristatus *Ama.* B
2, 1.
HIERONIMUS, *St. Jerome (ca. 347-419/20): Laud.* 356; divus *Ama.* 27, 3.
HIPPOCRATES, *the celebrated Greek physician (fifth century BC): Ama.* 25, 5.
[HIPPOCRENE], *a spring on Mount Helicon, sacred to the Muses: Nar.* 14, 1; *Laud.* 241.
HIPPOLYTUS, *see Hyppolitus.*
HOMEREIOS Ὁμήρειος, ον, *Homeric:* τύχη *Nar.* 34, 12.
HOMERICUS, a, um, *Homeric:* fatum *Nar.* 29, 2; thema *Nar.* 5, 16.
HOMERUS *(see also Meonis), Homer (eighth century BC): Nar.* 5, 6-8; 5, 12; 26, 3; *Laud.*
392; *Ama.* 27, 2; [35, 80]; magnus *Buc.* B 1, 7; sublimis *Laud.* 459.
HOPELLUS, GEORGIUS, *Georg Hoppel (d. 1533): Nar.* 24, 12.
[HORATIUS] FLACCUS, *see Flaccus.*
HORLAEUS, IACOBUS, *Jakob Horle (Hurle) of Frankenberg (d. 1519): Nar.* 6, 5; [6, 6-
9]; 6, 12; [6, 13-14].
HORRISONUS, *the Hörselberg, a mountain east of Eisenach: Buc.* [4, 77-78]; 4, 79; [4,
99-109].
HUNUS, MARTINUS, *Martin Hune of Gittelde in Brunswick: Nar.* 17, 10.
HUTTENUS, ULRICHUS, *Ulrich von Hutten (1488-1523): Laud.* B 3, tit.; B 4, 1; [B
4, 2-6].
HYBLE, *a mountain in Sicily, famous for its honey:* Sicula *Buc.* 6, 26.
HYBLAEUS, a, um, *of Mount Hybla:* nectar *Laud.* 107.
HYDRA, *the many-headed Lernaean serpent, killed by Hercules:* torva *Laud.* 216.
HYPERBOREUS, a, um, *Hyperborean, arctic:* frigus *Rec.* 200.
HYPPOLITUS, *Hippolytus, the chaste son of Theseus and Hippolyte, who rejected the
advances of his stepmother Phaedra:* castus *Laud.* 304.

IARBAS *(see also Crotus Rubianus), a pastoral name for Crotus Rubianus: Buc.* 8, tit.; 8,
passim as speaker; doctus *Buc.* 7, 99; improbus *Buc.* 8, 13.
IASON, *the son of Aeson, leader of the Argonauts who set off in quest of the Golden Fleece,
husband of Medea: Ama.* 35, 39.
IBIS, *pseudonym for a bitter enemy of Ovid: Laud.* 382; 392.
IDA, *mountain range in Phrygia, near Troy:* Phrygia *Buc.* 7, 150; B 2, 41.
IESSEUS *or* IESSAEUS, a, um, *begotten by Jesse:* vates *(David) Buc.* 6, 90.
IESUS *or* IESUS CHRISTUS *(see also Christus): Nar.* 5, 15; [6, 7]; 7, 14; 13, 10; 15, 1; 20,
8; 21, 8; 25, 4; *Buc.* 11, 78.
ILIACUS, a, um, *Trojan:* Paris *Ama.* 35, 20; *Buc.* B 2, 40.
ILIAS, *The* Iliad *of Homer: Nar.* 26, 3; *Laud.* B 1, 12; [*Ama.* 35, 80].
INDI, *the Indians:* nigri *Buc.* 2, 37.

INDIA, *the subcontinent India:* dives *Ama.* 32, 66.

IOACHIMICI, *the silver coins known as Joachimstaler: Nar.* 10, 16.

IOBUS DE DOBENECK, *Job (Hiob) von Dobeneck, bishop of Pomesania (1501-1521): Nar.* 7, 5-6; [7, 7-12; 11, 8].

IODOCUS ISENNACHUS, *Jodocus Trutfetter of Eisenach (d. 1519): Laud.* 126.

IOLAS *(see also Guilielmus), a pastoral name for William II of Hesse: Buc.* [9, *passim*]; 9, 38; 9, 62; 9, 71; 9, 78; 9, 110; amatus *Buc.* 9, 73; extinctus *Buc.* 9, 29; 9, 67; magnus *Buc.* 9, 66; nobilis 9, 21; sublimis *Buc.* 9, 48.

IOLE, *a princess loved by Hercules:* [*Ama.* 35, 32]; callida *Ama.* 35, 35.

IONAS, IUSTUS (IUDOCUS) *(see also Vernus), Justus Jonas (1493-1555): Nar.* 16, 4-5; [16, 6]; 16, 8; *Buc.* B 9, tit.

IONIUS, a, um, *Ionian:* mare *Ama.* 35, 72.

IOVIS *(see also Iuppiter), an Italian sky-god identified with Zeus: Nar.* 17, 13; *Laud.* 74; *Buc.* 2, 16; 10, 123; 10, 131; B 4, 2; B 5, 1; [B 5, 3; B 5, 5]; B 5, 8; immortalis *Ama.* 13, 1; — *the sky:* rapidus *Pug.* 32; — *Pluto, god of the underworld:* Stygius *Buc.* B 11, 8.

ISENNACHUS, IODOCUS, *see Iodocus Isennachus.*

ISIDIS LIBURNA, *pseudo-etymological name for Eisenach: Buc.* 4, 81.

ISTER, *the lower course of the Danube: Laud.* 408.

ISTRICOLA, ae, *living along the lower course of the Danube:* Daci *Laud.* 452.

ITALIA, *Italy: Nar.* 13, 4; 20, 1; 20, 10; 20, 12; [*Laud.* 23; 68; 408].

ITALICUS, a, um, *Italian:* disciplina *Nar.* 12, 13; luxus *Ama.* 22, 4.

ITALUS, a, um, *Italian:* artes *Laud.* 26.

IUCUNDUS, *a pastoral name ("delightful"), possibly for Crotus Rubianus: Buc.* 9, tit.; 9, *passim as speaker;* 9, 7.

[IULIUS II], *pope from 1503 to 1513: Buc.* 10, 131.

IULIUS, a, um, *Julian; promulgated by Caesar Augustus (the adopted son of Julius Caesar):* lex *Laud.* 431.

IULUS, *son of Aeneas: Laud.* 199.

IUNO, *the sister and wife of Jupiter:* regia *Buc.* B 2, 42.

IUPPITER *(see also Iovis), an Italian sky-god identified with Zeus: Ama.* B 2, 29; *Buc.*, ded. 7; *Buc.* 2, 3; 7, 100; B 5, 7; [B 10, 1]; immortalis *Ama.* 12, 12; — *the Christian God: Laud.* 441.

IUSTICIA, *Justice (personified): Laud.* 437.

IXIONIUS, a, um, *of Ixion, a king of the Lapiths who tried to seduce Juno and was bound with snakes to a perpetually turning wheel in the underworld:* furores *Pug.* 37.

[KETZMANN], *see Chezimanus.*

LABEONES, *men like the teacher of law M. Antistius Labeo (d. AD 10/11): Laud.* 445.

LAEANDER, *Leander of Abydos, who swam the Hellespont to see his mistress Hero in Sestos:* [*Ama.* 35, 17]; Abidenus *Laud.* 183.

LAETHAEUS, a, um, *of Lethe, a river in the underworld, the water of which induced oblivion in those who drank it:* flumen *Laud.*, ded. 3; somnus *Buc.* 9, 29.

LAEUS, *Edward Lee (ca. 1485-1544): Nar.* 15, 14; 17, 16.

LANGUS, IOHANNES, *Johann Lang of Erfurt (ca. 1486-1548): Nar.* 17, 3; 19, 8; [19, 9]; 25, 3.

LANUS, *the Lahn River in Hesse: Buc.* 9, 41; pulcher *Buc.* 9, 57.

LARES, *household gods; hence, home, homeland:* ignoti *Rec.* 121; Phrygii *(Troy) Ama.* 35, 74; sui *Rec.* 70.

LASPHE, *a small town in modern Nordrhein-Westfalen:* vulgata *Laud.* 123.

LASPHE, IOANNES, *the suffragan bishop Johann Bonemilch of Laasphe (d. 1510): Laud.*, ded., tit.; [ded., *passim*]; *Laud.* [121-123; 507-532]; 508.

LATERANUM, *the house in Erfurt where the Eberbachs lived and operated a pharmacy:* *Ama.* A 1, 11.

LATIALIS, e, *Latin:* vulgus *Laud.* 461.

LATINE, *in Latin: Nar.* 22, 4.

LATINI, *the Latins, Romans: Laud.* 97.

LATINITAS, *Latinity, the Latin language:* recta *Ama.*, ded. 8.

LATINUS, a, um, *Latin:* carmen *Nar.* 28, 6; facundia *Laud.* 116; fraternitas *Ama.* 22, 6; lingua *Nar.* 2, 3; 18, 1; *Buc.* B 2, 36; pecus *Buc.*, lim. 5; scriptio *Ama.* B 3, 1; elegiae *Nar.* 26, 5; Musae *Laud.* 542; *Buc.* 10, 159; nymphae *Rec.* 51; Pierides *Buc.* 10, 173; vaccae *Buc.* B 10, 3; versus *Nar.* 25, 8; 26, 3.

LATIUM, *Latium in central Italy; hence, Rome, Italy: Laud.* 25; *Buc.* B 2, 20; venerabile *Laud.* 37.

LATIUS, a, um, *Latin, Roman:* carmen *Buc.* B 7, 6; grex *Buc.* B 6, 13; lingua *Laud.* 115; nomen *Buc.* 4, 79; rus *Buc.*, lim. 4; *Buc.* B 11, 22; vigor *Laud.* 422.

[LAURENTIUS], *St. Laurence: Pug.* 78.

LAURENTIUS USINGENIUS *or* USINGEN, *Lorenz Arnoldi of Usingen (d. 1521): Rec.* 83-84; B 1, tit.; B 1, 5.

LEANDER, *see Laeander.*

[LEE, EDWARD], *see Laeus.*

LEMNII, *the inhabitants of Lemnos: Ama.* 23, 1.

LEO, *the constellation Leo:* calidus *Buc.* 8, 45; — *Heinrich Löwe: see Enricus.*

LEOBURGIUS, a, um, *see Herebordus.*

LERNAEUS, a, um, *of the Lernaean Hydra:* venenum *Rec.* 105; *Laud.* 390.

LETHAEUS, *see Laethaeus.*

LEUCAS, *the promontory of Leucas, an island in the Ionian Sea: Ama.* 10, 10.

LIBETRIS, idis, *of Libethra, a spring on Mount Helicon sacred to the Muses:* undae *Ama.* 25, 8.

LIBS, *the south-west wind: Buc.* 7, 178.

LICAMBES, *Lycambes, a Theban whom Archilochus attacked in such bitter lampoons that he hanged himself:* miser *Pug.* B 1, 25.

LICIUS, a, um, *of Lycia, a country in the south of Asia Minor:* Chymera *Laud.* 365.

LICURGI, *men like Lycurgus, the lawgiver of the Spartans:* celebres *Laud.* 421.

LINCUS, VINCILAUS, *Wenceslaus Linck of Colditz (1483-1547): Nar.* 24, 5.

LIPS, LIPSIA, *Leipzig: Nar.* 7, 11-12; 11, 1; 12, 1; 15, 1; 17, 4; 18, 3; amplificata Musis Latinis *Laud.* 542.

LIPSICUS, a, um, *of Leipzig:* Academia *Nar.* 11, 2; congressus *Nar.* 18, 3.

LIVOR, *Envy (personified): Buc.* 4, 95; B 9, 1; edax *Laud.* 579; *Buc.* B 1, 5.

[LÖWENBURG], *the country estate of the Von der Marthen family: Buc.* 4, 27-33.

LUCIFER *(see also Phosphorus), the morning star; hence, a new day:* tercius *Buc.* 7, 1; 11, 9.

LUCRETIA, *the wife of Collatinus; she committed suicide after being raped by Sextus Tarquinius:* casta *Buc.* B 2, 43.

LUDOVICUS, *see Christianus, Ludovicus.*

LUDOVICUS MOELSINGENSIS, *Ludwig Platz of Melsungen (d. 1547): Rec.* 81-83; 152.

LUNA *(see also Diana), the moon-goddess, the moon: Buc.* 7, 148; Cynthia *Laud.* B 1, 4.

LUPAMBULUS, *Wolfgang Staffel (d. 1505): Rec.* [99-146]; 102; 137.

LUTHERUS, MARTINUS, *Martin Luther (1483-1546): Nar.* 17, 17-18; 18, 3.

LYCAEUM, *the gymnasium near Athens where Aristotle taught; hence, a university:* nescio quale *Buc.* 7, 106.

LYCAMBES, *see Licambes.*

LYCIA, *a country in the south of Asia Minor: Ama.* 24, 5.

LYCIUS, a, um, *see Licius.*

LYCORIS, *a poetical name for the mistress of the poet Gallus: Ama.* B 2, 66; — *a shepherdess:*

non ulla *Buc.* 6, 62.
LYCURGI, *see Licurgi.*
LYDIA, *girl celebrated in a poem attributed to Vergil: Ama.* B 2, 61.

MAECENAS, *see Moecenas.*
MAEDAEA *(see also Phasias), the sorceress Medea of Colchis:* saeva *Laud.* 409.
MAEONIS, *see Meonis.*
MANNUS, *a pastoral name for Eobanus Hessus (or perhaps Hermann Trebelius): Buc.* 10, tit.; 10, *passim as speaker;* 10, 42; 10, 50.
MANTOUS, a, um, *of Mantua:* poaetae *(Vergil and Baptista Mantuanus) Buc.* 3, 29.
MANTUA, *the city in Italy where Vergil and Baptista Mantuanus were born:* [*Buc.* B 11, 23-24]; foelix *Buc.* 3, 18.
MANTUANUS, BAPTISTA *(see also Faustus), the Italian humanist Giovanni Battista Spagnolo of Mantua (1447-1516): Ama.* 25, 8; [B 2, 67-72; *Buc.*, lim. 2; *Buc.* 3, 17-29]; magnus *Ama.* B 2, 73; noster *Ama.* B 2, 67.
[MARBURG], *see Marpurgum.*
MARCELLUS REGIOMONTANUS, IOANNES, *Johann Marcellus of Königsberg (1510-1552): Nar.* 13, 7.
MARCI, *orators like Marcus Tullius Cicero (106-43 BC): Laud.* 443.
MARGARITANUS, a, um *(see also Gerlach, Herebordus, Martinus), belonging to the Von der Marthen family:* stirps *Laud.* 151; 464.
MARGARITUS, *see Herebordus.*
MARIA, *the Virgin Mary: Rec.* [12; 55]; 56; 195; *Buc.* [5, *passim;* 11, *passim*]; B 6, 1.
MARO, *see Vergilius Maro.*
MARPURGUM, *Marburg in Hesse: Nar.* 26, 1-2; 26, 5; 29, 2; [*Buc.* 9, 56-57; 9, 115].
MARS, *the god of war: Ama.* 25, 7; B 2, 30; favens *Pug.* 92; — *battle:* furibundus *Pug.* 62; iuratus *Pug.* 22; novus *Pug.* 89; speratus *Pug.* 68; 100.
MARSIA, *Marsyas, a satyr who challenged Apollo to a flute-playing contest, but was defeated and flayed alive: Buc.* 5, 50; [6, 97].
MARSILIUS FICINUS, *see Ficinus, Marsilius.*
[MARTIALIS, M. VALERIUS], *see Bilbilitanus.*
MARTINUS, *Martin von der Marthen (d. 1552): Laud.* [462-467]; 465.
MARTIUS, a, um, *of Mars, martial, warlike:* amor *Pug.* 44; hostis *Buc.* 11, 97; taela *Pug.* 20.
MATERNUS PISTORIUS, *Maternus Pistoris of Ingwiller in Alsace (d. 1534): Nar.* 19, 2; *Laud.* 137-138; 178-179.
MAUSOLUS, *ruler of Caria in the fourth century BC, whose wife Artemisia built the Mausoleum for him: Laud.* 79.
[MAXENTIUS], *Roman emperor (306-312): Laud.* 526.
MEBESIUS, IOHANNES, *Eobanus's kinsman and teacher in Gemünden, Johann Mebes (Mebessen, Mehessen): Nar.* 6, 4.
[MECKBACH], *see Megobachus.*
MEDEA, *see Maedaea.*
[MEDUSA], *see Phorcis.*
MEDUSEUS, a, um, *of Medusa, whose snake-haired visage turned all those who looked on it into stone; cut off by Perseus, her head adorned the aegis of Athena:* capilli *Pug.* 61.
MEGOBACHUS, *Johann Meckbach (1495-1555): Nar.* 18, 1.
MELANCHTHON, PHILIPPUS, *Philip Melanchthon (1497-1560): Nar.* 17, 20; 21, 8; 26, 4; 28, 4.
MELES, *a river in Ionia, on whose banks Homer was said to have been born: Nar.* 5, 7.
MELSUNGEN, *see Moelsingen.*
MEMPHIS, *a city of Middle Egypt, where the sacred bull Apis was worshiped:* barbara *Laud.* 78.

PANES, *gods of the woods and fields: Ama.* 32, 30.

PANISCUS *(see also Christianus [Ludovicus]), a pastoral name ("little Pan") for Ludwig Christiani: Buc.* 1, tit.; 1, *passim as speaker;* 1, 26; 1, 38; 8, 65; [8, 66-68; 8, 96].

PANOMPHEUS, *a title of Jupiter ("author of all oracles"): Pug.* 8.

PAPHIUS, a, um, *of Venus, sacred to Venus:* lupanar *Laud.* 241; sordes *Ama.* B 2, 68; faces *Ama.* B 2, 34; fores *Ama.* 35, 50.

[PARADISE], *the earthly Paradise, located on a high mountain in the east: Buc.* 2, 16-19; 2, 94-95.

PARCAE *(see also Fatum), the Fates:* [*Rec.* 120; *Buc.* 9, 22-28]; fatales *Buc.* 9, 22.

PARIS, *a son of Priam, king of Troy. While still a shepherd on Mount Ida he was chosen to judge a beauty contest among Hera, Athena, and Aphrodite. After deserting his lover Oenone, he seduced Helen and abducted her to Troy:* Iliacus *Ama.* 35, 20; *Buc.* B 2, 40; servans pecudes *Buc.* 7, 149.

PARNASSIS, idis, *of Mount Parnassus:* umbrae *Laud.* 161.

PARNASSUS, *a twin-peaked mountain in Phocis, sacred to Apollo and the Muses: Rec.* 75; *Buc.* 2, 31.

PARRHASIUS, *a painter from Ephesus (early fourth century BC): Laud.* 363.

PATAREUS, a, um, *of Patara in Lycia, with a famous oracle of Apollo:* Apollo *Laud.* 468.

PATROCLUS, *the friend of Achilles: Laud.* 318.

PENATES, *household gods; hence, home, homeland:* longinqui *Laud.* 90; patrii *Rec.* 66; *Laud.* 558; Phrygii *Laud.* B 3, 29.

PENEIUS, a, um, *begotten by the river-god Peneius:* Daphne *Laud.* 160.

PERGAMA, *the citadel of Troy:* clara *Laud.* B 1, 11.

PERICLES, *the Athenian orator and statesman (fifth century BC):* magnus *Laud.* 117.

PERMESSIS, *a spring and river on Mount Helicon, sacred to Apollo and the Muses: Buc.* 8, 47; vitreus *Laud.* 249.

PESTANUS, a, um *(see also Poestum), of Paestum in Lucania, famed for its roses:* rosa *Buc.* 10, 9.

PHAEDRA, *the wife of Theseus, who tried to seduce her stepson Hippolytus:* omnis *Laud.* 304.

PHALERNUM, *Falernian wine: Rec.* B 1, 8.

PHASIAS *(see also Maedaea), the sorceress Medea of Colchis: Ama.* 35, 39; Colchis *Laud.* 185.

PHILAEGON *or* PHYLAEGON, *a pastoral name ("fond of goats") for Crotus Rubianus: Buc.* 3, tit.; 3, *passim as speaker;* 3, 6; 3, 76; [7, 172]; magnus *Buc.* 7, 47; meus *Buc.* 7, 166.

PHILEREMUS *(see also Herebordus), a pastoral name ("fond of the wilderness") for Herbord von der Marthen: Buc.* 4, tit.; 4, *passim as speaker;* 4, 1; 4, 5; 4, 34; 4, 57; 4, 71; 4, 89; 11, 6.

PHILIPPUS *(see also Nisus), Count Palatine Philip II (1448-1508):* [*Buc.* B 2, 28]; Palatinus *Laud.* 541; — *Philip I of Hesse (1504-1567): Nar.* 26, 1-2; [27, 1-3]; 28, 4; [29, 6; 30, 1-2; 33,2; *Buc.* 9, 83-120].

PHILLIRIDES *(see also Chyron), the centaur Chiron, son of Philyra: Buc.* 5, 27.

PHILLIS, *a shepherd girl:* mammosa *Buc.* 1, 90; nulla *Buc.* 6, 62; mammosae *Buc.* 1, 87.

PHLEGETHON, *river of fire in the underworld; hence, the underworld: Buc.* 5, 31.

PHOEBEUS *or* PHOEBAEUS, a, um, *of Phoebus:* lampas *Buc.* 9, 95; cultores *Laud.* 253; sorores *(the Muses) Ama.* 36, 3; suggesta *Laud.* 331.

PHOEBUS *(see also Apollo, Phoibos, Titan), the sun-god, patron of poetry and the Muses: Rec.* 74; 196; 216; *Laud.* 13; 128; 158; 167; 259; 327; *Ama.* 9, 7; 32, 61; B 2, 26; [*Buc.*, ded. 28]; *Buc.* 5, 103; 6, 30; 8, 19; 8, 47; comosus *Laud.*, lim. 4; intonsus *Laud.* 72; triumphans *Laud.* 399; victor *Buc.* 5, 50.

PHOIBOS Φοῖβος *(see also Phoebus), Apollo, the patron god of poetry: Nar.* 34, 1.

PHORCIS, *Medusa, a daughter of Phorcys and mother of Pegasus by Poseidon: Ama.* B 2, 30.

SYSIPHUS, *Sisyphus, a king of Corinth, notorious for his trickery:* stultus *Pug.* 38.

TACITUS, CORNELIUS, *the Roman historian (b. around AD 56): Ama.* 22, 5.

TANAIS, *the Don River:* nivalis *Laud.* 209; Scythicus *Buc.* 10, 3.

TANTALEUS, a, um, *of Tantalus:* furores *Pug.* 37.

TANTALUS, *a Lydian king, son of Zeus; after he betrayed the gods' secrets, he was punished in Hades by having fruit and water close at hand, yet forever out of his reach: Ama.* B 2, 24.

TARTARA *(see also Orcus), Tartarus, hell:* fumantia *Laud.* 222.

TARTAREUS, a, um, *of Tartarus, hell:* numen *Buc.* 8, 39; venena *Buc.* 4, 108.

TEMPE, *the beautiful valley of the Peneus in Thessaly; hence, a beautiful valley:* sanctissima *Laud.* 305; suavissima *Buc.* 6, 25.

TERENTIUS, *the Roman playwright Terence (second century BC): Nar.* 21, 4.

[TEREUS], *legendary king of Thrace, husband of Procne, whose sister he raped. He was eventually changed into a hoopoe: Pug.* 39.

TETHYS, *a sea-goddess; hence, the sea:* vaga *Laud.* 340.

TEUTONICUS, *a German: Laud.* 27.

TEUTONICUS, a, um *(see also Germanus), Teutonic, German:* lingua *Nar.* 31, 20; nomen *Nar.* 5, 10; orbis *Buc.,* lim. 5; poeta *Buc.* B 9, 17; Athenae *Laud.* 413; laudes *Laud.* 277; orae *Buc.* 3, 32; urbes *Laud.* 49; 69; vates *Laud.* 162; *Buc.* B 10, 6.

TEUTONIS, idos *(see also Germanus), German: Buc.* B 9, 21.

TEUTONUS, a, um *(see also Germanus), German:* pascua *Buc.* 6, 7.

THAIS, *famous Athenian courtesan: Laud.* 244.

THALIA, *the Muse of light verse:* nostra *Buc.,* ded. 32.

THAMIRAS, *Thamyras, a legendary Thracian bard: Buc.* 1, 41; 1, 50.

THEBAIS, *The* Thebaid *of P. Statius (ca. 40–ca. 96): Laud.* B 1, 14.

THEBE, *Thebes, the ancient capital of Upper Egypt:* antiqua *Laud.* B 1, 13.

THEOCRITUS, *the Greek pastoralist (third century BC): Nar.* 22, 4; 22, 11; [*Buc.,* lim. 1; *Buc.* B 7, 10].

THERSITES, *people like Thersites, the ugliest and most scurrilous of the Greeks before Troy:* loquaces *Laud.* 329.

THESEUS, *a legendary king of Athens, friend of Pirithous: Laud.* 318.

THESPIADES *(see also Musa), the Muses, so called because the town of Thespiae lay at the foot of Mount Helicon: Laud.* 246; *Buc.* 5, *passim.*

THISBE, *see Thysbe.*

THRAX, *a Thracian:* Orpheus ille *Ama.* 33, 6.

THREICIUS, a, um, *Thracian:* vates *(Orpheus) Laud.* 221.

THURIGNUS (THURINGUS), *see Duringus.*

THURINGIA , *see Turingia.*

THYSBE, *Thisbe, the lover of Pyramus: Ama.* 10, 9; [35, 22].

TIBRIS, *see Tybris.*

TIBULLUS, *the Roman poet (55/48-19 BC):* [*Laud.* B 3, 31]; Rhomanus *Ama.* B 2, 65.

TIMOLUS, *Mount Tmolus in Lydia, famous for its wines and saffron:* viridis *Laud.* 106.

TIPHERNUS, *see Typhernus.*

TIRYNTHIUS, *see Tyrinthius.*

TITAN *(see also Phoebus), the sun-god Helios: Buc.* 8, 1; 11, 10.

TITYRUS *(see also Vergilius Maro), Vergil as a pastoral poet: Buc.* 3, 15; [3, 16-29]; 6, 11; meus *Buc.* 3, 23.

TONANS *(see also Deus), the Thunderer, God: Buc.* 11, 41.

TRAGOCOMENSIS, e, *from the village of Bockendorf in Hesse: Nar.* 5, 10.

TRANQUILLUS *(see also Mutianus), a pastoral name ("tranquil") for Mutianus Rufus: Buc.* 2, 104; [2, 105-106]; *Buc.* 5, tit.; 5, *passim as speaker;* 5, 9; 5, 33; 5, 56; senior *Buc.* 5, 7.

VIRTUS, *Virtue (personified):* inclyta *Laud.* 436.
VISTULA, *a river in present-day Poland: Nar.* 7, 5.
VISURGIS, *the Weser River in western Germany: Nar.* 5, 2.
VORHEMIUS, GEORGIUS HELTUS, *see Heltus Vorhemius, Georgius.*
VORHEMIUS, GEORGIUS PAETUS, *Georg Petz of Forchheim (d. 1522): Nar.* 19, 3; [19, 4].
 [VULCANUS], *Vulcan, the god of fire (identified with Hephaestus): Ama.* B 2, 30.

[WEINMANN, SEBASTIAN], *see Sebastianus.*
WERLERUS, *see Berlerus.*
WERTERUS, *see Berterus.*
[WILLIAM II OF HESSE], *see Guilielmus, Iolas.*
WITEBERGA *(see also Albioris), Wittenberg: Nar.* 18, 3.
[WORMS], *see Vangiones.*

XANTUS, *a river near Troy: Rec.* 168.
XENOCRATES, *Greek philosopher of Chalcedon, head of the Academy from 339 to 314 BC: Ama.*, ded. 8.

ZEPHIRUS *or* ZEPHYRUS *(see also Favonius), the warm west wind, harbinger of spring: Buc.* 2, 46; 4, 69; 5, 47; 5, 79; leves *Buc.* 7, 152.
ZEUSINUS, a, um, *of the painter Zeuxis of Heraclea in Lucania (third/second century BC):* botri *Laud.* 364.
ZOILUS, *a sophist of the fourth century BC who poked fun at Homer's errors and inconsistencies; hence, a spiteful critic:* [*Pug.* B. 1, *passim*]; *Laud.* 393; 577; *Buc.* B 1, 8; bilinguis *Pug.* B 1, 1; turpis *Rec.* B 2, 3-4.

GENERAL INDEX

This index combines names and subjects. Names that do not appear in the text, or references to such names, are enclosed in brackets. All references are to the page numbers. References to Camerarius's biography and Eobanus's works are to the English translation. For names in the Latin texts consult the Glossarial Index.